Origins

Canadian History to Confederation

Fifth Edition

Origins

Canadian History to Confederation

Fifth Edition

R. Douglas Francis
University of Calgary

Richard Jones

Donald B. Smith
University of Calgary

THOMSON

NELSON

Australia   Canada   Mexico   Singapore   Spain   United Kingdom   United States

THOMSON

NELSON

Origins: Canadian History to Confederation
Fifth Edition

by R. Douglas Francis, Richard Jones,
and Donald B. Smith

Editorial Director and Publisher:
Evelyn Veitch

Executive Editor:
Chris Carson

Marketing Manager:
Lenore Taylor

Senior Developmental Editor:
Rebecca Rea

Managing Production Editor:
Susan Calvert

Production Coordinator:
Helen Jager Locsin

Copy Editor/Proofreader:
Gail Marsden

Creative Director:
Angela Cluer

Interior Design
Sarah Battersby

Permissions Coordinator:
Cindy Howard

Cover Design:
Peter Papayanakis

Cover Images:
Main image: George Simpson
McTavish/National Archives of
Canada/C-75911
Inset image: The United Church of
Canada/Victoria University Archives,
Toronto/Acc. no. 76.001 P/790N

Compositor:
Carol Magee

Printer:
Transcontinental

**National Library of Canada
Cataloguing in Publication Data**

Francis, R.D. (R. Douglas), 1944-
  Origins: Canadian history to
Confederation/R. Douglas Francis,
Richard Jones, Donald B. Smith.–
5th ed.

Includes bibliographical references
and index.

ISBN 0-17-622434-3

  1. Canada–History–To 1763 (New
France)—Textbooks. 2. Canada–
History–1763-1867—Textbooks. -
I. Jones, Richard, 1943- II. Smith,
Donald B., 1946- III. Title.

FC161.F73 2004   971
C2003-905760-7

We dedicate this fifth edition to our Ph.D. supervisors:
Ramsay Cook
the late Jean Hamelin
J.M.S. Careless and the late Edward S. Rogers

PREFACE

THE NATURE OF HISTORY

The word "history" refers to both the events of the past and the historian's study of them. While many naturally assume that what the historian tells us about past events is definitive, students of history realize that no conclusive or final study of any event in the past is possible. Historians constantly search for a deeper and richer understanding of, and new perspectives on, past events. That is why history is always being revised and rewritten.

The rewriting of history occurs for many reasons. New evidence, for example, constantly emerges through the discovery of new sources or documents. The work of scholars in other humanities and social science disciplines — such as archaeology and anthropology for Native history, or demography, sociology, and geography for social history — leads to new insights. As well, new perspectives result from historians asking new questions. When, for example, historians were preoccupied with the study of political figures and events, this perspective dictated the sources they consulted and the questions they asked of those sources. When a new generation of historians desired to learn more about the lives of "ordinary people" or of social events, they located different sources, and asked new questions of traditional ones. Today, the study of history has expanded significantly to include a host of sub-disciplines: such as women's, ethnic, Native, working-class, intellectual, military, and cultural history, to mention only a few. Such a multiplicity of approaches enriches our understanding of the past.

Adding complexity to the study of history today, besides the unearthing of new sources and the emergence of new varied types of history, are new theoretical approaches. Theories of relativism, Marxism, feminism, and, more recently, post-modernism, force historians to question the nature of history, the role of the historian, and, in some cases, even the ability to write history if seen as some kind of objective study of the past. Still, historians continue to study the past in the belief that it provides knowledge essential for understanding the present, and for providing a perspective on the future. The current debates over the nature of history have influenced and shaped the writing of history within Canada and elsewhere.

THE NATURE OF THIS TEXT

Origins and *Destinies*, the companion volumes of Canadian history, cover the study of Canada's past from the beginnings to the present. The texts reflect and incorporate the new trends in historical writing. First, we include the most recent and up-to-date research by Canadian historians. In a format and style that is clear and engaging for students interested in studying Canada's history, we present as comprehensive and rich a study of Canada's past as possible in a two-volume text. Secondly, we introduce students to the new types of history broadly defined as the "new social history" and the "new cultural history," while also providing them with the more traditional political and economic accounts. Thirdly, we include the historical development and contribution of the Aboriginal people, French-speaking and English-speaking Canadians, recent immigrants, women, and minority groups, realizing that together they make up Canada's rich past. As well, we include the history of each of the country's regions, while keeping Canada as the focal point. Finally, up-to-date annotated bibliographies appear at the end of each chapter to identify the major historical writings on the events covered in the chapter.

To review Canadian historians' lively debate on important events, issues, or trends in historical writing, *Origins* and *Destinies* provide a series of boxed inserts entitled "Where Historians Disagree" that highlight differing views. These debate boxes remind students that the writing of Canadian history is an ongoing process. To show that history is the action of individuals, we include "Historical Portraits" that highlight the life of well-known, and not-so-well-known, persons who made their mark in history. Individuals seldom act alone, however, but are part of a community. Thus, in this new edition of *Origins* and *Destinies*, "Community Portraits" appear to demonstrate the contribution of selected communities to Canada's history.

In terms of format, *Origins* and *Destinies* are divided into thematic sections, each one introduced by a brief overview of themes highlighted in the chapters within the section. Each chapter treats a major topic or period and begins with a "Time Line" listing the key events discussed. *Origins* and *Destinies* follow a chronological approach to help students understand how events developed through time. As well, headings and subheadings throughout the chapters assist in organizing the material. At the end of each chapter a section entitled "Linking to the Past" directs students to additional information for selected topics on the World Wide Web. As well, a section entitled "Related Readings" identifies useful articles in the sixth edition of R. Douglas Francis and Donald B. Smith, eds., *Readings in Canadian History*, volume 1, *Pre-Confederation*, and volume 2, *Post-Confederation*.

In terms of content, *Origins*, the first volume, tells the story of pre-Confederation Canada — of the Native peoples and of the coming of the Norse, the Portuguese, the Spanish, the Basques, and particularly the French and the British who eventually established permanent European settlements. Anyone seeking to understand our diversity must first examine the era when our present regional personalities first formed in Atlantic Canada, the St. Lawrence River valley, the Great Lakes, the Red River, and the Pacific coast.

Destinies, the second volume, takes Canada's story from 1867 to the present day. Unlike the United States, Canada did not experience a uniform wave of expansion westward from the Atlantic seaboard. In many cases, the European communities in Canada began as pockets of settlement, independent of one another, founded at different times, and with people of various European backgrounds. In *Destinies*, we show how Canada came to take the transcontinental form it did, and how the various groups within its boundaries united together. We focus on various regional, ethnic, and social tensions as well as including references to more harmonious events.

We hope that *Origins* and *Destinies* will provide students of Canadian history with a knowledge of Canada's past, a desire to explore that past in greater depth in more specialized courses in Canadian history, and an appreciation of the multilayered, vibrant, and exciting nature of the writing of Canadian history in keeping with the discipline of history as a whole.

Students seeking more extensive bibliographical information are directed to the following works. Important annotated bibliographical guides to the study of Canadian history include M. Brook Taylor, ed., *Canadian History: A Reader's Guide*, vol. 1, *Beginnings to Confederation* (Toronto: University of Toronto Press, 1994); Doug Owram, ed., *Canadian History: A Reader's Guide*, vol. 2, *Confederation to the Present* (Toronto: University of Toronto Press, 1994); Carl Berger, ed., *Contemporary Approaches to Canadian History* (Toronto: Copp Clark Pitman, 1987); and John Schultz, ed., *Writing about Canada: A Handbook for Modern Canadian History* (Scarborough, ON: Prentice-Hall, 1990). An invaluable bibliography (without annotation) is Paul Aubin and Louis-Marie Côté's *Bibliographie de l'histoire du Québec et du Canada/Bibliography of the History of Quebec and Canada*, published (in several volumes) by the Institut québécois de recherche sur la culture in Quebec City. Easy to use, it contains more than 100 000 titles, all published between 1946 and 1985. Current bibliographies of the most recent publications are published in every issue of the *Canadian Historical Review* and the *Revue d'histoire de l'Amérique française*.

ACKNOWLEDGEMENTS

In preparing five editions of *Origins* and *Destinies*, we have benefited enormously from the advice and suggestions of a large number of Canadian historians. They have read chapters and often the entire manuscript, providing us with useful criticism within their respective research areas. In particular, we wish to thank the following teachers and researchers: William Acheson (University of New Brunswick); Gratien Allaire (Faculté Saint-Jean, University of Alberta); Douglas Baldwin (Acadian University); Jean Barman (University of British Columbia); John Belshaw (University College of the Cariboo); Phillip Buckner (University of New Brunswick); Anne Buffam (Open University); Robert Burkinshaw (Trinity Western University); Robert A. Campbell (Capilano College); Sarah Carter (University of Winnipeg); Joseph Cherwinski (Memorial University of Newfoundland); Gail Cuthbert-Brandt (York University); Jean Daigle (Université de Moncton); George A. Davison (College of New Caledonia); A.A. den Otter (Memorial University); Olive Dickason (University of Alberta); Mark Dickerson (University of Calgary); John English (University of Waterloo); A. Ernest Epp (Lakehead University); Robin Fisher (Simon Fraser University); Rae Fleming; Gerald Friesen (University of Manitoba); Donald Fyson (Université Laval); Michael Granger; Roger Hall (University of Western Ontario); John David Hamilton; James Helmer (University of Calgary); James Hiller (Memorial University of Newfoundland); Raymond Huel (University of Lethbridge); Bonnie Huskins (University College of the Fraser Valley); Helen Towser Jones (Capilano College); Jeffrey Keshen (University of Ottawa); Douglas Leighton (University of Western Ontario); Ernest LeVos (Grant MacEwan College); Ingeborg Marshall; Marcel Martel (York University); Bea Medicine (University of Calgary); James Miller (University of Saskatchewan); Dale Miquelon (University of Saskatchewan); William Morrison (Brandon University); Suzanne Morton (McGill University); Ken Munro (University of Alberta); the late Howard Palmer (University of Calgary); Martin Pâquet (Université Laval); Margaret Prang (University of British Columbia); Colin Read (University of Western Ontario); Keith Regular; Daniel Richter (Dickinson College); Patricia Roome (Mount Royal College); R. H. Roy (University of Victoria); Eric Sager (University of Victoria); Phyllis Senese (University of Victoria); Thomas Socknat (University of Toronto); Donald Swainson (Queen's University); M. Brook Taylor (Mount Saint Vincent University); John Herd Thompson (Duke University); Jill Wade (Open University); Keith Walden (Trent University); and William Westfall (York University). Douglas Francis thanks Michael Brookes for his indomitable enthusiasm to see this book in print (and his name in it).

At Nelson, we benefited enormously from a dedicated and enthusiastic editorial team. In particular, we wish to thank Chris Carson, Executive Editor; Rebecca Rae, Senior Developmental Editor; Susan Calvert, Managing Production Editor; and Gail Marsden, Copy Editor and Proofreader. It was our pleasure to work with each of them.

We also wish to thank our wives Barbara Grant, Lilianne Plamondon, and Nancy Townshend for sharing our enthusiasm as well as enduring our, of course, only occasional bouts of ill humour throughout this project, which has been on-going for the past... twenty years.

We wish to dedicate this fifth edition to our thesis advisers of long ago, Ramsay Cook (for R. Douglas Francis), the late Jean Hamelin (for Richard Jones), and J. M. S. Careless and the late Edward S. Rogers (for Donald Smith). These individuals, excellent teachers and researchers, left an indelible mark upon each of us.

CONTENTS

PART TWO ☙ BRITISH NORTH AMERICAN COLONIAL SOCIETIES, 1760 TO 1815

PART THREE ◈ THE CANADAS, 1815 TO THE 1860s

PART FOUR   COMMUNITIES EAST AND WEST, 1815 TO THE 1860s

LIST OF MAPS

Origins

Canadian History to Confederation

Fifth Edition

THE FIRST PEOPLES

TIME LINE

70 000– 14 000 years ago	A land bridge between North America and Siberia, known as Beringia, exists
c. 15 000 years ago	The glaciers begin to melt and to retreat
c. 12 000 years ago	A human settlement exists in the southernmost portion of the Americas, Monte Verde, Chile
10 000 years ago	Humans live throughout large sections of what is now Canada
5000 years ago	The glacial ice recedes to approximately its present northern position, and the climate becomes similar to today's
3500– 2000 years ago	Civilizations develop in Mexico, Central America, and Peru
A.D. 1–500	Mound Builders' culture arises in Ohio
c. 500	The First Nations of southern Ontario begin to grow corn, resulting in the development of societies based on agriculture
c. 700– 1000	Rise of Mississippian culture in the Mississippi valley
c. 1500	A variety of peoples reside within what is now Canada, with more than 50 languages, belonging to 11 linguistic families (1 Inuit and 10 First Nations)
c. 1730	The Plains people on what is now the Canadian prairies acquire the horse

The first question of Canadian history remains unanswered: What was the place of origin of the first inhabitants of what would become Canada? First Nations elders believe that their ancestors emerged from this continent; while most archaeologists contend that early humans migrated to the Americas across the land bridge that then spanned the Bering Strait. They disagree, however, as to when this migration first occurred, although consensus exists that the original inhabitants of North America lived on this continent at least 10 000 years before the Europeans' arrival.

ORIGIN OF THE FIRST PEOPLES OF NORTH AMERICA

Many First Nations elders accept as a spiritual truth — one revealed in sacred myths, dreams, and visions — that their ancestors originated in North America. This spiritual belief offers an insight into the First Peoples' vision of their cultures and their rights to the land. Young Blackfoot-speaking children in present-day southern Alberta and Montana, for example, learn many stories about Napi or "Old Man," the creator of the world. Other First Nations have their own explanations of the earth's beginnings, but the Blackfoot's is one of the most descriptive and complete.

In the beginning, water covered the entire world. One day, the curious Napi decided to find out what lay below. He sent a duck, then an otter and a badger, but they all dived in vain. Then Napi asked a muskrat to plunge into the depths. He was gone so long that Napi feared he had drowned. At last the muskrat surfaced, holding a ball of mud. The Old Man took this lump and blew on it until it was transformed into the earth. Napi then piled up rocks to make mountains, dug out river and lake beds and filled them with water, and covered the plains with grass. He made all the birds and animals and, finally, people. He taught the men and women how to hunt and how to live. His work completed, the Old Man climbed a mountain and disappeared. Some say Napi's home is in the Rocky Mountains at the head of the Alberta river that bears his name — The Oldman.[1]

Modern scientists base their theories exclusively on observable data in the natural world. On the basis of archaeological and geological evidence, archaeologists, some of whom are members of contemporary First Nations, argue that humans did not evolve independently in the Americas but migrated from Siberia.[2] A few archaeologists propose that other migrations occurred by sea, principally to South America from across the Pacific.

Archaeologists believe that *Homo habilis*, the first direct ancestor of modern-day human beings, appeared nearly 2 million years ago in Africa. A more advanced form, *Homo erectus*, followed, approximately 1.5 million years ago, in Asia, Africa, and Europe. About 100 000 years ago, *Homo sapiens neanderthalensis*, or Neanderthal man, emerged. (Canadian archaeologist Robert McGhee has written, "Only within the past 100 000 years have there existed people, who if appropriately clothed and barbered, could walk down a city street without being suspected of having escaped from a zoo."[3]) Physical evidence of hominid bones, dating back up to 40 000 years, have been found in Africa, Asia, and Europe, but not in the Americas. Physical and genetic data link Aboriginal peoples in the Americas to Asian populations. Thus, archaeologists conclude that the human species originated outside the Americas.

Most archaeologists believe that the early inhabitants of North America crossed from Siberia during the last Ice Age, when sea levels dropped and the continental shelf became exposed. This land bridge, known as Beringia, existed from 70 000 to 14 000 years ago. At one point, the expanse of open grassland and tundra was more than 2000 km wide. Beringia served as a highway for animals passing back and forth between Asia and the Americas. To date no evidence has been found of an ice-free corridor that may have existed along the eastern slope of the Rocky Mountains, thus providing the animals — and, later, humans — with a pathway southward. But an ice-free coastal corridor may have been present. Thus, human hunters, after crossing

Beringia, may have travelled by water between the unglaciated pockets of land. Whether by foot or boat or a combination of the two, humans gradually advanced southward throughout North, Central, and South America, eventually crossing more than 15 000 km from Alaska to Patagonia, at the tip of South America. The possibility of human migration across the South Pacific from Polynesia to South America is regarded as most unlikely due to unfavourable ocean current and wind patterns, as well as an absence of adjacent islands. Again the obvious proba-bility remains that humans entered the Americas from northeastern Siberia to Alaska. Canada's high Arctic was the last region to be populated, roughly 4000 years ago, as the ice retreated.

ARCHAEOLOGICAL HYPOTHESES

 Scientists disagree as to when the migration from Siberia occurred. Supporters of the more con-troversial claims contend that humans possibly entered the Americas as early as approximately 100 000 years ago, although no incontrovertible evidence of such an early arrival exists. Most

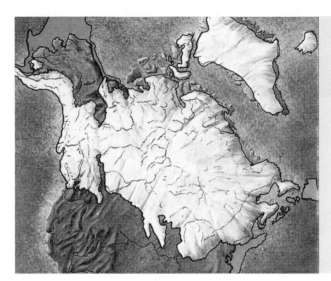

Canada between approximately 80 000 and 20 000 years ago. At this time, almost all of Canada was buried beneath a kilometre or more of glacial ice. A large ice-free area known as the Bering Land Bridge con-nected Siberia and Alaska. Animals and human hunters moved between the Old World and the New across this arctic landscape.

Canada about 12 000 years ago. At this time, the rapidly retreating glaciers were fringed by large lakes of glacial melt-water. The ancient beaches of some of these lakes reveal the remains of camps occupied by First Nations peoples who moved north to occupy the land that is now Canada.

Canada today.

Source: © Canadian Museum of Civilization, illustrator Gilles Archambault, 1989, image nos. 598-10739, 598-10741, 598-10742.

archaeologists place the earliest migration in a much more recent time span. They refer to sites, such as that at Monte Verde in Chile, that show evidence of human occupation more than 12 000 years ago. (This, of course, indicates a human occupation of North America at least several thousand years earlier, if one accepts the northern migration route.) Most archaeologists accept as evidence only those artifacts found in sealed deposits with organic matter that can be radiocarbon-dated. In addition, they require evidence of distinctively styled artifacts. One example is the "fluted point," a stone projectile point with one or more flutes, or hollowed-out channels, that allowed for the attachment of the point to a wooden or bone shaft.

By the "conservative" criteria, there are four Canadian sites — at Debert, Nova Scotia; at Vermilion Lakes, Banff National Park; at Charlie Lake Cave, north of Fort St. John, British Columbia; and Wally's Beach (St. Mary's Reservoir) in southwestern Alberta — that confirm the presence of humans in Canada at least 10 000 years ago.

About 8000 B.C., a drastic change in climate occurred in the northern hemisphere. For reasons still not fully understood, the great ice sheets (more than 3 km thick) that once covered 97 percent of Canada began to melt. The run-off raised the sea level, causing the Beringian Plain to disappear and the Bering Strait to form.

The absence of ice sheets in formerly glaciated territories meant that wind and rainfall patterns shifted. Forests replaced grasslands, and deserts developed. Some animals now became extinct, especially large grazing animals such as mammoths (giant elephants), American camels, and a very large race of bison that foraged on the grasslands.

CIVILIZATIONS OF THE AMERICAS

About 5000 years ago, the ice receded to approximately its present northern position and the climate became similar to today's. The Bering Strait attained its present width of approximately 80 km, and land animals could no longer cross between Siberia and Alaska. People still made that journey, but no longer from Asia's inland centres; they were sea-mammal hunters and fishers who traded across the strait. The Native American nations grew largely as a result of natural population increase, rather than migration.

From 3500 to 2000 years ago, the First Nations population of the Americas underwent major economic and social developments. The peak of technological and social complexity was achieved in present-day Mexico, Central America, and the Andes of Peru, where permanent communities had the highest population densities on the two continents. In central and southern Mexico, a series of great classical civilizations developed. The dominant one, the Aztec, emerged around A.D. 1200. Agriculture (corn, beans, and squash) and rich sea resources formed the basis of these civilizations. Centres with temples and other large structures such as plazas, chiefs' houses, and highways, all constructed with carved and painted stone, appeared as well.

These civilizations developed without the aid of Europe's domesticated animals — horses, oxen, and donkeys. They had discovered the wheel (wheeled toys have been found in various parts of Mexico), but without animals for transport (other than the dog and, in the Andes, the llama) they had no use for it. They also lacked sufficient supplies of usable copper and tin, to allow for the replacement of stone tools. The Peruvians made a few tools from metal that had washed down in the streams, but in Mexico and Central America only stone tools existed.

Despite the absence of the wheel and of metal tools, the Native peoples of the Americas became well-advanced in science and arts. The Maya in Central America, whose civilization flourished between A.D. 300 and 900, developed a sophisticated system of mathematics, applying the concept of zero 500 years before the Hindus did. The Maya, being knowledgeable about astronomy, developed a 365-day annual calendar and plotted the cycle of the planet Venus. They calculated eclipses and recorded their calculations in a writing system that was both pictographic and phonetic. In the Andes, the Incas between A.D. 1200 and 1530 developed irrigation systems, built bridges and roads, erected stone walls using enormous rocks cut to fit so tightly that a knife blade could not be pushed between two blocks, and did metalwork of the highest quality, in gold and silver. First Nations farmers developed more than 100 species of plants that are routinely farmed today, including two of the world's basic food crops: corn (maize) and potatoes (the other two are wheat and rice).

THE MOUND BUILDERS

w(w)w About 2000 years ago, immediately south of the Great Lakes, farming and a sedentary way of life replaced gathering and hunting in the Ohio and later the Mississippi valleys. The "Mound Builders" of the Ohio River valley (the Hopewell culture) constructed gigantic sculptured earthworks — some nearly 25 m high — in geometric designs, sometimes in the shape of humans, birds, or serpents.

Archaeologists have located thousands of mounds used as burial sites and have excavated several earthen-walled enclosures, including one fortification with a circumference of more than 5 km, enclosing the equivalent of 50 modern city blocks. The Ohio peoples had an extensive trading network. Archaeologists have found, among the artifacts in the burial mounds, large ceremonial blades chipped from obsidian (a volcanic glass) from deposits in what is now Yellowstone National Park in Wyoming; embossed breastplates, ornaments, and weapons made from copper nuggets from the Great Lakes; decorative objects cut from mica sheets from the southern Appalachians; and ornaments made from shells and shark and alligator teeth from the Gulf of Mexico.

The Mound Builders' culture evolved slowly, reaching its peak roughly 2000 years ago. The Ohio mounds may have been the model for the Great Serpent burial mound, near present-day

Peterborough, Ontario. Approximately 2000 years ago, the local people built the earthworks, 400 m long, 15 m across, and rising half a metre to a metre above the surface.

About A.D. 500, the Mound Builders' culture declined, perhaps as a result of attacks by other nations or of severe changes in climate that undermined agriculture. A similar culture farther west, around present-day St. Louis, also based on agriculture, replaced that of the Mound Builders. It extended over most of the Mississippi watershed, from Wisconsin to Louisiana and from Oklahoma to Tennessee. From A.D. 700 to 1200, this Mississippian culture influenced the less technologically advanced Aboriginal nations to the east. Indeed, its example led the Iroquoian-speaking peoples of the lower Great Lakes and the St. Lawrence valley to adopt agricultural techniques similar to those of the Mound Builders and the Mississippians.

POPULATION GROWTH

Agriculture could support a larger population than hunting and gathering. The cultivation of as little as 1 percent of the land, in fact, could greatly increase the food supply. Recent estimates of the Aboriginal population of the Americas in the mid-fifteenth century indicate numbers as high as 100 million people, or approximately one-sixth of the human race at that time. The population north of Mexico may have reached 10 million before European contact. Native populations reached such numbers because they lived in a relatively disease-free zone. The Iroquoians, for instance, in present-day southern Ontario and southwestern Quebec, domesticated high-yield cereals and tubers, which allowed them to feed a large population. Approximately half a million people (the most widely accepted estimate) lived within the boundaries of present-day Canada. Roughly half of them lived along the Pacific coast, with its abundant and easily available resources, and in present-day southern Ontario and Quebec, where the Iroquoians practised farming.

The Europeans reduced the Native populations dramatically by unintentionally exposing them to diseases new to the Americas. The Native population lacked defences against such contagious diseases as smallpox and measles. Environmental historian Alfred Crosby has written that "the initial appearance of these diseases is as certain to have set off deadly epidemics as dropping lighted matches into tinder is certain to cause fires."[4] Aboriginal healers had never before encountered these epidemic diseases. They could not combat them, nor could the Europeans, until the twentieth century — long after the Native population had been repeatedly devastated. After European contact, death rates in some areas of the Americas reached as high as 90–95 percent. By the early twentieth century, the entire First Nations population in Canada and the United States had been reduced to less than 1 million, or one-tenth of the estimated population at the time of European contact. Historian Olive P. Dickason has noted that in the seventeenth century, "the lands that appeared 'vacant' to the new arrivals were either hunting areas or else had been recently depopulated because of introduced epidemics."[5]

CLASSIFYING THE FIRST NATIONS

 The First Nations population has been classified according to three distinct categories: linguistic, national, and cultural. None is satisfactory. A linguistic division in Canada reveals twelve separate indigenous language units. One is Eskimo–Aleut, the language spoken by the Inuit; the other eleven are First Nations linguistic groups. Seven of them (Salishan, Tsimshian, Haidan, Wakashan, Tlingit, Kutenaian, and Athapaskan) are found in British Columbia. The Siouan speakers are found on the prairies and in the foothills of the Rockies. The Iroquoian speakers live in eastern Canada. The Algonquian (or Algonkian) linguistic family, the largest group, extends from the Atlantic coast to the Rockies. The Athapaskan language group can be found throughout Yukon and the Northwest Territories and the northern sections of the four western provinces. As nearly as can be determined, the First Nations spoke about 50 different languages.

This linguistic classification unfortunately leads to the linking together of widely disparate groups that had little in common except language. The language of one could differ as much from another as English from German or Portuguese from Romanian. Within the same linguistic family, groups often had different ways of life. The Mi'kmaq of the Maritimes and the Blackfoot of the Prairies, for instance, although separated by 4000 km, are joined together in the Algonquian linguistic family. But they lived entirely different lives, totally unaware of each other's existence. Conversely, the Haidas of the Queen Charlotte Islands culturally resembled their mainland neighbours, the Tsimshians, in everything except their completely unrelated language.

To classify Canada's original inhabitants by political categories also poses problems. Nations — that is, groups of people bound together by a common culture and language and acting as a unit in relations with their neighbours — certainly existed. But among some groups, the ties between the various bands were not strong. The more remote bands diverged considerably in dialect and, in some cases, had so thoroughly assimilated the customs of alien peoples around them that they lost all sense of political unity with their distant relatives.

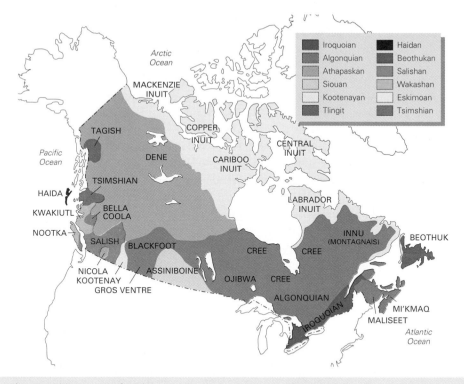

Aboriginal language families within the boundaries of present-day Canada: an approximate guide for the period from the sixteenth to the eighteenth centuries.

Source: Adapted from P.G. Cornell, J. Hamelin, F. Ouellet, and M. Trudel, *Canada: Unity in Diversity* (Toronto: Holt, Rinehart and Winston, 1967), p. 14.

NATIVE CULTURE AREAS

 A better classification of Native North Americans is that by cultural areas because it recognizes how climate and regional resources influence the development of societies and technologies. According to this classification, Native societies in Canada consisted of six culture areas: Northwest Coast, Plateau, Plains, Subarctic, Arctic, and Northeast. The cultural areas tend to coincide with ecological zones. None of these cultural areas stopped at what is now the Canada–U.S. border.

Gradually each band fitted itself to a culture area. They adapted to new environmental conditions, especially climate change. The First Nations developed extensive trading networks. The peoples of northern North America belonged to a larger world than their own communities. The peoples of Aboriginal Canada were not isolated, but part of a hemisphere-wide civilization. Over

Aboriginal culture areas. Rather than being an authoritative representation of actual territories at any one time, this map should be regarded as a rough guide to contiguous groups that had or have similar cultures and histories.

Source: Based on *Handbook of North American Indians*, vol. 4, *History of Indian–White Relations* (Washington: Smithsonian Institution, 1988).

Gitsaex village, a Tsimshian community on the Pacific, around 1750, as depicted in a painting by Gordon Miller in 1983.

R. Cole Harris, ed., *Historical Atlas of Canada*, vol. 1, *From the Beginning to 1800* (Toronto: University of Toronto Press, 1987), plate 13. Reprinted by permission of the University of Toronto Press Incorporated.

time, Native societies dynamically changed. As archaeologist Robert McGhee has written: "Native North American cultures were not fixed in ancient traditions, any more than were those of Old World peoples, and were remarkably flexible to change in response to new ideas or circumstances."[6]

THE NORTHWEST COAST

Archaeologists believe that the ancestors of the Native peoples of the Pacific coast had resided there for thousands of years before European contact. The linguistic complexity of the coastal region, with its nineteen distinct languages, suggests that it is an "old area," and thus the most likely starting point for migrations of successive groups to the east and south.

Yet, despite their different histories, the Northwest Coast peoples' ways of life resembled each others in many aspects. Evidence exists of wide-scale adaptation to a similar environment. All along the coast, groups shared knowledge and techniques.

The coastal inhabitants relied on the abundant fish for their livelihood: herring, smelt, oolichan (candle-fish), halibut, and several species of cod. Salmon, which they speared, netted, and trapped in large quantities, then sun-dried or smoked, became their basic, year-round staple. In addition, they hunted sea mammals, such as whales, seals, sea lions, porpoises, and sea otters. Such an abundant food supply made the Pacific coast region the most densely populated area in Canada.

The Northwest Coast peoples used the giant cedars and firs of the coastal rain forest to build houses and to make dugout canoes and woodwork, such as carved boxes, bowls, dishes, and ladles. They lived the year round in villages located in sheltered island coves or on channels near the mouths of rivers. Each village was self-contained, but on occasion, particularly in times of war, several settlements joined together. Their communal activities included the potlatch, a large ceremonial feast, which they used to mourn the dead, to celebrate the investiture of new chiefs, or to mark the completion of a new house.

A hierarchical social structure based on wealth and heredity evolved on the Northwest Coast, with chiefs, nobles, and commoners. Social grading existed within each class. Below the commoners were slaves, who in some villages apparently made up a third of the population. Historian Olive P. Dickason observed that slaves "were usually prisoners of war, but sometimes individuals who had lost status because of debt; one could also be born into slavery, one of the few regions in North America where this happened. In any event, slaves had no rights of any kind and could be put to death at the will of their masters."[7]

THE PLATEAU

The Plateau culture area, the smallest of the six regions, takes in the high plateau between the Coast Range and the Rocky Mountains in the south–central interior of British Columbia. It extends southward through western Montana, Idaho, and eastern Washington and Oregon. The Canadian portion of the Plateau area is a region noted for its hot, dry summers and cold winters. In Canada the Plateau cultural area includes the Kutenai (or Kootenay) in the east, the Interior Salish in the west, and the Athapaskan-speaking groups to the north. These nations depended on salmon, and thus their populations were concentrated downriver, where the fish were most abundant. Their Northwest Coast neighbours influenced them greatly. But, after the arrival of the horse in Plateau society in the early eighteenth century, they had more contact with the Plains people. In dress, customs, and religion, the Plateau people came to resemble, in many ways, those on the Plains.

THE PLAINS

East of the Plateau region lies the Plains (or Great Plains) culture area, the broad central region of North America west of the Mississippi and Red River valleys and east of the Rockies. The open grasslands, with tall grass in the east and short grass in the west, extend on a north–south axis from northern Alberta and Saskatchewan and western Manitoba to Texas. The region has a continental climate — hot, dry summers and cold winters.

Throughout the buffalo era, the northernwestern Plains attracted Native communities from all directions. Knowledgeable and experienced, the Natives pursued the vast herds. Often several local bands belonging to different First Nations formed a single encampment. Mixing, merging, and amalgamation were common. Relations between Native communities spanned the spectrum from peaceful to hostile.

In the eighteenth century, First Nations belonging to three linguistic families lived on the Canadian Plains: the Algonquian, the Athapaskan, and the Siouan. As the Plains became a crossroads for many First Nations, a sign language developed to allow people to communicate. These Plains Native peoples specialized in the communal hunt of the buffalo, or bison, an animal that was central to their way of life. They ate its flesh and used the hide to make teepee covers, clothing, and robes. From the thick hide of the buffalo's neck they made shields, from the horns they fashioned spoons and drinking cups, and from the sinew they created thread and bow string. On the treeless Great Plains, dried buffalo dung provided fuel.

Natives hunted the buffalo on foot in small nomadic bands of roughly 50 to 100 people. Finding the buffalo required a knowledge of their migratory habits. Large herds existed in abundance, but one could go for days or weeks without seeing a single animal. Hunting also required considerable skill in approaching the animals because neither the lance nor the bow was effective against them except at close range. Buffalo also could run at speeds of over 50 km per hour, making it impossible for hunters on foot to run them down.

Over the millennia, the Plains people developed increasingly effective subsistence strategies. The drive became the best way of harvesting the herds. The Plains Native peoples lured the buffalo into corrals or pounds of poles and brush in small valleys where they could ambush them. Where the land was uneven, as in the foothills to the west, the ambush frequently took the form of a jump, where the hunters stampeded the animals over a cliff or steep cutbank.

One such location is Head-Smashed-In Buffalo Jump, a UNESCO World Heritage Site in the Oldman River valley, 130 km south of Calgary in southwestern Alberta. Used for at least 6000 and possibly for 9000 years, it is one of the oldest, largest, and best-preserved of all the buffalo jumps in North America. Evidence remains of several of the drive paths, marked by rock piles about a metre in diameter and a third of a metre high, stretching back, in one case, as far as 8 km from the cliff.

A Blackfoot couple with horse-drawn travois. A horse could pull a load four times as great twice as far as a dog.

Edward S. Curtis/Glenbow Archives, Calgary, Canada/NA-1700-156.

The arrival of the horse on the northern prairie in the early eighteenth century provides perhaps the most dramatic example of the ability of Plains people to adapt to new situations, to take advantage of new opportunities. The horse originally existed in the Americas, but then it disappeared, until reintroduced by the Spaniards into Mexico in the sixteenth century. Quickly the horse replaced the dog as the chief transporter of goods. The Plains peoples adopted the dog travois (two trailing poles on which was attached a platform or net for holding a load) for use with the horse. Their horse-drawn travois carried a load of 150 kg, in contrast to 35 kg pulled by a dog travois. As well, a horse could travel 20 km a day — twice as far as a dog. With the horse, the Plains peoples could take more than just the basic necessities as they moved from one hunting camp to another and to keep extra suits of clothing, additional buffalo robes for winter, and more dried provisions. The horse transformed the buffalo hunt. Mounted hunters simply surrounded a buffalo herd, without having to drive it into an enclosure or over a cliff.

THE SUBARCTIC

To the north lies the Subarctic culture area, a sparsely populated region. A low-lying region covered with coniferous trees, it extends across the Canadian Shield, from the Labrador coast to the mouth of the Yukon River, covering over a quarter of present-day Canada. Its northern boundary is below the tree line. The winters are long and harsh, but the forests provide shelter for its human inhabitants. Members of two linguistic families lived in the Subarctic: in the west, the Athapaskan-speaking groups, or "Dene" (pronounced "de-ne" or "de-nay" and meaning "the people"); and in the east, the Subarctic Algonquians.

In the summer, the Subarctic peoples lived in communal encampments of several hunting bands (about 100 people) situated at good fishing sites. In the autumn they divided into individual hunting bands of approximately 25 people, closely related either by family ties or by marriage, to hunt for food. A senior male directed the group and, in consultation with the other men, decided where and when they would hunt and camp. Many Dene and Algonquians relied on the moose, whose importance to them was comparable to that of the buffalo to the Plains peoples. Because of the thin distribution of game animals over vast areas of the boreal forest, the Subarctic human population was among the lowest in the world.

THE ARCTIC

Immediately north of the Subarctic, above the tree line, lies the Arctic culture area. Today, this area includes much of Alaska, all of the Canadian North above the tree line, and Greenland. The region has one of the world's harshest climates. For about eight months of the year it remains snow-covered and its seas frozen.

The Subarctic peoples have left numerous rock painting sites across northern Canada.

Manitoba Museum of Man and Nature.

Today, the various Inuit groups speak related languages, which suggests that these languages derived from a single ancestral tongue. Their languages also have similarities to those of the Chukchi, Koryak, and Itel'men peoples of northeastern Siberia. Racially as well, the Inuit resemble First Nations. This suggests that the Inuit originated in Asia.

About 4000 years ago, humans developed skills and technologies to hunt and to fish to enable them to survive winters on the treeless tundra of Arctic Canada. They constructed dog sleds, snow houses, and soapstone lamps. They killed sea mammals with harpoons attached to retrieving lines, and used barbed stone spears to fish and hunt birds. They also used the bow and arrow expertly. Although fewer species of animals exist in this region, they are relatively larger. In certain areas, migration and the availability of food lead to dense seasonal concentrations of many mammals, such as caribou, walrus, and seals.

By A.D. 1000, an Alaskan people, the Thule — the direct ancestors of the modern Inuit — had entered the central Arctic. Four hundred years later, a sparse Thule population occupied most of Arctic Canada north of the tree line. In the relatively mild weather conditions at the time of their arrival, they were able to adapt their rich maritime hunting culture to the Canadian Arctic. After perfecting the techniques of hunting on the open seas, they could take even large sea mammals, like the bowhead whale. The colder climate of the sixteenth century onward made this life untenable and they developed the well-known classic Inuit culture. Modern Canadian and Greenlandic Inuit are descended from them.

Copper Inuit archers in the early twentieth century. Their bows had an effective range of 30 to 40 m.

Sir G. Hubert Wilkins/Canadian Museum of Civilization/51165.

THE NORTHEAST

The Northeast (or Eastern Woodlands) culture area extended roughly from the Atlantic to the Great Lakes, and north to the Subarctic. The Northeast Native peoples hunted a variety of large game, particularly deer, as well as smaller game. They also fished and gathered edible wild plants and roots. Dramatic changes followed when hunters in southern Ontario adopted the bow and arrow from the Ohio region, about 1500 years ago. Climate and soil conditions south of the Canadian Shield allowed some nations to grow corn, beans, and squash. Two linguistic families lived in the Northeast: the Algonquians, a migratory people primarily dependent on hunting and fishing; and the Iroquoians, a semi-nomadic and agricultural people. The Algonquians occupied the northern part of the region, while the Iroquoians inhabited much of present-day southern Ontario and neighbouring New York State.

THE ALGONQUIANS

The Algonquian-speaking peoples were widespread on the eve of European contact. The Mi'kmaq (Micmac) lived in the Maritimes, and the closely related Maliseet (Malecite) in what is now western New Brunswick. North of the St. Lawrence and east of the St. Maurice River dwelt the Montagnais (Innu). The Algonquins (Algonkins), the group that gave its name to the Algonquian linguistic family, lived in the Ottawa valley. (Note that the tribal name ends in "-quin" and that of the linguistic family in "-quian.") Still farther west lived the Nipissings on Lake Nipissing, the Ottawas (Odawa) on Manitoulin Island in Lake Huron, and the Ojibwas (Ojibways, Chippewas) around Lake Superior. The Beothuk, now extinct, lived in Newfoundland. They might have been Algonquian speakers, but the evidence is inconclusive.

Ojibwa (Anishinabeg) birchbark canoe, photographed about 1895, probably in northern Minnesota.

Smithsonian Institution, National Anthropological Archives.

Although many Algonquian groups grew crops, those north of the Great Lakes chiefly hunted and fished. During the winter they broke up into family groups to hunt deer, elk, bear, beaver, and other animals. In the early spring they met at maple groves to gather and boil the tree sap. In the summer, the women undertook agricultural work, while the men fished. During the fall they gathered wild rice, and, farther south, harvested corn.

Several winter hunting groups joined together for summer fishing. According to anthropologist Bruce Trigger, each fishing band had its own name, territory, and leader. The leader, however, had relatively little power or authority.[8] The men of these male-centred hunting groups usually married women from neighbouring bands, thus maintaining friendly ties. Adjacent bands, sharing a common language and customs, constituted a local community. Their unity was more cultural than political, since the band was the only clearly defined political unit. They traded extensively with their neighbours.

THE IROQUOIANS

Initially, the Northeast peoples were hunters and gatherers, but gradually many in the area south of the Canadian Shield became Aboriginal farmers. Crops that originated in Mexico and Central America played an important role in the development of Iroquoian culture. About a.d. 500, corn spread northward via the Ohio and Illinois areas to southern Ontario. It adapted to the shorter growing season and the more rigorous climate. Tobacco probably entered eastern Canada 2500 years ago, and beans about 1000 years ago. Beans, high in protein, partially freed the Iroquoians from having to supplement their corn diet with animal protein. This new food supply contributed to rapid population growth.

At first, small-scale gardening supplemented hunting and fishing, but later the opposite was true. By the time of European contact the Iroquoian farming nations of the lower Great Lakes depended on their crops for up to four-fifths of their food. Every 10 to 15 years, they moved their village sites as the soil and firewood became depleted. Iroquoian women assumed the tasks of planting, cultivating, and harvesting the crops, thus freeing the men for clearing the land for farming, and for hunting, fishing, trading, and warfare.

Where Social Scientists Disagree

How Much Power Did Women Have in Northern Iroquoian Society?

The question of women's authority in Iroquois society has long fascinated scholars. Much of the discussion centres on information provided by the Jesuits in their annual reports, or *Relations*, published from the early seventeenth century to the 1670s, and Jesuit writings in the early eighteenth century. Ethnologists a century ago noted that the Iroquois organized their societies on different lines than did the patrilineal western Europeans. The American ethnologist Lucien Carr, for instance, believed that Iroquois women controlled their societies. In 1884, he wrote that the Iroquois woman, "by virtue of her functions as wife and mother, exercised an influence but little short of despotic, not only in the wigwam but also around the council fire."[1] Another American ethnologist J.N.B. Hewitt, himself of Iroquois background (Tuscarora), agreed. In 1933, he wrote: "She indeed possessed and exercised all civil and political power and authority. The country, the land, the fields with their harvests and fruits belonged to her ... her plans and wishes molded the policy and inspired the decisions of council."[2]

Scholars in the mid-twentieth century returned to this topic, re-examining the same material but arriving at different conclusions. Anthropologist Cara E. Richards, for instance, argued that Iroquois women enjoyed little real power in the seventeenth century.[3] It was only in the eighteenth and nineteenth centuries, when population losses and other post-contact pressures necessitated a change to the early-seventeenth-century power structure, that women's power and influence prevailed.

In her book *Chain Her by One Foot: The Subjugation of Women in Seventeenth-Century New France*, Canadian sociologist Karen Anderson took a middle position arguing that before Huron contact with the French, equality existed between males and females. The Jesuit fathers, however, upset this balance by imposing Christianity and European standards on male–female relations. By 1650, Anderson notes, "Women, especially, had been profoundly changed, accepting the domination of their husbands and fathers." Elsewhere she emphasizes, "What is astonishing is how quickly women's status was changed once Christianity was established."[4]

Controversy had also centred on the sources that Anderson and others used: the Jesuit *Relations*. Anthropologist Judith K. Brown points out that "the *Relations* cover an extended period of time and are anecdotal rather than descriptive. They are the work of many authors, whose prime purpose was to describe not the customs they found, but their own missionary activities."[5]

In the 1970s, the Iroquoianist William N. Fenton and French-language specialist Elizabeth L. Moore made available an English translation of the early-eighteenth-century ethnological classic *Moeurs des sauvages ameriquains, Comparees aux moeurs des premiers temps* (1724) by Joseph-François Lafitau. While Lafitau's remarks on male–female relations apply to only one Iroquois community near Montreal, at a specific period of time, the 1710s, it is invaluable. The Jesuit missionary lived for nearly six years (1712–17) with the Christianized Iroquois converts at Sault St. Louis (later known as Caughnawaga or Kahnawake). He based his study on his own observations, information from another Jesuit who had worked in New France for over half a century, and on the Jesuit *Relations*. Lafitau summarized the status of Iroquois women in this manner: "Nothing is more real [...] than the women's superiority. It is they who really maintain the tribe, the nobility of blood, the genealogical tree, the order of generations and conservation of the families. In them resides all the real authority: the lands, fields and all their harvest belong to them; they are the soul of the councils, the arbiters of peace and war; they hold the taxes and the public treasure; it is to them that the slaves are entrusted; they arrange the marriages; the children are under their authority; and the order of succession is founded on their blood."[6]

Anthropologist Elisabeth Tooker added a fresh new geographical dimension to this topic in her 1984 essay, "Women in Iroquois Society." She emphasized the importance of the two different domains of Iroquois societies: the clearing — the domain of females; and the forest — that of males: "As the women did all the agricultural work of planting, tending, and harvesting of crops, the whole clearing (village and fields) also was regarded as the domain of women. The land beyond the clearing, the forest, was the domain of men."[7]

Over a hundred years after it began, the debate over the balance of power between Iroquois men and women in the seventeenth century continues.

---

[1] Lucien Carr, "On the Social and Political Position of Woman among the Huron–Iroquois Tribes, *16th and 17th Annual Reports of the Trustees of the Peabody Museum*, 3, 3–4 (1884): 211; reprinted in William Guy Spittal, ed., *Iroquois Women: An Anthology* (Ohsweken, ON: Iroqrafts, 1990), p. 13.

[2] J.N.B. Hewitt, "Status of Women in Iroquois Polity before 1784," *Annual Report of the Board of Regents of the Smithsonian Institution for the year ending June 30, 1932*, p. 487; reprinted in Spittal, ed., *Iroquois Women*, p. 67.

[3] Cara E. Richards, "Matriarchy or Mistake: The Role of Iroquois Women through Time," in V.F. Kay, ed., *Cultural Stability and Cultural Change, Proceedings of the 1957 Annual Spring Meeting of the American Ethnological Society*, reprinted in Spittal, ed., *Iroquois Women*, pp. 149–59. (The quote appears on p. 153.)

[4] Karen Anderson, *Chain Her by One Foot: The Subjugation of Women in Seventeenth-Century New France* (London and New York: Routledge, 1991), pp. 52 and 162.

[5] Judith K. Brown, "Economic Organization and the Position of Women Among the Iroquois," *Ethnohistory*, 17, 3–4 (1970); 165, footnote 5, reprinted in Spittal, ed., *Iroquois Women*, p. 196.

[6] Joseph-François Lafitau, trans., *Customs of the American Indians Compared with the Customs of Primitive Times*, 2 vols. (Toronto: Champlain Society, 1974 and 1977), vol. 1, p. 69.

[7] Elisabeth Tooker, "Women in Iroquois Society," in *Extending the Rafters: Interdisciplinary Approaches to Iroquoian Studies* (Albany: State University of New York Press, 1984), pp. 109–23; reprinted in Wendy Mitchinson et al., eds., *Canadian Women: A Reader* (Toronto: Harcourt Brace, 1996), p. 28.

With the development of agriculture, larger Native confederacies formed. Two Iroquoian confederacies existed in the Great Lakes area at the time of European contact: the Huron, an alliance of four nations; and the Five (later Six) Nations or Iroquois. The territory of the Five Nations, or as they called themselves, the League of Hodenosaunee (People of the Longhouse), south of Lake Ontario, was more extensive than the lands of the Huron, south of Georgian Bay on Lake Huron. The languages of the Five Nations (from east to west, Mohawk, Oneida, Onondaga, Cayuga, and Seneca) were more distinct from each other than those of the Huron nations. Each member nation had its own council, which met in the group's largest village. The national councils sent representatives to the League, or Confederacy Council, which governed the confederacies. By the mid-1530s, another group of Iroquoians — neither Huron nor

Iroquois — occupied the St. Lawrence River valley: the St. Lawrence Iroquoians.

The Iroquoian peoples lived in stockaded villages of up to 1500 inhabitants. From ten to thirty families belonging to the same clan lived together in "longhouses," some the size of half a football field in length, and consisting of a framework of saplings, often arched in a barrel shape, covered with sheets of bark. The Iroquoians divided the longhouses into apartments, occupied by closely related families. A corridor ran down the middle of the house, and families on each side shared fireplaces.

The core of any household consisted of a number of females descended from a common ancestor. When a man married, he moved to his wife's home, where authority was invested in an elderly woman. In Iroquoian society the older women had real social and political power. The matrons of the appropriate families elected the chiefs, who were men; these women could also vote out of office any chief who displeased them.

At the time of European contact, First Nations groups lived in six culture areas that parallel Canada's major environmental areas: the West Coast, the interior of British Columbia, the Prairies, the Canadian Shield, the eastern woodlands, and the Arctic. Linguistic diversity also existed, with more than 50 different languages being spoken in six culture areas. On the eve of European contact, the Aboriginal peoples had achieved full occupation and use of North America.

In each cultural area, nature and the availability of natural resources largely dictated the lifestyle of the particular groups. First Nations communities often traded across linguistic and cultural boundaries. These exchanges sealed political and social relationships. In some cases, hostile groups went to war against each other. Individuals considered themselves part of their family, their band, and their nation, but did not look upon all Aboriginal groups as one.

Caroline Parker, a Seneca woman, around 1850, wearing beaded clothing she made herself.

Courtesy of The Southwest Museum, Los Angeles. Photo # N.24963.

NOTES

1. This paraphrasing of the Blackfoot origin story is based on the account given in John Ewers, *The Blackfeet* (Norman: University of Oklahoma Press, 1958), pp. 3–4.
2. Alice Kehoe discusses this subject in her book *North American Indians: A Comprehensive Account*, 2nd ed. (Englewood Cliffs, NJ: Prentice-Hall, 1992), pp. 2–3; and also in her *America Before the European Invasions* (London: Pearson Education, 2002), pp. 9, 20.
3. Robert McGhee, *Ancient Canada* (Ottawa: Canadian Museum of Civilization/Libre Expression, 1989), p. 12.
4. Alfred W. Crosby, "Virgin Soil Epidemics as a Factor in the Aboriginal Depopulation in America," *William and Mary Quarterly*, 3rd series, 33 (1976): 290.
5. Olive P. Dickason, *Canada's First Nations: A History of the Founding Peoples from Earliest Times* (Toronto: McClelland & Stewart, 1992), p. 43.

6. Robert McGhee, "Canada YIK: The First Millennium," *The Beaver*, December 1999/January 2000, p. 10.
7. Dickason, *Canada's First Nations*, p. 67.
8. Bruce G. Trigger, *The Indians and the Heroic Age of New France* (Ottawa: Canadian Historical Association, 1977), p. 6.

LINKING TO THE PAST   w(w)w

Aboriginal Canada: Antiquity
http://www.ucalgary.ca/applied_history/tutor/firstnations/antiquity.html

An overview of the First Nations within the present-day boundaries of Canada before European contact.

A History of the Native People of Canada
http://www.civilisations.ca/archeo/hnpc/npint00e.html

A study of the history of the Native peoples in present-day Canada from 12 000 years ago to European contact, based upon archaeological evidence.

EarthWorks
http://www.earthworks.uc.edu

Virtual reconstructions of some of Ohio's mounds and other earthworks, plus a bibliography of works on the Ohio Valley prehistoric architecture.

Native Civilizations
http://www.ucalgary.ca/applied_history/tutor/firstnations/civilisations.html

An introduction to regional, cultural, and linguistic approaches to classifying the First Nations in Canada, complete with maps, images, and links to other sites of interest.

Stones Unturned
http://www.civilization.ca/aborig/stones/engfrm.htm

A virtual exhibition of native clothing, musical instruments, games, and toys from the Canadian Museum of Civilization. This site also contains brief descriptions and maps of the main Native language groups.

An Iroquoian Longhouse in RealSpace VR
http://www.thinedge.com/longh-rs.htm

Explore the inside of a longhouse in 3-D (you will need Java and Live Picture Viewer to view this page).

RELATED READINGS

R. Douglas Francis and Donald B. Smith, eds., *Readings in Canadian History: Pre-Confederation*, 6th ed. (Toronto: Nelson Thomson Learning, 2002), contains an important article relating to this chapter: Richard White and William Cronon, "Ecological Change and Indian–White Relations," pp. 4–21.

BIBLIOGRAPHY

Three valuable overviews by anthropologists are Alice B. Kehoe, *North American Indians: A Comprehensive Account*, 2nd ed. (Englewood Cliffs, NJ: Prentice-Hall, 1992); R. Bruce Morrison and C. Roderick Wilson, eds., *Native Peoples: The Canadian Experience*, 2nd ed. (Toronto: McClelland & Stewart, 1995); and Alan D. McMillan, *Native Peoples and Cultures of Canada: An Anthropological Overview*, 2nd ed. (Vancouver: Douglas

& McIntyre, 1995). While Diamond Jenness's study *The Indians of Canada* (Ottawa: King's Printer, 1932) should still be consulted, by far the best survey is Olive P. Dickason, *Canada's First Nations: A History of* the *Founding Peoples from Earliest Times*, 3rd ed. (Don Mills, Ontario: Oxford University Press, 2002). Useful overviews include Arthur J. Ray, *I Have Lived Here Since the World Began: An Illustrated History of Canada's Native People* (Toronto: Key Porter Books, 1996); and Bruce G. Trigger and Wilcomb E. Washburn, eds., *The Cambridge History of the Native Peoples of the Americas: Volume 1, North America* (Port Chester, NY: Cambridge University Press, 1996).

Alice Kehoe provides a splendid account of the development of human cultures in North America in *America Before the European Invasions* (London: Pearson Education Limited, 2002). A valuable popular account of the archaeological record is Robert McGhee's *Ancient Canada* (Ottawa: Canadian Museum of Civilization/Libre Expression, 1989). A very speculative work, by a non-specialist, is Elaine Dewar's *Bones: Discovering the First Americans* (Toronto: Random House, 2001).

Henry F. Dobyns, *Native American Historical Demography: A Critical Bibliography* (Bloomington: Indiana University Press, 1976) provides demographic information. For details on the impact of disease consult Alfred W. Crosby, "Virgin Soil Epidemics as a Factor in the Aboriginal Depopulation in America," *William and Mary Quarterly*, 3rd series, 33 (1976): 289–99, and his *Ecological Imperialism: The Biological Expansion of Europe, 900–1900* (Cambridge: Cambridge University Press, 1986). Recently David Helge challenged Dobyns's estimates on the magnitude of the demographic decline in *Numbers from Nowhere: The American Indian Contact Population Debate* (Norman: University of Oklahoma Press, 1998).

Short reviews of Native culture areas appear in Morrison and Wilson, *Native Peoples*; Kehoe, *North American Indians*; and McMillan, *Native Peoples and Cultures of Canada*. Very helpful are the well-researched essays included in Paul Robert Magocsi, ed., *Canada's Aboriginal Peoples. A Short Introduction* (Toronto: University of Toronto Press, 2002). Six volumes in the series *Handbook of North American Indians* (Washington, DC: Smithsonian Institution) are invaluable: vol. 1, David Dumas, ed., *Arctic* (1985); vol. 6, June Helm, ed., *Subarctic* (1981); vol. 7, Wayne Suttles, ed., *Northwest Coast* (1990); vol. 12, Deward E. Walker, ed., *Plateau* (1998); vol. 13, Raymond J. Demaillie, ed., *Plains* (2001); and vol. 15, Bruce G. Trigger, ed., *Northeast* (1978). Useful studies of Native languages are Michael K. Foster's "Canada's First Languages," *Language and Society* 7 (Winter–Spring 1982): 7–16, and his entry "Native People, Languages" in *The Canadian Encyclopedia*, 2nd ed., vol. 3 (Edmonton: Hurtig, 1988), 1453–56.

The early maps in R. Cole Harris, ed., *Historical Atlas of Canada*, vol. 1, *From the Beginning to 1800* (Toronto: University of Toronto Press, 1987), are based on the most recent archaeological discoveries. This atlas contains a wealth of new information about the first inhabitants of present-day Canada. The most up-to-date summary of our current understanding is Dickason's *Canada's First Nations*. A survey of developments in Ontario appears in Edward S. Rogers and Donald B. Smith, eds., *Aboriginal Ontario: Historical Perspectives on the First Nations* (Toronto: Dundurn Press, 1994); and in Peter A. Baskerville's chapter, "Change and Exchange: 9000 B.C.E.–1500 C.E.," in his *Ontario, Image, Identity, and Power* (Don Mills, Ontario: Oxford University Press, 2002), pp. 1–11. One of the best overviews on First Nations groups embracing change is Theodore Binnema's *Common and Contested Ground. A Human and Environmental History of the Northwestern Plains* (Norman: University of Oklahoma Press, 2001). For bibliographical information consult Shepard Krech III, *Native Canadian Anthropology and History: A Select Bibliography*, rev. ed. (Winnipeg: Rupert's Land Research Centre, University of Winnipeg, 1994).

PART ONE

EARLY EUROPEAN SETTLEMENT
TO 1760

INTRODUCTION

When western Europeans first crossed the North Atlantic Ocean in the fifteenth and sixteenth centuries they entered a new world, one that was remarkably different from that of Europe. The First Nations' ancestors had already occupied what would become known as Canada for over 10 000 years. The two groups — First Nations and Europeans — interacted sometimes peacefully, more often through conflict, as they both sought to use the vast natural resources to their own advantage. Fish and furs brought the Europeans back annually, eventually leading the French to establish permanent settlements in what they called New France. French settlements prevailed in Acadia (the present-day Maritimes) and in the St. Lawrence valley. New France was large, but in comparison with the colony of New England to the south, founded about the same time, the population remained quite small, numbering only 65 000 people at the time of the Conquest in 1760, almost 150 years after Champlain founded Quebec in 1608.

New France inherited French institutions, such as the French administrative and judicial systems, but because of differing geography and historical circumstances, they were modified to meet North American circumstances. Conflict with the Iroquois and the English helped to forge a common identity among the French settlers. By the mid-eighteenth century, the contours of the Canadian and Acadian identities were evident. The British conquest in 1760 ended the French regime in North America, but not the French fact in the St. Lawrence valley or in the Maritimes.

THE EUROPEANS' ARRIVAL

TIME LINE

985 — Eric the Red establishes Norse settlements in Greenland

1001 — Leif, son of Eric the Red, leads an expedition to northeastern North America but within a decade the attempts to establish permanent Norse settlements fail

1492 — Christopher Columbus reaches North America; in the belief that he is in Asia, he calls the inhabitants, "Indians"

1497 — Giovanni Caboto (John Cabot), an Italian navigator in the English service, lands in northeastern North America

1524 — Giovanni da Verrazzano, an Italian navigator in the French service, explores much of the Atlantic coast between Florida and the Gulf of St. Lawrence

1534 — Jacques Cartier, on his first voyage for the king of France, enters the Gulf of St. Lawrence

1535–
1536 — Cartier makes a second voyage, during which he visits Hochelaga (Montreal) and winters at Stadacona (Quebec City)

1540s — Basque whalers begin to operate whaling stations on the south coast of Labrador

1542 — The Cartier–Roberval expedition, begun in 1541, ends disastrously with the abandonment of the attempted French settlement

1576 — Martin Frobisher makes the first of a number of attempts to find the Northwest Passage

1583 — Humphrey Gilbert claims Newfoundland for England

1588 — Britain defeats the Spanish Armada, which contributes to the decline of the Basque whaling operation on the south coast of Labrador

The strange boat amazed the Aboriginal hunters along the Labrador and Newfoundland coast. They believed that the world ended beyond the horizon and that they were the only inhabitants. Never before had anyone seen such a sight emerging from the edge of the world. Upon the small sea monster's back arose a tall leafless tree from which hung a gigantic white blanket. Around the tree stood ugly beings with facial hair and skin the colour of the underbelly of a fish. The year was about A.D. 1000, and the newcomers were the Norse. After an interval of nearly five centuries, other Europeans followed in quick succession: the English, the Portuguese, the French, the Spanish, and the Basques.

The absence of written source materials makes the narration of the Europeans' arrival a formidable task. No accounts by the original inhabitants are available, and only a few Norse sagas and the occasional European explorer's journal exist for the period before 1600. Morris Bishop, a biographer of Samuel de Champlain, the founder of Quebec in 1608, put it best when he wrote, "In reading history one must always be impressed by the fact that our knowledge is only a collection of scraps and fragments that we put together into a pleasing design, and often the discovery of one new fragment would cause us to alter utterly the whole design."[1] What follows is a short summary of current knowledge of the Europeans' arrival in northeastern North America subject to amendment.

THE ARRIVAL OF THE NORSE

Irish monks were probably the first European navigators both interested in voyaging westward and capable of reaching North America. They travelled in curraghs, wood-framed boats covered with sewn ox-hides, powered by oars and a square sail. In the early Middle Ages, tales circulated about the celebrated Irish saint, Brendan, who was said to have found new lands by sailing west in the sixth century. But no medieval claim that he reached lands to the west has ever been discovered.

 From the ninth to the twelfth centuries, Scandinavia led the European sea powers with a commercial empire extending from Russia in the east to Sicily in the south and Normandy in the west. The Norse occupied small coastal areas on the southwestern coast of Greenland, as part of their voyages from the European mainland. Eric the Red (Eirikr Thorvaldsson) founded the Norse settlements in Greenland in A.D. 985. Exiled from his native Norway as punishment for committing murder, he escaped to Iceland, only to become involved in a feud there. Banished for more killings, he fled farther west to a vast uninhabited subcontinent. On its southwestern coast he found that the land had green, reasonably level pastures and impressive fiords and headlands, all of which reminded him of his native Norway. Finding it rich in game animals, with a sea full of fish and large mammals such as seals and walrus, he believed that the land could support many Icelanders. Eric named the country "Greenland." On returning to Iceland, Eric encouraged others to migrate with him. Accompanied by fifteen shiploads of Icelanders, the Norse adventurer founded two settlements, where they raised cows, horses, sheep, pigs, and goats. Recent excavations of the remains of Eric's own farm revealed a surprisingly large and comfortable establishment, built with thick walls of stone and turf.

In A.D. 986, Bjarni Herjōlfsson, the owner of a ship that traded between Norway and Iceland, went to join Eric in Greenland. En route, he and his crew met with stormy weather, which drove them off course for several days. When the thick mists cleared they sighted a flat land covered with woods. As this country did not fit the description that he had of Greenland, Bjarni sailed north. Bjarni thus became the first known European to sight eastern North America (probably Labrador), although he never landed there.

 Eric's second son, Leifr (or Leif) Eiriksson, grew up hearing tales about Bjarni's discovery. In A.D. 1001, he assembled a crew of 35 and set out to explore the lands southwest of Greenland.

Viking ships, or *knarrs*, around A.D. 1000, a reconstruction by Louis S. Glanzman. These ships were propelled principally by one big square sail, made out of coarse woollen cloth. For auxiliary power, the men pulled on long oars, for which there were holes in the uppermost plank of the ship.

National Geographic Society Image Collection.

He sailed past Baffin Island, which he called "Helluland" (Flat Stone Land). Farther south, he landed in a forested area — probably the coast of central Labrador — that he called "Markland" (Wood Land). Continuing on, he reached an attractive location with a moderate climate, which he named "Vinland" (Wineland) for its plentiful "wineberries" (probably wild red currants, gooseberries, or mountain cranberries). Scholars have placed Vinland at different locations between Labrador and Florida. A year later Leif and his crew loaded a cargo of timber and "wineberries" and set sail for Greenland. They had not encountered any other humans during their stay.

CONFLICT BETWEEN THE NORSE AND THE FIRST PEOPLES

Leif's brother, Thorvaldr, led the next voyage to Vinland. With his crew of 30 he reached the Vinland houses and settled there for the winter, catching fish to supplement provisions brought from Greenland.

During the second summer, Thorvaldr and his crew apparently followed the coast northward, where they encountered nine *skraelings* (barbarians), as the Norse called them, sleeping under three "skin boats" on shore (because of this reference in the Vinland Sagas, some experts believe these *skraelings* were not First Nations but Inuit using kayaks). The Norse murdered eight of the nine. The one individual who escaped later returned with others in a fleet of skin boats. In the skirmish that ensued, Thorvaldr was killed. The crew returned to Vinland and then to Greenland. Similar skirmishes occurred on subsequent expeditions, preventing the establishment of a permanent colony.

THE HISTORICAL VALUE OF THE NORSE SAGAS

We know of the journeys of Eric the Red, Bjarni Herjõlfsson, Leif Eiriksson, and the later Viking explorers from sagas, or adventure stories, that were passed on orally from generation to generation, for about 300 years before being written down. Expert storytellers told these sagas to hold an audience spellbound. In the retelling, they no doubt embellished many of the original facts, but the sagas have great value.

 In 1960, Helge Ingstad and his archaeologist wife, Anne Stine Ingstad, used the sagas to locate the first known site of European settlement in North America, L'Anse aux Meadows, on the northeastern tip of the Great Northern Peninsula of Newfoundland. Here they unearthed the remains of eight sod-walled structures (the largest is 25 m long) similar to those constructed by the Norse in Iceland and Greenland. Excavation led to the discovery of Norse artifacts, including a bronze cloak pin, used by the Norse to fasten their cloaks on the right shoulder in order to leave their arms free to wield a sword, and a soapstone disk, the weight from a spindle used in spinning yarn from wool. Radiocarbon-dating of Norse artifacts found at the site indicated occupancy in the vicinity of A.D. 1000 — the date of the Vinland expeditions. The absence of a midden (or refuse heap) containing bones and other debris, together with the fact that none of the buildings had been rebuilt or had major repairs, hints at a short occupancy. Today L'Anse aux Meadows is designated a World Heritage Site by UNESCO. It is the only authenticated Viking site in northeastern North America.

THE NORSE IN GREENLAND

For nearly 500 years, the Norse occupied Greenland. Their economy was based on raising stock, hunting, and fishing. They travelled to the west for timber and to the north to trade with the Inuit along the Greenlandic coast, and Baffin and Ellesmere Islands. Norse specimens, including ship rivets, chainmail pieces, two items of woven woollen cloth, barrel-bottom fragments, and many copper and iron artifacts have been excavated on the east coast of Ellesmere Island.

The Greenland settlements prospered in the twelfth century, when an estimated 2000–4000 people, and perhaps as many as 6000, lived there. Then, in the thirteenth century, Greenland's climate became colder, which threatened agriculture. Furthermore, the settlements' prosperity, precariously built on the walrus-ivory trade, declined when the Portuguese imported African elephant ivory. As well, the Black Death of 1349, struck Norway and Iceland severely. The epidemic of bubonic plague killed one-third of the population — a loss that cost the Norse their command of the seas. Thereafter, the annual ship that brought vital supplies from Norway no longer appeared. By 1450, the Greenlandic settlements had disappeared.

A reconstruction of the turf houses originally built by the Norse at L'Anse aux Meadows around A.D. 1000.

J. Steeves/Canadian Heritage/Parks Canada East.

THE ENTRY OF THE PORTUGUESE AND THE SPANISH

The Portuguese replaced the Scandinavians as the leading European sea power by the fifteenth century, as a result of their fast and efficient sea-going vessels known as caravels (their long, narrow ships with two masts).

By 1420 they had reached Madeira, and by 1427 the Azores. But then their voyages across the Atlantic ceased, for they had reached latitudes at which strong westerly winds made sailing dangerous. Instead they focussed on discovering a sea route around Africa to India. In 1488, Bartholomeu Dias rounded the Cape of Good Hope and reached India.

EUROPE'S INTEREST IN EXPANSION

No doubt curiosity, the desire to find a "New World," a better land than that in which they lived, led the Portuguese — and later the Spanish, French, English, and Dutch — to expand beyond Europe. Economic motives also played an important role. The Turks' capture in 1453 of Constantinople, the key city in Europe's trade with the Orient, caused a desperate search to find a new route to "the Indies," as China, Japan, Indonesia, and India were then collectively called, for spices to preserve their meat. As well, they came to convert the "heathen" to Christianity.

Why did the Europeans become the great explorers at the end of the fifteenth century? Why not the Chinese or the Arabs, who both had extensive maritime experience? The Arabs living on the western and northwestern shores of the Indian Ocean, for example, were as far advanced as their European contemporaries in the sciences required for seafaring (astronomy, geography, mathematics, and navigation). Long before the Portuguese had begun to travel along the west coast of Africa, Arabs had explored the east coast of that continent to the island of Madagascar. But

A bronze ringed pin found at L'Anse aux Meadows. Cloak pins like this one were fashionable in the Viking settlements in Scotland, Ireland, and Iceland.

G. Vandervloogt/Canadian Heritage/Parks Canada East.

the Arabs felt no need to go farther, since their territories included the rich variety of tropical plants and animals, as well as minerals, that Europe sought. In essence, then, the Arabs on the Indian Ocean were "already there."

Similarly, well over a 1000 years before European exploration, the Chinese had evolved a strong maritime tradition. The Chinese had introduced the compass to Europe and developed elaborate navigational charts showing detailed compass bearings. By the fifteenth century, they had already built a remarkable navy that had traded with the Islamic world for at least 500 years. But beginning in the mid-1430s, the Chinese withdrew under orders from the emperor to suppress all seafaring. An austere isolationism was imposed. So, just at the moment when Europeans were embarking on their great explorations, China turned inward. It no longer felt the need to venture abroad.

THE VOYAGE OF COLUMBUS, 1492

In ancient times, Europeans believed that Asia could be reached by sailing westward. Aristotle, the Greek philosopher, said that it was possible to sail westward from Spain to "the Indies." Two thousand years later, many Europeans held the same view. When the Italian mariner Christopher Columbus proposed his expedition to the king and queen of Spain, he did so essentially in these terms: Let the Portuguese take the long eastward route around Africa to the Indies; I will find the direct route across the Atlantic.

At the age of 41, Columbus already had extensive seafaring experience. Under the Portuguese flag he had sailed from above the Arctic Circle almost to the equator, and from the eastern Mediterranean west to the outer Azores in the mid-Atlantic. In 1492 he sailed south to the Canary Islands, avoiding the strong westerly winds of the North Atlantic, and then west, reaching the Caribbean. Convinced that he had reached islands near mainland Asia, he named the original inhabitants of the Americas "Indians."

Columbus's voyage led to fierce rivalry between Spain and Portugal. In 1493, the king and queen of Spain approached Pope Alexander VI and asked for exclusive rights over the territories they had recently "discovered." The Spanish-born pope drew a line of division through the mid-Atlantic, from the north pole to the south. By the Treaty of Tordesillas in 1494, Spain and Portugal agreed to move the Pope's line of division one hundred leagues farther west. All the land to the west of the line belonged to Spain, while the land to the east belonged to Portugal. (This division brought Newfoundland and much of Brazil into Portugal's sphere.)

THE ENGLISH AND THE FRENCH CROSS THE NORTH ATLANTIC

When news of Columbus's first two Atlantic voyages to "Asia" reached England, King Henry VII sponsored his own expedition. In 1496, he chose John Cabot (Giovanni Caboto), an experienced Italian mariner, to lead it. He instructed Cabot to "seek out, discover, and finde, whatsoever isles ... and provinces of the heathen and infidelles," and to claim them for England. The merchants of the English port of Bristol, anxious to secure direct access to the spices of the east, sponsored the expedition.

Cabot set sail in late May 1497. Unlike the Norse, the Italian navigator had the benefit of compass, quadrant, and traverse table. On June 24 he reached land, probably the eastern coast of Newfoundland. Here he planted the flags of England and his native Venice and claimed the territory for Henry VII. He discovered that the seas swarmed with fish, by letting down and drawing up baskets weighted with stones. They had found the great continental shelf of Newfoundland, the shallow areas called banks, favourite breeding places of the cod. Cabot also entered the Gulf of St. Lawrence, believing it to be a direct route to China and India.

Encouraged by this information, Henry VII sponsored a second voyage. In May 1498, Cabot sailed again from Bristol with five ships. Shortly out of port, one vessel turned back in distress to Ireland, but the other four were lost. Cabot's disappearance, followed shortly afterwards by the death of Henry VII, caused English interest in the search for a Northwest Passage to lapse temporarily. Nevertheless, John Cabot's first voyage announced England's interest in the Americas. The voyage also brought to Western Europe's attention the Grand Banks fishery. Possibly, Bristol fishers had fished the Grand Banks since the 1480s, but now their secret was out. Fishing — the first great European business in North America — had begun.

In 1997, the 500th anniversary of Cabot's voyage, a reconstructed *Matthew* faced the same perils as did Cabot's ship.

Photo courtesy *The Telegram*, St. John's, Newfoundland.

THE PORTUGUESE IN THE NORTH ATLANTIC

 Soon after Cabot came the Portuguese. Until the early sixteenth century, Portugal concentrated on the discovery of a sea route around Africa and on Brazil, which it claimed in 1500. But in hope of finding a Northwest Passage, Portugal sponsored three North Atlantic expeditions. In 1500 João Fernandes, a *lavrador* (small farmer), reached Greenland. When he first sighted the huge land mass, Fernandes humorously called it "Tierra del Lavrador," Land of the Farmer. A century later, when mapmakers learned of the old Norse name "Greenland," they revived it and shifted the name Labrador to the southwest.

In the same year, Gaspar Corte-Real sailed to Newfoundland. The Azorean sea captain kidnapped 57 First Nations people and sent them back to Europe with his brother Miguel. Their fate in Europe remains unknown. As well, Gaspar Corte-Real and his crew never returned. Like Cabot and his four ships, he was lost with all hands, as was Miguel when he came back to search for his brother.

Despite the dangers of navigating the uncharted North Atlantic, the Portugese annually fished the Grand Banks and the coastal waters of Newfoundland. Several place names, now corrupted in English or French versions, testify to their travels: Cape Race (from *raso*, shaved), at the southeastern corner of Newfoundland; Fermeuse Harbour (from *fremoso*, beautiful), about halfway from the cape to St. John's harbour; and Cape Spear (from the Portuguese *de espera*, hope), just south of St. John's harbour.

Since the Corte-Real expeditions did not produce any riches, the Portuguese lost interest in North Atlantic exploration for two decades. But around 1520, João Alvares Fagundes made a voyage along the south coast of Newfoundland and into the Gulf of St. Lawrence. Upon his return, he obtained colonists from Portugal and the Azores and established a colony, probably on the eastern coast of Cape Breton Island. After a year or so, difficulties arose with the local First Nations, and the settlement — the first European settlement since the Norse — died out. After Fagundes's failure the Portuguese lost interest, apart from the cod fisheries in the North Atlantic.

FRENCH INTEREST IN THE NORTH ATLANTIC

Of all the European powers in the early sixteenth century, France was perhaps the best situated to dominate northeastern North America. It had twice the population of Portugal and Spain together, and six times that of England. It also had more ocean-facing territory, at least as many seaports as England, and far greater wealth. Yet, due to its involvement in European conflicts, France did not become involved in North Atlantic exploration until 1524.

France was interested in a westerly route to Asia. Two possible entry points existed: between Florida and Newfoundland (the most promising) and between Labrador and Greenland. The French selected Giovanni da Verrazzano, an Italian navigator, as commander of their expedition. He searched the North American coast from the Carolinas to Gaspé. At one point, just north of what is now North Carolina, beyond a narrow strip of coastline, he thought he had seen an immense, oceanlike body of water, but it was a mirage. The error had a long life. For years afterward, cartographers placed the Pacific Ocean just north of Florida, almost reaching the Atlantic. Gradually, as more became known about the continent, mapmakers placed the Pacific farther west. But as late as the mid-eighteenth century, one European map still showed a sea connected to the Pacific covering much of present-day western Canada.

Despite Verrazzano's failure to find a passage to Asia, France had a better understanding of the eastern North American coastline. But France did not follow up Verrazzano's discoveries, because of war against the Hapsburgs (the rulers of Austria, the Low Countries, and Spain).

JACQUES CARTIER'S THREE VOYAGES

 Jacques Cartier, a mariner from the wealthy port of Saint-Malo in Brittany, northwestern France, succeeded Verrazzano. Fishers from Saint-Malo and other northern French ports were already sailing to the Grand Banks. Cartier probably gained his first maritime experience on these runs. In April 1534, Cartier left Saint-Malo with two ships and 61 men in search of a passage to China and India. The expedition reached the Strait of Belle Isle between Labrador and Newfoundland a month later. Unimpressed with the area, Cartier called it "the land God gave to Cain," after the biblical wasteland.

Cartier entered the Gulf of St. Lawrence and landed at present-day Prince Edward Island. Next, he sailed north to Chaleur Bay, which divides Quebec from New Brunswick, and met Mi'kmaq traders. Cartier's journal contains the first reference since the Vinland Sagas to a trading exchange between Native peoples and Europeans — initiated by the Natives. They "set up a great clamour and made frequent signs to us to come on shore, holding up to us some furs on sticks," a clear indication that they had already participated in a previous exchange, or exchanges.

As the French moved north to Gaspé they encountered Iroquoians who had come from the interior to fish. Unaccustomed to trading with Europeans, they had brought no furs with them. The French gave the Iroquoians "knives, glass beads, combs, and other trinkets of small value" to win their friendship. Then the French kidnapped two sons of the chief, Donnacona, and took them back to France to learn French, so that they could serve as guides on the next voyage.

It was standard practice among early Europeans in the Americas to capture the inhabitants and take them back to Europe as proof of having reached the new lands. Often, the First Nations did not survive the voyage across the Atlantic; those who did often died in Europe, unable to fight off illnesses that did not exist in the Americas and to which they had not developed immunities. In this instance, Donnacona's sons, Taignoagny and Domagaya, lived and assisted Cartier in his next expedition.

CARTIER'S YEAR IN THE ST. LAWRENCE VALLEY, 1535–1536

In 1535, Cartier returned with three ships and sailed up the St. Lawrence to the Native village of Stadacona (present-day Quebec), the home of his guides, Taignoagny and Domagaya. Cartier recorded a word that they used to refer to their home: "They call a town, *Canada*."[2] En route, the French sea captain gave the name "St. Lawrence" to a cove at which the French stopped, after the Christian martyr whose feast day it was (August 10). The entire gulf and the great river later obtained the same name.

The Iroquoians at Stadacona saw the French as powerful and valuable trading partners. Thus, when Cartier told Chief Donnacona that he intended to travel inland, the chief strongly objected. The Stadaconans wanted to monopolize the trade with the French and to barter the interior groups' furs for the precious European iron tools.

Cartier paid Donnacona no heed and travelled west in early October. By his own estimate, more than 1000 people greeted him at Hochelaga, a palisaded town of 50 longhouses, much more impressive than Stadacona. That afternoon, Cartier climbed the large hill he called Mont Royal (which eventually became "Montréal"). From the summit he had a magnificent view of the well-cultivated cornfields and longhouses below, but he also sighted the Lachine rapids to the west, which no boat larger than a canoe could pass. The French stayed just one day, then returned downriver. It was too late in the year to depart safely for France, so Cartier and his men wintered at Stadacona.

Tension prevailed at Stadacona throughout the winter of 1535–36. By travelling upriver without Donnacona's permission, Cartier had interfered with the Stadaconans' trading rights. In addition, the French who had been left behind built a small fort during Cartier's absence — an act that infringed on the Stadaconans' land rights, which the French did not recognize.

The winter, much longer and colder in Canada than in France, proved a nightmare for the French. By January and February, ice — nearly 4 m thick — locked in the ships. On land the snow lay more than a metre deep. To add to the sailors' problems, scurvy, a disease caused by insufficient vitamin C in the diet, broke out. Twenty-five men (one-quarter of Cartier's crew) died before the French learned the Native cure for the disease: boiling the bark and leaves of the *annedda* (white cedar) to make a brew with a high content of ascorbic acid (vitamin C).

Despite the Stadaconans' help, Cartier remained antagonistic to Donnacona and his people. Anxious to obtain more information about the lands to the west, particularly the rich "kingdom of the Saguenay" that Taignoagny and Domagaya had spoken of, the French mariner kidnapped them, their father, Donnacona, and three of his principal supporters. The French believed this fabulous land to be rich in gold and silver — a second Mexico. (In reality, the stories of the Saguenay probably referred to copper deposits around Lake Superior.) After promising to return his hostages the following year, Cartier left in the spring of 1536. Four children presented to Cartier by Donnacona and the chief of a neighbouring village went along as well. The ten First Nations captives never saw "Canada" again.

Cartier entered Saint-Malo in July 1536, after an absence of 14 months. Although he had not discovered great wealth, he had nonetheless made some important contributions: he proved that Newfoundland was an island, charted much of the Gulf of St. Lawrence, and recorded in his journal the existence of a great river flowing from deep in the interior — the St. Lawrence. His geographical exploration remained unsurpassed by any other French explorer until Champlain, in the early 1600s.

THE CARTIER–ROBERVAL EXPEDITION, 1541–1542

War between France and Spain delayed Cartier's third voyage until 1541. This time, the French navigator left with a mandate to found a colony and locate the famed "kingdom of the Saguenay" and the Northwest Passage. The expedition split into two groups. Cartier led the first group to Cap Rouge, about 15 km upstream from Stadacona. Here he unloaded cattle and supplies and planted crops, making it quite clear that he and the 150 French colonists intended to stay. Very little information has survived regarding the settlement that winter, but it was later reported that First Nations killed at least 35 settlers.

By the spring, Cartier had had enough. With a cargo of iron pyrites and quartz that he thought were gold and diamonds, he sailed for France. A French proverb still used in Brittany and Normandy owes its origin to this episode: *"Faux comme un diamant du Canada"* (fake as a Canadian diamond).

Cartier's superior, Jean-François de La Rocque de Roberval, arrived at Cap Rouge with the second part of the expedition, just after Cartier's hasty departure. He had with him some 200 settlers; they too experienced a terrible winter at the site of Cartier's settlement, which they rebuilt. Fifty colonists died from scurvy. The next summer Roberval also returned to France. An inscription on a French map of 1550 explains the reasons for the colony's failure: "It was impossible to trade with the people of that country because of their austerity, the intemperate climate of said country, and the slight profit."

France, still at war with Spain, was torn in the 1560s by religious wars. For thirty years Catholics battled Protestants, until the Edict of Nantes in 1598 solved the religious problem. It acknowledged Catholicism as the official religion of France, while allowing the Hugenots, as the Protestants were called, the right to worship, and to enjoy political privileges, including the right of holding public office.

During the French Wars of Religion (1562–1598), France left Canada to its Native inhabitants. French fishers, whalers, and traders continued to come in great numbers to northeastern North America, but France did not attempt colonization again for another half-century. The harsh climate, hostile relations with the Native peoples, and the failure to find gold combined to give the French a poor image of Canada. In the late 1550s, France directed its colonization efforts toward Brazil instead and, in the early 1560s, toward the present-day southeastern United States. By the late sixteenth century, the French monarchy was too busy fighting the Wars of Religion to establish settlements overseas.

FISHING AND TRADING OFF THE EAST COAST OF NORTH AMERICA

European fishers maintained contact with Newfoundland. Between March and October of each year, large fishing fleets — Portuguese, Basque, French, and English — gathered there. They supplied the markets of western Europe and the Mediterranean with the "beef of the sea" (cod). The Newfoundland fishery had become big business by the mid-sixteenth century. With an estimated 10 000 individuals visiting annually, it provided a livelihood for twice as many fishers as did the fisheries of the Gulf of Mexico and the Caribbean combined, where the great Spanish fleets sailed.

The success of the Newfoundland cod fishery initially depended on the harvesting of salt left by the evaporation of seawater. This salt was better than the mineral variety for curing fish because it was more uniform in quality. France, Spain, and Portugal produced an abundance of "solar salt," but England, not as blessed with sunshine, did not. This hurt England in the age of the "green fishery," the term sailors used to describe a method of salting fish immediately upon catching them, then transporting them back to Europe for drying. To compensate for their lack of solar salt, the English developed "dry fishing" — drying their lightly salted fish before

Part of Mercator's Map, 1569.

Source: D.G.G. Kerr, ed., *A Historical Atlas of Canada* (Toronto: Thomas Nelson & Sons, 1961), p. 11.

returning home. The sun-cured codfish lasted indefinitely if kept dry, and could be reconstituted by soaking it in water.

English fishing expeditions to Newfoundland became an annual event. From December to February the English cleaned, overhauled, and completely fitted their ships. Then in March they left from the great ports in southwestern England — Plymouth, Poole, Dartmouth — with sufficient provisions and stores for eight months. Estimates of the number of English ships involved in Newfoundland expeditions around the year 1600 vary from 250 to 400, and the number of men from 6000 to 10 000. These expeditions made good England's claims to the Avalon Peninsula on Newfoundland's east coast, the location of the best English fishing and processing sites.

The English practised inshore fishing methods that they had first used off the coast of Iceland. They fished from open boats or from barrels suspended over the ship's side. Before the fishing began, they searched for the most convenient "room" — a tract of land on the waterfront of a cove or harbour adjacent to their fishery. There they constructed the sheds, drying racks ("flakes"), wharves ("stages"), and other facilities where they landed their boats and processed their catch. A large fishing room was called a "plantation," and its owner, if he lived permanently on it, a "planter." Most of the ships carried a crew of twenty, of whom a dozen fished while the rest cured the fish on shore. The fishing day was an arduous one. Up before dawn, the men fished until 4:00 P.M. Then, at about 6:00 P.M., the first boat reached the staging to unload the catch. The men worked 18 to 20 hours a day to take advantage of the run of fish. The method of curing involved splitting, lightly salting, and drying the cod, producing an excellent "stock" fish that did not spoil during the long voyages to the Caribbean.

England profited greatly from the decline of Spanish naval strength after the defeat of the Spanish Armada in 1588. No longer was Spain the great power it had been in the mid-sixteenth century. England, in the seventeenth century, gained a market for its dried cod in southern Europe, including Spain. The English sold the firmest and whitest cod in the Mediterranean. They classified slightly damaged fish as second grade and also shipped it to overseas buyers. They packed the poorest-grade fish in casks and sold it to slave owners in the West Indies.

THE BASQUE WHALING STATIONS

 Basque whalers, from their homeland in the border region of France and Spain, joined the cod fishers in the early sixteenth century and carried out whaling in the Strait of Belle Isle. Europe's first commercial whalers came prepared to set up a long-distance fishery. The south coast of Labrador became the first region of northeastern North America to undergo extensive exploitation by Europeans. Whaling stations flourished there for half a century. Sixteenth-century Europeans treasured whale oil as a fuel for lamps, an all-purpose lubricant, an additive to drugs, and a major ingredient of scores of products, such as soap and pitch. At its peak, the fishery employed about 2000 men, who remained in Newfoundland–Labrador waters for 6 months each season, from June until January. At the Basque shore stations, Inuit and First Nations groups could obtain European materials on an annual basis from fixed locations in southern Labrador, and perhaps on the Gaspé coast as well. Marc Lescarbot, the early French chronicler, noted that the Native people trading along the Gaspé shore during the first decade of the seventeenth century spoke a Basque–Algonquian trade language that was "half Basque." This became a "contact" language, one used in speaking to the Europeans. Other trade languages would later develop elsewhere, such as Chinook on the Pacific coast.

ENGLISH ACTIVITY IN THE NORTH ATLANTIC AND ARCTIC

England sponsored a number of expeditions north of Newfoundland in the late sixteenth and early seventeenth centuries. In 1576, only a few months before Sir Francis Drake left to plunder Spanish shipping in the Pacific Ocean, Martin Frobisher, 37 years old and a mariner of great repute, sailed northerly in search of a Northwest Passage to India and China. Off southern Baffin Island, Frobisher encountered Inuit, who came to trade meat and furs for metal objects and clothing. The Inuit showed that they were no strangers to European ships by doing gymnastic exercises in the ship's rigging. They indicated that they wanted to trade. Evidently they had already encountered vessels of the Newfoundland fishing fleet and had probably traded with the fishers, from whom they obtained iron. Frobisher himself discovered this when, in a skirmish with the Inuit, he was struck by an iron-tipped arrow.

Community Portrait

The Basque Whaling Community of Red Bay, Labrador, 1550–1600

In the mid-1970s, Selma Barkham, a researcher employed by the Public Archives (now the National Archives) of Canada, discovered a forgotten chapter of Canadian history. While it had long been known that Basque whalers had hunted off the Labrador coast, the extent of their operations, and the location of their whaling stations, was not known. While examining wills, lawsuits, mortgages, and insurance policies in Basque archives in Spain, Barkham came across a wealth of information on the whale fishery in the Strait of Belle Isle, separating Labrador from the northern tip of Newfoundland. The Strait was excellent for whale hunting, as it acted as a funnel through which migrating whales passed in great numbers.

Barkham made a preliminary investigation of the southern Labrador coast with James Tuck, an archaeologist from Memorial University of Newfoundland, and several other scientists in the summer of 1977. All down the coastline they found evidence that the Basques had been in the region. At several locations they found red patches on the beaches, the remains of the imported red roof tile used by the Basque whalers for their buildings. Tuck returned in the summer of 1978 to excavate the most promising site, on Saddle Island in Red Bay, one of the finest harbours in the Strait of Belle Isle. On the harbour side of the island he found fragments of old stone walls stained with a black material, later identified as burnt whale oil. The archaeologist had discovered the remains of the ovens where whale blubber was tried (boiled down) into oil. During future visits to Saddle Island, Tuck and his team located additional evidence of Basque activity. They found the remains of houses and of the workshops where the coopers (barrel-makers) constructed the barrels to ship whale oil.

In 1978, Robert Grenier, head of marine archaeology for Parks Canada, began underwater investigations that greatly complemented Barkham's archival research and Tuck's archaeological work on Saddle Island. He discovered the well-preserved remains of a sunken Basque ship only thirty metres offshore of the Saddle Island station. It had gone down in a squall with a load of nearly 1000 barrels of whale oil. Subsequent investigations in the icy waters led to the location of the ship's compass, anchor, rudder, and loaded swivel gun. In 1979, the Historic Sites and Monuments Board of Canada designated the forgotten Basque whaling station of Red Bay a place of national historic interest.

Red Bay appears to have been the Basque whalers' favourite whaling station. Normally about ten galleons arrived in Red Bay every summer in the late sixteenth century. Depending on a ship's tonnage, crews ranged from 50 to 120 men. During the whaling season, the men harpooned whales from small open whale boats. Once killed, the dead whales were towed back to the galleon left moored in the harbour. After the men removed large strips or slabs of blubber, they hauled it ashore. At the whaling station they rendered it into whale oil in huge ovens or tryworks, containing several ovens, sheltered by roofs of red tile brought to Red Bay for that purpose.

An artist's reconstruction of Basque galleons riding at anchor in Red Bay, Labrador, the largest whaling port on the Strait of Belle Isle. Smoke billows forth from the massive stone tryworks built by the Basques to render blubber into whale oil. Painting by Richard Schlecht.

"Discovery in Labrador: A 16th-Century Basque Whaling Port and Its Sunken Fleet," *National Geographic*, 168, 1 (July 1985): 42–43. Richard Schlecht.

The graves located at Red Bay reveal that the tradespeople were sturdy and relatively young. Basque males of all ages, some as young as 11 or 12, participated. The captains hired in the late winter and early spring, and they did allow females to join their crews. Each crew member had to produce, at personal expense, essential items, such as clothing, suitable for great variations in climate. The Basque crews earned shares in the season's catch rather than fixed salaries. Constant upward mobility allowed individuals to climb the shipboard hierarchy and, with special training, to become harpooners or pilots themselves. For food the ships brought large amounts of cider, wine, and ship's biscuit. At Red Bay the men enjoyed a diet based largely on cod and salmon, with an occasional piece of caribou or a wild duck.

Between mid-June and early July the whaling ships left for Labrador. An average Atlantic crossing in the sixteenth century normally took a month. Basque whalers commonly stayed in Labrador well into the winter, returning to Spain by the end of January, by which time the Strait of Belle Isle had normally frozen over. Their residency in Labrador in winter required solid buildings, hence the Basques imported large amounts of Iberian tile for the construction of their buildings.

The whaling effort at stations such as Red Bay proved so effective that it led to a massive depletion in northwestern Atlantic whale stocks. Another factor that helped to put an end to the Basque Labrador whale fishery by the end of the sixteenth century was the ill-fated Spanish Armada of 1588, the attempted Spanish naval invasion of Britain, a disaster that claimed many Basque ships and sailors' lives. One written source indicates that perhaps another contributing factor was Native resistance, particularly by the Inuit, to the Basque presence on the southern Labrador coast. In any event, the Basque whaling community at Red Bay vanished shortly after the beginning of the seventeenth century.

Further Reading

Selma Barkham, "The Basques: Filling a gap in our history between Jacques Cartier and Champlain," *Canadian Geographical Journal*, 96, 1, (Feb./March, 1978): 8–19.

Robert McGhee, "Chapter 10. The Grand Bay," *Canada Rediscovered* (Ottawa: Canadian Museum of Civilization, 1991): 141–153.

James A. Tuck and Robert Grenier, *Red Bay, Labrador. World Whaling Capital*, A.D. *1550–1600* (St. John's, Newfoundland: Atlantic Archaeology Ltd., 1989).

Frobisher failed to find a passage to the Orient, either on this first journey or on two subsequent voyages in 1577 and 1578. Ten years later, John Davis followed up on Frobisher's work in three successive summers (1585–87), but without success. The necessary maritime technology for the penetration of the Arctic Archipelago simply did not exist in the late sixteenth century. It was as impossible a goal for that age as a landing on the moon would have been for the nineteenth century.

EUROPEAN TRADE WITH THE FIRST NATIONS

Unfortunately, little contemporary information has survived about how the First Nations and Inuit perceived the first Europeans they met. The information that does exist attests to the Native peoples' amazement at the range and abundance of material goods that the newcomers possessed. The Hurons of the Great Lakes called the French "Agnonha," Iron People.

The First Nations retained their superbly crafted bark canoes, snowshoes, toboggans, and bark-covered wigwams, because they were superior to what the Europeans could offer. They willingly traded, however, many animal skins in exchange for the Europeans' metal tools and weapons. The newcomers' steel axes lightened the labour of gathering firewood. Their copper cooking pots were not fragile like pottery vessels or perishable like wooden boxes and birchbark kettles. Steel knives proved more durable than stone knives. Steel awls and needles made sewing and the working of hides and leather much easier.

European trade goods entered the extensive Native trading networks, and interior groups obtained them long before they ever saw a European. Archaeology has confirmed, for example, the presence, by the early sixteenth century, of European trade goods among the Seneca south of Lake Ontario, an Iroquoian nation located hundreds of kilometres from the Atlantic.

Yet, if the Native peoples of North America initially regarded the European newcomers with awe (interpreting their possession of metal objects as evidence of some great supernatural power), the amazement quickly passed. Missionary reports from the early seventeenth century reveal that First Nations soon noted the slowness of the French in mastering Native languages and in learning to use canoes, snowshoes, and everything else that seemed to them to be commonplace.

Encounter with Eskimos, a watercolour by John White, an English artist who travelled with Martin Frobisher on his second expedition to Baffin Island in 1577.

A Historical Portrait

☞ Martin Frobisher

Martin Frobisher was one of the most famous mariners of Elizabethan England. In the late sixteenth century, his name was as well known as that of Francis Drake and John Hawkins. Brave and impetuous, a man of action, he became the first English pioneer of northern Canadian exploration. His first Arctic voyage of 1576 marked the beginning of a more than two-century-long quest to find the Northwest Passage, the route to Asia through Arctic waters. Historian Leslie Neatby has written of him, that, as his original achievements were all in Canadian waters, "he may justly be recognized as the first Anglo-Canadian"[1]

As a boy he does not appear to have received much schooling. All his life he was an atrocious speller. On documents his name appears in several versions, including "Furbiser," "Frobiser," "Furbisher," and even "Flourbyssher." In 1553, at the age of 14, young Martin left on his first sea voyage. Frobisher survived the trip to West Africa, although three-quarters of the expedition did not. Other African voyages followed, as well as privateering ventures seizing enemy vessels on the high seas.

For years the veteran sea rover dreamt of leading a search for the Northwest Passage. Finally, in 1576, a group of London merchants financially backed his proposed expedition. Of the three vessels that left England, only Frobisher's made it to the huge bay on Baffin Island that now bears his name. He travelled up the bay for 200 km, which he took to be a strait with the Americas on one side and Asia on the other. Before returning to England, he took back samples of ore that he believed contained gold. Several London assayers pronounced the ore as valueless, but one was found who stated that it contained gold. That single upbeat report sufficed to send Frobisher back the next year to search for more ore. He returned with 200 tonnes and a gold rush began.

Frobisher's third voyage in 1578 consisted of 15 ships, the largest naval fleet that has ever been used in Arctic exploration. In spite of a hazardous journey, all but two of the vessels reached Frobisher Bay. The sailors spent the following weeks gathering and loading ore. On Kodlunarn Island, one of the mining sites at the southeastern tip of Baffin Island, they built a house of stone and lime. Expecting to return, they wanted to test the durability of the structure over the winter. Believing that they had struck pay dirt, the expedition then returned with 1350 t of ore.

Disaster awaited the expedition's return. All attempts to smelt precious metal out of the rock failed. Frobisher's "gold" created a huge scandal when it turned out to be only pyrite. Financial ruin followed for Frobisher's backers. The veteran sea captain's reputation fell momentarily, but then rose when he took a leading role in repelling the Spanish Armada in 1588. Frobisher died six years later while storming an enemy fort in France.

During all of his voyages Frobisher had been in contact with the Inuit. Nearly three centuries later, in the early 1860s, the American Charles Francis Hall found the ruins of the expedition's house on Kodlunarn Island. He also discovered that the Inuit, with whom Frobisher had hostile relations (he kidnapped several of them and took them back to England, where they quickly died from disease), had an accurate oral record of his voyages three centuries earlier. Their stories, which had been passed on from generation to generation, confirmed many of the details found in the written record. On account of the lengthy court cases after the return of the third voyage in 1578, the written records on the Frobisher expeditions are considerable.

[1] Leslie H. Neatby, "Martin Frobisher," *Arctic* 36 (3) (Sept. 1983): 374.

The original inhabitants of present-day Atlantic and Arctic Canada witnessed the arrival of the first Europeans — the Norse — around A.D. 1000, and that of the English, Portuguese, French, Spanish, and Basques five centuries later. The early European navigators crossed the North Atlantic at great personal risk. John Cabot, the Corte-Real brothers, and Sir Humphrey Gilbert (who claimed Newfoundland for England in 1583) lost their lives during their explorations. In the words of the American maritime historian Samuel Eliot Morison, "North America became a graveyard for European ships and sailors."[3] Yet the Europeans persisted. Some came in search of a profitable Northwest Passage to China and the Indies. Others — the vast majority — were lured by the promise of economic gain in the ruthless exploitation of the cod and whale fisheries, and later in the fur trade. Yet, as late as 1600, no permanent European settlement existed in northern North America.

A view of Quebec, showing First Nations cooking with a large metal kettle and wearing European cloth or blankets, which indicates the Native peoples' growing reliance on European goods. Cartouche of a manuscript map of North America by Jean-Baptiste-Louis Franquelin (1699), reproduced by A.L. Pinart in 1893.

National Archives of Canada/C-15791.

NOTES

1. Morris Bishop, *Champlain: The Life of Fortitude* (Toronto: McClelland & Stewart, 1963 [1948]), p. 26.
2. H.P. Biggar, ed., *The Voyages of Jacques Cartier* (Ottawa: King's Printer, 1924), p. 245. For an important discussion of other possible origins of the word "Canada" see Olive P. Dickason, "Appendix 1: Origin of the Name 'Canada,'" in *The Myth of the Savage and the Beginnings of French Colonialism in the Americas* (Edmonton: University of Alberta Press, 1984), pp. 279–80.
3. Samuel Eliot Morison, *The European Discovery of America: The Northern Voyages, A.D. 500–1600* (New York: Oxford University Press, 1971), p. xi.

LINKING TO THE PAST

Early Exploration and Settlement of Newfoundland and Labrador
http://www.heritage.nf.ca/exploration/early_ex.html

An account of exploration and early settlement from the arrival of the Norse to John Cabot's voyages; includes information on geographical knowledge and navigation methods.

Leif Eiriksson
http://viking.no/e/people/leif/e-leiv.htm

An overview of the lives and adventures of Eric the Red, Leif Eiriksson, and Thorvaldr, Leif's brother.

L'Anse aux Meadows
http://collections.ic.gc.ca/vikings

Information pertaining to the L'Anse aux Meadows historic site, including discovery, history, and reconstruction. For more information, visit http://www.pc.gc.ca/lhn-nhs/nl/meadows/index_E.asp.

Later Exploration and Settlement of Newfoundland and Labrador
http://www.heritage.nf.ca/exploration/later_ex.html

An overview of exploration after Cabot, including contributions of Portuguese, English, and French explorers, as well as an illustrated section on cartography.

Jacques Cartier's Voyages
http://www.civilization.ca/vmnf/explor/carti_e1.html

An account of Jacques Cartier's voyages and colonization efforts.

Basque Whaling at Red Bay, Labrador
http://www.labradorstraits.net/redbay.shtml

An introduction to Basque whaling at Red Bay in the sixteenth century. For a closer look at what life at a whaling station was like, go to http://www.civilization.ca/hist/canp1/ca04eng.html.

RELATED READINGS

R. Douglas Francis and Donald B. Smith, eds., *Readings in Canadian History: Pre-Confederation*, 6th ed. (Toronto: Nelson Thomson Learning, 2002), contains the following essays relevant to this topic: Keith Matthews, "The Nature and the Framework of Newfoundland History," pp. 113–119; Richard White and William Cronon, "Ecological Change and Indian–White Relations," pp. 4–21; and Arthur J. Ray, "Fur Trade History as an Aspect of Native History," pp. 51–60.

BIBLIOGRAPHY

Well-written summaries of the early European explorers' accounts include Samuel Eliot Morison, *The European Discovery of America: The Northern Voyages,* A.D. *500–1600* (New York: Oxford University Press, 1971); Daniel J. Boorstin, *The Discoverers: A History of Man's Search to Know His World and Himself* (New York: Random House, 1983); and Robert McGhee, *Canada Rediscovered* (Ottawa: Canadian Museum of Civilization/Libre Expression, 1991). The primary texts are available in David Quinn, ed., *New American World: A Documentary History of North America to 1615*, 5 vols. (New York: Arno Press, 1979). Economic aspects are briefly reviewed by Michael Bliss in *Northern Enterprise: Five Centuries of Canadian Business* (Toronto: McClelland & Stewart, 1987). The *Dictionary of Canadian Biography*, vol. 1, *1000–1700* (Toronto: University of Toronto Press, 1966), contains biographical portraits. It is now available online: www.biographi.ca. Ralph T. Pastore provides a bibliographical guide to the secondary literature in his essay "Beginnings to 1600," in M. Brook Taylor, ed., *Canadian History: A Reader's Guide*, vol. 1, *Beginnings to Confederation* (Toronto: University of Toronto Press, 1994), pp. 3–32.

For the Norse experience in Greenland and North America see Robert McGhee, "Contact between Native North Americans and the Medieval Norse: A Review of the Evidence," *American Antiquity* 49(1) (1984): 4–26. Helge and Anne Stine Ingstad tell the story of the discovery of L'Anse aux Meadows in *The Viking Discovery of America. The Excavation of a Norse Settlement in L'Anse aux Meadows, Newfoundland* (St. John's, Newfoundland: Breakwater, 2000). Peter Schledermann's "Inuit Prehistory and Archaeology," in Morris Zaslow, ed., *A Century of Canada's Arctic Islands* (Ottawa: Royal Society of Canada, 1981), pp. 245–56, reviews the finds of Norse objects on Ellesmere Island. Joel Berglund reviews the end of the Norse Greenlandic communities in "The Decline of the Norse Settlements in Greenland," *Arctic Anthropology* 23(1–2) (1986): 109–35. Peter E. Pope reviews the various theories of where Cabot landed in *The Many Landfalls of John Cabot* (Toronto: University of Toronto Press, 1997). Another study is Peter Firstbrook's *The Voyage of the Matthew: John Cabot and the Discovery of North America* (Toronto: McClelland & Stewart, 1997).

Bruce G. Trigger, *The Children of Aataentsic: A History of the Huron People to 1660*, vol. 1 (Montreal/Kingston: McGill-Queen's University Press, 1976), provides background information on the St. Lawrence Iroquoians' reactions to Cartier and Roberval. See also Trigger's *Natives and Newcomers: Canada's "Heroic Age" Reconsidered* (Montreal/Kingston: McGill-Queen's University Press, 1985). For an understanding of the Cartier–Roberval expeditions consult the following two surveys: Olive P. Dickason, *The Myth of the Savage and the Beginnings of French Colonialism in the Americas* (Edmonton: University of Alberta Press, 1984); and Marcel Trudel, *The Beginnings of New France, 1524–1663* (Toronto: McClelland & Stewart, 1973). Ramsay Cook has edited H.P. Biggar's translation of Cartier's journeys; see Jacques Cartier, *The Voyages of Jacques Cartier* (Toronto: University of Toronto Press, 1993). Cornelius Jaenen reviews the cultural interaction between the French and the Native peoples in *Friend and Foe* (Toronto: McClelland & Stewart, 1976). Ralph Pastore reviews "The Sixteenth Century: Aboriginal Peoples and European Contact" in Phillip A. Buckner and John G. Reid, eds., *The Atlantic Region to Confederation: A History* (Toronto: University of Toronto Press, 1994), pp. 22–39. Leslie C. Green and Olive P. Dickason examine the ideology that motivated the European occupation of the Americas in *The Law of Nations and the New World* (Edmonton: University of Alberta Press, 1989).

On Basque activity in northeastern North America see Selma Barkham, "A Note on the Strait of Belle-Isle during the Period of Basque Contact with Indians and Inuit," *Etudes/Inuit/Studies* 4 (1980): 51–58; and "The Basque Whaling Establishments in Labrador, 1536–1632: A Summary," *Arctic* 37 (1984): 515–19. A well-illustrated series of articles (including contributions by James A. Tuck and Robert Grenier) entitled "Discovery in Labrador: A 16th-Century Basque Whaling Port and Its Sunken Fleet" appeared in *National Geographic* 168(1) (July 1985): 40–71. Jean-Pierre Proulx reviews the Basque arrival in *Basque Whaling in Labrador in the 16th Century* (Ottawa: National Historic Sites, Parks Services, 1993). Peter Bakker has written on the Basque–Algonquian trade language in "Basque Pidgin Vocabulary in European–Algonquian Trade Contacts," in William Cowan, ed., *Papers of the 15th Algonquian Conference* (Ottawa: Carleton University, 1988), pp. 7–15. Laurier Turgeon examines First Nation and French contact in "French Fishers, Fur Traders, and Amerindians during the Sixteenth Century: History and Archaeology," *William and Mary Quarterly*, 3rd series, 55 (4) (October 1998): 585–610. The ecological consequences of the European arrival in the waters off northeastern North America are described by Farley Mowat in his popular study *Sea of Slaughter* (Toronto: McClelland & Stewart, 1984). A delightful book is Mark Kurlansky's *Cod: A Biography of the Fish That Changed the World* (London: Penguin Books, 1998).

The impact of the Europeans on the First Nations' relationship to nature is reviewed by Calvin Martin in *Keepers of the Game: Indian–Animal Relationships and the Fur Trade* (Berkeley: University of California Press, 1978). This controversial study must be supplemented by Shepard Krech III, ed., *Indians, Animals and the Fur Trade: A Critique of Keepers of the Game* (Athens: University of Georgia Press, 1981).

A survey of the Frobisher and Davis expeditions in Arctic waters appears in L.H. Neatby, In *Quest of the North West Passage* (Toronto: Longmans, 1958). Robert McGhee's *The Arctic Voyages of Martin Frobisher* (Montreal/Kingston: McGill-Queen's University Press, 2001) provides a readable introduction to the story of early British Arctic exploration. William W. Fitzhugh's essay, "Early Contacts North of Newfoundland before A.D. 1600," in William W. Fitzhugh, ed., *Culture in Contact: The European Impact on Native Cultural Institutions in Eastern North America, A.D. 1000–1800* (Washington, DC: Smithsonian Institution Press, 1985), pp. 23–43, reviews the period between the Norse expeditions and those of Davis and Frobisher. Susan Rowley has written a fascinating article on the Inuit oral accounts of the Frobisher expeditions: "Frobisher Miksanut: Inuit Accounts of the Frobisher Voyages," in William W. Fitzhugh and Jacqueline S. Olin, eds., *Archeology of the Frobisher Voyages* (Washington: Smithsonian Institution Press, 1993).

For excellent maps of early European exploration see: R. Cole Harris, ed., *Historical Atlas of Canada*, vol. 1, *From the Beginning to 1800* (Toronto: University of Toronto Press, 1987); and Derek Hayes, *Historical Atlas of Canada. Canada's History Illustrated with Original Maps* (Vancouver: Douglas and McIntyre, 2002).

THE BEGINNINGS OF NEW FRANCE

TIME LINE

1603 – Samuel de Champlain accompanies the Gravé expedition to northeastern North America

1605 – Champlain and Pierre Du Gua de Monts establish Port-Royal, a French post on the Bay of Fundy in present-day Nova Scotia, but abandon it in 1607

1608 – Champlain builds a new fortified trading post at Quebec

1609 – For the first time Champlain and the French clash with the Iroquois or Five Nations initiating a nearly century-long conflict

1627 – Establishment of the Company of One Hundred Associates, formed to speed up the development of the colony of New France

1629 – The English seize and hold Quebec for three years

1632 – The Jesuit order obtains a monopoly over the mission work in New France

1634 – The settlement of Trois-Rivières is founded

1635 – Champlain dies on Christmas Day

1639 – Marie de l'Incarnation and two Ursuline sisters arrive at Quebec

1642 – Ville-Marie, later known as Montreal, is founded

1645 – Establishment of the Habitants' Company to replace the debt-ridden Company of One Hundred Associates

I n the late sixteenth century, no fabric then available rivalled the warmth, wearability, and beauty of furs. Persons of importance in Europe wore them to display their rank and wealth. As beaver had become almost extinct in Europe, merchants eagerly sought even cast-off First Nations beaver robes. When the robes were worn or slept in, the long guard hairs of the beaver pelts loosened and fell out, leaving only the soft underfur. Hat makers could then process the underfur into a smooth felt unequalled by any type of woven cloth. By the end of the sixteenth century, hundreds of French traders sailed to Tadoussac, at the mouth of the Saguenay River in Quebec, to bargain for pelts.

Jacques Cartier's three voyages established a French claim to the Gulf of St. Lawrence, but international recognition of France's claim would come only with successful occupation. It was the fur trade in the early 1580s that led to France's return, and to its permanent occupation of the St. Lawrence valley. In the Gulf of St. Lawrence and along the Atlantic coastline, the fur trade began as a by-product of the fishing industry. By returning each year to the same locality, the French established good trading relationships with the local First Nations. In the 1580s, French merchants sent out ships commissioned solely to trade for furs. The French government decided to bring the trade under the control of fur-trading companies. For a private fur-trading company to obtain a monopoly, it had to fulfil two promises: to promote settlement and to send Roman Catholic missionaries to Christianize the Native peoples.

THE RISE OF THE FUR TRADE

Fur coats, muffs, wraps, gloves, fur-trimmed garments, and most important, wide-brimmed beaver hats all commanded high prices. Fur proved an ideal product for the European traders.

Initially, the First Nations did not perceive the fur trade as posing any danger to their independence. By the early seventeenth century, however, the Algonquians on the Atlantic coast had lost much of their self-sufficiency and become reliant on the Europeans. The fur trade transformed the coastal groups from hunters and fishers into trappers. Prior to European contact, the Mi'kmaq spent more than half the year living on the coast, since the sea supplied as much as 90 percent of their diet. Now they spent long periods each year hunting inland for fur-bearing animals. This change in their traditional activities affected their winter diet. They no longer accumulated their usual summer food stores and instead relied partly on the dried foods they received in trade.

Tadoussac, at the mouth of the Saguenay River, became France's principal trading centre on the Gulf of St. Lawrence. Pre-existing trading networks led from there to Hudson Bay and the Great Lakes. In the mid-1580s, as many as 20 vessels at a time called at Tadoussac in the summer.

Trade reached such a volume by the 1590s that the French Crown established a monopoly to control it. But the monopolists' colonization schemes were expensive. All early attempts failed: the French colonists suffered a disastrous winter at Tadoussac in 1600–01, when only five of the sixteen settlers survived the winter. An outpost established in 1598 on Sable Island (about 200 km off the coast of Nova Scotia, close to the fishing grounds) also failed.

In 1603, François Gravé Du Pont, an experienced captain who had already made fishing voyages up the St. Lawrence, became the French monopolists' representative. Could the St. Lawrence valley support a settlement? On Gravé's ship in 1603, as a sort of observer-chronicler, sailed Samuel de Champlain, a young mariner in his twenties. The two men remained partners for nearly 30 years and together helped establish the first permanent French settlement in the Americas.

SAMUEL DE CHAMPLAIN

Considering Champlain's key role in the history of New France from 1608 to his death in 1635, surprisingly little is known about his background. He was probably born about 1580; most likely he came from Brouage, on the Bay of Biscay in western France — one of the principal sources of salt for the fishing fleet. At an early age he went to sea and became a competent ship's captain and an authority on navigation. The earliest references to him document his service in the royal army. As a soldier in his mid-teens, young Samuel was toughened by service in a Renaissance European army whose soldiers' actions, in the words of French historian E. Pocquet, could be summarized by five phrases: to steal possessions, to carry off cattle, to burn homes, to kill men, and to rape women.[1]

After his army service, Champlain undertook a voyage to the West Indies that kept him away from France for two and a half years. He returned to France in 1601, and two years later was invited to sail with Gravé.

Much had changed in the St. Lawrence valley since the journeys of Cartier and Roberval. Champlain saw large numbers of Montagnais and Algonquins, both Algonquian-speaking groups, at Tadoussac and small groups at several encampments along the St. Lawrence, but the peoples of Stadacona and Hochelaga had mysteriously left.

Unfortunately, we have only hypotheses, and no complete accounts, of the St. Lawrence valley from the time of Cartier and Roberval in the mid-sixteenth century to Champlain's visit in 1603. Canadian economic historian Harold Innis believed that eastern Algonquian nations drove out the St. Lawrence Iroquoians. They had obtained iron weapons before the St. Lawrence Iroquoians, which gave them a technological advantage in warfare.

In the 1970s, Bruce Trigger, an anthropologist who has done extensive research on the ethnohistory of northeastern North America, advanced another theory. Trigger speculates that the landlocked New York Iroquois wanted European trade goods, but found them difficult to obtain from either the Saint Lawrence Iroquoians or the Algonquians. Consequently, the Iroquois raided and dispersed their neighbours, the St. Lawrence Iroquoians, some of whom may have moved west to join the Hurons on Georgian Bay on Lake Huron. Archaeologists, Trigger states, have established that European goods reached all of the New York Iroquois groups by 1600. These, he surmises, must have been largely obtained as booty from the St. Lawrence Iroquoians. Although both explanations for the disappearance of the St. Lawrence Iroquoians are plausible, the data are lacking to reach any definite conclusions. It is also possible that European diseases, inadvertently introduced by Cartier, Roberval, and the French settlers, wiped out these people.

Following Cartier's route as far as Montreal, Gravé and Champlain made a careful examination of the St. Lawrence valley during the summer of 1603. They heard much about the *pays d'en haut* (literally, upper country), north and west of the St. Lawrence valley from the Algonquians who had a good working knowledge of the lower Great Lakes since their trading network reached inland to the Hurons' country. They also learned for the first time of a nation called the "good Iroquois" (the Hurons) who lived by a great lake to the northwest (Lake Huron). The Native peoples also told them about the existence of Lakes Ontario and Erie, and the extraordinary Niagara Falls.

THE FRENCH IN ACADIA

Today we take for granted that Quebec was the natural site for France's first permanent settlement in present-day Canada. In reality, however, the French initially rejected this location. From 1604 to 1607 Pierre Du Gua de Monts, the new fur-trade monopolist, accompanied by Gravé

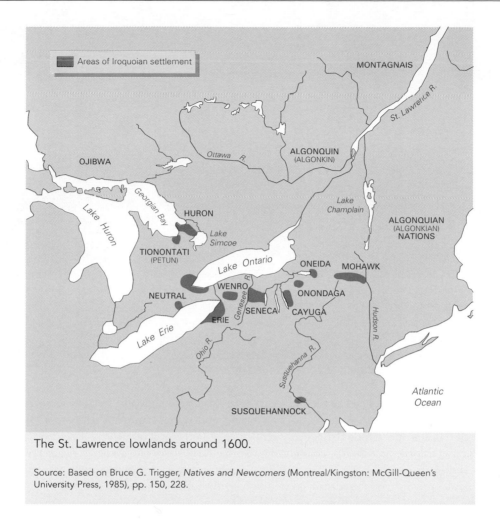

The St. Lawrence lowlands around 1600.

Source: Based on Bruce G. Trigger, *Natives and Newcomers* (Montreal/Kingston: McGill-Queen's University Press, 1985), pp. 150, 228.

and Champlain, searched elsewhere for the best place to establish a colony. To escape the competition of traders who refused to respect de Monts's monopoly of the St. Lawrence fur trade, the French sailed south to the present-day Maritime provinces, a region with a climate milder than that of the St. Lawrence region and one potentially rich in minerals. They also searched for a more southerly location for the colony in the hope that they might still find a route to Asia.

Armed with vice-regal powers and a 10-year fur-trading monopoly, de Monts led his colonists to the south coast of Nova Scotia. They sailed up the Bay of Fundy and entered the Annapolis Basin, which Champlain named Port-Royal. The party crossed to the New Brunswick shore, passed a large river (which they named the Saint John River), and wintered on a small island near the mouth of the St. Croix River, now on the border between Maine and New Brunswick. Roughly half of the expedition's 79 men died of scurvy before spring, and many more were close to death.

THE FRENCH AT PORT-ROYAL

After a summer exploring the coastline, the French stayed the next winter on the mainland at Port-Royal. This colony became the first European agricultural settlement in what is now Canada. The French continued to explore the coastline the following summer and then wintered again at Port-Royal.

The Port-Royal settlement was rebuilt based on historical and archaeological evidence. Many visitors come to this historic site in Nova Scotia today.

Tourism Nova Scotia.

   In 1606–07, the French had their first successful Acadian winter and, in fact, enjoyed themselves, thanks largely to the Order of Good Cheer founded by Champlain. The order, the first social club in Canada, required that every gentleman at Port-Royal take turns at becoming chief steward and caterer for a day. Ceremoniously wearing the chain of office, each steward prepared meals and made out the next day's menus. In friendly rivalry, each man vied with the others to serve game and fish in abundance, in addition to the usual bread and salt cod. They sang familiar songs and composed new ones on the spot. In 1606 Marc Lescarbot, a lawyer in the party, presented *Théâtre de Neptune*, the first theatrical production in Canadian history.

Despite the improved situation that winter, de Monts decided to abandon Port-Royal. After three years of considerable expenditures, unsuccessfully searching for mineral resources and the Northwest Passage, de Monts realized the area's limitations. He could not enforce his fur-trade monopoly along the winding and indented coasts of the Maritimes. A rival needed only a ship, a crew, and a supply of trade goods to sail to the Maritimes and make his fortune. Annually, about 80 ships poached on de Monts's domain. Furthermore, he made insufficient profit to justify the cost of maintaining a post at Port-Royal. Ironically, the very year that the French abandoned Acadia (the name given to the area of what is now Maine, New Brunswick, and Nova Scotia), the English established their first permanent settlement at Jamestown in Virginia.

THE FOUNDING OF QUEBEC

 In 1608 Champlain and Gravé returned to the St. Lawrence valley, to find a location where they could control access to the interior and prevent competition from other traders. At the point where the St. Lawrence narrows before widening out again, and in the shadow of a towering cliff, Champlain constructed a *habitation*, a collection of wooden buildings built in the form of a quadrangle and surrounded by a stockade and moats. He called it Quebec — Kebec being the Algonquian word for "strait" or "narrow passage." Champlain's *habitation* became the heart of the first permanent and continuous French settlement in Canada.

Gravé left Quebec with a load of furs in mid-September. Once again, the French were badly prepared for a severe Canadian winter. Twenty of the 28 Frenchmen died, two-thirds from scurvy and the other third from dysentery. Champlain himself was stricken with scurvy but survived.

In hindsight, one might ask why the Native peoples welcomed the French occupation of Quebec. Like other Europeans, the French did not recognize the First Nations' rights to the land. They officially claimed the St. Lawrence valley for France on the basis of Jacques Cartier's "discovery" of it. And, as a Christian nation, the newcomers assumed they had the right to occupy non-Christians' lands. In fact, they soon began to provide land to colonists. In 1627, for instance, they simply granted all of North America then not occupied by a Christian prince to the newly created Company of One Hundred Associates.

The First Nations of northeastern North America regarded the land as theirs. Each Montagnais (Innu) band around Tadoussac and Quebec, for example, occupied a specific territory; the boundaries were well known and usually well defined by recognizable geographical features. Fortunately for the French, however, they had entered a war zone. The Montagnais welcomed the French traders because they saw them as potential allies who possessed muskets. The Montagnais could use help against the Iroquois raiders. The trading post at Quebec also ensured that the Montagnais could obtain badly needed iron goods, at advantageous rates. As historian Arthur J. Ray notes, "The Montagnais obtained their furs from their partners in the interior at much lower prices than they charged the Europeans for them."[2]

The *habitation* at Quebec, from Champlain's *Voyages*, 1613. The walls have loopholes, and a moat and drawbridge surround the wooden buildings. Today Notre-Dame-des-Victoires, one of the oldest churches in Canada, located at the Place-Royale in Quebec's Lower Town, raises its spire almost on the site of Champlain's habitation.

Rare Book Collection/National Library of Canada/8759.

EARLY FRENCH–NATIVE RELATIONS

No sooner had the French established Quebec and concluded an alliance with the Algonquians than the Montagnais and Algonquins asked Champlain to join their war parties against the Iroquois. As the French depended on these nations for furs, they complied. In 1609, Champlain and the French joined the Algonquians and some Hurons in an attack on the Iroquois to the southwest. The French firearms so frightened the Iroquois that they lost the battle at the lake the French named Lake Champlain. The French and their Native allies again defeated a Mohawk war party near the mouth of the Richelieu River the next summer.

The Franco–Algonquian alliance proved invaluable to the French. The Montagnais and Algonquins taught them how to adapt to winter and supplied them with invaluable geographical information about the interior. The French learned the value of birchbark canoes, and when the waterways froze, of toboggans and snowshoes. As well, they relied on the First Nations for food. As late as 1643, Quebec depended almost entirely on Native hunters for its supply of fresh meat. The French also gathered wild berries, particularly blueberries, and learned from the Native peoples how to make maple sugar.

In Brazil in the mid-sixteenth century, the French began the practice of sending young men to live with the Aboriginal peoples to learn their languages and ways of life. Champlain wanted to establish the same practice in New France. He arranged for cultural go-betweens known as coureurs de bois (literally, "runners of the woods"), who could reinforce France's economic and political alliance with the Algonquians and Hurons.

In 1610, Champlain arranged an exchange with the Hurons. He sent Étienne Brûlé, a young Frenchman, to live with them. In return, Champlain took Savignon, brother of a Huron headman and roughly the same age as Brûlé, into his custody.

Indian Preparing Birch Bark Map for Professor Hind, by Henry Youle Hind, 1861–62. A scene from a mid-nineteenth-century expedition across what is now northern Quebec and Labrador. For more than three centuries, Europeans relied on the Native peoples for geographical information about the Americas.

J. Ross Robertson Collection/Toronto Reference Library/T31956.

From Brûlé and Savignon the French learned about the Huron Confederacy, an alliance of several nations with a population of up to 30 000 on Lake Huron. The Hurons' trading area extended as far west as Lake Superior and as far north as James Bay. Huron, in fact, was the trading language of the entire Upper Great Lakes.

Champlain made his last journey into the interior in the summer of 1615, for the purpose of strengthening the Franco–Huron alliance. While in Huronia, Champlain concluded treaties in friendship with individual Huron leaders, affirming French support in their wars — provided that the Hurons continued to trade with the French. By joining a large war party of Hurons and Algonquins against the Iroquois, he convinced the Hurons of his support. Henceforth, the French could live securely as guests among their Huron allies. And although the Hurons still had to pay compensation to the Algonquins for using the Ottawa River, they took their own furs to New France. By the 1620s, the Hurons supplied from one-half to two-thirds of the furs obtained by the French.

THE COMPANY OF ONE HUNDRED ASSOCIATES

New France grew slowly. During the winter of 1620–21, no more than 60 people lived at Quebec. Thanks to the co-operation of the Native peoples, the fur trade required few Europeans. Furthermore, no incentive existed for Europeans to settle and farm in the northern colony. To whom would farmers have sold their produce? No market existed.

New France remained pathetically small compared with other European settlements in areas of greater agricultural potential. The English colony of Virginia, for example, with its

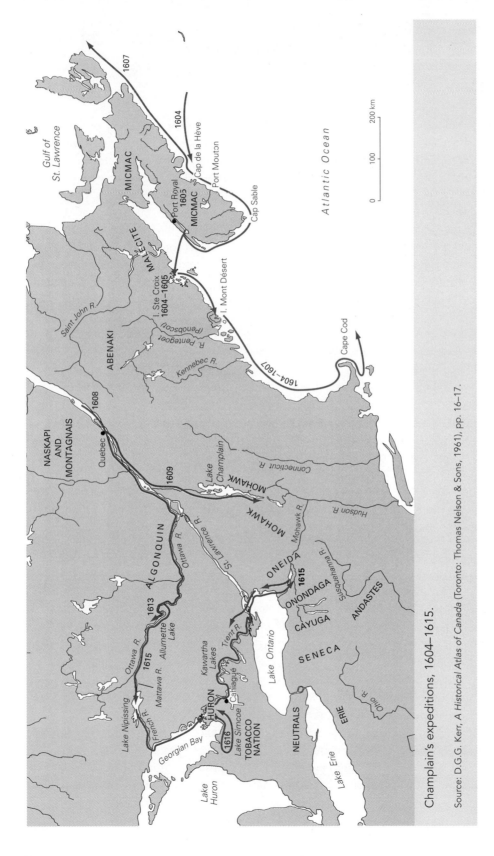

Champlain's expeditions, 1604–1615.

Source: D.G.G. Kerr, *A Historical Atlas of Canada* (Toronto: Thomas Nelson & Sons, 1961), pp. 16–17.

A Historical Portrait 🖎

🖝 Jean Nicollet

Very little is known about Jean Nicollet, one of the most colourful characters of early New France. None of his own accounts survive; there are just a few references to him in the Jesuit *Relations*, their annual reports back to France, and in church and legal records. Apparently the priests valued him greatly. As Father Barthélemy Vimont wrote in 1643, "His disposition and his excellent memory led one to expect worthwhile things of him."

Nicollet's father was the king's postal courier between the French port of Cherbourg on the English Channel and Paris. At the age of about 20, in either 1618 or 1619, Jean came to the infant colony of New France, then just the tiny trading post of Quebec. Samuel de Champlain, badly in need of interpreters and representatives to consolidate his First Nations alliances, immediately dispatched him to Allumette Island, a strategic Algonquin community on the Ottawa River. He was the first European to live with the important Algonquin trading chief Tessouat and his followers, where he learned both Algonquin and Huron, the trading language of the Upper Great Lakes. Father Vimont wrote of him: "He tarried with them two years, alone of the French, and always joined the Barbarians in their excursions and journeys."

Impressed by his wilderness skills and his ability to promote the fur trade, Champlain next sent Nicollet among the Nipissings, an Algonquian-speaking group who lived north of the Algonquins by the lake that bears their name, between the Ottawa River and Lake Huron. Nicollet became extremely close with these people, who were important intermediaries with the First Nations south of James Bay. Father Vimont tells some of the story: Nicollet lived "eight or nine years with the Algonquin Nipissiriniens, where he passed for one of that nation, taking part in the very frequent councils of those tribes, having his own separate cabin and household, and fishing and trading for himself."

The Jesuits found his behaviour superior to that of other Frenchmen in the interior, such as the coureur de bois Étienne Brûlé, detested by the priests for what they regarded as his loose moral conduct. Vimont, at least, overlooked the fact that while among the Nipissing, Nicollet took a Native wife, outside of Christian marriage, and had at least one daughter by her, whom he brought with him to the colony in 1633. At this point, according to Father LeJeune, Nicollett asked to stay in the settlement, "to assure his salvation." He became an interpreter and fur-trade clerk at Trois-Rivières.

In 1637 he married Marguerite, the Canadian-born daughter of Guillaume Couillard and Guillemette Hébert. At the time of their marriage, the average age of women in New France was nearly 22, and the legal age 12. Marguerite was only 11. Nevertheless, on account of their esteem for Nicollet, the Jesuits allowed the ceremony to proceed. The couple had a son and a daughter. The children would have few memories of their father. Unable to swim, Nicollet drowned after his boat was overturned by a strong gust of wind near Quebec in late 1642.

Jean Nicollet is best remembered for the voyage in 1634 to the Winnebagos, a Siouan-speaking group in Wisconsin. A statue of him, the first European to reach

Lake Michigan, commemorates his arrival at Green Bay, Wisconsin. A National Forest in Wisconsin bears his name. In reality, however, the voyage never occurred. It appears that Nicollet did make a western voyage in the mid-1630s, but it was to the north shore of Lake Superior and not to Lake Michigan. The error was due to a misreading of a passage in the *Relations* by mid-nineteenth-century American historian John Gilmary Shea.

Other scholars over the next century simply repeated the error and ignored the original reference, until Canadian historians Marcel Trudel[1] and Jacques Gagnon[2] corrected this error.

Recently, Quebec genealogist Pierre Boileau discovered that among Nicollet's descendants (through his Nipissing daughter) is René Lévesque,[3] Quebec's first separatist premier.

[1] Marcel Trudel, "Jean Nicollet dans le lac Supérieur et non dans le lac Michigan," *Revue d'histoire de l'Amérique française*, 34 (2) (septembre 1980): 183–196.

[2] Jacques Gagnon, "Jean Nicollet au lac Michigan. Histoire d'une erreur historique," *Revue d'histoire de l'Amérique française*, 50, 1 (été 1996): 95–101.

[3] Pierre Boileau, *Précis de généalogie: Le Temple des Ancêtres de René Lévesque* (Montreal: Guerin, 1995) planche 50, p. 64.

tobacco-based economy, had 2000 inhabitants by 1627, or twenty times New France's population. Even the newly established Dutch colony of New Netherlands in the Hudson River valley had 200 settlers by 1625.

In 1627, the French government, observing the success of other European settlements in America, decided to end New France's total dependency on furs. Cardinal Richelieu, Louis XIII's prime minister, made that decision.

From his appointment in 1624 to his death in 1642, the cardinal worked to unify France under the Crown and to make France the leading nation in Europe, with strong colonies overseas. He extended French overseas commerce and authority through mercantile trade. Mercantilism, the dominant economic philosophy of Europe, held that colonies existed for the mother country's benefit. They would supply those things she needed and provide a market for those things she produced, particularly manufactured goods. Like every other European government of the day, the French looked upon their colonies as areas to be exploited. Direct trade by foreigners with the colonies was forbidden. The mother country and the colonies monopolized shipping. Only French ships could carry the goods to and from the colony. From its overseas settlements, Richelieu believed that France could draw strength and riches to increase its stature in Europe.

The cardinal sponsored a new company called the Compagnie des Cent-Associés ("Company of One Hundred Associates"), which obtained working capital from 100 investors to develop and exploit New France's resources and to encourage Roman Catholic missionary activity. (Despite the promises of the Edict of Nantes, Protestants were barred from participation and were henceforth officially excluded from the colony.) The company became the seigneur of all the lands France claimed in North America. It had a monopoly on all commerce, including the fur trade, and the right to cede land to settlers in seigneurial tenure. In return for its trade monopoly, the company promised to bring out 4000 settlers, all French and Roman Catholic, within 15 years and to promote missions to the First Nations.

Unfortunately for New France, the project began at the worst possible time: war had just broken out between France and England. In 1627 the Kirke brothers, English privateers, seized

Tadoussac and captured, off the shores of the Gaspe, the French ships that were bringing 400 settlers to New France. In 1629, the English attacked Quebec itself. Cut off from France and their provisions long exhausted, Champlain and his starving garrison surrendered in July 1629. Champlain, the ailing Gravé, and the garrison left Quebec.

Still New France's greatest champion and lobbyist, Champlain urged the French ambassador in England to begin negotiations for the return of Quebec. For three years, the St. Lawrence remained closed to the French, which meant heavy losses for the One Hundred Associates. England's king, Charles I, who had married Louis XIII's sister, refused to return the captured territories until his French brother-in-law paid his sister's full dowry. In 1632, Louis XIII settled his debts and the English left the St. Lawrence. Champlain returned to New France and undertook one last initiative: he founded a fur-trading post above Quebec in 1634 at Trois-Rivières.

Champlain deserves full credit for establishing New France, their Laurentian colony in northeastern North America. The French leader served, in effect if not in title, as New France's governor. Through his numerous alliances with the Algonquins and Hurons, managed by young Frenchmen like Jean Nicollet, he kept the tiny trading post of Quebec alive. Rightly, he is considered "the founder of New France." With the founder's death on Christmas Day, 1635, the effective leadership of the fur-trading colony passed into the hands of the religious orders, particularly the Jesuits.

THE CONTRIBUTIONS OF THE FRENCH RELIGIOUS ORDERS

For nearly a century, France had been rent by civil strife between Catholics and Protestants, or Huguenots. In reaction to an increasingly corrupt and seemingly unredeemable papacy, church reformers, led by Martin Luther, a German priest who broke with Rome in 1517, began what is called the Protestant Reformation. The followers of Luther and other reformers like the Frenchman John Calvin in Geneva came to be known as "Protestants," individuals who no longer recognized the spiritual and moral authority of the pope. By the mid-sixteenth century a number of Protestant churches had arisen in many parts of northern Europe (most of Germany, Switzerland, Holland, Scandinavia, Scotland, and England), and a substantial Huguenot minority existed in France.

To resist the resurgent Protestants, southern Europeans, including the Catholic majority in France, fought back. They launched a "Counter-Reformation," first to root out the corruption in the Catholic church, and then to win back those lost to the Protestant heretics. The Jesuits, the papacy's most expert missionaries, led the struggle. Other groups, such as the Ursulines, a female teaching order, followed them. Both the Jesuits and the Ursulines extended their mission to convert non-Christians throughout the world.

Champlain wanted the neighbouring Algonquians on the St. Lawrence to convert to Christianity, form settlements, and farm, as the French did. Ultimately he hoped that the French and the Christianized First Nations would amalgamate, through intermarriage, into a single people. The first French missionaries assigned the task of transforming the Native peoples into a French people were the Récollets, a branch of the Franciscan Friars, who lacked a large financial base. At first they believed the task would be relatively easy. Three Récollet priests and a lay brother arrived at Quebec in 1615, and five years later they opened a monastery close to the settlement. The Récollets initially hoped their seminary would train a Native clergy for the colony, but they found the First Nations had no desire to assimilate into French society. The seminary soon closed for lack of students and funds.

THE JESUIT ORDER

 In an attempt to solve their financial problems, the Récollets sought to collaborate with the Society of Jesus (commonly known as the Jesuits), a wealthy and powerful order founded by Ignatius Loyola a century earlier. From 1625 to 1629, the Jesuits assisted the Récollets in establishing missions in New France. This highly disciplined order, renowned for its ability to attract able candidates, often of high rank, was also known for its willingness to take on the most dangerous tasks. Thanks to their *Relations*, or annual reports back to France, we know a great deal about their activities in New France.

In 1632, Cardinal Richelieu gave the Jesuits a monopoly over the Canadian mission field. Their work then began in earnest. Yet when they opened a school for Native children, they encountered the same problems as the Récollets had.

Enlisting Native students was difficult because their parents often refused to let the children go. The priests had to give presents to the parents in order to gain students for the seminary. Many students ran away, and others became ill and died. The deaths increased the parents' resistance to their children's schooling, as did the French custom of physically punishing children, a practice foreign to the Natives' approach to child-rearing.

The arrival of the Ursuline nuns in Quebec in 1639 marked the beginning of their outreach to the First Nations. The Jesuits invited them to Christianize and to "civilize" the young Native girls. But the Ursulines, despite determined efforts on their part, had little success. In 1668 Marie de l'Incarnation, founder of the Ursuline Order in New France, wrote, "We have observed that of a hundred that have passed through our hands we have scarcely civilized one. We find docility and intelligence in these girls but, when we are least expecting it, they clamber over our wall and go off to run with their kinsmen in the woods, finding more to please them there than in all the amenities of our French house."

The Ursulines proved more successful in their hospital work. A number of First Nations people agreed to leave their aged and infirm at what they called the "house of death" (the mortality rate being so high) rather than to abandon them to die while travelling to their hunting territories.

The Arrival of the Ursulines at Quebec, August 1639, painted by Frank Craig (1874–1918) in the early twentieth century.

National Archives of Canada/C-1549.

THE JESUITS' WORK WITH THE ALGONQUIANS

Like the Récollets before them, the Jesuits encouraged the Algonquians to abandon their migratory ways, which the priests regarded as contrary to the laws of the church and incompatible with Christian life. They urged them to live in the French manner, in settled agricultural communities, or *réductions*, adjacent to French settlements in the St. Lawrence valley. These became, in effect, the first reserves in Canada.

To accomplish their goal, the Jesuits hired workmen to help the Montagnais clear farmland and build a small village between the St. Lawrence and the cliff of Cap aux Diamants (where Jacques Cartier's men had mined for diamonds a century earlier), about 6 km west of Quebec. The Jesuits called the 3500 ha *réduction* St. Joseph de Sillery, after a former minister and ambassador of the king, who donated his fortune to establish a model Native settlement.

A Jesuit preaching to the Algonquians of the Great Lakes. The Ojibwa (Anishinabeg) called the French *Wa-mit-ig-oshe*, "men who wave a piece of wood over their heads." This drawing is by C.W. Jefferys (1869–1951), well known for his reconstructions of Canadian history.

National Archives of Canada/C-5855.

By 1641 the Sillery reserve contained some 30 families — about 150 baptized First Nations people. Some Algonquians from Trois-Rivières joined them in clearing land and planting crops. The village became divided into a Christian faction and a somewhat larger non-Christian faction. The Jesuits' limited financial support and the constant threat of Iroquois attacks, however, checked the development of the community. Throughout the 1640s, the village men frequently left for long periods on war parties, at which time those left behind abandoned the village for the safety of Quebec. Sillery then became a ghost town. Disease also struck, carrying away a number of the important converts. An Iroquois raid in 1655 and a fire in 1656 that destroyed the mission residence, the church, and most of the small houses ended the experiment. It never recovered. By 1663, French farmers occupied most of the Sillery land.

The Jesuits contributed greatly to education in New France. In 1635, they established a college for First Nations boys at Quebec. It became the first institution of higher learning north of Mexico, established a year before Harvard University in Massachusetts. Four years later, in 1639, the Jesuits encouraged the Ursulines and the Hospital nuns of Dieppe to begin a school for girls and a hospital at Quebec. They were also in contact with the Société de Notre-Dame, an association of priests and laypeople founded in 1639 in Paris.

THE JESUITS BRING INDENTURED WORKERS TO NEW FRANCE

The church, in effect, became the second industry of the colony. The Jesuits, Ursulines, and the Hospital nuns came in number to serve the Native peoples and in turn brought out *engagés*, or indentured workers, on three-year contracts, to help them. These newcomers created a market for agricultural produce in the colony. Upon being discharged, many left to return to France, rather than stay on in a land that had little to offer in terms of security or creature comforts, with its formidable winters, heavily forested land to clear, and shortage of marriageable women. But some engagés stayed and began to farm.

THE FOUNDING OF MONTREAL

wⓦw The Société de Notre-Dame planned a mission settlement remote and independent from the main settlement at Quebec. It believed that once it had built a church, a school, and a hospital, the First Nations would come and settle, and be converted to Christianity. The organizers chose the former site of Hochelaga, on the island of Montreal, at the crossroads of the Ottawa and the St. Lawrence rivers, a location that could be easily reached by the Algonquian-speaking nations.

Paul de Chomedey de Maisonneuve, a 33-year-old career soldier, led the first settlers to establish what they hoped would become a model Christian community. The citizens at Quebec did their best to discourage Maisonneuve and his band of 40 colonists from continuing up the St. Lawrence, then beset by Iroquois attacks. Maisonneuve replied that even if every tree on the island were changed into an Iroquois, his honour would oblige him to establish the new religious colony. Go they did, and in mid-May 1642 they founded Ville-Marie, the future Montreal.

The first settlers farmed on the grassy areas where the villages of the Laurentian Iroquoians once stood. The only sizable influx of new settlers, 100 in all, arrived in 1653. Despite an initial

Statue of Chomedey de Maisonneuve and Notre-Dame Church, Place d'Armes, Montreal. Sculptor Philippe Hébert's monument to the founder of Montreal was unveiled in Place d'Armes in 1895. It was on this spot that French soldiers laid down their arms on September 9, 1760, after the capitulations of New France the previous day.

Comstock © John Jacquemain.

burst of enthusiasm, the outpost grew slowly, and chronic underpopulation remained a problem until the late 1660s. Two factors prevented the colony's expansion: the Société's quick loss of enthusiasm for its missionary enterprise, and the repeated raids by the Iroquois, who resented the founding of a French village in their northern hunting grounds. It took a large dose of courage to settle in the centre of the battle zone. In 1663 the Sulpicians, another French religious order, took over the direction of the settlement and became the seigneurs of the island of Montreal.

THE HABITANTS' COMPANY

The Company of One Hundred Associates never overcame the effects of the English occupation of Quebec between 1629 and 1632. By the early 1640s, it stood on the verge of bankruptcy, heavily in debt and unable to supply the funds needed to maintain and defend the colony. The leading settlers in 1645 — a group of about fifteen businesspeople — took matters into their own hands and formed the Compagnie des habitants ("Habitants' Company"). While reserving its rights of ownership over all of New France, the Company of One Hundred Associates ceded the fur monopoly to them. Henceforth the Habitants' Company had to pay the costs of administering the colony, including payments to the governor and the military officers for the maintenance of forts and garrisons, the upkeep of the clergy, and the responsibility of bringing twenty male and female settlers to the colony each year.

NEW FRANCE IN THE MID-1640S

In 1645 — a decade after Champlain's death — the French colony in the valley of the St. Lawrence contained only 600 residents and a few hundred *engagés*. Clerical intervention in the 1630s had helped, but the colony's population still remained smaller than a single large Iroquoian village. This modest growth is puzzling, considering the advantages of emigrating

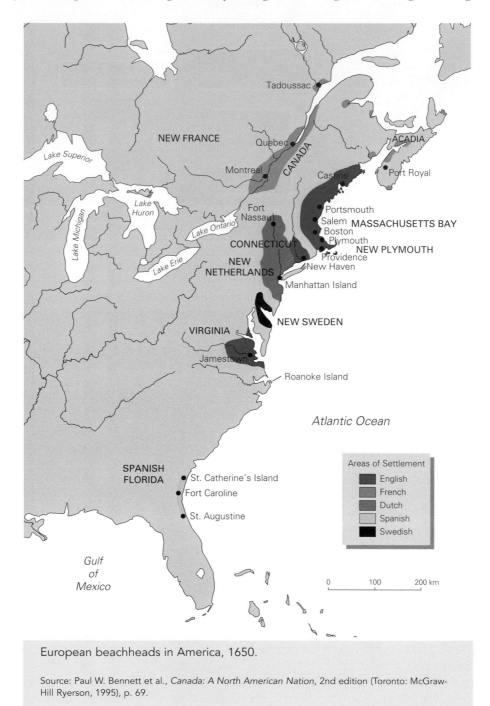

European beachheads in America, 1650.

Source: Paul W. Bennett et al., *Canada: A North American Nation*, 2nd edition (Toronto: McGraw-Hill Ryerson, 1995), p. 69.

from France. Landless peasants or workers settling in Canada could obtain all the land they wanted. Moreover, they could enjoy privileges denied their class in France, and they could avoid paying royal taxes.

Nevertheless, French emigration to New France remained unpopular. The French government offered little incentive to emigrate. French Protestants who might have been tempted to leave certainly had no incentive to do so after 1627, when both Protestant worship and teaching were forbidden in "Canada," as the French now termed the St. Lawrence valley. Stories about the Canadian climate and the hostile Iroquois discouraged immigration. The obvious dangers and discomfort of emigrating also influenced others. First, the would-be colonists faced the dangers of crossing the North Atlantic, a journey that took anywhere from three weeks to more than three months. On these voyages, if headwinds continued too long, food supplies would sometimes run out, and then scurvy would take its toll. (If fewer than 10 percent of the ship's company died during a crossing, the captain considered the voyage a success.)

The peasants and artisans who arrived safely faced the challenge of clearing the virgin forest. A man could clear one hectare a year at best. Much of this difficult work had to be performed in the summer months, when the black flies and mosquitoes made life intolerable. Then, too, the new arrivals faced the danger of Iroquois raids, which resumed in earnest in the 1640s. Every man — and many women — capable of bearing arms had to be ready at all times to fight for their lives. Furthermore, the early settlers, at least initially, still failed to dress warmly enough and found the winters excruciatingly cold.

All this having been said, hundreds of emigrants did leave France for the Americas in the 1630s and 1640s. They settled in the French Antilles, in the Caribbean, and in the islands of Martinique and Guadeloupe in particular, where, despite warfare with the local Caribs, employment could be had. Unlike the northern fur trade, tobacco and cotton farming required a great deal of unskilled labour. Within a decade, the European population of the French Antilles was estimated at 7000. Emigrants from France continued to see little economic opportunity in New France in the mid-1640s, and this best explains the colony's small population.

The fur trade made the colony. New France depended on the Algonquians and Hurons who hunted, trapped, and prepared the beaver pelts, and then carried them hundreds of kilometres to Quebec. Within a generation, France had advanced 1000 km into the interior, establishing a firm trading alliance with the Hurons. But in early 1649 it was doubtful whether New France, with a resident population of barely 1000, could survive in the face of determined Iroquois attacks.

Notes

1. E. Pocquet, *Histoire de Bretagne*, vol. 5, p. 310, cited in Morris Bishop, *Champlain: The Life of Fortitude* (Toronto: McClelland & Stewart, 1963 [1948]), p. 8.
2. Arthur J. Ray, *I Have Lived Here since the World Began: An Illustrated History of Canada's Native People* (Toronto: Key Porter Books, 1996), p. 56.

Linking to the Past

Living in Canada in the Time of Champlain, 1600–1635
http://www.civilization.ca/vmnf/expos/champlain/indexeng.htm
A virtual exhibition featuring Champlain's voyages, as well as commerce, warfare, farming, and other aspects of life in New France during this period.

The Foundation of Quebec, 1608
http://www.fordham.edu/halsall/mod/1608champlain.html
Read Champlain's own account of the founding of Quebec.

Jean Nicollet
http://www.civilization.ca/vmnf/explor/nicol_e1.html
A brief account of the contributions of Jean Nicollet.

The Jesuit *Relations* and the History of New France
http://www.nlc-bnc.ca/jesuit-relations/index-e.html
Information and an essay on the importance of the Jesuit *Relations*, along with scans of each page
of the original edition of the *Relations*.

The Jesuit *Relations* and Allied Documents, 1610 to 1791
http://puffin.creighton.edu/jesuit/relations
Searchable full text of seventy volumes of the Jesuit *Relations*.

Old Montreal: Centuries of History
http://www.vieux.montreal.qc.ca/histoire/eng/introa.htm
A brief history of Montreal, from its founding as Ville-Marie to the present.

BIBLIOGRAPHY

Marcel Trudel provides an overview of the period in *The Beginnings of New France, 1524–1663* (Toronto: McClelland & Stewart, 1973). A shorter summary appears in W.J. Eccles, *The Canada Frontier, 1534–1760* (Toronto: Holt, Rinehart and Winston, 1969). His later work, *France in America*, rev. ed. (Markham, ON: Fitzhenry & Whiteside, 1990 [1972]), also contains information on the early French colonies in the Caribbean as well as New France and Acadia. Bibliographical guides include Jacques Rouillard, ed., *Guide d'histoire du Québec du régime français à nos jours: Bibliographie commentée* (Montreal: Éditions du Méridien, 1991); and Thomas Wien, "Canada and the Pays d'en haut, 1600–1760," in M. Brook Taylor, ed., *Canadian History: A Reader's Guide*, vol. 1, *Beginnings to Confederation* (Toronto: University of Toronto Press, 1994), pp. 33–75. Contemporary maps and illustrations appear in André Vachon, in collaboration with Victorin Chabot and André Desrosiers, *Dreams of Empire: Canada Before 1700* (Ottawa: Public Archives of Canada, 1982); and Derek Hayes, *Historical Atlas of Canada. Canada's History Illustrated with Original Maps* (Vancouver: Douglas and McIntyre, 2002).

For First Nations affairs, Bruce G. Trigger's *The Children of Aataentsic: A History of the Huron People to 1660*, 2 vols. (Montreal/Kingston: McGill-Queen's University Press, 1976), and his *Natives and Newcomers: Canada's "Heroic Age" Reconsidered* (Montreal/Kingston: McGill-Queen's University Press, 1985) are invaluable; a shorter summary appears in his booklet *The Indians and the Heroic Age of New France* (Ottawa: Canadian Historical Association, 1989 [1977]). Denys Delâge's *Bitter Feast: Amerindians and Europeans in Northeastern North America, 1600–64*, trans. Jane Brierley (Vancouver: University of British Columbia Press, 1993), also provides a complete overview. An older study, A.G. Bailey's *The Conflict of European and Eastern Algonkian Cultures, 1504–1700* (Toronto: University of Toronto Press, 1969 [1937]), is still valuable. Arthur J. Ray, *Indians in the Fur Trade* (Toronto: University of Toronto Press, 1974); and Carolyn Gilman, *Where Two Worlds Meet: The Great Lakes Fur Trade* (St. Paul: Minnesota Historical Society, 1982) cover the economic aspects of early Native–European contact. An excellent overview of early French–First Nation relations is the chapter, "The Native People and the Beginnings of New France," in John A. Dickinson and Brian Young's *A Short History of Quebec*, 3rd ed. (Montreal/Kingston: McGill-Queen's University Press, 2003), pp. 3–27. J.B. Jamieson reviews the disappearance of the St. Lawrence Iroquoians in "Trade and Warfare," *Man in the Northeast* 39 (1990): 79–86. A more recent treatment is James F. Pendergast, "The Confusing Identities Attributed to Stadacona and Hochelaga," *Journal of Canadian Studies*, 3, 4 (Winter 1998): 149–167. Two examinations of the early French missionaries' policies toward First Nations women include: Eleanor Leacock, "Montagnais Women and the Jesuit Program for Colonization," in Mona Etienne and Eleanor Leacock, eds., *Women and Colonization. Anthropological Perspectives* (Brooklyn, N.Y.: J.F. Bergin Publishers, 1980): 25–42; and Carol Devens, *Countering Colonization. Native American Women and Great Lakes Missions, 1630–1900* (Berkeley: University of California Press, 1992).

Two well-written biographies of Champlain are available: Morris Bishop, *Champlain: The Life of Fortitude* (Toronto: McClelland & Stewart, 1963 [1948]); and Samuel Eliot Morison, *Samuel de Champlain: Father of New France* (Boston: Little, Brown, 1972). Marcel Trudel has contributed the entry on Champlain in the *Dictionary of Canadian Biography*, vol. 1, *1000–1700* (Toronto: University of Toronto Press, 1966), pp. 186–99. For an understanding of Champlain's Native policy one must, however, supplement these studies with Trigger's *Children of Aataentsic* and his *Natives and Newcomers*. Champlain's "real" birth date (most likely around 1580, not 1570 or 1567) is analyzed by Jean Liebel in "On a vieilli Champlain," *Revue d'histoire de l'Amérique française* 32(2) (septembre 1978): 229–37.

Valuable sources on the subject of the Algonquians in the St. Lawrence valley include Alain Beaulieu, *Convertir les fils de Caïn: Jésuites et Amérindiens nomades en Nouvelle-France, 1632–1642* (Quebec: Nuit blanche, 1990); Marc Jetten, *Enclaves amérindiennes: les "réductions" du Canada 1637–1701* (Sillery, PQ: Septentrion, 1994); John A. Dickinson, "Native Sovereignty and French Justice in Early Canada," in Jim Phillips, Tina Loo, and Susan Lewthwaite, eds., *Essays in the History of Canadian Law*, vol. 5, *Crime and Criminal Justice* (Toronto: University of Toronto Press, 1994), pp. 17–40; James P. Ronda, "The Sillery Experiment: A Jesuit–Indian Village in New France, 1637–1663," *American Indian Culture and Research Journal* 3(1) (1979): 1–18; and Cornelius J. Jaenen, *Friend and Foe: Aspects of French–Amerindian Cultural Contact in the Sixteenth and Seventeenth Centuries* (Toronto: McClelland & Stewart, 1976). François-Marc Gagnon examines early French racial attitudes in *Ces hommes dits sauvages: L'histoire fascinante d'un préjugé qui remonte aux premiers découvreurs du Canada* (Montreal: Libre Expression, 1984). Olive P. Dickason's *The Myth of the Savage and the Beginnings of French Colonialism in the Americas* (Edmonton: University of Alberta Press, 1984); John Webster Grant's *Moon of Wintertime: Missionaries and the Indians of Canada in Encounter since 1534* (Toronto: University of Toronto Press, 1984); and James Axtell's *The Invasion Within: The Contest of Cultures in Colonial North America* (New York: Oxford University Press, 1985) are very useful for their review of early missionary activities in New France. For a review of European opinions about the land rights of Aboriginal peoples in the Americas see Leslie C. Green and Olive P. Dickason, *The Law of Nations and the New World* (Edmonton: University of Alberta Press, 1989); and Cornelius Jaenen, *The French Relationship with the Native Peoples of New France and Acadia* (Ottawa: Department of Indian and Northern Affairs, 1984). Biographical articles appear in the *Dictionary of Canadian Biography*, vol. 1; see in particular the entries on Jacques Noël, p. 520; François Gravé Du Pont, pp. 345–46; Pierre Du Gua de Monts, pp. 291–95; Étienne Brûlé, pp. 130–33; Marie Guyart, *dite* Marie de l'Incarnation, pp. 351–59; and Paul de Chomedey de Maisonneuve, pp. 212–22.

The early history of the settlement of Quebec is reviewed in John Hare, Marc Lafrance, and David Thiery Ruddel, *Histoire de la Ville de Québec, 1608–1871* (Montreal: Boréal Express, 1987). Hubert Charbonneau et al., *The First French Canadians: Pioneers in the St. Lawrence Valley*, trans. Paola Colozzo (Newark: University of Delaware Press, 1993), discusses the first French settlers in the St. Lawrence valley. For the early history of Montreal consult Robert Prévost, *Montréal: A History*, trans. by Elizabeth Mueller and Robert Chodos (Toronto: McClelland & Stewart, 1993); Gustave Lanctôt, *Montreal under Maisonneuve, 1642–1665*, trans. Alta Lind Cook (Toronto: Clarke Irwin, 1969); and the beautifully illustrated *Pour le Christ et le Roi: La vie au temps des premiers Montréalais*, sous la direction d'Yves Landry (Montreal: Libre Expression/Art Global, 1992).

Valuable maps of early Acadia and New France are contained in R. Cole Harris, ed., *Historical Atlas of Canada*, vol. 1, *From the Beginning to 1800* (Toronto: University of Toronto Press, 1987). Jacob Ernest Cooke et al., eds., *The Encyclopedia of the North American Colonies*, 3 vols. (New York: Scribner's, 1993), contains many useful articles on New France.

THE IROQUOIS, THE HURONS, AND THE FRENCH

TIME LINE

c.1475–	
1525	League of the Iroquois (Five Nations) is established
1609	The first clash occurs between the French and the Iroquois
1615	The first Roman Catholic missionaries reach the Hurons
mid-1630s	A series of epidemics sweeps the Hurons' country
1639	The Jesuits build Sainte-Marie, a permanent mission headquarters in Huronia
1649	The fall of Huronia, the Iroquois defeat the Hurons in a quick military campaign
1653	French coureurs de bois replace the Hurons as the middlemen of the fur trade
1660	Dollard's last stand at Long Sault
1665	The Carignan–Salières regiment is dispatched from France to fight the Five Nations
1667	Truce between the French and the Iroquois League of Five Nations, the beginning of two decades of peace
1680	Death of Kateri Tegakwitha, a famous Iroquois Christian convert
1687	The resumption of conflict between New France and the League of Five Nations, which ends in 1701
1701	The Great Peace of Montreal of 1701

From Champlain's first encounter with the Mohawks in 1609 to the Great Peace of Montreal of 1701, the Five Nations were a major concern — frequently *the* major concern — of the French settlers. Sometime between 1475 and 1525, most authorities agree, the confederacy of Mohawk, Oneida, Onondaga, Cayuga, and Seneca formed. Over the course of the sixteenth century they consolidated their position across what is now upstate New York. The league co-ordinated Iroquois affairs with other First Nations groups, and, in the seventeenth century, with the European newcomers. Much discussion has followed on the nature of their union: was it a warlike league to expand their power or a union formed to secure peace in the Great Lakes area? The French, the Algonquians, and the "good Iroquois" — as Champlain called the Hurons, a friendly Iroquoian power — were convinced that war was the Five Nations' objective. Although the Iroquois and Huron confederacies belonged to the same linguistic family and shared the same culture, the Jesuit fathers and early French chroniclers like Marie de l'Incarnation condemned the Iroquois and praised the Huron.

The French first learned of the existence of the Five Nations from the Algonquians. The very name the Montagnais attached to them indicates the animosity they felt toward them. Linguist Peter Bakker has translated the word "Hirokoa" as "the killer people." The word originated in the Algonquian–Basque trade language, a mixture of Basque and Algonquian that developed in the late sixteenth century from New England to Labrador between the Basque fishers and whalers, and the Algonquians. From the Algonquians, Basque fishers first learned of the "Hirokoa," the Algonquians' formidable enemies, who lived in the distant interior. When the French heard the word they revised the spelling to fit their own language, and the word "Iroquois" was born. It was not the Five Nations' name for themselves. But like so many names applied to First Nations groups, it was their enemies' designation. The name "Mohawk" was itself derived from a New England Algonquian word meaning "eater of human flesh."

In any discussion of the conflict of the Iroquois with the French and their Algonquian and Huron allies, one must keep in mind the highly biased nature of the written source materials. No contemporary accounts by the Iroquois exist, but we do have a story, handed down by word of mouth from generation to generation, of the Iroquois's perception of their enemies. The account, in several variations, tells of the founding, in what is now upstate New York, of the League of Five Nations, or the League of the Iroquois, by the following nations from east to west: the Mohawks, the Oneidas, the Onondagas, the Cayugas, and the Senecas. After the Tuscaroras, from the Carolinas, joined the confederacy in the early eighteenth century, the Five became the Six Nations. The story of how these nations formed a political union in which each preserved the essentials of sovereignty provides a rich source of information about the values of the Ho-dé-no-sau-nee ("people of the longhouse"), as the Iroquois call themselves.

THE FORMATION OF THE LEAGUE OF THE IROQUOIS

The founders conceived their league as the nucleus of a larger union. Historians now generally agree that it was established by the late fifteenth century. Paul A.W. Wallace studied various versions of the founding story of the Confederacy of the Iroquois and consulted with members of the Six Nations to write *The White Roots of Peace*, the story of how Dekanahwideh, the Peacemaker, the culture hero of the Iroquois, brought the Great Peace to Iroquoia.

The core of the narrative begins with Dekanahwideh's arrival in the country of the Iroquois. The Iroquoian nations at this time often raided each other's villages and suffered attacks by the powerful Algonquians as well. Order and public safety had broken down. Only a short distance inland, Dekanahwideh found his way into Iroquoia blocked by a man who had fallen to the lowest level that the Native mind could conceive — a notorious cannibal.

A rare photo of an Iroquois trail, taken a century ago in the territory of the Seneca, near Conesus Lake, New York. Generally, the paths followed the ridges, where the forest was not so thick.

National Anthropological Archives/Smithsonian Institution/947A.

Immediately the Peacemaker went to the cannibal's cabin and, finding it empty, climbed onto the bark roof and waited. Lying on the roof, he peered down through the smoke hole to create his own reflection on the surface of the water in the kettle below.

When the cannibal returned, he cut up and placed his victim's body in his cooking pot. But while bending over the kettle, he saw Dekanahwideh's calm, strong face reflected from the water's surface. Thinking the image of wisdom and strength was his own, he became greatly disturbed, because he had never dreamed that he possessed such noble qualities. He stepped back and began to think about the brutal life he led. In revulsion, the cannibal emptied the kettle and resolved to stop his killing. Just then, the Peacemaker came down from the roof and explained his Good News of Peace and Power. The man "took hold of the message" and offered himself as a disciple. Dekanahwideh gave him the name Hiawatha, which meant "he who combs," for he would comb the twists out of people's perverted minds.

The lawgiver and his new spokesperson visited the five warring nations and, with varying degrees of difficulty, persuaded each of them to come under the Tree of Peace and to form the union of the Ho-dé-no-sau-nee. Dekanahwideh then planted the Tree of Peace, a great white pine with healthy white roots that extended to the four corners of the earth, allowing all nations of good will to follow those roots to their source and to take shelter with the others under the great tree. On top of the tree, he placed the Eagle That Sees Afar, a symbol of military preparedness. Then he put antlers on the heads of the 50 chiefs representing the Five Nations and gave them the Words of the Law.

A new political structure was thus created to maintain peace among the Iroquois and gradually to draw the surrounding nations into the league. Well-routed pathways extended the Iroquois Peace over a vast area. Carrying gifts of deerskin and wampum, ambassadors travelled the trails to settle disputes between the member nations. War parties used the forest paths to attack outsiders who encroached on Five Nations lands. In the eyes of the Iroquois, the Hurons' refusal to come under the Tree of Peace proved their hostile, evil intent.

This story of the founding of the Iroquois Confederacy helps explain the Iroquois's feelings of superiority over their neighbours: it was among the Iroquois that the Tree of Peace was first planted. The Five Nations stood at the centre of the universe. In the late 1640s, this belief gave them great self-confidence and a strong sense of purpose.

THE MISSIONARIES' ARRIVAL IN HURONIA

At the time of French–First Nations contact in the seventeenth century, the Hurons and the Iroquois were at war. A desire for war honours and prestige contributed to the hostility. Participation in a war party, if successful, raised a man's standing in his clan and village. It increased his chances of an advantageous marriage and his hopes of one day becoming a village leader. Moreover, the necessity of avenging the dead led to more warfare, since the Iroquois and the Hurons believed the souls of the dead would not rest in peace until they had been avenged. This led to an escalation of the feud between the two hostile groups.

With the arrival of the Europeans, economic motives joined those of prestige and the blood feud as causes of Native warfare. Both the Iroquois and the Hurons needed a steady supply of furs to buy European trade goods. By the 1620s, the Hurons had become the principal economic partners of the French, exchanging furs for corn and European goods with the neighbouring Algonquians, who, in turn, traded as far north as James Bay and along the shores of Lakes Michigan and Superior. As elsewhere on the continent, the fur trade and the goods that it brought enriched Huron culture. The Hurons began to decorate their pottery with more elaborate patterns and to use iron knives to make more intricate bone carvings.

THE JESUITS AND THE HURONS

After establishing an economic alliance with the Hurons, the French obtained permission to send Roman Catholic priests to Huronia. Champlain dispatched Récollet missionaries in 1615 and Jesuit fathers in 1627. As a condition for renewing the Franco–Huron alliance after the English ended their occupation of Quebec in 1632, the French insisted that the Hurons allow Jesuits to live in Huronia. Reluctantly, the Hurons agreed. In 1634, Jean de Brébeuf and two companions reopened the Huron mission. Dressed in black gowns, wearing broad-brimmed black hats, and with iron chains and black beads hanging from their belts, the "Black Robes" went from village to village to spread the Christian gospel. The Hurons met them with apprehension and a growing fear, particularly after the outbreak of European diseases.

The Jesuit order put great effort into building up its mission. It used French lay workers (*donnés*), whose contracts assured them of lifetime support but no wages. The Jesuits mastered the Huron language and then communicated their ideas to the would-be converts. They also used non-verbal methods: pictures of holy subjects or of the sufferings of lost souls; religious statues; coloured beads as prizes for successful memorization; ceremonies, chants, and processions on holy days and on such occasions as baptisms, marriages, and funerals. They decorated the churches with crosses, bells, and candles, creating a colourful visual display.

CULTURAL DIFFERENCES BETWEEN THE HURONS AND THE FRENCH

In this initial period the Jesuits made some progress, but the gulf between the two societies remained great. For the Hurons, the meaning of existence was to maintain harmony with nature. They did not consider humans superior to other entities in the natural world, but rather equal partners. Their sacred stories explained their perception of the universe: the relationship between humanity and the earth, between people and animals, between the sun and the moon, between sickness and health. Christianity differed from the Hurons' religion in viewing the world as provisional and preparatory to the afterlife. John Webster Grant, the Canadian religious historian, wrote that if the First Nations religious symbol was the circle, the Christian's "might well be an arrow running from the creation of the world through God's redeeming acts in history to the final apocalypse."[1]

To gain an audience among the Hurons, the Jesuits emphasized the similarities between the Hurons' faith and their own. They pointed out that both believed in a supernatural power that influenced their lives, one which the Hurons located in the sun or sky and the Jesuits in heaven. Both Huron shamans and Roman Catholic priests encouraged personal contact with the supernatural. At puberty, every young Huron man was expected, through fasting and a vision quest, to find his own guardian spirit. The Jesuits also encouraged spiritual quests and valued fasts and vigils. The common reliance on prayer revealed a shared conviction that divine power controlled warfare, caused rain or drought, and gave health or disease. Finally, both Jesuits and Hurons

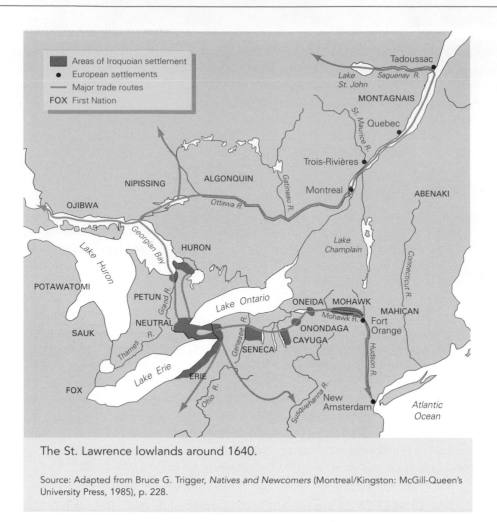

The St. Lawrence lowlands around 1640.

Source: Adapted from Bruce G. Trigger, *Natives and Newcomers* (Montreal/Kingston: McGill-Queen's University Press, 1985), p. 228.

accepted the idea of an afterlife; for the Hurons it was a pleasant place where life continued essentially as on earth, and for Christians it was heaven.

These common elements aside, the two religions had enormous differences. The Christian insistence that only one deity ruled the universe conflicted with the Huron belief in many supernatural beings. Furthermore, the Hurons had nothing remotely close to the Jesuits' concepts of the Trinity and the Incarnation. Marriage was another controversial issue. The Jesuits found the Hurons' sexual behaviour aberrant. Among the Hurons, divorce was easy and frequent, in contrast with the Jesuits' ideal of the indissolubility of marriage. Since Huron children by custom belonged to the mother, divorce did not endanger family stability. The Hurons also failed to see lifetime marriage as superior to their own custom. Moreover, they could not understand the Jesuits' practice of celibacy and sexual self-denial.

The two cultures also disagreed on issues of human sinfulness and the need for salvation. Although the Hurons distinguished between good and evil, they had no concept similar to the missionaries' idea of universal guilt, of a fundamental inadequacy in human nature. Like most Native North Americans, the Hurons believed that almost all people would experience the same pleasant afterlife, regardless of how they had lived on earth. For the Jesuits, there was both a heaven and a hell. The only way to escape hell was through Christianity. This concept of a place of torment proved very difficult to convey to the Hurons.

The Jesuits tried to convince the Hurons of the worthiness of biblical standards. They insisted that the Hurons curtail easy divorce, marry for life, and end their undue reliance on dreams. To the Hurons, the missionaries threatened to subvert the very customs and beliefs essential to successful hunting, good health, and survival. As a Huron chief complained to Brébeuf, "You are talking of overthrowing the country."

NEW EPIDEMICS STRIKE HURONIA

The French brought with them more than European trade goods and a Christian missionary message. Unknowingly, they brought European diseases that devastated the Hurons and their neighbours. By 1639 smallpox raged throughout Huronia, killing more than half the Huron population and reducing their numbers to 10 000. Since old people and children died in the greatest numbers, the Hurons lost much of their traditional religious lore, which tended to be the preserve of the elderly, and suffered a shortage of warriors in the next decade with the deaths of so many children.

By the late 1630s, the Hurons concluded that the Jesuits were sorcerers who brought disease. The Hurons recognized three major sources of illness: natural causes, unfulfilled desires of a person's soul (alleviated by a form of dream-fulfilment), and witchcraft. Not surprisingly, the Hurons blamed the new diseases on their visitors, since the Jesuits alone seemed immune to the diseases. The Jesuits' celibacy also suggested that the "white shamans" nurtured great supernatural power for the purposes of witchcraft. Furthermore, they seemed to cause death by their rituals: after they touched sick babies with drops of water, many died.

As the epidemics spread, the Hurons' fear of the Jesuits increased. They denied the Jesuits entry into their longhouses and villages. The Hurons harassed and threatened the Jesuits. On at

Model of a Huron village, based on historical and archaeological information. The Hurons located their settlements on slightly elevated ground by streams, and close to sandy, well-drained soil, in which they could grow corn.

© Canadian Museum of Civilization. Photographer Jim Wright, 1965, image no. J10162.

least two occasions, in 1637 and 1640, general Huron councils discussed the death penalty for the missionaries or at least the possibility of forcing "the sorcerers" to return to Quebec. Yet they pursued neither course of action. Many of the leading chiefs realized that the Hurons depended on the French for European hardware and dry goods and that they could not live without them. Thus, trading relations with the French forced the Hurons to tolerate the missionaries.

HURON CHRISTIAN CONVERTS

During the epidemics of the mid-1630s, the missionaries under Jean de Brébeuf's direction worked in selected Huron villages, spending most of their time mingling with the villagers. Jérôme Lalemant, the new superior of the Huron mission, changed this policy in 1638. He constructed a permanent mission headquarters of stone and timber buildings. Begun in 1639, Sainte-Marie included residences, chapels, workshops, and a hospital within its fortified walls. Adjacent to Sainte-Marie, the Jesuits cleared fields and planted crops.

Inspired by accounts of the Jesuits' mission in Paraguay, Lalemant hoped that the Huron converts would settle at Sainte-Marie and adopt French customs. When they refused to leave their villages and abandon their clans, he established permanent Jesuit residences in the major Huron towns. The priests visited other villages on assigned circuits.

In the early 1640s, conversions increased. Several factors contributed to this. No doubt the Jesuits' repeated explanations of the two faiths' common themes helped, and the Jesuits' unquestioned bravery during the Iroquois attacks influenced others to convert. But simple economics also influenced many Huron traders. As anthropologist Bruce Trigger has pointed out, French traders and government officials accorded Native Christians far greater honour and gave them additional presents at Quebec and Trois-Rivières. Another incentive to convert came from the French policy of selling guns only to First Nations people who were baptized. In 1648, when only 15 percent of the Huron population had been baptized, half of those in the Huron trading fleet were already Christians or were receiving instruction. By 1646, the Christian Huron community numbered 500 and was growing.

The development of a Christian faction in Huronia, however, seriously divided the community. Jesuit priests forbade Huron converts to participate in Native feasts and celebrations. To avoid involvement in Huron rituals, Christian warriors often refused to fight alongside traditionalists. Conversion on occasion also resulted in divorce and in the Christian warriors' expulsion from their wives' or mothers' longhouses.

Huron Christians praying. In the mid-1640s, a growing number of Hurons accepted Jesus and his teachings. From Bressani's map of New France, *Novae Franciae Accurata Delineatio* (1657).

National Archives of Canada/C-71502.

THE FINAL STRUGGLE BETWEEN THE HURONS AND THE IROQUOIS

At the time when disease had weakened them and their internal cohesion had been reduced by the growth of a Christian faction, the Hurons faced their greatest military threat from the Iroquois. An Iroquois invitation to the Hurons to join the Five Nations Confederacy had been refused. Furthermore, the Iroquois looked for new sources of furs. The Huron country bordered the fur-rich areas around the upper Great Lakes that the western Iroquois wanted to exploit. They coveted the hunting grounds of southern Ontario.

Guns made the Iroquois a formidable foe. By 1639, they obtained firearms from English traders in the Connecticut valley and then directly from Dutch traders on the upper Hudson River. The longer and heavier

Where Historians Disagree
Why the Hurons Accepted Christianity

In the 1640s an extraordinary event occurred; large numbers of Hurons in good health accepted Christianity. Before 1639, the Jesuits' attempts to Christianize the Hurons met with limited success mostly with individuals who were on the point of death, yet by 1648 they had converted several thousand people. Had it not been for the Iroquois defeat of the Hurons in 1649–50 and their subsequent dispersal, the Jesuits' dream of establishing a Roman Catholic Huronia might have been realized. The massive conversion of Hurons to Christianity in the last years of Huronia has recently aroused new interest among historians.

The impact of disease offers one explanation for the Hurons' sudden receptiveness to Christianity. From 1635 to 1640, a series of epidemics carried away more than half the population. The Hurons lost many of their most skilful leaders and craftspeople, and this had the effect of increasing their dependence on trade with the French. Anthropologist Bruce G. Trigger, in his article "The French Presence in Huronia," identified the economic motives, among other factors, that led many Hurons to convert. They sought, through conversion, "to receive preferential treatment in their dealings with traders and officials in New France," and in particular, to be able to secure guns, which were given only to converts. In fact, as Trigger points out, "in 1648, when only 15 percent of the Hurons were Christian, half of the men in the Huron [trading] fleet were either converts or were preparing for baptism."[1]

Trigger's secular explanation of the Jesuits' success in his later two-volume work[2] greatly annoyed historian Lucien Campeau, a Jesuit. Referring to Trigger's work as "mal-heureusement biaisée et peu exacte sous l'aspect historique" [unfortunately biased and not very historically accurate], Campeau wrote a full account of his order's work among the Hurons in order to prove that the Hurons understood the Christian message as it was preached to them and that this message was the primary reason for their conversion.[3] In reply, Trigger pointed out that Campeau had failed to examine the most recent ethnohistorical research in preparing his study. Moreover, he was too ready to accept, uncritically and at face value, the Jesuits' account of their mission work. "What we have here is splendid hagiography but very old-fashioned historiography."[4]

Biography can be useful in humanizing historical controversies such as this by putting a human face on the discussions. Yet, in the case of the Hurons, the would-be biographer faces incredible obstacles. As Trigger has written, "For the majority of Indians whose names have been preserved, only a few isolated events are recorded and even a skeletal life history of such individuals remains beyond our grasp."[5] Fortunately, however, Trigger was able to use the Jesuit *Relations* to provide an account of the Christian convert Joseph Chihoatenhwa.[6] Expanding upon Trigger's sketch, John Steckley, an anthropologist and student of the Huron language, has completed a short biography.[7] In Chihoatenhwa's case, economic factors apparently played very little part in his decision to accept Christianity, as he traded with the neighbouring Petuns and not with the French. Steckley argues, as does Trigger, that Joseph Chihoatenhwa converted in 1637 for reasons deep within his First Nations culture. "As a Christian,

Chihoatenhwa did have, or believed he had, a source of power on which he could draw, a spiritual source not unlike that upon which a pre-contact Huron shaman could rely. . . . The priest appeared to have an effective medicine when no other was forthcoming; a preventative or cure which Chihoatenhwa accepted much [as] he would have in earlier times accepted the curing vision or dream of a powerful shaman."[8]

Historians, anthropologists, and ethno-historians radically differ about the causes of the Hurons' conversion to Christianity, but all agree on the importance of the phenomenon and on the richness of the Jesuits' descriptions of their efforts to convert the Hurons.

[1] Bruce G. Trigger, "The French Presence in Huronia," *Canadian Historical Review* 49 [1968]: 134, reprinted in R. Douglas Francis and Donald B. Smith, eds., *Readings in Canadian History: Pre-Confederation*, 6th ed. [Toronto: Nelson Thomson Learning, 2000], p. 35.

[2] Bruce G. Trigger, *The Children of Aataentsic: A History of the Huron People to 1660*, 2 vols. (Montreal/Kingston: McGill-Queen's University Press, 1976).

[3] Lucien Campeau, *La Mission des Jésuites chez les Hurons, 1634–1650* (Montreal: Éditions Bellarmin, 1987), p. 18.

[4] Bruce G. Trigger, "Review of *La Mission des Jésuites chez les Hurons, 1634–1650* by Lucien Campeau," *Canadian Historical Review* 69 (1988): 102.

[5] Trigger, *The Children of Aataentsic*, vol. 1, p. 22.

[6] Ibid., vol. 2, pp. 550–51, 565–67, 594–95, 598–601.

[7] One of the three biographies included in John Steckley's *Untold Tales: Three 17th Century Huron* (Ajax, ON: R.A. Kerton, 1981).

[8] Steckley, *Untold Tales*, pp. 9–10.

Dutch guns were superior to those that the French sold to their Christian converts. Thus equipped, the Iroquois could raid the nations to the north much more easily than before.

Bruce Trigger estimates that in 1648 the Iroquois had more than 500 guns, while the Hurons probably had no more than 120. These guns were crude, awkward to handle, and in many ways little better than the bow and arrow, but their thunderous noise and their ability to inflict mortal wounds made them a source of terror. They also increased the self-confidence of those who owned them.

The successful Iroquois attacks of the early 1640s caused some Huron traditionalists to question whether peace with their enemies the Iroquois, with whom they shared common customs and speech, was not preferable to cultural extinction through association with the Jesuits. In the end, however, the majority of the traditionalists mistrusted the Iroquois more than they did the French, and remained with the Christian Hurons in alliance with the French. The defeat of the anti-Jesuit Hurons ended organized resistance to the missionaries.

THE FALL OF HURONIA

In mid-March 1649, a large Iroquois army struck a small Huron village, killing or capturing all but ten of the 400 inhabitants. They then used the village as a base camp to destroy other settlements. Hurons who had earlier been captured and adopted by the Iroquois played a leading role in the attacks. The adopted Hurons, together with the Iroquois, tortured the French priests they captured, regarding them as sorcerers responsible for Huronia's destruction. Familiar with the frequent baptizing of dying children, the attackers repeatedly baptized Father Jean de

Brébeuf and Gabriel Lalemant (the nephew of Jérôme Lalemant, now the superior of all the Jesuits in Canada) with boiling water, then further tortured and finally executed them.

Over the course of the campaign, several hundred Hurons died or were captured. The attacks threw the surviving settlements into chaos. The Hurons, seeing their position as untenable, burned their villages and deserted them. Hunger and contagious diseases claimed many Huron refugees, who spent the winter on Christian Island, in Georgian Bay. A small number of survivors eventually accompanied the Jesuits to Quebec, where the order established a fortified mission for them on Île d'Orléans, just east of the town. Others joined the Algonquians to the north. In the next few years, a number of Hurons voluntarily joined the Iroquois. The Hurons' dispersal marked the end of Huronia.

THE IMPACT OF THE FALL OF HURONIA

The fall of Huronia led to Iroquois attacks on other Iroquoian-speaking peoples. The League of Peace looked increasingly like a League of War. As historian Daniel Richter has written, "Iroquois ideals, like those of most peoples in history, did not always conform to reality."[2] Richter feels that the urgency behind this warfare was a result of the severe depopulation from epidemics after the mid-1630s. Economic motives played a part, but the demand for captives to replace the deceased relatives was equally important.

The Five Nations' subsequent victories over the Hurons' neighbours to the west, the Petuns, and to the south, the Neutrals, greatly disrupted the fur trade. Yet, as Bruce Trigger notes, "The situation would have been far worse for the French if the Huron traditionalists had been able to conclude an alliance with the Iroquois."[3] The diversion of furs to the Dutch on the Hudson River and the consequent bypassing of the St. Lawrence would have ruined the fur-trading colony. As it was, only in the short run did the dispersal of the Hurons hurt the colony's economy — in the long run, it helped it. Because the Hurons could no longer supply food to the northern Algonquians, the latter became a new market for the colony's farmers. Historian John Dickinson has noted also that in the 1650s the majority of the *engagés* began to stay in the colony after their contracts had expired. Farming expanded, as did the French fur trade.

By 1653, the French coureurs de bois had replaced the vanquished Huron intermediaries in the fur trade. They went inland to live with the Algonquians of the upper Great Lakes, or the "Ottawa," as the French called them, and to take their furs to New France. In 1654, Médard Chouart Des Groseilliers canoed into the interior, returning two years later with a rich cargo of furs. (Des Groseilliers' brother-in-law, Pierre-Esprit Radisson, accompanied him on later journeys, including one in 1659 to the far end of Lake Superior, where they heard of a "Bay of the North Sea" hundreds of kilometres to the north.)

RENEWED IROQUOIS ATTACKS ON NEW FRANCE

In the early 1650s, New France suffered greatly and almost collapsed from Iroquois attacks. Between 1650 and 1653, the Iroquois killed 32 French settlers and captured 22. A mere 50 settlers held Montreal, the advance guard of the settlements. Even at Trois-Rivières and Quebec, few went out to work their fields because of the ever-present danger. When they did, they left with sickles in their hands and firearms slung across their backs. The Iroquois's use of guerrilla war tactics, their avoidance of open combat in favour of ambush, and the speed and unexpectedness of their attacks demoralized many colonists in the three tiny French settlements. Marie de l'Incarnation, the founder of the Ursuline order in New France, recalled in a letter to her sister that the Iroquois "made such ravages in their regions that we believed for a time that we should have to go back to France."

A Historical Portrait ☙

☛ Marie de l'Incarnation

In the mid-sixteenth century, France became the focal point for the Roman Catholic Reformation. Hundreds of missionaries left France in the seventeenth century in the hope of beginning a renewed form of Christianity. The situation of women in France was also changing, as the Counter-Reformation offered women, through the practice of new life in Christian perfection, equal rights. In the distant Canadian missions Catholic French women, like Marie de l'Incarnation, could live side by side with men and work together to build a better Christian world.

Marie Guyart, the founder of the Ursuline order in New France, was born in 1599 in Tours, a textile town of almost 20 000 people in the centre of France's rich Loire valley. Her father was a baker. From early childhood, she received religious visitations: when she was a small girl, Jesus had visited her and kissed her in a dream. Even as a girl she had wanted to become a nun.

Pressed by her parents, Marie reluctantly married Claude Martin, a master silkworker. A jealous mother-in-law and financial difficulties that led to her husband's bankruptcy contributed to a troubled marriage. But it was short. After two years of married life, Claude Martin died, leaving his 19-year-old wife destitute and with a son only 6 months old.

The young widow went with her son to live with her sister and her sister's husband. Marie was able to help her brother-in-law, a successful merchant wagoner who transported goods throughout the kingdom. She did everything from grooming horses to keeping the accounts. Shortly after joining

him, the extremely capable businesswoman literally ran his office. But all these years she patiently waited, until her son was old enough and she could finally join a convent.

Marie secretly took a vow of chastity and began to prepare herself for what she called a "mystic union" with Christ. Away from work she abandoned herself to solitude and meditation. She yearned for full union with God. Dreams, visions, and interior voices came to her. To discipline her flesh she wore harsh clothing, slept on a bed of boards, and sometimes rose at night to whip herself first with thongs, then with nettles. By suffering pain she believed she shared, in a small way, the sufferings of Jesus on the cross.

When her son Claude reached the age of 12 she believed him ready for the separation. She arranged for her sister and brother-in-law to look after his education, and she entered the Ursuline convent. Madame Martin became an Ursuline nun under the name of Marie de l'Incarnation and took her final vows two years later in 1633. Although on at least one occasion her son came to the convent door yelling: "Give me back my mother, I want my mother," she remained inside.

Marie de l'Incarnation learned about the Canadian missions from the Jesuit *Relations*. She wanted to bring knowledge of Jesus Christ to the First Nations. Fortunately, a patron, the wealthy Madeline de la Peltrie, came forward to pay for a women's convent in Quebec. Marie de l'Incarnation and two other Ursulines arrived in 1639 at a tiny hamlet of only a few houses. They immediately began their school for

First Nations girls and for an increasing number of settlers' children, who came to predominate in number (the school still exists today). At the time of Marie's death in 1672 the Ursuline community numbered over 20, and Quebec had hundreds of houses and several substantial buildings.

It is estimated that Marie de l'Incarnation wrote approximately 13 000 letters in her lifetime. Unfortunately only several hundred survive, many of them saved by her son, Claude Martin, who became a Benedictine monk. After his mother's death, he wrote her life story. Thanks to Canadian writer Joyce Marshall's translation of a number of the surviving letters, in her book *Word from New*

France: The Selected Letters of Marie de l'Incarnation (Toronto: Oxford University Press, 1967), English-Canadian students can gain access to her thoughts. Marshall writes of this remarkable woman:

> Above all, the personality that emerges is her own and it is unmistakable. She is one of the bare handful of personalities that walk out from among the shadowy stereotypes that are all the chroniclers of the time have sent down to us. Hers was a personality that grew and matured, that we can watch growing and maturing as life worked upon it, and it was permitted a serenity and tenderness at the last that are very moving. (p. 20)

Only with the outbreak of war between the Iroquois and the Eries to the west did New France obtain a 5-year truce with the Iroquois in the mid-1650s. However, fighting resumed in 1658. Fortunately for the French, their population had increased by this time: the population had tripled, from 1050 permanent French residents in 1651 to nearly 3300 by 1662, thanks largely to new farming opportunities. The French had also developed more effective measures against Iroquois attacks. A small detachment of soldiers patrolled the St. Lawrence from Trois-Rivières to Montreal, the most exposed settlement. The French organized militia units and erected stockades. They also came to realize that the Iroquois could best be fought by using guerrilla tactics, and so adopted them.

DOLLARD DES ORMEAUX

The settlers made their first advance against the Iroquois in the spring of 1660. The military force consisted of Adam Dollard Des Ormeaux, an ambitious young soldier recently arrived from France, and sixteen other young Frenchmen, along with Annaotaha, an experienced Huron warrior, with several dozen warriors. They left Montreal intending to ambush a small Iroquois party on the Ottawa River.

To his complete surprise, Dollard encountered at Long Sault, northwest of Montreal, an Iroquois invasion army of some 300 warriors on their way to rendezvous with 400 more who awaited them at the Richelieu River. The Iroquois besieged the French and their Native allies, and then waited for reinforcements before making the final assault. In the interim, some of the adopted Hurons in the Iroquois camp persuaded a number of the Hurons with Dollard to join them. Since the French had turned over several Huron refugees to the Iroquois not long before, most of the Hurons felt no obligation to fight to the death. Only five Frenchmen remained alive when the final Iroquois attack came. All five died at the torture stake. But three Hurons escaped to recount the tragedy to the French.

Historian André Vachon thus summarized the accomplishment of Dollard and his companions in repelling an attack on Montreal: they "diverted the Iroquois army temporarily from

The battle of Long Sault on the Ottawa River assumed epic proportions for French-Canadian nationalists in the early twentieth century. Writers such as Abbé Lionel Groulx (1878–1967) wrote of Dollard Des Ormeaux as the soldier-saint who saved Montreal in 1660. This painting by the famous Quebec artist M.-A. de Foy Suzor-Côté (1869–1937), completed in 1926, is entitled *Le combat de Dollard Des Ormeaux 1660*.

National Archives of Canada/C-3108.

its objective in 1660, thereby allowing the settlers to harvest their crop and escape famine and allowing Radisson to reach Montreal safe and sound with a load of furs."[4] (In the late nineteenth and early twentieth centuries, French-Canadian historians resurrected Dollard as a national French-Canadian hero. In French-speaking Quebec, May 24 was popularly known as Dollard Day throughout most of the twentieth century.)

Security finally came for the habitants when, in 1663, King Louis XIV elevated the tiny colony to a royal province of France. The previous year he had sent 100 troops to New France, and in 1665 he dispatched the Carignan-Salières regiment, over 1000 strong. In 1666, the French made two overland attacks on the Mohawks in present-day New York State. The Iroquois, who were also then involved in a war with the Susquehannock (Iroquoian-speaking First Nations living in present-day Pennsylvania), made peace with the French in 1667. Upon their regiment's recall to France in 1668, some 400 officers and men of the Carignan-Salières took their discharge in New France. The officers received large tracts of land in the exposed region along the Richelieu River and near Montreal. Twenty years of peace followed, during which the colony greatly advanced.

THE IROQUOIS AND THE FRENCH, 1667–1701

Tension continued between the Five Nations and the French in the Great Lakes area. To obtain furs, the Iroquois sent raiding parties in the late 1660s to the Illinois country, but this interfered with

French exploration of the Mississippi valley. The Illinois nation refused to accept the Iroquois invitation to ally themselves with the Iroquois League and turned to the French, who promised aid and protection. Relations between the Five Nations and the French deteriorated every year as the Iroquois increased their raids against the Illinois, now French allies.

At the same time that the Five Nations attacked the Illinois to the west, they attempted to improve their relations with the northern Algonquians in order to obtain their furs. This seriously troubled the French, whose policy, succinctly put, aimed to keep their Algonquian allies at peace among themselves but at war with the Five Nations. The establishment of Hudson's Bay Company posts on James Bay and Hudson Bay in the 1670s had already diverted northern furs to the English. If the Iroquois took more furs from north of the Great Lakes to the Atlantic seaboard, New France would lose its leading export.

The Iroquois had colonized the north shore of Lake Ontario in the 1660s, and they used their settlements as bases for trading with the northern Algonquians. These developing trade links led the French to establish the post of Cataraqui, or Frontenac (at present-day Kingston), in 1673 to control the trade at the eastern end of Lake Ontario. Around 1680, the French also briefly maintained a fort at Niagara to control the trade at the western end of Lake Ontario.

The French ended their truce with the Iroquois in the mid-1680s. They wanted the Five Nations to cease their attacks on the Illinois and to stop trading the northern Algonquians' furs to the English. Governor Le Febvre de La Barre's attempted invasion of the Iroquois country proved a fiasco. When provisions ran out and fever ravaged the governor's troops, he signed a humiliating peace treaty with the Iroquois that led to his dismissal as governor.

In 1687, the French persuaded the Algonquians to join nearly 2000 French troops on a second expedition to the Iroquois country. The invaders burned a number of villages, destroyed cornfields, and looted graves. The war was now fully underway. In 1689 the Iroquois, with the aid of the English, retaliated by attacking the French settlement at Lachine, about 15 km west of Montreal. According to a French account, 1500 Iroquois laid waste the open country: "The ground was everywhere covered with corpses, and the Iroquois carried away six-score captives, most of whom were burned." Historian José António Brandão estimates that the Iroquois captured or killed close to 600 French colonists from 1687 to 1697.[5]

The early 1690s marked the high point of the Iroquois's success against the French — but then their fortunes turned. The settlers (by necessity now skilled in the techniques of guerrilla warfare), together with 1500 regular troops sent from France, gained the upper hand. By 1693, the Five Nations were suffering very heavy losses as a result of both war and disease. In the face of the Algonquians' attacks, they could no longer maintain their forward position on the north shore of Lake Ontario. Their numbers fell from more than 10 000 in the 1640s to less than 9000 at the turn of the century, despite the massive adoptions of other Iroquoians.

IROQUOIS CHRISTIAN CONVERTS

A major break in the unity of the League came in the late seventeenth century. The presence of Jesuit priests in their villages during the truce weakened the Iroquois, especially from 1668 to

Abbé Lionel Groulx, in a photo taken in 1960, holds his book *Dollard, est-il un mythe?* (*Dollard, Is He a Myth?*) published in Montreal that same year. For this nationalist historian, Dollard served as an example of what French Canadians should all strive to become.

National Archives of Canada/C-16657.

An eighteenth-century Iroquois warrior, an engraving of a sketch by Jacques Grasset St. Sauveur. Although he left Canada in 1764 at the age of 7, Grasset, who became a fashionable novelist in France, vividly remembered the Iroquois. He had seen them in his native Montreal, where his father was involved in trading with the First Nations.

National Archives of Canada/C-3165.

1686. The priests attracted war captives who had previously encountered missionaries and others to move from the Iroquois villages in present-day New York State to their mission on the island of Montreal (later moved to the Lake of Two Mountains, to Oka, in 1717), and at Sault St. Louis (Caughnawaga, now Kahnawake) southwest of Montreal.

Perhaps the most famous convert was Kateri Tegakwitha (pronounced Teg-gah-kweet-ha), the daughter of a Mohawk father and an Algonquian mother. After her conversion she escaped to Sault St. Louis where she organized, with two other Iroquois women, a special society of devotion. Until her death, in 1680, Kateri's band of devout women flourished. In 1980, three centuries after her death, Pope John Paul II beatified Kateri, which is just one step away from sainthood in the Roman Catholic church.

By 1700, an estimated two-thirds of the Mohawks, the most easterly of the Five Nations or Iroquois Confederacy, lived in the Montreal area. In the early 1690s, Canadian Iroquois fought beside the French against the League Iroquois.

Conversion to Christianity weakened the indigenous belief systems of the Iroquois. The Jesuit *Relations* report, for example, that when ritual demanded that Garakontié, a leading Christian convert, recite "the genealogy and origin of the Iroquois ... he always protested that what he was about to say was merely a formula which is usually followed on such occasions, but that it was not true"; indeed, he said it was "simply a story, and that Jesus was the sole Master of our lives."

Many of the Jesuits' Iroquois converts were recently adopted Hurons and other prisoners, a fact that indicates the Five Nations had not yet had enough time to assimilate fully all their growing number of adoptees. In the mid-1660s, several Jesuit missionaries established that adoptees constituted two-thirds or more of the population of many Iroquois villages. The recently adopted Iroquois no doubt weakened the unity of the Five Nations' communities.

THE SOUTHWARD MIGRATION OF THE ALGONQUIANS

The Algonquians considered themselves the allies, not the subjects, of France. In 1671, the French had claimed possession of the Great Lakes in the presence of a great convocation at Sault Ste. Marie. Fourteen nations witnessed the raising of a cross and of a post bearing France's coat of arms. The Algonquians, however, had an entirely different understanding of the proceedings, as evidenced by their oral history of the event, which William Warren, a nineteenth-century Native historian, later recorded. The First Nations believed that the French had simply asked "for permission to trade in the country," and that the French king's representative had, in return, "promised the protection of the great French nation against all their enemies."[6]

Having secured their ties with the French and having seen the Five Nations Confederacy in such a weakened state, the Algonquians advanced south from Lake Superior and the north shore of Lake Huron to occupy the former Huron, Petun, and Neutral homelands. By coming south, the Algonquians acquired rich new hunting and fishing grounds. Some even acquired a new name: The English colonists on the Atlantic coast termed all the newcomers in the area bounded by Lakes Ontario, Erie, and Huron either Chippewa or Ojibwa. But they reserved a new name,

Mississauga, for the Ojibwa on the north shore of Lake Ontario. In 1640, the Jesuit fathers first recorded the term *omisagai* (Mississauga) as the name of an Algonquian band near the Mississagi River on the northwestern shore of Lake Huron. For unknown reasons, the French, and later the English, applied this name to all the Algonquians settling on the north shore of Lake Ontario. Only a tiny fraction of these Native people could have been members of the actual Mississauga bands, but once recorded in the Europeans' documents, the name became the one most commonly used. The Ojibwa, of course, continued to call themselves by their own name of *Anishinabeg*, meaning "human beings."

PEACE ESTABLISHED, 1701

The English made peace with the French in 1697. This truce led the Iroquois to reconsider their own conflict with the French. In 1700 they made an offer to the French, who convened a council with them at Montreal. Combat fatalities, the exodus of Roman Catholic converts to New France, and disease had all greatly weakened the Iroquois. The Five Nations had had approximately 2570 warriors in 1689; by 1700, there were only 1230.

The Iroquois south of Lake Ontario made peace with the French and the western nations in August 1701. First Nation representatives travelled to Montreal for the ratification of the treaty. To ensure that the Iroquois continued to serve as a buffer between the English colonies and New France, the French allowed them to continue to trade some northern furs with the English. (The Christian Iroquois at Kahnawake became the intermediaries in the lucrative Albany–Montreal trade route.) In turn, the Five Nations promised their neutrality in any future colonial war between France and England. The Great Peace ended the Iroquois wars that had menaced New France for decades.

In the short term, the non-Christian Iroquois had seriously hindered the expansion of New France. The colony's very existence was in question after the dispersal of the Hurons and after the Iroquois raids on the tiny French settlements in the St. Lawrence valley in the early 1650s. Yet, in the long term, the destruction of Huronia actually contributed to New France's growth. Agriculture became more profitable as the colony inherited the Hurons' former role as the Algonquians' "provisioners." In addition, the French in the late 1650s and early 1660s entered the interior themselves to trade directly for the Algonquians' furs, and the coureurs de bois helped reinforce the existing Franco–Algonquian alliance. Together, the French and their Algonquian allies gained the upper hand over the Five Nations in the late 1680s and 1690s, which led to the Great Peace of 1701.

NOTES

1. John Webster Grant, *Moon of Wintertime: Missionaries and the Indians of Canada in Encounter since 1534* (Toronto: University of Toronto Press, 1984), p. 24.
2. Daniel K. Richter, *The Ordeal of the Longhouse: The Peoples of the Iroquois League in the Era of European Colonization* (Chapel Hill: University of North Carolina Press, 1992), p. 38.
3. Bruce G. Trigger, *Natives and Newcomers: Canada's "Heroic Age" Reconsidered* (Montreal/Kingston: McGill-Queen's University Press, 1985), p. 335.
4. André Vachon, "Dollard Des Ormeaux," in *Dictionary of Canadian Biography*, vol. 1 (Toronto: University of Toronto Press, 1966), p. 274.
5. José António Brandão, *Your Fyre Shall Burn No More: Iroquois Policy toward New France and Its Native Allies to 1701* (Lincoln: University of Nebraska Press, 1997), p. 125.
6. William M. Warren, *History of the Ojibway Nation* (Minneapolis: Ross & Haines, 1957 [1885]), p. 131.

LINKING TO THE PAST www

De-Ka-Nah-Wi-Da and Hiawatha
http://www.indians.org/welker/hiawatha.htm

The story of Dekanahwideh and Hiawatha from the Indigenous Peoples' Literature site.

Huron and Iroquois History
http://www.tolatsga.org/hur.html and http://www.tolatsga.org/iro.html

These pages from the First Nations Histories site feature a wealth of information on these two confederacies, including detailed accounts of the wars between them, and of the influence that French settlers and French trade had on their relations.

The Native People of Simcoe County, Ontario
http://innisfil.library.on.ca/natives

A detailed account of the Native history in the heart of former Huronia; topics covered include interaction with the Europeans, wars, migration, and disease.

Sainte-Marie among the Hurons
http://www.saintemarieamongthehurons.on.ca

Detailed information on life in this seventeenth-century Jesuit mission in present-day Ontario. For additional information, visit http://www.sfo.com/~denglish/wynaks/wn_stmar.htm.

The Early Years of the Hudson's Bay Company
http://www.hbc.com/hbc/e_hi/historic_hbc/earlyyears.htm

The first two sections of this site from the Hudson's Bay Company cover early exploration, establishment of posts on James Bay and Hudson Bay, and the granting of the Royal Charter.

Fort Frontenac
http://www.carf.info/kingstonpast/fortfrontenac.php

This page from the Cataraqui Archaeological Research Foundation provides an illustrated overview of the history and archaeology of Fort Frontenac (located in present-day Kingston).

RELATED READINGS

R. Douglas Francis and Donald B. Smith, eds., *Readings in Canadian History: Pre-Confederation*, 6th ed. (Toronto: Nelson Thomson Learning, 2002), includes Bruce G. Trigger, "The French Presence in Huronia: The Structure of Franco–Huron Relations in the First Half of the Seventeenth Century," pp. 21–47; and W.J. Eccles, "Society and the Frontier," pp. 78–91.

BIBLIOGRAPHY

A number of studies exist on the relationship between the People of the Longhouse and the French. William N. Fenton provides an overview in "The Iroquois in History," in Eleanor Burke Leacock and Nancy Oestreich Lurie, eds., *North American Indians in Historical Perspective* (New York: Random House, 1971), pp. 129–68. This essay is reprinted in his encyclopedic work, *The Great Law and the Longhouse: A Political History of the Iroquois Confederacy* (Norman: University of Oklahoma Press, 1998). On First Nation–European relations in general during this period see Bruce G. Trigger, ed., *Northeast*, vol. 15 of the *Handbook of North American Indians* (Washington, DC: Smithsonian Institution, 1978); and Denys Delâge, *Bitter Feast: Amerindians and Europeans in Northeastern North America, 1600–64*, trans. Jane Brierley (Vancouver: University of British Columbia Press, 1993).

Bruce G. Trigger's summary in *Natives and Newcomers: Canada's "Heroic Age" Reconsidered* (Montreal/Kingston: McGill-Queen's University Press, 1985) covers the early period of contact to 1663.

Trigger has also written *The Indians and the Heroic Age of New France* (Ottawa: Canadian Historical Association, 1989 [1977]). The best short introduction to the Five (later Six) Nations, or Iroquois, remains Dean R. Snow, *The Iroquois* (Oxford: Blackwell, 1994). Francis Jennings reviews the period from the 1600s to 1744 in *The Ambiguous Iroquois Empire* (New York: W.W. Norton, 1984), and in his sequel, *Empire of Fortune: Crowns, Colonies and Tribes in the Seven Years War in America* (New York: W.W. Norton, 1988). A useful study of the Iroquois and their relations with neighbouring First Nations groups is Daniel K. Richter and James H. Merrell, *Beyond the Covenant Chain: The Iroquois and Their Neighbors in Indian North America, 1600–1800* (Syracuse: Syracuse University Press, 1987).

Paul A.W. Wallace relates the story of the founding of the League of the Iroquois in *The White Roots of Peace* (Philadelphia: University of Pennsylvania, 1946; reprinted Ohsweken, ON: Iroqrafts, 1998). A shorter version by the same author entitled "Dekanahwideh" appears in the *Dictionary of Canadian Biography*, vol. 1, *1000–1700* (Toronto: University of Toronto Press, 1966), pp. 253–55. Christopher Vecsey comments on other versions in "The Story and Structure of the Iroquois Confederacy," *Journal of the American Academy of Religion 54* (1986): 79–106. William Engelbrecht relies on archaeological as well as oral data to determine the league's origins in his article "New York Iroquois Political Development," in William W. Fitzhugh, ed., *Cultures in Contact* (Washington, DC: Smithsonian Institution Press, 1985), pp. 163–83. Anthony F.C. Wallace (son of Paul A.W. Wallace) has written a complete study of one of the Iroquois nations in *The Death and Rebirth of the Seneca* (New York: Alfred A. Knopf, 1969). On the status of women in Iroquois society see the collection of essays edited by W.G. Spittal, *Iroquois Women: An Anthology* (Ohsweken, ON: Iroqrafts, 1990). A very good summary of the culture of the Iroquois is Hazel W. Hertzberg's *The Great Tree and the Longhouse* (New York: Macmillan, 1966).

There are a number of studies on the Hurons. Bruce G. Trigger, *The Huron Farmers of the North*, 2nd ed. (Fort Worth, TX: Holt, Rinehart and Winston, 1990); and Elisabeth Tooker, *An Ethnography of the Huron Indians, 1615–1649* (Syracuse, NY: Syracuse University Press, 1991), are the best starting points. See also Conrad Heidenreich, *Huronia: A History and Geography of the Huron Indians, 1600–1650* (Toronto: McClelland & Stewart, 1971). Bruce G. Trigger provides the fullest review in *The Children of Aataentsic: A History of the Huron People to 1660*, 2 vols. (Montreal/Kingston: McGill-Queen's University Press, 1976). Georges E. Sioui has written *Les Wendats: Une civilisation méconnue* (Quebec: Les presses de l'Université Laval, 1994).

Good short summaries of the Jesuits' contact with the Hurons are contained in Henry Warner Bowden, *American Indians and Christian Missions* (Chicago: University of Chicago Press, 1981), pp. 59–95; and in James Axtell, *The Invasion Within: The Contest of Cultures in Colonial North America* (New York: Oxford University Press, 1985). These can be supplemented by John Webster Grant's *Moon of Wintertime: Missionaries and the Indians of Canada in Encounter since 1534* (Toronto: University of Toronto Press, 1984). A full review is provided by Father Lucien Campeau in *La Mission des Jésuites chez les Hurons, 1634–1650* (Montreal: Éditions Bellarmin, 1987). S.R. Mealing has edited *The Jesuit Relations and Allied Documents* (Toronto: McClelland & Stewart, 1963), a one-volume anthology of selections from the Jesuit *Relations*. Dean R. Snow, Charles T. Gehring, and William A. Starna provide a good selection of documents, including several translated from Dutch, in *Mohawk Country: Early Narratives about the Native People* (Syracuse, NY: Syracuse University Press, 1996). Cornelius Jaenen has edited a useful collection of French documents, *The French Regime in the Upper Country of Canada during the Seventeenth Century* (Toronto: Champlain Society, 1996). In her book *Chain Her by One Foot: The Subjugation of Women in Seventeenth-Century New France* (London: Routledge, 1991), Karen Anderson argues that the Jesuits introduced the subjugation of women by men in the Hurons' egalitarian society. For a complete biography of an important Jesuit priest in Huronia see René Latourelle, *Jean de Brébeuf* (Montreal: Éditions Bellarmin, 1993). Carole Blackburn's *Harvest of Souls: The Jesuit Mission and Colonialism in North America, 1632–1650* (Montreal/Kingston: McGill-Queen's University Press, 2000) is a recent study.

Important books on the Iroquois and the Great Lakes Native peoples include Daniel K. Richter, *The Ordeal of the Longhouse: The Peoples of the Iroquois League in the Era of European Colonization* (Chapel Hill: University of North Carolina Press, 1992); Richard White, *The Middle Ground: Indians, Empires, and Republics in the Great Lakes Region, 1650–1815* (Cambridge: Cambridge University Press, 1991); Gilles Havard, *The Great Peace of Montreal of 1701. French–Native Diplomacy in the Seventeenth Century* (Montreal/Kingston: McGill-Queen's University Press, 2001); Alain Beaulieu and Roland Viau, *The Great Peace: Chronicle of Diplomatic Saga* (Montreal: Libre Expression, 2001); Brian J. Given, *A Most Pernicious Thing: Gun Trading and Native Warfare in the Early Contact Period* (Ottawa: Carleton University Press, 1994);

Matthew Dennis, *Cultivating a Landscape of Peace: Iroquois–European Encounters in Seventeenth-Century America* (Cooperstown, NY: Cornell University Press, 1993); José António Brandão, *Your Fyre Shall Burn No More: Iroquois Policy toward New France and Its Native Allies to 1701* (Lincoln: University of Nebraska Press, 1997).

Information on the First Nations in the St. Lawrence valley is contained in Marc Jetten, *Enclaves amérindiennes: les "réductions" du Canada 1637–1701* (Sillery, QC: Septentrion, 1994). In his collection of five biographies of First Nations women, John Steckley tells the story of the important Iroquois convert to Catholicism, Kateri Tegakwitha, in his *Beyond Their Years. Five Native Women's Stories* (Toronto: Canadian Scholars' Press Inc., 1999), pp. 13–67. Another interesting essay on her is Allan Greer's "Savage/Saint: The Lives of Kateri Tegakwitha," in Sylvie Dépatie et al., *Vingt ans après. Habitants et Marchands. Twenty Years Later* (Montreal/Kingston: McGill-Queen's University Press, 1988), pp. 138–159. William N. Fenton and Elizabeth L. Moore have edited and translated the Jesuit Father Joseph-François Lafitau's perceptive study of the Iroquois at Sault St. Louis (Kahnawake) near Montreal in the early eighteenth century, *Customs of the American Indians Compared with the Customs of Primitive Times*, 2 vols. (Toronto: Champlain Society, 1974). For a fascinating account of a New England captive at Kahnawake see John Demos, *The Unredeemed Captive: A Family Story from Early America* (New York: Vintage Books, 1995). Gerald R. Alfred's *Heeding the Voices of our Ancestors: Kahnawake Mohawk Politics and the Rise of Native Nationalism* (Toronto: Oxford University Press, 1995) contains one chapter on the history of Kahnawake in the late seventeenth and early eighteenth centuries.

The best treatment of Dollard is by André Vachon in the *Dictionary of Canadian Biography*, vol. 1 (Toronto: University of Toronto Press, 1966), pp. 266–75. Terry Crowley has collected a number of primary and secondary accounts of this famous son of New France in his edited work *Clio's Craft: A Primer of Historical Methods* (Toronto: Copp Clark Pitman, 1988), pp. 253–303. Patrice Groulx reviews interpretations of Dollard in *Pièges de la mémoire: Dollard des Ormeaux, les Amérindiens et nous* (Hull, QC: Editions Vents d'Ouest, 1998).

For French views of the Iroquois see Joyce Marshall, trans. and ed., *Word from New France: The Selected Letters of Marie de l'Incarnation* (Toronto: Oxford University Press, 1967). Studies on Marie de l'Incarnation and the First Nations include Natalie Zemon Davis, "Marie de l'Incarnation, New Worlds," in *Women on the Margins: Three Seventeenth-Century Lives* (Cambridge, MA: Harvard University Press, 1995), pp. 63–139, 259–95; Françoise Deroy-Pineau, *Marie de l'Incarnation. Marie Guyart, femme d'affaires, mystique, mère de la Nouvelle-France (1599–1672* (Montreal: Fides, 1999); and Claire Gourdeau's *Les délices de nos coeurs: Marie de l'Incarnation et ses pensionnaires amérindiennes* (Sillery, QC: Septentrion, 1994).

Useful maps showing France's inland expansion appear in R. Cole Harris, ed., *Historical Atlas of Canada*, vol. 1, *From the Beginning to 1800* (Toronto: University of Toronto Press, 1987).

PROVINCE DE FRANCE, 1663–1760

From the 1650s onward, the small French colony in the St. Lawrence valley grew steadily. A new market for French farm produce opened up among the Algonquians after the scattering of the Hurons in 1649–50. French traders entered the interior to gather and bring out furs, thus expanding the trade. Decades of warfare with the Iroquois forged a sense of unity among the settlers. More than 70 years of intermittent struggle with England's American colonies, from 1689 to 1760, also helped to fashion a new Canadian identity. The military support, given by both France's Algonquian allies and the First Nations at mission stations in the St. Lawrence valley, helped to protect New France against the English colonies.

Between 1663 and 1672, the French Crown strengthened the colony's economic infrastructure and introduced new political institutions that lasted nearly a century. Three individuals transformed New France: King Louis XIV; Jean-Baptiste Colbert, the king's minister of the marine; and Jean Talon, the first intendant, and the official responsible for the civil administration of the colony. They worked to transform the St. Lawrence valley into La Nouvelle France — a new France overseas. By the early eighteenth century, however, a distinct, new people was emerging, the *Canadiens*.

THE FIRST HALF-CENTURY OF ROYAL GOVERNMENT

In 1661, Louis XIV became king of France. He created an absolute monarchy in which all authority descended from him (*"L'état c'est moi,"* he said in his famous phrase). The "Sun King," as he became known, ruled France for the next half-century, until his death in 1715.

The new monarch sought to create a dynamic French presence in North America by making New France a *province de France*, a colony directly under his personal rule. New France now acquired the same administrative structures that the French provinces had, but New France was under the supervision of Jean-Baptiste Colbert, the minister of the marine, or to use the more modern term, minister of colonies.

As did other contemporary Western European governments, the French looked upon their colonies as existing exclusively for the profit of the metropolis. Whatever manufactured goods the settlers needed, they must buy from France. The colonists, in turn, were expected to supply France with natural products and to sell their exports only in France. Only French ships could transport goods to and fro. This was mercantilism. Colbert believed that if New France produced more than it cost to administer, the colony could help to make France rich.

From New France, the mother country wanted furs, minerals, and timber (including ship masts), which France formerly had to import from Scandinavia and Russia. In addition, Colbert sought to develop a triangular trade network among New France, the French possessions in the Caribbean, and France itself. New France could export fish, wheat, peas, and barrel staves to France and the French West Indies; the islands could export rum, molasses, and sugar to Canada and France; and France could send its textiles and manufactured goods to Canada and the West Indies.

New France had to become more self-sufficient before the master plan could succeed. Colbert dreamed of making New France into a much more self-reliant, defensible colony, with a prosperous agricultural base in the St. Lawrence valley and its own basic domestic industries. The minister wanted it to become a "compact colony," one centred in the St. Lawrence valley, without unnecessary forts and outposts on the periphery. He also opposed western expansion. Colbert's first objective was to strengthen the colony militarily. In the mid-1660s, he dispatched regular troops to New France, the Carignan-Salières regiment. When the Iroquois made peace in 1667, Colbert's program to transform New France into a profitable and well-populated colony based in the St. Lawrence valley began.

THE REFORM OF THE SEIGNEURIAL SYSTEM

In fashioning this new royal province of France, the minister of the marine reformed the system of land holdings. French immigrants to the colony were familiar with it because it formed the basis of land tenure in France. Peasant settlers, or *censitaires*, depended on seigneurs, or lords (or, more appropriately, squires or gentry), in turn themselves vassals of the king. Title to all the land rested with the king, who granted fiefs, or estates, as he saw fit. The soil belonged to the seigneur, but the mineral or subsoil rights and all oak trees on the property belonged to the monarch. Landowners who acquired large domains and who did nothing to improve them lost their lands to more energetic seigneurs.

In 1627, the king granted the Company of One Hundred Associates legal and seigneurial rights over the territory of New France. The company in turn granted to favoured individuals — usually nobles or religious bodies such as the Jesuits, the Ursulines, or the Sulpicians — large tracts of land, called "seigneuries," along the St. Lawrence between Quebec and Montreal. In return for their rectangular estates fronting on the river and usually extending into the foothills behind, the seigneurs undertook to bring out the *censitaires* (or habitants, to employ Canadian usage), who in turn paid them rent and dues.

Under royal government, the intendant, among his other administrative duties, granted seigneuries and supervised the seigneurial system. On his arrival in 1665, Jean Talon, the first intendant of New France, implemented Colbert's plan. He made actual occupancy a condition of all future grants. Talon and his immediate successors also kept the size of the seigneuries relatively small to prevent the rise of a class of large landowners who might challenge royal authority. Nearly 200 seigneuries were open for settlement by 1715, most of them along the St. Lawrence from Montreal to below Quebec.

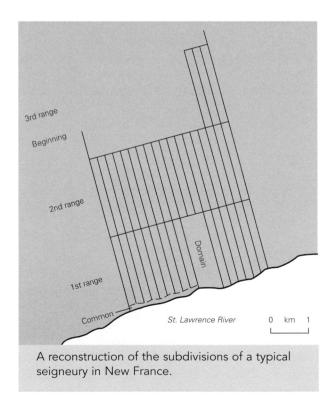

A reconstruction of the subdivisions of a typical seigneury in New France.

THE OBLIGATIONS OF THE SEIGNEURS AND THE *CENSITAIRES*

Both the seigneurs and the *censitaires* had obligations to fulfil under the seigneurial system. The seigneurs had to clear some of their seigneury, maintain a manor house, and reside there or have a responsible person living there throughout the year. They had to make land grants of up to 80 ha to any genuine settlers who applied. Finally, on part of their land, they had to establish a flour mill for the use of their *censitaires*. Some seigneurs also maintained a court of law to settle minor disputes.

The *censitaires*, or habitants, also had responsibilities. They had to build their own house, clear their land, and pay their seigneur the *cens* (a small cash payment) and *rentes* (another money payment). Together, these two charges amounted to less than one-tenth of a *censitaire's* annual income. They had to take their wheat to the seigneurial mill, paying the seigneur one sack of flour out of every fourteen for this privilege. In a few seigneuries, the seigneur had the *droit de corvée* (right to forced labour), usually three days per year, determined in the contract with the *censitaire*. As well, the *censitaires* were required by the Crown to work without pay for a day or two a year, doing general maintenance work on any seigneurial roads or bridges. In return for their grant of land, the habitants had to maintain the portion of road that passed through their farms. If they met these requirements, the habitants became virtual owners of their land, which they could pass on to their children. If they sold their land outside their families, however, they must pay the seigneur a portion of the money they obtained, somewhat like a real-estate sales tax.

Under royal government, the settlers became part of a well-organized social unit and gained title to a tract of land. In time, the seigneur built a manor house, a church, and a mill on the seigneury. Many seigneurs in pioneer times lived and worked as their habitants did, and this blunted the social distinctions that had prevailed in France between lord and peasant. In the colony's early years, in fact, a handful of enterprising and ambitious settlers themselves became seigneurs. Pierre Boucher, a pioneer of modest means, managed to become a seigneur in early New France; in 1654, he was elevated to the governorship of Trois-Rivières. As historians Louise Dechêne and Fernand Ouellet argue, however, social distinctions did become important as the seigneuries became heavily settled and the opportunity for social mobility declined.

THE GROWTH OF SETTLEMENT

To help populate the seigneuries, Colbert and Jean Talon worked to correct a social imbalance in the colony: the abundance of eligible bachelors and shortage of French women. In Montreal in 1663, for example, there was only one marriageable woman for every eight eligible men. Before 1660 the average age of first-time French brides in the colony was fifteen. Most widows remarried within a year of their husband's death.

THE DAUGHTERS OF THE KING

Colbert sought women who were strong enough for work in the fields and who had a good moral character. At first the French Crown selected orphanage girls, but when they proved not to be rugged enough, it recruited young, healthy country girls. A number of the *filles du roi* ("daughters of the king") were not much older than sixteen. The king provided substantial dowries — "the king's gift" — usually consisting of clothing or household supplies. When the young women arrived in Quebec, the Ursulines and Hospital sisters looked after them. In all, the state sent out nearly 800 *filles du roi* between 1663 and 1673.

Where Historians Disagree

◈ The Nature of the Seigneurial System in New France

French-Canadian historians have debated the nature of the seigneurial system in New France for more than a quarter of a century. Earlier historians, such as François-Xavier Garneau, held that the system was neither harsh nor oppressive. According to them, the institutions that France established in the St. Lawrence valley, including the seigneurial system, had been purified in the new setting, their negative aspects removed by the French Crown. In 1899, historian Benjamin Sulte suggested that the seigneur in New France was not an exploiter but a "colonization agent."[1] This traditionalist interpretation of New France as an open, egalitarian society dominated in Quebec until the mid-twentieth century.

A new, critical view of the seigneurial system emerged in the 1960s and 1970s. In 1974, Louise Dechêne published a meticulous local study of the Montreal area that pointed to the oppressive nature of the seigneurial system in the late seventeenth century.[2] She thus sided with fellow historian Fernand Ouellet, who, in his numerous writings from the 1960s to the 1980s, argued that in the eighteenth century New France was a class-bound society. Both Dechêne and Ouellet maintained that seigneurial practices in the St. Lawrence valley conformed to French patterns. In some cases, the customs in Canada were more outdated than those in France. As Ouellet wrote in 1981, "In brief, the *ancien régime* society that had developed in the St. Lawrence valley, far from being a modernized or purified version of that of the mother country, was in a sense more archaic."[3]

Anglophone historians are equally divided on the seigneurial system. R. Cole Harris, for instance, agrees with traditionalist French-Canadian historians. He questions the interpretation that farmers in New France occupied a position comparable to that of peasants in rural France during the last two centuries of pre-revolutionary France. "Rural Canada provided relative opportunity (cheaper land and higher wages) for ordinary people, and relative disincentive (higher labour costs, land of little value, and weak markets) for a landed elite."[4] Harris argues that the rural population of New France was independent and self-reliant, and that it had opportunities for upward mobility. To a certain extent, the late W.J. Eccles, the leading anglophone historian on New France, in the 1970s and 1980s, sided with the traditionalists. He wrote, "The seigneurs were little more than land settlement agents and their financial rewards were not great."[5]

Historian Allan Greer, in a monograph,[6] has challenged the traditionalists' viewpoint. Greer contends that "exploitation, domination, and the clash of interests were characteristics of rural Canada since the early years of the French regime."[7] More recently, he elaborated further: "By the end of the French regime, a substantial proportion of the surplus production, that is, of the grain not needed to keep family members alive, was being siphoned off by the colony's seigneurs. All in all, seigneurial exactions did tear a significant chunk out of the habitant household economy."[8]

[1] Benjamin Sulte, "Le système seigneurial," in *Mélanges historiques*, vol. 1 (Montréal, 1918), p. 80; cited in Serge Jaumain et Matteo Sanfilippo, "Le Régime seigneurial en Nouvelle-France: Un débat historiographique," *The Register* 5,2 (Autumn 1984): 227.

[2] Louise Dechêne, *Habitants et marchands de Montréal au XVIIe Siècle* (Paris: Les Edition Plons, 1974).

[3] Fernand Ouellet, "The Formation of a New Society in the St. Lawrence Valley: From Classless Society to Class Conflict," in Jacques A. Barbier, ed. and trans., *Economy, Class and Nation in Quebec: Interpretive Essays* (Toronto: Copp Clark Pitman, 1991), p. 33; originally published in French in the *Canadian Historical Review* 62, 4 (1981): 407–50.

[4] R. Cole Harris, in the new preface to *The Seigneurial System in Early Canada: A Geographical Study*, 2nd ed. (Montreal/Kingston: McGill-Queen's University Press, 1984), p. xix.

[5] W.J. Eccles, *The Canadian Frontier 1534–1760* (Toronto: Holt, Rinehart and Winston, 1969), p. 68.

[6] Allan Greer, *Peasant, Lord, and Merchant: Rural Society in Three Quebec Parishes, 1740–1840* (Toronto: University of Toronto Press, 1985).

[7] Ibid, p. xiv.

[8] Allan Greer, *The People of New France* (Toronto: University of Toronto Press, 1997), p. 38.

The girls, kept under supervision in one place, chose their husbands themselves, usually within two weeks after arrival. A young man in search of a wife had to declare his possessions and means of livelihood to the "directress" in charge of the girls. To encourage marriage, the government fined bachelors and denied them trading rights. Thus, men sought brides, and women had a good deal of choice. Usually they first wanted to know whether the suitor had a farm.

Even if the young man had built a home, a difficult life awaited these women, whose marriage contract bound them for life. They faced relentless work in clearing and maintaining their new family farms, for women in New France toiled in the fields alongside the men. The severity of Canadian winters also came as a shock to the young French women. In northern France, snow covered the ground for a few days, at most. In New France, it remained for over four months — then there was the extreme cold, the freezing of lakes and rivers. Fortunately, though, by the time the *filles du roi* arrived, the French settlers had learned to adjust to winter conditions. They now slaughtered animals at the onset of winter and hung the meat in icy cellars. By eating fresh meat and the past season's vegetables through the winter, they escaped scurvy. They also learned to construct houses in ways that improved heat retention and heating efficiency, by digging cellars first and by putting fireplaces in the centre of the houses. In addition, they built roofs with steep angles that readily shed the snow. In the late seventeenth century, the settler introduced another improvement: iron fireboxes that produced four times more heat than conventional fireplaces. They built larger barns to store fodder for the winter and to keep domestic animals inside during the coldest weather.

To make the settlers' lives easier, Colbert sent livestock to Canada at the Crown's expense. The first horses arrived in 1665. The First Nations, who had never seen such animals, called them the "moose of France." Horses thrived in the colony. The habitants developed a particular fondness for them, and by the eighteenth century even the poorest settler tried to keep one. By the 1720s, there was one horse for every five settlers.

THE *ENGAGÉS*

In the mid- to late 1660s, the Crown sent several hundred *engagés*, or indentured workers, to the colony annually. These immigrants constituted the majority of the arrivals from France in the seventeenth century. Bound by a three-year contract, or *engagement*, to a settler, merchant,

FRENCH IMMIGRANTS BY SEX AND DECADE, 1608–1759

PERIOD	MEN	WOMEN	TOTAL
Before 1630	15	6	21
1630–1639	88	51	139
1640–1649	141	86	227
1650–1659	403	239	642
1660–1669	1075	623	1698
1670–1679	429	369	798
1680–1689	486	56	542
1690–1699	490	32	522
1700–1709	283	24	307
1710–1719	293	18	311
1720–1729	420	14	434
1730–1739	483	16	499
1740–1749	576	16	592
1750–1759	1699	52	1751
Unknown	27	17	44
Total	6908	1619	8527

Source: R. Cole Harris, ed., *Historical Atlas of Canada*, vol. 1, *From the Beginning to 1800* (Toronto: University of Toronto Press, 1987), plate 45. Reprinted by permission of the University of Toronto Press Incorporated.

or religious community, they received a modest wage. They were nicknamed "Thirty-six Months," since after that period they became free. Apparently, beginning in the 1650s, more than half stayed in the colony after their term of service ended. In the early days of Royal Government, the *engagés* performed much of the colony's heavy labour, doing dockwork and construction and clearing more land for farming. The system proved advantageous to both the seigneur, who used them to open up more land, and to the *engagés*, who gained valuable knowledge of local conditions before they began farming on their own.

In total, the Crown sent nearly 4000 men and women to Canada by 1672. Many died from disease, either on the voyage or in the colony itself. A number returned to France. Nonetheless, New France's population grew rapidly from roughly 3000 in 1663 to almost 10 000 a decade later. Most settled along the St. Lawrence River from below Quebec to Montreal, and they cleared more land east of Montreal along the Richelieu River.

AN EARLY FRENCH IMMIGRANT

To put a human face on the early immigrants who came to New France, let us look at the experience of one man, Étienne Trudeau, from the city of La Rochelle in western France. This robust fellow, a master carpenter at eighteen, signed a contract for five years of military service in New France. Upon arrival in Montreal in 1659, he began service with the Sulpician Fathers, who had hired him. Three years later he and two others were ambushed by 50 Iroquois. They fought back bravely and survived the attack.

In 1667, the year of the Iroquois peace treaty, the 26-year-old Étienne married Adrienne Barbier, the daughter of a carpenter who was one of the original twelve colonists to arrive at

Montreal in 1642. Étienne and Adrienne had four children; one child eventually settled in Louisiana, while three became voyageurs and went to the Great Lakes before their marriages. Étienne lived an active life as a farmer, carpenter, and stonemason. He died in 1712 at Montreal; his wife died several years later. Étienne Trudeau was the ancestor of all the Trudeaus of New France, including a ninth-generation descendant — Pierre Elliott Trudeau, prime minister of Canada from 1968 to 1979 and from 1980 to 1984.

THE SETTLEMENT OF THE ST. LAWRENCE VALLEY

 Throughout the French regime, the St. Lawrence River remained the colony's main thoroughfare, both in summer by canoe or small boat and in winter by sleigh over the ice. Frontage along the water highway was always most sought after. In addition, the settlers wanted to be close to one another, within hailing distance of their neighbours, in the event of Iroquois attacks. Around Quebec, the shores of the St. Lawrence already looked like one sprawling, unending village street, with the habitants' whitewashed farmhouses huddled closely together. The narrow farms extending back from the river were often twenty times as long as they were wide.

This modern photograph, taken along the Richelieu River east of Montreal in 1976, shows the long strips of farmland reaching back from the river, evidence of the continued impact of the seigneurial system on land formation.

Bernard Vallée/Archives nationales du Québec à Québec, E10/D76-533/P19A.

    The French state achieved significant population growth in the colony from 1663 to 1672.  The women sent out in Colbert's great wave of immigrants married and produced large families. In the late seventeenth century, the state encouraged births by offering what might be viewed as Canada's first baby bonuses. Couples with ten or more living children received a substantial gift of money. The sexes became evenly balanced in New France. By 1700, women were an average age of 22 when they were married, an age seven years higher than it had been 40 years earlier! Their spouses tended by 1700 to be older; the males averaged 28 years of age. Despite disasters, such as the smallpox epidemic of 1701, which killed 1000 people, New France's rapid population increase continued: it doubled every 25 years, almost entirely as a result of the high birth rate rather than immigration. The fact that women married earlier than their European counterparts effectively gave them more child-bearing years.

    In the colony's early years, women gave birth to eight or nine children on average (after 1700, the figure dropped to seven). One out of every five children, however, died before the age of one; hence the average "completed" family in the eighteenth century consisted of 5.65 children per couple. Midwives delivered babies at home. A new mother might have a woman friend stay for a week or so after the birth, and her own mother usually stayed with her for at least a month.

    The remarkable example of the Tremblay family dramatically underlines the prodigious population increase that occurred in New France. Pierre Tremblay arrived in the colony in 1647, and married 10 years later at Quebec. When he died, he left behind 12 children, 4 of whom were boys. His sons in turn had 15, 14, 14, and 6 children, respectively, and their descendants similarly had large families. By 1957, the 300th anniversary of Pierre Tremblay's marriage, there were 60 000 Tremblays in North America, all descended from this one marriage in New France.

COLBERT'S ADMINISTRATIVE REFORMS

To mark New France's new status as a royal colony, Colbert established administrative structures identical to those already existing in the provinces of France. At the top was the king, Louis XIV.

THE POLITICAL ADMINISTRATION OF NEW FRANCE

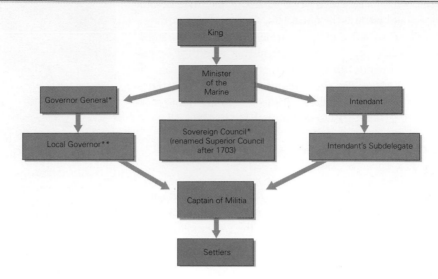

*The governor general, the intendant, the bishop, and the appointed councillors all belonged to the Sovereign Council.
**There was a local governor for each of the following: Acadia, Quebec, Trois-Rivières, Montreal, Louisiana, Île-Royale.

Source: Adapted from Marcel Trudel, *Introduction to New France* (Toronto: Holt, Rinehart and Winston, 1968), p. 156.

He, however, delegated enormous powers to his ministers, particularly to Colbert. In effect, the government of New France resided with the minister of the marine, assisted by his *commis*, or secretary (the equivalent of a twentieth-century deputy minister in Canada). The colony was administered by the Sovereign Council, which was headed by a governor and an intendant, both appointed by the king.

THE GOVERNOR

The governor general held supreme authority. Almost without exception, he was a noble and a soldier. He ensured that the other officials discharged their responsibilities honestly and efficiently.

He had undisputed control over military and diplomatic affairs. Military officers in the colony could not marry without first securing his permission. He also conducted diplomatic relations with the neighbouring First Nations and the English colonies. The administration of Daniel de Rémy de Courcelle, governor of New France from 1665 to 1672, was marked by important campaigns against the Iroquois. His successor, the Comte de Frontenac (1672–82 and 1689–98), also spent much of his time dealing with the First Nations and with the English colonies.

The most celebrated governors of the eighteenth century included Philippe de Rigaud de Vaudreuil (1703–25) and his son, Pierre de Rigaud de Vaudreuil de Cavagnial (1755–60), the latter being the only Canadian-born governor of New France. The towns of Montreal and Trois-Rivières also had local governors answerable to the governor general (who also served as the governor of the Quebec area). They functioned chiefly as military leaders. Claude de Ramezay, governor of Montreal in the early eighteenth century, remains one of the best-known local governors and his residence, the Château de Ramezay, built on Notre Dame Street in 1705, still stands. (This jewel of Montreal's heritage now houses an excellent museum.)

THE INTENDANT

The intendant — the official responsible for justice, public order, and finance — was the second-ranking official in the colonial hierarchy. A skilled administrator with a good educational background and, usually, extensive legal training, he ran most of the daily affairs of New France. He managed the budgets of both the army and the colony. The intendant headed the police and looked after road construction and maintenance. He was also responsible for the construction and maintenance of fortifications. As the population increased, the Crown appointed deputy intendants at Montreal, Trois-Rivières, and, later, Detroit. They were answerable to the intendant at Quebec.

The governor and intendant quarrelled often in the early years of royal government, largely because of their overlapping powers. These conflicts led the minister of the marine to define more clearly their respective roles and those of the other justice officers. Although the governor remained the supreme authority, the powers of the intendant were considerably enhanced. He quickly became, for example, the dominant figure in the Sovereign Council (renamed the Superior Council in 1703), the senior tribunal of the colony. Although ranked behind the governor and the bishop, the intendant came to preside over the council meetings. Three of the best-known intendants of New France were Jean Talon (1665–68, 1669–72), Gilles Hocquart (1731–48), and François Bigot (1748–60).

Portrait of Bishop François de Laval (1623–1708), a copy of an engraving by Claude Duflos (1708), painted in 1788. Bishop Laval, the colony's first bishop, directed the diocese of Quebec from 1659 to 1684 and founded the Séminaire de Québec in 1663.

Pierre Soulard/Musée de la civilisation, dépôt du Séminaire de Québec, 1995.3480.

THE BISHOP

The bishop played a role in the political life of the colony, even though the powers of the office were significantly reduced after 1663. When the Sovereign Council was first established, the bishop ranked directly behind the governor. Thus, the first bishop, François de Laval, initially shared with the governor the responsibility of selecting the other council members from among the leading colonists. But after Laval clashed with the governor, he lost this right. Thereafter, the bishop's influence declined, and his attendance at the council became infrequent. The Crown respected the social and religious role of the church, but opposed any political authority it might claim.

The puritanical Jean-Baptiste de La Croix de Chevrières de Saint-Vallier (1688–1727), who served for nearly 40 years, followed Laval. He waged war against drunkenness, blasphemy, dancing, and immodest dress. Laval had spoken against women appearing in church wearing fashionable gowns that revealed naked arms and bosoms, but Saint-Vallier went farther and tried to stop women from wearing low-cut gowns in their homes.

At the beginning of the period of royal government, Louis XIV and Colbert feared the excessive authority of the clergy in New France. The Jesuits had, in effect, run the colony for 30 years. Thus, the minister of the marine instructed the governor and the intendant to subordinate the church to the authority of the state. After 1663, the king nominated the bishop and contributed 40 percent of the colonial church's finances in order to control the church.

The opening of the Sovereign Council. The governor appears in the centre, the bishop on the governor's right and the intendant on the governor's left, with the other sovereign councillors around them at the council table. This painting, an historical reconstruction by Charles Huot, hangs in the Quebec National Assembly.

Commission de la Capitale Nationale.

THE SOVEREIGN COUNCIL

The Sovereign Council, after 1703 known as the Superior Council, both made laws and heard criminal and civil cases. The members of the tribunal sat around a large table, with the governor, bishop, and intendant at the head — the governor in the centre, the bishop on the governor's right, and the intendant on the governor's left. As the amount of litigation in the colony increased, the council restricted itself to legal functions, and the intendant enacted legislation.

THE CAPTAIN OF MILITIA

Colbert also established the office of captain of militia. In 1669, the intendant organized the entire male population between the ages of 16 and 60 into militia units. He formed a company in each parish and appointed a captain from among the most respected habitants to command it. The office carried with it no salary, but it brought considerable status and prestige; the captains became the most influential men in their communities. In addition to drilling the militia, supervising their equipment, and leading them in battle, the captains acted locally as the intendant's agents, communicating his regulations and ordinances to the habitants and seeing that they were carried out. They also directed the *corvées* for work on bridges and roads. During a *corvée*, even the local seigneur came under the militia captain's command. This new office thus prevented the seigneurs from becoming too powerful.

PUBLIC MEETINGS

Colbert made no provision for local self-government. New France had no municipal governments, nor mayors or town councils. Furthermore, people could not call a meeting or arrange a public assembly. Government came from above, not from below. Even the magistrates of the Sovereign Council were appointed and paid stipends, and were, therefore, dependent on the governor and the intendant. The only elected office in the late seventeenth century (and for the remainder of the French regime) was church warden.

Yet, a little flexibility did exist. Occasionally the governor and the intendant consulted the public on issues of general interest. They called together seventeen assemblies between 1672 and 1700. On at least one occasion, the intendant subsequently acted on the assembly's requests. Thus, the people of New France had a tiny say in the administration of their affairs. The authorities did legislate in accordance with public opinion, although they were not bound to do so. In 1709 in Quebec and in 1717 in Montreal, the governor and the intendant also permitted the merchants to establish chambers of commerce. These bodies nominated a member to inform the governor and the intendant of how best to promote commerce in their towns.

THE LOWER COURTS

The lower courts in Quebec, Montreal, and Trois-Rivières stood below the Sovereign Council. The judges of these courts applied the municipal legislation drawn up by the Sovereign Council, such as regulations on street traffic, road maintenance, garbage disposal, and fire prevention. A few of the most populated seigneuries also had seigneurial courts, which heard minor civil disputes. In 1664 the law for the area around Paris, the so-called Custom of Paris (*coutume de Paris*), officially became the colony's legal code. Today's Civil Code in Quebec evolved from this "law of Canada."

In reforming New France's justice system, Colbert ensured that justice would be provided with minimal expense to the state. First, he banned lawyers from practising in the colony; citizens argued their own civil cases in court. Notaries — not lawyers — drew up legal contracts. By 1700, the colony supported four notaries at Quebec, three at Montreal, and one at Trois-Rivières. Second, the Crown enforced a tariff of modest fees that legal officials, from judges down to bailiffs, could charge.

The courts operated as they did in France. When a crime was committed, the local magistrate or the attorney general of the Sovereign Council ordered the gathering of evidence. The judge, or a member of the Sovereign Council delegated by the attorney general, interrogated anyone thought to have knowledge of the crime. If the evidence revealed a suspect, that person was apprehended and put in jail. The judge or attorney general then interrogated the prisoner under oath (at this point, the suspect still had not been informed of the charge against him).

This questioning and the taking down of statements was known as the *question ordinaire*. If, in important cases, the defendant proved reluctant to talk, torture could be used to extract a confession or the names of accomplices. This procedure, the *question extraordinaire*, was employed against at least 30 men and women during the century of royal government.[1] The *maître des hautes oeuvres*, or master of the means of torture, bound boards to the defendant's shins, inserted wedges, and then struck them with a hammer, painfully crushing the bones of the accused. After each hammer blow the interrogators restated their questions until they believed the prisoner was telling the truth. As legal historian Douglas Hay writes, "If the truth had to be sought in the bones, nerves and sinews of an unwilling witness, that was unfortunate," but the investigator "considered it much as a surgeon would his exploratory operation."[2]

If the Sovereign Council heard the trial, the attorney general received all the evidence and testimony, laid it before the court, and added a summation. The members of the council subsequently discussed the report and gave their opinions. The intendant then delivered the verdict. The sentence was carried out either the same day or within a day or two.

The Failure of Colbert's Plan for a "Compact Colony"

Having set up a new administrative structure, Colbert sought capable men to fill the senior posts so as to establish a self-reliant colony, or "a compact colony," in the St. Lawrence valley. Intendant Jean Talon, a man of about 40 who had been an intendant in France as well, began investigating New France's economic possibilities — discovering what the soil would grow, surveying the forests, and sponsoring expeditions to search for minerals. He also tried to develop a shipbuilding industry in the colony. The Crown sent skilled ship carpenters, tar-makers, blacksmiths, and foundry workers, as well as the necessary supplies. Three ships were built, but the industry never became profitable. The imported skilled workers demanded high wages; iron had to be imported; and the industry required heavy capital out-lays. In the end, ships cost much more to build in Canada than in France, and the program was curtailed.

New France also failed to develop a large overseas trade with the West Indies. The loss of two of Talon's ships at sea helped to cut short the experiment. Other difficulties arose as well. Ships out of New France could sail south only in the summer months — the hurricane season in southern waters. These ships had to run the gauntlet of English privateers in wartime, and other nations' privateers at all times. As well, the Canadians had to compete with New England mariners, who could sell wheat and fish at lower prices year round. For these reasons, then, New France failed to secure a foothold in the West Indies market.

Of the industries in New France, fishing offered the greatest promise. Colbert subsidized the necessary equipment. But Canadian fishers faced several disadvantages, the foremost being the failure to establish salt works in the colony. This meant a reliance on France for a supply of salt. In addition, French merchants in France sent their ships directly to the Grand Banks, and they returned directly to France without ever landing in New France and purchasing Canadian fish.

One of Talon's enterprises that did succeed was a brewery at Quebec. Cheap beer brewed in the colony proved popular. Other industries he promoted included the production of hats and shoes. Unfortunately for Colbert's hopes, everything Canada produced, except for furs and beer, could be obtained more cheaply elsewhere.

When Jean Talon left the colony in 1672, the industries he had promoted died. The Crown allocated no more funds because France had begun a costly war with the Dutch. New France had to depend solely on the fur trade, which remained its main economic activity.

Colonial administrators in New France also contributed to the failure of Colbert's "compact colony" ideal by using their positions to advance their own interests instead of those of the colony. As business historian Michael Bliss writes, "The idea that people with power should *not* use it to enrich themselves is a very modern notion. In the seventeenth and eighteenth centuries virtually all administrators of government — in Britain, France, and all their colonies — expected to gain personally from possession of their offices."[3]

Economic Development after the Treaty of Utrecht

In 1713, the British and French signed the Treaty of Utrecht, which inaugurated a 30-year truce. This "30 years of peace" enabled New France to consolidate itself economically and socially. Many French-Canadian historians look upon the 30 years of peace as New France's Golden Age.

Once again, the French government supported economic initiatives in New France. This time they proved more successful. The number of flour mills in the colony increased by 50 percent between 1719 and 1734. The fishing industry also grew, with fish and seal oil becoming export products. Gilles Hocquart, the intendant from 1731 to 1748, established tanneries at Quebec, Lévis, and Montreal.

The Crown also improved transportation. In 1737, the intendant completed the "Chemin du Roi" (King's Highway), which connected Montreal and Quebec for the first time. It greatly facilitated travel. A return trip by water from Montreal to Quebec might take several weeks, while the trip by coach over the King's Highway could be completed in as little as nine days. The highway opened up new lands north of the St. Lawrence to settlement. It would also become the colony's lifeline in the summer of 1759, when the British fleet gained control of the St. Lawrence.

Private citizens also worked to develop the colony's industrial resources. Beginning in the 1720s, local contractors established small shipyards along the St. Lawrence. Intendant Gilles Hocquart helped with subsidies and assisted in establishing state-owned shipyards where workers were employed in sailmaking, rope manufacturing, tar works, foundries, sawmills, and tool and machinery making. He also encouraged the building of large ships, even though Canada's resources were better suited for small ones. In the 1740s, for example, the royal shipyard at Quebec constructed nine warships. The labour costs were too high, however, and in the 1750s the shipyard cut back to only five naval vessels.

In 1729, François Poulin de Francheville established Canada's first heavy industry, the St. Maurice Forges, or ironworks, 15 km north of Trois-Rivières. But by 1741, as a result of serious technical errors and lax administration, the company declared bankruptcy, at which point the Crown, which had given large subsidies, took control. Production under royal administration fluctuated greatly from year to year, but for a few years profits were reported. The ironworks employed about 100 workers, who produced sizable quantities of cooking pots, pans, and soup ladles, as well as cannons and cannonballs. They also made the first Canadian stoves.

By 1700, agriculture replaced the fur trade as the leading economic activity in New France, with three out of four Canadian families involved in farming. This greatly changed the colony's economic structure. Between 1706 and 1739, the Canadian population increased 250 percent and the amount of land under cultivation increased 430 percent. Wheat accounted for about three-quarters of the cultivated farmland, so the colony became self-sufficient in wheat and flour. (Wheat, in fact, made up one-third of the colony's exports by the 1730s.) The habitants also grew peas, oats, rye, barley, buckwheat, and maize. Surprisingly, the vegetable that in the early nineteenth century became the staple food of the habitants' diet was not grown in the colony: the English introduced the potato to the St. Lawrence valley after 1760.

Market conditions limited the production of produce and the growth of livestock. The towns of New France were not large, and many town dwellers kept their own gardens and livestock. But, in the eighteenth century, an increase in the population and the opening of an export market improved the situation. Flour, biscuits, and peas were exported regularly to the new French fortress at Louisbourg on Île Royale (now Cape Breton Island) as well as to the French West Indies. The habitants needed to produce a surplus to pay church tithes and seigneurial dues and to purchase the things they could not make themselves.

The unlimited supply of land and the high productivity of the new soil discouraged farmers from applying the intensive agricultural methods then commonly used in France, where land was scarce and expensive. When the good land became exhausted, the farmers cleared more with no concern for conservation. They avoided elaborate crop rotations, heavy manuring, and selective breeding of their cattle.

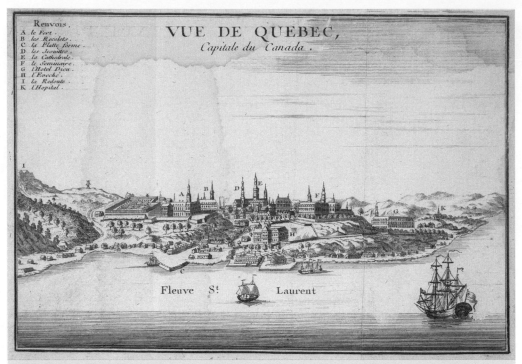

View of Quebec, about 1730. Note the Fort, "A"; the Cathedral, "E"; the Hotel Dieu, "G"; and the Bishop's Residence, "H."

National Archives of Canada/C-43730.

THE SOCIETY OF NEW FRANCE IN THE EIGHTEENTH CENTURY

During the eighteenth century, about one-quarter of New France's inhabitants resided in towns. At the end of the French regime, in 1760, nearly 8000 people lived in Quebec, with Montreal having only one-half of Quebec City's population. Quebec was the seaport and administrative capital, Montreal was a secondary town on the westernmost edge of French settlement. Trois-Rivières remained a small service centre with fewer than 1000 inhabitants.

From the St. Lawrence, the church spires, the religious communities' residences, the governors' and intendants' homes, the stone warehouses along the waterfront, all gave the towns of New France an impressive look. But appearances were deceiving. Well into the eighteenth century, pigs rooted among the refuse citizens dumped in the narrow streets. On a few streets open sewers carried garbage down to the river during heavy rains and the uncobbled streets became quagmires. There was no street lighting.

ROYAL ADMINISTRATORS AND MILITARY OFFICERS

Royal officials and military officers dominated life in Quebec, Montreal, and Trois-Rivières. In terms of social ranking, these senior administrators stood at the top. The metropolitan French predominated in the Sovereign Council and held the top positions in the civil-service hierarchy. At the local level, however, the greater number of judges were Canadian born.

The nobility kept alive the military and aristocratic values of Old France in Canada. In general, the sons of the nobles became military officers, obtaining commissions in the Troupes de la Marine, or colonial regular army.

The military formed a vital part of the community, especially considering that the St. Lawrence valley had enjoyed only 50 years of complete freedom from war in the course of New France's 150-year existence. Every year, the Crown spent large sums for the maintenance of about 1500 regular French soldiers in New France, many of whom were stationed in the towns. Most of the soldiers were billeted in private homes. Within the army, tension arose between the French and the Canadian-born officers. Canadian leaders enjoyed greater popularity with the Canadian troops than did the metropolitan French officers. Unlike the French soldiers, Canadian troops had adapted to, and preferred, a different type of warfare — what in the twentieth century would be called guerrilla warfare.

THE MERCHANTS

The merchants, or bourgeoisie, constituted an important social group in New France. But historians in the 1950s and 1960s debated the nature, size, and strength of this group. They questioned whether New France had a significant class of French-Canadian entrepreneurs that existed in the colony. Some historians, among them Maurice Séguin, Guy Frégault, and Michel Brunet, argued that it did; others, such as Jean Hamelin and Fernand Ouellet, disagreed. Hamelin and Ouellet contended that the existence of monopolies and state control over the economy had stunted the development of a national bourgeoisie.

Was French Canada's dynamic entrepreneurial class wiped out as a result of the British conquest, or did such a class even exist prior to the fall of New France? Although a conclusive answer is not possible, it would appear that the metropolitan French controlled the biggest commercial operations connected with the profitable wholesale trade. They had the necessary funds and contacts to obtain adequate supplies in France. These French merchants provided most of the imported manufactured goods at Louisbourg and at Quebec. French merchants and their Quebec agents handled about two-thirds of the colony's external trade.[4] The Canadian merchants dominated only the smaller-scale retail operations. Thus, while much work remains to be done on this subject, a picture emerges of a strong metropolitan French presence in large-scale commerce.

How did the metropolitan French react to life overseas? Little information survives, but it is clear that two French Protestant merchants, François Havy and his cousin, Jean Lefebvre, had a difficult time during their residence at Quebec. If they had converted to Catholicism they might have been accepted into the community, but they did not. Being Protestants, neither man could marry in New France nor bring a wife and family from France; since from 1627 onwards, Protestants had been banned from settling permanently in the colony. The tolerance for French

A French-Canadian couple in their Sunday clothes.

Ville de Montréal. Gestion de documents et des archives.

Protestants, recognized in the Edict of Nantes, completely ended in 1685 when Louis XIV revoked the Edict. Although in the 1740s a few French Protestant import–export merchants were tacitly allowed to live at Quebec, they remained total outsiders in the colony.

French Canadians dominated in smaller-scale trading. In the eighteenth century, scores of small partnerships participated in the fur trade. The companies usually consisted of three or four partners who obtained a three-year lease on the trade at a particular fur-trading post, and shared in the profits or losses according to the percentage of the capital they had invested. The partners obtained trade goods from the large Montreal merchants, usually on credit at 30 percent interest. These Montreal merchants in turn marketed the furs through their agents at home in France.

WOMEN IN THE COLONY

Historian Jan Noel has argued that a number of women in New France enjoyed freedom from "traditional" gender roles; certainly the examples of Marie de l'Incarnation and Marguerite Bourgeoys of Montreal — the founder of the teaching order the Sisters of the Congregation of Notre-Dame — prove the point. Noel calls such women *"les femmes favorisées."*[5] But, by the eighteenth century, the status of women in New France came to resemble more closely that in France. As historian Allan Greer states: "In a general sense, men ruled in New France, just as they did in old France."[6] There were important exceptions, however, in the female religious orders and in business.

Women in eighteenth-century New France frequently ran small businesses that sold cloth, clothes, furs, brandy, and utensils. During their husbands' absences in the interior, the fur traders' wives and daughters often looked after their stores and accounts. A number of widowed merchants' wives continued their husbands' businesses. Well-versed in the affairs of her fur-trader husband, Marie-Anne Barbel continued his business after his death in 1745. She also expanded his real estate holdings and began a pottery works. She was one of Quebec's well-to-do merchants until the Seven Years' War ruined her fur-trade operation. Much of her property was destroyed in the British bombardment of Quebec's Lower Town in 1759.

Other women also began successful commercial careers. Agathe de Saint-Père, Madame de Repentigny, headed a textile firm — New France's first — in the early eighteenth century. This energetic businesswoman ransomed nine English weavers held prisoner by the First Nations and hired them to teach Canadian apprentices the trade. Soon she had twenty looms operating, turning out coarse cloth and canvas. Marie-Charlotte Denys de la Ronde, the widow of Claude de Ramezay, governor of Montreal, operated a sawmill, a brick factory, and a tile works. Her daughter, Louise de Ramezay, owned a flour mill, a tannery, and sawmills. After François Poulin de Francheville's death in 1733, his widow, Thérèse de Couagne, continued to operate the St. Maurice ironworks, at least until 1735.

Throughout New France, married women shared in the work of their husbands. At busy times of the year, they helped in the fields. In the urban areas, artisans' and merchants' wives assisted their spouses. Both rural and urban women often kept the family accounts and managed the servants (if there were any) or the apprentices, in the case of artisans.

Under the *coutume de Paris*, married women had a status inferior to their husbands. The patriarchal ideal of French society made marriage sacrosanct. Divorce did not exist in Roman Catholic New France. In the case of abusive relationships, legal separations were difficult to obtain. As historian Peter Moogk writes: "Since wife beating was tolerated in this society, occasional physical abuse was not sufficient proof of a murderous hatred." As he notes: "Women bore the burden of preserving the union of husband and wife, and it could be a heavy yoke to bear."[7]

THE *ENGAGÉS* IN THE FUR TRADE

Small-scale fur traders and the voyageurs, or *engagés*, ranked below the middle-sized French-Canadian retail merchants. These individuals carried the products of the country to the town, and vice versa; the voyageurs, under contract as *engagés* (as was increasingly the case after 1700), travelled thousands of kilometres from the St. Lawrence valley.

Every year, 400 to 500 people received permission to enter the fur trade around the Great Lakes or in the upper Mississippi valley. Possibly many more went without permission. Little is known of these people. According to historian Gratien Allaire, the trading firms recruited the majority around Montreal.[8] His research also reveals that the *engagés* tended to be habitants from rural areas seeking to supplement their farm incomes.

TRADESPEOPLE

The colony had about 2000 trades workers by the 1740s. The most numerous in the construction industry were carpenters and masons; in transportation, navigators and carters; and in the food industry, bakers and butchers. As a rule, craftsworkers owned all their own tools and worked in small workshops attached to their homes. The French authorities often accused Canadian workers of being headstrong and insubordinate; their self-confidence and independence were frowned upon by the administrators from Old France, where the average person had little, if any, personal freedom or opportunity for personal advancement.

THE HABITANTS AND THEIR WAY OF LIFE

The habitants comprised the largest group in the colony. By the 1740s, the oldest seigneuries had two (in some cases, three) rows of farms stretching back from the river. The habitants' lots, or *rotures*, were rectangular in shape and generally had a ratio of width to length of one to ten. The habitants paid no direct taxes, apart from the occasional tax for local improvements, whereas in France the peasants paid between one-third and one-half of their income in taxes. In addition, the habitants paid only half the rate for the church tithe that was required at the time in northern France.

The majority of the habitants apparently ate well. They enjoyed almost daily pork and game, particularly venison and wild hare. Gradually, though, wild game came to be relied on less and less as it became harder to obtain near the settled areas. The pig remained a mainstay of the habitants' diet because it was inexpensive to keep (it would eat anything from acorns to kitchen scraps) and because, as the old folk saying in both France and New France put it, "You can eat everything but the squeal." Fish formed part of the core diet of the French settlers, as did buckwheat, a hardy cereal used to make bread, pancakes, and porridges. Maple syrup was used for sweetening.

Vegetables from the garden, particularly peas and fèves (the large tough-fibred beans from Normandy that were brought to the St. Lawrence valley), were favourites. Dried peas and beans could be stored for years and then made into tasty soups. And because legumes absorbed the flavour of either smoked or salted pork fat well, the habitants frequently used pork in their recipes for pea soup and baked beans.

The *Canadiens* also enjoyed such fruits as apples, plums, and cherries. Apple trees, brought from the northwest of France, thrived in the cool, moist Canadian climate. Wild fruits, especially raspberries, red and black currants, and cranberries, were to be had for the picking.

As for beverages, wealthy habitants could obtain expensive tea and coffee from the traders. Milk, in contrast, was cheap and plentiful. Cider was drunk at all meals. The well-to-do could afford wine imported from France, while the habitants drank the cheaper beer brewed in the colony or, indeed, beer that they brewed themselves.

Farmers in New France detested being called "peasants." As the Finnish traveller Pehr Kalm noted in 1749, "The gentlemen and ladies, as well as the poorest peasants and their wives, are called Monsieur and Madame." The habitants had more personal freedom than did their counterparts in France. The royal officials in New France repeatedly complained that the independent-minded Canadians always pleased themselves and paid little attention to the administrators' directives.

The habitants' lives centred on their farms, which they cultivated with their families' help. The *curé* and the captain of militia served as the habitants' links with the outside world. As in France, the *curés* registered the births, deaths, and marriages in their parish.

THE CHURCH IN NEW FRANCE

During the years of royal government, and particularly during the years of the great migration from France in the late 1660s and early 1670s, the church suffered from an acute shortage of priests. As late as 1683, the intendant reported that three-quarters or more of the habitants heard mass only four times a year. This problem remained until well into the nineteenth century.

The parish priests played an important role in those communities they could regularly visit. As sociologist Jean-Charles Falardeau notes: "The Canadian curés were pastors of communities lacking resources, organization and, most of the time, local leaders. They soon became also the real leaders of these communities."[9]

Yet historians such as W.J. Eccles and Cornelius Jaenen, while not denying the church's central role, distance themselves from such an interpretation. They stress that the people of New France showed a surprising independence from the church. When, for instance, the Crown decided that the populace should pay tithes (or ecclesiastical taxes) for the support of a secular clergy, and the bishop stipulated that it be at the rate of one-thirteenth of the produce of the land, the people protested. The bishop reduced his demand to one-twentieth, and eventually had to accept only one twenty-sixth of the grain. To make up the difference, the Crown provided the clergy with annual subsidies. Only when more land came into production in the early eighteenth century did many parish priests become relatively well off.

The frequent *ordonnances* of the intendant directed to the inhabitants of the parishes with priests provide further proof of the independence of many *Canadiens* from the clergy. The ordinances prohibited walking out of church as soon as the priest began his sermon, standing in the lobby arguing, brawling during the service, and even bringing dogs into church.

The clergy did, however, enjoy the respect of the community for what today would be called social services. During the early history of New France, the clergy were actively involved in teaching, nursing, and other charitable work. In 1760, the nearly 100 diocesan or parish priests in the colony were assisted by 30 Sulpicians (a religious order that had begun work in the colony in 1657), 25 Jesuits, 24 Récollets (who had returned in 1670), and more than 200 nuns belonging to six religious communities. The clerically administered social institutions endured, in many cases, into the twentieth century.

EDUCATION AND SOCIAL WELFARE

The church controlled schooling in the colony, and all the religious communities assumed some responsibility for education. Urban dwellers benefited most from the schools, as most schools were located in the major towns. In a study of three rural parishes in mid-eighteenth-century New France, historian Allan Greer discovered that only 10 percent of the men and women could sign their marriage act. In the urban centre of Trois-Rivières, in contrast, it was approximately 50 percent.[10] The Quebec Seminary ran the Petit Séminaire, the most important elementary school in the colony. The Jesuit College at Quebec provided male students with a postsecondary education equivalent to that which could be obtained in a provincial town in France. The Congrégation de Notre-Dame and the Ursuline order established elementary schools for girls in the larger centres.

The church also provided welfare services and maintained charitable institutions. Three female and two male religious communities became involved in this work. Each of the three principal towns in New France had a Bureau of the Poor, which served as a relief centre and employment agency. Those persons who were too elderly or too infirm to work, and who were not being cared for by their children at home, were placed in institutions at Montreal or Quebec, along with the chronically ill, the insane, and women of "loose morals" (the latter were put there to be reformed by the hospital nuns). To help pay for these institutional services and for their hospitals, the church held initially about one-tenth of the seigneurial lands in the St. Lawrence valley, and by the 1750s about one-quarter of the land. In 1760, more than one-third of New France's population lived on church seigneuries, providing the clergy with a substantial revenue.

POPULAR RELIGION

Popular religion remained strong in New France. Many *Canadiens* in the rural areas believed in magic and witchcraft. Canadian children heard tales of flying canoes, werewolves, and encounters with the devil. Individuals who today would be considered mentally ill were then believed to be possessed by demons and were considered sorcerers. The clergy frequently performed exorcisms on such individuals with the aid of prayers, candles, and holy water, and refused them burial in sanctified ground. New France, however, never knew the hysteria that swept through part of New England in the 1690s, as exemplified by the infamous witchhunts of Salem. No executions occurred in New France as punishment for occult practices.

THE CANADIANIZATION OF THE CLERGY

Gradually, the clergy became "Canadianized." The formation of a native-born Canadian secular clergy had long been an objective of the church. The seminary in Quebec trained Canadian priests at its theological college.

During the eighteenth century, Canadians increasingly staffed the parishes in New France. By 1760, Canada had about 100 parishes, most of them run by diocesan clergy, about four-fifths of whom were Canadian. Tensions, however, existed between the Canadian-born clergy at the lower levels of the church's administration and the French-born clergy who dominated at the top.

THE FIRST NATIONS POPULATION

In many regards New France was a multicultural society, with a considerable First Nations population and an African community. The Native presence was greatest in the Montreal area where, from the 1670s to the 1710s, the "mission" First Nations outnumbered the French settlers.

Marguerite Bourgeoys (1620–1700), founder of the famous teaching order the Congrégation de Notre-Dame de Montréal. She opened the first school in Montreal in a stable in 1658. This, her only authentic portrait, was painted by Pierre LeBer shortly after her death in 1700.

Archives de la Congrégation de Notre-Dame de Montréal.

This painting by French-Canadian illustrator Henri Julien (1852–1908) is entitled *La Chasse-Galerie* (1906). It depicts a very popular tale of the fur trade, which involved Satan's promise to a group of voyageurs to return them to their homes in New France for New Year's Eve on condition that they did not utter the name of God or touch a cross or a church steeple along the way. If they did, the Devil would claim their souls. The tale allowed for all kinds of variation: sometimes Satan won; at other times he failed. The legend never lost its appeal, as listeners never knew how it would end.

Jean-Guy Kérouac/Musée du Québec/34.254.

Several thousand First Nations people lived in four major *réductions*, or missions, in the St. Lawrence valley in the late seventeenth and early eighteenth centuries: the Hurons at Lorette, near Quebec; the Abenakis from present-day Maine at Saint-François, east of Montreal; and the Iroquois at Sault St. Louis (Kahnawake), and the Lake of Two Mountains (Kanesatake or Oka), both west of Montreal. The Catholic missionaries did not insist on Native amalgamation with French civilization. As long as Aboriginal customs did not conflict with Christianity, they were accepted.

These First Nations communities acted as a buffer against Iroquois and English invaders. But their existence had an unanticipated side-effect. It speeded up the expanding contraband fur trade between New France and the American colonies, in which both the Roman Catholic Iroquois and the Abenakis participated. The "mission" First Nations did not consider themselves subjects of French law.

Historian Peter Moogk has noted that the Christian First Nations of New France sometimes raised the children of French Canadians, as a consequence of the fact that unmarried pregnant women in the colony faced prosecution as criminals.[11] Some women concealed their pregnancies, then left their babies to perish. The death penalty could be imposed in such cases. A few unwed mothers gave their babies to the First Nations to raise instead. The midwives who assisted these women with their deliveries helped them escape detection.

Natives also adopted and raised American children who had been taken as captives during Franco-Indian raids. At Kahnawake, the captives received Christian and Mohawk names, and were assimilated into the community. The Mohawk political scientist Gerald Alfred adds that many assumed "leadership roles in both the political and military sphere."[12]

As the French needed the resident First Nations for protection and assistance in their raids against the English, they could not antagonize them by rigorously enforcing French laws. Thus, although they regarded the First Nations in the colony as French subjects, they granted them what might best be termed "special status." As historian W.J. Eccles has written, the French avoided addressing the basic question of whether or not the Natives were subject to French law "by tacitly granting [them] something akin to diplomatic immunity." The French did not usually prosecute Natives for breaches of the peace, "for one good reason; to have attempted to do so with any degree of vigour would have alienated the Indians, and this the French could not afford to do."[13]

FIRST NATIONS AND AFRICAN SLAVES

A slave class existed in Canada to help meet an acute labour shortage. From the late 1680s, Native slaves from the upper Mississippi valley began arriving in New France on a regular basis. These *panis*, or Pawnees (the name of a single nation, was used despite the fact that the slaves were taken from many other groups as well), were sold to the French by other First Nations. Africans captured during raids on the English colonies or brought in from the French West Indies also increased the number of slaves in the colony. The few African slaves were sold at an average price twice as high as that received for the more numerous Native captives, because Africans had greater resistance to disease than did the First Nations. Montreal, the centre of New France's fur trade, had the largest number of slaves in the colony — several hundred by the mid-eighteenth century.

The Canadians traded slaves like cattle, at the marketplace and at auctions. Three-quarters of the slaves lived in towns, where they worked mainly as domestic servants. The governors owned slaves: Rigaud de Vaudreuil, governor from 1703 to 1725, owned 11 slaves, while the Marquis de Beauharnois, in office from 1726 to 1746, owned 27. But the biggest slave owners were merchants, traders, and the clergy. First Nations and African slaves also worked at the convents and hospitals operated by nuns in Quebec and Montreal.

While no exact census of New France's slave population exists, local records reveal that approximately 3600 slaves lived in the colony from its origin to 1759; of these, about two-thirds were First Nations, and one-third were African. They lived short lives: for Native slaves, the average age at death was about 18, and for Africans, 25.

THE RISE OF A *CANADIEN* IDENTITY

By the early eighteenth century, the colonists called themselves *Canadiens*. Some families had already resided in Canada for two or three generations. A new French people, self-confident and increasingly conscious of their separation from the French in France, emerged. As well, the regional dialects of France eventually died out in the St. Lawrence valley, as the newcomers from various areas of France intermingled, settling together in one area and speaking a common French language. They spoke *canadien–français*, a language with its own distinct expressions to describe Canadian realities — for example, *poudrerie* (drifting or powdering of snow), *cabane à sucre* (a cabin used at maple sugar time), and First Nations words such as *canoë* and *toboggan*.

By 1754, New France's French-Canadian population had reached 55 000. What had begun as an offshoot of Old France became a new community in Canada. Little by little, the French had

A Historical Portrait 🌾

☛ Marie-Joseph-Angélique

Marie-Joseph-Angélique, an African household slave of François Poulin de Francheville (a wealthy Montreal merchant and part owner of the St. Maurice ironworks), was about 21 years old when baptized on June 28, 1730. She gave birth to three children by César, the African slave of Ignace Gamelin, a business associate of Francheville. Twins followed a year later.

Like many Native and African slaves in New France, Angélique did domestic work. She washed dishes, cleaned house, ran errands. Her meals were basic, and she slept in a corner of the kitchen, on the floor. Montreal, the centre of New France's fur trade, had the largest number of slaves in the colony — several hundred by the mid-eighteenth century.

On the evening of April 10, 1734, Angélique deliberately set fire to the Francheville house, which stood near the Hôtel-Dieu Hospital. The fire spread quickly, and within minutes Montreal became a fiery inferno. The blaze, Montreal's worst disaster since the Iroquois attacks, destroyed 46 houses, as well as the hospital.

Why did the slave woman set the fire? Probably because of a love interest and the threat of her sale to a West Indian plantation. Several months earlier Angélique had run away with Claude Thibault, a French-Canadian servant in the Francheville household. Captured by the authorities, Angélique was sent back to her owner, Madame Francheville, Thérèse de Couagne, now a widow because her husband had died in November 1733. Upon her return, Angélique's conflicts with Madame Francheville continued unabated. Finally, Madame Francheville decided to sell the slave woman to a West Indian plantation as soon as the ice broke up and navigation resumed.

Painting by Alan Daniel in Janet Lunn and Christopher Moore, *The Story of Canada* (Toronto: Lester Publishing/Key Porter Books, 1992), p. 67.

Fearful of being sold, Angélique apparently started the fire to distract her owner, allowing her, in the confusion, to escape south with Claude to New England. But she was caught not far from Montreal.

On June 4, the Montreal court read its judgement. Angélique would first be interrogated under torture to reveal her accomplice. She was then required to make a full honourable apology for the fire, have her hand cut off, and be burnt alive. An appeal to the Superior Council in Quebec, the colony's court of appeal, moderated the sentence slightly. After torture to reveal her accomplice, she was to be taken to the parish church in a rubbish cart to confess her guilt. Immediately afterwards, she would be hanged, and her body burnt.

The authorities attempted to carry out the sentence in Montreal on June 21. But Angélique confessed her guilt only during the fourth round of torture; at no point did she reveal the name of an accomplice. She was hanged, her body burned, and her ashes were thrown into the wind. The authorities never found Claude Thibault.

become *Canadiens*, with values, manners, and attitudes that differentiated them more and more from the metropolitan French. The *Canadiens* resented the assumption of superiority by the military and ecclesiastical leaders of Old France. The French officer Louis-Antoine de Bougainville, who came to Quebec in 1757, was struck by the increasing differences between the French and the *Canadiens*: "We seem to belong to another, even an enemy, nation."[14]

NOTES

1. André Lachance, "Tout sur la torture," *Le Magazine Maclean* (décembre 1966): 38.
2. Douglas Hay, "The Meanings of the Criminal Law in Quebec, 1764–1774," in Louis A. Knafla, ed., *Crime and Criminal Justice in Europe and Canada* (Waterloo, ON: Wilfrid Laurier University Press, 1981), p. 77.
3. Michael Bliss, *Northern Enterprise: Five Centuries of Canadian Business* (Toronto: McClelland & Stewart, 1987), p. 44.
4. Bliss, *Northern Enterprise*, 70.
5. Jan Noel, "New France: Les femmes favorisées," in R. Douglas Francis and Donald B. Smith, eds., *Readings in Canadian History: Pre-Confederation*, 6th ed. (Toronto: Nelson Thomson Learning, 2002), pp. 91–110.
6. Allan Greer, *The People of New France* (Toronto: University of Toronto Press, 1997), p. 74.
7. Peter N. Moogk, *La Nouvelle France. The Making of French Canada — A Cultural History* (East Lansing, Michigan: Michigan State University Press, 2000): 231, 229.
8. Gratien Allaire, "Fur Trade Engagés, 1701–1745," in Thomas C. Buckley, ed., *Rendezvous: Selected Papers of the North American Fur Trade Conference, 1981* (St. Paul, MN: North American Fur Trade Conference, 1984), p. 22.
9. Jean-Charles Falardeau, "The Seventeenth-Century Parish in French Canada," in Marcel Rioux and Yves Martin, eds., *French-Canadian Society*, vol. 1 (Toronto: McClelland & Stewart, 1964), p. 27.
10. Allan Greer, "The Pattern of Literacy in Quebec, 1745–1899," *Histoire sociale/Social History* 11(22) (November 1978): 299.
11. Peter N. Moogk, "*Les Petits Sauvages*: The Children of Eighteenth-Century New France," in Joy Parr, ed., *Childhood and Family in Canadian History* (Toronto: McClelland & Stewart, 1982), p. 27.
12. Gerald R. Alfred, *Heeding the Voices of Our Ancestors: Kahnawake Mohawk Politics and the Rise of Native Nationalism* (Toronto: Oxford University Press, 1995), p. 200.
13. W.J. Eccles, *The Canadian Frontier, 1534–1760* (Toronto: Holt, Rinehart and Winston, 1969), p. 78.
14. Bougainville quoted by Guy Frégault, *Canada: The War of the Conquest*, trans. Margaret M. Cameron (Toronto: Oxford University Press, 1969), p. 64. On this important point see the comments of

George F.G. Stanley in *New France: The Last Phase, 1744–1760* (Toronto: McClelland & Stewart, 1968), p. 272.

LINKING TO THE PAST www

Virtual Museum of New France
http://www.civilization.ca/vmnf/vmnfe.asp

Extensive information on the exploration of and life in New France during the seventeenth and eighteenth centuries. Look at "People" to learn all about those who lived in New France: habitants, *filles du roi*, voyageurs, coureurs de bois, and more.

Tracing the History of New France
http://www.archives.ca/05/0517_e.html

Topics discussed include land, First Nations, administration, seigneurial regime, economy, population, religion, and wars. Play the interactive game to test your knowledge of New France.

Jean Talon
http://www.statcan.ca/english/about/jt.htm

Read about Jean Talon and North America's first census, which he administered during the winter of 1665–66.

The St. Lawrence River
http://collections.ic.gc.ca/stlauren/sl.htm

A look at the St. Lawrence, the maritime seaway and economic centre of Canada. Click on "History" to learn about the St. Lawrence's rich heritage. "Nouvelle France (1608–1760): French Control over the St. Lawrence" is of particular relevance to this chapter.

A Century of New France: 1663–1763
http://www.canadianheritage.org/books/canada3.htm

An overview of the growth of New France, including a discussion of the life of its inhabitants, as well as political and military issues.

The Black Community in the History of Quebec and Canada
http://www.qesn.meq.gouv.qc.ca/mpages/unit1/u1p3.htm

This site offers a brief look at the introduction of black slaves into Canada, some decrees related to slavery, and the case of Marie-Joseph-Angélique.

RELATED READINGS

R. Douglas Francis and Donald B. Smith, eds., *Readings in Canadian History: Pre-Confederation*, 6th ed. (Toronto: Nelson Thomson Learning, 2002), contains two articles that deal directly with this topic: W.J. Eccles, "Society and the Frontier," pp. 78–91; and Jan Noel, "New France: Les femmes favorisées," pp. 91–110.

BIBLIOGRAPHY

Allan Greer provides an excellent introduction to the social history of New France in *The People of New France* (Toronto: University of Toronto Press, 1997); also consult Dale Miquelon *The First Canada: To 1791* (Toronto: McGraw-Hill Ryerson, 1994); Jacques Mathieu, *La Nouvelle-France: Les Français en Amerique du Nord XVIe-XVIIIᵉ siècle* (Quebec: Les Presses de l'Université Laval, 1991); and John A. Dickinson and Brian Young, *A Short History of Quebec*, 3rd ed. (Montreal/Kingston: McGill-Queen's University Press, 2003), pp.

3–104. More detailed treatments include W.J. Eccles, *Canada Under Louis XIV, 1663–1701* (Toronto: McClelland & Stewart, 1964); and Dale Miquelon, *New France, 1701–1744* (Toronto: McClelland & Stewart, 1987). Older works include W.J. Eccles, *The Canadian Frontier, 1534–1760* (Toronto: Holt, Rinehart and Winston, 1969), and his *France in America*, rev. ed. (Markham, ON: Fitzhenry & Whiteside, 1990); Marcel Trudel, I*ntroduction to New France* (Toronto: Holt, Rinehart and Winston, 1968); and R. Cole Harris, "The French Impact in Canada and Acadia," in R. Cole Harris and John Warkentin, eds., *Canada Before Confederation* (Ottawa: Carleton University Press, 1991 [1974]), pp. 19–63.

Two invaluable bibliographical works for all aspects of New France's history, particularly its social and economic past, are Thomas Wien, "Canada and the *Pays d'en haut*, 1600–1700," in M. Brook Taylor, ed., *Canadian History: A Reader's Guide*, vol. 1, *Beginnings to Confederation* (Toronto: University of Toronto Press, 1994), pp. 33–75; and Jacques Rouillard, ed., *Guide d'histoire du Québec du régime français à nos jours: Bibliographie commentée* (Montreal: Éditions du Méridien, 1991).

Michael Bliss reviews the economic life of New France in *Northern Enterprise: Five Centuries of Canadian Business* (Toronto: McClelland & Stewart, 1987). Twenty-two essays by John F. Bosher, chiefly on the business history of the French colony, appear in his *Business and Religion in the Age of New France, 1600–1760* (Toronto: Canadian Scholars' Press, 1994). An excellent business history is Dale Miquelon's *Dugard of Rouen: French Trade to Canada and the West Indies, 1729–1770* (Montreal/Kingston: McGill-Queen's University Press, 1978). A short summary of the fur trade by W.J. Eccles, "The Fur Trade in the Colonial Northeast," appears in Wilcomb E. Washburn, ed., *Handbook of North American Indians*, vol. 4, *History of Indian–White Relations* (Washington, DC: Smithsonian Institution, 1988), pp. 324–34. Martin Fournier has written a biography of the best known coureur de bois of New France, *Pierre-Esprit Radisson. Merchant Adventurer, 1636–1701*. Translated by Mary Ricard (Montreal/Kingston: McGill-Queen's University Press, 2001).

A number of important articles by W.J. Eccles have been reprinted in his *Essays on New France* (Toronto: Oxford University Press, 1987). Terence Crowley, in "'Thunder Gusts': Popular Disturbances in Early French Canada," *Historical Papers/Communications Historiques* (1979): 11–32, reviews civil discontent in the colony. Louise Dechêne describes Montreal in the seventeenth century in *Habitants and Merchants in Seventeenth Century Montreal*, trans. Liana Vardi (Montreal/Kingston: McGill-Queen's University Press, 1992). John Hare, Marc Lafrance, and David Thiery Ruddel review urban life at Quebec in *Histoire de la Ville de Québec, 1608–1871* (Montreal: Boréal Express, 1987). André Lachance has written a study of urban life in the French regime, *La vie urbaine en Nouvelle-France* (Montreal: Boréal Express, 1987). Recent contributions by the same author include his two books: *Juger et Punir en Nouvelle-France* (Montreal: Libre Expression, 2000); and *Vivre, Aimer et Mourir en Nouvelle-France* (Montreal: Libre Expression, 2000). Peter N. Moogk's *La Nouvelle France: The Making of French-Canada—A Cultural History* (East Lansing, Michigan: Michigan State University Press, 2000), a series of exploratory articles on various aspects of French-Canadian culture before 1760, is invaluable.

For further information on other aspects of the social history of New France see the following pamphlets published by the Canadian Historical Association: Marcel Trudel, *The Seigneurial Regime* (Ottawa, 1956); W.J. Eccles, *The Government of New France* (Ottawa, 1965); and Cornelius J. Jaenen, *The Role of the Church in New France* (Ottawa, 1985). Jaenen's full study of religious life in New France is also entitled *The Role of the Church in New France* (Toronto: McGraw-Hill Ryerson, 1976). Several important essays on New France's society appear in Fernand Ouellet, *Economy, Class and Nation in Quebec: Interpretive Essays,* ed. and trans. Jacques A. Barbier (Toronto: Copp Clark Pitman, 1991). R. Cole Harris, in *The Seigneurial System in Canada: A Geographical Study,* 2nd ed. (Montreal/Kingston: McGill-Queen's University Press, 1984), reviews the seigneurial system. Roger Magnuson examines the important topic of schooling in *Education in New France* (Montreal/Kingston: McGill-Queen's University Press, 1992). Patricia Simpson has published a biography of an important Montreal educator, *Marguerite Bourgeoys and Montreal, 1640–1665* (Montreal/Kingston: McGill-Queen's University Press, 1997). Nadia Fahmy-Eid's essay, "The Education of Girls by the Ursulines of Quebec during the French Regime," appears in Wendy Mitchinson et al., eds., *Canadian Women: A Reader* (Toronto: Harcourt Brace, 1996), pp. 33–48. The first chapter of Robin W. Winks, *The Blacks in Canada: A History* (Montreal/Kingston: McGill-Queen's University Press, 1971), entitled "Slavery in New France," pp. 1–23, is helpful. For a view of New France in 1749 see Pehr Kalm's *Travels into North America*, 2 vols. (New York: Dover, 1966) for descriptions of Canadian life and customs. A delightful account of early French-Canadian food and cooking customs is Jay A. Anderson's "The Early Development of French-Canadian Food Ways," in Edith Fowke, ed., *Folklore of Canada* (Toronto: McClelland & Stewart, 1976), pp. 91–99.

For the activities of women in New France consult Micheline Dumont et al., *Quebec Women: A History* (Toronto: Women's Press, 1987); and Lilianne Plamondon, "A Businesswoman in New France: Marie-Anne Barbel, The Widow Fornel," in Veronica Strong-Boag and Anita Clair Fellman, eds., *Rethinking Canada: The Promise of Women's History* (Toronto: McClelland & Stewart, 1986), pp. 45–58. A good overview is "Women in New France," Chapter 2 of Alison Prentice et al., *Canadian Women: A History* (Toronto: Harcourt Brace, 1996), pp. 33–57, but the fullest account appears in Allan Greer, *The People of New France*, pp. 86–88. The best study of the "King's Daughters" is Yves Landry, *Les Filles du roi au XVIIe siècle* (Montreal: Leméac, 1992). André Vachon tells the fascinating story of the black slave Marie-Joseph-Angélique in the *Dictionary of Canadian Biography*, vol. 2, *1701–1740* (Toronto: University of Toronto Press, 1969), pp. 457–58. Jan Noel has written *Women in New France* (Ottawa: Canadian Historical Association, 1998), which among its other virtues contains an up-to-date bibliography. In a recent article, "Caste and Clientage in an Eighteenth-Century Quebec Convent," *Canadian Historical Review* 82 (2001): 465–490, Noel examines the influence of convents in New France. Jan Noel has also edited an interesting collection of articles, *Race and Gender in the Northern Colonies* (Toronto: Canadian Scholars Press, Inc., 2000), which contains essays on women in New France and New England.

Peter N. Moogk studies the children of eighteenth-century New France in *"Les Petits Sauvages,"* in Joy Parr, ed., *Childhood and Family in Canadian History* (Toronto: McClelland & Stewart, 1982), pp. 17–43. One can find in the previously cited collection of articles by J.F Bosher, *Business and Religion in the Age of New France, 1600–1760*, his important essay "The Family in New France," pp. 93–106. The story of the Tremblay family is told in Jacqueline Darveau-Cardinal's "De l'origine et de l'histoire de quelques patronymes Canadiens," *La revue française de Généalogie* 11 (1981): 20–23. Another interesting family history is the review of the Trudeau family in Canada in Thomas J. Laforest, *Our French-Canadian Ancestors* (Palm Harbour, FL: USI Press, 1981).

Two studies of the population of New France are: Hubert Charbonneau et al., *The First French Canadians: Pioneers in the St. Lawrence Valley*, trans. Paola Colozzo (Newark: University of Delaware Press, 1993); and *Frenchmen into Peasants: Modernity and Tradition in the Peopling of French Canada* (Cambridge, MA: Harvard University Press, 1997). Peter N. Moogk's "Reluctant Exiles: Emigrants from France in Canada before 1760," *William and Mary Quarterly*, 46(3) (July 1989): 463–505, should also be consulted.

For biographies of prominent individuals in New France see the *Dictionary of Canadian Biography*, vols. 1–4 (Toronto: University of Toronto Press, 1966, 1969, 1974, 1979). It is now also available online: www.biographi.ca. For valuable maps of the St. Lawrence colony consult R. Cole Harris, ed., *Historical Atlas of Canada*, vol. 1, *From the Beginning to 1800* (Toronto: University of Toronto Press, 1987). Jacob Ernest Cooke, ed., *The Encyclopedia of the North American Colonies*, 3 vols. (New York: Charles Scribner's Sons, 1993), contains a wealth of information about various aspects of the social and economic history of New France. For bibliographical references to the First Nations in the St. Lawrence valley, see the bibliographies provided in Chapters 3, 4, and 7 of this book.

THE ACADIANS

TIME LINE

1605 – The French found Port-Royal, and remain there until 1607

1632 – France begins its first serious attempt to colonize Acadia

1686 – The number of French settlers in present-day Nova Scotia grows to 800

1710 – The English capture Port-Royal and rename it "Annapolis Royal"

1713 – In the Treaty of Utrecht, France cedes "Acadia" to England

1720 – France begins the construction of its fortress Louisbourg on Île Royale (Cape Breton Island)

1749 – The British found Halifax

1755 – The expulsion of the Acadians begins

1758 – Louisbourg falls to the British

The deportation of the Acadians from Île Saint-Jean (Prince Edward Island)

The French used the name "Acadia" to distinguish the eastern or maritime part of New France from the valley of the St. Lawrence, which they called Canada. Under French rule, Canada and Acadia remained separate colonies. Just where Acadia ended and Canada began was never clearly defined, but certainly Acadia included present-day New Brunswick, Nova Scotia, and Prince Edward Island. It was located in a war zone between the English- and French-dominated areas.

Since France's interests lay largely in Canada, with its fur trade and agricultural settlement, France neglected Acadia. Little contact existed between the two colonies. Gradually, cultural differences emerged between the Acadians and the Canadians despite their common French origins and shared Roman Catholic faith. By the mid-eighteenth century, the Acadians (the majority of whom lived under British rule, after the Treaty of Utrecht of 1713 ceded mainland Nova Scotia to England) had become a people distinct from both the Canadians and the French. Nonetheless, the English regarded them, along with the French, as a threat to British Nova Scotia, and in 1755 they deported the Acadians from their homeland.

THE BEGINNINGS OF FRENCH ACADIA

 The roots of French Acadia go back to 1604, when the French wintered on an island in the St. Croix River, on the present-day boundary between Maine and New Brunswick. The following two winters they stayed at Port-Royal in present-day Nova Scotia. But with Champlain's founding of Quebec in 1608, France focussed its colonization efforts on Canada, although its interest in Acadia never waned entirely.

 Jean de Biencourt, Sieur de Poutrincourt, a French nobleman, arrived with the first expedition of 1604 and left in 1607. In 1611 Poutrincourt brought back his family, several settlers, and two Jesuit priests, but his settlement failed after the pirate Samuel Argall struck from his base at Jamestown, Virginia, and destroyed Port-Royal. L'Acadie, as a European settlement, almost completely vanished until the 1630s. With the arrival of Governor Isaac de Razilly in 1632, France began its first serious attempt to colonize Acadia. Many of the settlers came from the west coast of France, near the Atlantic port of La Rochelle. Labourers skilled in harvesting salt joined the contingent of several hundred colonists.

In Acadia, rather than clear the forested upland areas, they built dikes to reclaim the fertile marshland that the Bay of Fundy's strong tides flooded twice daily. To ensure the effective drainage of the diked marshlands, the Acadians also constructed a system of drainage ditches, combined with an *aboîteau* (a hinged valve in the dike itself), which allowed fresh water to run off the marshes at low tide and at the same time prevented salt water from flowing onto the diked farmland when the tide rose. For two to four years, the Acadians let snow and rain wash away the salt from the tidal marshes. At the end of that period they planted crops on the fertile, stone-free plains.

Razilly's death in 1636 proved catastrophic for the colony. Years of strife and confusion followed, as three men vied for control of Acadia: Charles de Menou d'Aulnay, Nicolas Denys, and Charles de Saint-Étienne de La Tour. Each governed his own territory and claimed exclusive trading rights. A small civil war broke out among them, ending only in the mid-1640s. Then, in 1654, the English conquered Acadia and held it until 1670. They saw it chiefly as a strategically located fishing and fur-trading area.

Acadians repairing a dike in the early eighteenth century. This re-creation by Azor Vienneau is based on archaeological and historical evidence.

History Collection/Nova Scotia Museum, Halifax/NSM 87.120.2.

ACADIAN SOCIETY IN THE LATE SEVENTEENTH CENTURY

During the period of occupation, the Acadians initially sought to accommodate their English rulers. Some Acadians learned to speak English. The generation of Acadian children born during the occupation had little knowledge of France.

The descendants of the immigrants of 1632 intermarried and developed a tightly knit community. At Port-Royal, the average Acadian couple usually married in their early twenties, and had ten or eleven children, most of whom survived to adulthood. The population doubled every 20 years, a faster rate than in New France. By 1670, the colony had a population of about 500. The absence of war, famine, or epidemics (such as typhoid, smallpox, and cholera) contributed to the rapid population increase.

Blood ties, common beliefs, and a system of mutual aid and solidarity united these first Europeans in Acadia. They developed their own speech patterns in an amalgam of various dialects — mostly French, a few English, and one or two Native — that merged and adapted into a single new language that reflected the Acadians' distinctive way of life and their need for a special vocabulary to describe it.

Although Port-Royal was Acadia's largest settlement, there were other small outlying communities on the Bay of Fundy and along the eastern coastline of present-day Nova Scotia. Acadian settlements were established in the 1670s and 1680s at Beaubassin (Amherst), Grand Pré (Wolfville), and Cobequid (Truro). With the addition of about 40 families brought out after 1671, the population grew to more than 800 by 1686.

By the end of the seventeenth century, the Acadians had established themselves in the region's fertile marshlands. Wheat and peas became their principal field crops. Every farm included a plot of vegetables. Most farms had a small orchard of cherry, pear, and apple trees. Almost all farmers kept cattle and sheep. Their pigs roamed freely in the forest behind their houses. Judging by the names they gave their settlements along the Bay of Fundy and the Chignecto Isthmus, which connects present-day Nova Scotia and New Brunswick, they were

Saltmarsh haying on an Acadian farm in the early 1700s, a re-creation by Azor Vienneau. Recently, on the upper Belleisle marsh in Annapolis County, Nova Scotia, archaeologists discovered evidence of two farmhouses with outbuildings like the ones shown in the background of this scene.

History Collection/Nova Scotia Museum, Halifax/NSM 87.120.4.

contented: Beaubassin ("beautiful pond"), Cocagne ("land of plenty"), and a settlement near Port-Royal called Paradis Terrestre ("earthly paradise," or "Garden of Eden"). Historical geographers R. Cole Harris and John Warkentin noted that "like the Canadians [the Acadians] achieved a far higher standard of living than all but the most privileged French peasants."[1]

In Acadian society, the family and the church, rather than the seigneurial system that dominated Canadian society, became the most powerful institutions. The Crown granted seigneuries at Port-Royal, at Beaubassin (the first major village settled after Port-Royal), and along the Saint John River, but the seigneurs had practically no influence on the settlers' daily life. In the St. Lawrence valley the intendant enforced the system, but in Acadia no such official existed. Acadia was much more egalitarian than Canada, the latter with its clearly stratified society.

The church was much more influential in Acadia than it was in the St. Lawrence valley. No single religious order dominated Acadian development; the Jesuits, Capuchins, Récollets, and Sulpicians all took part in religious and educational work among the Acadians. The inhabitants often sought the advice of their priests, who acted as unofficial judges in the disputes that arose among them. But the clergy did not rule the settlements. As in New France in the late seventeenth and eighteenth centuries, the Acadian clergy had limited authority over the populace.

The Acadians produced small agricultural surpluses to trade for items they did not make or grow themselves. They traded mainly with New England, rather than Canada or France. In many respects, the Bay of Fundy colony became a commercial dependency of New England. Acadian governors were unable to prevent the entry of American merchants and fishers to the area. British merchants even built warehouses at Port-Royal. There they purchased furs and surplus Acadian wheat and oats in return for West Indian sugar, molasses, and rum. In turn, the Acadians bought European manufactured goods, knives, needles, dishes, and cloth from the American merchants. The Acadians also travelled to Boston to sell their wheat and furs. They brought back cloth, tobacco, and pipes. In the late 1680s, even the governor of Acadia bought stockings and shoes in Boston for his garrison at Port-Royal.

RELATIONS WITH THE NATIVE PEOPLES

 At first the Acadians maintained good relations with the Mi'kmaq, in part because they used the tidal flats, lands of little interest to the First Nations. Unlike the New England settlers, who antagonized the Native peoples by seizing their lands and clearing away the forests, the Acadians initially posed little threat. Indeed, a few Acadian men married Native women. The community of La Hève (now LaHave, in Lunenburg County, Nova Scotia) became a Métis (mixed-blood) settlement. But, as historian William C. Wicken has pointed out, the relationship became strained in the mid-eighteenth century. As the Acadian population increased, it began to compete with the Mi'kmaq for the same natural resources. The Acadian population multiplied by nearly 30 times between 1671 and 1755,[2] whereas the Mi'kmaq numbers during the same time period stayed relatively stationary.

ACADIA BECOMES NOVA SCOTIA

New England wanted political as well as economic control over Acadia. When war broke out in Europe in 1689, the New Englanders led by William Phips attacked Port-Royal in 1690. They easily overpowered the garrison of 100 troops, and sacked Acadia's capital. The New Englanders held on to Acadia for seven years, until the signing of the Treaty of Ryswick in 1697, when France regained the colony.

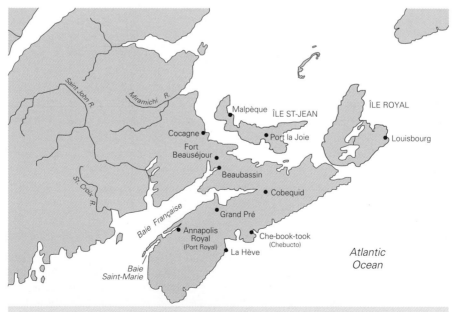

Acadia in the mid-eighteenth century.

Acadians trading with New Englanders in the early 1700s, a re-creation by Azor Vienneau. Some of the details in this painting are based on the inventory lists of ships that traded in Acadia during this period; other details are based on artifacts discovered at the archaeological dig of an early-eighteenth-century Acadian farmsite at Belleisle, Nova Scotia.

History Collection/Nova Scotia Museum, Halifax/NSM 87.120.3.

With the outbreak of war in Europe in 1702, Acadia again became easy prey for seafaring raiders from New England. Despite repeated attacks and looting, Acadians, with little help from France, held their ground against the English until 1710. That year, Britain supplied New England with money, arms, munitions, and naval aid to re-conquer Acadia. The American colonies provided additional men and supplies. An expedition of 3400 men and 36 ships arrived at Port-Royal in September 1710. The French governor held only a ramshackle fort with fewer than 300 men. The French resisted for three weeks, then accepted the inevitable and surrendered in mid-October.

THE TREATY OF UTRECHT

The Treaty of Utrecht in 1713 put to rest the question of the ownership of the peninsula. Acadia became Nova Scotia, and the English changed the name of Port-Royal to Annapolis Royal. But Louis XIV did obtain certain guarantees for the Acadians. One clause of the treaty stipulated that they had the right to leave Nova Scotia and settle elsewhere. Originally, they had one year in which to make up their minds, but this was later changed to allow slightly more time.

A rivalry for the allegiance of the Acadians began. France retained Île Royale (Cape Breton Island), where it began in 1720 to build a fortified town to protect the Gulf of St. Lawrence. They called their new fortress, Louisbourg. Anxious to establish a strong colony there, the French tried to attract the Acadians. The Acadian community did send representatives to inspect the lands on Cape Breton, but the delegates reported negatively on the rocky soil. Few Acadians liked the idea of having to leave their rich farmlands and comfortable houses to pioneer once again. The English tried to prevent Acadians from leaving by forbidding them to construct boats or to sell their property and cattle. From the English vantage point, French immigration to Cape Breton would only reinforce the French presence there and weaken Nova Scotia, which would lose successful farmers and their livestock. The British also feared that the Acadians might destroy their homesteads and the restraining dikes as they left.

THE NEUTRAL ACADIANS

The English administrators of Annapolis Royal faced a major problem: how should a minority govern a majority? They insisted that the Acadians become British subjects by swearing an oath of allegiance. This was customary practice, both after the succession of a new monarch to the throne and after a war. On five occasions, the governors of Nova Scotia tried to force the Acadians to swear an oath. Each time, the Acadians insisted on remaining neutral. As a border people between two rival empires, the Acadians wanted to proceed cautiously. In particular, the Acadians feared reprisals from the Mi'kmaq, firm allies of the French, if they appeared to ally themselves with the British.

Finally, in 1717, the Acadians worked out the terms on which they would remain under British government: they would have the right to practise their Catholic faith and the right to maintain neutrality in future wars against France. In 1730 the British agreed to their terms, and required in return only that the Acadians take this mild oath:

> I sincerely promise and swear on my faith as a Christian that I will be utterly loyal, and will truly obey His Majesty King George the second, whom I recognize as the sovereign lord of Acadia or Nova Scotia. May God so help me.

The Acadians took the oath, and thereafter were identified as "the neutral French." But for maintaining their right to neutrality, they earned the wrath of both the French and the English. As historian Naomi Griffiths notes, "In 1748, the Acadians considered themselves Acadian, the French considered them unreliable allies, and the English, unsatisfactory citizens."[3]

THE ACADIANS' GOLDEN AGE, 1714–1744

For these 30 years, the Acadians prospered. Their high birth rate and longevity led to a phenomenal population increase. In Port-Royal, 75 percent of the population reached the age of 21, at a time when only 50 percent reached that age in France. In 1711, there were approximately 2500 Acadians; in 1750, more than 10 000; and in 1755, more than 13 000 (Louisbourg excluded). The Acadian population spread into settlements along the present-day New Brunswick shoreline, as well as Île Saint-Jean (Prince Edward Island) and even into areas of present-day Nova Scotia that had been surveyed and reserved for future English immigration.

The Acadians continued their traditional lifestyle: farming, fishing, hunting, and trading. Women played a vitally important role. They joined the men in the fields at seeding time and during harvest. While the young men built and repaired the dikes, women were responsible for poultry raising and the orchards. The women also made their family's clothing. Along with the men, women passed on to the next generation their Acadian oral culture in songs, poetry, and stories.

The Acadians relied on their local priests or on the village patriarchs to solve problems of land boundaries, cattle theft, and other legal matters. The text of the Treaty of Utrecht guaranteed them the free exercise of Roman Catholicism "insofar as the laws of Great Britain allowed."

Although this guarantee was a contradiction in terms because English laws made the practice of Roman Catholicism in Britain difficult, the British authorities in Nova Scotia allowed a broad interpretation of the clause and granted the Acadians religious freedom.

The Roman Catholic church ministered to both the French and the Mi'kmaq populations. The missionaries gained great influence among the Mi'kmaq, who numbered about 1000 in the early 1740s in peninsular Nova Scotia and probably another 1000 on Île Saint-Jean, Cape Breton, and the mainland side of the Bay of Fundy. By the first half of the eighteenth century, the Roman Catholic religion had become an integral part of their identity. Abbé Pierre Maillard developed a Mi'kmaq alphabet, allowing them to learn selected prayers and chants and the catechisms. The Catholic priests, anthropologist Harald Prins writes, probably "had something to do with the fact that the Mi'kmaq term for a Protestant person was mu alasutmaq ('he who does not pray')."[4]

INCREASING TENSIONS BETWEEN THE ACADIANS AND THE ENGLISH

The British paid little attention to the colony in the late 1730s. They left the melancholic Major Lawrence Armstrong in charge at Annapolis Royal from 1731 to 1739. Historian George Rawlyk describes him as "probably insane for much of the time."[5] Then, in 1744, war broke out between England and France once again. The conflict lasted four years, and during it the English captured Louisbourg. But the peace treaty of 1748 restored the status quo. The English returned Louisbourg to France, an act that angered the New Englanders who, at great expense and loss of life, had captured it.

England consequently felt obliged to fortify Nova Scotia, to make it a proper counterbalance to Louisbourg. The English had earlier committed themselves to making Nova Scotia an effective part of their North American empire. Now they sought to make the Acadians into completely trustworthy subjects, to populate Nova Scotia with Protestant settlers, and to replace Annapolis Royal with a new military and administrative centre.

The new governor, Edward Cornwallis, then 36 years old (the uncle of the Lord Cornwallis who would surrender to the Americans at Yorktown in 1781), transported 2000 colonists to the port the Mi'kmaqs knew as "Che-book-took" (at the biggest harbour), a name the English rendered as "Chebucto." Cornwallis renamed it Halifax, after the Earl of Halifax, the president of the English Board of Trade and Plantations, which was a committee of Crown appointees in London who handled the administration of Britain's North American colonies until 1768.

In 1750–51, the British also brought in approximately 1500 "foreign Protestants," largely Germans, whom they settled at Lunenburg on the south shore of the peninsula, within easy reach of Halifax. Lunenburg became the first British settlement in Nova Scotia outside Halifax. British authorities then transferred the seat of government from Annapolis Royal to Halifax. Cornwallis introduced British institutions and laws to Nova Scotia, and fortified the new settlement to equal the strength of Louisbourg. These measures, together with the construction of roads to the Acadian settlements and the introduction of a large English garrison, completely changed the balance of power in the colony.

Simultaneously, the French strengthened their position in what is now New Brunswick. While the English were constructing their naval and military base at Halifax and bringing Protestant immigrants into Nova Scotia, the French increased their garrison at the mouth of the Saint John River and occupied the Chignecto Isthmus, building Fort Beauséjour (near present-day Sackville, New Brunswick) in 1750. Beauséjour protected their overland communications from Canada to Louisbourg.

An aerial photograph of the restored mid-eighteenth-century fortress of Louisbourg. It shows Porte Dauphine, the main entrance to the fort, and (upper right) the King's Bastion and the barracks.

J. Steeves/Canadian Heritage/Parks Canada East.

THE FIRST NATIONS AND THE ENGLISH

The French had maintained their alliance with the Mi'kmaq and Maliseet (from present-day western New Brunswick) in the hope of using them against the English. The Mi'kmaq needed little encouragement, since they were resentful of English encroachments on their hunting grounds. In addition, unlike the French, the British had refused to give them annual gifts in return for the use of their land. The English seldom took the Mi'kmaqs into account when the question of land ownership arose. As far as they were concerned, France had ceded its title to the land with the Treaty of Utrecht in 1713, and it belonged to Britain. As anthropologist Harald Prins has observed, the French might look upon the Mi'kmaq as proxy warriors, but in the Mi'kmaqs' eyes they were "freedom fighters trying to liberate their homeland from the British intruders."[6]

Years of Mi'kmaq raids and harassment followed the Treaty of Utrecht, with many of the attacks against the British taking place at sea. (The Mi'kmaqs had purchased European longboats after their first contact with French fishers.) They captured dozens of English trading and fishing boats in the course of these attacks. With the outbreak of war between England and France in 1744, the Mi'kmaq raids against the British in Nova Scotia reached a new level of intensity. Cornwallis responded by proposing drastic measures. One plan was to recruit 50 rangers locally and bring in another 100 from Boston to kill Mi'kmaqs. On October 2, 1749, the English governor issued his proclamation commanding all "to Annoy, distress, take or destroy the Savages commonly called Mic-macks, wherever they are found." In wartime the French paid the First Nations for English

Indian Camp, New Brunswick, painted by William Robert Herries (1818–1845) in the mid-nineteenth century. The Maliseets' hunting and fishing territory once stretched from the Saint John River valley to the lower Saint Lawrence River, opposite Tadoussac. The Mi'kmaqs lived in the more easterly portion of what is now New Brunswick and in Nova Scotia, Prince Edward Island, and (by the 1700s) southern Newfoundland.

Beaverbrook Art Gallery, Fredericton.

scalps, just as the English paid for Native scalps. Cornwallis again promised payment and added that any person found helping the First Nations would this time be treated as one.

Cornwallis's drastic measures, however, never went into effect. London advised a milder policy, adding that experience in other parts of North America had indicated that "gentler Methods and Offers of Peace have more frequently prevailed with Indians than the Sword, if at the same Time, that the Sword is held over their Heads."

BRITAIN'S GROWING ANXIETY ABOUT THE ACADIANS

As frontier incidents and Mi'kmaq raids increased, Cornwallis became ever more doubtful of the Acadians' loyalty to Britain in the event of another war. In 1749 the governor commanded them to swear an oath of unconditional allegiance to Britain or risk deportation. But when the Acadian delegates replied negatively to Cornwallis's ultimatum, he did not expel them, preferring to wait until British power became stronger in Nova Scotia.

The Acadians entered a period of great tension in the early 1750s. Between 1500 and 2000 Acadians left peninsular Nova Scotia by choice or by coercion — many were forced by French raiding parties to move to French territory north of the isthmus. Yet the four-fifths of the Acadians who remained in the colony believed that the governor, by his refusal to remove them, had, like other English governors before him, accepted their "neutral" status.

When Charles Lawrence became lieutenant governor of Nova Scotia in 1753, the Acadians expected the situation to remain the same. This time, however, they were wrong. First and foremost, Colonel Lawrence was a soldier. Like most soldiers, he knew only allies and enemies, not "neutrals." To him, the Acadians posed a definite threat in the event of another full-scale war between France and Britain. In the early months of 1754, Lawrence did not consider expulsion to be justified. He believed that if the British confronted the Acadians firmly, they would yield and agree to take the oath of total unconditional loyalty.

THE EXPULSION OF THE ACADIANS

The outbreak of war in North America in 1754 and General Braddock's campaign in 1755 altered the military situations. In June 1755, Colonel Robert Monckton, with a force composed largely of New England troops, captured Fort Beauséjour and the rest of the French garrisons on the Chignecto Isthmus.[7] Sufficiently impressed by the English victories, the Native peoples stopped their attacks. This allowed Lawrence to turn his attention to the Acadian question.

In July, Lawrence ordered representatives of the Acadians to appear before the Halifax Council, which advised the governor. He probably believed that the Acadians would capitulate quickly and agree to the oath. The council, dominated by military officers, insisted on an iron-clad oath from the Acadians that they would support Britain in the event of war. (The council may have had ulterior motives in setting such strict terms: some of the twelve council members were perhaps eyeing the Acadians' rich lands along the Bay of Fundy; there were profits to be made in the evacuations, as well as in the resettlement of New Englanders in Nova Scotia.)

On July 23, two days before the first Acadian delegates from the villages arrived, the news of General Braddock's catastrophic defeat near Fort Duquesne in the Ohio country reached Halifax. Casualties approached 40 percent, and the British commander himself had been killed. Nova Scotia's need for the Acadians to make a declaration of unequivocal allegiance to Britain, to recognize themselves as unconditional subjects of the British Crown, became all the more urgent.

The Acadian delegates pointed out that they had always been loyal to George II and agreed to present all their firearms to the English as proof of their loyalty. They were prepared to abide by the oath they had sworn earlier, but not to take a new one. They asked to be considered as a neutral people, pointing out that between 1713 and 1755 they had never fought for France. Throughout the discussion, none of the delegates foresaw the catastrophe impending if they refused to swear the required oath. They underestimated the determination of Lawrence's council.

The final confrontation came on July 28. After hearing the delegates one last time, the council reached a decision. It endorsed the deportation of all Acadians under British jurisdiction who had refused to take the unqualified oath. Now, in the general hysteria after Braddock's defeat, the British were prepared to remove them. The Acadians' fate passed into the hands of 2000 hostile, anti-Catholic New England militiamen working under the instructions of Lieutenant Governor Charles Lawrence.

THE DEPORTATION BEGINS

The deportation began immediately after the council's decision. Lawrence attempted initially to prepare carefully for the evacuation, providing adequate cabin space on the ships and ample provisions for the duration of the journey. But, in the end, the evacuation was brutal and poorly planned. The English first herded the Acadians together at Annapolis Royal, Grand Pré,

Beaubassin, and other settlements. Since sending them to Cape Breton or Canada would only serve to build up the French militia in the two French colonies, the English dispersed most of them among the Thirteen Colonies and sent some to England. Lawrence's troops, including those commanded by Colonel Robert Monckton, the victor at Fort Beauséjour, burned houses and barns to deprive those who escaped of shelter. Within hours, the work of more than a century of toil had become ashes.

THE DESTRUCTION OF ACADIAN SOCIETY

The expulsion destroyed Acadian society. It broke up communities and dispersed closely knit families. Some fought back — for the most part, ineffectively. Abbé François Le Guerne, who remained in what is now southern New Brunswick until August 1757, reported that women and children took to the woods to escape deportation and to flee the English soldiers who had burned their property. Some 86 Acadians escaped by digging a tunnel from their barracks in their prison camp near Fort Beauséjour. On board a ship bound for the American colonies, an Acadian group seized their captors, sailed back to the Bay of Fundy, and then fled overland to the upper reaches of the Saint John River. An estimated 2000 Acadians fled to Île Saint-Jean (Prince Edward Island). The refugees outnumbered the original Acadian residents on the island three to one.

The exodus brought confusion to Île Saint-Jean. Many Acadian refugees came with only the clothes on their backs. Starvation was general as the islanders had enjoyed only one good harvest over the previous five years. But, despite the hardships, the Acadian refugees felt that this

The Expulsion of the Acadians from Île Saint-Jean, 1758, a painting by Lewis Parker, one of Canada's foremost painters of historical scenes. It depicts the arrival of ten British warships sent to evacuate the Acadian population of Île Saint-Jean (now Prince Edward Island).

Painting by Lewis Parker. © Parks Canada.

Where Historians Disagree
The Expulsion of the Acadians: Was It Necessary?

Canadian historians have long discussed the necessity and the degree of cruelty of the British expulsion of the Acadians in 1755. The controversy owes as much to the complexity of the question and the contradictions in the evidence as to differing perspectives. As historian Naomi Griffiths wrote: "Acadian history 1710–1755 provides endless questions of fact and interpretation, problems about what actually happened and whether it was brought about intentionally or not.... As the years lead on to 1755, the problems which divide historians multiply, and the events of the expulsion itself have been so diversely treated that one sometimes wonders whether the authors are writing about the same events."[1] Some condemn the English; others believe the Acadians themselves were to blame for their misfortunes. A third group contends that interference from Quebec and Louisbourg resulted in the tragedy.

The argument that the deportation was necessary was still being made in the 1950s. As late as 1956, popular historian Joseph Lister Rutledge summarized this position: "If ever a conquered people were treated with consideration by their captors, it was the Acadians.... The net result was generous and understanding treatment for people who represented a very stubborn breed indeed. This conquered people retained their land and freedom and the assurance of the exercise of their religion. The loyalty oath required of them was generous to a fault."[2]

Several English-language writers have argued that the expulsion should be seen solely as a military operation necessary for Nova Scotia's defence. Archibald McKellar MacMechan, professor of English at Dalhousie University, for instance, wrote as follows in 1913: "Before passing judgement on the men who conceived and executed this removal of an entire population, it should be remembered that they acted as did Louis XIV in expelling the Huguenots from France and the United States in expelling the tories. All were precautionary measures dictated by the need of national self-preservation; and they were regarded by those who took them as imperative in a dangerous crisis. Lawrence acted like the commander of a fort expecting a siege, who levels trees and houses outside the walls in order to afford the enemy no shelter and to give the garrison a clear field of fire."[3]

Most French-language historians have rejected the arguments advanced in defence of the expulsion. In the 1920s, French historian Émile Lauvrière noted of Governor Lawrence's actions that "only a criminal soul could devise such a plot in all its details."[4] French-Canadian writer and Roman Catholic priest Henri Beaudé (who wrote under the pseudonym of Henri d'Arles) considered the deportation order entirely undeserved and "conceived in hate, a prejudice of race and religion."[5]

While not overlooking the cruelty of the expulsion, two English-language historians have tried to understand more fully the British decision to evict an entire people. In 1979, Naomi Griffiths wrote that the imposition in 1755 of a "declaration of unequivocal allegiance to British interests" was "reasonable enough" because war with France had begun.[6] Historian Stephen E. Patterson has commented as well on the circumstances, or the context, in which the deportation occurred: "It took place in a time of war, a bitter war between inveterate enemies for whom possession of Nova Scotia had become symbolic of their power and prestige in the international world."[7]

A recent resolution, passed unanimously in June 2002 in the Quebec National Assembly, proves, however, that intense feelings remain on this issue. The Quebec legislators expressed their support for the Acadian people in Canada's demand, "that the British Crown officially recognize the historical wrongdoing in the deportation of their ancestors."[8] In mid-December 2003, the governor general officially acknowledged the Acadian expulsion in a royal proclamation. It acknowledged the wrongs done to the Acadians during the expulsion. It also stated that, beginning in 2005, and then annually thereafter, July 28 would become a commemorative day to mark the deportation.

[1] Naomi Griffiths, ed., *The Acadian Deportation: Deliberate Perfidy or Cruel Necessity?* (Toronto: Copp Clark, 1969), p. 3.

[2] Joseph Lister Rutledge, *Century of Conflict* (Toronto: Doubleday, 1956), p. 409. *Century of Conflict* was published in the popular *Canadian History Series*, edited by Thomas B. Costain.

[3] Archibald McKellar MacMechan, in A. Shortt and A.G. Doughty, eds., *Canada and Its Provinces*, vol. 13. (Toronto: Glasgow Brook, 1914), p. 98.

[4] N.E.S. Griffiths, "The Acadians," in the *Dictionary of Canadian Biography*, vol. 4, *1771–1800* (Toronto: University of Toronto Press, 1979), p. xxvi.

[5] Henri d'Arles [Henri Beaudé] *La déportation des Acadiens* (Montreal: Bibliothèque de l'Action française, 1918), pp. 21–26, translated and quoted in Griffiths, *The Acadian Deportation*, p. 156.

[6] Griffiths, "The Acadians," p. xxvi.

[7] Stephen E. Patterson, "1744–1763: Colonial Wars and Aboriginal Peoples," chapter seven of Phillip A. Buckner and John G. Reid, eds., *The Atlantic Region to Confederation: A History* (Toronto: University of Toronto Press, 1994), p. 145.

[8] Rhéal Séguin, "Britain made a mistake with Acadians, Quebec says," *The Globe and Mail*, June 14, 2002.

life was preferable to that of banishment from the Maritimes. After the fall of Louisbourg in 1758, however, the British landed on the island and began to deport all the Acadians they could capture.

Many died, victims of malnutrition and exposure in the deportations from the Maritimes. Storms at sea, a shortage of food and drinking water, and poor sanitary conditions meant that many ships lost more than one-third of their Acadian passengers. The *Cornwallis*, which left Chignecto with 417 Acadians on board, docked at Charleston, South Carolina, with only 210 still alive. The expulsions continued for seven years, until 1762.

The British military occasionally sent ships from the same village to different destination points. Inevitably, family members were separated. Massachusetts, New York, Pennsylvania, Maryland, Virginia, the Carolinas, and Georgia all received Acadians. For the most part, the Americans provided support and tried to settle the exiles in various small towns and villages, but these efforts proved to be largely unsuccessful. Despite all prohibitions to the contrary, the Acadians, footsore and half-clad, wandered from town to town, looking for family and friends. They remained outsiders in the communities where they were settled. Their mortality rate in the American colonies was high. An estimated one-third of those deported died from diseases that had been practically unknown to them before 1755 — smallpox, typhoid, and yellow fever.

It is extremely difficult to determine the number of Acadians expelled between 1755 and 1763. Historians estimate that the British deported nearly three-quarters of the Acadian population of roughly 13 000. Approximately 7000 were deported in the first year, 1755, alone. By the time the policy ended in 1762, the British had exiled perhaps another 3000 Acadians.

The Acadians from peninsular Nova Scotia were split into small groups. The British rounded up many who escaped to Île Royale (Cape Breton) and Île Saint-Jean (Prince Edward Island) after they took these two islands in 1758. (Of the 2000 captives taken on Île Saint-Jean in 1758, 700 drowned when three transport vessels were lost at sea.) Some Acadians sought refuge in the isolated Miramichi River valley, in what is now northeastern New Brunswick. About 1500 Acadians also fled to New France to establish homes near Quebec, Trois-Rivières, and Montreal. Others successfully made their way to St. Pierre and Miquelon, the two small islands off the coast of Newfoundland that France was able to retain under the peace treaty of 1763.

THE ACADIANS IN FRANCE AND LOUISIANA

One thousand Acadians were sent to Virginia in 1756 and then immediately dispatched to England. The Virginians argued that the Acadians were British subjects, which therefore entitled them to England's support. About one-quarter of them died from an epidemic of smallpox during their first summer in England. The remainder spent seven years in internment camps in England, until France took them in 1763.

Many of the Acadians who settled in France in 1763 had difficulty adjusting to French society, which suggests that, although they spoke French and practised Catholicism, they were a people distinct from the French. Acadians were not accustomed to the limitations that restricted ordinary French people in the eighteenth century: the *corvée* (enforced days of unpaid labour) and restrictions on travel within the country. The way of life in France was alien to them, and seemed harsh.

Not finding comfortable homes in France, seven shiploads of Acadians — nearly 1600 people — sailed for New Orleans, Louisiana, in 1785, where they joined other Acadians who had settled there earlier. Some 300 had arrived in 1764–65. Of those, some had initially sought refuge at Saint-Domingue (present-day Haiti), the French sugar island, but had eventually crossed over to New Orleans. In addition, about 700 Acadians from Maryland and Pennsylvania had arrived in Louisiana by ship between 1766 and 1770.

Although it was at that time a Spanish possession, Louisiana's main language was French, and the colony was officially Roman Catholic. Like the Bay of Fundy area, Louisiana had large marshes that needed draining — work at which the Acadians had prior experience. Today, Louisiana is home to more than 1 million descendants of the Acadians. As the Acadian settlements spread across the Louisiana bayous and prairies, their neighbours shortened the French name *Acadien* to "Cadien" and, eventually, to "Cajun."

THE RETURN OF SOME ACADIANS

In 1764, the British permitted the Acadians to resettle in Nova Scotia. A steady stream of wanderers returned — in all, an estimated 3000. But since New Englanders now owned their farms, they could not regain their land.

By 1800, the Acadians in Nova Scotia numbered 4000 and in the new colonies of New Brunswick and Prince Edward Island, 3800 and 700 respectively — a result of high birth rates rather than the return of more exiles. They were concentrated around Baie Sainte-Marie (St. Mary's Bay) in southwestern Nova Scotia and Chéticamp on Cape Breton Island. They also settled around Malpèque on Prince Edward Island. Since present-day New Brunswick contained vacant land, especially along its east coast, the majority of returned Acadians went there. They joined a group of Acadians who had previously sought refuge in this area during the expulsion. Finding themselves in many of these locations on infertile land, most of the Acadians became fishers rather than farmers. Subsequently they made a living from these lands, but it was at a much lower standard than what they had known on their well-developed farms before 1755.

Buffeted about for a generation, from 1755 to the late 1780s, the Acadians finally established a new Acadia, but one that was much less cohesive than the original one. They tried to rebuild their shattered communities, but many family units had been broken up. In the new Acadia, the Roman Catholic clergy represented the only remaining French institution.

The Martin house, originally from Ste. Anne, New Brunswick, was built around 1770. It was moved to the Acadian Historical Village near Caraquet, New Brunswick, and restored. Note the pitch of the roof of this old Acadian house.

Village Historique Acadien.

It became customary in Acadian villages for the older people to tell of their experiences in the deportation. Indeed, the expulsion became the unifying event of Acadian experience. The tradition remained an oral one until American poet Henry Wadsworth Longfellow, who first heard the story in the early 1840s, recorded it in his poem *Evangeline*, which was subsequently published in several French translations. The story centres on Evangeline Bellefontaine, a 17-year-old *Acadienne* who is separated in the deportation from her lover, Gabriel Lajeunesse. When, after a lifelong search, she finds him again, he is a broken old man. As she holds him in her arms, he dies. *Evangeline* confirmed for Acadians that they were a unique people with an identity of their own.

In 1979 Antonine Maillet, Acadia's great novelist, wrote a more convincing tale, *Pélagie-la-Charrette*. This is the story of an unconquerable woman, Pélagie, who, after the expulsion, spent a decade travelling in a cart drawn by a cow. With others she met along the way, she journeyed from Georgia back to Acadia. "When they built their carts," Maillet wrote, "they were just families. By the time they returned to Acadia they were a people."

It is tragic that the first European immigrant group to establish itself successfully in the present-day Maritime provinces received such treatment. But the Acadians lived in a war zone, an area contested by two great European powers. Geography not only isolated them from their natural allies — the Canadians in the valley of the St. Lawrence — it also linked them closely with New England. The Acadians tried to maintain a balance between the two competing powers by keeping a strict neutrality. They succeeded for more than a century, until wartime hysteria won out and the British felt it necessary to expel the "neutral French."

NOTES

1. R. Cole Harris and John Warkentin, eds., *Canada Before Confederation: A Study in Historical Geography* (Ottawa: Carleton University Press, 1991 [1974]), p. 30.
2. William C. Wicken, "Re-examining Mi'kmaq–Acadian Relations, 1635–1755," in Sylvie Dépatie et al., eds., *Vingt ans après: Habitants et marchands. Twenty Years Later* (Montreal/Kingston: McGill-Queen's University Press, 1998), p. 96.
3. Naomi Griffiths, *The Acadians: Creation of a People* (Toronto: McGraw-Hill Ryerson, 1973), p. 37.
4. Harald E.L. Prins, *The Mi'kmaq Resistance, Accommodation, and Cultural Survival* (Fort Worth, TX: Harcourt Brace, 1996), p. 122.
5. George Rawlyk, "Cod, Louisbourg, and the Acadians," chapter six of Phillip A. Buckner and John G. Reid, eds., *The Atlantic Region to Confederation* (Toronto: University of Toronto Press, 1994), p. 113.
6. Prins, *The Mi'kmaq Resistance*, p. 135.
7. Ironically, the largest Acadian community today is in Moncton, New Brunswick — named in honour of Robert Monckton, who became lieutenant governor of Nova Scotia in 1755.

LINKING TO THE PAST w(W)w

Musée Acadien de l'Université de Moncton

http://www.umoncton.ca/maum

Permanent online exhibit offers a concise discussion of Acadian history illustrated with images from the museum's collection.

Acadian and French-Canadian Ancestral Home
http://www.acadian-home.org

A compendium of articles and images relating to the Acadians, organized by topic.

The Acadian Odyssey
http://collections.ic.gc.ca/acadian/english/toce/toce.htm

An overview of the Acadians' roots with a description of daily life in Acadia.

Mi'kmaq Portraits Collection
http://museum.gov.ns.ca/mikmaq

This site features hundreds of images related to the Mi'kmaq from the 1500s to the present.

Nova Scotia: Acadian Historical Atlas
http://collections.ic.gc.ca/neo-ecossaise

Modern and historical maps of regions of Nova Scotia, along with a list of people who lived there before the deportation.

Acadian–Cajun Genealogy and History
http://www.acadian-cajun.com

An extensive site depicting the history of Acadia and Acadian settlement in Louisiana, and featuring information on genealogy research in this area.

RELATED READINGS

Naomi Griffiths's article "The Golden Age: Acadian Life, 1713–1748," reprinted in R. Douglas Francis and Donald B. Smith, eds., *Readings in Canadian History: Pre-Confederation*, 6th ed. (Toronto: Nelson Thomson Learning, 2002), pp. 120–131, is a valuable introduction to the topic.

BIBLIOGRAPHY

Naomi Griffiths has written two good summaries of Acadian history: *The Acadians: Creation of a People* (Toronto: McGraw-Hill Ryerson, 1973); and *The Contexts of Acadian History, 1686–1784* (Montreal/ Kingston: McGill-Queen's University Press, 1992). Barry Moody provides bibliographical suggestions in M. Brook Taylor, ed., *Canadian History: A Reader's Guide*, vol. 1, *Beginnings to Confederation* (Toronto: University of Toronto Press, 1994), pp. 76–111. For the early period consult John G. Reid, *Acadia, Maine, and New Scotland: Marginal Colonies in the Seventeenth Century* (Toronto: University of Toronto Press, 1981). Andrew H. Clark provides a historical geographer's view in *Acadia: The Geography of Early Nova Scotia to 1760* (Madison: University of Wisconsin Press, 1968). See also Naomi Griffiths's "The Acadians," in the *Dictionary of Canadian Biography*, vol. 4, *1771–1800* (Toronto: University of Toronto Press, 1979), pp. xvii–xxxi. Jean Daigle's account, "Acadia, 1604–1763: An Historical Synthesis" in Jean Daigle, ed., *The Acadians of the Maritimes* (Moncton: Centre d'études acadiennes, 1982), pp. 17–46, is very useful. Cornelius Jaenen and Cecila Morgan, eds., *Documents in Pre-Confederation History* (Don Mills, Ontario: Addison-Wesley, 1998) contains valuable documents in "Topic 3: The Acadians—A Neglected or Persecuted People?" pp. 49–70. Valuable studies of the Acadians on Île Saint-Jean (Prince Edward Island) include D.C. Harvey, *The French Regime in Prince Edward Island* (New York: AMS, 1970 [1926]); and Georges Arsenault, *The Island Acadians, 1720–1980* (Charlottetown: Ragweed, 1989). Bibliographical references to Louisbourg appear in the bibliography of this text's chapter 7.

Guy Frégault's "The Deportation of the Acadians, 1755–62," chapter 6 in his book *Canada: The War of the Conquest*, trans. Margaret M. Cameron (Toronto: Oxford University Press, 1969), pp. 164–200, provides a French-Canadian historian's interpretation of events in Acadia in the 1750s. Various opinions on the issue of the expulsion appear in Naomi Griffiths, ed., *The Acadian Deportation: Deliberate Perfidy or Cruel Necessity?* (Toronto: Copp Clark, 1969). T.G. Barnes provides a good historiographical review in his "Historiography of the Acadians' *Grand Dérangement*, 1775," *Quebec Studies* 7 (1988): 74–86.

Several interesting articles on the Acadians appear in Phillip A. Buckner and David Frank, eds. and comps., *Atlantic Canada Before Confederation*, vol. 1, *The Acadiensis Reader* (Fredericton: Acadiensis Press, 1985): Gisa Hynes, "Some Aspects of the Demography of Port-Royal, 1650–1755," pp. 11–25; Naomi Griffiths, "Acadians in Exile: The Experiences of the Acadians in the British Seaports," pp. 26–43; and Graeme Wynn, "Late Eighteenth-Century Agriculture on the Bay of Fundy Marshlands," pp. 44–53. Robert G. Leblanc provides a short review of the expulsion in "The Acadian Migrations," *Canadian Geographical Journal* 81 (July 1970): 10–19. For the Acadians' arrival in Louisiana see Carl A. Brasseaux, "A New Acadia: The Acadian Migrations to South Louisiana, 1764–1803," *Acadiensis* 15 (1985): 123–32. His more specialized studies on the topic include: *The Founding of New Acadia: The Beginnings of Acadian Life in Louisiana, 1765–1803* (Baton Rouge: Louisiana State University, 1987); and *Acadian to Cajun: Transformation of a People, 1803–1877* (Jackson: University Press of Mississippi, 1992).

The history of the Mi'kmaqs in Acadia under French and British rule is recounted in Olive P. Dickason, "Louisbourg and the Indians: A Study in Imperial Race Relations," *History and Archaeology* 6 (1976): 1–206; L.F.S. Upton, *Micmacs and Colonists: Indian–White Relations in the Maritimes, 1713–1867* (Vancouver: University of British Columbia Press, 1979); Harald E.L. Prins, *The Mi'kmaq: Resistance, Accommodation, and Cultural Survival* (Fort Worth, TX: Harcourt Brace, 1996); and Jennifer Reid, *Myth, Symbol, and Colonial Encounter: British and Mi'kmaq in Acadia, 1700–1867* (Ottawa: University of Ottawa Press, 1995). Daniel N. Paul takes a critical view of both French and English policies toward the Mi'kmaq in *We Were Not the Savages: A Micmac Perspective on the Collision of European and Aboriginal Civilizations* (Halifax: Nimbus, 1993). William C. Wicken seriously challenges the presentation of Acadian–Mi'kmaq relations as harmonious at all times in "Re-examining Mi'kmaq-Acadian Relations, 1635–1755," in Sylvie Depatie et al., eds., *Vingt ans après: Habitants et marchands. Twenty Years Later* (Montreal/Kingston: McGill-Queen's University Press, 1998), pp. 93–114. In his recent study, *Mi'kmaq Treaties on Trial: History, Land, and Donald Marshall, Junior* (Toronto: University of Toronto Press, 2002), Wicken examines a series of British–Mi'kmaq treaties (1726, 1749, 1752, and 1760–1). Stephen E. Patterson has written "Indian–White Relations in Nova Scotia, 1749–61: A Study in Political Interaction," *Acadiensis* 23(1) (Autumn 1993): 23–59.

Léon Thériault provides an overview of Acadian history since the expulsion in "Acadia, 1763–1978: An Historical Synthesis," in Jean Daigle, ed, *The Acadians of the Maritimes* (Moncton: Centre d'études acadiennes, 1982), pp. 47–86. A recent popular survey of the entire sweep of Acadian history, before the expulsion and up to the present, is Nicolas Landry and Nicole Lang's *Histoire de l'Acadie* (Sillery, Quebec: Septentrion, 2001). The story of the founding of Halifax is told in Judith Fingard, Janet Guildford, and David Sutherland, *Halifax: The First 250 Years* (Halifax: Formac Publishing, 1999). Biographical portraits of seventeenth- and eighteenth-century Acadians appear in the *Dictionary of Canadian Biography*, vols. 1–4 (Toronto: University of Toronto Press, 1966, 1969, 1974, 1979).

Maps of Acadian marshland settlement and of the Acadian deportation and return appear in R. Cole Harris, ed., *Historical Atlas of Canada*, vol. 1, *From the Beginning to 1800* (Toronto: University of Toronto Press, 1987). For a complete overview of the area in the seventeenth and eighteenth centuries consult the early chapters of Phillip A. Buckner and John G. Reid, eds., *The Atlantic Region to Confederation: A History* (Toronto: University of Toronto Press, 1994).

THE ANGLO-FRENCH STRUGGLE FOR A CONTINENT

TIME LINE

1670 –	Establishment of the Hudson's Bay Company
1689– **1697** –	War between England and France
1701– **1713** –	War between England and France resumes
1711 –	English expedition against Quebec fails
1713 –	Signing of the Treaty of Utrecht. France gives up her claim to Hudson Bay and Newfoundland, and cedes "Acadia" to England
1744– **1748** –	The English and French are again at war
1755 –	General Braddock is defeated
1756 –	Beginning of the Seven Years' War
1759 –	Wolfe's victory on the Plains of Abraham, leading to the fall of Quebec
1760 –	The British conquer New France and establish a military government until the signing of the peace treaty in 1763, which ends the war

At approximately the same time that the French settled Quebec, England established its first colonies in North America: Virginia in 1607, Newfoundland in 1610, and Massachusetts in 1620. Others followed on the Atlantic seaboard, and in 1664 the Dutch colony of New Netherland passed into English hands and was renamed New York. The English also sponsored expeditions into Hudson Bay. Henry Hudson in 1610–11 first located the immense body of water the size of the Mediterranean Sea. A little more than half a century later, an English company established a string of fur-trading posts around Hudson Bay. Conflict between England and France arose in the late 1680s, when the two empires confronted each other in the North American interior. The struggle continued, with several interludes of peace, until 1760, when the French forces capitulated at Montreal.

THE ENGLISH CHALLENGE FROM THE NORTH

w(w)w English interest in finding the Northwest Passage revived in the early seventeenth century. In
June 1610, Henry Hudson entered an ice-bound strait previously noted (in the 1570s and 1580s) by English Arctic explorers Martin Frobisher and John Davis. Both the strait and the inland sea into which it led were later named after him. Although Hudson and his men spent a terrible winter on the east coast of James Bay, they continued their search for the Northwest Passage the following spring. Hudson's crew mutinied and seized him, his son, and seven others, and set them adrift. Eight of the twelve mutineers returned alive to England, where they falsely reported that the expedition had found the Northwest Passage. Nothing is known of Henry Hudson's fate. The Welsh navigator Sir Thomas Button crossed Hudson Bay in 1612 but failed to find Hudson or a passage to the Indies.

Other English expeditions followed until 1631, when it became clear that, even if the Northwest Passage existed, it would not be a commercially viable trade route. Since both the Dutch and the English had already begun to make the longer but less hazardous journey around Africa to India and China, the lure of the Northwest Passage diminished.

Ironically, two renegade French traders, Pierre-Esprit Radisson and Médard Chouart Des Groseilliers (Mr. Radishes and Mr. Gooseberry, as the English called them), who had found no support in New France for their plan to expand their operations into the rich fur country south of Hudson Bay and James Bay, directed the English to that area. In 1668, a group of English merchants under the patronage of Prince Rupert, a cousin of King Charles II, sponsored Groseilliers' expedition, which was to winter on Hudson Bay and return with a cargo of fur. The enterprise proved so successful that in 1670 Charles II gave the Hudson's Bay Company exclusive trading rights and property ownership to "Rupert's Land," all the lands within the area drained by the rivers flowing into Hudson and James Bays (nearly half the area of Canada today).

FRENCH EXPANSION TO THE NORTH AND WEST

The English now threatened New France's fur trade from two sides: New York and Hudson Bay. The collapse of the French trading system with the Hurons in 1649 had left a vacuum and greatly facilitated the English dominance of Hudson Bay. In response, the French in the early 1670s sent overland expeditions to Hudson Bay, Lake Superior, and the Mississippi River.

Frontenac, who became governor in 1672, openly promoted further westward expansion into the Mississippi valley. His ally was René-Robert Cavelier de La Salle, a daring and ambitious fur trader, who in 1682 reached the Mississippi delta. He raised the royal arms of France and claimed all the land drained by the Mississippi River and its tributaries for the king of France. He named the huge valley Louisiana, after Louis XIV. La Salle attempted to found a colony in

Louisiana, but his efforts ended in failure — and his assassination in 1687 — although the French established a successful settlement 20 years later.

In the mid-1670s, Montreal traders built Michilimackinac at the junction of Lakes Michigan and Huron, which became the starting point for the fur trade along the upper Mississippi River and beyond Lake Superior. Soon the French built trading posts from the Ohio River to Lake Superior and north to Hudson Bay. A mixed First Nations and French (Métis) population arose at these western posts, particularly at the larger centres like Michilimackinac, and later Green Bay and Detroit. First Nations, Métis, and Canadians lived as neighbours. They shared cultural traits and developed a new trade language, accommodating words and expressions from Native languages and from French. Historian Richard White describes the new culture as "the middle ground."[1]

THE FIRST ROUND OF CONFLICT WITH THE ENGLISH COLONIES, 1689–1713

Frontenac's successors faced an increasingly difficult military situation in the 1680s. After the French ended their truce with the Iroquois in the mid-1680s, the Five Nations, with the encouragement of the English, resumed their raids on New France. Few in number and scattered over a vast area, the French realized the importance of co-operation with their Algonquian allies. The

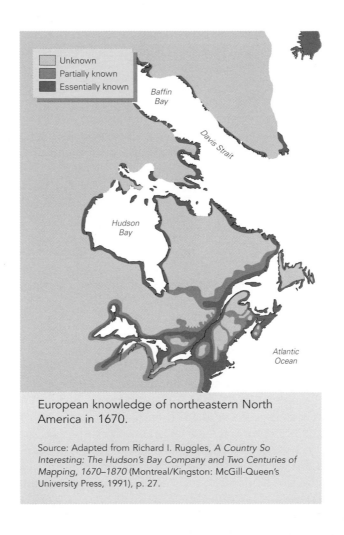

European knowledge of northeastern North America in 1670.

Source: Adapted from Richard I. Ruggles, *A Country So Interesting: The Hudson's Bay Company and Two Centuries of Mapping, 1670–1870* (Montreal/Kingston: McGill-Queen's University Press, 1991), p. 27.

coureurs de bois now became the colony's greatest strength, as they linked New France with its Native allies in the interior.

The Iroquois raid in 1689 on Lachine, a settlement just west of Montreal, sent in retaliation for earlier French attacks, led to a new round of conflict between the French and the Iroquois, and their allies, the English colonies. Sent back to New France as governor in 1689, Frontenac launched French-Canadian and First Nations guerrilla raids against the English settlements. At Schenectady, New York, and Salmon Falls, New Hampshire, the French and Native raiding parties broke into homes. They scalped men, women, and children and took (in the raids between the 1690s and 1713, and then again between 1744 and the fall of New France in 1760), hundreds of prisoners. They brought them back to the Native communities or to the French settlements in the St. Lawrence valley. While many eventually returned to New England, others (particularly those taken as young children) refused to leave, and remained with their new Native or French-Canadian families.

The Canadian militia and their Algonquian allies under the direction of regular French officers successfully waged *la petite guerre*, the war of ambush and surprise, or in modern usage, guerrilla warfare. It continued for nearly a decade, until 1697, when the Treaty of Ryswick between England and France brought four years of peace. But in 1701, the very year that New France's long conflict with the Iroquois ended, war broke out again with England.

Canadian on Snowshoes Going to War Over the Snow, the only known late-seventeenth-century illustration of a militiaman in New France.

National Archives of Canada/C-113193.

FRANCE'S NEW NORTH AMERICAN STRATEGY, 1701

France developed a new North American strategy in 1701 and held to it for the remainder of the French regime. With a glut of furs in France, the fur trade no longer was of any real economic benefit. But rather than retreat from the Great Lakes and the Mississippi valley, the French chose to stay in order to keep the First Nations in the French alliance and thus prevent English expansion into the West. As a result, the French retained their fur-trading empire for strategic rather than economic reasons. No more attention was paid to Colbert's idea of a "compact colony" on the banks of the St. Lawrence. Instead, the French began preparations for a chain of posts linking the Great Lakes to the Gulf of Mexico. Louis XIV also ordered the building of a new settlement, to be named *Détroit* ("the straits"), at the narrows between Lakes Erie and Huron. Detroit would bar English access to the northwest and maintain French control of the upper Great Lakes. With their Native allies, the French planned to contain the English within the coastal strip between the Alleghenies and the Atlantic.

NEW FRANCE IN WARTIME

The war that began between the English colonies and New France in 1689 was ultimately resolved only in 1760 — more than three-quarters of a century later. In the initial struggle, New France had three limitations. First, it had a small population in comparison with the English colonies, being outnumbered by nearly twenty to one. A second weakness lay in New France's precarious economy. Only one export industry existed — the heavily subsidized fur trade — and it was extremely vulnerable in wartime when the transport of furs from the interior could be cut off. The colony's third weakness lay in the relatively small scale of its agriculture, also vulnerable to disruption in wartime. Even in good years, the habitants produced only a small surplus.

In wartime, they had a deficit, because militia service took farmers off the land. War also meant increased dependence on France for food and war materials at a time when the sea lanes to and from France became exposed to English attack.

The French colony did, however, have a number of strengths. It had effective political leadership. Royal government in 1663 had left New France with a unified command structure in times of war. Subject only to annual review, the governor had complete control over the marshalling of the colony's resources, its negotiations with the Native peoples, and the planning of its war strategy. Nature had provided New France with a second strength: natural defences. The Adirondacks of New York, the Green Mountains of Vermont, and the White Mountains of New Hampshire and Maine all protected the French colony from a direct attack from the south. Two of the three gateways to the St. Lawrence — the river itself (closed half of the year by ice) and the Hudson River–Lake Champlain–Richelieu River waterway — could be sealed. Quebec commanded the St. Lawrence River, and a system of forts existed on the Richelieu River (later complemented by French fortifications at the southern end of Lake Champlain). The western approach from Lake Ontario only remained open. Inadvertently the Iroquois had built up the third strength of the French, by teaching the habitants the techniques of guerrilla warfare. A cadre of tough and versatile French raiders had emerged from the wars with the Iroquois in the Illinois country — individuals who subsequently became Frontenac's most valued troops in his raids against English frontier settlements in New England and New York.

NEW FRANCE'S FIRST NATIONS ALLIES

New France's Native allies constituted her fourth great asset. The French had very close trading (and, hence, military) ties with the Abenakis from Maine, many of whom had sought refuge in Canada at Odanak (St. François) and Bécancour. These Catholic converts now joined the other First Nations groups in the St. Lawrence valley, living beside the French. The "mission" First Nations included the Iroquois near Montreal: at Kahnawake (Caughnawaga), Kanesatake (Oka), and Akwesasne (St. Regis); as well as the Algonquins at Kanesatake, and Hurons at Lorette (Wendake) near Quebec. The close French allies, who numbered approximately 4000 individuals

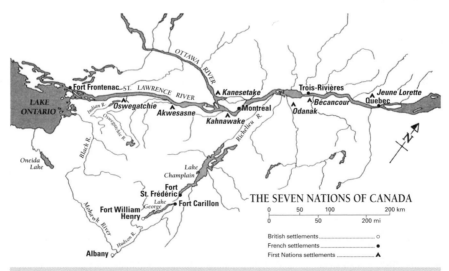

Source: William R. Constable, Map 2: *The Seven Nations of Canada*, in D. Peter MacLeod, *The Canadian Iroquois and the Seven Years' War* (Toronto: Dundurn Press, 1996).

in the mid-eighteenth century, helped to protect the St. Lawrence valley. The French "mission" First Nations formed an alliance network known as the Seven Nations of Canada. Anxious not to antagonize these allies, the French left them with a surprising degree of independence. They were, for example, largely excluded from the application of the French legal system.

New France also had alliances with the Great Lakes Algonquians: the Ojibwa, Ottawa, Potawatomi, Miami, and Illinois. Canadian fur traders and fort commanders cultivated the friendship of the Great Lakes Algonquians by giving them gifts and presents. While the English benefited from the Five Nations' support in the 1680s and 1690s, the majority of the Native groups in northeastern North America sided with the French.

DIVISION AMONG THE ENGLISH COLONIES

The French also benefited from divisions within the English colonies. A great deal of friction existed in English America, arising in part from differences in origin and religion. Thus the numerical superiority of the English colonies was more apparent than real. Furthermore, not all the colonies felt threatened by the French, and therefore not all were prepared to fight. The colonies of the Carolinas, Virginia, Maryland, and Pennsylvania, for instance, believed themselves quite safe behind their mountain barriers. New York and Massachusetts shielded Rhode Island and Connecticut. In the north, only two highly populated colonies — Massachusetts and New York — supported the struggle.

Of the two English colonies that fought New France, New York might have proved Canada's match had the colony's non-Native population not been divided in the 1690s between the descendants of the original Dutch colonists and the new English settlers. The Dutch in the north showed little enthusiasm for offensive operations in the name of the English king, and consequently New York posed little threat to New France. Massachusetts, though, did launch a naval attack on Quebec in 1690.

This mid-twentieth century promotional poster for Canadian Pacific's magnificent Château Frontenac, built in 1893, recalls the governor's famous answer to the English demand to surrender the city: You will obtain my reply from "the mouths of my cannon and muskets."

Archives of the Canadian Pacific. Reprinted by permission of Fairmont Hotels.

TWO DISASTROUS ENGLISH NAVAL EXPEDITIONS

Two English attempts to seize Quebec by naval attack failed. Sir William Phips of Massachusetts, after taking Port-Royal in Acadia in 1690, returned to Boston to take command of a naval expedition of more than 30 vessels with 2300 men. Fortunately for the survival of Canada, Phips's ships took two months to reach Quebec: en route, smallpox broke out and swept through his ranks. He also faced a determined French defence force at Quebec. When Phips demanded that Frontenac surrender, the governor informed the invader that he would obtain his reply "from the mouths of my cannon and muskets." Having arrived at Quebec late in the season, and fearing entrapment in the ice during a lengthy siege, Phips withdrew. Frontenac's blistery response had its intended effect. After Phips's retreat grateful residents of Quebec named the newly built parish church at Place Royale, Notre-Dame-de-la-Victoire.

Luck intervened again 21 years later at the end of the first round of the Anglo–French struggle for northeastern North America. In 1711, Sir Hovenden Walker organized an armada of some 7500 troops, while an additional 2300 troops worked their way up the Lake Champlain route by land. New France thus faced an invasion force equal to half the total French population of the St. Lawrence valley. Once again, disaster struck the invaders. In fog and gales at the mouth of the St. Lawrence, the English lost ships and nearly 900 men. The Walker expedition turned back. Quebec's thankful citizens rejoiced by renaming the little church in the lower town — this time, Notre-Dame-des-Victoires, in honour of both victories. (A church still stands on this site today.)

THE TREATY OF UTRECHT

The Treaty of Utrecht in 1713 settled the war. By the end of the struggle, the French had more than held their own ground. They occupied York Factory, the most important Hudson's Bay Company post on Hudson Bay. They retained Detroit and their forts on the Great Lakes. The establishment of Louisiana had consolidated their position in the Mississippi valley. Yet the peace treaty did not reflect these strengths.

At the bargaining table at Utrecht, New France paid for Louis XIV's European losses. France had to make concessions, and the French monarch decided to make them in North America. France ceded all claims to Newfoundland, except for fishing rights on the north shore, and renounced its claims on Hudson Bay. The French recognized British suzerainty over the Iroquois Confederacy and surrendered control over what the English called Nova Scotia, handing the major French Acadian settlements over to the English. Thus, without losing a single major battle, the Canadians were defeated in the Treaty of Utrecht.

MILITARY PREPARATIONS, 1713–1744

France's forfeiture of Acadia and Newfoundland was a serious setback for New France. But the French still held Île Royale (Cape Breton Island), whose cod fishery was worth more to France's economy than the entire fur trade of New France. In an attempt to redress the strategic situation, they began the construction of the military fortress of Louisbourg there in 1720. It also served as the administrative centre for Île Royale and Île St-Jean (Prince Edward Island). Although essentially a garrison town, Louisbourg also became an important fishing port and trading centre among France, Quebec, and the West Indies. As one of the busiest seaports in colonial America — fourth after Boston, New York, and Charleston — it was visited in the 1740s, on average, by 130 to 150 vessels every year. By the 1740s, its year-round population was 2500 to 3000. Soldiers made up about one-quarter of the population in the 1740s, and in the 1750s they constituted nearly one-half.

To protect the major towns in the St. Lawrence valley, Governor Philippe de Rigaud de Vaudreuil built fortifications at Quebec and Montreal. The French also moved to strengthen their military position on the Great Lakes and on Lake Champlain. They built Fort Saint-Frédéric on Lake Champlain, at the narrows of the lake near its southern end to close off the main invasion route into Canada from New York.

THE WAR AGAINST THE FOX

While strengthening their military position on the Great Lakes, the French became involved in a Native war west of Lake Michigan. The Fox nation, wishing to retain their position as intermediaries in the fur trade, prevented the French from making direct contact with the Dakota (Sioux), the Fox's neighbours and enemies immediately to the west. Friction with the French turned into open warfare from 1714 to 1717. The first campaigns checked the Fox only temporarily, and conflict broke out again in 1728. For the first and only time in the Great Lakes

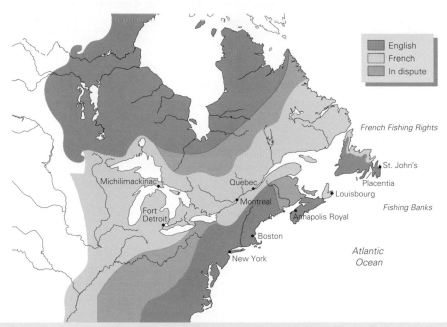

Declared French and English spheres of interest after the Treaty of Utrecht, 1713.
Beyond the palisades of the French and English forts, the Native peoples controlled all
of the interior.

Source: Adapted from P.G. Cornell, J. Hamelin, F. Ouellet, and M. Trudel, *Canada: Unity in Diversity* (Toronto: Holt, Rinehart and Winston, 1967), p. 38.

area, the French incited neighbouring nations to kill off the Fox. This annihilation policy, however, proved impossible. In 1737 the French authorities conceded the futility of continued military action and granted the Fox a pardon.

The strength of the French in the interior rested on the "gift diplomacy" they so skilfully practised. Each year at Detroit, Niagara, Michilimackinac, and other posts around the Great Lakes and Lake Winnipeg, the French gave their Native allies gifts of guns, ammunition, and supplies. The First Nations regarded the annual gifts as a form of rent for the use of the land on which the French forts stood and also as a fee for the right to travel across their territory. They controlled their lands and limited the French to the confines of their trading posts, and to their towns and settlements in the St. Lawrence valley.

THE SECOND ROUND OF CONFLICT WITH THE ENGLISH COLONIES, 1744–1760

Apart from the war with the Fox to the west and the Mi'kmaq raids against the British in Nova Scotia, peace prevailed in the period 1713–44. This tranquillity ended in 1744 with the outbreak of war in Europe between France and England. The New England business community welcomed the opportunity to attack Île Royale. If it fell, they could secure a monopoly of the North Atlantic fisheries.

Governor William Shirley of Massachusetts organized an expedition of over 4000 colonial militia to attack the French fortress of Louisbourg. In spite of the many years spent on construction, the walls on the town's southern and northern flanks remained extremely weak. The French also lacked adequate provisions and munitions. The attackers bombarded the town heavily for nearly seven weeks, reducing it to ruins. When no help came from France, the defenders surrendered.

Louisbourg's fall caused great anxiety in Canada. It revealed the precariousness of France's position in the interior. It also opened the gates of the St. Lawrence, clearing the way to Quebec. Fortunately for New France, England could not mount an invasion of Quebec in 1745. Prince Charles Edward Stuart, "Bonnie Prince Charlie," had just rallied his Highland forces in Scotland. Until the English defeated Prince Charles at Culloden Moor in April 1746, they did not have troops to send elsewhere.

France, realizing the importance of Louisbourg, attempted to retake it in the summer of 1746. The invasion, however, proved to be one of the most unfortunate ever undertaken by the French. Scurvy and smallpox took their toll. Nearly 600 of the 7000 soldiers died and another 1500, stricken with disease, could not fight. The force returned to France without having attained a single one of its objectives.

England's possession of Louisbourg continued to hurt the French. It prevented supplies of ammunition and trade goods, so badly needed for the Native trade, from reaching the interior. This led to the defection of many of France's Great Lakes First Nations allies. Fortunately, hostilities with England ceased in 1748 and the French rushed trade goods to the interior, ending the Natives' hostility.

France now knew that without its leading Atlantic port it would lose the interior of North America, and perhaps the St. Lawrence valley as well. During the peace treaty negotiations at Aix-la-Chapelle in 1748, France therefore sacrificed its conquests in the Netherlands as well as the city of Madras in India in order to regain Louisbourg.

RIVALRY IN THE OHIO COUNTRY

The Treaty of Aix-la-Chapelle in 1748 was no more than a glorified ceasefire. The next clash came in the Ohio country. In 1753 the Marquis Duquesne, the new governor of New France, made French control of the Ohio River, the natural highway to the West, a top military priority. He sent a French military expedition to clear a route from Lake Erie to the forks of the Ohio River. The following year he commanded French soldiers to build Fort Duquesne at the forks of the river.

In early 1754, Virginia's governor sent George Washington, a 22-year-old militia officer, and a number of Native allies to expel the French from the Ohio. Washington's party ambushed a small French detachment in the Ohio country. Washington then withdrew to Fort Necessity, about 100 km from Fort Duquesne. The French retaliated with a force of 500 French, Canadians, and First Nations. They attacked the Virginians and soon overpowered them. The French allowed Washington and the Virginians to return home, but their defeat brought all the wavering Native bands into the French alliance. These skirmishes, in essence, began the Seven Years' War, two years before the first shots were fired in Europe.

NEW FRANCE AT THE OUTSET OF THE SEVEN YEARS' WAR

 By the mid-1750s, New France had built up its military strength considerably. The population of Canada tripled after 1713, to more than 55 000 in 1755, thus enlarging the militia. As well, settlers cleared new farmland along the Richelieu River, southeast of Montreal; along the Ottawa River, northwest of Montreal; and along the Chaudière River, south of Quebec, providing

The French military position in the interior depended on its alliances with the First Nations. As this historical reconstruction by the famous American artist Frederic Remington shows, the French had to win over First Nations support by first following their protocols of diplomacy.

National Archives of Canada/C-011198.

additional food for the army. In addition, extensive road building allowed expansion back from the waterfront, thereby facilitating better communication.

Many weaknesses existed, however. First, New France's elongated frontier was a liability; for example, it took a year to exchange letters between Quebec and New Orleans. To protect French interests, the Crown built a string of forts from Louisbourg to Fort Duquesne, but many of these outposts were simply trading posts grown into wooden forts. Second, Canadian control of the interior depended on the precarious support of the Great Lakes First Nations. Third, although the population of New France had increased to more than 55 000, the population of the American colonies now exceeded 1 million. American settlement extended nearly 200 km from the coastline. Fourth, although the 8000 militia of the colony could be called up quickly, few of them knew the guerrilla techniques that their grandfathers and great-grandfathers had mastered. Fifth, the growing friction between the French and the Canadian-born in the army officers' ranks weakened New France.

A sixth weakness of New France lay in its economy. Although agricultural productivity had improved, the colony still could not feed its more than 6000 regular troops, as well as varying numbers of First Nations and militia who had to be supplied in wartime. Another problem existed as well: the need for farm labour to harvest crops made it impossible for the French to go on lengthy offensives.

More troubling than all these shortcomings was the new unity of the American colonies. The co-ordination of strategy under a British commander-in-chief did much to draw the English colonies together. In addition, the colonists wanted to defeat New France in order to end the border raids and to gain access to the rich farmlands of the Ohio valley. Nine colonies, each with populations larger than that of New France, gave the English colonists a labour-force advantage of roughly twenty to one. The foodstuffs available to them were enormous. In 1755, the governor of Pennsylvania claimed that his colony alone produced enough food to provide for an army of 100 000.

NEW FRANCE'S SUCCESSES, 1754–1757

In its early years, however, the war for North America went badly for the British. In 1755, General Edward Braddock planned a four-pronged offensive aimed at taking four French forts: Duquesne, Niagara, Saint-Frédéric, and Beauséjour (on the Isthmus of Chignecto, between present-day Nova Scotia and New Brunswick). Braddock took command of the assault on Fort Duquesne, with a strike force of 1000 regulars and 1500 colonial troops. It took two months for the force to make its long march over the mountains. As they travelled they constructed a road, a technique of war totally foreign to the French and Native allies, who valued speed and the surprise attack. The advance column of 1450 men had high spirits when they finally arrived within 15 km of Fort Duquesne. Then came the ambush at the Monongahela River. The French and their Native allies unleashed a barrage of gunfire at the scarlet-coated regulars and blue-coated Virginians, inflicting 1000 casualties. They killed Braddock and destroyed his army.

Upon receiving news of the defeat at Fort Duquesne, the British postponed their expedition against Fort Niagara. Meanwhile, in their attack on Fort Saint-Frédéric in the Lake Champlain area, they did no better than a draw. The newly appointed Canadian-born governor, Pierre de Rigaud de Vaudreuil de Cavagnial (the Marquis de Vaudreuil), immediately built Fort Carillon at the northern end of Lake George. Carillon, so named because it was located where the falling waters produced the sound of bells, became New France's first line of defence for the St. Lawrence valley.

The Anglo-Americans scored their only clear-cut success in Acadia. Thanks to the assistance of Thomas Pichon, a traitorous French officer, the British took Fort Beauséjour and, with it, French Acadia. On the grounds of military necessity, the British captured and expelled nearly 10 000 Acadians, who numbered approximately one-sixth of the population of New France.

With the exception of their loss of Fort Beauséjour, the French and their Native allies humiliated the larger English colonies and the British army in 1755. Governor Vaudreuil wanted to keep up the momentum. In 1756, he sent out more than 2000 First Nations warriors and Canadians in raids from Fort Duquesne. The Canadian guerrilla bands caused so much terror in Virginia and Maryland that these two colonies stayed out of the war until 1758, fearing that the raids might trigger slave uprisings. The French gained control of the Great Lakes by capturing Fort Oswego, at the eastern end of Lake Ontario, in 1756. The following year Vaudreuil attempted to take Fort William Henry, south of the French stronghold of Carillon (or Ticonderoga, as the English called it). This was a greater challenge, as Fort William Henry — unlike Oswego — lay at the end of a short and easy supply line and could be reinforced speedily from Albany. In addition, grain shortages proved to be severe and persistent in Canada, and the limited provisions would not permit a long siege of the English fort.

A final problem surfaced: a growing rift arose between Governor Vaudreuil and the Marquis de Montcalm, the new French military commander in Canada. When Fort William Henry fell, Vaudreuil wanted to march against Fort Edward, the English post on the Hudson River, 25 km to the south, but Montcalm opposed such a strategy. He wanted to concentrate French and Canadian troops in the St. Lawrence valley in order to protect Montreal and Quebec against the

A reconstruction by Edwin Willard Deming of General Braddock's defeat by the French and their Native allies at the Battle of Monongahela, 1755.

State Historical Society of Wisconsin/WHi (X3) 29984.

next English invasion. The French ministry resolved the dispute in late 1758 by putting Montcalm in command over Vaudreuil in military matters.

BRITAIN GAINS THE UPPER HAND

The entire aspect of the war changed in 1757 with the accession of William Pitt the Elder, the self-styled saviour of the British empire, to the prime ministership of England. He inspired the nation to make a greater effort, and made the American war and the conquest of Canada his major objectives. The British offensive of 1758 aimed at the same four localities as that of 1755, but on this occasion, the results proved quite different.

Several factors explain the improvement in England's fortunes. First, Pitt decided in 1758 to commit large numbers of regular soldiers to America, men reliable under fire in set-piece European-style battles. Second, by 1758 the Royal Navy had effectively blockaded France to prevent "escapes" of French support squadrons to Canada. Finally, Pitt greatly increased Britain's financial commitment to the war. More men, more ships, and more money made a significant difference in British fortunes in 1758 and 1759.

FRANCE'S REVERSES IN 1758

The first English objective in 1758 was to retake Louisbourg. On account of the effectiveness of the British blockade on France, Louisbourg lacked the protection of a fleet. The combined naval and army force numbered approximately 27 000, outnumbering the defenders three to one.

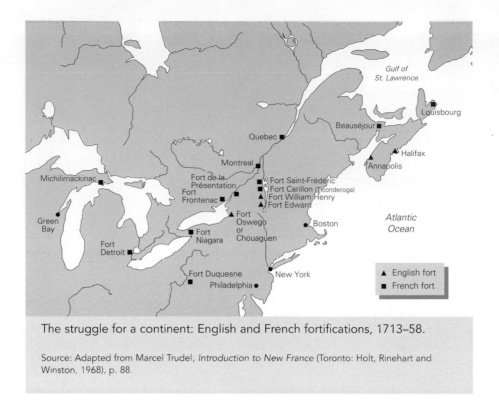

The struggle for a continent: English and French fortifications, 1713–58.

Source: Adapted from Marcel Trudel, *Introduction to New France* (Toronto: Holt, Rinehart and Winston, 1968), p. 88.

The British believed that Louisbourg had to be taken quickly if Quebec was to be captured in the same season. The defenders, however, held out for seven weeks — just long enough to rule out an expedition against Quebec before winter arrived.

The successful French defence at Carillon also served to prevent an attack on Canada in 1758. Montcalm faced an English army of 15 000 with only 3500 men. Yet, Montcalm won. But the French success had its price. Indirectly, it cost the French both Fort Frontenac on Lake Ontario and Fort Duquesne in present-day Pennsylvania. Since Fort Frontenac, with its small garrison and inadequate walls, could not be defended against an English attack, the French themselves destroyed the important post in August 1758. They also blew up Fort Duquesne and retreated. The English renamed the site "Pittsburgh," after their prime minister.

The largest single explanation for the English success in 1758 was the Royal Navy. It allowed the English colonies to obtain troop reinforcements and supplies, while also blockading New France. In 1759, New France faced odds of nearly three to one in ships, four to one in regular soldiers committed to North America, and ten to one in money.

THE FALL OF NEW FRANCE

In 1759, Pitt concentrated all his efforts on taking the French colony. With the great resources England had in America, it could attack both Quebec and Carillon in equal strength. New France, by contrast, with its limited resources, had to concentrate its defence forces in the most vital area, Quebec. At the capital, white-haired men and beardless boys turned out to defend their homeland. The Franco–Canadian army that gathered at Quebec in the summer of 1759 numbered about 15 000, an impressive force for a colony of only about 60 000.

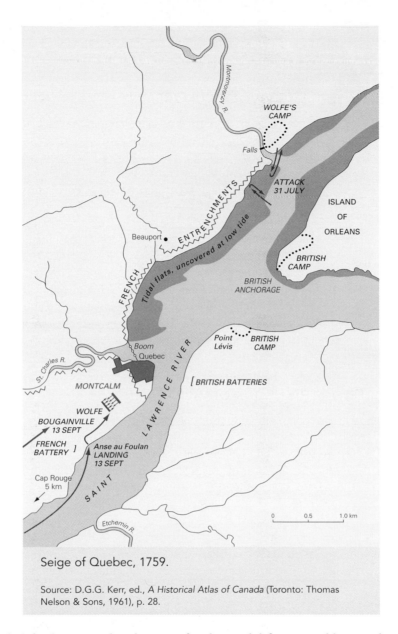

Seige of Quebec, 1759.

Source: D.G.G. Kerr, ed., *A Historical Atlas of Canada* (Toronto: Thomas Nelson & Sons, 1961), p. 28.

The French defenders at Quebec, however, faced several defensive problems in the summer of 1759. First, the city walls on the western side facing the Plains of Abraham had no gun emplacements, seriously weakening the city's defence. Second, the French made a monumental error: they left undefended the south bank of the river opposite the city. Worse still, under cover of this fire, the Royal Navy could transport its ships up the river beyond Quebec. In effect, the British army could land either above or below Quebec for an assault on the walled town.

All that summer, inland French-held garrisons continued to fall into enemy hands. By the end of June 1759, the British had reoccupied Fort Oswego. Fort Niagara succumbed to a British attack in late July. Rather than see the British take Fort Rouillé, France's small outpost in the area that the First Nations called Toronto, the French burned it to the ground. (An obelisk on the grounds of Toronto's Canadian National Exhibition marks the fort's location.) The French now

The Notre-Dame-des-Victoires Church after the naval bombardment of Quebec by the British in 1759. Note the extent of the war damage shown in this engraving by A. Bennoist, from a sketch by Richard Short, an English naval officer.

National Archives of Canada/C-357.

lost control of Lakes Ontario and Erie, and the Ohio country. In addition, they abandoned Forts Carillon and Saint-Frédéric and retreated northward to the head of Lake Champlain.

JAMES WOLFE AT QUEBEC

James Wolfe, a 32-year-old professional soldier who had performed well at Louisbourg, commanded the British invasion force of some 13 500 men against Quebec. An excellent battalion commander, he had never led an army before. At the time of the attack on Quebec, Wolfe looked ill and indeed was. Frequently in pain, he was often depressed to the state of despair.

The Canadian historian C.P. Stacey aptly called James Wolfe a "Hamlet-figure" — because of his enormous difficulty making up his mind.[2] Only after several weeks of indecision did he decide to strike Montcalm and his forces at Montmorency, just east of Quebec. Wolfe's frontal attack on the French army's entrenchments failed, and the British retreated. The English commander spent the remainder of the summer systematically devastating the parishes around Quebec. On the south shore of the St. Lawrence, the British destroyed a thousand buildings as well as the French Canadians' harvest.

THE BATTLE OF THE PLAINS OF ABRAHAM

Wolfe knew he had to obtain a foothold on the north shore and then force Montcalm into an open, European-style battle. Fortunately, he found a small cove, Anse au Foulon, from which a narrow path led up the steep, 65 m cliffs. Believing that an invasion force could not climb the heights on the tiny path, the French had left it lightly guarded. Equally surprising, the French had failed to establish a password for a French convoy expected to bring supplies on the night of September 12. As well, Montcalm believed the British attack would come on the other side of the city or at its centre — never at Anse au Foulon to the west. Thus, the British achieved complete surprise.

The French sentries on the shore believed that the boats gliding past them belonged to the French convoy expected that night. (In fact, the convoy had been cancelled.) The British commander placed his few French-speaking officers in the forward vessels; in the dark, they answered the sentries' challenges satisfactorily. A half-hour before dawn on September 13, the British landed near the cove. Three waves of landing ships reached the shore in total darkness. The advance party, two abreast, then walked up the steep pathway and, without detection, gained the summit of the cliffs.

A series of risks paid off for Wolfe: the difficult naval landing succeeded and his advance guard of Scottish Highlanders overpowered the French post, securing a foothold on the cliffs. If the French sentries had identified the British in time, they could have sounded the alarm and easily eliminated the advance guard as they climbed the cliffs.

By daybreak, Wolfe had deployed 4500 highly trained British troops on the Plains of Abraham, the grassy field close to the unarmed western walls of the citadel. At this point, Montcalm made a fatal mistake. Instead of waiting for Colonel Louis-Antoine de Bougainville to arrive with his 3000 regulars stationed at Cap Rouge, about 15 km upstream, he attacked. The decisive battle lasted less than half an hour. Wolfe was ready: to ensure accurate and concentrated fire power, he had deployed three-quarters of his men in a single line confronting the French. The

A Historical Portrait ✒

☞ The Marquis de Montcalm

Louis-Joseph de Montcalm was born in 1712 at the Château of Candiac in the south of France, near Montpellier. He came of a noble background. The Montcalm family had turned Protestant during the sixteenth century. When the persecution of French Protestants intensified in the mid-1680s, Montcalm's uncle took refuge in the Protestant stronghold of Geneva, Switzerland, while his father converted to Catholicism and thus was permitted to inherit the family's confiscated estates.

At the age of 20, Louis-Joseph began his active military career. In 1736 he married Angélique Talon de Boulay, whose family had powerful connections at court, which, no doubt, helped her husband to obtain his rapid promotions. Before his call to Canada in 1756 he fought in eleven European campaigns and was wounded five times. In the intervals between campaigns he spent much of his time at Candiac, with his wife and children (four of the ten children died in infancy). He truly loved his wife. Just four months before the fateful battle on the Plains of Abraham, he wrote to her: "I think that I should have given up all my honours to be back with you, but the king must be obeyed; the moment when I shall see you again will be the finest of my life. Good-bye, my heart, I believe I love you more than ever."

As the commander of French regular soldiers (*troupes de terre*) in New France,

In October 2001, 242 years after his death, the remains of Louis-Joseph, Marquis de Montcalm, were disinterred from their resting place in the chapel of the Ursuline convent in Quebc, and reburied in a specially-built mausoleum in the Seven Years' War Cemetery, a National Historic Site. Photo by Marc-André Grenier, Commission de la capitale nationale du Québec.

Photo by Marc-André Grenier, Commission de la Capitale Nationale du Québec.

Montcalm was subordinate to Governor Vaudreuil, who directly controlled the colonial troops (*troupes de la marine*) and the militia, as well as relations with the First Nations allies. The two men did not get along at all. Montcalm viewed the Canadian-born governor as a civilian playing at war. In turn, Vaudreuil found Montcalm pompous and arrogant. Despite their differences, New France won three great battles from 1756 to 1758: Oswego (1756), William Henry (1757), and Carillon (1758).

Montcalm advocated a cautious strategic policy, whereas the Canadian-born Vaudreuil favoured boldness. The French general wanted all of New France's forces withdrawn from the interior and concentrated in the St. Lawrence valley. But Vaudreuil refused to abandon the outer defence lines.

The threat of a massive British invasion of the St. Lawrence valley in 1759 led the king to intervene. He made Montcalm supreme commander, responsible for all French forces at Quebec, in 1758. The marquis was a brave and experienced soldier, but at the important battle of the Plains of Abraham on September 13, 1759, he made the mistake of rushing forward, without waiting for nearby reinforcements, to fight the British on the Plains. He paid with his life for that serious tactical error. Mortally wounded in the battle, Montcalm died at the age of 47 in the early morning of September 14. He was buried by torchlight that evening, in a shell crater under the floor of the Ursuline chapel. The Church of the Ursulines was the only church in Quebec not completely destroyed by shell-fire.

British held their fire until the French army was within 40 m of them. Then the British officers gave the order, "Fire." The muskets roared, and a second volley followed, breaking the French attack and causing the French army to retire in disorder. Wolfe, leading a picked force of grenadiers, was shot down and died on the battlefield. In the confusion after Wolfe's death the French army retreated up the St. Lawrence by a circuitous route. Mortally wounded in the battle, Montcalm died the next morning from wounds received in battle. Both sides suffered about 650 casualties. On September 18, Quebec, short of provisions and soldiers and weakly fortified, surrendered.

NEW FRANCE'S FINAL YEAR, 1759–1760

The loss of Quebec was a serious blow to the French, but they still controlled the rest of the St. Lawrence valley. Their army remained intact.

New France's fate was not decided on the Plains of Abraham. The loss of Quebec was a serious blow to the French. But they still controlled the rest of the St. Lawrence valley and their army remained intact. Ironically, the decisive battle for New France was a naval battle fought at Quiberon Bay, off the coast of France. The Royal Navy's destruction of the French fleet meant that France could not send, even if it wished to do so, a reserve force to save Canada. The success of the French army's offensive against Quebec in the spring of 1760 depended on the dispatch of a French armada, with fresh troops and supplies. But help would not arrive.

Before the ice left the rivers in April, the Chevalier de Lévis, Montcalm's successor as French commander, marched his 7000 troops to Quebec. James Murray, the British commander, had experienced a terrible winter, in which scurvy had reduced his garrison to only 4000. Lévis

The Death of General Wolfe. This dramatic and richly colourful painting by Benjamin West (1738–1820), unveiled in London in 1771, has become one of the world's most famous historical paintings. Its fame endures even though as early as 1901 A.G. Doughty and G.W Parmelee, in their exhaustive documentary collection *The Siege of Quebec*, pronounced it "absolutely valueless as a historic representation." Wolfe died, they claimed, not in the centre of the action, but in a corner of the battlefield, attended by not more than four men.

National Gallery of Canada, Ottawa. Transfer from the Canadian War Memorials, 1921 (Gift of the 2nd Duke of Westminster, Eaton Hall, Cheshire, 1918).

The details of "The Death of Wolfe" by Benjamin West (left) might well be historically inaccurate, but ethnologists regard the representation of this First Nations warrior as reasonably accurate. Note the scalp lock ornamented with feathers, the silver earrings, the wool with beaded chevron designs, the sash, the pipe tomahawk, and the warrior's tattooed body and face. (The artist had observed First Nations people while growing up in colonial Pennsylvania.)

Detail from *The Death of General Wolfe* by Benjamin West. National Gallery of Canada.

defeated him at Ste. Foy, immediately west of the city (near the site of Université Laval today). This battle proved bloodier than the Plains of Abraham, with about 850 casualties on the French side and nearly 1100 on the English side.

Lévis then besieged Quebec. But short of ammunition and supplies, Lévis — and all of New France — prayed for French ships to reach Quebec. Unfortunately for New France, it was English, not French, ships that arrived first at Quebec in mid-May. Lévis had to abandon his plans to retake Quebec. The rest of the year's operations were a foregone conclusion. General Jeffery Amherst, British Commander-in-Chief in America, advanced toward Montreal from the south, with a huge invasion army.

At Montreal that September, Lévis and 2000 troops confronted 17 000 British and American troops. The French capitulated on September 8, 1760, and the British took possession of Montreal. Canada passed into British hands.

Where Historians Disagree

≈ Was Montcalm an Asset or a Liability for New France?

Historians have long debated the abilities of Montcalm as a military leader. Nineteenth-century French-Canadian historians like François-Xavier Garneau and the Abbé J.B.A. Ferland had little use for him. Vaudreuil, the first Canadian-born governor of New France, is their hero, active and energetic — in contrast to the apathetic, defeatist Montcalm. But in the early twentieth century, the French-Canadian historian Thomas Chapais stepped forward to defend the French general. In *Le Marquis de Montcalm*, a full-length biography published in 1911, Chapais argued that Montcalm had energy, courage, and ability. He also loved, not detested, the Canadian people. Up until the 1950s, both French- and English-Canadian historians regarded the book as thorough, objective, and well-researched. Montcalm's reputation was intact when Lucien Bouchard, the future sovereignist premier of Quebec, attended secondary school. Years later Bouchard remembered his history lessons in the 1950s: "There was the battle of Wolfe against Montcalm. That was the big thing. We spent weeks on that. The battle, before the battle, during the

battle, after the battle. The sense of loss and sadness and mourning. It was so sad when Montcalm died — we didn't care much about Wolfe."[1]

Chapais's study was eventually challenged. In 1955, Guy Frégault, one of the first university-trained French-Canadian historians, published a lengthy study, in which he questioned the competence of Montcalm.[2] English-Canadian historian W.J. Eccles later supported Frégault in his denunciations of the French general. In his negative sketch of Montcalm,[3] Canadian military historian George F.G. Stanley added balance to the discussion when he wrote: "Criticism of Montcalm, two centuries later, may smack of hindsight — that wonderful advantage possessed by historians over people about whom they write." Stanley, however, then added, "but even Montcalm's contemporaries were similarly critical."[4] The best summary on the subject is probably that of C.P. Stacey, who wrote in his postscript to his *Quebec, 1759: The Siege and the Battle* "The last word will never be said on the remarkable happenings at Quebec in 1759."[5]

[1] Lucien Bouchard, quoted in Jeffrey Simpson, *Faultlines: Struggling for a Canadian Vision* (Toronto: HarperCollins, 1993), p. 279).

[2] Guy Frégault, *La guerre de la conquête* (Montreal: Fides, 1955); translated by Margaret M. Cameron, as *Canada. The War of the Conquest* (Toronto: Oxford University Press, 1969).

[3] W.J. Eccles, "Louis-Joseph de Montcalm, Marquis de Montcalm," *Dictionary of Canadian Biography*, vol. 3: *1741–1770* (Toronto: University of Toronto Press, 1974), pp. 458–469.

[4] George F.G. Stanley, *New France: The Last Phase 1744–1760* (Toronto: McClelland & Stewart, 1968), p. 233.

[5] C.P. Stacey, *Quebec, 1759: The Siege and the Battle* (Toronto: Macmillan, 1959), p. 167.

In 1760, the imperial conflict for mastery of northeastern North America ended. France lost New France essentially because of the low ranking it assigned the colony. Half a century earlier, at the Treaty of Utrecht, it had traded New France's gains in North America to win back lost territory in Europe. During the Seven Years' War, Europe, the Caribbean, and India remained France's priorities. Compared to England and the Thirteen Colonies, France supplied little assistance to New France in the late 1750s.

NOTES

1. See Richard White, *The Middle Ground: Indians, Empires, and Republics in the Great Lakes Region, 1650–1815* (Cambridge: Cambridge University Press, 1991).
2. C.P. Stacey, *Quebec, 1759: The Siege and the Battle* (Toronto: Macmillan, 1959), p. 171.

LINKING TO THE PAST   www

Henry Hudson
http://www.ianchadwick.com/hudson

An illustrated biography of Henry Hudson, by Ian Chadwick, which includes detailed information about his voyages.

The Fortress of Louisbourg
http://collections.ic.gc.ca/louisbourg

This site offers a virtual tour of the reconstructed fort and recounts the history of Louisbourg, with extensive information on its eighteenth-century inhabitants.

The Seven Years' War
http://www.militaryheritage.com/7yrswar.htm

This site, sponsored by the Discriminating General, a company that specializes in military replicas, includes descriptions of the regiments on both the French and English sides, relevant articles, and sound clips.

Braddock's Defeat
http://www.nationalcenter.org/Braddock%27sDefeat.html

A letter written by George Washington to his mother in July 1755 describing the defeat of General Braddock's forces near Fort Duquesne.

Carillon and the Plains of Abraham
http://www.mohicanpress.com/mo08006.html

A description of Montcalm's defence at Carillon and the battle on the Plains of Abraham.

RELATED READINGS

Two articles in R. Douglas Francis and Donald B. Smith, eds., *Readings in Canadian History: Pre-Confederation*, 6th ed. (Toronto: Nelson Thomson Learning, 2002), are useful for this topic: W.J. Eccles, "The Preemptive Conquest, 1749–1763," pp. 135–153; and Elizabeth A. Fenn, "Biological Warfare in Eighteenth Century North America: Beyond Jeffrey Amherst," pp. 153–175.

BIBLIOGRAPHY

For an overview of French expansion into the interior of North America and New France's conflict with the English colonies see the following works by W.J. Eccles: *The Canadian Frontier, 1534–1760* (Toronto: Holt, Rinehart and Winston, 1969); *France in America*, rev. ed. (Markham, ON: Fitzhenry & Whiteside,

1990); and *Essays on New France* (Toronto: Oxford University Press, 1987). Bibliographical guides include Jacques Rouillard, ed., *Guide d'histoire du Québec du régime français à nos jours: Bibliographie commentée* (Montreal: Éditions du Méridien, 1991); and Thomas Wien, "Canada and the Pays d'en haut, 1600–1760," in M. Brook Taylor, ed., *Canadian History: A Reader's Guide*, vol. 1, *Beginnings to Confederation* (Toronto: University of Toronto Press, 1994), pp. 33–75.

Excellent volumes on the military events of the late seventeenth and eighteenth centuries include I.K. Steele, *Guerillas and Grenadiers: The Struggle for Canada, 1689–1760* (Toronto: Ryerson Press, 1969), and his more recent book, *Warpaths: Invasions of North America* (New York: Oxford University Press, 1994); George F.G. Stanley, *New France: The Last Phase, 1744–1760* (Toronto: McClelland & Stewart, 1968); C.P. Stacey, *Quebec, 1759: The Siege and the Battle* (Toronto: Macmillan, 1959); and Guy Frégault, *Canada: The War of the Conquest*, trans. Margaret M. Cameron (Toronto: Oxford University Press, 1969). On French relations with the Fox see R. David Edmunds and Joseph L. Peyser, *The Fox Wars: The Mesquakie Challenge to New France* (Norman: University of Oklahoma Press, 1993). The first four volumes of the *Dictionary of Canadian Biography* (Toronto: University of Toronto Press, 1966–1976) also contain important biographical sketches; of particular interest are C.P. Stacey, "James Wolfe" in vol. 3, pp. 666–74; W.J. Eccles, "Louis-Joseph de Montcalm," in vol. 3, pp. 458–69; and W.J. Eccles, "Pierre de Rigaud de Vaudreuil de Cavagnial," in vol. 4, pp. 662–74. Christopher Hibbert has written the popular biography, *Wolfe at Quebec* (New York: Cooper Square Press, 1999), which first appeared in 1959. Donald W. Olson et al. have recently published a new look at the background to the battle of the Plains of Abraham, "Perfect Tide, Ideal Moon: An Unappreciated Aspect of Wolfe's Generalship at Quebec, 1759," *William and Mary Quarterly* 59, 4 (2002): 957–974. Jay Cassel reviews the French military in New France in Jacob Ernest Cooke, ed., *Encyclopedia of North American Colonies*, vol. 2 (New York: Charles Scribner's Sons, 1993), pp. 499–507. Summaries of the two respective armies in the 1750s appear in vol. 3 of the *Dictionary of Canadian Biography*; see the essays by W.J. Eccles, "The French Forces in North America during the Seven Years' War," pp. xv–xxiii; and C.P. Stacey, "The British Forces in North America during the Seven Years' War," pp. xxiv–xxx. Martin L. Nicolai reviews the French forces in "A Different Kind of Courage: The French Military and the Canadian Irregular Soldier during the Seven Years' War," *Canadian Historical Review* 70 (1989): 53–75. A beautifully illustrated volume on the Plains of Abraham has been prepared by Jacques Mathieu and Eugen Kedl, *Les Plaines d'Abraham: Le culte de l'idéal* (Sillery, QC: Septentrion, 1993). Naval historian Geoffrey Marcus has written, *Quiberon Bay: The Campaign in Home Waters* (London: Hollis and Carter, 1960).

Two overviews of the history of Louisbourg are J.S. McLennan, *Louisbourg from Its Foundation to Its Fall, 1713–58* (Halifax: Book Room, 1990 [1918]); and the short, up-to-date booklet by Terry Crowley, *Louisbourg: Atlantic Fortress and Seaport* (Ottawa: Canadian Historical Association, 1990). *Louisbourg: An 18th Century Town* by A.J.B. Johnston et al. (Halifax: Nimbus, 1991) is a lively popular account. A.J.B. Johnston has written two important volumes on Louisbourg, *Life and Religion at Louisbourg, 1713–1758* (Montreal/Kingston: McGill-Queen's University Press, 1996); and *Control and Order in French Colonial Louisbourg, 1713–1758* (East Lansing, Michigan: Michigan State University Press, 2001). Olive P. Dickason explains Louisbourg's alliances with the First Nations in "Louisbourg and the Indians: A Study in Imperial Race Relations," *History and Archaeology* 6 (1976): 1–206. Students will enjoy the five well-crafted biographies of ordinary Louisbourg citizens in Christopher Moore's *Louisbourg Portraits* (Toronto: Macmillan, 1982).

For background on the Native involvement in the Seven Years' War see Francis Jennings, *Empire of Fortune: Crowns, Colonies and Tribes in the Seven Years War in America* (New York: W.W. Norton, 1988); D. Peter MacLeod, *The Canadian Iroquois and the Seven Years' War* (Toronto: Dundurn Press, 1996); Jean-Pierre Sawaya, *La Fédération des Sept Feux de la vallée du Saint-Laurent* (Sillery, QC: Les Editions du Septentrion, 1998); and Richard White, *The Middle Ground: Indians, Empires and Republics in the Great Lakes Region, 1650–1815* (Cambridge: Cambridge University Press, 1991). D. Peter MacLeod reviews the impact of smallpox on France's First Nations allies in "Microbes and Muskets," *Ethnohistory* 39(1) (Winter 1992): 42–64. Jan Grabowski underlines the independence of the "mission" First Nations in "French Criminal Justice and Indians in Montreal, 1670–1760," *Ethnohistory* 43(3) (Summer 1996): 405–29. An interesting look at the impact of the British invasion on the south shore of the St. Lawrence (east of Quebec, from Beaumont to Kamouraska) is Gaston Deschênes, *L'Année des Anglais: La Côte-du-sud à l'heure de la conquête* (Sillery, QC: Septentrion, 1988). I.K. Steele reviews the crucial battle of Fort William Henry in 1757 in *Betrayals: Fort William Henry and the "Massacre"* (New York: Oxford University Press, 1990).

Valuable maps depicting events of the Seven Years' War and the battles for Quebec, 1759–60, are contained in R. Cole Harris, ed., *Historical Atlas of Canada*, vol. 1, *From the Beginning to 1800* (Toronto: University of Toronto Press, 1987)

PART TWO

BRITISH NORTH AMERICAN COLONIAL SOCIETIES, 1760 TO 1815

INTRODUCTION

New colonial societies emerged in British North America between the end of the Seven Years' War in 1763 and the War of 1812. Quebec became Britain's first new colony in 1763. The Conquest had required tremendous adjustment for the French inhabitants as they came under British rule. And yet, in light of the upheaval that occurred, the French inhabitants adjusted well. By 1791, they retained many aspects of their former lifestyle, including their Catholic religion, the seigneurial system, and their language.

The British government shifted its policy toward its newly acquired colony of Quebec three times between 1760 and 1815. In the Proclamation of 1763, the British aimed to assimilate the French. Then in the Quebec Act of 1774, the authorities publicly accepted the "French fact" and recognized French-Canadian institutions. What caused Britain to alter its policy had less to do with the internal dynamics of the colony of Quebec and the reaction of French Canadians to British rule, and more to do with external circumstances. When the hoped-for immigration of New Englanders to Quebec after the Conquest did not occur in significant numbers, and as the Thirteen Colonies became more rebellious, the British government realized the advantages of winning over the French-Canadian population. Then in the 1780s the desired immigration from the south of a large Loyalist population made it imperative to make another alteration. The Constitutional Act of 1791 led to the creation of Upper Canada out of the western portion of the Province of Quebec as a new Loyalist homeland.

The first governor of Upper Canada, John Graves Simcoe, aimed to make Upper Canada a "model British colony" in hopes of attracting more Loyalists from the south. Late Loyalists did come, although more often in search of cheap land than from any desire to remain loyal to Britain. On the eve of the War of 1812, probably four-fifths of the population of Upper Canada was of recent American origin, without any Loyalist connections. The American invasion in the

War of 1812 helped to promote among a number of the newcomers an identification with their new home, an emotional link with Upper Canada.

In Nova Scotia, a dominant English-speaking society emerged after the deportation of the Acadian population in the mid-1750s. A group of New Englanders, known as the Planters, moved north in the post-Conquest era to settle in Nova Scotia. By the beginning of the American Revolution, over 60 percent of Nova Scotia's population consisted of New Englanders. Initially, it seemed that Nova Scotia might join the revolution as the fourteenth American colony in 1775–76; instead, it remained neutral.

When the Loyalists arrived in the immediate post-revolutionary period, most settled in the Saint John River valley. They appealed to the British government for their own government, free from the control of Halifax. Britain complied with the creation of the new colony of New Brunswick in 1784 for the newly arrived Loyalists. Prince Edward Island had enjoyed separate colonial status since 1769. Cape Breton, a separate colony since 1784, would join Nova Scotia in 1820. Newfoundland would only formally be constituted a colony in 1824.

Chapter 8

The Aftermath of the Conquest of Quebec, 1760–1774

Time Line

1760 – The British proclaim military rule over Quebec

1763 – The Treaty of Paris cedes Canada to Britain; James Murray named governor of Quebec

A Royal Proclamation creates a vast "Indian Territory" south of the Great Lakes and establishes governmental institutions for Quebec

Pontiac organizes a Native resistance against the British

1764 – Military rule ends in Quebec

1765 – Fire ravages Montreal

1766 – Jean-Olivier Briand named Roman Catholic Bishop of Quebec, with British approval

1768 – Sir Guy Carleton (later Lord Dorchester) becomes governor of Quebec

1774 – The Quebec Act extends Quebec's boundaries, modifies the structures of the colony's government, and bestows official recognition upon the Roman Catholic church and the seigneurial system

With thousands of British troops massed at the gates of Montreal in early September 1760, the Marquis de Vaudreuil, governor general of New France, saw no sense in continuing the struggle. Wishing to spare the colony further devastation and bloodshed, he resolved to surrender and set about drawing up the conditions to offer the attackers. Certain of victory, General Jeffery Amherst, the British commander-in-chief, was not, however, about to accept indiscriminately all the demands of the losers; in particular, he refused to accord the French the "honours of war" — the privilege, often conceded in that age to a defeated army, of marching out under arms with colours flying and drums beating. Vaudreuil capitulated anyway, thereby bringing upon himself the wrath of the French government, which was apparently far more interested in the fate of the French army than in that of the *Canadiens*. On September 22, 1760, General Amherst proclaimed British military rule over Quebec. The British Conquest thus became a reality, at least militarily. But only the final peace treaty would determine the ultimate fate of the colony — whether it would be retained by Britain or restored to France.

British Military Rule, 1760–1763

The roughly 70 000 *Canadiens* living in the St. Lawrence valley faced harsh wartime conditions. Quebec City was in ruins. During the prolonged siege of the fortress in the summer of 1759, Wolfe's troops also laid waste the south shore of the St. Lawrence as far as Kamouraska, 150 km downstream. The next year, James Murray continued the ravages at Sorel and elsewhere. This devastation resulted in such severe food shortages that Murray, named military governor of the district of Quebec after the surrender, intervened to force merchants to sell hoarded grain stocks at uninflated prices.

The Articles of Capitulation

The French Canadians may have considered the terms of capitulation mild. Certainly they had feared worse. Henri-Marie de Pontbriand, Bishop of Quebec, had warned them in 1755 that, if they lost, they risked suffering the fate of the Acadians — expulsion. Whether the British conquerors were practising enlightened self-interest or magnanimity, the results were the same: rather than encourage New France's inhabitants to depart, the British sought to make them loyal subjects of the Crown. The British refused to guarantee the survival of French laws, customs, and institutions, but His Majesty's new subjects were allowed to retain their "entire peaceable property and possession of their goods, noble and ignoble, moveable and immoveable." They could also continue to practise the Roman Catholic religion. Priests and female (but not male) religious orders were permitted to perform their functions.

Colonials wishing to return to France could do so. About three-quarters of the 2200 French troops that remained in Vaudreuil's desertion-plagued army sailed home with their officers. Perhaps another 2000 French and *Canadiens*, including the richest members of colonial society, joined them. New France thus lost its political and military elites.

War and its aftermath disrupted the colony's economy. Some merchants returned to Europe. Others were forced into bankruptcy. François Havy and Jean Lefebvre, French Huguenots, started transferring their assets from Quebec to La Rochelle when the Seven Years' War officially broke out in 1756. Hostilities made it virtually impossible for them to ship their furs across the sea, and after the battle of Ste. Foy, in 1760, the French government's decision to suspend payments on all colonial paper money consummated their ruin. Moreover, the shelling of Quebec's Lower Town had destroyed much of the property of the local merchants. For them the Conquest was a disaster.

How the French and English forces might have appeared on the day of capitulation at Montreal, September 8, 1760. Canadian artist Adam Sherriff Scott (1887–1980) painted this scene two centuries after the event.

Scott, Adam Sherriff, National Archives of Canada/C-011043.

The Conquest also placed the Roman Catholic church in a disadvantageous position. First, the church suffered substantial property losses during the military campaign; then, numerous ecclesiastics returned to France. When Bishop Pontbriand died in June 1760, he left no successor. Without a bishop, no new clergy could be ordained. Worse, the Church of England now became the established church and the colony's Roman Catholic church could no longer count on the government to support it financially and legally.

THE ROYAL PROCLAMATION OF 1763

The Treaty of Paris, signed in 1763, formally ended the Seven Years' War. France ceded Canada to the British, who were not really sure that they wanted it. During the discussions of the terms of peace, British Prime Minister William Pitt allegedly pleaded with his cabinet: "Some are for keeping Canada, some the West Indian sugar-producing island of Guadeloupe. Who will tell me what I shall be hanged for not keeping?" In the end, the British government decided to retain Canada, if only to avoid another series of wars with France in northeastern North America. The following year, civil rule began. The three military districts of Montreal, Trois-Rivières, and Quebec were united into the Province of Quebec, with James Murray as governor.

The peace treaty confronted Britain with a difficult dilemma. It now administered a large French population in North America whose loyalty would naturally be doubtful in the event of renewed war with France. The new colonial masters therefore hoped that the French population might be quickly assimilated, with the anticipated arrival of large numbers of English-speaking Protestant immigrants. But rather than move north to Quebec, with its harsh climate and "foreign" population, New England migrants headed west to more fertile lands. The assimilationists' program was doomed from the beginning. Thus, by the outbreak of the American Revolution some 15 years later, not only were the habitants still Catholic and French-speaking, they were also, thanks to a high birth rate of 55 per 1000 annually, much more numerous.

PONTIAC'S RESISTANCE

With the return of peace, the First Nations question posed a greater problem for Britain than the treatment of the *Canadiens*. The Proclamation of 1763 dealt specifically with growing unrest in the vast territories acquired south of the Great Lakes and west of the Allegheny Mountains.

Pontiac, an Ottawa chief in the Detroit region, organized a pan-Indian confederacy and mounted the most formidable Native resistance that the British had ever faced. The First Nations resented settler encroachments on their lands. Dissatisfaction also arose from another source — a fundamental difference in French and English policy toward the Native peoples.

The French practised "gift diplomacy," the custom of making generous annual payments to First Nations people. The English in the Thirteen Colonies preferred treaties or one-time-only purchases for the First Nations' lands. Sir William Johnson, the British "superintendent of northern Indians," understood the need for the annual payments and urged a return to the French policy. General Amherst refused, and he paid dearly for his stubbornness.

In May 1763, the First Nations attacked British garrisons and frontier settlements throughout the upper Mississippi and Ohio River basins. Pontiac and his confederacy captured every British post west of Niagara with the exception of Detroit, killing or taking captive an estimated 2000 settlers. So relentless was the Native resistance that Amherst contemplated waging biological warfare. In a letter he advised one commander: "You will do well to try to inoculate the Indians (with smallpox) by means of blankets, as well as to try every other method that can serve to extirpate this execrable race." No evidence exists that Amherst actually attempted to carry out this policy.

Several factors finally led the First Nations to make peace. First, the key fort of Detroit still remained in English hands. Also, by autumn the Native peoples had to resume their hunting to bring in winter food supplies. Then came word of the peace treaty between the French and the English, signifying that Pontiac could not expect French military aid from Louisiana. In addition, old rivalries resurfaced, destroying the unity of Native alliance. By late 1764, British military expeditions succeeded in quelling lingering Native opposition.

The resistance justified British plans, already drawn up by the Board of Trade and Plantations in London, to satisfy Native grievances. The Proclamation of 1763, issued by the British in October, at the height of the resistance, set aside a huge reserve west of the Allegheny Mountains for "the several nations or tribes of Indians with whom we are connected, and who live under our protection." The British agreed not to colonize First Nations territory without prior purchase by the Crown and the consent of the affected band. Colonial governors were forbidden to make any land grants to colonists or to survey within the area of the reserve. London alone was to manage trade relations with the First Nations.

This "ambitious programme of imperial control," as historian Pierre Tousignant describes the proclamation,[1] became the first legal recognition by the British Crown of Aboriginal rights. Events soon showed, however, that the policy was unenforceable without a substantial British military presence in the interior. In defiance of the British government, thousands of land-hungry Americans began to push over the mountains into First Nations' land, notably the fertile Ohio country.

IMPACT OF THE PROCLAMATION OF 1763

In creating the "Indian Territory," the Royal Proclamation drastically reduced Quebec's territory to a rough quadrilateral along both sides of the St. Lawrence River, extending from what is today eastern Ontario to Gaspé. It also provided the new province with governmental institutions, among them a council to assist the governor.

Where Historians Disagree
The Impact of the Conquest of 1760

The debate over the effects of the British Conquest on Quebec started when serious historical writing began in Quebec in the 1840s. It arose in part from historians stressing different aspects and asking different questions. What kind of society was New France before the Conquest? What was the fate of such groups as the seigneurs, the clergy, and the commercial elites? What repercussions did the Conquest have on economic and social development? How did life change for the habitants? Historians' evaluations have also changed because they have used different frames of reference and have written at different time periods. In addition, subjective factors such as ideological orientation and political beliefs undoubtedly added to the controversy, making it strongly polemical. These last factors assumed considerable importance as the debate over the future of Quebec heated up in the 1960s.

In the aftermath of the Rebellions of 1837–38, the nationalist François-Xavier Garneau, recognized as French Canada's first major historian, portrayed the Conquest as a tragedy, the beginning of his people's "sufferings and humiliations."[1] But historian Benjamin Sulte, who revered British liberties, concluded in 1905 that, on the contrary, it signified the passage from "a reign of absolute subjection under the Bourbons to the free and untrammelled life of constitutional government."[2]

English-speaking historians have also differed substantially on the impact of the Conquest. A.L. Burt noted: "The years of this military régime are of supreme importance in the history of Canada, for they planted in Canadian hearts that trust in British justice which has preserved the country with its dual nationality from splitting asunder."[3] Historian Arthur Lower disagreed. He wrote of the "bitter agony of Canada" in 1760: "If the French in Canada had had a choice of conquerors, they could not have selected more happily than fate did for them. But conquerors are conquerors: they may make themselves hated or they may get themselves tolerated; they cannot, unless they abandon their own way of life and quickly assimilate themselves, in which case they cease to be conquerors, make themselves loved. As long as French are French and English are English, the memory of the Conquest and its effects will remain."[4]

Many French-Canadian clerical historians, horrified by the excesses of the French Revolution, suggested that the British, by conquering the colony, saved Quebec from the atheism of republican France. But Abbé Lionel Groulx, whose historical writings spanned more than six decades of the twentieth century, viewed the Conquest as the "supreme catastrophe," from which French Canada would recover through the actions of the church, and also thanks to the qualities (and especially the fertility!) of rural families.[5]

In the 1950s and 1960s, historians Maurice Séguin, Guy Frégault, and Michel Brunet argued that the Conquest had "decapitated" New France's bourgeoisie; in their view the return to France of many of the colony's bourgeoisie inevitably condemned French Canada to economic inferiority. Other historians disagreed. In his study of Canadian merchants involved in the fur trade, José Igartua concluded that the new British system of business competition was responsible for the economic decline of the

French. "The Montreal merchants were not 'decapitated' by the Conquest; rather, they were faced in very short succession with a series of transformations in the socioeconomic structure of the colony to which they might have been able to adapt had these transformations been spread over a longer period of time."[6] Fernand Ouellet, for his part, questioned the very existence of a significant Canadian bourgeoisie prior to the Conquest. He contended that the Conquest had the positive effect of opening up new markets for wheat for Quebec farmers. When French Canadians later fell behind economically, Ouellet blamed their traditional ideas and their inability to adapt to new circumstances.[7]

Historian Susan Mann, writing from a feminist perspective, has captured in one trenchant phrase what might have been the sentiments of many *Canadiens* as they faced the realities of defeat and foreign takeover: "Conquest is like rape."[8] Yet at the same time Mann takes pains to demonstrate that, for most people, the woes of political change surely took second place to the problems of everyday existence.

In recent years, the great majority of historians have preferred to debate more contemporary issues. Those few historians who have shown interest in the eighteenth century have tended to be more preoccupied with specific aspects of life at the time of the Conquest than with global interpretations. Donald Fyson and others, for example, have examined the evolution of justice, a sphere in which the Conquest, by introducing English law, brought considerable disorder. Still, the fact that one event has stimulated so much interest and controversy is surely proof of its immense significance in French Canada's history.

[1] François-Xavier Garneau, *Histoire du Canada*, 8th ed., vol. VI (Montreal: Éditions de l'Arbre, 1945), p. 82.

[2] Benjamin Sulte, quoted in Ramsay Cook, *The Maple Leaf Forever: Essays on Nationalism and Politics in Canada* (Toronto: Macmillan, 1971), p. 102.

[3] A.L. Burt, *The Old Province of Quebec*, vol. I (Toronto: McClelland & Stewart, 1968 [1933]), p. 50.

[4] Arthur Lower, *Colony to Nation: A History of Canada*, 3rd ed. (Toronto: Longmans, 1957), p. 64.

[5] Lionel Groulx, *La naissance d'une race* (Montreal: Action française, 1919), p. 229.

[6] José Igartua, "A Change in Climate: The Conquest and the *Marchands* of Montreal," *Canadian Historical Association, Historical Papers* (1974), reprinted in R. Douglas Francis and Donald B. Smith, eds., *Readings in Canadian History: Pre-Confederation*, 5th ed. (Toronto: Harcourt Brace, 1998), p. 220.

[7] Fernand Ouellet, *Histoire économique et sociale du Québec, 1760–1850* (Montreal: Fides, 1966), p. 76.

[8] Susan Mann, *The Dream of Nation: A Social and Intellectual History of Quebec* (Montreal/Kingston: McGill-Queen's University Press, 2002, [1982]), p. 31.

Other stipulations in the Proclamation gave *Canadiens* good reason to worry about the future: for one thing, as Roman Catholics, they were to be excluded from all offices. Elected assemblies were promised, with a view to attracting English Protestant immigrants from the New England colonies. While awaiting the expected wave of settlers that would permit the British to remake Quebec into an English colony, those few English-speakers already living in Quebec could rely on "the enjoyment of the benefit of the laws of our realm of England."

In the view of historian Philip Lawson, the Royal Proclamation of 1763 had "all the appearance of a hasty public compromise" that contained "many inadequacies and mistakes."[2] The government's priority was to satisfy British settler opinion; it therefore sought to establish British institutions and law in the colony. Certainly it did not wish to be seen as overly concerned about the fate of the colony's overwhelming French-speaking Roman Catholic population. It was left to the colonial governors in Quebec to deal with the practical realities and to find appropriate compromises.

THE JUDICIAL SYSTEM

After 1759, the British military commanders set up military tribunals to judge all important cases. These courts were most concerned with offences committed by soldiers, including desertion, insubordination, theft, and rape. Some cases involved civilians accused of criminal offences. One case in particular struck French Canadians' imagination. When Louis Dodier of St. Vallier, east of Quebec City, was found axed to death, suspicion first fell upon Joseph Corriveau, his father-in-law, who was tried and found guilty. Corriveau then accused his own daughter, Marie-Josephte, Dodier's wife, and a new trial took place. At this trial, a jury composed entirely of English-speaking army officers found Marie-Josephte guilty of having murdered her husband, and the judge condemned her to death. After her execution, her corpse was hanged in chains in a cage and exhibited for several weeks on a road in Lauzon, across the river from Quebec City. "La Corriveau" became a central figure in Quebec folklore for nearly two centuries.

Outside the large towns, the militia officers functioned, as historian A.L. Burt put it, as "the hands, the eyes, the ears, and the mouth of the government."[3] Among other responsibilities, they acted as magistrates, applying French law and, more generally, in accordance with Amherst's instructions, the principles of "due justice and equity." The Royal Proclamation of 1763, however, introduced the law and legal system of England into the colony. Historian Evelyn Kolish sees the Proclamation as an "attempt to transform the colony, in its form of government, its laws and its customs, to make it conform to the model of other British colonies."[4] Historian Donald Fyson, for his part, emphasizes the fact that it was the governor's instructions, not the Proclamation itself, that actually spoke of the changes to be put into place.

With the coming of civil government in 1764, the militia captains were cast aside and replaced by Protestant justices of the peace, often merchants or half-pay officers, and by bailiffs, many of them French-speaking habitants. Under English law, these new officials could seize homes for minor debts and imprison debtors, although such punishments seem to have been rare in Quebec. As in the days of New France, in some prosecutions for assault, the alleged victims were bailiffs. Some justices of the peace were accused by their detractors of deliberately stirring up feuds so that they might charge fees to settle them. Sir Guy Carleton, who was sent to Quebec as lieutenant governor in 1766, resented the opposition shown to his administration by the merchant community, which included several judges. In one famous comment, he vented his frustrations: "Not a Protestant butcher or publican became bankrupt who did not apply to be made a justice." Such accusations were probably groundless, and Carleton did admit that many judges were indeed worthy individuals. Earlier historians mistakenly thought that the *Canadiens* boycotted the system of justice after the Conquest; more recent research suggests that they actually had frequent recourse to the courts. Still, they probably often relied on local

A First Nations council with the British. The Native peoples of northeastern North America made wampum (cylindrical beads made of shell) belts. The wampum belt served as a mnemonic device to recall to the speaker a previous agreement or treaty. This is an engraving from a painting by Benjamin West, found in William Smith's *An Historical Account of the Expedition Against the Ohio Indians* (Philadelphia, 1766).

priests, notables, or even former militia captains, who still retained their moral authority, to settle disputes informally. Whether they did this more than in the days of New France remains a moot point.

Important criminal cases were heard by the court of King's Bench, but relatively few *Canadiens* went before it. A significant number of cases concerned alleged misconduct by soldiers. Trials in this court were held chiefly in English before English-speaking jurors, but interpreters were used when the accused was French-speaking. No laws actually disqualified French-speaking Roman Catholics from serving as jurors, but in some cases juries were entirely English-speaking. When French-speaking Catherine Sauvage was brought before a court in 1766 and accused of attempted arson, 12 English jurors listened to the translated testimony of the French-speaking prosecutor and witnesses.

In practice, French civil law remained largely intact in the new province, but English law was also admitted, a situation that on some occasions provoked serious legal disorder. On questions related to marriage and inheritance, for example, decisions based on French law by lower courts were sometimes reversed by the court of King's Bench, which relied on English law. Yet, because of their relatively minor importance and also because of the cost of appeals, most verdicts of the lower courts were not appealed. Juries in civil suits as well as in some criminal cases often included both English-speakers and French-speakers, particularly in lower courts. The demographic context also forced Murray to authorize Roman Catholic barristers to practise in the courts.

THE ROMAN CATHOLIC CHURCH IN THE PROVINCE OF QUEBEC

Murray found British policy pertaining to the Roman Catholic church contradictory. Both the articles of capitulation and the Treaty of Paris granted freedom of worship, though only "as far as the laws of Great Britain permit." (Although there was little overt persecution of Roman Catholics in England after 1689, anti-Catholic legislation remained in force until 1829.) Moreover, London had instructed Murray to take measures to ensure that the *Canadiens* "may by degrees be induced to embrace the Protestant religion, and their children be brought up in the principles of it."

During the war, Murray had identified the clergy as "the source of all the mischiefs which have befallen the poor Canadians." In particular, he was suspicious of the French-born members of male religious orders such as the Jesuits and the Sulpicians. In time, however, Murray adopted a pragmatic attitude toward the Catholic church. He realized that, even with all the support of the colonial administration, the handful of Protestants in the conquered colony had no chance of converting the *Canadiens*. He also judged that the church enjoyed considerable influence with the habitants. By avoiding any open oppression of Roman Catholics and rewarding loyal priests, the British administration, Murray reasoned, might even be able to rally the church's support. Thus, he made no attempt to close the churches. Instead, he and his officials simply kept a watchful eye on their activities and administration.

THE PRECARIOUS STATE OF THE CHURCH

The period immediately after the Conquest was a difficult one for the Roman Catholic church. The male clergy, numbering close to 200 at the time of the Conquest, quickly declined to fewer than 140 by 1762, as a result of deaths and departures to France. Furthermore, male religious orders were forbidden to recruit. The British army was quartered at the Jesuit property at Quebec, and the fate of the wealthy Sulpician community in Montreal was in doubt.

The Jesuit College and chapel in 1760, located in the Upper Town on the site of Quebec City's present city hall. During the military regime, the college served as a barracks for British troops. This engraving is by Richard Short.

National Archives of Canada/C-354.

The female orders, also with about 200 members in 1760, enjoyed greater tolerance, perhaps because most of the nuns had been born in Canada and also because the authorities appreciated the usefulness of their hospital work and other kinds of social assistance. The nuns were obliged to care for wounded soldiers, though they were explicitly warned not to minister to their patients' souls. Yet tolerance did not bring prosperity: the religious community of the Hôpital Général de Québec verged on bankruptcy and that of the Hôtel-Dieu de Montréal envisaged returning to France. Anxious to consolidate good relations with the British, the Ursulines at Quebec elected as their superior Esther Wheelright, an American captive who had been rebaptized Marie-Joseph and had become an Ursuline nun 45 years earlier.

THE SELECTION OF A NEW BISHOP

The most delicate problem that had to be solved was the replacement of Bishop Pontbriand, who died in 1760. London instructed Murray not to re-establish the "Popish hierarchy." But when the New Englanders failed to come north, the governor needed someone with whom he could deal as the leader of French-Canadian society. Murray, an aristocrat, believed that such a leader should come from the church. He was thus ready, in spite of London's directives to the contrary, to accept a "superintendent of the Romish religion." But when the Quebec cathedral chapter chose Étienne Montgolfier, superior of the Sulpicians, as candidate for bishop, Murray balked and made known his preference for Jean-Olivier Briand, vicar general of the diocese of Quebec, who had shown great respect for British authority. The chapter capitulated and nominated Briand for the position instead.

With Murray's support and some rule-bending, the nominee for bishop sailed for London to lobby the British government for its approval. After obtaining London's agreement, Briand went to France, where Rome, conveniently overlooking the government meddling that had gone into his selection, named him bishop. In June 1766, six years after Pontbriand's death, the Canadian church at last had a new leader.

With a bishop installed, priests could now be ordained, though training them was another matter. Discipline among the clergy could also be more easily maintained; indeed, a firmer hand at the helm was necessary. Too many priests had committed serious offences, and other petty breaches of the rules were even more common. Nor were the faithful above reproach, at least in the critical eyes of their clergy. Bishop Briand ceaselessly bemoaned wayward members of his flock who "confessed Christianity with their mouths while contradicting it by their conduct." Exasperated, he sometimes wondered if he would not have been happier ministering as a humble parish priest.

Co-operation with the British brought the church obvious benefits. Bishop Briand, for example, even obtained an annuity from the governor for his "good behaviour." But the British exacted a high price for their concessions. After all, the governor had effectively chosen the bishop, and this represented a significant limitation of ecclesiastical authority. Furthermore, when Briand named priests to *cures* he sought the governor's approval. Murray consistently refused Briand's requests to recruit foreign priests. When, after eight years, Briand was finally permitted to name a coadjutor with the right to succeed him as bishop of Quebec, Carleton forced him to choose a man five years his senior who would attempt to run the diocese from the seclusion of his presbytery on the Île d'Orléans.

The governor used the church to communicate with the general population and to keep French Canadians loyal to the government. The church in turn issued pastoral messages in support of the state whenever Murray desired them. Priests made government announcements from the pulpits and on church steps. In 1762, Briand even prescribed special public prayers on the occasion of the coronation and wedding of King George III. To his critics, who thought him too obliging, he replied that the British "are our rulers and we owe to them what we used to owe to the French."

CANADIEN SOCIETY IN THE AFTERMATH OF THE CONQUEST

Although the time when Britain ruled Quebec was hardly a golden age for French Canadians, their survival was possible. Pressures on the land in the old seigneurial region along the St. Lawrence were not yet intense, and new concessions could be had with relative ease. Nor did the habitants feel threatened by an increase in the "foreign," English-speaking population: excluding soldiers, the barely 500 British in the colony in 1765 hardly posed a threat to the 70 000 *Canadiens*.

Moreover, the presence of British troops prevented any serious uprising among the French Canadians, especially at a time when they could not expect any help from France. In a realistic assessment, Murray commented that the *Canadiens* "hardly will hereafter be easily persuaded to take up arms against a nation ... who will have it always in their power to burn or destroy."

THE SEIGNEURS

The seigneurs faced difficult times after the Conquest. With the end of the French regime, they lost their privileged links with the state, as well as their military commissions. Many were not wealthy, as their sparsely populated seigneuries produced little income. Some, however, seized the opportunity to buy lands abandoned by seigneurs who had returned to France.

A few succeeded remarkably well in managing the transition and in adjusting national loyalties to personal interests. Gaspard-Joseph Chaussegros de Léry, son of the famous engineer who built the fortifications of Quebec City, offers a case in point. After the Conquest, he emigrated to France, hoping for a commission in the French army. Unsuccessful, he decided to return to Canada in 1764, going by way of London, where he was the first Canadian seigneur to be presented to King George III. Yet, Governor James Murray received him coldly because Chaussegros had left two sons in France, where they were preparing for careers in the French army.

A despairing Chaussegros considered selling his lands at a loss and returning to France, until he learned that the French authorities were questioning his loyalty and that he was in danger of being arrested should he set foot on French soil. His luck changed when Guy Carleton replaced Murray as governor. Carleton befriended him, gave him a pension and positions, and even named him to his Legislative Council in 1775. Chaussegros also became prosperous. He acquired several seigneuries with flour mills and sawmills. (As for his sons left behind in France, one of them, François-Joseph Chaussegros de Léry, served with distinction in the French army for nearly half a century, fighting in 35 campaigns and 70 battles and sieges. Napoleon named him a baron in 1811. The name of this celebrated Quebec-born Marshal of France is inscribed on the Arc de Triomphe in Paris.)

Michel Chartier de Lotbinière, a military officer, married Louise-Madeleine, a sister of Gaspard-Joseph Chaussegros de Léry. He did less well. Although he acquired several seigneuries after the Conquest, he lost two of them when the Royal Proclamation of 1763 situated them within the boundaries of the colony of New York. Incapable of paying his debts, he was compelled to cede most of the remaining lands to his son. He hoped for a restoration of the seigneurs' social status through the creation of a House of Assembly grouping all large landowners, British as well as French. When the Quebec Act failed to create such a body, he bitterly denounced Governor Carleton's "despotism" and emigrated to France.

In general, both Murray and Carleton showed favour toward the seigneurs, believing that they had great influence with the habitants. Recognizing that the "nobles" had been deprived of "their honours, their privileges, their revenues and their laws," Carleton recommended that the British show them sympathy in return for their loyalty. London agreed, and by 1771 additional royal instructions had been issued to ensure the perpetuation of the seigneurial system.

URBAN LIFE

The degree of satisfaction among urban dwellers is more difficult to judge. Even the term "urban" must be put in context. Barely 20 percent of the Province of Quebec's citizens lived in towns, and even the largest of these were tiny communities by today's standards. Quebec, the largest centre, had scarcely more than 7000 inhabitants in 1765; Montreal had barely 5000. Beyond the new borders, the Detroit area contained perhaps another 2000 *Canadiens*.

Although these townspeople had access to certain goods and services that their country cousins lacked, they suffered important disadvantages. Wageworkers, for example, had to contend with the seasonal nature of much of the available employment. Disease and fire also caused untold misery. Epidemics due to contaminated water supplies and poor hygiene took many lives, especially among the old and the very young.

Fires devastated urban areas. On May 18, 1765, Montreal suffered a great conflagration when a fire that began near the waterfront expanded to destroy more than 100 houses as well as the Hôpital général, run by the Grey Nuns, and many commercial establishments. Colonial authorities and charities distributed assistance to families who had lost all their possessions, but the loss of dwellings led to an acute housing crisis. Three years later, another fire destroyed 90 houses. The town was rebuilt, but the rising cost of land within the small city, with the ensuing increase in rents, pushed less affluent citizens, such as artisans and labourers, beyond the town

Eastern view of Montreal, drawn by Thomas Patten in 1762.

National Archives of Canada/C-2433.

walls. Although the bourgeois rebuilt their homes from stone, the poor continued to use wood, which was much cheaper. In spite of ordinances requiring regular sweeping of chimneys and forbidding the use of wooden shingles, fires continued to occur regularly.

THE COMMERCIAL ELITES

Several hundred merchants involved in a wide variety of commercial pursuits, including the fur trade, vied for influence in Quebec. Many of these merchants were French-speaking. Some, however, were English-speaking, having arrived after the Conquest from Britain or the American colonies. This group quickly carved out for itself an important place in the local economy.

The respective fates of both groups have long nourished historical controversy. On one side, historian Hilda Neatby maintained that French-speaking merchants had no difficulty in adjusting to British rule; they could get the credit they needed and, far from being worse off after the Conquest, participated in the general prosperity. On the other side, Michel Brunet saw the Conquest as establishing a new set of rules that placed the French at a decided disadvantage. For his part, Fernand Ouellet admitted that the French merchants suffered a relative decline; indeed, research shows that British investments in the fur trade as well as in other sectors appear to have surpassed French investments by the early 1770s. But Ouellet asserted that the French merchants themselves were much to blame for their own fate: they were too individualistic to build up the powerful associations that would have enabled them to remain competitive, and they were too conservative in their investments.

The difficulty of trade relations with France forced Canadian merchants to try to adapt to the new conditions. A few continued to import French merchandise to be sold in Canada. Others, like François Baby, successfully made arrangements to shift their commercial relations from France to England. (Baby later became an important public official in the colony.) But most French-speaking merchants possessed only meagre financial resources with which to undertake the post-Conquest struggle for control of the fur trade, the most dynamic sector of the economy. Moreover, the British army handed over its lucrative provisioning contracts in Quebec to leading English merchants.

A Historical Portrait 🖙

🖙 Louise de Ramezay and Marie-Anne Barbel

The effects of the British Conquest on the inhabitants of New France varied widely for reasons linked to social class, place of residence, occupation, and even gender. French law gave women, especially unmarried women and widows, considerable latitude in managing business activities. Indeed, prior to the Conquest, several women distinguished themselves in that sector of activity.

Louise de Ramezay, daughter of Claude de Ramezay, governor of Montreal, was born in 1705. She never married and spent most of her life in Montreal. Her earliest business interests were linked to a very profitable sawmill that her father built on the seigneury of Chambly, south of Montreal. This sawmill was well situated, taking delivery of logs from the upper Richelieu valley and Lake Champlain, and selling boards and planks to shipyards in Quebec City. In 1745, Louise de Ramezay entered into an association with Marie-Anne Legras, wife of Jean-Baptiste-François Hertel de Rouville, and built a sawmill and a flour mill on the seigneury of Rouville. She also owned a third sawmill at a site west of Lake Champlain. In addition, she became an important landowner, with an interest in five seigneuries. She had a tannery on the island of Montreal as well. Her commercial activities appear to have flourished, partly because of Louise de Ramezay's own administrative talents, partly also because of favours obtained thanks to her high position within the colonial aristocracy.

With the British Conquest and the redrawing of the borders of Quebec, she lost the seigneury that colonial authorities had granted her in upper New York state, as well as the sawmill situated on it. She continued, however, to manage her other activities for a time, but had sold these off by the time of her death in 1776. The Conquest appears to have had little to do with her departure from business.

Marie-Anne Barbel, daughter of a well-known royal notary, was born in 1703. In 1723, she married Jean-Louis Fornel, a well-to-do merchant. The colonial governor and the intendant were among the guests at the wedding. These connections would later be highly useful to the couple.

Fornel had interests in the fur trade and, when absent from Quebec City, he gave his wife power of attorney to manage his affairs. When Fornel died in 1745, Marie-Anne Barbel continued to develop the family business. She retained the warehouse at Place Royale, in Quebec City's Lower Town, and, in addition, she obtained grants of two fur-trading posts on the St. Lawrence River. She joined with French merchants François Havy and Jean Lefebvre to promote exports of furs to France. She also owned several houses and considerable land in Quebec City and on the outskirts.

After 1756, when the Seven Years' War began, the presence of the British in the Gulf of St. Lawrence disrupted Barbel's fur-trading activities. The Conquest itself proved disastrous for Barbel: her properties in Quebec City were heavily damaged or destroyed. She withdrew from commerce and borrowed heavily to reconstruct her houses. She then rented these in order to pay off her debts. Barbel died in 1793. She was surely a capable businesswoman, but her links with the colonial administration in New France gave her significant advantages. With the Conquest, these advantages disappeared.

Even British merchants in Quebec experienced difficulties in the 1760s establishing themselves in business. They lacked capital, credit, and lines of supply. Yet they apparently benefited from various types of favouritism. When shipping space was scarce, for example, they were able to get their shipments aboard government vessels. The English and Scottish merchants were accustomed to the greater competitiveness that accompanied British trade policy, while in New France trade had been well ordered and more state regulated. Still, the French did enjoy one advantage: the Great Lakes First Nations preferred doing business with French families, such as the Cadots (Cadottes), St. Germains, and Grignons, who had intermarried with them and had Métis families.

The arrival in Quebec of large numbers of English-speaking merchants, as well as officers and administrators, helps explain the rising numbers of mixed marriages in the colony. New arrivals were willing, even eager, to marry *Canadiennes*, but mercantile ambitions were in evidence. Merchant Justin Franck advertised in the *Quebec Gazette* for "a good woman for a wife." He wanted her to be healthy (he specified her ideal weight) and wealthy — "a genteel English, Scotch, Dutch or French girl, of middle size and age, fit for the care of a house and a shop, used to confinement and the keeping of her tongue." He promised that if she showed "good behaviour," she would be entitled to a housekeeper.

THE CONFLICT BETWEEN THE MERCHANTS AND THE GOVERNOR

The English-speaking merchants in Quebec did not necessarily enjoy the favour of the aristocratic colonial governors. Murray, for example, clearly preferred gentlemen such as the French-Canadian seigneurs (with whom he could converse in excellent French) to English tradesmen, whom he considered to be "in general the most immoral collection of men I ever knew and of course little calculated to make the new subjects enamoured with our laws, religion and customs."

In return, the local English-speaking merchants viewed Murray as a despot. Did he not favour the agents of the London-based merchant houses over them? They condemned him for the strict controls he imposed on the fur trade, conveniently ignoring the fact that British policy severely limited the governor's options. They denounced him for being too conciliatory to the colony's French-speaking Roman Catholic population, who happened to constitute more than 95 percent of the total, and they agitated for an assembly in which no Roman Catholic would be allowed to sit. Finally, they petitioned the king for Murray's recall.

Murray's troubles were compounded by the fact that, in the colony, authority was divided between himself, as civilian governor, and Ralph Burton, as military commander. Friction between the two, who formerly were warm friends, rapidly intensified. Murray sailed for England in June 1766, and, even though he successfully defended

James Murray, first governor of the Province of Quebec (1763–68).

National Archives of Canada/ C-26065.

himself against the accusations of the local resident British merchants in Quebec and officially remained governor until 1768, he never returned to Quebec.

Murray's successor, Sir Guy Carleton, appeared to want to do a better job of redressing the English-speaking merchants' grievances. He endorsed Britain's decision to lift the constraints imposed on the fur traders and to leave control of trade relations with the First Nations to the colonial governments. English-speaking Canadian merchants were pleased but began to complain increasingly of competition from wealthier traders from New York and Pennsylvania. Moreover, in responding to the anglophone merchants' complaints concerning Quebec's laws, taxes, and system of justice, Carleton could not overlook the necessity of ensuring the loyalty of the overwhelming majority of the population who, he prophesied, would people this country "to the end of time," barring some unforeseen catastrophe. Before long, the merchants vigorously censured his moderate policies and his sympathy for the seigneurs and higher clergy.

THE QUEBEC ACT

 From the late 1760s, pressures in North America began to force London to consider changes in its administration of Quebec. Within the colony itself a tiny but vocal minority, mostly merchants, urged England to grant Quebec the liberties and representative institutions it had given the Thirteen Colonies. This group was convinced that appointed officials from London, many of them army officers, were incapable of recognizing that the local resident commercial class constituted the very backbone of the colony and thus merited special consideration. French merchants supported some of their grievances, particularly in opposition to the seigneurs' own pretensions, but language and religion constituted a barrier to common action. While English-speaking merchants demanded that British commercial law apply to the colony, the *Canadiens* agitated in favour of a return to "our customs and usages." The English felt that, by right of conquest, only Protestants should occupy administrative positions in the colony. For the *Canadiens*, more equitable arrangements between the king's old — that is, British — subjects and his new, French-speaking Roman Catholic subjects were needed.

THE QUEST FOR SECURITY

For Britain, security in North America was paramount. The Quebec Act of 1774, which spelled out Britain's new policy, extended Quebec's frontiers into the Ohio region. The British hoped by this means to put an end to the virtual anarchy and ferocious competition among traders that plagued the territory. Quebec's economy depended far more on furs than did New York's, and giving the West to Quebec would thus preserve the economic balance. London also viewed annexation of the Ohio region to Quebec as a wise decision because the St. Lawrence traders and merchants had generally maintained good relations with the First Nations who lived there. Perhaps more important, they appeared to be the only traders capable of successfully competing with the original French traders who worked along the Mississippi.

Not surprisingly, the extension of Quebec's boundaries embittered the Americans. They viewed it as a measure that effectively continued to seal off the West, which had been officially closed since the Proclamation of 1763. They also bitterly resented the recognition that the Quebec Act bestowed on the colony's despised "papists" by conceding "the free exercise of the religion of the Church of Rome" and by firmly recognizing the right of the Roman Catholic church to collect tithes. The "tyrannical act" figured prominently among the grievances of the Americans when they launched their rebellion in April 1775, three weeks before the Quebec Act was officially proclaimed.

The Quebec Act retained the application within Quebec of English criminal law, with its "certainty and lenity ..., and the benefits and advantages resulting from the use of it," as the act put it. It was presumed that French Canadians were happy with English law. The French probably did find the judicial system relatively lenient, thanks to high rates of acquittal and discharge. But punishments, such as whipping and fines, appear to have been of roughly equal severity with those meted out in the days of New France.

In civil matters, the act put into law the significant concessions that Governors Murray and Carleton had already made to the seigneurs. In particular, it reintroduced French civil law with regard to property. This was an attempt to resolve the uneasy co-existence of two completely different legal systems. The return of French civil law enraged the English-speaking merchants but pleased the seigneurs. Britain now legally confirmed the existence of the seigneurial system and gave it a much-needed boost through the restoration of seigneurial dues.

Finally, this new constitution for Quebec substantially modified the structures of government in the province. It established an appointive Legislative Council that could make laws with the governor's consent. The governor could suspend or remove councillors. Significantly, these councillors could now be Roman Catholics.

REACTION TO THE QUEBEC ACT

The English merchants, while satisfied with the colony's new boundaries, were furious that Parliament had denied them the elective assembly for which they had so often petitioned. But the British Parliament refused to place the colonial government in the hands of a few hundred English Protestant merchants, nor was it willing to countenance the establishment of a representative assembly that would be dominated by French-speaking Roman Catholics whose ethnicity and religion made them quite untrustworthy in the eyes of British Protestants.

The higher clergy and seigneurs may well have looked upon the Quebec Act as a veritable charter of French-Canadian rights as well as a vindication of their dominant role in society. In addition, the seigneurs were probably pleased that no representative legislative body had been created. Carleton reported that the seigneurs, whom he described as "the better sort of Canadians," feared a popular assembly whose inevitable consequence would be to make the people "refractory and insolent." As for the habitants, the legal recognition given to the tithe and seigneurial dues was surely disappointing. Nevertheless, restoration of their system of colonization, which enabled the habitants to obtain land without having to purchase it, no doubt pleased them.

In an editorial written in March 1999 to condemn Catalan (and especially Quebec) separatism, *The Globe and Mail* newspaper waxed enthusiastic over the Quebec Act. That legislation, together with later acts, demonstrated that "the genius of Canada has always been its acceptance, nay celebration, of non-sovereign nationality within the bosom of the Canadian state." But what have historians (who of course can be equally subjective) concluded? Some have indeed noted the humanity and "liberality" of the Quebec Act. Thomas Chapais wrote in 1919 that the act was a "victory" for the cause of French Canadians because it freed them from a "precarious toleration" and put them in possession of a "legal guarantee."[5] More recently, Hilda Neatby argued that the act simply "confirmed ... what had already been conceded in practice."[6] Historian Pierre Tousignant, for his part, cautions that expediency also played a role in Parliament's adoption of the Quebec Act: any generosity shown toward Britain's new subjects had to "reinforce, not weaken, metropolitan authority."[7]

SECRET INSTRUCTIONS

The Quebec Act, however, cannot be fully appreciated without considering the secret instructions that accompanied it and in many ways contradicted it. These instructions required the governor to weigh the possibility of law reform that would gradually introduce English civil law. They also explicitly detailed plans to subordinate the church to strict state control. Appeals to

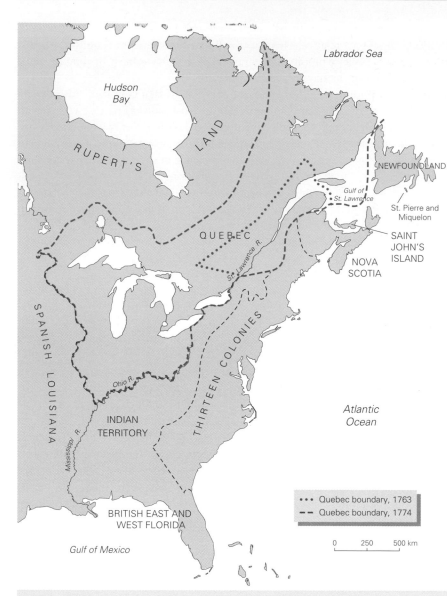

The Quebec boundary before and after the Quebec Act, 1774.

Source: Based on *The Integrated Atlas: History and Geography of Canada and the World* (Toronto: Harcourt Brace, 1996), p. 114.

any "foreign ecclesiastical jurisdiction" — that is, to the pope — were forbidden. Protestant ministers could at some future date collect tithes from Roman Catholics. Clergy were to be permitted to marry. The government was to oversee the bishop's performance of all his official functions and to regulate seminaries. The religious orders were to disappear, with the Jesuits being given an extra push through the outright suppression of the order and the confiscation by the state of all its holdings. Once all of these initiatives had been carried out, the church itself would gradually wither away. That, at least, was the hope of the authors of the secret instructions.

Bishop Briand appears to have learned of these proposals, and they must have horrified him. Had all his efforts to improve the lot of the church in the years since the Conquest and establish it as the leading French-Canadian institution been to no avail? Were the British now going to push for the full Protestantization of the colony?

Carleton reassured Briand that he disapproved of the instructions and intended to ignore them. Understandably, Carleton's major preoccupation was with the security of the colony he governed. His conservative and aristocratic bias led him to favour the clergy and the large landowners, who would support the government if the Americans invaded. Carleton's preferences, however, caused him to exaggerate the influence of these elites on the general population. But did he have an alternative? Had he chosen to promote the objectives of the largely anti-French and anti-Catholic English-speaking merchants and thus deliberately attempted to undermine the colony's traditional social institutions, his success with the rather independent-minded habitants would surely not have been greater.

Fifteen years after the Conquest, official British policy toward the new colony of Quebec was modified for a second time in the Quebec Act of 1774. Publicly, Britain gave the appearance of yielding to French and Roman Catholic desires. George III declared that the act would have "the best effects in quieting the minds and promoting the happiness of my Canadian subjects." The French could now play at least a minority role in the administration of the province. The Quebec Act also showed that the British believed the Roman Catholic church was powerful and held considerable sway over the *Canadiens*. There was no quick way in which to Anglicize and Protestantize a colony that had attracted but a few hundred English-speaking Protestant immigrants, largely merchants. Not that the British rejected assimilation as their ultimate aim; it was simply not a realistic policy in 1774. A year later, with the outbreak of revolution to the south, it was even less feasible. Eventually, with the arrival of thousands of Loyalists who wished to cast their lot with Britain, the hopes of the assimilationists would revive. But for the moment, Quebec's population remained overwhelmingly French-speaking and Roman Catholic.

NOTES

1. Pierre Tousignant, "The Integration of the Province of Quebec into the British Empire, 1763–91. Part 1: From the Royal Proclamation to the Quebec Act," *Dictionary of Canadian Biography*, vol. 4 (Toronto: University of Toronto Press, 1980), pp. xxxii–xlix.
2. Philip Lawson, *The Imperial Challenge: Quebec and Britain in the Age of the American Revolution* (Montreal/Kingston: McGill-Queen's University Press, 1989), pp. 36–37.
3. A.L. Burt, *The Old Province of Quebec*, vol. 1 (Toronto: McClelland & Stewart, 1968 [1933]), p. 28.
4. Evelyn Kolish, *Nationalismes et conflits de droits: le débat du droit privé au Québec, 1760–1840* (LaSalle, QC: Hurtubise HMH, 1994), p. 30.
5. Thomas Chapais, *Cours d'histoire du Canada* (Quebec: J.P. Garneau, 1919), vol. 1, p. 167.
6. Hilda Neatby, *The Quebec Act: Protest and Policy* (Scarborough, ON: Prentice-Hall, 1972), p. 137.
7. Pierre Tousignant, "The Integration of the Province of Quebec into the British Empire, 1763–91. Part 1: From the Royal Proclamation to the Quebec Act," *Dictionary of Canadian Biography*, vol. 4 (Toronto: University of Toronto Press, 1980), p. lii.

LINKING TO THE PAST www

The Treaty of Paris, 1763
http://www.yale.edu/lawweb/avalon/paris763.htm

The full text of the 1763 Treaty of Paris. Articles IV to VII are of particular relevance to this chapter.

The Royal Proclamation of 1763
http://www.solon.org/Constitutions/Canada/English/PreConfederation/rp_1763.html
The full text of the Royal Proclamation of 1763.

Chief Pontiac and the Siege of Detroit
http://www.detroitnews.com/history/pontiac/pontiac.htm
This illustrated article from the *Detroit News* traces the story of Pontiac's life and the uprising he led against the British.

After the Proclamation of 1763
http://www.canadianheritage.org/books/canada4.htm
A discussion of the effects of the Treaty of Paris and the Royal Proclamation on life in British North America and Quebec.

Court Structure of Quebec and Lower Canada, 1764 to 1860
http://www.hst.ulaval.ca/profs/dfyson/courtstr
A detailed look at the courts during this period.

The Quebec Act, 1774
http://www.solon.org/Constitutions/Canada/English/PreConfederation/qa_1774.html
The full text of the 1774 Quebec Act.

RELATED READINGS

R. Douglas Francis and Donald B. Smith, eds., *Readings in Canadian History: Pre-Confederation*, 6th ed. (Toronto: Nelson Thomson Learning, 2002), contains three articles relevant to this chapter: S. Dale Standen, "The Debate on the Social and Economic Consequences of the Conquest: A Summary," pp. 203–10; José Igartua, "A Change in Climate: The Conquest and the *Marchands* of Montreal," pp. 211–25; and Allan Greer, "The Fall of New France," pp. 225–31.

BIBLIOGRAPHY

Although first published more than half a century ago, A.L. Burt, *The Old Province of Quebec* (Toronto: McClelland & Stewart, 1968 [1933]) is the standard general work on the post-Conquest decades. Hilda Neatby incorporated new research into her book *Quebec: The Revolutionary Age, 1760–1791* (Toronto: McClelland & Stewart, 1966). An excellent study of the framing of British policy toward Quebec is Philip Lawson, *The Imperial Challenge: Quebec and Britain in the Age of the American Revolution* (Montreal/Kingston: McGill-Queen's University Press, 1989). See also Pierre Tousignant's useful essay, "The Integration of the Province of Quebec into the British Empire, 1763–91. Part 1: From the Royal Proclamation to the Quebec Act," *Dictionary of Canadian Biography*, vol. 4, *1771–1800*, pp. xxxii–xlix. James H. Lambert provides bibliographical references for the period from 1760 to Confederation in his essay "Quebec/Lower Canada," in M. Brook Taylor, ed., *Canadian History: A Reader's Guide*, vol. 1, *Beginnings to Confederation* (Toronto: University of Toronto Press, 1994), pp. 112–83.

Fernand Ouellet reviews economic aspects of the period in *Economic and Social History of Quebec, 1760–1850* (Toronto: Macmillan, 1980). Several articles on the same topic are included in his *Economy, Class and Nation in Quebec: Interpretive Essays*, ed. and trans. Jacques A. Barbier (Mississauga, ON: Copp Clark Pitman, 1991). Important surveys of life in Quebec at this time include Allan Greer, *Peasant, Lord, and Merchant: Rural Society in Three Quebec Parishes, 1740–1840* (Toronto: University of Toronto Press, 1985); and David Thiery Ruddel, *Quebec City, 1765–1832: The Evolution of a Colonial Town* (Ottawa: Canadian Museum of Civilization, 1987). The evolution of religious rites is studied in Ollivier Hubert, *Sur la terre comme au ciel: la gestion des rites par l'Église catholique du Québec (fin XVIIe-mi-XIXe siècle)* (Quebec: Presses de l'Université Laval, 2000). Law and justice are examined in Donald Fyson's Ph.D. thesis, "Criminal Justice, Civil Society, and the Local State: The Justices of the Peace in the District of Montreal,

1764–1830" (Université de Montréal, 1995), to be published in 2005. See also Evelyn Kolish, *Nationalismes et conflits de droits: le débat du droit privé au Québec, 1760–1840* (LaSalle, QC: Hurtubise HMH, 1994); and, in addition, two articles by Douglas Hay, "The Meanings of the Criminal Law in Quebec, 1764–1774," in Louis A. Knafla, ed., *Crime and Criminal Justice in Europe and Canada*, 2nd ed. (Waterloo, ON: Wilfrid Laurier University Press, 1985), pp. 77–110; and "Civilians Tried in Military Courts, 1759–64," in F. Murray Greenwood and Barry Wright, eds., *Canadian State Trials, vol. I: Law, Politics, and Security Measures, 1608–1837* (Toronto: University of Toronto Press, 1996), pp. 114–128.

Historiographical studies of the impact of the Conquest are available in Cameron Nish, ed., *The French Canadians, 1759–1766: Conquered? Half-conquered? Liberated?* (Toronto: Copp Clark, 1966); and Dale Miquelon, ed., *Society and Conquest: The Debate on the Bourgeoisie and Social Change in French Canada, 1700–1850* (Toronto: Copp Clark, 1977); Paul W. Bennett and Cornelius J. Jaenen, *Emerging Identities: Selected Problems and Interpretations in Canadian History* (Scarborough, ON: Prentice Hall, 1986), pp. 76–105; two volumes by Serge Gagnon, *Quebec and Its Historians, 1840–1920* and *Quebec and Its Historians: The Twentieth Century* (Montreal: Harvest House, 1982, 1985); and Ronald Rudin, *Making History in Twentieth-Century Quebec* (Toronto: University of Toronto Press, 1997). See also Claude Couture, "La Conquête de 1760 et le problème de la transition au capitalisme," *Revue d'histoire de l'Amérique française* 39 (1985–86): 369–89; and S. Dale Standen, "The Debate on the Social and Economic Consequences of the Conquest: A Summary," listed in the preceding "Related Readings" section.

Linda Kerr presents a new view of the initial difficulties of the resident English-speaking merchants in Quebec in her Ph.D. thesis, "Quebec: The Making of an Imperial Mercantile Community, 1760–1768" (University of Alberta, 1992). The fate of French-speaking merchants is examined in José Igartua, "The Merchants of Montreal at the Conquest: A Socio-Economic Profile," *Histoire sociale/Social History* 8 (1973): 275–93, and in "A Change in Climate: The Conquest and the *Marchands* of Montreal," listed in this chapter's "Related Readings" section. Ronald Rudin provides a short review of Quebec's embryonic English-speaking community in *The Forgotten Quebecers: A History of English-Speaking Quebec, 1759–1980* (Quebec: Institut québécois de recherche sur la culture, 1985). Lorraine Gadoury examines family relationships within the French-speaking colonial elite in *Échanges épistolaires au sein de l'élite canadienne du XVIIIe siècle* (Montreal: Hurtubise, 1998). Finally, the major figures of these years all have biographies in various volumes of the *Dictionary of Canadian Biography*, an essential tool for this and other periods. It is now also available online: www.biographi.ca. One sketch not to be missed is the biography of Marie-Josephte Corriveau, "La Corriveau," by folklorist Luc Lacourcière, in vol. 3: *1741–1770*, pp. 142–43. For important maps of Quebec in this period see R. Cole Harris, ed., *Historical Atlas of Canada*, vol. 1, *From the Beginning to 1800* (Toronto: University of Toronto Press, 1987).

The following books and articles provide a good introduction to the Native history of the period: Francis Jennings, *Empire of Fortune: Crowns, Colonies and Tribes in the Seven Years War in America* (New York: W.W. Norton, 1988); Howard H. Peckham, *Pontiac and the Indian Uprising* (Chicago: University of Chicago Press, 1961 [1947]); Richard White, *The Middle Ground: Indians, Empires and Republics in the Great Lakes Region, 1650–1815* (Cambridge: Cambridge University Press, 1991); W.J. Eccles, "Sovereignty-Association, 1500–1783," in his *Essays on New France* (Toronto: Oxford University Press, 1987), pp. 156–81; Jacqueline Peterson, "Many Roads to Red River: Métis Genesis in the Great Lakes Region, 1680–1815," in Jacqueline Peterson and Jennifer S.H. Brown, eds., *The New Peoples: Being and Becoming Métis in North America* (Winnipeg: University of Manitoba Press, 1985), pp. 37–71; and Harriet Gorham, "Families of Mixed Descent in the Western Great Lakes Region," in Bruce Alden Cox, ed., *Native People, Native Lands: Canadian Indians, Inuit and Metis* (Ottawa: Carleton University Press, 1988), pp. 37–55. Specific developments in the province of Quebec are mentioned in Daniel Francis, *A History of the Native Peoples of Québec, 1760–1867* (Ottawa: Indian and Northern Affairs Canada, 1983). On Native history of the St. Lawrence Valley, see Jean-Pierre Sawaya, *La Fédération des Sept Feux de la vallée du Saint-Laurent, XVIIe-XIXe siècles* (Sillery: Septentrion, 1998); and Denys Delâge, "Les Iroquois chrétiens des 'réductions,' 1677–1770," *Recherches amérindiennes au Québec* 21(1–2) (1991): 59–70; 21(3) (1991): 39–50.

QUEBEC SOCIETY IN THE LATE EIGHTEENTH CENTURY

TIME LINE

1775 – American armies invade Quebec; Montreal capitulates

1776 – The Thirteen Colonies declare their independence from Great Britain

The arrival of British reinforcements forces an American retreat from Quebec

1782 – Loyalists begin to assemble in New York while awaiting evacuation, many to British North America

1783 – The Treaty of Paris ends the war between Britain and the United States; peace returns to North America

1784 – Loyalists of the Six Nations Confederacy resettled along the Grand River in southwestern Ontario

A smallpox epidemic sweeps Quebec

1786 – Guy Carleton, now Lord Dorchester, returns to Quebec as governor

1788 – Poor harvests cause famine in many regions of Quebec

1791 – The Constitutional Act

The Province of Quebec divided, by executive order, into the separate provinces of Upper and Lower Canada

The impact of the American Revolution on Quebec was virtually as great as that of the British Conquest. In the aftermath of the Conquest, the British failed in their attempts to attract English-speaking settlers to Quebec. In contrast, the American Revolution led to the arrival of a sizable English-speaking population. Those people in the Thirteen Colonies who wanted to live under the British flag or who had supported Britain during the revolution were forced to leave the United States. Some First Nations people also migrated north: nearly 2000 Iroquois who had been living in New York state settled in present-day Ontario, then part of the Province of Quebec. All told, 15 000 Loyalists came to Quebec (whose territory then included much of present-day Ontario), giving the colony a significant English-speaking minority. This "peaceful invasion" of English-speaking Protestants set the stage for the heightened ethnic and religious tensions that followed and resulted in significant political change.

Quebec society underwent other changes during this period. Both the Roman Catholic church and the seigneurs strengthened their position, although an increasing number of seigneurs were wealthy English-speakers who had purchased lands. Merchants had to adapt to new political and economic realities, and their influence in the colony increased. The habitants, French-speaking small farmers, faced uncertain conditions, with some good crops but many poor harvests that, on occasion, provoked famine. Epidemics were frequent and death rates, especially for children, were high.

THE AMERICAN INVASION

From the early 1770s, American radical propaganda denouncing British tyranny, lauding elective institutions, and proclaiming the people's rights and liberties circulated widely in Quebec. American agents roamed the countryside, appealing to the French Canadians to choose between making the rest of North America their "unalterable friends" or their "inveterate enemies." French-born expatriate Fleury Mesplet, sent to Quebec by Benjamin Franklin, set about printing and distributing pamphlets on liberty. He took up residence in Montreal where, except for three years he spent in prison for sedition, the founder of *The Gazette* defended democratic ideals, first American, and then, after 1789, French.

 The Continental Congress in Philadelphia decided early in the revolutionary war to invade Canada in order to prevent the British from concentrating their forces there and then sweeping down into the Thirteen Colonies. In May 1775, the Americans raided St. Jean, on the Richelieu River, thereby demonstrating British military weakness as well as the Canadian militia's lack of enthusiasm. Then, in September, General George Washington's armies advanced into Quebec by way of Lake Champlain and Maine. Both the clergy and the seigneurs upheld the traditional order that the American revolutionaries threatened. They urged the habitants to support the British cause and, indeed, to enlist. Few came forward. Bishop Briand complained to one parish priest: "My authority is no more respected than yours. They tell both of us that we are Englishmen."

CARLETON'S ROLE

Governor Guy Carleton abandoned Montreal to the invading Americans in late 1775. After narrowly escaping the advancing enemy forces, he succeeded in reaching Quebec, although he doubted that that city could long hold off the besiegers. As he put it: "We have so many enemies within, and foolish people, dupes to those traitors (i.e. the American rebels) ... [that] I think our fate extremely doubtful, to say nothing worse."

The Americans, for their part, were confident of success. General Richard Montgomery boasted that he would eat Christmas dinner in Quebec City or in hell. In fact, he ate it in neither

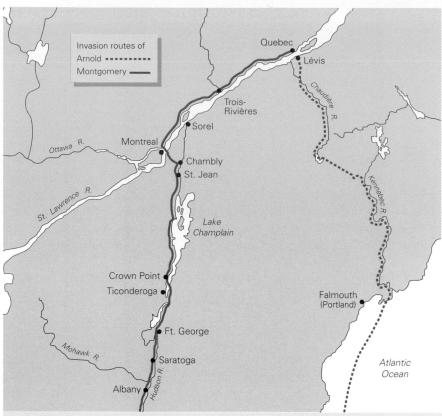

The American invasion of Canada, 1775–76.

Source: Based on C.W. Jefferys, *The Picture Gallery of Canadian History*, Vol. 2 (Toronto: The Ryerson Press, 1945), p. 5.

Sir Guy Carleton, Lord Dorchester.

place. The assault came in the early morning of December 31, and Montgomery was killed in a vain attempt to take the city.

In London, the British government prepared for an expedition to relieve Quebec. An angry George III declared that "when such acts of vigour are shown by the rebellious Americans, we must show that the English lion when aroused has not only his wonted resolution, but has added the swiftness of the racehorse." Five months later, in May 1776, a fleet of British ships sailed up the St. Lawrence, and the ill-equipped and demoralized Americans hastily departed.

Several British politicians demanded Carleton's recall for not preventing the American retreat up the Richelieu River and for not retaking the important fortress of Ticonderoga on Lake Champlain in preparation for the invasion of the Hudson River valley. Historian A.L. Burt also believed that the governor's inaction "ruined the campaign of 1776 and possibly altered the outcome of the war."[1] Actually, Carleton did try to march after the Americans but his troops, after weeks spent on crowded transport ships, needed frequent rest. Moreover, they appear to have consumed too many fresh vegetables and were plagued by an outbreak of the "flux." The British also lacked supplies, again through no fault of

Death of General Montgomery in the Attack on Quebec, 31 December 1775, by John Trumbull (1786), a highly imaginative and romanticized version of Montgomery's death. In 1819, the capital of the state of Alabama was named after this revolutionary war hero.

Trumbull Collection/Yale University Art Gallery.

Carleton's. According to historian R.A. Bowler, Carleton may have been overprudent, but he does not seem to have made strategical errors, and he should certainly not receive all the blame for the failures of the campaign.[2]

In 1777, the British conceived a plan to crush the revolt by striking down from Quebec to New York City, thus cutting the rebellious colonies in two. These hopes were dashed when a numerically superior American force surrounded and defeated the British at Saratoga, north of Albany. Thereafter, the British launched no more large-scale expeditions southward from the St. Lawrence.

The alliance of France with the American colonies in February 1778 changed the face of the war. A secret clause of the arrangement stipulated, however, that France would not invade Canada or Acadia; the Americans wanted no restoration of New France. Louis XVI, for his part, wanted to weaken British power by assisting the Thirteen Colonies in gaining their independence, but he did not favour an American conquest of Canada. Indeed, he hoped that a British Canada, by posing a continual threat to the Americans, would ensure the latter's dependence on France. Clearly, neither France nor the United States wished the other to possess Canada.

THE FRENCH CANADIANS' RESPONSE TO THE AMERICAN INVASION

During the American expedition into Canada, some people, often English-speaking merchants, welcomed the invading revolutionaries with enthusiasm. One French merchant who also did so was Christophe Pélissier, director of the Forges du Saint-Maurice, who provided American troops with munitions for their march on Quebec City.

Some habitants, for their part, also seem to have given support to the Americans. But in most cases, communities disagreed over what position to adopt. In January 1776, Michel Blais, a seigneur and militia captain, announced on the church steps of St. Pierre, a village near Montmagny, east of Quebec City, that a certain Pierre Ayotte was in the area to recruit for the American cause. He later insisted, in his defence, that he had spoken with such an ironical tone that no one came forward. Still, several inhabitants of the village and the surrounding area joined the rebel ranks. In March, British authorities ordered a former French army officer to assemble the royalist forces in the Montmagny region and to attack an American outpost at Lévis, across the river from Quebec. The house of Michel Blais at St. Pierre became the head-quarters of the British. The Americans, warned by their *Canadien* followers, arrived on the scene with nearly 250 men, including 150 French Canadians, and a pitched battle was fought around Blais's house. The Americans won the skirmish and took several prisoners, one of whom was Charles-François Bailly de Messein, future bishop of Quebec, then a young priest who had joined the British ranks as a chaplain in order to preach loyalty to England.

Perhaps some habitants were swept up by the Americans' heady notions of liberty and equality; more likely they listened receptively to the Americans' denunciations of tithes and sei-gneurial rents, both firmly established by the Quebec Act. But linguistically and religiously, the invaders were akin to the conquerors, not the conquered, and there was little love lost for the *Bastonnois*, or "people of Boston," as the French Canadians called the Americans. In general, like the First Nations, the habitants felt little interest in this struggle; most preferred to keep their neutrality as long as possible. When American fortunes improved and American soldiers were willing to pay good prices in coin for supplies, the habitants sympathized with them. But when the invaders failed to take Quebec and the long winter siege dragged on, and — even worse — when they began to pay for their provisions with paper money or simply not at all, the pur-ported liberators' popularity fell precipitously.

The habitants' behaviour embittered Carleton; after all, scarcely a few months before the invasion, he had written that the French Canadians rejoiced over the Quebec Act and that the formation of a French-Canadian regiment "would complete their happiness." Nevertheless, after the American withdrawal, Carleton acted in a relatively conciliatory fashion. Perhaps he was too weak to do otherwise. He sent a commission into the rural parishes to inquire into the disloy-alty of the habitants. The commissioners interviewed priests; they inspected local militias, revoking officers' commissions in most parishes; they confiscated weapons; and they harangued the population on their duty to be loyal to Britain.

Throughout the war, military *corvées* (forced labour for the government), previously levied under the French regime, were common, with the habitants being called on to furnish and transport materials for various construction works. They were not paid for their labour unless they were artisans. Moreover, army and militia officers were often arbitrary in their application of the ordinance on *corvées*. The correspondence of Frederick Haldimand, appointed governor of Quebec in 1777, shows that desertions from the military *corvées* became frequent and that the governor often imposed fines and prison sentences on recalcitrant workers.

The church, too, attempted to reassert its authority. In a pastoral letter that he ordered read in all churches in the colony, Bishop Briand condemned the rebellion as "contrary to religion as well as to good sense and to reason." Most priests, on Briand's orders, refused the sacraments to rebels, even at the hour of death. Pro-American priests such as the Jesuit Pierre-René Floquet were suspended from their functions. When the Americans departed, Briand demanded that parishioners who had sided with the Americans repent publicly. In one case, twelve rebel sympathizers, after being released from the Quebec City prison, went to the cathedral steps after high mass and pleaded that God and the king pardon their scandalous behaviour.

Those habitants left in peace by troops on both sides, and able to cultivate their farms, benefited from a tripling of agricultural prices. In part, speculators caused this inflation by going out into the countryside and buying up crops. In an effort to control prices the government intervened, just as it had in earlier days, by prohibiting exports and hoarding. But due to the determination of the grain speculators, the government's actions were generally ineffective.

The rise in prices encouraged the habitants to clear and sow new land in order to increase their production of wheat and other crops. Prosperity came to the countryside, but the towns suffered greatly as prices for flour and other basic necessities soared. Harvests were generally abundant but, in view of war needs, most of the crops were sold on the local market. Thus, grain exports to both the West Indies and Britain fell off considerably.

THE AMERICAN REVOLUTION AND THE FIRST NATIONS

Like the *Canadiens*, the Native peoples, particularly the Six Nations, were threatened and cajoled by both sides in the struggle. At the beginning of the American Revolution, the Six Nations Confederacy council declared its neutrality in what it perceived as a "family feud" between the British and their American offspring. Later on, however, the Native peoples could not avoid being drawn into the feud. The cost of their involvement in the conflict was heavy: the Iroquois League, which was several hundred years old, collapsed, and the Mohawks lost their lands along the Mohawk River in central New York state and elsewhere. Britain's defeat led 2000 Iroquois to abandon their homelands and migrate to the western section of the Province of Quebec that would become Upper Canada.

 After the defeat of Pontiac, the British had cultivated good relations with the First Nations to ensure their military assistance. William Johnson, a large landowner in the Mohawk valley who spoke Mohawk and served as the British government's northern superintendent of Indian affairs, was instrumental in carrying out this policy. Johnson, whose companion was Molly Brant, the sister of Six Nations war chief Joseph Brant (Thayendanegea), played an important role in the lengthy negotiations to define a boundary for the "Indian territory" that took place after the Proclamation of 1763 and Pontiac's resistance. After his death in 1774, his nephew and successor, Guy Johnson, argued that the annexation of First Nations territory to the Province of Quebec (by the Quebec Act) showed the British government's solicitude for its Native subjects and its desire to protect their territory from settlement.

In 1775, the British instructed Guy Johnson to pressure the Iroquois to "take up the hatchet against His Majesty's rebellious subjects." Johnson failed, however, to neutralize American efforts to enlist the aid of the Oneidas and Tuscaroras. Johnson then came to Montreal and attempted to build up support for the British cause among the several thousand Iroquois living at Kahnawake, southwest of Montreal, at Kanesatake (Oka), about 50 km west of Montreal, and at St. Régis (Akwesasne), a settlement on the St. Lawrence River about 100 km west of Montreal.

Thanks largely to the efforts of Joseph Brant, the Mohawks and some Senecas supported the British. The Onondagas and the Cayugas, though, declared their neutrality, while many Oneidas and Tuscaroras, as well as some of the Iroquois in the Montreal area, showed a preference for the Americans. In 1779, however, American troops under General John Sullivan invaded the Six Nations territory, indiscriminately punishing the Iroquois by burning crops and destroying villages. These attacks on the hitherto neutral Onondagas and Cayugas brought them over to the British side. One thousand Iroquois warriors retaliated by burning and pillaging American farms throughout the immense territory between the Ohio and Mohawk rivers.

By 1782, with the British on the verge of final defeat, Frederick Haldimand, the governor of Quebec, instructed commanders to limit themselves to purely defensive actions. The First

Community Portrait

⇐ The Community of Odanak

Often overlooked in discussions of the Native history of the St. Lawrence valley in the eighteenth century are the Algonquian-speaking communities, one of the most prominent being the Abenaki of Odanak. Located on the banks of the St. Francois River, near Sorel, just east of Montreal, "Odanak" means "at the village" in the Algonquian language of the Abenaki. The name "Abenaki" itself is an alteration of "Wabanaki," meaning "land of the dawn," or "country lying to the east." Here today live descendants of the original inhabitants of the northern and central New England states. The community of Odanak was one of four major Roman Catholic mission stations in the St. Lawrence valley, in the French regime, along with Lorette (Hurons) at Quebec, Kahnewake (Iroquois), and Kahnesatake (Iroquois and Algonquian), in the Montreal area. It was a community of great ethnic diversity.

The majority of the Abenaki at Odanak arrived in New France as refugees from Northern New England's Indian Wars. Apparently the Soroki nation originally constituted a majority in the refugee community, founded in the early eighteenth century. But Odanak was swept by smallpox in 1730, and the losses in the raids to the south proved great. Then another important nation, the Abenaki proper, arrived and gained predominance in the community. In total, the members of perhaps as many as twenty Algonquian-speaking First Nations made their way as refugees from the encroaching American settlements to the south. At Odanak they all gradually lost their separate identity. As the majority, the Abenaki proper gave their name to the others in the community.

Abenaki war parties went forth from the St. Francois River against the "Bastoniak" (people from Boston), as the Abenaki called the New England settlers. These loyal French allies served the French to the end of the French regime. Odanak warriors joined other First Nations and the French in the ambush of British General Braddock in 1755, and fought beside the French at Quebec in 1759. In retaliation for their repeated raids on New England settlements, the British made an assault on the "St. Francis Indians" a priority in 1759. Only weeks after their victory on the Plains of Abraham, a company of American frontier rangers led by Major Robert Rogers made a surprise attack on Odanak, during which they burned the village church and all the houses to the ground, and killed Abenakis at random.

Welcome to Odanak, the entry to the community on Highway 132 near Sorel, Quebec, 1984.

Paul-Émile Rioux, Reproduction autorisée par Les Publications du Québec.

In his report to General Amherst, the British Commander, Major Rogers claimed his rangers killed 200 Abenaki, but French sources state that only 30 died. What explains the discrepancy? Anthropologist Gordon Day's investigation of Abenaki oral traditions helped demystify the event. Two hundred years after the horrific raid a vivid oral memory of it remained with several of the eldest members of the community. After evaluating the oral memories with the same degree of care used in documentary analysis, he identified a valuable addition to our knowledge of the raid. At Odanak in the late 1950s he spoke with several elderly people who remembered traditions told to them as children by their grandparents, themselves born in the early nineteenth century. According to these informants, a First Nations person serving with the American forces came to the village the night before the attack to give warning. This allowed the community to move their children, women, and old people into places of safe refuge. The Odanak Abenaki regrouped shortly thereafter and the next year raided an American settlement in New Hampshire. Peace came late that year, and they re-established their village at the same location on the banks of the St. François.

Strangely it was to this same First Nation village that Rev. Eleazar Wheelock sent recruiters in 1774 to obtain students for his Moor's Indian Charity School at Hanover, New Hampshire (today's Dartmouth College). Normally Odanak would have had nothing to do with the detested "Bastoniak," who had occupied the Abenaki homeland. But at the time of their visit an individual then in office as a principal chief proved very sympathetic: Joseph-Louis Gill, "The White Chief of the Abenakis," the son of two New England captives. Gill was of European descent only in a biological sense. In the early eighteenth century the Abenaki had captured two English children, a boy and a girl, from the New

England coast. Adopted into Abenaki families at Odanak, and raised as Abenakis and as Catholics, these captives later married at Odanak where they lived their entire lives. Joseph-Louis, the eldest of their seven children, became a chief in the community around 1750. His first wife, an Abenaki woman, died during Rogers's raid; his second wife was French-Canadian. During the British regime he met with the British authorities in 1764 to complain of encroachments by settlers in the Odanak area on the Abenakis' hunting territories. Toward the end of his life Gill became prayer leader at Odanak, which meant he was the most important person in the Odanak church after the Catholic missionary.

Although a staunch Roman Catholic, Gill wanted his family to obtain an education, even if the welcoming school was Protestant and in "Bastonki," as the Abenakis called New England. The chief sent four of his relatives to Dartmouth. Although none of the Abenaki young men he sent to the school converted to Protestantism, several Abenaki students from Odanak did, after Chief Gill's death in 1798. These Protestant Abenaki and their converts in the community added an additional layer of complexity to the already multi-ethnic Aboriginal community, made up of descendants of approximately twenty First Nations.

Further Reading
Thomas M. Charland, "Joseph-Louis Gill, known also as Magouaouidombaouit," *Dictionary of Canadian Biography*, vol. 4: *1771–1800* (Toronto: University of Toronto Press, 1979): 293–94.

Gordon M. Day, "Oral Tradition as Complement," *Ethnohistory* 19, 2 (Spring 1972): 99–107.

Gordon M. Day, "Western Abenaki," in Bruce G. Trigger, ed., *Handbook of North American Indians*, vol. 15, *Northeast* (Washington: Smithsonian Institution, 1978), pp. 148–59.

Nations however, were not prepared to capitulate, and only with difficulty did Haldimand's orders prevail.

THE NATIVE PEOPLES AND THE RETURN OF PEACE

Peace came, first in preliminary fashion at the end of 1782 and finally in September 1783 with the Treaty of Paris. The First Nations were not mentioned in the treaty, and the British showed no interest in their fate. The British recognized the area south of the Great Lakes, from the Appalachian mountains to the Mississippi River, as American territory. The Iroquois, though, had never acknowledged direct British sovereignty over their land or the Crown's right to dispose of it. Outraged, Brant and the Iroquois were described as being prepared to "defend their own just rights or perish in the attempt.... They would die like men, which they thought preferable to misery and distress if deprived of their hunting grounds." John Johnson (William's son), who had just replaced his cousin Guy as the British superintendent of northern Indian affairs, went with much trepidation to Niagara to negotiate with Brant. For his part, an embarrassed Governor Haldimand wanted to mollify the Iroquois and the Great Lakes First Nations in order to prevent them from taking revenge on the British, whom they now saw as their betrayers. The governor therefore urged the British to delay the surrender of the western posts of Oswego, Niagara, Detroit, and Michilimackinac, now in American territory.

The First Nations' attempts to convince the Americans to recognize the boundary of the Proclamation of 1763 (and as later extended in the Treaty of Fort Stanwix in 1768) were fruitless because the Americans intended to open the eastern part of the "Indian territory" to settlement. In fact, hundreds of settlers had already crossed the former boundary line. The First Nations, now greatly outnumbered, thus had little choice but to cede extensive lands to the states of New York and Pennsylvania.

A disheartened Joseph Brant, backed by John Johnson, prevailed upon Haldimand to grant new lands to the Iroquois in the area north of Lakes Ontario and Erie. In 1783–84, the Indian Department purchased vast tracts of land from the Mississaugas, as the British called the Ojibwa (Anishinabeg) on the north shore of Lake Ontario. It gave part of this territory, a long narrow strip of land along the Grand River, to the Six Nations "to enjoy forever." The poverty of the reserve's new inhabitants, however, brought Brant to sell off large portions of lands for European settlement. Brant personally received land at what is now Burlington, as well as a house and a military commission. His sister Molly was also given a house, and her daughters married English military men and officials.

Joseph Brant, 1786. Painting by Gilbert Stuart.

Fenimore Art Museum, Cooperstown, New York. Photo credit: Richard Walker.

LOYALIST IMMIGRATION

 During and after the revolution, thousands of Loyalists, bitterly denounced as un-American by the victorious revolutionaries, fled north across the border. Haldimand was overwhelmed and, at least with regard to tardy arrivals, suspected that they were more often land-hungry immigrants than genuine Loyalists. Many came to Quebec from upper New York and New England. They would immediately have settled in the area that was to become the Eastern Townships had not Haldimand, unsure of the location of the international border and perhaps fearing to settle an English-speaking population along it, forbidden them to do so. (The ban was lifted only in 1791.)

Nor did Haldimand wish the Loyalists to settle on the seigneurial lands along the St. Lawrence River where, he feared, conflicts with French Canadians might erupt. He preferred that they move on to Nova Scotia, or that they migrate to the western portion of the Province of Quebec that was to become Upper Canada in 1791. The Crown bore the costs of transporting the Loyalists and, after making the necessary agreements with the Mississaugas, assisted them in establishing their own farms.

 The arrival of the Loyalists encouraged those British administrators who wanted to make Quebec into an English-speaking colony. For the first time since the Conquest, a significant contingent of English-speaking immigrants settled in the province. Quebec's population of British origin increased to at least 10 percent of the total non-Native population, estimated at about 160 000 in 1790.

Guy Carleton, now Lord Dorchester, had commanded the evacuation of nearly 30 000 Loyalists from New York City in 1782–83. He had developed a great sympathy for them, and subsequently showed a much more English outlook during his second tour of duty as governor of Quebec from 1786 to 1796. He had also been greatly disappointed by the habitants' failure to rally to the British cause during the invasion of 1775, and was convinced that they had not been governed with a sufficiently firm hand. He took as his principal adviser William Smith, a prominent Loyalist and former chief justice of New York (1780–83), whom he named chief justice of the Province of Quebec. Smith looked forward to the day when the French would be assimilated by waves of English-speaking settlers from the United States. Dorchester himself no longer believed that Quebec was destined to remain predominantly French Canadian "to the end of time."

The Life of the Habitants

The departure of the Americans and the return of peace did not guarantee prosperity for the habitants. Agriculture, of course, depended largely on the weather, and yields were highly uncertain. After a prosperous period in the mid-1770s came several very lean years. Drought ruined the crop in 1779, and the harvests of the early 1780s were also poor, spoiled by late springs or early autumn frosts. Only in the mid-1780s did the situation improve, and then not for long. In 1788, rust or smut resulted in a serious drop in production, and the large surplus of 1787 had already been shipped away by the time the extent of the damage was realized. The results were catastrophic. In the wake of the shortage, prices more than doubled and both the urban and the rural poor suffered. Many died from famine, particularly in the Montreal area. Not until 1791 did harvests return to prewar levels.

Increased production after 1791 necessitated larger markets, both at home and abroad. Fortunately for the colonial economy, the accelerating pace of industrialization, urbanization, and population growth in Britain meant that that nation would buy virtually all surplus grain available in Canada. In the aftermath of the American Revolution and the Napoleonic Wars in Europe, Canada's economy became ever more tightly integrated into the imperial economic system.

Even in relatively prosperous times, illness haunted the habitants. On several occasions, they fell victim to smallpox, typhoid fever, and other diseases transmitted through the water supply. In the disastrous epidemic of 1784, the death rate climbed to an extremely high rate of 45 per 1000. Syphilis, one of the diseases for which no treatment existed, was prevalent in the

Thomas Davies (c. 1737–1812), an English military artist, completed this painting of Château-Richer on the Côte de Beaupré, east of Quebec City, in 1787. It offers an excellent view of a mature rural landscape along the St. Lawrence River in the eighteenth century. The wooden enclosures in the river and the tidal marshes are traps for eels.

National Gallery of Canada, Ottawa. Purchased, 1954.

port city of Quebec. Stricken individuals came from all social classes, from the recent immigrant to a top British administrator of the Province of Quebec — General Henry Hope, military commander-in-chief and lieutenant governor of Quebec, who died of the disease in April 1789. Historian A.J.H. Richardson cites one contemporary source that indicated that this reputedly handsome soldier died from "his improper Gallantries.... [He had become] the most shocking object that can be imagined — his Features & the greatest part of his Face entirely destroy'd."[3]

Medical practitioners in the colony (most of them without diplomas) numbered but a few dozen in the late eighteenth century. The majority were English-speaking and lived in towns, at a time when 80 percent of the population remained rural. Moreover, the number of inhabitants per doctor was rising sharply and the colony had no school of medicine to train new doctors. The profession lacked prestige (except perhaps for medical officers in the army), and doctors seem to have had difficulty finding paying clients: they often ran notices in the newspapers requesting payment. In rural areas, folk medicines, many obtained from the Native people during the French regime, remained in use.

TOWNSPEOPLE

After a period of stagnation due to war, agricultural crises, and epidemics, Quebec City and Montreal developed more rapidly, particularly after 1785, thanks to increased trade with Britain. Yet Quebec City's population reached only 7300 by 1795, and Montreal's was even more modest. Urban development proceeded according to the commercial interests of property owners. Poor areas of town were neglected. Roads into town were kept up by the habitants who used them. An ordinance in 1778 ordered farmers transporting wood, hay, fur, and other provisions into Quebec City to carry shovels, picks, and hoes in their carts to repair the road. Militia officers were often hired to supervise the work, but rules were difficult to enforce.

COLONIAL ELITES

In his relations with the merchants in the early 1780s, Governor Haldimand was simply treading the well-worn path of hostility already established by Murray and Carleton. All three were conservative, authoritarian, and generally unwilling to share power in the colony with any group. The scorn of government officials for the merchants was certainly increased by the merchants' behaviour during the American invasion, when many supported the Americans with enthusiasm. The governors had the Legislative Council at their disposal, to which they appointed mostly government supporters, including some French-speaking seigneurs. They also had a few close advisers, such as the chief justice and the attorney general. But many of these administrators were inept, and few had any sensitivity toward the colony's French-speaking majority.

Security became the major preoccupation of the governors in this troubled period. They treated the French seigneurial and clerical elites with a certain deference. They assumed that these elites exercised great influence over the *Canadiens*, and they favoured individuals they viewed as belonging to the upper ranks of society.

MERCHANTS

Although most of Quebec's inhabitants survived by cultivating the land, the fur trade still remained the province's principal source of commercial wealth. In the late 1780s, furs represented more than half of total exports — even though the fur trade was undergoing radical changes at the time. Government regulations in wartime, such as the preference accorded military cargoes on transport ships, had provoked numerous complaints from traders. Following the American Revolution, Albany ceased to be a centre for fur exports to Britain, a development that boosted the fortunes of the Montreal traders. But after 1794, when the British formally relinquished the Ohio country to the Americans in Jay's Treaty, the Montreal merchants lost an enormously productive fur-trading region and now had to look to the Northwest.

Most importantly, the industry became concentrated in the hands of fewer and fewer traders. The new barons of the North West Company, formed in the early 1780s, were almost all English-speaking. The French, who tended to work alone or in small associations, were being pushed out; by 1789, they supplied only 15 percent of the trade goods sent inland. The surviving *Canadien* merchants could not pay the capital investment required for expeditions to the western posts. But *Canadiens* continued to provide most of the labour required in the trade.

At the same time, relations between the merchants and the colonial authorities went from bad to worse. The merchants' bitterness toward the Quebec Act intensified, and they petitioned London for its repeal. As noted earlier, they maintained that the province needed an elected assembly to defend their interests. As well, they demanded the granting of English commercial law, which would liberate them from French "custom and usage," as recognized in the Quebec Act. They sought recognition of legal rights, such as the right to trial by jury in civil cases, to protect them from the arbitrary authority exercised by the governor and appointed officials. The merchants also managed to arouse the ire of several public officials, whom they personally attacked. Although the government did make some effort to redress their grievances, Haldimand in particular felt that most British merchants were making their representations without considering the rest of society.

THE SEIGNEURS

Historians have emphasized the governors' sympathies for the colony's traditional elites. The Quebec Act helped confirm the social and economic status of the seigneurs. Some, such as the military engineer Gaspard-Joseph Chaussegros de Léry, the military officer René-Amable Boucher de Boucherville, and the businessman François Baby, were named to the Legislative Council; several others received civil-service or judicial appointments. When Carleton re-established the militia in 1777, seigneurs such as Baby, who had been loyal to Britain during the American invasion, regained their traditional military role.

The growth of Quebec's population and the increases in wheat production should have brought the seigneurs important economic benefits. The development of new lands and investments in roads and mills, however, required capital that most seigneurs did not possess. Seigneuries, therefore, began to pass into the hands of the British, to individuals such as Gabriel Christie, whose properties in the upper Richelieu valley assured his family material security with minimal risk. By 1784, more than one-quarter of the seigneuries, including the most lucrative, had British owners. The *censitaires* remained almost exclusively French, with English-speaking settlers preferring the freehold system of land tenure. Thus, despite the declining prestige of the seigneurs, the system itself appears to have served as a bulwark against assimilation.

The seigneurs belonging to Governor Carleton's councils often voted together as a sort of conservative French party, resisting plans for immigration and for the conversion of seigneurial grants to freehold tenure. When talk of enacting a new constitution that would introduce a popularly elected assembly increased in the late 1780s, seigneurs such as Baby and Boucher de Boucherville pleaded against setting up a body that would surely boost the fortunes of the anglophone merchants and thus endanger religion and property.

After the establishment of the Assembly, however, several seigneurs ran for office and, except for the merchants, they constituted the most numerous group in Lower Canada's first elected house. They also tended to speak of themselves as the representatives of the French-Canadian nation, although French-Canadian merchants hotly disputed this claim. Moreover, a slowly rising group of professionals, at first consisting of a few notaries and lawyers, more frequently challenged the seigneurs' attempts to assume leadership.

THE ROMAN CATHOLIC CHURCH IN LATE-EIGHTEENTH-CENTURY QUEBEC

The Roman Catholic church provided a much more complex problem for the British authorities. Although it had been loyal to the Crown during the American Revolution, the British tried to prevent it from becoming too powerful and independent. Also, many of the strongly Anglican administrators of the colony scorned "Romanism" and hoped that the French might eventually convert to Protestantism. While waiting for this transition, they certainly did not intend to support the institutions of the Roman Catholic church. While the government did not persecute the Roman Catholic church in the usual sense of the term in the period 1784 to 1791, it did intervene constantly in church affairs in an effort to weaken and control the institution.

Ecclesiastical succession continued to pose a serious problem. Briand resigned in 1784 so that his elderly assistant, coadjutor Louis-Philippe Mariauchau d'Esgly, might become bishop and choose his own coadjutor before he died. D'Esgly picked the relatively youthful Jean-François Hubert, but Haldimand, in England at the time, was furious at not having been consulted. London's candidate was an elderly and somewhat senile Sulpician priest who fortunately declined the nomination. Hubert was finally accepted and became bishop upon d'Esgly's death in 1788. Lord Dorchester then imposed as coadjutor the ambitious and worldly Charles-François Bailly de Messein, a strongly pro-British cleric whose relations with Hubert were often sorely strained.

The church confronted other equally serious problems, among them the perennial question of clerical recruitment. Immediately after the Conquest, Quebec had 3 priests per 1000 people.

By 1788, this ratio had declined to only 1 per 1000. Seventy-five parishes lacked priests, and the bishops worried greatly about the quality of parish religious life. The government opposed any attempts to relieve the shortage by bringing in priests from France, or even French-speaking priests from the Duchy of Savoy who were not of French nationality. Only after 1791 were some French priests, driven by the French Revolution to England, allowed to come to Canada. British interference ensured the Canadianization of the clergy. Of 64 new priests appointed between 1784 and 1792, 58 were born in Canada.

Male orders such as the Jesuits and the Récollets were still prohibited from recruiting; together, the two orders accounted for only 16 priests in 1790. Upon the death of the last Canadian Jesuit in 1800, the properties of that order were forfeited to the Crown. The Crown thus assumed title to the Jesuits' mission lands at Kahnawake. Since the Sulpician order remained intact, however, the British allowed it to keep its mission at the Lake of Two Mountains, or Kanesatake (Oka).

Although female communities could continue to recruit, in practice they received few candidates because of their insistence on a dowry. The number of nuns in 1790 — about 230 — was scarcely higher than it had been in 1760. Church officials lamented the lack of discipline in the communities, complaining of nuns who were discourteous to their superiors, who maintained small business operations for their private needs, and who played cards too much. Some priests also caused problems. A few were alcoholics, or they gambled, or they read frivolous books. Some went to balls, and even participated in the dances, or they fought in public. Others were libertines. A few engaged in commercial sidelines to augment their stipends. Yet such cases were exceptional, and most priests appear to have behaved well.

In the late eighteenth century, the church contributed greatly to Quebec's cultural heritage through the work of artists and sculptors hired to create religious art for churches. The Baillairgés, father and son, founders of a dynasty that occupied a prominent place in Quebec's art and architecture for four generations, executed the interior decoration of the reconstructed Notre-Dame cathedral in Quebec City. Philippe Liébert, a painter and sculptor, devoted his considerable talents to church decoration in the Montreal region. Goldsmiths such as François Ranvoyzé showed imagination and versatility in the fabrication of hundreds of chalices and other religious objects.

PROPOSALS FOR POLITICAL CHANGE

While the church showed little interest in the colony's constitutional future, the English-speaking merchants discussed it with increasing urgency. They wanted a Legislative Assembly, preferably controlled by the province's tiny English-speaking minority. They saw themselves as responsible for economic growth and thus deserving of greater political power. Attorney General James Monk agreed that any Assembly would have to overrepresent the English to avoid French domination. But Chief Justice William Smith felt that the English element had to be strengthened through immigration before representative government could be established.

Many French-Canadian merchants and professionals also desired an Assembly, since the French, as the majority, hoped to control this part of government. The merchants and professionals tried to persuade the habitants that an Assembly would decide on the *corvées* and on militia laws — the implications being that a French-dominated legislative body would be unfavourable to both. But the seigneurs, who linked their interests and privileges to the maintenance of the status quo, warned that an Assembly could be dangerous for the colony, for it might tax land. Moreover, the seigneurs were outraged by the prospect of their tenants' becoming their political equals with the advent of elections.

A Historical Portrait

☞ The Baillairgés

The late eighteenth century saw art and architecture flourish in Quebec. Much of this cultural growth occurred as a result of the patronage of the Roman Catholic church, which was recovering slowly from the effects of the Conquest. One family dynasty in particular, the Baillairgés, became noted for its contribution to the development of sculpture, painting, and architecture in Quebec City and the surrounding region. Four generations of this dynasty were active in these domains from the last days of New France until the beginning of the twentieth century.

Jean Baillairgé (1726–1805), a builder and carpenter from Poitou, France, settled in Quebec City in 1741. Without formal training, he gained his knowledge on site. After the Conquest, the parish authorities of Notre-Dame-de-Québec asked him to prepare plans for the reconstruction of the cathedral, which had been burned during the British bombardment of 1759. Bishop Briand objected to Baillairgé's plans for a simplified structure that he judged unbecoming for a cathedral. Disappointed, Baillairgé announced in 1769 that he was leaving Quebec. He changed his mind, however, when he obtained the contract to build the cathedral's spire. In a career that lasted 60 years, he built and decorated churches in Quebec City and its environs. His most notable work was the interior decoration of Quebec City's cathedral after 1787, a task in which he was ably assisted by his son, François. Art critics recognize that Baillairgé filled a void in the domains of architecture and sculpture created by the death or departure of artisans who had been active before the Conquest. Art historian Luc Noppen describes Baillairgé's work as "traditional," most of his models having been works done before the Conquest.

Jean's son, François (1759–1830), spent three years in Paris, studying at the Royal Academy, but probably learning more at various workshops. Primarily a sculptor, he devoted his talents to the interior decoration of churches, an activity in which he demonstrated considerable originality. Between 1787 and 1793, he worked with his father in decorating the interior of Quebec City's cathedral. The fruit of his labour was destroyed when fire ravaged the cathedral in 1922. Fortunately, during extensive restoration work just prior to the fire, a great number of photographs of the interior of the church had been taken. These photographs made it possible to rebuild the cathedral's interior exactly as it had been before the fire.

Thomas (1791–1859), son of François, became Lower Canada's best-known church architect of his day. He was particularly noted for his harmonious facades with two towers, in which he synthesized French and English neoclassical styles. Thomas's close relations with the diocese of Quebec, and perhaps the colony's tiny number of practising architects, guaranteed him the contracts he needed. Finally, Charles (1826–1906), architect and engineer, a member of the fourth generation of the Baillairgés, contributed, in his role as municipal engineer, to the beautification of Quebec City. His works still abound in the city and its environs, where he designed more than 200 buildings, including parts of the old Université Laval, the neo-Gothic church of Sainte-Marie, then the diocese's most sumptuous church, and the Quebec City prison. Charles's relations with the church were not always good, but he could turn to the Department of Public Works, the other major employer of architects. Charles also contributed through his writings to the diffusion of technical knowledge in his fields of expertise.

The Woolsey Family, by William Berczy, Sr. (1809). John William Woolsey, a prominent member of Quebec City's English-speaking business community, was the son of an English merchant and his French-Canadian wife. Canadian art historian Dennis Reid termed Berczy's exceptionally well-crafted family portrait "one of the masterpieces of Canadian art."

National Gallery of Canada, Ottawa. Gift of Major Edgar C. Woolsey, Ottawa, 1952.

Petitions and counter-petitions circulated. In reality, the great majority of the province's 150 000 "new subjects" (the *Canadiens*) probably had little understanding of, and even less interest in, the question. Their main preoccupation was simply in subsisting, an objective not easily attained in these often difficult years.

THE CONSTITUTIONAL ACT OF 1791

Although not thoroughly familiar with social conditions in Quebec, the imperial government had to arbitrate often contradictory pressures and draw up the new constitution. William Grenville, secretary of state for the colonies, drafted the Constitutional Act of 1791. At the same time, the Province of Quebec was divided by executive order into two sections, the provinces of Upper and Lower Canada, with the upper part possessing an English-speaking Loyalist majority. The reasons for the partition of Quebec were not economic or geographic, for the colony functioned effectively as a single unit. Rather, Westminster's motivation was, as Grenville explained, to reduce "dissensions and animosities" among two "classes of men, differing in their prejudices, and perhaps in their interests."

The Constitutional Act of 1791 established an elective Legislative Assembly in each of the Canadas. Besides giving a voice to the population, this body could raise money through taxes for local expenditures, thus reducing the burden on the imperial treasury. At the same time, wary of what had happened in the American colonies, London moved to place the Assembly under strong executive control that would apply restraint if the people's representatives got out of hand. A lieutenant governor was to be appointed in each province. He would name the members of the

Legislative Council, the upper house. The Legislative Council's membership was intended eventually to be hereditary, like that of the British House of Lords. Thus, the "right men" — landowners — would be assured of a place in power. The Executive Council, also composed of appointed officials, would be the governor's personal cabinet. The governor enjoyed extensive veto powers and a measure of financial autonomy, thanks to the revenues from the Crown lands set aside by the Constitutional Act of 1791. Other lands were reserved for the maintenance of a "Protestant clergy," intended to mean the Church of England. Over the years, this system proved inefficient and increasingly unworkable. Both the appointed executive branch and the elected Assembly possessed considerable powers and frequently used them to thwart each other's will.

On account of property qualifications in England at this time, relatively few people there (less than 3 percent of the population) could vote in elections. Essentially the same qualifications applied in Lower Canada, but because of that colony's very different social structure, the great majority of non-Aboriginal male farmers, or habitants, obtained the right to vote. Still, suffrage was far from universal. Most urban labourers and domestics were disqualified because they neither owned property nor paid sufficient rent. The property qualification eliminated most women from the rolls, although it was only in 1834 that the Assembly of Lower Canada specifically disenfranchised women.

The British colonies in North America, 1791.

Source: Adapted from Ralph Krueger, Ray Corder, and John Koegler, *This Land of Ours: A New Geography of Canada* (Toronto: Harcourt Brace Jovanovich, 1991), p. 130. Used with permission.

The electoral arrangements disappointed Lower Canada's English Protestants. They had petitioned for an Assembly from which the French would be excluded, or at least in which there would be an English-speaking majority bolstered by further immigration. Montreal merchant Adam Lymburner lobbied in London for an arrangement in which the towns, where most of the English-speaking population lived, would get half the seats, even though they contained only about one-fifth of the total population. His avowed aim was to avoid putting the Assembly in the "power of ignorant and obstinate men" who held "the absurd idea that it is the landholders' interest to oppress commerce." In fact, although the towns obtained only 10 of the 50 seats, about 20 of the candidates elected in the first elections, held in 1792, were merchants, including a number who were French-speaking. There were also 14 seigneurs representing rural seats. Most members were from the upper bourgeoisie and, indeed, 21 were justices of the peace. Though the merchants would face opposition in the legislature, coming from the seigneurs and a handful of French-speaking notaries and lawyers, the assembly as a whole was a "docile instrument in the hands of the governor."[4]

After the Proclamation of 1763 and the Quebec Act of 1774, Quebec obtained, with the Constitutional Act of 1791, its third constitution in fewer than 30 years. The American Revolution and the arrival of thousands of Loyalists had made change imperative. Reactions to the new legislation varied widely. In Britain there was satisfaction that the new colony of Upper Canada would be free to grow under British law and British liberty, while the French majority in Lower Canada, confined to the House of Assembly, could do little damage. Some, like William Pitt, even hoped that the French, seeing the British system at work in Upper Canada, would gradually adopt English laws and customs. In the meantime, no force would be required.

Certain Lower Canadian groups, such as the seigneurs, the professionals, and the merchants, thought that they could use the new institutions profitably. Most disappointed as a group were Lower Canada's 10 000 English. The Constitutional Act of 1791 led to their separation from the growing English-speaking population in the new colony of Upper Canada. Moreover, the English-speaking inhabitants of what now became Lower Canada obtained few of the reforms for which they had agitated and did not even succeed in getting the Quebec Act repealed. The only real compensation received was the provision for the freehold system of land tenure in the area outside the seigneurial zone, in what became the Eastern Townships. Furthermore, the English were unsure of what to expect from the Assembly. The maintenance of a strong executive under British control was small consolation to the merchants. After all, the government had been in British hands since 1760, and yet the merchants were more often than not at loggerheads with the colonial administrators. Nevertheless, regardless of political changes, the English merchants' economic power continued to increase. In the 1790s, in fact, they had reason to be optimistic about the future.

NOTES

1. A.L. Burt, *The Old Province of Quebec*, vol. 1 (Toronto: McClelland & Stewart, 1968 [1933]), p. 218.
2. R. Arthur Bowler, "Sir Guy Carleton and the Campaign of 1776 in Canada," *Canadian Historical Review* 55 (1974): 131–40.
3. A.J.H. Richardson, "Henry Hope," *Dictionary of Canadian Biography*, vol. 4, *1771–1800* (Toronto: University of Toronto Press, 1979), p. 367.
4. F. Murray Greenwood, *Legacies of Fear: Law and Politics in Quebec in the Era of the French Revolution* (Toronto: University of Toronto Press, 1993), p. 52.

LINKING TO THE PAST w@w

Revolution Rejected: Canada and the American Revolution
http://www.warmuseum.ca/cwm/expo/index_e.html

Historical background, images of artifacts, and a quiz related to the American Revolution as it affected Canada.

Sir William Johnson
http://www.canadiana.org/ECO/mtq?id=d46f607295&doc=08342

Full text of *Sir William Johnson and the Six Nations*, an 1891 book by William Elliot Griffis.

Arriving in Canada
http://www.civilization.ca/hist/canp1/ca15eng.html

A brief look at the Loyalists' arrival; follow the links on this page for more information.

Index to Ontario Loyalists
http://www.rootsweb.com/~canmil/uel/indexloy.htm

These pages from the Canadian Military Heritage Project include a brief history of the Loyalists and Loyalist regiments, as well as resources for genealogical research.

Notre-Dame Cathedral, Quebec City
http://collections.ic.gc.ca/relig/ndamq/ndamqexe.htm

Read about the history of this cathedral, including Jean and Thomas Baillairgé's contribution to its reconstruction. Follow the link for Thomas Baillairgé's biography.

Constitutional Act of 1791
http://www.uni.ca/1791_ca.html

Full text of the Act. For a summary of its implications, go to http://www.nlc-bnc.ca/2/18/h18-2088-e.html.

RELATED READINGS

The following articles from R. Douglas Francis and Donald B. Smith, eds., *Readings in Canadian History: Pre-Confederation*, 6th ed. (Toronto: Nelson Thomson Learning, 2002), are helpful for topics studied in this chapter: S. Dale Standen, "The Debate on the Social and Economic Consequences of the Conquest: A Summary," pp. 203–10; José Igartua, "A Change in Climate: The Conquest and the *Marchands* of Montreal," pp. 211–25; and Allan Greer, "The Fall of New France," pp. 225–31.

BIBLIOGRAPHY

Hilda Neatby's synthesis, *Quebec: The Revolutionary Age, 1760–1791* (Toronto: McClelland & Stewart, 1966), reviews the political developments. Chapters 4 and 5 of Fernand Ouellet's *Economic and Social History of Quebec, 1760–1850* (Toronto: Macmillan, 1980) are also very useful. On the American invasion see Robert M. Hatch, *Thrust for Canada: The American Attempt on Quebec in 1775–1776* (Boston: Houghton Mifflin, 1979); George A. Rawlyk, *Revolution Rejected, 1775–1776* (Scarborough, ON: Prentice-Hall, 1968); and George F.G. Stanley, *Canada Invaded, 1775–1776* (Toronto: Hakkert, 1973). A critical examination of Carleton's wartime conduct may be found in R. Arthur Bowler, "Sir Guy Carleton and the Campaign of 1776 in Canada," *Canadian Historical Review* 55 (1974): 131–40.

L.F.S. Upton, ed., *The United Empire Loyalists: Men and Myths* (Toronto: Copp Clark, 1967) contains useful documents, while David V.J. Bell, "The Loyalist Tradition in Canada," *Journal of Canadian Studies* 5 (1970): 22–33, evaluates the impact of the arrival of the Loyalists.

The best study on the Six Nations is by Barbara Graymont, *The Iroquois in the American Revolution* (Syracuse: Syracuse University Press, 1972). Isabel Thompson Kelsay has written *Joseph Brant, 1743–1807: Man of Two Worlds* (Syracuse: Syracuse University Press, 1984), the most complete biography of the important Mohawk war chief. For Native affairs in the St. Lawrence valley in this period see Daniel Francis, *A History of the Native Peoples of Quebec, 1760–1867* (Ottawa: Department of Northern and Indian Affairs, 1984).

Françoise Noël has studied the management of an important group of seigneuries in *The Christie Seigneuries: Estate Management and Settlement in the Upper Richelieu Valley, 1760–1854* (Montreal/Kingston: McGill-Queen's University Press, 1992). On the seigneurs' links with the military see Roch Legault, "L'organisation militaire sous le régime britannique et le rôle assigné à la gentilhommerie canadienne (1760–1815)," *Revue d'histoire de l'Amérique française* 45 (1991–92): 229–50. Lorraine Gadoury examines family relationships within the French-speaking colonial elite in *Échanges épistolaires au sein de l'élite canadienne du XVIIIe siècle* (Montreal: Hurtubise, 1998). Useful studies on the evolution of justice and the legal system are Evelyn Kolish, *Nationalismes et conflits de droits: le débat du droit privé au Québec, 1760–1840* (LaSalle, QC: Hurtubise HMH, 1994); and Donald Fyson's Ph.D. dissertation, "Criminal Justice, Civil Society, and the Local State: The Justices of the Peace in the District of Montreal, 1764–1830" (Université de Montréal, 1995), to be published in 2005. An article that examines how the legal system was used against pro-American rebels is Jean-Marie Fecteau and Douglas Hay, "'Government by Will and Pleasure Instead of Law': Military Justice and the Legal System in Quebec," in F. Murray Greenwood and Barry Wright, eds., *Canadian State Trials, vol. I: Law, Politics, and Security Measures 1608–1837* (Toronto: University of Toronto Press, 1996), pp. 129–71.

Church history is examined by Lucien Lemieux, *Histoire du catholicisme québécois: Les XVIIIe et XIXe siècles,* tome 1: *Les années difficiles (1760–1839)* (Montreal: Boréal, 1989). See also Marcel Trudel, "La servitude de l'Église catholique du Canada français sous le régime anglais," *Canadian Historical Association Report* (1963): 42–64; and Jean-Pierre Wallot, "Religion and French-Canadian Mores in the Early Nineteenth Century," *Canadian Historical Review* 52 (1971): 51–94. Attempts to bring French-speaking priests from Savoy to Quebec are described in Luca Codignola, "Le Québec et les prêtres savoyards, 1779–1784: les dimensions internationales d'un échec," *Revue d'histoire de l'Amérique française* 43 (1989–90): 559–68. Some information on women in late-eighteenth-century Quebec is available in Micheline Dumont et al., *Quebec Women: A History* (Toronto: Women's Press, 1987). The history of Quebec's English-speaking population is reviewed in Ronald Rudin, *The Forgotten Quebecers: A History of English-Speaking Quebec, 1759–1980* (Quebec: Institut québécois de recherche sur la culture, 1985).

Pierre Tousignant studies the genesis of the Constitutional Act in "Problématique pour une nouvelle approche de la constitution de 1791," *Revue d'histoire de l'Amérique française* 27 (1973–74): 181–234. David Milobar shows how British needs and perceptions determined the nature of reform in Quebec in "Government and the Nature of Reform in Quebec, 1782–1791," *International History Review* 12 (1990): 45–64. Also very useful is Philip Lawson, *The Imperial Challenge: Quebec and Britain in the Age of the American Revolution* (Montreal/Kingston: McGill-Queen's University Press, 1989). F. Murray Greenwood has written an account of political developments in the 1790s, *Legacies of Fear: Law and Politics in Quebec in the Era of the French Revolution* (Toronto: University of Toronto Press, 1993).

Important studies of life in rural and urban Quebec include Allan Greer, *Peasant, Lord, and Merchant: Rural Society in Three Quebec Parishes, 1740–1840* (Toronto: University of Toronto Press, 1985); and David T. Ruddel, *Quebec City, 1765–1832: The Evolution of a Colonial Town* (Ottawa: Canadian Museum of Civilization, 1987). Lorraine Gadboury examines family relationships within the French-speaking colonial elite in *Échanges épistolaires au sein de l'élite canadienne du XVIIIe siècle* (Montreal: Hurtubise, 1999).

Useful maps of the St. Lawrence valley in the late eighteenth and early nineteenth centuries appear in the first two volumes of the *Historical Atlas of Canada*. vol. 1, R. Cole Harris, ed., *From the Beginning to 1800* (Toronto: University of Toronto Press, 1987); and vol. 2, R. Louis Gentilcore, ed., *The Land Transformed, 1800–1891* (Toronto: University of Toronto Press, 1993).

The following books and articles provide a good introduction to the Native history of the period: Francis Jennings, *Empire of Fortune: Crowns, Colonies and Tribes in the Seven Years' War in America* (New York: W.W. Norton, 1988); Howard H. Peckham, *Pontiac and the Indian Uprising* (Chicago: University of Chicago Press, 1961 [1947]); Richard White, *The Middle Ground: Indians, Empires and Republics in the Great Lakes Region, 1650–1815* (Cambridge: Cambridge University Press, 1991); W.J. Eccles, "Sovereignty-

Association, 1500–1783," in his *Essays on New France* (Toronto: Oxford University Press, 1987), pp. 156–81; Jacqueline Peterson, "Many Roads to Red River: Métis Genesis in the Great Lakes Region, 1680–1815," in Jacqueline Peterson and Jennifer S.H. Brown, eds., *The New Peoples: Being and Becoming Métis in North America* (Winnipeg: University of Manitoba Press, 1985), pp. 37–71; and Harriet Gorham, "Families of Mixed Descent in the Western Great Lakes Region," in Bruce Alden Cox, ed., *Native People, Native Lands: Canadian Indians, Inuit and Métis* (Ottawa: Carleton University Press, 1988), pp. 37–55. Specific developments in the Province of Quebec are mentioned in Daniel Francis, *A History of the Native Peoples of Québec, 1760–1867* (Ottawa: Indian and Northern Affairs Canada, 1983). On Native history of the St. Lawrence valley, see Jean-Pierre Sawaya, *La Fédération des Sept Feux de la vallée du Saint-Laurent, XVIIe-XIXe siècles* (Sillery: Septentrion, 1998); and Denys Delâge, "Les Iroquois chrétiens des 'réductions,' 1677–1770," *Recherches amérindiennes au Québec* 21(1–2) (1991): 59–70; 21(3) (1991): 39–50.

Finally, the major figures of these years all have biographies in various volumes of the *Dictionary of Canadian Biography*, an essential tool for this and other periods. One sketch not to be missed is the biography of Marie-Josephte Corriveau, "La Corriveau," by folklorist Luc Lacourcière, in vol. 3: *1741–1770*, pp. 142–43.

MARITIME SOCIETY, 1760–1815

TIME LINE

1759 –	The Planters from New England begin arriving in great numbers in Nova Scotia
1760– **1761** –	Mi'kmaq and Maliseet sign peace treaties with the British
1764 –	The British allow Acadians to return to Nova Scotia
1767 –	St John's Island, named Prince Edward Island in 1799, is granted by lottery to British proprietors
1776 –	Jonathan Eddy's pro-American force unsuccessfully attacks Fort Cumberland
	Henry Alline begins his career as an itinerant preacher
1783 –	The American Revolution ends
1784 –	New Brunswick and Cape Breton (to 1820) are established as separate jurisdictions
1785 –	Parrtown, New Brunswick, is incorporated as the city of Saint John
1793– **1815** –	The French Revolutionary Wars, followed by the Napoleonic Wars
1812– **1814** –	The War of 1812

After the British conquest of Canada, the Thirteen Colonies moved toward independence. The United States, however, would not include all of British North America. Nova Scotia, the new colony of Saint John's Island (created in 1769 and renamed Prince Edward Island in 1799), Newfoundland, and the former French colony of Quebec remained part of the British empire.

Britain easily maintained control of the small, isolated colony of Saint John's Island, with its settler population of only 1000 recent British arrivals and Acadians. As for Newfoundland, its Anglo-Irish population looked eastward to Britain rather than southward to the Thirteen Colonies. In contrast, over half of Nova Scotia's approximately 20 000 inhabitants came from New England. They maintained strong economic and cultural ties with their former homeland.

Nova Scotia, which then comprised the whole of present-day Nova Scotia and New Brunswick, faced a difficult decision concerning which side to support in the American Revolution. Initially, it looked as if Nova Scotia might become the fourteenth insurgent colony. Why did Nova Scotia not become a state in the American union? Why did it choose to stay in the British empire in 1775–76, and again in the War of 1812?

NEW ENGLAND'S OUTPOST

With the deportation of the Acadians in 1755 and the capture of Louisbourg in 1758, Americans began moving north. The British authorities wanted to attract loyal Protestant settlers in order to prevent the deported Acadians' return. In October 1758, Governor Lawrence issued a proclamation throughout British America that invited settlers to claim the unoccupied Acadian farmlands. The circular described Acadia's 80 000 ha of "Plowlands producing Wheat, Rye, Barley, Oats, Hemp, Flax ... cultivated for more than a Hundred Years past, and never fail of Crops, nor need manuring." The Nova Scotia government agreed to pay for New Englanders' transportation to and give grants of 40 ha of land to each family head and 20 ha for each additional family member.

In crowded, heavily settled southeastern Massachusetts, eastern Connecticut, and Rhode Island, the invitation had great appeal among the poorer farmers. Hundreds of fishers anxious to locate closer to the Grand Banks also came. These New England farmers and fishers became known as the Planters. Between 1759 and 1767, some 8000 Planters from New England settled in Nova Scotia. Most of the immigrants went to the Annapolis valley in peninsular Nova Scotia, to fertile lands previously cleared and diked by the Acadians, and to the area around Cumberland, near present-day Sackville, New Brunswick. A much smaller number entered the Saint John River valley, forming small frontier communities at the mouth of the river and at Maugerville (just south of present-day Fredericton), along the lower Saint John River. On account of the difficult conditions in what became known as "Nova Scarcity," a number of the recent arrivals returned to their homes in New England in the 1760s.

The Planters who remained worked to create a new English-speaking Nova Scotia. But the lack of roads linking the settlements prevented regular communication. As historian George Rawlyk noted, "on the eve of the American Revolution, Nova Scotia was little more than a political expression for a number of widely scattered and isolated communities."[1] Nevertheless, on the eve of the American Revolution, New Englanders constituted about half of Nova Scotia's total population of nearly 20 000.

Americans were still migrating to the forested lands north of the Bay of Fundy when hundreds of Acadians returned. In 1764, the British government permitted them to settle in Nova Scotia, providing that they dispersed throughout the colony. Many returned not to their farms, which were now occupied by New Englanders, but to the Bay of Chaleur, on the present-day border between Quebec and New Brunswick. The settlement of Caraquet became a focal point for the region. Other Acadians lived on farms along the lower Saint John River.

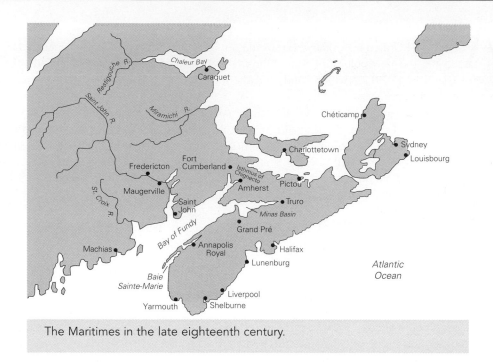

The Maritimes in the late eighteenth century.

British immigrants came to Nova Scotia in the 1760s and 1770s: some 2000 settlers from Ulster in Northern Ireland; more than 750 from Yorkshire, England, many of whom settled on the Isthmus of Chignecto; and, in 1773, nearly 200 Scots who settled at Pictou. They joined the original British residents of Halifax, the 1500 or so Acadians, and the approximately 1500 "foreign Protestants," largely Germans, who resided south of Halifax in the area around Lunenburg.

HALIFAX'S PREDOMINANCE IN NOVA SCOTIA

Halifax, as the only urban centre, became the colony's capital. It housed the military establishment and published the province's only newspaper. The upper level of Halifax society, headed by the governor, included his senior officials, and a group of merchants who had grown rich from army and navy contracts. A handful of smaller merchants and professional people also lived in the colony's capital. The rest of the city's population consisted of poor fishers, carpenters, mechanics, and labourers.

Nova Scotia obtained an elected assembly in 1758, but few rural members could afford to take their seats as unpaid legislators. As a result, a small clique of Halifax merchants controlled both the Assembly and the Governor's Council. So influential were the merchants that they secured the recall of Governor Francis Legge to England. Sent to the colony in 1773, the would-be reform governor attempted to expose the spoils system operated by the large Halifax merchants. They, in turn, protested to London, threatening that Nova Scotia would join the American Revolution if Legge's investigations continued. Already fearful of developments in the Thirteen Colonies, London overlooked the evidence of corruption that Legge had unearthed and ordered the governor home in early 1776.

NOVA SCOTIA AND THE AMERICAN REVOLUTION

The rebellion rhetoric in the Thirteen Colonies in 1775–76 found an audience in rural Nova Scotia. Many New Englanders resented Britain's unfulfilled promises of constitutional rights. At annual town meetings, New England voters elected their officers and decided local issues. But in Nova Scotia in the 1760s, this form of township democracy did not exist; instead, London built a tightly controlled, centralized government structure. The merchant-controlled Assembly in Halifax, which strongly supported the governor, worked to eliminate local township government. It appointed justices of the peace to administer the local areas and did not allow the election of township officials.

As tensions mounted in the Thirteen Colonies, settlements throughout Nova Scotia began holding town meetings similar to those held in the American colonies. When Governor Legge called out one-fifth of the provincial militia in November 1775 and levied new taxes to meet the cost, petitions from the settlements of Truro, Cumberland, and Onslow voiced opposition to military service. The Chignecto settlers objected to the new tax and to the idea that the governor might force them to "march into different parts in Arms against their friends and relations." Like the Acadians of 20 years earlier, most Nova Scotian settlers sought neutrality. On December 8, 1775, the inhabitants of Yarmouth, for example, sent this memorandum to the governor:

> We were almost all of us born in New England, we have Fathers, Brothers, & Sisters in that Country, divided betwixt natural affection to our nearest relations, and good Faith and Friendship to our King and Country, we want to know, if we may be permitted at this time to live in a peaceable State, as we look on that to be the only situation in which we with our Wives and Children, can be in any tolerable degree safe . . .

Realizing the seriousness of the discontent, Legge retreated. He suspended compulsory military service, allowed the militia to stay at home unless an actual invasion occurred, and cancelled the new taxes, thus effectively neutralizing much of the discontent.

RESPONSES TO THE AMERICAN REVOLUTION

The communities farthest from Halifax showed the greatest enthusiasm for the American cause. The town of Machias, on the vaguely defined border between Nova Scotia and Maine, the Maugerville settlement on the lower Saint John River, and the Chignecto–Cumberland region at the head of the Bay of Fundy became active centres of support for the American Revolution. Jonathan Eddy, a New Englander who farmed in the Chignecto region, took the lead in organizing the revolutionary movement there. His invasion force of about 180 men attacked British-held Fort Cumberland (the reconstructed French fort of Beauséjour) in 1776. But they had no artillery to mount a siege. Few New Englanders on the isthmus openly supported Eddy's small, poorly trained, undisciplined, and badly led army. With the arrival of British reinforcements, Eddy's troops fled in disarray. The British burned the homes and barns of his supporters. The following summer, British naval vessels entered the Bay of Fundy and took control of the area.

The insurgents' attempt to capture Fort Cumberland failed for a number of reasons. Historian John Bartlet Brebner points out that General George Washington, whom Eddy approached for support, refused because he knew that the Americans had "little energy or material available for side shows, no matter how admirable the cause and its proponents."[2] As well, the presence of the Royal Navy discouraged the Americans from making such an attempt. Brebner believes the Americans' lack of a navy and their failure to win sufficient support among Nova Scotians best explain Britain's success in expelling the revolutionaries.

Micmac Encampment, by Hibbert Newton Binney, completed around 1790.

History Collection/Nova Scotia Museum, Halifax/NSM 79.146.1.

FIRST NATIONS AND ACADIAN RESPONSES

The British also obtained the neutrality of most of the thousand or so Mi'kmaqs and Maliseets who held the balance of power north of the Bay of Fundy. By now the British had adopted the French techniques of gift diplomacy, giving their Native allies presents of food, medicine, and ammunition. In addition, Britain appeared to be the stronger of the two opponents after it extended its control over the Bay of Fundy and captured the coastline of northern Maine from the Americans. Thanks to the First Nations, the upper Saint John River valley remained in the British zone of influence throughout the war. The Acadians, for their part, had no interest in becoming involved in the civil war between the two English-speaking groups.

GROWING ANTAGONISM TOWARD THE AMERICAN REVOLUTIONARIES

While the American insurgents consolidated their hold on the former Thirteen Colonies, Nova Scotia moved in a different direction. American raids on Nova Scotia made many once-sympathetic Nova Scotians antagonistic to the American revolutionaries. No Nova Scotia port (except Halifax) escaped the raiders, who seized anything they could carry away. These attacks alienated wealthy citizens in Yarmouth, Lunenburg, and Liverpool, and prompted them to launch their own retaliatory attacks against American shipping. By 1781, settlements in the Minas Basin and the Bay of Fundy area, which in 1775–76 had opposed increased taxes for military defence, now willingly accepted militia service and taxes to meet the cost of defending the colony.

HENRY ALLINE AND THE NEW LIGHT MOVEMENT

The unwillingness of many New Englanders in Nova Scotia to support the American Revolution can also be explained by what some historians call the "missing decade" thesis.[3] Although these recent immigrants held many New England values and still possessed an attachment to their homeland, they had been absent during a crucial decade in New England's political development.

No doubt they heard a little of the revolutionary rhetoric of the early 1770s about the growing British oppression and the need to defend New Englanders' liberties, but they were more concerned about the need to clear land and develop the fisheries. They simply wanted political agents from both Maine and Halifax to leave them alone.

Nonetheless, during this period of acute disorientation and confusion, these settlers needed direction. In the late 1770s and early 1780s, a religious gospel rather than a political one monopolized the attention of Nova Scotians. They became part of a great religious revival that centred on a charismatic young man named Henry Alline.

Born and raised in Rhode Island, Alline belonged to the Congregational church, the church to which most New England immigrants in Nova Scotia adhered. Henry received his early education at Newport, before his family moved to Nova Scotia in 1760. They settled in one of the richest farming areas in the colony — the Minas Basin, near present-day Windsor. The 12-year-old received no further schooling, for no school existed in his township. Nor was there a church. Families maintained their religion through family prayer, Bible reading, and religious discussions at home. But Alline came into contact with an evangelical group that emphasized the need for an intensely emotional conversion experience known as the "New Light."

In 1776, at the age of 28, Alline began his career as an itinerant preacher. From the reminiscences of one of his early listeners, we know that Alline appeared "mighty in prayer" and never talked "about the world at all, except as urged by necessity." Committed to music as a means of teaching the faith, he was "a good singer and loved singing." Physically, he was of "middling size; straight, and very thin; of light complexion, with light curly hair, and blue eyes, with a solemn expression"; his dress was "neat but plain."

Initially, Alline confined his activities to the Minas Basin, but three years later several Annapolis valley churches ordained him as their minister. Convinced that God had selected him to carry His message, he travelled constantly. The evangelist often rode as far as 80 km a day, bringing religion to rural people. His willingness to preach under all conditions struck a responsive chord among the economically impoverished rural Nova Scotians on their frontier farms. They heard Alline and believed him when he told them that Nova Scotia had become the new centre of Christendom.

Alline's religious revival filled the spiritual vacuum in the new settlements far away from the revolutionary struggle. Very effectively, he spread his message that good Christians should work to secure their spiritual salvation rather than to fight military battles. He convinced many Nova Scotians that they were performing a special role — bringing the world back to God — and that Christ merited their allegiance, not the British or the revolutionaries. As a result, Nova Scotia's "New Light" communities chose political neutrality and worked instead to perfect their spiritual condition.

Alline died of tuberculosis in early February 1784, leaving behind scores of disciples and hundreds of followers. After his death, his manuscript journals were copied and recopied by hand and circulated among his followers until they were published in 1806. George Rawlyk regards them as "one of the two or three most illuminating, honest, introspective accounts available concerning the spiritual travails of any eighteenth-century North American mystical evangelical."[4] Alline's disciples, popularly referred to as Allinites, later became members of the Baptist church and carried on the teachings of the "Apostle of Nova Scotia."

THE NEW ENGLAND LOYALISTS

Throughout the Thirteen Colonies, a substantial number of Americans opposed the American Revolution and wanted to remain loyal to Britain. Historians now estimate that approximately 20 percent of the white American population in 1776 (roughly half a million people) became

Where Historians Disagree

Why Didn't Nova Scotia Join the American Revolution?

On the eve of the American Revolutionary War in 1775–76, about half of Nova Scotia's 20 000 settlers were New Englanders. The colony appeared to be a northern outpost of New England. Why, then, did it refuse to join the revolution?

Historian Beamish Murdoch offered the first explanation. New England farmers, who had been given land previously owned by the Acadians when they arrived after the Conquest, were, as a result, "full of intense loyalty and affection to the British government."[1] Some 70 years later, in the 1930s, Professor Viola Barnes added an economic motive: Halifax merchants and Governor Francis Legge kept Nova Scotia loyal to the Crown because it was in their best interest to do so. When the Americans boycotted West Indies trade, Halifax merchants saw their opportunity to appropriate the trade themselves. "In short," she wrote, "Nova Scotia remained loyal because the merchant class in control believed the Province profited more than it lost by the connection with the mother country, and because the Governor, with their help, was able to prevent the radicals from stirring the people to revolt."[2]

Other historians now entered the fray. Professor W.B. Kerr challenged Barnes's interpretation. He questioned why Nova Scotia merchants would object to New Englanders carrying a monopoly of their trade, since they were New Englanders themselves. Furthermore, they were free to pursue their own trade if they so desired. Kerr then offered his own explanation, "the almost total want of sympathy among artisans, fishermen, and farmers for the American cause." Furthermore, the Nova

Scotia legislature, made up of a majority of New Englanders, expressed their loyalty to the king on the eve of the revolution, acknowledging him to be the "supreme Legislature of the province and it is our indispensable duty to pay a due proportion of the expense of this great Empire."[3] Nova Scotia historian D.C. Harvey added yet another explanation: Nova Scotians "were inclined to submit to the will of the stronger."[4] Simply put, British naval power surpassed that of the rebels.

In 1937, noted historian J.B. Brebner argued that geographical isolation, as well as close economic ties to Britain through mercantile trade, kept Nova Scotia insulated from activities elsewhere on the continent. As he concluded: "Nova Scotia had insulated and neutralized the New England migrants so thoroughly that as Nova Scotians they had henceforth to look eastward to London for direction and help rather than southward to Boston as they had done in the past."[5]

Beginning in the 1940s, historians became interested in religious revivalism as a factor in keeping Nova Scotians neutral. M.W. Armstrong saw the "Great Awakening" (as this revival was called) as "an expression of democratic ideals and spiritual independence" that raised the minds of Nova Scotians above worldly concerns. How could "King George" and the revolution compete with "King Jesus" and redemption, he queried?[6] In 1959, sociologist S.D. Clark applied Frederick Jackson Turner's frontier thesis to an understanding of Nova Scotia's neutrality during the revolution.[7] He saw the New Light religious revival in the outposts of Nova Scotia as a frontier movement of social protest that strengthened the spirit of local autonomy and resolved their determination to be politically independent of both Britain and its Halifax political agents, and New England.

Professors Gordon Stewart and George Rawlyk introduced their "Missing Decade" thesis. They argued that those New Englanders who migrated to Nova Scotia in the early 1760s missed the rebellious rhetoric that occurred between 1765 and 1775. Therefore they could not identify with their arguments.[8] Rawlyk then went on to explore the role of Henry Alline, the charismatic leader of the religious revival in Nova Scotia, in keeping Nova Scotians neutral. Rawlyk argued that Alline's message to Nova Scotia "Yankees" that they had a divine mission "to lead the world back to God" gave them a purpose above and beyond that of worldly revolution.[9]

More recently, J.M. Bumsted has questioned both the size and the importance of the New England population in Nova Scotia during the American Revolution. He argues that as the war got underway, Nova Scotia "Yankees" who supported the rebel cause returned to New England and therefore played no part in Nova Scotia's decision. As well, the strong British military presence in the colony, and resentment among Nova Scotians at the destructive behaviour of the American rebels within the colony, kept them neutral.[10] The question as to why Nova Scotia did not become the fourteenth state continues to intrigue historians.

[1] Beamish Murdoch, *History of Nova Scotia or Acadie*, vol. 2. (Halifax, N.S.: J. Barnes, 1865–67), p. 562.

[2] V.F. Barnes, "Francis Legge, Governor of Loyalist Nova Scotia, 1773–1776," *New England Quarterly*, July 1931, quoted in George A. Rawlyk, ed., *Revolution Rejected, 1775–1776* [Scarborough, ON: Prentice-Hall, 1968), pp. 32–33.

[3] W.B. Kerr, "The Merchants of Nova Scotia and the American Revolution," *Canadian Historical Review*, 33 (1932): 22.

[4] D.C. Harvey, "The Struggle for the New England Form of Township Government in Nova Scotia," *Canadian Historical Association Report* (1933): 22.

[5] John Bartlet Brebner, *The Neutral Yankees of Nova Scotia* (Toronto: McClelland & Stewart, 1969), p. 310.

[6] M.W. Armstrong, "Neutrality and Religion in Revolutionary Nova Scotia," *New England Quarterly* (March 1946): 57–58.

[7] S.D. Clark, *Movements of Political Protest in Canada, 1640–1840* (Toronto: University of Toronto Press, 1959).

[8] Gordon Stewart and George Rawlyk, *A People Highly Favoured of God* (Toronto: Macmillan, 1972).

[9] G.A. Rawlyk, *Ravished by the Spirit: Religious Revivals, Baptists, and Henry Alline* (Montreal/Kingston: McGill-Queen's University Press, 1984).

[10] J.M. Bumsted, "1763–1783: Resettlement and Rebellion," in P.A. Buckner and J.G. Reid, eds., *The Atlantic Region to Confederation: A History* (Toronto: University of Toronto Press, 1994), pp. 156–83.

Loyalists.[5] They were strongest in New York, partly because New York had a strong British aristocracy, and weakest in Connecticut, Massachusetts, and Virginia. Loyalists came from every class, race, occupation, religion, and geographical region. They supported Britain for many diverse reasons, ranging from personal loyalty to the Crown to a fear that the revolution would threaten individual freedoms.

Loyalists who had served as colonial office holders often had a vested interest in maintaining the status quo. But a high proportion of Loyalists also came from religious and cultural minorities. Not yet having joined mainstream American society, recent immigrants from Europe (Germany, the Netherlands, and the British Isles) and members of religious minorities (such as the French Huguenots, Maryland Roman Catholics, and Quaker pacifists) held on to the British

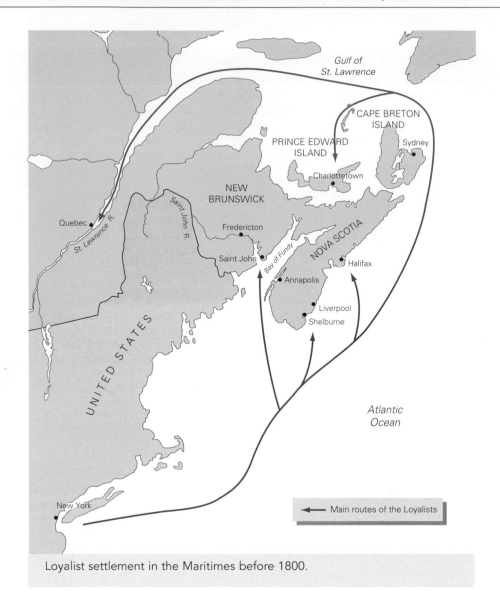

Loyalist settlement in the Maritimes before 1800.

connection for fear that increased American power could result in a loss of their religious freedoms. The First Nations, particularly the Iroquois, looked upon Britain as the lesser of two evils, since Britain wished to slow the advance of the American settlers westward, anxious as it was to avoid the increased expenditures of more wars with the Native peoples. African Americans saw an opportunity to free themselves by joining the British and fleeing their owners.

PERSECUTION OF THE LOYALISTS

Persecution of the Loyalists began as early as 1774, when it became more and more difficult to maintain neutrality in face of the approaching struggle. Appropriately, the term "lynch law," an informal system of law enforcement, originated to describe the treatment of Loyalists in Virginia. A favourite pastime was tarring and feathering outspoken Loyalists. The victim was stripped naked, smeared with a coat of tar and feathers, then paraded through the streets.

With the passing of the Declaration of Independence, the local revolutionary committees stepped up their activities against Loyalists. According to historians Wallace Brown and Hereward Senior, the committees' means of persuasion "ranged from mild social pressure to murder."[6] Various states disenfranchised, put in prison, banished, and fined "Tories" and confiscated their property as well. In Loyalist-controlled areas, outrages were also committed against, and restrictions of civil liberties imposed on, those believed to be supporters of the revolution.

The decisive battle of the revolutionary war was fought on October 19, 1781, when Britain's Lord Cornwallis surrendered his army of 7000 at Yorktown, Virginia. This battle really ended the war, although the general peace was made two years later.

For many Loyalists, the two years between the disaster at Yorktown and the final signing of peace was the worst time of all. As the war ended, the British evacuated southern ports such as Wilmington, Charleston, and Savannah, to which the Loyalists had fled for protection. Persecution reached new levels. Several of the newly independent states subjected the Loyalists to double and triple taxation, and Congress encouraged the states to confiscate their property. Physical violence against Loyalists continued. It became clear that Britain had to do something for them. The British continued to hold New York City and Long Island, and many Loyalists (at one point, 30 000) assembled there, awaiting evacuation.

At the peace negotiations, the American commissioners agreed that no further persecutions of Loyalists would take place. But while Congress urged the states to grant restitution and amnesty, it had no power to enforce its requests. Except in one or two states, every clause in the Treaty of Paris relating to the Loyalists was abrogated. When news of the preliminary peace reached the United States in the spring of 1783, the proscriptions, confiscations, and harassment of Loyalists began again.

THE GREAT LOYALIST MIGRATION TO NOVA SCOTIA

The exodus of thousands of Loyalists and their families began even before the peace treaty. Historian Ann Gorman Condon has written of them: "Looked at from the perspective of the late twentieth century, it is clear that the Loyalists were the first mass movement of political refugees in modern history."[7]

Traditionally, the number of exiles has been estimated at 100 000, but this figure is probably inflated. Wallace Brown and Hereward Senior believe that British North America received more than 50 000 white, black, and First Nations Loyalists. The British Isles received approximately 10 000, several thousand went to the British West Indies, and a small number (mainly Germans), returned to the Rhine valley. The overwhelming majority of the Loyalists were of European background, as Brown and Senior note, but approximately 6000 African-American Loyalists migrated to the Maritimes, the West Indies, and Sierra Leone in West Africa. Some 2000 Iroquois also left New York. In all, 70 000 people — approximately the population of New France at the time of the conquest — left the United States.[8]

Both during and after the war, the more influential Loyalists, such as royal officials, wealthy merchants, landowners, professionals, and high military officers, sailed directly for England to press their claims for compensation. The humbler element settled in the remaining British North American colonies.

The Loyalists favoured Nova Scotia over Quebec at a ratio of roughly two to one. Nova Scotia's fisheries, its large tracts of empty land, and the potential trade with the West Indies attracted them. Nova Scotia, too, was the shorter trip by sea. Small groups of Loyalists had been finding their way to Halifax since 1775. The evacuation of New York in 1783, though, led to an unanticipated invasion. On April 26, 1783, the first or "spring" fleet set sail, carrying no fewer than 7000 men, women, and children. Half the vessels went to Port Roseway, about 150 km south of Halifax, and the other half sailed to the mouth of the Saint John River. They went ashore at Saint John on May 18, now commemorated in New Brunswick as "Loyalist Landing Day." Other fleets followed in the summer and autumn.

THE LOYALISTS' FIRST SETTLEMENTS

 About 15 000 Loyalists went to what became New Brunswick in 1784; about the same number to peninsular Nova Scotia, and about a thousand each to Prince Edward Island and Cape Breton, with a few families to Newfoundland. The great migration to the Atlantic colonies more than doubled their population with the arrival of over 30 000 civilian refugees and disbanded soldiers.

The smallest group of those who made their way to Nova Scotia came, surprisingly, from New England. Historian Neil MacKinnon noted that "the New England states seem to have been represented more by quality than quantity, leadership than numbers."[9] He estimated that of those who came to Nova Scotia, at least 40 percent came from New York state, 15 percent from the other middle colonies (particularly New Jersey), 20 percent from New England, and about 25 percent (black and white) from the southern colonies.

Arrival proved a mixed blessing. In spite of the British government's promises, the colonists found that almost no preparations had been made to receive them at Saint John. No shelter had been prepared, provisions were in short supply, and the land along the river was unsurveyed. Elizabeth Morgan later recalled her thoughts immediately after landing: "I climbed to the top of Chipman's Hill and watched the sails disappearing in the distance, and such a feeling of loneliness came over me that, although I had not shed a single tear through all the war, I sat down on the damp moss with my baby in my lap and cried." (Her future great-grandson would be Samuel Leonard Tilley, one of New Brunswick's Fathers of Confederation.)

Many Loyalists brought with them vivid memories of American injustices. The Dribblee family of Long Island had experienced particularly harsh treatment. As Polly Dribblee recorded in a letter to her brother in England, rebels had plundered their house and forced her and her five children out "naked into the streets." Two more times before they left Long Island, they were "plundered and stripped." Their misfortune continued in New Brunswick. During their first year at Saint John, Polly's husband, Filer Dribblee, who had spent six months in prison during the war, entered a deep depression, and finally took his own life. As well, the Dribblees' log-cabin home burnt twice in one year.

Port Roseway, quickly renamed Shelburne after the current British prime minister, became the largest Loyalist settlement. By 1784, the population had reached 10 000. About half of Nova Scotia's 3000 African-American Loyalists settled in Shelburne's suburb of Birchtown. But the following year the town's population declined sharply, shrinking to 600 by 1815. The inexperienced Loyalist settlers had initially picked Shelburne for its magnificent long, narrow harbour, but soon discovered that it had little else: the soil and timber were poor, the inland communications primitive, and the whaling and fisheries in the area disappointing.

THE BLACK LOYALISTS

 For the African-American Loyalists, far more disappointments than the conditions of Shelburne awaited them. Among their ranks were men and women who had heeded the British proclamation of 1779 that offered freedom to any slaves who left their American masters and rallied to support the Crown. Some blacks had taken part in combat; others had served as spies, guides, nurses, and personal servants.

The Loyalist boomtown of Shelburne, Nova Scotia, in 1789. Along with the Saint John River valley in New Brunswick, Shelburne was one of the first major areas of Loyalist settlement. This drawing is by William Booth.

National Archives of Canada/C-10548.

In 1783, some 3000 African-American Loyalists arrived in the Maritimes, having won their freedom during the American Revolution by crossing over to the British lines. The British government might have promised them freedom, but it did not grant them equality. They were given smaller and less fertile grants than the other Loyalists, and substantially fewer provisions and tools. They could not vote, sit in non-segregated sections of churches, or even fish in the Saint John harbour.

Thomas Peter, an African-American Loyalist from North Carolina, went to England to protest. Here he met a group of English reformers promoting a "back to Africa" campaign for distressed blacks from all parts of the British empire. More than 1000 African Americans took advantage of the opportunity to go to Sierra Leone on the West African coast in 1792. In 1800, another 550 blacks arrived in Sierra Leone from Nova Scotia. These individuals were Maroons, descendants of slaves who had escaped from the Spanish two centuries earlier, and had lived free lives in the interior of Jamaica. Fearing the support they might give to a slave revolt in Jamaica, such as that which had broken out in neighbouring Haiti, the British expelled them to Nova Scotia in 1796. Now four years later, hoping to save the cost of keeping them in Halifax, Britain deported them to Sierra Leone in West Africa.

Many of the white Loyalists also found economic conditions in Nova Scotia difficult. In one stroke, the colony's population had doubled and the resources of "Nova Scarcity" proved insufficient to meet the demand. Eventually, over half the Loyalists who came to Nova Scotia went elsewhere. Some moved to Upper Canada, others went to England, a number returned to the United States, and, as previously mentioned, many free African-American Loyalists resettled in British West Africa.

THE FOUNDING OF NEW BRUNSWICK

Shortly after the arrival in what is today New Brunswick, elite Loyalists from the St. John River petitioned London to have the section north of the Bay of Fundy removed from Nova Scotia and made a separate Loyalist province. They argued that the distance of the Saint John settlements from Halifax made it difficult to transact business with the capital. No doubt they also realized that the creation of a new colony would provide administrative offices for themselves.

In the summer of 1784, Britain created the new colony of New Brunswick. Colonel Thomas Carleton, the younger brother of Quebec governor Sir Guy Carleton, became the colony's first governor, a position he held for 30 years. In 1785, the major settlement at the mouth of the great river was named Saint John. The new capital, approximately 100 km north of Saint John, received the name of Frederick's Town (the "k," "s," and "w" were dropped shortly thereafter), in honour of Frederick Augustus, Duke of York, the second son of George III.

Thomas Carleton selected Fredericton as the capital to promote inland settlement. Moreover, the upriver location had a military advantage, as Carleton could garrison his two regiments of British troops there, safe from a sudden coastal attack.

The possibility of an American attack was a real one, because the Americans claimed one-third of the province. The Treaty of Paris of 1783 established the St. Croix River as the boundary between Maine and New Brunswick. Unfortunately, identification of the St. Croix proved difficult, as three rivers flowed into Passamaquoddy Bay. The Americans pressed for the most easterly river as the boundary, while the British claimed the westerly river. Britain won its case by proving that Champlain and de Monts had wintered in 1604–05 on Dochet's Island at the mouth of the most westerly river, thus claiming it to be the true St. Croix. They confirmed the site by conducting excavations on the island and revealing the ruins of the buildings as described by Champlain in his journal. New Brunswick thus emerged in roughly the form its founders had envisioned.

BUILDING A LOYALIST PROVINCE

 The Loyalists gradually built a new society in the Saint John River valley. It was hard work even for the affluent, for New Brunswick had a severe shortage of labour. As the New Brunswick historian W.S. MacNutt wrote, "Judges of the Supreme Court and other Loyalist patricians took to the fields to raise the fruits and vegetables necessary to livelihood."[10] Slowly a series of largely self-sufficient agricultural communities developed on favourable coastal locations and in the lowland river valleys. The town of Saint John became the major urban centre, with a population of 3500 in 1785. The Acadians' settlements, formed originally by those who had fled to the Miramichi to escape deportation between 1755 and 1758, were located along the eastern and northern shores of New Brunswick. But, elsewhere the forests prevailed. Historical geographer Graeme Wynn notes that by 1800 the settlers had "done no more than trim part of the forest edge."[11]

Ironically, the First Nations, whose allegiance had been critical in retaining western Nova Scotia for the Crown, suffered the most. The Loyalists encroached on their hunting and fishing territories. They helped themselves to Mi'kmaq and Maliseet land, fish, game, and timber. The British confiscated portions of their territories as Crown land without financial compensation. As historian Leslie Upton points out, the Mi'kmaqs and Maliseets in 1782 "were no longer of account as allies, enemies, or people." The correspondence connected with the arrival of 35 000 immigrants contained "not one word about the Indians who would be dispossessed by the new settlers."[12] In the Great Lakes area the Royal Proclamation of 1763 protected First Nations land rights, but the British ruled that the Royal Proclamation did not apply in the Maritime colonies.

Chief Justice Ludlow's House on the River St. John, New Brunswick, by George Herriot.
"Spring Hill," the rural estate near Fredericton of the first chief justice of New
Brunswick, seems quite stately, but life, even for Loyalist patricians, was difficult because
of the labour shortage in the colony.

Royal Ontario Museum.

Britain assumed that the French had already dealt in the Maritime area with the issue of Native
title, but they had not.

THE LOYALISTS IN PRINCE EDWARD ISLAND

About 800 Loyalists travelled to Saint John's Island, soon to be renamed Prince Edward Island.
They formed about one-fifth of the population. In Nova Scotia and New Brunswick, the authorities eventually supplied the Loyalists with free land, government timber, and tools. On Prince
Edward Island, however, the hapless newcomers became tenant farmers on land granted to
absentee proprietors.

In 1767, the British government had divided the entire island into long belts of land,
stretching from north to south. It then proceeded to grant all 67 townships of roughly 8000 ha
each to favourites of the Crown. The new landlords had to pay a small annual fee, or quitrent,
for their land; they also had to promise to bring over settlers.

To attract Loyalists to their lands, the landowners promised them grants of land with secure
titles. But once the settlers had cleared their lands, erected buildings, and planted orchards, the
proprietors refused to grant land title to those who wanted to become landowners. Many settlers obtained no redress and left in disgust. Those who remained fought for 75 years for justice. Only in 1860 would a land commission recommend that free grants be made to those who
could prove that their ancestors had been attracted to the island by the original promises made

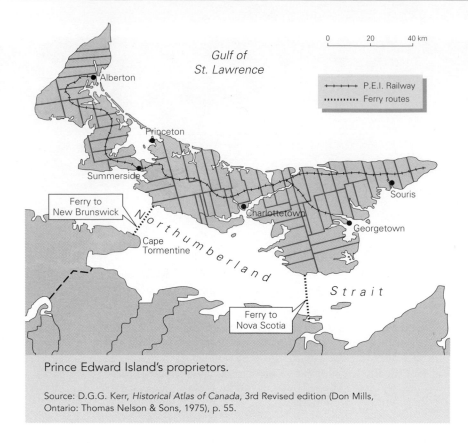

Prince Edward Island's proprietors.

Source: D.G.G. Kerr, *Historical Atlas of Canada*, 3rd Revised edition (Don Mills, Ontario: Thomas Nelson & Sons, 1975), p. 55.

to the Loyalists. A final attempt to resolve the land question was made in 1873, in conjunction with Prince Edward Island's entry into Confederation.

CAPE BRETON ISLAND

About a thousand Loyalists came to Cape Breton Island. David Mathews, a former mayor of New York, and Abraham Cuyler, a former mayor of Albany, New York, convinced the British government to make the island a separate colony, essentially to obtain for themselves coveted government jobs. Mathews became the new colony's attorney general, and Cuyler, its secretary and register. The new capital was named Sydney after the British colonial secretary. But the British government provided little financial support for the colony, which languished as a result, despite the fact that Sydney lay at the centre of the richest coal field in the Maritimes. London did not even establish an assembly for the island. In 1820 the colonial office, without any consultation with the inhabitants, decided to re-join Cape Breton to Nova Scotia.

The prosperity of the War of 1812 gave the island several good years economically. The major social and economic development, however, came with the arrival of Scottish immigrants from 1802 onward — Catholic Scots from the Hebrides, the coastal islands off the west coast of Scotland, many of whom spoke only Gaelic. The magnificent hills and seacoast reminded them of their homeland. They became fishers and farmers. By the mid-nineteenth century the Scots had become the dominant community on Cape Breton Island, outnumbering the Mi'kmaqs, Acadians, and Loyalist descendants combined. The Scots brought with them their passion for piping, fiddle music, singing Gaelic songs, and stepdancing, traditions that remain strong among their descendants on the island two centuries later.

THE MARITIME ECONOMY FROM THE REVOLUTIONARY WAR TO THE WAR OF 1812

For more than a century before the American Revolution, trade linked New England, Britain, and the West Indies. New England sold fish, lumber, and foodstuffs to the West Indies, which in turn supplied molasses to New England and sugar to Britain. The mother country provided New England with manufactured goods. The Maritime region stood decidedly on the periphery of this imperial trade: while it was of strategic importance on the Gulf of St. Lawrence, the Maritime region was not of economic importance, apart from its fish. After the United States gained independence, Britain looked to the Maritime colonies to replace New England in the triangular trade between itself and its Caribbean colonies. To this end, Britain closed its West Indian ports to American ships.

TRADE WITH THE WEST INDIES

Initially, the Maritime colonies lacked the resources and the economic infrastructure needed to supply the British West Indies. They could provide only a limited amount of the islands' needs in fish and lumber; they could not meet their demand for foodstuffs at all. Nova Scotia and New Brunswick themselves had to import American farm products. The Maritimes' expensive labour, its inadequate transportation system, and its land-granting system (which encouraged a general dispersal of the population) all contributed to the slow development of agriculture. Moreover, with cheap imported food from the United States, little incentive existed to begin full-time farming.

Direct trade between Nova Scotia and the British West Indies decreased still further in the 1790s, when Britain met the Caribbean planters' demands for cheap foodstuffs by allowing American shipping access to the West Indies.

THE IMPACT OF THE NAPOLEONIC WARS

Real economic growth in the Maritimes began only after the outbreak of war between Britain and France in 1793 and, particularly, after the rise of Napoleon in the late 1790s. The British government now spent lavishly on fortifications in Halifax, constructing public and military buildings. Halifax became the strongest fortress outside Europe and the main supply base for the British West Indies.

After the beginning of the Napoleonic Wars, a flourishing timber industry developed in British North America. Britain required a safe supply of masts and spars for building war ships, and it needed timber for construction. The imperial government gave tariff preferences for British American timber. This led to a lumber boom in New Brunswick, the Maritime colony with the greatest timber resources. The exports of fir and pine timber from New Brunswick increased twentyfold between 1805 and 1812. Wood products would dominate New Brunswick's export economy for the next half-century. Every winter, armies of lumberjacks cut down the trees and then, every spring, tied them into huge rafts and floated them down the Saint John, St. Croix, and Miramichi rivers. Heavily forested New Brunswick, being closer to Britain, was better situated than were the Canadas for this trade.

Inadvertently, the United States also promoted the prosperity of the Maritimes. After France and Britain imposed blockades on each other in 1806, President Thomas Jefferson, in retaliation against both countries' restrictions on neutral trade, prohibited all commerce out of American ports. The policy backfired, however, for by closing American ports in 1807, the president ruined New England's trade — and enriched that of the Maritimes.

Since Britain depended on American foodstuffs as much as the United States needed British manufactured goods, Anglo–American trade continued, but now through illegal channels. An

In a short, fierce battle off Boston harbour in 1813, the HMS *Shannon* captured the larger American frigate the *Chesapeake*. The arrival of the two vessels at Halifax was a highlight of the sea war. This print is by J.C. Schetky, from a design by R.H. King.

Collection of the Nova Scotia Archives and Records Management.

active smuggling trade developed, with cargoes being transferred at sea or carried overland across the British–American frontier. In defiance of their government, American ship captains sailed into British ports, making the Maritimes in 1808 into a great clearinghouse for international trade. The Maritime colonies now purchased American produce and goods and then re-exported these materials as if they were their own. Similarly, they sold British manufactured goods to the Americans. This thriving trade continued throughout the War of 1812.

The long-standing trade between the fish-exporting houses of Halifax and the British West Indies also expanded at the time of the American embargo acts. Britain encouraged this trade by paying bounties on fish exported from Nova Scotia and New Brunswick to the West Indies. It provided convoy protection, for after the British defeated the French navy at Trafalgar in 1805 the threat of a French naval invasion of Britain ended, and the admiralty could spare ships for convoy duty. The shipping of smuggled American flour, beef, and dry goods to the West Indies via the Maritime provinces began.

If the Anglo-American trade war benefited the Maritimes, the War of 1812 itself brought more economic blessings. Throughout the war, New England, in effect, was neutral. The legislatures of the New England states had openly condemned the war that had ruined their commerce. As Washington lacked the military capacity to impose its will on New England, its trade with Britain and its Maritime colonies continued, so much so that the Halifax newspaper, the *Acadian Recorder*, wrote on May 14, 1814: "Happy state of Nova Scotia! Amongst all this tumult we have lived in peace and security; invaded only by a numerous host of American doubloons and dollars, which have swept away the contents of our stores and shops like a torrent." Only naval activity on the high seas reminded Maritimers that they still lived in a war theatre. The occupation by the British in 1814 of part of the coast of present-day Maine allowed more opportunities for commerical profit.

THE EMERGENCE OF A DISTINCT IDENTITY

Within a generation, New England, the ancestral home of many of Nova Scotia's and New Brunswick's inhabitants, became a "foreign country." In the early 1780s, the bitterness on both sides remained strong. Gradually, though, as time erased memories of their struggles, the Loyalists accepted the newly independent United States. The Americans welcomed Loyalists back. A number of Loyalists returned to the United States in the late 1780s, particularly when Britain allowed half-pay officers to receive their pensions while living outside the empire. Cadwallader Colden, for example, the grandson of a royal lieutenant governor of New York, returned from self-imposed exile and was later elected mayor of New York City.

Gradually, the Loyalists and the New Englanders in the Maritimes lost many of their Yankee customs. One important cultural trait, though, did remain: their speech patterns. The New Englanders and the Loyalists spoke American English, which by the time of their arrival in the Maritimes in the mid- and late eighteenth century was noticeably different from British English.

The American Revolution had a profound influence on Nova Scotia. It forced the colony's inhabitants, many of whom were emigrants from New England, to choose sides: the insurgent Thirteen Colonies or the empire? Initially, like the Acadians before them, they attempted to remain neutral. Circumstances, however, shifted that neutrality toward a commitment to Britain.

At the end of the revolutionary war, tens of thousands of Loyalists came from the newly independent, former Thirteen Colonies to live in the Maritimes. They had a great impact. Their arrival led to the creation of two new colonies: New Brunswick and Cape Breton Island (a separate colony until 1820). Among the Loyalists were American colonists of many class, ethnic, racial, and religious backgrounds. This Loyalist legacy contributed to a deep affection for Great Britain in what became Maritime Canada. Loyalists also formed the backbone of the Maritime economy in the late eighteenth and early nineteenth centuries. Most significant of all, they contributed to a deep affection for Great Britain, which helped to ensure that the region remained loyal, and did not break away as the American colonies had.

NOTES

1. George A. Rawlyk, "The American Revolution and Nova Scotia Reconsidered," *Dalhousie Review* 43 (1963–64): 379.
2. John Bartlet Brebner, *The Neutral Yankees of Nova Scotia* (Toronto: McClelland & Stewart, 1969 [1937]), p. 285.
3. This thesis was first advanced by Gordon Stewart and George A. Rawlyk in *A People Highly Favoured of God* (Toronto: Macmillan, 1972); see especially pp. 3–4 and 43–44.
4. George A. Rawlyk, *Ravished by the Spirit: Religious Revivals, Baptists, and Henry Alline* (Montreal/Kingston: McGill-Queen's University Press, 1984), p. 13.
5. Paul H. Smith, "The American Loyalists: Notes on Their Organization and Numerical Strength," *William and Mary Quarterly*, 3rd series, 25 (1968): 269.
6. Wallace Brown and Hereward Senior, *Victorious in Defeat: The Loyalists in Canada* (Toronto: Methuen, 1984), p. 16.
7. Ann Gorman Condon, "1783–1800: Loyalist Arrival, Acadian Return, Imperial Reform," in Phillip A. Buckner and John G. Reid, eds., *The Atlantic Region to Confederation: A History* (Toronto: University of Toronto Press, 1994), p. 186.
8. The estimates of the Loyalists' numbers are taken from Brown and Senior, *Victorious in Defeat*.

9. Neil MacKinnon, *This Unfriendly Soil: The Loyalist Experience in Nova Scotia, 1783–1791* (Montreal/Kingston: McGill-Queen's University Press, 1986), p. 59.
10. W.S. MacNutt, *New Brunswick: A History, 1784–1867* (Toronto: Macmillan, 1963), p. 70.
11. Graeme Wynn, *Timber Colony* (Toronto: University of Toronto Press, 1981), p.18.
12. L.F.S. Upton, *Micmacs and Colonists: Indian–White Relations in the Maritimes, 1713–1867* (Vancouver: University of British Columbia Press, 1979), p. 78.

LINKING TO THE PAST   w(w)w

What Is a Loyalist?
http://www.uelac.org/whatis.html

Basic information about Loyalists as well as a summary of their immigration to the Maritime provinces and Quebec.

The American Revolution and the Fourteenth Colony
http://www.blupete.com/Hist/NovaScotiaBk2/Part2/Splash.htm

One account of why Nova Scotia did not support the American Revolution.

King's Landing Historical Settlement
http://www.kingslanding.nb.ca/home.html

Explore this Loyalist settlement in New Brunswick and look at reproductions of antiques from the period.

Black Loyalists
http://collections.ic.gc.ca/blackloyalists

An extensive, illustrated history of black Loyalists, from before the American Revolution to emigration to Sierra Leone. For information on one black settlement in Nova Scotia, Birchtown, visit http://museum.gov.ns.ca/arch/sites/birch.

From Slavery to Sierra Leone
http://collections.ic.gc.ca/port_royal/blkloyal.html

The story of a black Loyalist woman, from her escape from slavery and life in Nova Scotia to her decision to leave the continent.

History of Saint John, New Brunswick
http://www.city.saint-john.nb.ca/2.cfm?PageID=2-4-4

A look at the history of Canada's oldest incorporated city, from early exploration to the present.

RELATED READINGS

For articles of interest on this topic in R. Douglas Francis and Donald B. Smith, eds., *Readings in Canadian History: Pre-Confederation*, 6th ed. (Toronto: Nelson Thomson Learning, 2002), see George A. Rawlyk, "The American Revolution and Nova Scotia Reconsidered," pp. 179–190; and Ann Gorman Condon, "The Family in Exile: Loyalist Social Values after the Revolution," pp. 191–199.

BIBLIOGRAPHY

Valuable overviews of the Loyalists include Christopher Moore, *The Loyalists: Revolution, Exile, Settlement* (Toronto: Macmillan, 1984); and Wallace Brown and Hereward Senior, *Victorious in Defeat: The Loyalists in Canada* (Toronto: Methuen, 1984). The story of Polly Dribblee and her family is told in Wallace Brown, *The Good Americans: The Loyalists in the American Revolution* (New York: William Morrow, 1969). For an estimate of the number of Loyalists who came to Nova Scotia see William H. Nelson, *The American Tory* (Oxford: Clarendon Press, 1961); and Paul H. Smith, "The American Loyalists: Notes on Their Organization and Numerical Strength," *William and Mary Quarterly*, 3rd series, 25 (1968): 259–77.

For a general overview of Maritime history in this period see Phillip A. Buckner and John G. Reid, eds., *The Atlantic Region to Confederation: A History* (Toronto: University of Toronto Press, 1994), pp. 156–260; Margaret R. Conrad and James K. Hiller, *Atlantic Canada. A Region in the Making* (Toronto: Oxford University Press, 2001); and W.S. MacNutt's *The Atlantic Provinces, 1712–1857* (Toronto: McClelland & Stewart, 1965), pp. 76–102. Margaret Conrad has edited several collections of articles on the Planters, the New England settlers who moved to Nova Scotia in the 1760s: *They Planted Well: New England Planters in Maritime Canada* (Fredericton: Acadiensis Press, 1988); *Making Adjustments: Change and Continuity in Planter Nova Scotia, 1759–1800* (Fredericton: Acadiensis Press, 1991); and (with Barry Moody) *Planter Links: Community and Culture in Colonial Nova Scotia* (Fredericton: Acadiensis Press, 2001). In W. Brook Taylor, ed., *Canadian History: A Reader's Guide*, vol. 1, *Beginnings to Confederation* (Toronto: University of Toronto Press, 1994), consult the essays by Barry Moody, "Acadia and Old Nova Scotia to 1784," pp. 76–111; and Ian Ross Robertson, "The Maritime Colonies, 1784 to Confederation," pp. 237–79.

Nova Scotia's response to the American Revolution is reviewed by John Bartlet Brebner in *The Neutral Yankees of Nova Scotia* (Toronto: McClelland & Stewart, 1969 [1937]). George A. Rawlyk examines the question of Nova Scotia and the revolution in "Revolution Rejected: Why Did Nova Scotia Fail to Join the American Revolution?" in Paul W. Bennett and Cornelius J. Jaenen, eds., *Emerging Identities: Selected Problems and Interpretations in Canadian History* (Scarborough, ON: Prentice-Hall, 1986), pp. 133–57. Ernest Clarke reviews a specific incident in these troubled years, in *The Siege of Fort Cumberland 1776* (Montreal: McGill-Queen's University Press, 1995). For an overview of this period see J.M. Bumsted, "1763–1783: Resettlement and Rebellion," in P.A. Buckner and J.G. Reid, eds., *The Atlantic Region to Confederation*, pp. 156–83.

For an introduction to Henry Alline and his New Light movement see the booklet by D.G. Bell, *Henry Alline and Maritime Religion* (Ottawa: Canadian Historical Association, 1993). For fuller treatments consult: Gordon Stewart and George A. Rawlyk, *A People Highly Favoured of God: The Nova Scotia Yankees and the American Revolution* (Toronto: Macmillan, 1972); J.M. Bumsted, *Henry Alline* (Toronto: University of Toronto Press, 1971); and George A. Rawlyk, *Ravished by the Spirit: Religious Revivals, Baptists, and Henry Alline* (Montreal/Kingston: McGill Queen's University Press, 1984).

Two guides to the Loyalists and their influence on the development of the Maritimes are Robert S. Allen, *Loyalist Literature: An Annotated Bibliographic Guide* (Toronto: Dundurn Press, 1982); and J.M. Bumsted, *Understanding the Loyalists* (Sackville, NB: Centre for Canadian Studies, Mount Allison University, 1986). The impact of the Loyalists in New Brunswick is reviewed by Ann Gorman Condon in *The Envy of the American States: The Loyalist Dream for New Brunswick* (Fredericton: New Ireland Press, 1983). W. Stewart MacNutt surveys the same subject in the opening pages of *New Brunswick: A History, 1784–1867* (Toronto: Macmillan, 1963). In *Benedict Arnold: A Traitor in Our Midst* (Montreal/Kingston: McGill-Queen's University Press, 2001), Barry K. Wilson recounts the New Brunswick sojourn of America's most reviled traitor, Benedict Arnold, the American general who changed sides in the American Revolution. Neil MacKinnon examines the Loyalists' first decade in Nova Scotia in *This Unfriendly Soil: The Loyalist Experience in Nova Scotia, 1783–1791* (Montreal/Kingston: McGill-Queen's University Press, 1986). An older popular study, Thomas Raddall's *Halifax: Warden of the North*, rev. ed. (Toronto: McClelland & Stewart, 1971 [1948]), contains a lively review of the impact of the revolution and the Loyalists on Halifax. A more recent review of the city by three professional historians is Judith Fingard, Janet Guildford, and David Sutherland, *Halifax: The First 250 Years* (Halifax: Formac Publishing, 1999). Graeme Wynn, a historical geographer, looks at early New Brunswick in *Timber Colony* (Toronto: University of Toronto Press, 1981). J.M. Bumsted's *Land, Settlement, and Politics on Eighteenth-Century Prince Edward Island* (Montreal/Kingston: McGill-Queen's University Press, 1987) focusses on developments in Prince Edward Island. For a brief look at Cape Breton Island see Robert J. Morgan, "Cape Breton by Itself," *Horizon Canada* 100 (1987): 2390–95.

For information on the Native peoples of the Maritimes during the American Revolution see L.F.S. Upton, *Micmacs and Colonists: Indian–White Relations in the Maritimes, 1713–1867* (Vancouver: University of British Columbia Press, 1979); and Harald E.L. Prins, *The Mi'kmaq Resistance: Accommodation and Cultural Survival* (Fort Worth, TX: Harcourt Brace, 1996). In *We Were Not the Savages: A Micmac Perspective on the Collision of European and Aboriginal Civilizations* (Halifax: Nimbus, 1993), Daniel N. Paul provides a

Mi'kmaq perspective on Native–newcomer relations. William C. Wicken reviews early British treaties with the Mi'kmaq in *Mi'kmaq Treaties on Trial. History, Land and Donald Marshall Jr.* (Toronto: University of Toronto Press, 2002).

James W. St. G. Walker's *The Black Loyalists: The Search for a Promised Land in Nova Scotia and Sierra Leone, 1783–1870* (Toronto: University of Toronto Press, 1992 [1976]) is the most important secondary source on the experience of black Loyalists. Eleven portraits of Loyalists, including Phyllis R. Blakeley's "Boston King: A Black Loyalist," appear in Phyllis R. Blakeley and John N. Grant, eds., *Eleven Exiles: Accounts of Loyalists of the American Revolution* (Toronto: Dundurn Press, 1982).

Important maps of the Maritimes in the late eighteenth and early nineteenth centuries appear in the first two volumes of the *Historical Atlas of Canada*, vol. 1, R. Cole Harris, ed., *From the Beginning to 1800* (Toronto: University of Toronto Press, 1987); and vol. 2, R. Louis Gentilcore, ed., *The Land Transformed, 1800–1891* (Toronto: University of Toronto Press, 1993).

BRITAIN'S FIRST INLAND COLONY: UPPER CANADA, 1791–1815

TIME LINE

1781–1818	The Mississaugas surrender large tracts of land on the north shore of Lake Ontario and in the Niagara peninsula to the British
1784	Joseph Brant and the Six Nations (Iroquois) Loyalists settle on the Grand River in the western portion of the Province of Quebec
1791	The Constitutional Act of 1791 is followed by the division of the Province of Quebec into Upper and Lower Canada
1792	John Graves Simcoe arrives as the first lieutenant governor of Upper Canada
1793	Simcoe founds York (Toronto), which becomes Upper Canada's capital in 1796
1794	Signing of Jay's Treaty, which leads to the surrender of the western posts in 1796
1796	Opening of Yonge Street from York (Toronto) to the headwaters of Lake Simcoe
1803	Colonel Thomas Talbot begins the Talbot Settlement in the London District
1812–1814	The War of 1812
1812	General Brock is killed at the battle of Queenston Heights
1813	Tecumseh, the great First Nations leader, dies at the battle of Moraviantown
1814	The Battle of Lundy's Lane, the bloodiest encounter of the war, in which the Americans and the British each suffer 800 casualties
1815	Birth in Scotland of John A. Macdonald, Kingston's most famous elected representative and Canada's first prime minister after Confederation

In 1774, the Province of Quebec included the territory north of the Great Lakes and immediately south of the Canadian Shield. The only European settlement of any size was located on the outskirts of present-day Windsor, where French-Canadian farmers who supplied Fort Detroit, just across the river, had established farms. The remainder of the whole western portion of the Province of Quebec remained one continuous forest. As economic historians Kenneth Norrie and Douglas Owram point out, "In the normal course of events, it would have been another generation before significant European settlement intruded upon the area."[1]

The American Revolution, however, led directly to the creation of Britain's first inland colony in 1791. John Graves Simcoe, commander of the Queen's Rangers (a Loyalist corps) in the revolution became the first lieutenant governor of Upper Canada. He spent four years constructing the framework for a colony intended to be the ideal home for Loyalists. In the end, Americans in search of cheap land, not Loyalists, formed the majority of the settlers, outnumbering the Loyalists four to one at the beginning of the War of 1812. Could the northern colony resist American conquest? Many Upper Canadians asked themselves that question when war broke out between the British and the Americans in 1812.

THE ANISHINABEG

The Proclamation of 1763 had recognized the Great Lakes area as First Nations country; hence, the Native peoples had to surrender that land to the Crown before settlement could proceed. Until the early 1780s, three nations lived in what is now southern Ontario: the Ojibwas (Chippewas), the Ottawas (Odawas), and the Algonquins — the three Algonquian nations who called themselves the "Anishinabeg," meaning true human beings.

LAND PURCHASES MADE FOR LOYALIST SETTLEMENT, 1781–1784

Sir Frederick Haldimand, the governor of Quebec from 1778 to 1784, arranged for the purchase of the land from the Mississaugas, as the British called the Ojibwa along the north shore of Lake Ontario. The first settlement of Loyalist soldiers and refugees in the Niagara area began across the river from Fort Niagara, at what is now Niagara-on-the-Lake. In order to provide farms for these settlers, the British made their first treaty with the Mississaugas in 1781. They paid the Mississaugas "three hundred suits of clothing" for a strip of land 6.5 km wide on the west bank of the Niagara River.

Other Loyalists moved up the Hudson River valley to the St. Lawrence River, where Haldimand housed them in temporary camps, until he negotiated a treaty. In 1783, the Mississaugas surrendered all the land from roughly present-day Gananoque to the eastern end of the Bay of Quinte, extending back from Lake Ontario "as far as a man can travel in a day," in exchange for guns, powder, ammunition for the winter's hunt, clothing for all of their families, and "as much coarse red cloth as will make about a dozen coats and as many laced hats."

In 1784, the British purchased the Niagara peninsula and gave the Grand River valley to the Six Nations who had fought for Britain in the revolutionary war. The British believed that they had obtained title to the entire Niagara peninsula and the whole north shore of Lake Ontario, except for a large tract between the head of the lake (present-day Hamilton) and Toronto. The British regarded the transactions as simple real-estate deals — complete title to the surrendered area in exchange for trade goods, paid on a once-and-for-all-time basis.

Why did the Mississaugas accept these conditions? First, because they relied on the traders' European goods and on the gifts that the English had given them annually since the suppression of Pontiac's resistance. Second, it appears that they did not believe they were selling the land once and for all. The Native pattern of land ownership and use differed from

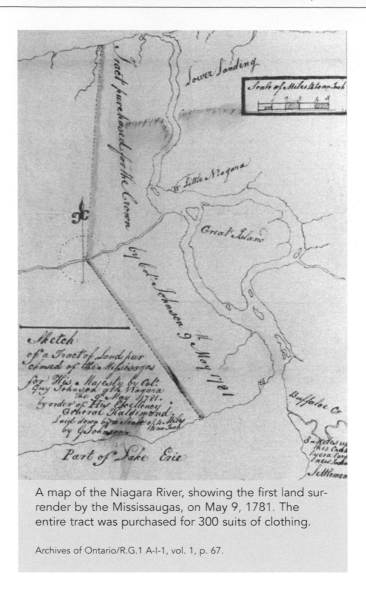

A map of the Niagara River, showing the first land surrender by the Mississaugas, on May 9, 1781. The entire tract was purchased for 300 suits of clothing.

Archives of Ontario/R.G.1 A-I-1, vol. 1, p. 67.

that of the British. Among the Great Lakes Algonquians, an individual family could use a recognized hunting ground, fishing place, or maple sugar bush, but as soon as the family ceased to go there, it reverted to the collective ownership of the entire band. Most likely, the Anishinabeg regarded the initial agreement as one with tenants for the use of the land as long as they practised good behaviour. Third, the Mississaugas had a small population of about 1000, divided into a dozen or more separate bands along the 500 km of lakefront. They could have resisted their British and Iroquois allies only with great difficulty. Thus, weakly organized, reliant on European trade goods, and believing that they would receive presents in perpetuity for the use of their land, the Mississaugas agreed to the proposals.

THE LOYALIST ARRIVAL IN 1784

The greatest number of Loyalist refugees arrived in 1784, the year after the peace treaty recognizing the Americans' independence was finalized. The Crown bore the costs of transporting them and provided them with free land, as well as food, clothing, tools, seed, and shelter. The

A Loyalist encampment at Johnstown (Cornwall) on the banks of the St. Lawrence River, June 6, 1784. Painted by James Peachy, a land surveyor working for the government.

National Archives of Canada/C-2001.

British allotted land according to status and rank. Each family head received 40 ha, with an additional 20 ha for each family member. Non-commissioned officers obtained 80 ha, field officers 400 ha, and captains 280 ha. Subalterns, staff, and warrant officers received 200 ha.

Loyalist settlements grew up throughout the province. In 1784, about 4000 Loyalists settled in the townships along the St. Lawrence–Bay of Quinte area. They gradually transformed the forest into orderly farms and settled communities. A large number of them were native-born Americans of German ancestry, and others were German regular soldiers who had fought as mercenaries for Britain.

Next in size to the St. Lawrence–Bay of Quinte settlements was the Niagara settlement, a haven for the first refugees from the frontier districts of Pennsylvania and New York. A relatively small number of Loyalists also settled on the northwestern shore of Lake Erie and in the towns of Sandwich (within the present-day boundaries of Windsor) and Amherstburg. In 1796, when Detroit passed into American hands, the population of these two towns greatly increased. Many of Detroit's French-Canadian citizens, wishing to retain their British allegiance, crossed to the Canadian side.

Some Loyalists settled in the lower Thames River valley (below present-day Chatham) once the Crown purchased the land from the Anishinabeg in 1790. The Long Point peninsula of Lake Erie became the last major centre of Loyalist settlement, the majority of its inhabitants having originally settled elsewhere.

IROQUOIS LOYALISTS

Approximately 2000 Iroquois Loyalists came to Upper Canada, leaving behind an equal number of their people. Of those that came, the majority were Mohawks, Cayugas, and Onondagas. Brant chose the location because of its proximity to their allies, the Senecas, most of whom decided to remain in western New York. A group of about 100 Mohawks antagonistic to Brant followed Chief John Deseronto and settled on a tract on the Bay of Quinte.

Anxious to retain Iroquois support in the event of another war with the Americans, the British provided the Six Nations on the Grand River with a church, a school, a sawmill, a gristmill, an allowance for a schoolmaster, and £1500 as general compensation for their war losses.

A Historical Portrait 🖋

☞ David Ramsay

In the 1790s David Ramsay, fur trader, revolutionary war soldier, guide — and Indian-killer — was one of the best-known individuals in Upper Canada. The colonial administrators and the Loyalist settlers respected him. In contrast, Joseph Brant, the Mohawk leader, regarded him as an "unworthy rascal." A number of the Mississaugas tolerated him — although he once killed and scalped eight Anishinabeg, including a woman and two children — because he provided a link with the dominant settler society. That the Mississaugas had to rely on this dangerous, unstable man, simply because he knew their language, shows their isolation from the British officials, and from the incoming settlers.

What little is known about Ramsay's early life comes from a land petition that he submitted to Governor Simcoe and from notes made by a British traveller, Captain Patrick Campbell, whom Ramsay guided in 1792 from Niagara to New York. Taking great interest in his fellow Scot's adventures, Captain Campbell stayed up with him one whole night to record his story, which he accepted completely because, as he wrote in his *Travels in North America*, "His honesty and fidelity is so well known, that he is entrusted with sums of money to any amount without requiring any token or receipt for the same." Ramsay claimed that he came from the town of Leven, Fifeshire, Scotland. As a young man he joined the crew of the British warship *Prince of Orange*, serving in the sieges of Louisbourg in 1758 and Quebec in 1759. After the Seven Years' War, he entered the Great Lakes fur trade, operating out of Schenectady, New York.

He spent the winter of 1771–72 on the north shore of Lake Erie with his 17-year-old brother, who had just arrived from Scotland. Ramsay alleged that he had been forced, in self-defence, to kill several Native people who, in a drunken state, attacked them. Sir William Johnson, the Indian Superintendent for the northern colonies had a different account. Johnson argued that Ramsay deserved "Capital punishment." He dismissed Ramsay's argument of self-defence because, "the Indians, whenever they meditate mischief, carefully avoid Liquor." But Johnson also realized that a jury would acquit him. As he wrote to an Indian Department assistant: "I don't think he will Suffer, had he killed a Hundred." Johnson was correct. In September 1773, a Montreal jury released Ramsay for "want of Evidence." Ramsay's brother, the only eyewitness of the killings present at the trial, supported his brother's story of self-defence. No Mississaugas were present.

The details of Ramsay's life confirm that he might have been a psychopath. After his military service with the Royal Navy on the Atlantic coast during the American Revolution, he went back to live among the First Nations people whose relatives he had killed a decade earlier. He learned to dress like them, to live like them, and to speak their language. Why he did so remains a mystery, especially as his dislike of them in no way appears to have diminished. He told Campbell, for example, in describing the killings of 1771–72: "After killing the first Indians, I cut lead, and chewed above thirty balls, and above three pound of Goose shot, for I thought it a pity to shoot an Indian with a smooth ball." Although in the late 1780s and early 1790s he received death threats from some Mississaugas, he remained among them.

Why did the Mississaugas tolerate him? First, probably because Ramsay followed their custom. He "covered the graves" of the murdered, paying a certain number of gifts to the relatives of those that he had killed. Secondly, and more important, a number of Mississaugas saw him as a valuable ally, perhaps their only ally. This "eccentric white man," as the Mississauga Methodist minister Peter Jones later described him, forwarded their grievances to the government. In a petition sent in their name to Governor Simcoe in the winter of 1793, for instance, Ramsay outlined the set-tlers' encroachments on their hunting territories and fishing grounds.

David Ramsay claimed that the Mississaugas in 1789 gave him a large tract of land at the mouth of the Twelve Mile (Bronte) Creek, between present-day Hamilton and Toronto as a gift. He stated that he and his heirs would allow the Mississaugas to use the land, to hunt and fish, and to plant orchards there, "forever as they now are or until they are half white. (But no black mixture allowed to inherit the above land)." The government never recognized the gift, but it did give Ramsay two substantial land grants elsewhere in Upper Canada, that were together roughly 500 ha in size. Ramsay died in New York City in 1810.

The Mohawks on the Bay of Quinte also obtained a school, a schoolmaster, and a church. In keeping with Indian Department policy, all the First Nations received annual presents and, like the other Loyalists, clothing, tools, and provisions.

LOYALIST SETTLEMENTS

Historian Bruce Wilson estimates that, in 1785, approximately 7500 Loyalists (5500 non-Native and 2000 Native) lived in the region extending west from Montreal into present-day Ontario. By 1791, the number had risen to perhaps 30 000. New settlements had been established throughout the area extending north from the St. Lawrence up the Ottawa River to the Rideau River. They were spread over 15 km around the Bay of Quinte and formed a narrow strip along the Lake Ontario shore from the Bay of Quinte to York, where farms extended 25 km up Yonge Street.

Settlers, mostly from rural New York and Pennsylvania, now occupied the narrow strip of good land below the escarpment around the Niagara peninsula and part way up the Lake Erie shoreline. From the concessions along the front of the Detroit River, settlement began to move along the south shore of Lake St. Clair, and into the lower Thames River valley.

THE LIFE OF THE LOYALISTS

The early Upper Canadian Loyalists came from many ethnic backgrounds, but most came from the same economic and social level — a humble one. Not until the wave of immigration from New Brunswick in the 1790s did Upper Canada receive what might be termed a Loyalist elite, composed of families such as the Robinsons, the Jarvises, and the Ryersons.

The early Loyalists lived in military tents until they built their first homes, usually very modest dwellings. They preferred sites by the lakes and rivers, the principal means of communication and

The oldest house of worship in Ontario is the Mohawk church built on the Six Nations territory on the Grand River in 1785. The building received a royal dedication in 1906 and is now known as "Her Majesty's Chapel of the Mohawks." Eliza Field Jones completed this sketch in the mid-nineteenth century. It appears in *History of the Ojebway Indians* (London: A.W. Bennett, 1861), a book written by her husband, the Rev. Peter Jones (Kahkewaquonaby), a Mississauga chief and Methodist missionary.

travel before roads. Native trails, although narrow (seldom exceeding 50 cm in width), were important for travelling in the immediate area.

To support themselves in the first year or so, Loyalist settlers relied heavily on the First Nations for food. On the open meadows, "Indian corn," or maize, became the most important first crop. Once the settlers cleared additional land, they planted wheat. Indeed, the destruction of the forest became an obsession for the settlers. Historical geographers R. Cole Harris and John Warkentin noted that "as a whole they were little interested in conservation or the long-term management of land and sought to maximize short-term profits."[2]

The average Loyalist home was a log cabin, with one or two rooms. These cabins had no cellar or foundation, an earthen floor, and roofs made of bark or small hollowed basswood logs that overlapped like tiles. They measured on average no more than 4 m by 5 m. Oil paper, not glass, usually covered the windows. Since bricks were not available, the chimneys were built of sticks and clay or rough, unmortared stones. Sometimes the houses lacked chimneys, and the smoke found its way out through a hole in the bark roof. Clay and moss filled the chinks between the logs. Occasionally furniture or family heirlooms survived the journey to Upper Canada, but most furniture was handmade. The settlers cooked on an open fireplace. In summer, flies and mosquitoes entered the houses. Field mice and rats (introduced from Europe) infested the towns.

Generally the settlers preferred the winter cold to the summer heat and fevers. They found the Upper Canadian winters only a little longer and colder than the winters most of them had known in New York and Pennsylvania.

The Loyalist settlers had one major complaint: Quebec's seigneurial land system. They wanted it changed immediately. The authorities obliged and illegally instituted a system of freehold tenure. The settlers could exchange land, by selling and purchasing it, well before the Constitutional Act of 1791 abolished the seigneurial system in the province it created: Upper Canada.

On a Bush Farm near Chatham, Upper Canada, 1838, by Philip John Bainbrigge.
Side by side, pioneer men and women shared in clearing the land, constructing log
houses, and planting, tending, and harvesting the crops.

National Archives of Canada/C-11811.

THE CONSTITUTIONAL ACT OF 1791

The Constitutional Act of 1791 brought the colony of Upper Canada into existence. It provided
for freehold tenure and free land. (Settlers paid only the fees for issuing and recording land
titles.) The legislation also set aside the equivalent of one-seventh of all lands granted in the
future for "the Support and Maintenance of a Protestant Clergy." Unfortunately, the act failed to
make explicit just what constituted the "Protestant Clergy" — the Church of England only, or
the Church of Scotland and other Protestant denominations as well? This caused confusion and
controversy. Initially, for instance, the provincial government interpreted the phrase to refer only
to the Church of England. In addition, the British government set aside another seventh of all
lands as Crown reserves; the revenues from the sale or rental of these lands were to be used to
fund the colonial government.

A "TRULY BRITISH" COLONY

John Graves Simcoe, an energetic and enthusiastic military officer in the revolutionary war, then
in his late thirties, became Upper Canada's first lieutenant governor. He wanted to make Upper
Canada a centre of British power in North America. To him, "democracy" and "republicanism"
were wicked words. Believing that many in the new republic to the south remained actively loyal
to England, he attempted to win Americans back to their old allegiance. He was convinced that
a new colony with "a free, honourable British Government" would remind Americans of what
they had lost in leaving the empire and of the benefits of returning to it. Free grants of land, he
reasoned, would also attract them.

Simcoe's choice of place names indicates his dream of transforming Upper Canada into a "little England." In 1793 he travelled through the colony, liberally choosing new designations. He went as far west as Detroit, confirming en route his choice of a site for the future capital at the place the Anishinabeg called "Ko-te-quo-gong" (At the Forks), at the headwaters of the Ashkahnesbe (Horn or Antler) River. Kotequogong became London. The river that the Anishinabeg had named Ashkahnesbe because its branches reminded them of a deer's antlers became the Thames. The governor selected the title of York from the Duke of York (the same Frederick Augustus, second and favourite son of King George III, whom New Brunswick had honoured in naming their capital Fredericton) to replace the Iroquoian word "Toronto." He named the river east of York the Don, and that to the west the Humber, after rivers in north-eastern England, a region that also furnished the name for the bluffs east of the townsite — Scarborough. To the north of York, he christened the large body of water the Anishinabeg called "Wah-we-ya-gahmah" (Round Lake) Lake Simcoe, after his father. When asked what he thought of the governor's contribution to the colony, Joseph Brant replied, "General Simcoe has done a great deal for this province; he has changed the name of every place in it."

The governor wanted to create a hierarchical society like that which existed in England. He firmly believed in the established Church of England. In his model British colony, the Anglican church alone would enjoy the right of performing marriages. Reluctantly Simcoe agreed that justices of the peace in remote areas might conduct marriage ceremonies, provided they followed the Anglican ritual. Only in 1798 was the right to solemnize marriages extended to Lutheran, Calvinist, and Church of Scotland ministers. Methodists remained excluded until 1831. The Upper Canadian administration regarded the Methodists, who had strong links until 1828 with their American parent church, as a dangerous American denomination.

ESTABLISHING A MILITARY PRESENCE

Simcoe placed the new colony on a firm military footing. War with the Americans threatened to break out in the early 1780s over the British-held "western posts" of Oswego, Niagara, Detroit, and Michilimackinac. By the peace treaty of 1783, Britain and the United States agreed to an international boundary that ran through the upper St. Lawrence and the Great Lakes to the lands claimed by Spain in the Mississippi and Missouri river basins. By the same treaty, the Americans promised to allow the Loyalists to return to their homes and collect their legitimate debts, but they failed to honour that promise.

Seizing upon this violation, Britain initially refused to vacate the "western posts." The British government allowed Simcoe to raise an infantry corps of 425 officers and men, the Queen's Rangers (the name of his old Loyalist regiment in the revolution) to protect Upper Canada. The Upper Canada Legislative Assembly subsequently passed a militia bill in 1793 requiring all able-bodied men from 16 to 50 years of age to enrol in and to drill for their local companies two to four times a year. By 1794, more than 5000 officers and men served in the militia. Only in that year did Britain agree to sign Jay's Treaty, which led to its withdrawal from the western posts by June 1, 1796.

LEGISLATING A COLONY INTO EXISTENCE

Initially Simcoe established his headquarters at Newark (now Niagara-on-the-Lake), only later changing it to York (Toronto). Then he called for elections to the Legislative Assembly. Very much the English squire, he complained about the social background of the elected members, once describing them as "of a Lower Order, who kept but one Table, that is, who dined in Common with their Servants."

York on Lake Ontario, Upper Canada, 1804, by Elisabeth Francis Hale (1774–1826). This watercolour shows the tiny capital of Upper Canada (population 435) hemmed in by the surrounding forest. Today's Front Street was then at the water's edge.

National Archives of Canada/C-40137.

The legislature created a judicial system. William Osgoode, a well-regarded English lawyer, became chief justice, with responsibility for the Court of King's Bench, the new superior court of civil and criminal jurisdiction. Within each district Simcoe created surrogate courts and a provincial court of probate. At a lower level, meetings for the courts of quarter sessions were organized. The justices of the peace presided over these and performed as well a wide range of administrative and judicial duties. At the township level the justices of the peace enjoyed considerable power, hearing court cases, supervising road and bridge construction contracts, and issuing various licences, including one for taverns. Township officials in Upper Canada were appointed, not elected as they were in New England.

THE SLAVERY QUESTION

While the majority of African-American Loyalists and slaves went to Nova Scotia after the revolution, some slaves, perhaps as many as 500, were brought to Upper Canada. Joseph Brant, the Iroquois war chief, for example, had several slaves, as did John Stuart, the first Anglican missionary at Kingston. Slavery, however, did not prosper in a northern area such as Upper Canada. The short Canadian growing season ruled out such crops as cotton, which required a cheap, plentiful labour force. Furthermore, owners had to feed, clothe, and house slaves throughout a long and unproductive winter. Finally, many Upper Canadians, including Simcoe, found slavery abhorrent.

Under the governor's direction, the Assembly adopted a bill that gradually abolished slavery in the province. Slaves already in Upper Canada had to remain slaves until death, but all children born after the act's passage would become free at the age of 25. Furthermore, no additional slaves could be brought to Upper Canada. After 1793, slavery steadily declined in the colony.

LAND GRANTS

Simcoe hoped to cultivate an aristocratic class in Upper Canada. He believed that he could legislate such an elite into existence through generous land grants. Members of the Executive and Legislative Councils received large grants of 1200–2000 ha, equivalent to those given the highest-ranked military officers. Their children could obtain 480 ha. But the plan rebounded. Few recipients had any intention of becoming country squires, preferring instead, as soon as they could, to sell their estates profitably. These grants locked up much valuable land and, to the resentment of many ordinary settlers, kept it out of their hands.

Upper Canada really had two systems of land tenure. The first applied to the "official" settlers, who obtained land on account of their past service to the Crown or because of their social position. The second consisted of immigrants obtaining grants of 80 ha of land on the promise to develop it. Once these individuals built their homes and fenced and cleared the road allowance, they gained title. This system involved mostly the "late Loyalists."

Simcoe's land policies continued after his departure from the colony in 1796. Most of the "late Loyalists" came, despite their name, not for political reasons, but rather for free land. Since the colony lay directly on the advancing American settlement frontier, it received settlers en route from New York to the Ohio and Mississippi valleys, who did not necessarily intend to stay in Upper Canada. Most of these Americans had little interest in Simcoe's plan for an elite British colony; indeed, in future years hostilities would arise in the colony between the "official" and the "immigrant" settlers.

COMMUNICATIONS

Simcoe contributed to the establishment of a road system in the colony. In 1793 he began a military road from Burlington Bay to the Thames River, which he named Dundas Street after Henry Dundas, then the secretary of state in the English cabinet. Simcoe believed that a second military road should be built from York to Lake Simcoe, to ensure rapid communication with the upper lakes. The Governor called this road, which he began in 1796, Yonge Street after Sir George Yonge, the British secretary of war.

Yonge and Dundas streets became the colony's principal pathways. Both roads allowed settlers to begin farms inland, away from the "front," at a time when most people clung tenaciously to the navigable waterways.

SIMCOE'S LEGACY

Simcoe left Upper Canada in mid-1796. While serving as governor, he had experienced many disappointments. While he may have considered the colony as something approaching the centre of the universe, the British government did not. It turned down his expensive schemes to build up Upper Canada economically and militarily. His proposal to create a provincial university also received little support, as did his attempt to establish the Church of England in the colony under a bishop's tutelage. In addition, he failed in his attempt to promote a hierarchical society in Upper Canada. Nevertheless, he did succeed in establishing a community. As historian Gerald Craig wrote, "Simcoe had helped to nurse a new province into being, but its inhabitants, busy with their own projects and their own local affairs, showed only a tepid interest in the goals he had set for them."[3]

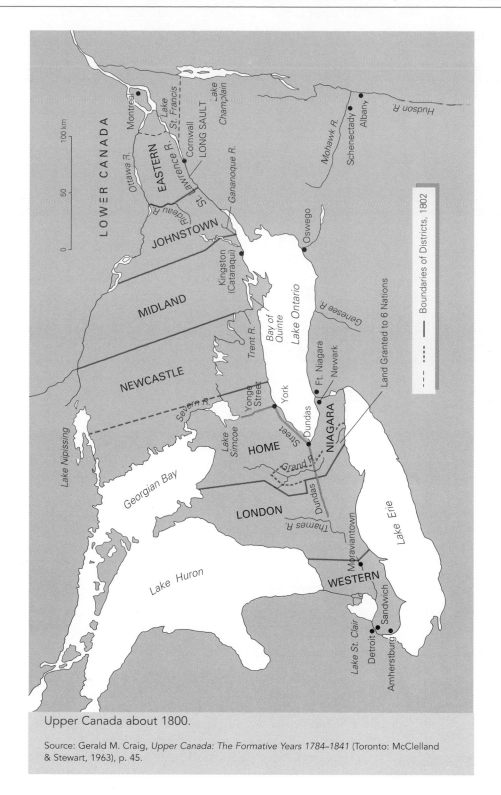

Upper Canada about 1800.

Source: Gerald M. Craig, *Upper Canada: The Formative Years 1784–1841* (Toronto: McClelland & Stewart, 1963), p. 45.

LOYALIST WOMEN IN EARLY UPPER CANADA

Mrs. Simcoe in Welsh dress, the only representation that survives of Elizabeth Simcoe, the wife of Upper Canada's first governor, John Graves Simcoe.

National Archives of Canada/C-81931.

Thanks largely to her diary and her drawings and sketches, Elizabeth Simcoe, the well-educated wife of Upper Canada's first governor, is remembered by historians. On the other hand, they have tended to ignore her female Loyalist contemporaries. Yet these women made important contributions. During the American Revolution, they had displayed exceptional courage. They took charge of their families and farms during their husbands' absences. Many had been harassed or persecuted. The insurgents had stolen their property and seized their homes, and in some cases jailed them. They had travelled, in many cases, with very young children through difficult wilderness to British refugee camps. Even here their struggles did not end. As historian Janice Potter writes, once behind British lines, "They had to fit once again into a patriarchal power structure in which their inferiority and dependence were assumed."[4] Men remained the decision-makers, the women and children being expected to follow their directions. A married woman had no legal identity separate from that of her husband. Some Loyalist women did submit claims for compensation to Britain after the war. Without fail, however, the all-male adjudicators of Loyalist claims awarded much more, proportionally, to men than to women.

    Few accounts mention Molly Brant, the Loyalist woman whose intervention helped prevent the Americans from gaining control of the entire Great Lakes area during the revolution, although the exploits of her brother Joseph Brant are well remembered. Molly Brant lived in Kingston from 1783 to her death in 1796. As a clan mother, she wielded considerable influence among the Six Nations, and she used that influence to keep her people loyal to the British Crown. As an Indian Department official put it, "One word from her goes farther with [the Mohawks] than a thousand from any white Man without Exception."

THE FIRST NATIONS: A DISPLACED PEOPLE

By 1796, the Native peoples understood that the land treaties meant the denial of a right of way across cleared fields, and if they camped on the settlers' lands, the farmers shot their dogs. The elders told the young people, such as Kahkewaquonaby (Sacred Feathers, known in English as Peter Jones), that when the British first came, they "asked for a small piece of land on which they might pitch their tents; the request was cheerfully granted. By and by they begged for more, and more was given them. In this way they have continued to ask, or have obtained by force or fraud, the fairest portions of our territory." Between 1805 and 1818, the Crown successfully pressured the Mississaugas to sell their last remaining tract, between Toronto and the head of the lake (present-day Hamilton). In two separate agreements, the British acquired the desired land.

    Other tragedies followed for the First Nations. Between the 1790s and the 1820s, smallpox, tuberculosis, and measles killed almost two-thirds of the Mississaugas at the western end of the lake. The band's population in that area dropped to 200 in the 1820s, down from more than 500 a generation earlier. The Iroquois also experienced difficult times in the 1790s and 1800s, as land sales eliminated much of their reserve on the Grand River. Chief Joseph Brant had welcomed settlers to the Grand River to teach European agricultural techniques. Not all his followers agreed. Many objected to the presence of the outsiders who, by 1798, controlled two-thirds of the Six Nations' original grant on the Grand River.

THE GROWTH OF SETTLEMENT

Upper Canada's non-Native population increased dramatically at the turn of the century. Many were "late Loyalists" in search of cheap land. By 1812, settlers lived on all the vacant townships along the north shore of Lake Ontario and on several townships on Lake Erie as well. Although few roads existed, the waterways allowed for the dispersal of settlement along an 800 km front in a period of less than 20 years.

THE PLAIN FOLK

Among the immigrants to Upper Canada were members of religious sects commonly called the "Plain Folk," because they believed in a pure religion and plain dress. They included Quakers, Mennonites, and Dunkards (a small group of Baptists who practised adult baptism by "dunking" the individual in water). Most of the Quakers originated in England, while the other sects came from Germany. But those that immigrated to Upper Canada came via the United States, mostly from Pennsylvania and New York. Many trekked north using heavy, broad-wheeled Conestoga wagons. They were pacifists who had remained neutral during the American Revolution. They also opposed taking oaths of allegiance to earthly rulers, believing that their allegiance was only to God. The prospect of good land, the hope for stability, and the promise of religious tolerance attracted them to Upper Canada.

The largest number of Plain Folk settled in the Niagara peninsula because of the easy access it afforded to the Quaker, Mennonite, and Dunkard settlements in Pennsylvania. The Bay of Quinte became another favourite area for religious minorities, as did Yonge Street, particularly in Markham and Vaughan townships. A sizeable number of Mennonites from Pennsylvania came later, and settled in Waterloo County. This community has remained the only locality in Ontario to retain the ethnic character of its early German-speaking settlers. The additional migration of the Amish directly from Germany in 1824 greatly strengthened the German character of the Waterloo area, as did the later arrival from Europe of German Lutherans and Roman Catholics.

The Plain Folk made ideal farmers. Historian G. Elmore Reaman has noted their three great strengths: "They were physically equipped both in knowledge of what to do in the wilderness and the strength to do it; they came with money and equipment; and they aided one another, whether Quaker, Huguenot, Lutheran, or Mennonite."[5]

On the eve of the War of 1812, the population of Upper Canada reached 75 000. Scattered along the St. Lawrence River and Lakes Ontario, Erie, and St. Clair, the settled areas rarely extended more than a few kilometres into the interior. The work of establishing farms and clearing new land took much of the settlers' time. The newcomers from the United States outnumbered the Loyalists and the British immigrants four to one. Like the Acadians of Nova Scotia a century earlier, these Americans lived in a British colony without really belonging to it. The War of 1812 would lead to enormous pressures on them to choose sides.

UPPER CANADA AND THE UNITED STATES, 1791–1812

As long as Britain retained the western posts, war with the United States appeared inevitable. Simcoe, in fact, had hoped that the First Nations south of the Great Lakes would defeat the

Old Fort Erie with the Migrations of the Wild-Pigeon in Spring, April 12, 1804, by Edward Walsh (1766–1832). In her diary entry for November 1, 1793, Elizabeth Simcoe commented that passenger pigeons were so numerous in Upper Canada in the spring and autumn that, at times, they darkened the entire sky. The pioneers put a stop to that. On both sides of the border, settlers trapped, clubbed, and shot the pigeons by the millions. The last recorded sighting of passenger pigeons in Ontario was in 1902. The last passenger pigeon in North America died in 1914 in a zoo in Cincinnati, Ohio.

Courtesy of Royal Ontario Museum, Toronto/952.218. © ROM.

Americans. For a short while, it appeared that they might. In 1791, the First Nations of the Ohio valley routed an American invasion army under General Arthur St. Clair, inflicting over 900 casualties. Canadian historian Olive Dickason has written of the battle, "As an Amerindian victory, it ranked second to that over Braddock in 1755; it was the worst defeat ever for Americans by Amerindians."[6] The Americans had to send another large military expedition to subdue them. In August 1794, General "Mad" Anthony Wayne defeated the Ohio First Nations at the Battle of Fallen Timbers, putting an end to Simcoe's dream of a Native buffer state.

International developments also contributed to Britain's decision to surrender the western posts. As a result of war with France, Britain needed to ease tensions with the United States. In 1794 the two countries signed Jay's Treaty, named for John Jay, the American chief justice who negotiated the agreement with the British. By its terms, Britain agreed to evacuate the forts on the south shores of the Great Lakes in 1796. With Britain's imminent withdrawal, the First Nations made peace with the Americans. In the Treaty of Greenville in 1795, they ceded their claims to most of the present-day state of Ohio. But Native resistance to the Americans' westward march continued.

CAUSES OF THE WAR OF 1812

In the first decade of the nineteenth century, Tecumseh, a Shawnee chief, and his brother, a religious leader, assembled a formidable Native confederacy. In 1811, Tecumseh was at open war with the Americans. Many Ohioans, Tennesseeans, and Kentuckians suspected — incorrectly — that the British continued to encourage and finance the First Nations raids. Many aggressive and intensely patriotic Americans judged it time to attack the British in the Canadas. At the same time, American "war hawks," anxious to begin a war with Britain, argued that the United States could use the opportunity to seize Upper Canada.

Two direct provocations by Britain led many Americans, including President James Madison, to support the pro-war group. In 1812, Napoleon's continental system closed all of western Europe, except Portugal, to British goods. Britain retaliated by imposing a naval blockade on France, preventing all ships, including American vessels, from trading with France. Officially neutral in the struggle, the Americans called for freedom of the seas. What right had England to board American ships on the high seas and prevent them from trading with countries on the continent? Madison considered this act the first provocation.

Without regard for neutral rights, British cruisers stopped and searched American ships on the North Atlantic. The British looked for British deserters who had gone over to American vessels to obtain higher wages, better food, and better working conditions. The Royal Navy seized thousands of sailors, alleging that they were British deserters. If a man produced his easily obtained certificate of American naturalization, the English ignored it, as their government did not recognize the right of a British subject to transfer allegiance to another country. "Free Trade and Sailors' Rights" became the cry of many Americans.

Forced, as he put it, to choose between war and degradation, Madison sent a message of war to Congress on June 1, 1812. Congress agreed and declared war against Britain.

The Odawa chief, Jean-Baptiste Assiginack, made this canoe model between 1814 and 1827 to represent his canoe and the Odawa warriors he led in the War of 1812.

© Canadian Museum of Civilization, artist Jean-Baptiste Assiginack, catalogue no. III-M-10a-n, image no. 589-1735.

THE WAR OF 1812

Throughout the first year of the war, the Americans believed that Upper Canada's American population would welcome them as liberators. Had not the majority of Upper Canada's population only recently arrived from the United States? Thomas Jefferson assured Americans that the conquest of Upper Canada would be a "mere matter of marching." This proved not to be the case at all.

Major General Isaac Brock, who had fought in the French wars in Europe and had then been stationed in North America, deserves much of the credit for Upper Canada's success in 1812. Before the war, Brock had built up the province's fortifications, trained the provincial militia, and maintained good relations with the Native peoples. As soon as war broke out, he took the offensive.

The First Nations' military contribution helps to explain Brock's success. For the Great Lakes First Nations, war did not break out in 1812; they had fought American frontiersmen for generations. Welcoming the outbreak of the second Anglo–American War in 1812, Tecumseh and hundreds of warriors joined the British in Upper Canada. At the outset, they assisted a small British force to take Michilimackinac, the leading fur-trading post in the Upper Great Lakes. Then they helped to cut the Americans' communication lines to Detroit, effectively winning that fort for the British. The fall of Detroit led to the embarrassing loss of all American territory west of Lake Erie.

Brock's unexpected victory at Detroit in August restored confidence among the loyal population that Upper Canada could be defended. He proved it again in October at Queenston Heights, but this time at the cost of his life: he was hit as he led a charge up the face of the heights. The attack, however, succeeded when 500 Iroquois joined 1000 British regulars and 600 Upper Canadian militia in retaking the strategic heights. Among the militia units was "Captain Robert Runchey's Company of Blacks," a force of former American slaves. The British victors captured 900 American prisoners. Having lost one army at Detroit, the Americans lost another on the Niagara frontier.

After the war, it was incorrectly believed that the civilian soldiers had won the contests at Detroit and Queenston Heights in 1812. In reality, regular soldiers constituted the first line of Britain's defence of Upper Canada, supplying the leadership and doing most of the fighting. Throughout the war, in fact, the Upper Canadian militia proved unreliable. Zeal for the fight always declined at harvest time or whenever news arrived of danger to the men's families from raiding parties. As historian George Sheppard has written: "Most Upper Canadian males, although obligated to fight, did not do so."[7]

THE CAMPAIGNS OF 1813 AND 1814

The Upper Canadians' worst moment in the war came in the spring and summer of 1813, when the gains of 1812 were reversed. The Americans twice briefly occupied York and launched a second invasion of the Niagara peninsula, forcing the British to withdraw to Burlington Heights at the head of the lake (present-day Hamilton). Desertions from the militia grew, and even two members of the Upper Canada Legislative Assembly joined the Americans. Only a surprise attack by British regular troops at Stoney Creek, immediately south of Burlington Heights, dislodged the Americans and saved Upper Canada. A second battle followed at Beaver Dams, where Iroquois from the Montreal area and from the Six Nations territory at the Grand River ambushed the Americans. The attackers benefited from vital information about the location of the American troops received from Laura Secord, a 37-year-old settler, who overheard American officers discussing their invasion plans. Slipping through the American cordon, she took a roundabout route to the British–First Nations camp with this information. Shortly after the Iroquois victory at Beaver Dams, the American invaders withdrew from the peninsula.

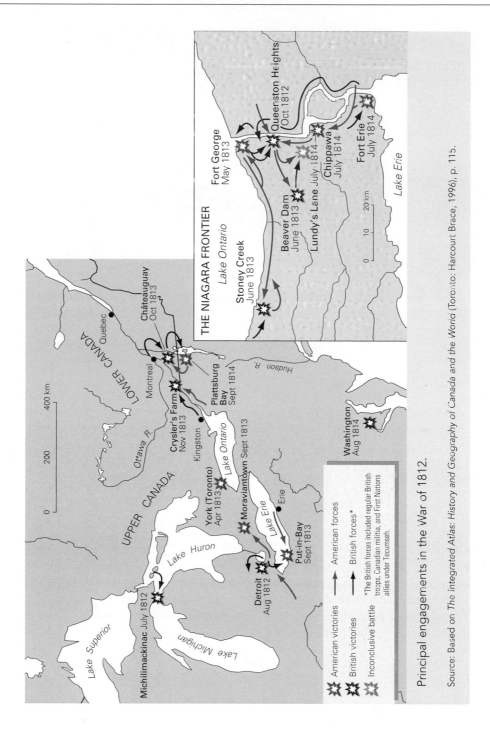

Principal engagements in the War of 1812.

Source: Based on *The Integrated Atlas: History and Geography of Canada and the World* (Toronto: Harcourt Brace, 1996), p. 115.

While their Niagara campaign in 1813 ended in failure, the Americans, that same year, proved successful in the Detroit sector of the conflict. The Americans' fortunes revived after Admiral Oliver Perry defeated the British at Put-in-Bay on Lake Erie. The lake, in effect, became an American possession, controlled by their naval forces for the remainder of the war. The British then withdrew from Detroit. At Moraviantown, on the Thames River, the Americans defeated the British regulars, the Upper Canadian militia, and the First Nations. The Americans held on to Southwestern Upper Canada until the end of the war. That fall, their two-pronged

Perry's Victory on Lake Erie, September 10th, 1813, drawn by J.J. Barralet and engraved by B. Tanner, 1814. At Put-in-Bay in September 1813, American naval officer Oliver H. Perry gained control over Lake Erie. With this short sentence he reported his victory: "We have met the enemy, and they are ours."

National Archives of Canada/C-7762.

attack on Montreal ended in defeat at Crysler's Farm in eastern Upper Canada, and at Châteauguay in Lower Canada.

Tecumseh was killed at Moraviantown on October 5, 1813. With his death, his confederacy collapsed. The link between the British and the Native peoples of the American Midwest was broken. Never again in the lower Great Lakes area did the First Nations constitute a serious military threat.

After Moraviantown, the battle lines consolidated for the remainder of the war. On July 25, 1814, the British defeated the Americans' last great attempt to capture Upper Canada, at Lundy's Lane in the Niagara peninsula. Lundy's Lane was the site of the bloodiest battle of the War of 1812. The six-hour battle lasted until darkness, and each side lost over 800 men. Although each side claimed victory, at the end of the battle the Americans had failed to dislodge the British. They withdrew, ending their final offensive in Upper Canada.

Outside Upper Canada, the British unsuccessfully took the offensive on Lake Champlain. In August 1814, a British expedition invaded Washington, burning the Capitol building and the president's house. The Americans halted the British, however, at Baltimore. The only other major battle of the war (at New Orleans) took place after the peace treaty had been signed on December 24, 1814.

The War of 1812 did not change the boundaries of Upper Canada. The peace treaty essentially confirmed the status quo. But, in one respect, the war had a very profound effect on Upper Canada: the unsuccessful and destructive attacks of 1812–14 engendered anti-American sentiment among a number of non-Loyalist settlers. Ironically, the American invasion contributed to the work that Simcoe had begun — the promotion of a loyalty to Upper Canada.

A desperate moment during the Battle of Moraviantown, October 5, 1813. Tecumseh's death marked the end of the Native peoples as a serious military force in northeastern North America.

National Archives of Canada/C-7763.

NOTES

1. Kenneth Norrie and Douglas Owram, *A History of the Canadian Economy* (Toronto: Harcourt Brace, 1991), p. 161.
2. R. Cole Harris and John Warkentin, *Canada Before Confederation: A Study in Historical Geography* (Ottawa: Carleton University Press, 1991 [1974]), p. 112.
3. Gerald M. Craig, *Upper Canada: The Formative Years, 1784–1841* (Toronto: McClelland & Stewart, 1963), p. 41.
4. Janice Potter, "Patriarchy and Paternalism: The Case of the Eastern Ontario Loyalist Women," *Ontario History* 81 (1989): 20.
5. G. Elmore Reaman, *The Trail of the Black Walnut* (Toronto: McClelland & Stewart, 1957), p. 147.
6. Olive P. Dickason, *Canada's First Nations: A History of Founding Peoples from Earliest Times* (Toronto: McClelland & Stewart, 1992), p. 219.
7. George Sheppard, *Plunder, Profit, and Paroles. A Social History of the War of 1812 in Upper Canada* (Montreal/Kingston: McGill-Queen's University Press, 1994), p. 5.

LINKING TO THE PAST

The Mississaugas of the New Credit First Nation
http://www.newcreditfirstnation.com/past2.htm
An overview of the history of this First Nation from the early 1700s to the present.

Her Majesty's Royal Chapel of the Mohawks
http://www.tyendinaga.net/hmrc/index.htm
Read about this historic chapel, also known as Christ Church, and learn about the historic events associated with it from the perspective of the Mohawks.

Molly Brant
http://collections.ic.gc.ca/wayfarers/molly.htm
A detailed biography of Molly Brant.

The Treaty of Greenville, 1795
http://www.ohiohistorycentral.org/ohc/history/h_indian/document/tgreenev.shtml
The full text of the Treaty of Greenville, 1795, between the United States and several First Nations.

The War of 1812 Website
http://www.militaryheritage.com/1812.htm
Links to many historical documents and articles about the War of 1812, as well as book reviews and information about British regiments.

The War of 1812: Traditions of Allegiance
http://collections.ic.gc.ca/heirloom_series/volume3/chapter6/chapter6.htm
An illustrated account of the War of 1812 from the perspective of Upper Canada.

RELATED READINGS

The following essays in R. Douglas Francis and Donald B. Smith, eds., *Readings in Canadian History: Pre-Confederation*, 6th ed. (Toronto: Nelson Thomson Learning, 2002), are of value to this topic: Jane Errington, "'Woman ... Is a Very Interesting Creature': Some Women's Experiences in Early Upper Canada," pp. 236–252; and Cecilia Morgan "'Of Slender Frame and Delicate Appearance': The Placing of Laura Secord in the Narratives of Canadian Loyalist History," pp. 252–265.

BIBLIOGRAPHY

For an understanding of early Upper Canada Gerald M. Craig's *Upper Canada: The Formative Years, 1784–1841* (Toronto: McClelland & Stewart, 1963) remains essential. J.K. Johnson underlines its importance in "Gerald Craig's *Upper Canada: The Formative Years* and the Writing of Canadian History," *Ontario History* 90(2) (Autumn 1998): 117–33. The period immediately before the establishment of Upper Canada is reviewed by A.L. Burt in "The Loyalists," chapter 15 of *The Old Province of Quebec,* vol. 2 (Toronto: McClelland & Stewart, 1968 [1933]), pp. 76–115. Other sources on the Loyalists who settled in Upper Canada include Bruce Wilson, *As She Began: An Illustrated Introduction to Loyalist Ontario* (Toronto: Dundurn Press, 1981); James J. Talman, ed., *Loyalist Narratives from Upper Canada* (Toronto: Champlain Society, 1946); Janice Potter, "Patriarchy and Paternalism: The Case of the Eastern Ontario Loyalist Women," *Ontario History* 81 (1989): 3–24; and Janice Potter-MacKinnon, *While the Women Only Wept: Loyalist Refugee Women in Eastern Ontario* (Montreal/Kingston: McGill-Queen's University Press, 1993). For a guide to the historical literature in general see Bryan D. Palmer, "Upper Canada," in M. Brook Taylor, ed., *Canadian History: A Reader's Guide*, vol. 1, *Beginnings to Confederation* (Toronto: University of Toronto Press, 1994), pp. 184–236. Peter A. Baskerville has written a useful overview of all of Ontario's history, *Ontario. Image, Identity and Power* (Toronto: Oxford University Press, 2001).

Simcoe's years in Upper Canada are reviewed in Stanley R. Mealing, "John Graves Simcoe," in the *Dictionary of Canadian Biography*, vol. 5, *1801–1820* (Toronto: University of Toronto Press, 1985), pp. 754–59. For an understanding of the mid-1790s in Upper Canada, Elizabeth Simcoe's diary is invaluable. John Ross Robertson's fully annotated version appeared as *The Diary of Mrs. John Graves Simcoe, Wife of the First Lieutenant-Governor of the Province of Upper Canada, 1792–6* (Toronto: Coles, 1973 [1911]). Mary Quayle Innis has edited an abridged version, *Mrs. Simcoe's Diary* (Toronto: Macmillan, 1965). For information on Molly Brant see Barbara Graymont's sketch in the *Dictionary of Canadian Biography*, vol. 4, *1771–1800* (Toronto: University of Toronto Press, 1979), pp. 416–19; Earle Thomas, *The Three Faces of*

Molly Brant (Kingston, ON: Quarry Press, 1996); and Gretchen Green, "Molly Brant, Catharine Brant, and Their Daughters: A Study in Colonial Acculturation," *Ontario History* 81(3) (1989): 235–50.

Several new studies have appeared on Upper Canadian women: Elizabeth Jane Errington, *Wives and Mothers, School Mistresses and Scullery Maids: Working Women in Upper Canada, 1790–1840* (Montreal/Kingston: McGill-Queen's University Press, 1995); Katherine M.J. McKenna, *A Life of Propriety: Anne Murray Powell and her Family, 1755–1849* (Montreal/Kingston: McGill-Queen's University Press, 1994); Janice Potter MacKinnon, *While the Women Only Wept: Loyalist Refugee Women in Eastern Ontario* (Montreal/Kingston: McGill-Queen's University Press, 1993); George Sheppard, "'Wants and Privations': Women and the War of 1812 in Upper Canada," *Histoire Sociale/Social History* 28 (May 1995): 159–79; and Cecilia Morgan, *Public Men and Virtuous Women: The Gendered Languages of Religion and Politics in Upper Canada, 1791–1850* (Toronto: University of Toronto Press, 1997). She has also written "'Of Slender Frame and Delicate Appearance': The Placing of Laura Secord in the Narratives of Canadian Loyalist History," *Journal of the Canadian Historical Association* (1994): 195–212; now expanded into a full book, Colin Coates and Cecilia Morgan, *Heroines and History: Representations of Madeline de Verchères and Laura Secord* (Toronto: University of Toronto Press, 2002).

For the early history of Upper Canada politics consult Elizabeth Jane Errington, *The Lion, the Eagle and Upper Canada: A Developing Colonial Ideology* (Montreal/Kingston: McGill-Queen's University Press, 1987); and David Mills, *The Idea of Loyalty in Upper Canada, 1784–1850* (Montreal/Kingston: McGill-Queen's University Press, 1988). Economic issues are examined in chapter 6 ("Upper Canada") of Kenneth Norrie and Douglas Owram's *A History of the Canadian Economy*, 2nd ed. (Toronto: Harcourt Brace, 1996), pp. 115–45. Consult also Douglas McCalla's *Planting the Province: The Economic History of Upper Canada, 1784–1870* (Toronto: University of Toronto Press, 1993); and Bruce G. Wilson, *The Enterprises of Robert Hamilton: A Study of Wealth and Influence in Early Upper Canada, 1776–1812* (Ottawa: Carleton University Press, 1983).

The experience of the Six Nations in early Upper Canada is reviewed in Isabel Thompson Kelsay, *Joseph Brant, 1743–1807: Man of Two Worlds* (Syracuse: Syracuse University Press, 1984); and Charles M. Johnston, ed., *The Valley of the Six Nations: A Collection of Documents on the Indian Lands of the Grand River* (Toronto: Champlain Society, 1964). For a discussion of the Ojibwas see Peter S. Schmalz, *The Ojibwa of Southern Ontario* (Toronto: University of Toronto Press, 1990); Donald B. Smith, *Sacred Feathers: The Reverend Peter Jones (Kahkewaquonaby) and the Mississauga Indians* (Toronto: University of Toronto Press, 1987); and Janet Chute, *The Legacy of Shingwaukonse: A Century of Native Leadership* (Toronto: University of Toronto Press, 1998). Five useful studies of the First Nations in the War of 1812 include John Sugden, *Tecumseh: A Life* (New York: Henry Holt, 1997); Robert S. Allen, *His Majesty's Indian Allies: British Indian Policy in the Defence of Canada, 1774–1815* (Toronto: Dundurn Press, 1992); Gregory Evans Dowd, *A Spirited Resistance: The North American Indian Struggle for Unity, 1745–1815* (Baltimore: Johns Hopkins University Press, 1992); Colin Calloway, *Crown and Calumet: British–Indian Relations, 1783–1815* (Norman: University of Oklahoma Press, 1987); and Carl Benn, *The Iroquois in the War of 1812* (Toronto: University of Toronto Press, 1998). Robert J. Surtees examines the early treaties in *Indian Land Surrenders in Ontario, 1763–1867* (Ottawa: Indian and Northern Affairs Canada, 1984). For land and justice issues consult as well, Sidney L. Harring, *White Man's Law. Native People in Nineteenth-century Canadian Jurisprudence* (Toronto: University of Toronto Press, 1998).

Daniel G. Hill's *The Freedom-Seekers: Blacks in Early Canada* (Agincourt, ON: Book Society of Canada, 1981) is a popular summary of the history of blacks in British North America. Robin W. Winks, *The Blacks in Canada: A History*, 2nd ed. (Montreal/Kingston: McGill-Queen's University Press, 1997) is very useful. In *The Trail of the Black Walnut* (Toronto: McClelland & Stewart, 1957), G. Elmore Reaman tells the story of the "Plain Folk" and their arrival in Upper Canada. Marianne McLean has written a well-researched monograph on Ontario's easternmost county, *The People of Glengarry: Highlanders in Transition, 1745–1820* (Montreal/Kingston: McGill-Queen's University Press, 1991).

A short summary of the War of 1812 appears in Wesley B. Turner, *The War of 1812. The War That Both Sides Won,* 2nd ed. (Toronto: Dundurn, 2000). A fuller overview is Victor Suthren, *The War of 1812* (Toronto: McClelland & Stewart, 1999). Pierre Berton has written two very readable accounts of the conflict: *The Invasion of Canada, 1812–1813* (Toronto: McClelland & Stewart, 1980), and *Flames Across the Border, 1813–1814* (Toronto: McClelland & Stewart, 1981). George F.G. Stanley provides the best scholarly account in *The War of 1812: Land Operations* (Toronto: Macmillan, 1983). George Sheppard has written a social history of the War of 1812 in Upper Canada, *Plunder, Profit, and Paroles* (Montreal/Kingston: McGill-Queen's University Press, 1994).

For early maps of Upper Canada see R. Louis Gentilcore and C. Grant Head, eds., *Ontario's History in Maps* (Toronto: University of Toronto Press, 1984); and consult R. Louis Gentilcore, ed., *Historical Atlas of Canada*, vol. 2, *The Land Transformed, 1800–1891* (Toronto: University of Toronto Press, 1993). Neil Forkey has written an environmental study of the Trent Valley, *Shaping the Upper Canadian Frontier. Environment, Society, and Culture in the Trent Valley* (Calgary: University of Calgary Press, 2002). Valuable portraits of early Upper Canadian figures appear in the *Dictionary of Canadian Biography*, vol. 4, *1770–1800*; vol. 5, *1800–1820*; and vol. 6, *1821–1835* (Toronto: University of Toronto Press, 1979, 1985, 1987).

PART THREE

THE CANADAS, 1815 TO THE 1860s

INTRODUCTION

All of the British North American colonies experienced a population boom in the period between the end of the War of 1812 and Confederation. Such phenomenal growth in population was particularly evident in the two Canadas. In Upper Canada, the population increase occurred as a result of large-scale immigration from the British Isles, thus reinforcing the already British American nature of this inland colony. In Lower Canada, the population growth — especially among the French Canadians — was a result of a high birth rate. Whatever immigration did occur into Lower Canada was English-speaking, thus heightening tension between the two cultural groups. Lower Canada also experienced a large out-migration of French Canadians in the 1850s and 1860s to the United States, mostly to work in the textile industries in the New England states or to farm in the American Midwest.

Population growth in the Canadas coincided with a period of economic prosperity, based on external trade. Until 1849, most of the trade occurred with the mother country through the mercantile system, by which the colonies supplied the raw materials in return for British manufactured goods. Once Britain dismantled its mercantile system in favour of free trade in the late 1840s, the British North American colonies looked increasingly to the United States for markets for their raw materials, especially during the period when the Reciprocity Treaty was in effect between 1854 and 1866.

The two Canadas benefited from increased trade with Britain and the United States through a system of canals and railroads that were in place by the mid-1850s and the 1860s. When this trade pattern was disrupted by the decision of the American government to end the Reciprocity Treaty in 1866, the British North American colonies looked for alternative trade relations among themselves — one of the factors leading to Confederation.

But prosperity in the Canadas was also the result of rapid internal growth, as these colonies experienced the beginnings of industrialization, symbolized by railroads, factories, and manufacturing centres in the growing towns and cities. An emerging middle class, especially in the commercial sector, both directed and benefited the most from the prosperity that industrialization and external trade provided.

Politically, the period begins with the struggle for responsible government. In both the Canadas, the privileged group around the governor opposed the elected members of the Assembly. In Upper Canada, the Rebellion of 1837 was a minor occurrence, but not so in Lower Canada, where it took on a greater intensity.

The British government commissioned Lord Durham to look into the reasons for the rebellions and to suggest solutions to the problems. One of Durham's more contentious recommendations was a union of the Canadas, which took place in 1841. The two colonies of Upper Canada, predominantly English-speaking, and Lower Canada, predominantly French-speaking, had some common interests, but in general were quite distinct. This resulted in tension. What developed was a *modus vivendi*, by which moderate political leaders from the two Canadas worked together to achieve responsible government in 1849.

CHAPTER

12

REBELLION AND CHANGE ON THE ST. LAWRENCE

TIME LINE

1792 – Lower Canada's elected Legislative Assembly meets for the first time

1806 – *Le Canadien* newspaper founded by four members of the Parti canadien, later the Parti patriote

1807 – Governor Sir James Craig's four-year "reign of terror" begins

1813 – A French-Canadian militia company defeats an American invading force at Châteauguay

1817 – Canada's first chartered bank, the Bank of Montreal, is established

1832 – The first of a series of cholera epidemics sweeps Lower Canada

1834 – The Patriotes' Ninety-two Resolutions of Grievances are adopted by the Assembly

The Assembly acts to end all female suffrage

1836 – Canada's first railway, running between Saint-Jean-sur-Richelieu and La Prairie, opposite Montreal, is inaugurated

1837 – Rebellion against the British colonial authorities breaks out in Lower Canada

1839 – In his report, Lord Durham recommends the union of Upper and Lower Canada

The half-century between the partition of Quebec in 1791 and the union of the two Canadas in 1841 is usually remembered for the political and military events of the late 1830s. Certainly, the rebellion that broke out in Lower Canada at the end of 1837 and flared up again in late 1838 stands out as the most dramatic occurrence of this period. The Patriotes — the rebels — shouted revolutionary rhetoric at mass meetings, laid plans to overthrow their British rulers, and took up arms. British troops intervened and brutally crushed the revolts. In the aftermath, the colonial authorities hanged, imprisoned, or exiled many Patriotes; hundreds more fled. The uprisings in Lower Canada were much more widespread and violent than those that occurred at the same time in Upper Canada.

Despite these dramatic events, the real revolution in Lower Canada lay in the transformation of the colony's economy, politics, society, and institutions. These profound changes had both positive and negative effects.

THE ECONOMIC REVOLUTION IN THE EARLY NINETEENTH CENTURY

 At the end of the eighteenth century, Quebec entered a period of intense, if uneven, economic growth, as Britain's industrialization and urbanization created new markets for the colony's foodstuffs and resources. The fur-trade era drew to a close, as profits slumped because of declining demand for furs overseas and ruinous competition at home. Yet some Montreal fur-trading firms survived by successfully diversifying their interests. Fur-trader Simon McTavish, for example, became a seigneur and owner of several businesses. Other traders became timber exporters, shipowners, importers, bankers, and railway promoters.

The rise of the timber industry offset the decline of the fur trade in Lower Canada. By 1810, wood products accounted for three-quarters of Quebec's exports (and the fur trade only one-tenth). Britain needed wood, especially to build ships. Napoleon's control of northern Europe from 1808 to 1810 cut Great Britain off from its traditional Baltic suppliers. As a result, Britain's imports of timber from Lower Canada and other North American colonies increased significantly. Then shipowners, working through the English Board of Trade, pressured the British government into doubling import duties on foreign, but not colonial, timber. This effectively guaranteed a highly profitable monopoly to colonial suppliers, even if the Baltic ports reopened. William Price, who came to Lower Canada in 1810, was one of several entrepreneurs who made his fortune selling timber. The company he founded would a century later become a pioneer in the development of the pulp and paper industry.

Other sectors of the economy experienced significant, though less spectacular, growth. Ships were built at nearly 80 localities along the St. Lawrence River. Quebec City had the biggest shipyards, and much of their production went overseas to Britain. Sawmills, candle and soap manufacturers, textile factories, flour mills, and an expanding construction industry contributed to this growth. Banks, beginning with the Bank of Montreal in 1817, were established to supply credit to new enterprises and commercial ventures.

URBAN LIFE IN LOWER CANADA

Lower Canada's rapidly expanding population provided the labour needed for the increased resource exploitation and manufacturing. Thanks largely to a birth rate that stayed slightly above 50 per 1000 throughout the period, as well as to substantial immigration, the population quintupled, rising from about 160 000 in 1790 to 890 000 in 1851. As early as the 1830s, demographic pressures resulted in increasing numbers of French Canadians emigrating to the United States in search of the land or work they could not find at home.

Community Portrait

The St. Maurice Forges, an Early Industrial Community

A few kilometres north of Trois-Rivières, Quebec, the tourist can spend a few pleasant and instructive hours visiting the Forges du Saint-Maurice National Historic Site. Set in rolling countryside along a small stream that drops through a gully to the St. Maurice River just below, it features the large reconstructed Grande Maison, the Master's House, built in 1738, and a modern blast-furnace interpretation centre describing the early development of the iron industry, from 1730 until 1883.

The Forges constituted a remarkable legacy from the era of New France. Already in this early period, the Forges produced large quantities of munitions for the army.

After the British conquered New France, they soon realized the importance of the ironworks and made certain that masters and skilled employees continued working and did not return to France. The British also used corvées to force the habitants to cut wood for charcoal.

The Forges attained their maximum development in the first decades of the nineteenth century, using wood charcoal in the process of ore reduction rather than the more modern, more efficient coke-fuelled technology. The ore used was bog ore, found in the form of nodules close to the surface in swampy areas. The Forges employed 400 people directly and also

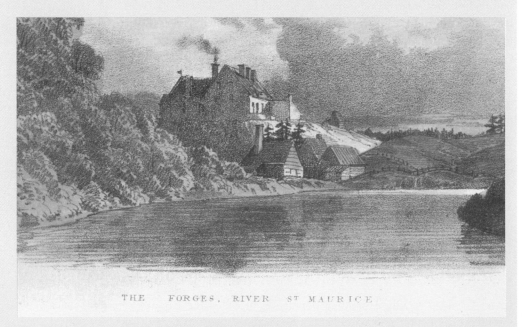

THE   FORGES,   RIVER   ST MAURICE

The iron forges on the St. Maurice River, 1832.

National Archives of Canada/C-004356.

provided work for the surrounding population, who were hired to collect, prepare, and
transport raw materials as well as products
and goods. Work "campaigns," during
which the blast furnace operated without
interruption, lasted six to eight months. The
pig iron that was produced supplied the
forges where blacksmiths fashioned tools
and implements, pots and kettles, stoves,
and munitions including cannonballs. From
the 1850s, the Forges sold huge quantities
of iron to the railway industry.

For most of the company's productive
life, the Forges were state-owned, marking
the great importance that the French, British,
and finally Canadian governments accorded
to this industry. Until 1863, the state granted
the Forges free access to vast timber and ore
resources, a privilege that ensured
profitability. When this privilege was withdrawn, and when the plant was forced to pay
the real costs of raw materials, it soon collapsed under an increasing load of debt.

Mathew Bell, a Scottish merchant, was
master of the Forges from 1793 until 1846,
when the government sold the enterprise.
The government set very favourable terms
for the tenants, who could run the business
for their profit. Bell used his influence as a
member of the Assembly and then as a legislative councillor to ensure that the Forges
disposed of adequate reserves of land for
procuring raw materials, including 10 000
cords of wood annually. Bell's monopolistic
control of huge tracts of land provoked substantial criticism. The Assembly even

accused him in one of the Ninety-two
Resolutions in 1834 of having been unduly
and illegally favoured by the Executive.

The community that grew up around
the Forges had a population of about 400
people, mostly workers and their families.
Five generations of workers lived on the
site, with fathers often passing on their
trade to their sons. Skilled workers and
craftsmen lived in houses, while the families
of unskilled labourers inhabited more
modest tenements. Most workers had
kitchen gardens, and kept livestock and
poultry. The village boasted a chapel while
the Grande Maison contained a well-
stocked store.

The St. Maurice Forges constituted the
first industrial village in Canada's history, its
character defined by its industrial vocation
and its population of skilled workers. The
community that grew up around the Forges
was a precursor of the numerous mining and
forestry communities that developed later,
particularly in northern regions of Canada.

Further Reading
Michel Bédard, André Bérubé, and Jean
Hamelin, "Mathew Bell," *Dictionary of
Canadian Biography, vol. 7 (1836–1850)*
(Toronto: University of Toronto Press, 1988):
70–75.

Roch Samson, *The Forges du Saint-
Maurice: Beginnings of the Iron and Steel
Industry in Canada, 1730-1883* (Quebec:
Les Presses de l'Université Laval and the
Department of Canadian Heritage — Parks
Canada, 1998), p. 10.

Lower Canada's two major cities developed rapidly as centres of both wealth and poverty.
In the early 1800s, the population of Quebec City grew at an annual rate of more than 5 percent. The Lower Town, around the seaport, was bustling, noisy, and dirty. A visitor wrote of a
"fearful scene of disorder, filth and intemperance," which he ascribed to the presence of a large
number of sailors, lumbermen, and Irish immigrants. The narrow streets, crowded houses, and
boarded roofs made the district "a most hazardous body of property," as one fire insurance agent
put it to explain his refusal to insure buildings in the area. In fact, fires were frequent throughout
the city and took a heavy toll.

The Fire in the Saint-Jean Quarter, Seen Looking Westward, 1845, a painting by Joseph Légaré (1795–1855). Fire was a constant danger in communities whose buildings were constructed largely of wood. In June 1845, a fire broke out in Quebec's Upper Town, destroying 1300 houses in the prosperous St. Jean quarter and leaving 10 000 people homeless. Only one month earlier, a fire in Quebec's working-class district of St. Roch in the Lower Town had demolished 1650 houses and left 12 000 people homeless.

Art Gallery of Ontario, Toronto. Purchased with assistance from Wintario, 1976/Acc. No. 76/210.

Many impoverished French Canadians settled in the industrial district of St. Roch, located on a seigneury held until 1805 by wealthy merchant William Grant. Grant had invested heavily in the purchase of properties disposed of by large landowners who returned to France after the Conquest. He also bought several large houses in Montreal, including the Château de Ramezay, and in Quebec, including Montcalm's former residence. In the 1790s, as St. Roch's population grew quickly, Grant ceded properties, developed industries and docks, and built mills, bakeries, and warehouses. When, in 1800, Quebec City put forth a plan for road development, Grant, together with religious communities and other private-property owners jealous of their prerogatives, had it overturned by the courts. Not until 1833 was a new plan presented. Grant was thus able to build roads substantially narrower than those in town and to locate them where he wished.

Seigneurial rents and dues brought Grant and succeeding owners of St. Roch an impressive income. In hard times, inhabitants often accumulated debts. During one of these periodic crises, in the fall of 1838, rumours circulated that the workers of St. Roch intended to sneak up to Quebec's Upper Town to strangle the bourgeois residents while they slept. Barrels of gunpowder and stocks of ammunition were discovered, and for some time thereafter the anxious burghers kept the city gates of Upper Town locked day and night.

Montreal also grew quickly. By 1825, it had 22 000 inhabitants. By the late 1830s it had overtaken Quebec, the administrative and ecclesiastical capital, and had become British North America's premier city, with a population of 37 000. Citizens of French origin constituted only a minority of its residents. Well over half of the city's anglophones were Irish immigrants, most of them poor labourers who settled in industrial areas such as Ste. Anne and Griffintown, near the port. The old city of Montreal, along the river, contained the markets, shops, and administrative buildings. Many of its streets were narrow, muddy in wet weather, and dusty in dry periods. Increasingly, Montrealers settled in the suburbs. Wealthy British residents built sumptuous residences with gardens on the verdant slopes of Mont Royal.

POPULATION GROWTH IN MONTREAL, HALIFAX, AND TORONTO, 1800–1850

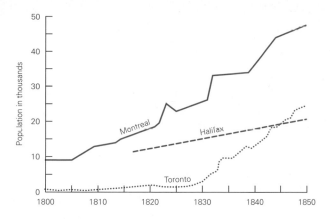

Source: R. Louis Gentilcore, ed., *Historical Atlas of Canada*, vol. 2, *The Land Transformed, 1800–1891* (Toronto: University of Toronto Press, 1993), plate 20. Reprinted by permission of the University of Toronto Press Incorporated.

Communications stimulated Montreal's growth. In 1836, Canada's first railway, linking St. Jean, on the Richelieu River, and hence Lake Champlain, to La Prairie, on the south shore of the St. Lawrence opposite Montreal, was inaugurated. Goods destined to and coming from increasingly prosperous Upper Canada passed through the port of Montreal. The city's merchants, mostly English-speaking and often from Scotland, sold imported goods or set up shops to manufacture such products as leather goods, clothing, barrels, and beer, or to process agricultural products from the fertile farm belt around the city. To supply his Montreal brewery with locally grown barley, industrialist John Molson brought seed barley from England and distributed it among farmers. He also owned the first steamer on the St. Lawrence (which he acquired in 1809), sat in the House of Assembly and later on the Legislative Council, and was president of the Bank of Montreal.

Most workers were unskilled. Many labourers had to spend more than half their earnings simply to feed their families. Prior to the 1830s, there were no unions, and legislation passed in 1802 authorized fines and prison sentences for striking employees.

WOMEN IN LOWER CANADA

Over one-quarter of the women of Lower Canada appeared to have been in the labour force in 1825, a figure higher than that at the end of the nineteenth century. They toiled in a wide variety of occupations. At least 13 000 were weavers. Others made soap, candles, and dresses. A census taken in 1825 showed that Montreal had female innkeepers, mercers, blacksmiths, and coachmakers. Some women earned money by taking in boarders, providing meals for them, and washing their laundry. Convents began to train a few women as teachers.

Many female labourers found jobs as domestics. In the eighteenth century, parents often placed their very young daughters as servants in the homes of more fortunate town-dwellers, where they would work until they married. They were paid no salary but received board, room, and clothing. By the early 1800s, however, domestic labour became salaried work, work that began at dawn and finished when the family went to bed. By 1820, about one family in five in Quebec City employed at least one servant.

Some women in Montreal and Quebec City worked as prostitutes; many were destitute Irish immigrants. Before 1839, as historian Mary-Anne Poutanen points out, prostitution was a crime only if street-walking and neighbourhood brothels annoyed passersby or neighbours. Then a new law stipulated that prostitutes could be apprehended and sentenced to hard labour and incarcerated for up to two months. Keeping a bawdy house was considered an indictable offence as a common nuisance by endangering the public peace.[1]

Women played a leading role in the early nineteenth century in the founding of charitable institutions intended to alleviate some of the problems associated with urban poverty. (Historian Jan Noel notes that after 1840, as gender roles hardened, men took control of most new social-welfare institutions while women provided the labour.) [2] Thérèse-Geneviève Coutlée was elected superior of the Sisters of Charity of Montreal's Hôpital Général in 1792. Particularly interested in assisting the poor and the sick, she was also, thanks to government assistance, drawn into caring for the mentally ill, who were housed within the hospital in tiny rooms with grated windows. Only in 1845 was a government asylum built at Beauport, near Quebec City.

Another major function of the hospital consisted of taking in abandoned newborn children, nearly three-quarters of whom died after being sent out to nurse. The nuns attributed the high mortality rate to the bad state of health of the children on arrival, "which proceeds from that shame which induces the mothers to resort to the utmost means of concealing the offspring of their crime from the eyes of the world." Legislators did not approve of these institutions, which they felt undermined marriage by encouraging unwed mothers to abandon their babies. Their existence, however, may have reduced the number of cases of infanticide.

Laywomen also engaged in philanthropy. Eleanor Gibb and other Protestant women, struck by the misery of poor Irish immigrants, founded the Female (later Ladies) Benevolent Society in 1815, while their Catholic counterparts established the Dames de Charité in 1827 to assist in providing housing, education, and employment to needy women and children.

SMALLPOX AND CHOLERA EPIDEMICS

In the early decades of the nineteenth century, disease posed a serious and constant threat to public health. This was particularly true in the towns, with their filthy living conditions and relatively concentrated populations.

In 1815, Lower Canada's Assembly provided for public vaccination against smallpox. The method proved controversial, however, and public apathy and distrust kept many people away. In addition, politics intervened to undermine the credibility of the Vaccine Board; the government appointed as president of the board a doctor favoured by the British establishment rather than the highly respected Dr. François Blanchet, a senior physician and prominent member of the Assembly. Disputes over regulations and payment of doctors helped seal the fate of the program, which was ended in 1823 with very serious consequences. Smallpox continued to be a major source of death in the St. Lawrence valley for many years; the last major outbreak, in 1885, killed 3000 people in Montreal.

In 1832, the first of a series of cholera epidemics provoked a wave of panic among Canadians. The disease, transmitted mainly through contaminated water supplies, had spread from the delta of the Ganges River in India across Europe to Britain. Its attacks were sudden, extremely painful, and very often fatal; death came within 48 hours, a result of complete dehydration of the victim's body. No known cure existed. In fact, most treatments probably hastened death: patients were bled, even when they were in a state of collapse; doctors administered laxatives, although the patients were suffering from uncontrollable diarrhea; and leeches and blisters were applied to the stomach. Fortunately for the victims of both the disease and the proposed remedies, physicians commonly prescribed opium as a painkiller.

The arrival in Canada of large numbers of immigrants, very often indigents from Ireland, caused much concern to the French Canadians living in the St. Lawrence valley. The Irish had been migrating in large numbers to Lower Canada since 1815, although most went on to Upper Canada or to the United States. Some 50 000 arrived in 1831. They were steerage passengers who had spent weeks on the boats, in filthy conditions, and often near starvation. Worried about the threat these immigrants posed to public health, the government of Lower Canada established a quarantine station on Grosse Île, a small island in the upper St. Lawrence River downstream from Quebec. The measure proved ineffective because regulations could not be enforced and medical services were totally inadequate. Among those who perished in Lower Canada, perhaps on Grosse Île, was the wife of an Irish farmer named John Ford, who himself escaped illness. Ford went on to Detroit, where he began to farm. He was the grandfather of Henry Ford, the founder of the modern automobile industry.

Conditions in Lower Canadian towns greatly contributed to the spread of infection. Houses were dirty and overcrowded, yards and streets were piled with refuse, and towns had open sewers. People emptied the remains of animal pens and latrines into the streets. Pigs and other animals ran loose. Slaughterhouses, often located in residential districts, dumped their waste into open water. In early spring 1832, the health board of Quebec City tried to force residents to clean up streets, houses, and yards. They were ordered to "scrape, wash and cleanse their premises and carry away all filth." Such regulations proved to be unenforceable, however, in the face of public indifference, if not outright hostility. In Montreal, city authorities had no choice but to sit back and wait for the expected onslaught of disease.

Cholera struck Quebec City at the end of the first week in June 1832. Hospitals overflowed with victims, while hundreds more lay in tents on the Plains of Abraham. Many panic-stricken residents fled to rural areas, often carrying the disease with them. To prevent despair, church bells were no longer rung for the dead. Police had to be called to enforce the rapid burial of the deceased. By the end of October, 7500 residents of Quebec and Montreal — more than one-tenth of the population of each city — had died.

The disease had important political, as well as economic and social, consequences. French Canadians, particularly in nationalist circles, hotly debated immigration policy; many, including the mayor of Quebec, blamed the British authorities for doing nothing to control the merchants and shipowners who profited by transporting immigrants who came with the disease. They denounced Governor Aylmer's administration for its inaction.

During a second, less severe, outbreak of cholera in Quebec City in 1834, Lord Aylmer fled to Sorel, and most of the Executive Council took up more healthy residence in the country. Even the rich, however, were not spared. Perhaps out of self-interest more than concern for the poor, they began to lobby for the public-health measures that, decades later, would dramatically reduce the incidence of deadly diseases.

RURAL QUEBEC

Nineteen out of twenty French Canadians in the early nineteenth century lived in rural areas, where they practised subsistence farming. Yet rural Quebec also underwent change. Thanks to the good harvests and high wheat prices of the 1790s and early 1800s, many habitants accumulated small surpluses of wheat that they sold to grain merchants for export abroad. For a short time, habitants saw their living conditions improve.

But yields varied enormously, and after 1815, crop failures became more frequent again. The productivity of even the best lands tended to drop after decades of cultivation without fertilization. New lands that had been opened up for colonization, especially those near the Canadian Shield, proved rocky and infertile. Crop diseases and insects posed a constant threat;

the wheat midge, for example, almost destroyed the entire harvests from 1834 to 1836, forcing Lower Canada to buy wheat from Upper Canada, where yields were increasing.

Farmers also had to contend with the effects of events abroad. The War of 1812 severely disrupted the grain trade, and depression in Britain from 1815 to 1820 caused prices to fall dramatically. Tariff barriers, such as Britain's Corn Laws of 1815, blocked the entry of colonial grain when the British price fell below a certain level.

Historians agree that the 1830s witnessed a rapid deterioration of economic conditions, with famine reported in 1837. Some, like Fernand Ouellet, have blamed the habitant for failing to adopt more modern agricultural techniques such as crop rotation and for depleting soil nutrients while doing nothing to restore them. Others, like Jean-Pierre Wallot and John McCallum, contend that the habitants' alleged backwardness was the consequence, rather than the cause, of their economic plight, and that farmers in Upper Canada and in the northeastern United States were no better versed in sound agricultural methods. Climatic factors and disease, as well as overpopulation, also seem to have played a part. Lacking the capital to invest in commercial substitutes for wheat, habitants turned more and more to peas, potatoes, and barley in order to avoid starvation. In despair, many of them supported the organizers of rebellion in 1837.

 Alexis de Tocqueville, the French social philosopher, confirmed the existence of rural unrest during a visit to Lower Canada in the late summer of 1831. The superior of the Sulpicians in Montreal assured him that there were no "happier people in the world than the French Canadians," and that they paid trifling rents and acquitted their dues to the church "ungrudgingly and easily." But when de Tocqueville rode into the countryside around Beauport, near Quebec City, and spoke with the habitants, he found them worried about immigration, resentful of the seigneurs, and envious of the wealth that the tithe placed in the hands of some clergy. The habitants had annual seigneurial dues to discharge. Those who bought land had to pay a heavy mutation fine (transfer fee) to the seigneur. They were also obliged to grind their grain at the seigneur's mills — a lucrative privilege for the landed gentry. Historian Allan Greer asserts that

The manor house of the Seigneurie des Aulnaies, 130 km east of Quebec City on the south shore of the St. Lawrence. Designed by Quebec City architect Charles Baillairgé, the manor was built between 1850 and 1853. The seigneurial mill and the manor are today historic sites.

Corporation touristique de la Seigneurie des Aulnaies.

this "feudal burden," while generally not crushing, made it difficult for the habitants to accumulate capital.[3]

By the mid-1830s, as most seigneurs rallied to the colonial government and the habitants increasingly criticized seigneurial privilege, the conflict between seigneurs and habitants deepened. For Greer, this conflict played "a major part" in the outbreak of the rebellions.[4]

THE CHURCH

During this period, two groups vied to obtain influence and prestige among the habitants: the Roman Catholic church, struggling to secure its independence from government dictates and implacably hostile to republican and liberal ideals; and a new professional elite composed of notaries, lawyers, and doctors. The professionals endorsed increasingly nationalistic ideas, particularly on political issues, and tended to be critical of the church; their forum was the colony's Assembly.

At the turn of the century, the church's position in Lower Canada was far from assured. In spite of what has been written by clerical historians about the habitants' profound religiosity, Quebec was not a theocratic society, and the clergy were neither very influential nor dominant. Contemporary accounts detail the spread of religious indifference and even of anti-clericalism, particularly among the bourgeoisie. Liberals read the works of French secular philosophers such as Rousseau and Voltaire. As for the habitants, they did not challenge official dogma, although many were probably more superstitious and conformist than pious and fervent. They were also strong-minded and independent. They attempted to avoid paying tithes and other religious contributions and they disputed over pews, the location of new churches, and other matters of a material nature.

For its part, the clergy often complained of disorders and immorality, although that, admittedly, was their duty. Serious sexual misdemeanours were apparently uncommon. Indeed, illegitimacy rates in Lower Canada were low by contemporary European and North American standards. Yet the habitants seem to have enjoyed their feast-days. Travellers reported frequently that the *Canadiens* danced, gorged themselves, got drunk to prepare themselves for Lent (which they scrupulously observed), then feasted again and got drunk to celebrate its passing. The church was even obliged to abolish several feast-days because of excesses, thus pleasing the British merchants, who did not approve of these kinds of pleasures nor of the loss of time that they entailed.

Habitants also commonly engaged in a popular custom known as the charivari, often a form of public rebuke for "mismatched" couples who appeared to marry for money or for mere sensual pleasure. Thus, for example, when an older man married a young woman, a crowd of young men would costume themselves and stage a noisy mock funeral on the couple's doorstep. They would return night after night beating old pots and kettles to harass the newlyweds until the victims finally sued for peace and paid a substantial fine. Part of the money would go to the poor, and the rest would buy drinks for the revellers. The clergy disapproved of this ritual, which they viewed as a challenge to their authority over marriage.

To increase its influence within French-Canadian society, the church needed more clergy. Indeed, at this time, it faced a veritable crisis: the number of priests declined from about 200 in 1760 to only 150 in 1790 and then increased to somewhat more than 300 by the time of the rebellion — but the population had mushroomed from 70 000 to 500 000 in the same period. Bishop Ignace Bourget of Montreal complained that "there are not enough workers to help us cultivate the vine." During his tenure as bishop of Quebec from 1806 to 1825, Monseigneur Joseph-Octave Plessis encouraged the establishment of classical colleges and succeeded in increasing the number of vocations.

EDUCATION AND THE CHURCH

The church, however, entertained serious doubts about the value of universal primary schooling. Many *curés* did not want to spend parish money on schools, and some saw education as dangerous. Jean-Jacques Lartigue, named first bishop of the new diocese of Montreal in 1836, said of the habitants: "It is better for them not to have a literary education than to risk a bad moral education." Since schools cost money and habitants generally did not want to pay for them, they tended to agree.

Some liberal French-speaking members of the Assembly saw education in a more positive light. So did the government, which in 1801 founded the Royal Institution for the Advancement of Learning (RIAL), a system of voluntary public education. The church, led by Plessis, was suspicious of the RIAL schools, since a Protestant government that still hoped for the assimilation and Protestantization of the habitants had established them; the church, therefore, chose to ignore the schools, and very few were actually established.

When, in 1818, the Assembly set up a board of trustees to oversee education, Plessis refused to participate in this essentially English-speaking Protestant body. The board did, however, authorize separate religious worship, visits to schools by priests, and French-language textbooks. It also appointed French-speaking Roman Catholic teachers in French-speaking areas of the province. Still, the local priests regarded the schools at best with indifference and sometimes with outright hostility. Many refused to become visitors, often on Plessis's orders.

In an effort to remodel educational legislation to make it more satisfactory to the church, the Assembly authorized the church to build its own schools, to be financed and directed by parish *fabriques* or councils. In the Legislative Council, Plessis urged state financing, but the government replied that, because of the Assembly's obstruction, no money was available. It was becoming more apparent, however, that French-speaking liberals favourable to non-confessional schools constituted as much a threat to clerical ambitions as did Anglo-Protestant government officials. Indeed, in 1829, the liberals supported a bill that gave control of schools to the Assembly and to local officials called *syndics*.

Within three years, many state-supported schools were built, leading to disputes between parish priests and town officials over their operation. Finally in 1836, in response to church pressure, the Assembly abrogated the Elementary Schools Act. The way was now open for clerical control of education.

THE CHURCH'S RELATIONS WITH GOVERNMENT

The church's major triumph in these years was the achievement of independence from government dictates. Until the 1830s, the government interfered with the nomination of bishops, although with decreasing success. When Bishop Bailly de Messein died in 1794, the governor gave the new bishop, Jean-François Hubert, a list of three names from which to choose a new coadjutor. But in 1825, the process was reversed: it was Bernard Claude Panet, the new bishop, who submitted a list of three names to the governor, Lord Dalhousie. Furthermore, only one of the candidates had indicated that he would accept the position. A somewhat humbled Dalhousie finally agreed to the only choice. By 1840, ecclesiastical nominations became purely a church matter.

On the issue of parish appointments, church and state also clashed. Here again the government sought to affirm its supremacy, examining lists of nominees and interfering occasionally, but aggressively, with the placement of priests. With the Constitutional Act of 1791, colonial administrators wanted amenable local clergy who could intervene to favour the election of pro-government candidates. Sir Robert Shore Milnes, sent to the colony in 1799 as the new lieutenant governor, prevented the entry into Lower Canada of French priests whose loyalty he doubted in these years of war. Ultimately, though, the church's use of its only weapon — passive resistance — brought it success, and the British permitted them to settle in the colony.

The church also prevailed on the question of the division of the large diocese of Quebec when, in 1836, Lord Gosford finally agreed to the establishment of the diocese of Montreal. A grateful Bishop Lartigue later wrote to Gosford to request his portrait "as a monument to your good deeds in this country."

The colonial government's principal administrators in the early nineteenth century made plans to subvert the Roman Catholic church. Herman Ryland, Governor Robert Prescott's profoundly anti-French and anti-Catholic secretary, hoped to undermine its influence through a reform of the educational system. Jacob Mountain, the Anglican Lord Bishop of Quebec, sought to raise the prestige of his church by increasing its status while decreasing that of the Roman Catholic church. He used his power as a legislative and executive councillor to block the creation of new Roman Catholic parishes and to prevent the immigration of priests from France. His cathedral, inaugurated in 1804, boasted a steeple which topped that of the nearby Roman Catholic cathedral by fully one metre! Attorney General (later, Chief Justice) Jonathan Sewell, more moderate and more patient, wanted to diminish gradually the powers of the Catholic bishops and, by giving Plessis and his coadjutor pensions and seats in the councils, make them obedient government servants. But by the time Sir George Prevost became governor in 1812, a good part of the momentum had gone out of these ambitious but dangerous projects. Plessis convinced the British government that an independent church could be a powerful ally during renewed war with the Americans.

TOWARD VICTORY

Undoubtedly, the local situation contributed to the church's ultimate victory in its long war with the state. Some governors were more willing to be flexible, and, in that, were perhaps more realistic than others. For their part, many church leaders were skilful diplomats who exploited every opportunity to assert the church's independence while at the same time giving the government full co-operation and assuring British authorities of their unbending loyalty. In addition, the English rulers' hopes for converting the habitants were fading. Groups such as the Methodists, who used Swiss French-speaking agents, vainly attempted to proselytize. Indeed, Protestants often appeared more preoccupied with their own denominational rivalries than with converting Catholics. Anglican Bishop Mountain, for example, tolerated Presbyterian and Lutheran ministers but disdained the Methodist clergy — the Methodists had left the Anglican church and founded a separate church — as "a set of ignorant enthusiasts whose preaching is calculated only to perplex the understanding and corrupt the morals, to relax the nerves of industry and dissolve the bonds of society."

International events afforded the church new opportunities to demonstrate its loyalty. The clergy had vigorously opposed the liberal ideals of the "anti-Christian" French Revolution that broke out with the storming of the Bastille prison in Paris on July 14, 1789. Horrified by the Reign of Terror that soon set in (among whose victims was King Louis XVI), Canadian prelates issued strong condemnations. These must have been all the more pleasing to the British authorities because war between Britain and France broke out in 1793. Then, while Napoleon's military campaigns provoked new suspicions of all things French, the War of 1812 gave the church a welcome opportunity to preach loyalty through pastoral letters and sermons. Led by the clergy, loyal French Canadians praised the exploits of Charles-Michel de Salaberry and his militia, who forced a numerically far superior American force to retreat at the battle of Châteauguay in 1813. Here were French-speaking troops winning a glorious victory for the British — undeniable

The Roman Catholic church in Quebec approved of the British victories over the French during the Revolutionary and Napoleonic Wars. Four years after Admiral Horatio Nelson's victory over the French at Trafalgar in 1805, the citizens of Montreal erected a column to honour him, at Place Jacques-Cartier in Montreal. The drawing was made in the mid-nineteenth century. The magnificent column still stands; in fact, several years ago the Parti Québécois government of Lucien Bouchard paid half the cost (with the city of Montreal) to restore and protect it.

From Montreal recueil iconographie la pictorial record, by Volpi. McGill University Rare Books and Special Collections.

proof of loyalty. Governor Prevost could well declare, "The Catholic clergy are my firmest supports." As for the events of 1837, except in some parishes where the Patriotes were well organized, they provoked additional manifestations of loyalty to the Crown, this time in the face of internal revolution.

The rise of the church in the early years of the nineteenth century took place partly at the expense of the colonial government, and partly at the expense of the new professional elite. The professional class was the church's only serious rival in the struggle for support and influence among the French-speaking population. The Rebellion of 1837 brought this conflict to a head and decided its outcome in the church's favour. By 1840 French Canada's clerical elite was poised to enter a golden age that would last for more than a century.

THE PROFESSIONAL ELITE

The new professional class was not so fortunate. Many of its members were sons of small farmers and, as such, could scarcely base their social aspirations upon family wealth. Politics became an outlet for this group's ambitions. Espousing liberal, democratic, and, ultimately, republican ideals, the group sought government reform through enlarging the powers of the lower house and curtailing those of the executive. These professionals were well aware of Lower Canada's colonial status and of French Canadians' lesser role in the economy and in government. They thus aimed to become champions of national values, and they easily associated the interests of French Canada with those of their own class. Not surprisingly, they framed their declarations of battle in the name of the French-Canadian nation.

This new middle class aspired to replace the seigneurs and, to a degree, compete with the clergy as leaders of French Canada. Many of its members viewed the seigneurs as exploiting the habitants when they raised seigneurial *rentes*, especially when the growing population in the seigneurial zone and better prices for timber enhanced the value of the seigneuries, more than half of which had passed to British owners. The French-speaking seigneurs also appeared as collaborators who bowed to the British to gain lucrative appointments and pensions. Many notaries and lawyers also condemned the church for its support of Britain. Some were openly anti-clerical, espousing the ideals of the French Revolution and American democracy. Bishop Plessis had denounced these radicals as early as 1809, accusing them of "tending to annihilate all principles of subordination and to set fire to the province."

Understandably, the French-speaking professionals who formed the backbone of the Parti canadien (later called the Parti patriote) had increasingly hostile relations with the British merchants. Well represented in the governor's inner councils, the really wealthy merchants numbered only a few hundred but, as historian Donald Creighton noted, they were "the most self-conscious, purposeful and assertive of all the Canadian social classes."[5] The merchants wanted to control Lower Canada's political institutions in order to introduce new laws to promote economic growth, commerce, and transportation. Some even demanded the abolition of the seigneurial system. Naturally, they accused the Assembly's French-speaking majority of systematically blocking necessary change. One solution they put forth was the union of the two Canadas, a measure intended to reduce the influence of the French. Twice, in 1022 and again in 1826, the British government examined such proposals, a harbinger of what was to come in 1840.

Members of the liberal professions anchored in rural Quebec had a very different view of Lower Canada's needs. Despite their political radicalism they were economic conservatives. While critical of many aspects of the seigneurial system, they did see it as a rampart against English-speaking farmers (anxious to gain freehold title to their lands) replacing the habitants in the St. Lawrence valley. The professionals defended traditional agriculture and denounced the threat of commercial capitalism, but, as political radicals, they called for greater autonomy for the colony and some even favoured rebellion.

Lower Canadian liberals were reticent when it came to recognizing the political rights of minority groups. In 1807, Ezekiel Hart, of Trois-Rivières, became the first Jew in the history of the British empire to be elected to a legislative assembly. Yet the Assembly refused to let him take his seat because he was a Jew, and also undoubtedly because he favoured the government party. A quarter of a century later, Hart and his sons were instrumental in having the Assembly adopt legislation according full political rights to Jews.

On the issue of women's suffrage, reformers in Lower Canada, in tune with those elsewhere in British North America and in Britain itself, wanted to deny women the right to vote. In the early decades of the nineteenth century, women appear to have voted in numerous instances in Lower Canada. In 1809, Louis-Joseph Papineau's mother was allowed to cast her vote for her son, whom she proudly described as "a good and faithful subject." But in 1820, after numerous complaints about voting by the wives of male property holders, the Assembly passed a resolution disenfranchising married women. Then, in 1834, it acted to end all female suffrage. Papineau and his party explained that electoral violence had reached such a point that "the public interest, decency, and the natural modesty of the sex" required that women not witness such scenes; also, it was alleged that the Patriotes did not always like the way that women voted! The legislation of 1834 was found to be *ultra vires* for reasons that had nothing to do with women; the right to vote was finally taken from women in 1849.

ASSEMBLY VERSUS GOVERNOR

The Rebellion of 1837 marked the failure of the Constitutional Act as a system of government for Lower Canada. Actually, the act's weaknesses had been apparent for at least a generation. Since the turn of the century, the increasingly French and Parti canadien–dominated Assembly had sought to strengthen the elective part of government and to weaken the all-powerful executive, whose members were appointed in London and Quebec.

The causes of the Rebellion of 1837 in Lower Canada were more complex than those in Upper Canada because of the colony's ethnic division. In part, this struggle pitted the English against the French, since Lower Canada's tiny English-speaking minority dominated the Executive Council and the Assembly represented the province's French-speaking majority. Yet the deterioration of French–English relations in the colony and the increasingly violent rhetoric on both sides did not prevent a small group of English-speaking Quebeckers from supporting the Patriotes. Some were Irish Catholics who had an intense hatred of England. Among these was the journalist Edmund Bailey O'Callaghan, a Patriote close to Papineau, whose anti-British prose in the *Irish Vindicator and Canada Advertiser* was as bitter as anything found in the French-language press. Others, such as brothers Wolfred and Robert Nelson, both supporters of reform, endorsed Patriote demands for an executive that would be responsible to the Assembly.

A Historical Portrait ✒

☞ Hortense Globensky

Women did not fight with the militia or even participate in direct political action during the Rebellions of 1837–38. Generally they showed their support behind the scenes. They manufactured bullets and cartridges, cared for wounded Patriotes, and took enormous risks in hiding rebels and their families in their own dwellings. Hundreds of women suffered from the consequences of the rebellions that had been led by men. Their houses were destroyed by British troops and "volunteers"; they found themselves reduced to misery. Charged with caring for their children and often their elderly parents, they were often without food as well, when the British destroyed supplies.

Yet some women became activists in the Patriote cause. Emmélie Boileau-Kimber, the wife of a doctor who was himself a strong Patriote supporter, held Patriote meetings at her *Tricolore*–flag-bedecked home in Chambly. Another Patriote set fire to her own house to demonstrate to the British that she did not fear them and to prevent them from pillaging her house before they destroyed it.

Hortense Globensky's case was different; she sided with the British even though she was French-speaking. Her father had immigrated from Poland and her mother, a French Canadian, belonged to a wealthy family. Her brother Maximilien had fought with the British against the Americans at Châteauguay and Ormstown during the War of 1812. His loyal participation brought him rewards that included a life-long pension and land. In 1837, the British military authorities asked him to form a unit of volunteers, whom he recruited from among society's "best known, most respectable, and most prosperous" members. His men participated in the ravages and reprisals around St. Eustache.

Like her brother, Hortense cast her lot openly with the British. In the election of 1834, she made no attempt to disguise her sympathies for the government party. In July 1837, friends warned her that Patriotes intended to attack her home at Ste. Scholastique, north of Montreal. One of her children had just died, and Globensky decided not to abandon the body. Upon the arrival of some 50 Patriotes one night, she took up position at a window with several pistols; seeing guns aimed directly at them, the attackers withdrew. As a souvenir of her exploit, friends styling themselves "loyal citizens of Montreal" gave her a silver teapot bearing the inscription: "in tribute for her heroism, greater than that expected of her sex, shown on the evening of July 6, 1837." Then, one Sunday in October 1837, after mass, as Patriotes attempted to encourage the parishioners to rebel, Globensky urged them to remain faithful to the government. When rebels sought to silence her, she drew a pistol and threatened them. A similar incident occurred in November. After the rebellion, she succeeded in obtaining the liberation of several rebel prisoners arrested by Colborne.

The uprising was also, in many ways, a struggle between the haves and the have-nots. Most defenders of authority, tradition, and wealth, including Roman Catholic prelates and seigneurs, opposed the reformers and disputed their claim to represent the French-Canadian nation and the majority of the population. Yet, even this generalization needs qualification, because the wealthy English-speaking merchants constantly attacked the economic status quo and lobbied for the economic reforms they judged beneficial to the colony's commercial development. At the same time, as members of a small minority, they obviously felt threatened by the French majority. Although they had previously been devoted advocates of an elected Assembly, they now defended their positions on the appointed Executive and Legislative Councils. They could not countenance political changes that would challenge their own economic dominance.

FINANCIAL QUESTIONS

In an effort to strengthen its role in government, the Assembly had for three decades sought greater control of the colony's finances. Constitutionally, it alone could initiate money bills concerning taxes and expenditures, but the executive itself also possessed revenues from Crown lands, from the military budget, and even from London, which enabled it to distribute patronage in the form of positions, salaries, and pensions to its supporters. Moreover, the Legislative Council could — and often did — refuse legislation that reached it from the Assembly. As a last resort, the governor possessed extensive veto powers. If the Legislative Council were elected, the governor would no longer be able to fill it with his own people; popular control would thus be enhanced.

The Assembly's disagreements with the governor on these basic issues were frequent and heated. As early as 1805, for example, a bill designed to raise money to build prisons provoked a debate that showed the intensity of growing English–French conflict. French members favoured paying for the prisons through higher import duties, while British merchants wanted to tax the land. Agriculture was arrayed against commerce, French against English. When the Assembly voted for import duties, the merchants appealed first to the Legislative Council, then to the governor, and finally to London. "If the [French] Canadians succeed in building so many churches, why couldn't they pay for the construction of prisons?" they argued. During this confrontation, a French-language newspaper, *Le Canadien*, was founded in November 1806. Edited by four members of the Parti canadien, it was intended to enable French Canadians to assert "the loyalty of their character and defy the designs of the opposition [British] party."

Relations between the Assembly and the governor deteriorated further during the mandate of Sir James Craig (1807–11). In the face of *Le Canadien's* vitriolic attacks on the beneficiaries of patronage and government land policies, and influenced by advisers such as the anti-Catholic Herman Ryland, Craig embarked upon a "reign of terror." When vocal Parti canadien members annoyed him, he dissolved the Assembly. When the election returned an almost identical body, he dissolved it again and went out campaigning. After *Le Canadien* denounced him, he had the paper's presses seized and its editors thrown in jail on charges of treason. When the second election brought back a reinforced Parti canadien, he attempted to frighten it into behaving, and he largely succeeded. As a long-term solution to the problem, he recommended assimilation through a union of the provinces, large-scale British immigration, the subordination of the Roman Catholic church, and the abolition of "the representative part of government." Craig then left the province, to the relief of the French-Canadian populace.

The question of provincial revenues had produced a deadlock in relations between the Assembly and the governor by the 1820s. Louis-Joseph Papineau piloted the attack. Foremost among the leaders of the Parti canadien (called the Parti patriote after 1826), Papineau entered the Assembly in 1809 and became its speaker in 1815. As one who had been brought up on a seigneury and was himself a seigneur, Papineau defended the values of tradition, nation, and family. Yet his education and political career had acquainted him with liberal thought. As the political crisis deepened after 1830, Papineau's early esteem for British institutions evolved into admiration for republicanism and American-style democracy. Liberal in his religious views, he nevertheless viewed the Roman Catholic church as an important national institution, and he attended mass to set an example for his tenants. Here, indeed, was a "divided soul," as historian Fernand Ouellet portrayed him.[6]

In 1828, believing that London would be more conciliatory once informed of the discontent in Lower Canada, the Assembly sent a petition bearing nearly 90 000 signatures and asking for curbs on the powers of the executive. But British politicians were convinced that a governor shorn of his powers would be unable to fulfil his constitutional obligations of responsibility to London.

Without saying as much, the Patriotes were apparently pushing for independence. At a time when the empire still formed a single tariff unit, London refused to consider the idea. Worse, perhaps, an independent Lower Canada might slide under the domination of the United States and risk pulling the rest of British North America along with it. Moreover, Britain's great interest in the emigration of its surplus population also made it imperative to retain the colony. In any case, the English population of Lower Canada did not want independence. As the *Quebec Gazette* warned in 1833, "Colonies biting the apple of independence will awake like Adam and Eve and find themselves naked."

Radicalization

The British Parliament adopted what it hoped would be perceived as a compromise solution. It gave the Assembly control of all expenditures on the condition that it agree to pay the civil list each year — that is, to pay for the civil administration of the colony, including the salaries of civil servants. But the mood among the Patriotes was uncompromising. In 1834 they drew up the Ninety-two Resolutions, in part a denunciation of the composition of the appointed Legislative Council and of its tendency to block legislation adopted by the elected Assembly. Certain resolutions appeared sufficiently threatening for the governor, Lord Aylmer, to conclude that the document was nothing less than a declaration of independence. To help resolve the executive's financial problems, London established the British American Land Company and granted it more than 400 000 hectares of land, in return for a commitment to build roads and make annual payments to the Crown. The company, however, showed little interest in colonization and much interest in speculation.

Britain's own political problems made the Lower Canadian question a very low priority for British politicians. The Whigs, then in power, opposed further concessions to Lower Canada's Assembly; at the same time, they wanted to appear conciliatory. Procrastination in the form of an investigation seemed the wisest policy. Unimpressed, the London *Times* in 1835 viewed this commission, headed by the Earl of Gosford, as "a frivolous and toad-eating embassy ... a temporizing mission, a bribe to the Radicals in the British Parliament to tolerate the Whig ministry."

Then, in March 1837, with the Ten Resolutions prepared by Lord John Russell, government leader in the British House of Commons, the Whigs announced an end to conciliation. This series of resolutions constituted a refusal by the Colonial Office of all of the Assembly's Ninety-two Resolutions. They authorized the government of Lower Canada, if necessary, to pay its administrative costs from the tax revenues without the Assembly's approval. There would be no elective Legislative Council, thus preserving the English-speaking minority's political influence.

A reconstruction by artist Charles Alexander Smith of the tumultuous meeting at St. Charles in 1837 at which the Patriotes called for an uprising against the British.

Charles Alexander Smith, "L'Assemblée des sixcomtés, in 1837," Oil on canvas, 300 x 690 cm., Musée national des beaux-arts du Québec, accession no. 37.54, photographer: Patrick Altman. Transferred from the Hôtel du Parlement, 1937. Restored at the Centre de Conservation du Québec with financial assistance from the Amis du Musée du Québec.

The Executive Council, representing wealth and enterprise, would, as before, continue to be responsible to the governor alone, not to the Assembly.

Papineau and his party thus failed to gain control over the executive's powers. So-called responsible government, which would oblige the governor to choose his ministers from the majority in the Assembly, could not be reconciled with the colonial relationship. The governor would continue to report to London, not to the local assembly. Momentarily, then, Canadian considerations were forgotten by Britain; the events of November and December of that same year, however, abruptly brought them back to the floor of the British Parliament.

THE LOWER CANADIAN REBELLIONS, 1837–1838

When they received news of Russell's resolutions, the Patriotes altered their tactics, since Britain apparently was not going to yield. For some, the time for revolt had arrived. More moderate views prevailed, though, and the plan agreed upon called for legal agitation that would bring the government to reconsider its positions. Revolution would be the ultimate recourse if this policy failed.

Throughout the tense days of summer and autumn 1837, the Patriote leaders worked on organization. They staged assemblies and collected funds. Patriote women established an association whose objective was "to assist, insofar as the weakness of their sex made it possible, in the triumph of the Patriote cause."[7] They organized boycotts of imported goods in an attempt to strike at British merchants. In September an association with military sections, the Fils de la liberté, was founded. At a public assembly at St. Charles on the Richelieu River east of Montreal, attended by perhaps 4000 people, Patriote orators called for revolt. The meeting adopted resolutions that included a declaration of independence. They developed plans to take Montreal and then move on to Quebec.

When the government issued warrants for their arrest, the principal Patriote leaders, Papineau included, fled to the countryside south of Montreal. The prospective urban uprising was suppressed.

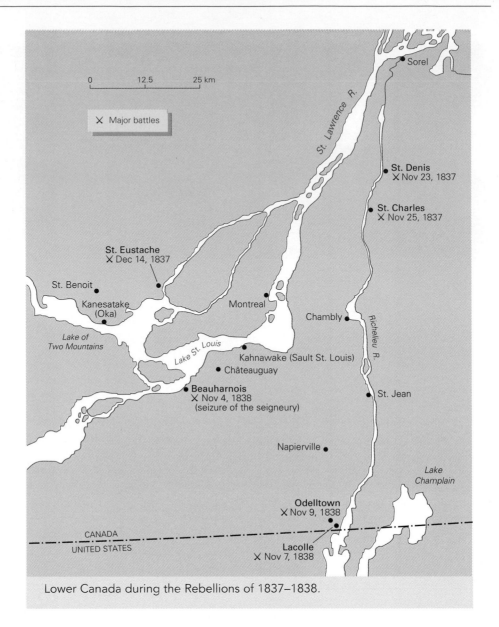

Lower Canada during the Rebellions of 1837–1838.

After an initial skirmish at St. Denis on November 23, which the Patriotes won, the British troops momentarily withdrew, awaited their second column, and then advanced. The fierce combat that ensued on November 25 at neighbouring St. Charles, in which Patriote forces were led by Wolfred Nelson, was catastrophic for the rebels. Between 50 and 150 Patriotes were killed, while the British lost only three men. Poorly armed civilians were no match for well-trained British regulars led by professional officers. Prisoners were then rounded up and sent to jail in Montreal. Throughout the St. Denis and St. Charles area, British troops also torched 20 houses and barns, adding to the atmosphere of terror.

Having pacified the Richelieu valley, Sir John Colborne, the former governor of Upper Canada who had just become commander-in-chief of all British troops in the Canadas, turned his attention to the area north of Montreal where Amury Girod, a Swiss immigrant, and Dr. Jean-Olivier Chénier headed the resistance movement. News of the Patriotes' defeat at St. Charles only hardened Chénier in his determination to "die fighting rather than surrender."

When Colborne approached St. Eustache in December 1837, Girod fled while Chénier and several insurgents took refuge in the church and other buildings. Some 70 Patriotes, including Chénier, died by gunfire or were burned to death. In total, 250 men died in battle in Lower Canada, in the Richelieu valley, and at St. Eustache, in late November and December 1837.

The victory won, the British imprisoned the rebel leaders they could catch and initiated a policy of home burning. St. Eustache was put to the torch, as was nearby St. Benoît, which had offered no resistance. One newspaper, which was usually favourable to the British, reported as follows: "For a radius of 15 miles around St. Eustache, not a building escaped being ravaged and pillaged by these new vandals" who displayed "no feelings of humanity."

By the time news of the insurrection reached London, just before Christmas, many of the rebel leaders had found asylum in the United States, where they attempted to muster support and regroup. Indeed, in February 1838, Robert Nelson led an incursion across the border. As provisional president of Lower Canada, he declared Canada's independence from Britain before fleeing back to safety on the American side.

This scene, painted by M.A. Hayes, a British officer, shows British troops with Patriote prisoners captured during the Rebellion of 1837.

National Archives of Canada/C-3653.

In November 1838, revolt broke out anew, this time southwest of Montreal. Momentarily the Patriotes at Beauharnois took control of the seigneury. In one incident resulting from years of mistrust and tense relations, a Patriote force raided the Mohawk community of Kahnawake (then also called Sault St. Louis). The raid failed, and the Mohawks captured some 60 Patriotes, whom they sent off as prisoners to Montreal.

British troops intervened in response to the new troubles and soon crushed all resistance at Beauharnois. Patriote raids from across the American border were easily turned back. Colborne — nicknamed *"le vieux brûlot"* ("the Old Firebrand") — was to be long remembered for his ruthlessness in ravaging and pillaging the countryside. After the rebellion, a grateful British government raised Colborne to the peerage as Lord Seaton — but many French Canadians chose to pronounce his new title "Lord Satan."

Intense historical controversy has surrounded the principal actors in this drama. Conservative clerical historians lauded the role of clergy such as Bishop Lartigue, who attempted to calm violent sentiment before it got out of hand. Others condemned the church for collaborating with the enemy. The Patriotes, too, have been the subject of differing judgements. Modern-day nationalists have seen them as heroes who struggled for Quebec's independence. Indeed, in 2002, the Parti Québécois government renamed the May 24 holiday, known first as Victoria Day and then later as Dollard des Ormeaux Day, the Journée des Patriotes.

Other historians such as Fernand Ouellet, have described the Patriotes as members of an ambitious professional elite, who sought political power and social prestige. Despite their revolutionary appearance, many Patriote leaders were social conservatives. For example, Papineau was a landowner, seigneur of

Defeat of the Insurgents by Sir John Colborne at St. Eustache, November 25, 1837, a reconstruction of the final assault on the church, by John Walker (1831–1898).

National Archives of Canada/C-6032.

Where Historians Disagree

Interpretations of the Rebellions of 1837–38 in Lower Canada

What were the causes of the uprisings of 1837–38 in Lower Canada? Despite decades of debate and discussion on the subject, no consensus exists.

Early-twentieth-century historians such as Thomas Chapais portrayed the rebellions in Lower Canada as the outcome of bitter political conflict between the British colonial governor and the Patriote-dominated elected Assembly. Chapais judged the insurrection to be "regrettable and unjustifiable," an "overreaction when weighted against our grievances."[1] Abbé Lionel Groulx, writing at about the same time, was torn by his various allegiances. As a conservative-minded priest, he reproved the Patriotes for their anti-clericalism and demagogic championing of "doctrinal fads" such as democracy and popular sovereignty. But, as a nationalist, he also saw in the events of 1837 "something extremely stimulating and healthy."[2] Later, nationalists such as Maurice Séguin interpreted the insurrections as a struggle for liberation, led by "the most advanced French Canadian nationalists against British domination."[3]*

By the 1960s, historians were casting their nets more widely in search of the underlying causes of the rebellions. Although they did not deny the existence of serious political quarrels, they asked other questions that enlarged the debate: Who were the Patriotes and what were their ambitions? How did the inhabitants react to the appeals of the rebels, and what explains their reaction? Was the rebellion really an English–French conflict, or was it mainly a struggle between classes?

Donald Creighton saw the rebellions as the final episode of a contest between agriculture and commerce. Progressive-minded but frustrated Montreal merchants attacked backward farmers and their political leaders, the Patriotes.[4] For his part, historian Fernand Ouellet meticulously traced the development of a severe agricultural crisis in Lower Canada in the early nineteenth century. He maintained that deteriorating economic conditions — and the fear that they bred — served to "unite the French Canadian lower and middle classes in a single nationalist movement" whose objective was the overthrow of the British colonial authority.[5] Ouellet also sought to show that the Patriotes comprised a growing professional elite ambitious for political power and social prestige.

In contrast, some historians, such as Jean-Pierre Wallot, have questioned the very existence of the agricultural crisis. In one study, Wallot and economist Gilles Paquet propose instead a "dynamic and entrepreneurial view of Lower Canada" during this period.[6] Historian Allan Greer has studied conditions in the lower Richelieu valley, a centre of Patriote activity and the scene of two important armed confrontations. He saw no precipitous decline in habitant wheat production there and concluded that this region simply did not "fit easily" into Ouellet's chronology.[7] Monographs focussing on other regions of the province could shed further light on the question of the existence of an agricultural crisis. Unfortunately, such monographs depend upon statistical series that are often incomplete and unreliable.

More recently, political scientist Daniel Salée has underlined the "revolutionary character" of the rebellions. According to Salée, the Patriotes were "bourgeois liberals" whose language placed them solidly within a broad current of opinion that was becoming increasingly influential throughout the western world at that time. Their economic program and their denunciations of the abuses of the seigneurial system enabled them to mobilize substantial support among the habitants.[8]

Allan Greer also sees the rebellions as a "classic revolutionary crisis."[9] He stresses the increasing involvement of the masses in the deepening crisis and maintains that their leaders well understood the necessity of securing the habitants' voluntary co-operation. F. Murray Greenwood sees the development of a "garrison mentality" among Lower Canada's English in the 1790s as having fatally destroyed any possibility of building harmonious relations with segments of the French population. Fearful of the external threat posed by Napoleon and equally fearful of a security threat within Lower Canada, the English elite attempted to introduce assimilationist polities in education and land tenure, to tighten control over the justice system, and to enforce royal supremacy over the Roman Catholic church.[10] Emphasis by Greenwood, Greer, and others on factors other than material conditions represents a useful widening of the debate.

* Translations from the French in this paragraph are by Richard Jones.

[1] Thomas Chapais, *Cours d'histoire de Canada*, vol. 4, *1833–1841* (Quebec: Bernard Valiquette, 1923), p. 226.

[2] Lionel Groulx, *Notre maître le passé*, vol. 2 (Quebec: Librairie Granger Frères, 1945), pp. 86–87.

[3] Maurice Séguin, *L'idée d'indépendance au Québec: genèse et historique* (Trois-Rivières: Boréal Express, 1968), p. 33.

[4] Donald Creighton, "The Economic Background of the Rebellions of Eighteen Thirty-Seven," *Canadian Journal of Economics and Political Science* 3 (1937): 322–34.

[5] Fernand Ouellet, *Lower Canada, 1791–1840: Social Change and Nationalism* (Toronto: McClelland & Stewart, 1980), p. 135.

[6] Jean-Pierre Wallot and Gilles Paquet, *Lower Canada at the Turn of the Nineteenth Century: Restructuring and Modernization* (Ottawa: Canadian Historical Association, 1988), p. 3.

[7] Allan Greer, *Peasant, Lord and Merchant: Rural Society in Three Quebec Parishes, 1740–1840* (Toronto: University of Toronto Press, 1985), p. 211.

[8] Daniel Salée, "Revolutionary Political Thought, the Persistence of the Old Order, and the Problem of Power in an Ancien Régime Colonial Society: Ideological Perspectives of Lower Canada, 1827–1838," *British Journal of Canadian Studies* 3[1] (1988): 52.

[9] Allan Greer, *The Patriots and the People: The Rebellion of 1837 in Rural Lower Canada* (Toronto: University of Toronto Press, 1993), p. 5.

[10] F. Murray Greenwood, *Legacies of Fear: Law and Politics in Quebec in the Era of the French Revolution* (Toronto: University of Toronto Press, 1993).

Montebello, who nonetheless spoke fervently about American democracy. But his revolutionary rhetoric became more ambivalent over time, and he denied with vehemence that he wanted revolution. Half an hour after the beginning of the Battle of St. Denis, he fled to the American border. (Robert Nelson replaced Papineau as the Patriote leader and introduced a truly radical program, which advocated the abolition of the seigneurial system as well as the abolition of the payment of the tithe to the Roman Catholic church.)

It is clear that the Patriote leaders, who were French-speaking merchants and professionals, had ambitions as a group, and that they saw the welfare of the masses as a function of their own interests. Church leaders also had ambitions. So did seigneurs such as Pierre de Boucherville, who calculated that he would have lost an annual revenue of 500 *louis* (gold coin pieces) if the revolution had succeeded. So did the English-speaking merchants, who, although a small minority, largely controlled the colony's economy. So did the British administrators, who believed that power should be entrusted to appointed officials, most of them English-speaking. So did the British Parliament, which still felt that colonies should be, and could be, useful to the mother country. And so, finally, did the habitants, who had many ideas of what was wrong with their situation and of what might better their lot, and who constituted the great majority — perhaps 95 percent — of the insurrection's active sympathizers.

CONSEQUENCES OF THE REBELLIONS

 To govern Lower Canada after it had suspended the colony's constitution, Britain set up a Special Council in 1838. It was composed of members of the English-speaking minority and included a few strongly loyalist French Canadians as well. During the rebellions, it suspended civil liberties and legal rights. Then it set up a police force in Montreal as well as a rural police force to pacify the habitants. The Council also weakened the hold of French civil law by giving new guarantees to landed property and by undermining seigneurial tenure on the Island of Montreal.

LORD DURHAM'S VISIT

For the longer term, London chose to address the Canadian problem by forming a royal commission to visit both Lower and Upper Canada. The future historian François-Xavier Garneau appealed to the commissioner on his arrival in Quebec: "Durham, close your ears to the counsels of vengeance; take upon yourself the defense of a helpless people." But Lord Durham was listening to other advice. Before he even left England, he had been lobbied by Canadian and British merchant groups who emphasized the ethnic aspect of the conflict; they urged union of the Canadas to save themselves from "the designs of the French faction, madly bent upon [the] destruction" of the rights, the interests, and the property of Lower Canada's British population.

Durham's concerns for economic development made him sympathetic to the merchants' views. In his report, submitted in 1839, he drew attention to the "deadly animosity" between French and English: "I found two nations warring in the bosom of a single state; I found a struggle, not of principles, but of races." A union of the two Canadas would yield a slight English majority, which immigration would further reinforce. As for the French, whom he viewed as innately inferior, Durham was convinced that "once placed, by the legitimate course of events and the working of natural causes, in a minority, [they] would abandon their vain hopes of nationality." Union with Upper Canada would thus assure the assimilation of the French — the ultimate solution to ethnic conflict in Lower Canada.

This drawing of a Patriote in the Rebellions of 1837–38 by Henri Julien was reproduced and distributed during the October Crisis in Quebec in 1970.

National Archives of Canada/C-17937.

The rebellion, then, brought Lower Canada to its knees and made it easy to overlook the enormous changes that the colony had undergone at virtually all levels since 1791. The colony lost its own government and was to be joined to Upper Canada in a union that the great majority of the French Canadians did not want. Moreover, the avowed purpose of this union, as expressed by Durham, by British parliamentarians, and by Lower Canadian merchants, was to break the power of French Canada and eventually to assimilate it. But like the proponents of the Constitutional Act a half-century earlier, the advocates of union proved to be poor prophets. So, too, did the French Canadians who viewed the prospect of union so darkly.

NOTES

1. Mary Anne Poutanen, "Reflections on Montreal Prostitution in the Records of the Lower Courts," in Donald Fyson et al., eds., *Class, Gender and the Law in Eighteenth- and Nineteenth-Century Quebec: Sources and Perspectives* (Montreal: McGill University, Department of History, 1993), pp. 99–125.

2. Jan Noel, " 'Femmes Fortes' and the Montreal Poor in the Early Nineteenth Century," in Wendy Mitchinson et al., eds., *Canadian Women: A Reader* (Toronto: Harcourt Brace, 1996), p. 69.

3. Allan Greer, *Peasant, Lord, and Merchant: Rural Society in Three Quebec Parishes, 1740–1840* (Toronto: University of Toronto Press, 1985), pp. 122–39.

4. Allan Greer, *The Patriots and the People: The Rebellion of 1837 in Rural Lower Canada* (Toronto: University of Toronto Press, 1993), p. 293.

5. Donald Creighton, *The Commercial Empire of the St. Lawrence, 1760–1850* (Toronto: Ryerson Press, 1937), p. 23, quoted in Gilles Paquet et Jean-Pierre Wallot, "Groupes sociaux et pouvoir: le cas canadien au tournant du XIXe siècle," *Revue d'histoire de l'Amérique française* 27 (1973–74): 539.

6. Fernand Ouellet, *Louis-Joseph Papineau: A Divided Soul* (Ottawa: Canadian Historical Association, 1960).

7. The original French text reads, "concourir, autant que la faiblesse de leur sexe peut le leur permettre, à faire réussir la cause patriotique." Quoted in Micheline Dumont et al., *L'histoire des femmes au Québec depuis quatre siècles* (Montreal: Le Jour, 1982), p. 145.

A reconstruction by Henri Julien of the hanging of five Patriotes on January 18, 1839: Joseph-Jacques Robert, François-Xavier Hamelin, Pierre-Théophile Décoigne, and Ambroise and Charles Sanguinet. The British, during the rule of the Special Council, executed 12 Patriotes and sent 58 to the penal colonies in Australia for their part in the 1838 uprising.

National Archives of Canada/C-20295.

LINKING TO THE PAST w⟨w⟩w

Canada after 1800
http://collections.ic.gc.ca/heirloom_series/volume1/chapter4/chapter4.htm

The first few pages cover political, economic, and social developments from early to mid-1850s.

Forges du Saint-Maurice National Historic Site
http://parkscanada.gc.ca/lhn-nhs/qc/saintmaurice/index_e.asp

An illustrated history of the Forges du Saint-Maurice covering the period from 1670 to the present, plus an online tour and a picture gallery.

John Molson (1763–1836)
http://collections.ic.gc.ca/heirloom_series/volume5/222-223.htm

A short biography of John Molson, who made significant contributions to the economic development of Quebec in the early nineteenth century.

Alexis de Tocqueville
http://www.mri.gouv.qc.ca/la_bibliotheque/AlToc_an.html

A brief description of Alexis de Tocqueville's visit to and observations of Lower Canada in 1831. Excerpts from his notebooks can be accessed at http://www.mri.gouv.qc.ca/la_bibliotheque/ATnotes_an.html.

Towards Confederation: Lower Canada (1791–1842)
http://www.nlc-bnc.ca/confed/lowercan/elowrcan.htm

An overview of the Lower Canada rebellions, with links to information on James Craig, Louis-Joseph Papineau, Lord Durham, the newspapers *The Quebec Mercury* and *Le Canadien*, and the British American Land Company.

Early Stages of Parliamentary Government
http://fc.lbpsb.qc.ca/~history/module4.htm

This history lesson from the History of Quebec and Canada Resource Page offers a succinct summary of social and economic conditions in Lower Canada in the early nineteenth century. Included is information on the Rebellion of 1837, with portraits of several Patriotes, maps and illustrations of the major struggles, and details of Lord Durham's report.

RELATED READINGS

R. Douglas Francis and Donald B. Smith, eds., *Readings in Canadian History: Pre-Confederation*, 6th ed. (Toronto: Nelson Thomson Learning, 2002), contains two important articles on the rebellions: Fernand Ouellet, "The Insurrections," pp. 269–80; and Colin Coates, "The Rebellions of 1837–38, and Other Bourgeois Revolutions in Quebec Historiography," pp. 280–91.

BIBLIOGRAPHY

Fernand Ouellet's *Lower Canada, 1791–1840: Social Change and Nationalism* (Toronto: McClelland & Stewart, 1979) is very useful for this period. His *Economic and Social History of Quebec, 1760–1850* (Toronto: Macmillan, 1980), and his *Economy, Class, and Nation in Quebec: Interpretive Essays*, ed. and trans. Jacques A. Barbier (Toronto: Copp Clark Pitman, 1991) should also be consulted. Jean-Pierre Wallot and Gilles Paquet criticize Ouellet's interpretations and provide a contrary view on several issues. See, for example, "The Agricultural Crisis in Lower Canada, 1802–12; *mise au point*. A Response to T.J.A. Le Goff," *Canadian Historical Review* 56 (1975): 133–61; "Stratégie foncière de l'habitant: Québec (1790–1835)," *Revue d'histoire de l'Amérique française* 39 (1985–1986): 551–81; and Gilles Paquet and Jean-Pierre Wallot, *Lower Canada at the Turn of the Nineteenth Century: Restructuring and Modernization* (Ottawa: Canadian Historical Association, 1988). Allan Greer, *Peasant, Lord, and Merchant: Rural Society in Three Quebec Parishes, 1740–1840* (Toronto: University of Toronto Press, 1985) is an important study of a region in which Patriote support was strong. John McCallum, *Unequal Beginnings: Agriculture and Economic Development in Quebec and Ontario until 1870* (Toronto: University of Toronto Press, 1980); Michael Bliss, *Northern Enterprise: Five Centuries of Canadian Business* (Toronto: McClelland & Stewart, 1987); and R. Cole Harris, "Quebec in the Century after the Conquest," in R. Cole Harris and John Warkentin, *Canada Before Confederation* (Ottawa: Carleton University Press, 1991 [1974]), pp. 65–109 are also helpful. Gérald Bernier and Daniel Salée argue in *The Shaping of Quebec Politics and Society: Colonialism, Power and the Transition to Capitalism in the 19th Century* (Washington, DC: Taylor and Francis, 1992) that social and class questions transcend ethnic issues in this period of Quebec's history.

Useful historiographical studies are Gérald Bernier and Daniel Salée, "Les insurrections de 1837–1838 au Québec; remarques critiques et théoriques en marge de l'historiographie," *Canadian Review of Studies in Nationalism/Revue canadienne des études sur le nationalisme* 13 (1986): 13–30; and Fernand Ouellet, "La tradition révolutionnaire au Canada: A Propos de l'historiographie des insurrections de 1837–1838 dans le Bas-Canada," *Revue de l'Université d'Ottawa/University of Ottawa Quarterly* 60 (1985): 91–124; and Allan Greer, "1837–38: Rebellion Reconsidered," *Canadian Historical Review* 76 (1995): 1–18. Bibliographical suggestions appear in James Lambert's essay, "Quebec/Lower Canada" in M. Brook Taylor, ed., *Canadian History: A Reader's Guide*, vol. 1, *Beginnings to Confederation* (Toronto: University of Toronto Press, 1994), pp. 112–83.

On the history of the Roman Catholic church see Lucien Lemieux, *Histoire du catholicisme québécois: les XVIIIe et XIXe siècles*, tome 1: *Les années difficiles (1760–1839)* (Montreal: Boréal, 1989). James Lambert has made a notable contribution to social and religious history in his regrettably unpublished Ph.D. thesis, "Monseigneur, the Catholic Bishop. Joseph-Octave Plessis, Church, State, and Society in Lower Canada: Historiography and Analysis," 3 vols. (Université Laval, 1980). On conflict between the clergy and the laity, see Christian Dessureault and Christine Hudon, "Conflits sociaux et élites locales au Bas-Canada: le clergé, les notables, la paysannerie et le contrôle de la fabrique," *Canadian Historical Review* 80 (1999): 413–39.

The impact of the French Revolution is discussed in Pierre Boulle and Richard-A. Lebrun, *Le Canada et la révolution française* (Montreal: Centre interuniversitaire d'études européennes, 1989); and in Michel Grenon, ed., *L'image de la Révolution française au Québec, 1789–1989* (Montreal: Hurtubise HMH, 1989). F. Murray Greenwood traces the development of a "garrison mentality" among Lower Canada's population in *Legacies of Fear: Law and Politics in Quebec in the Era of the French Revolution* (Toronto: University of Toronto Press, 1993).

Alexis de Tocqueville's Canadian journal offers a contemporary portrait of Lower Canada in the early 1830s; see Jacques Vallée, ed., *Tocqueville au Bas-Canada* (Montreal: Éditions du Jour, 1973); as well as Stéphane Dion, "La pensée de Tocqueville — L'épreuve du Canada français," *Revue d'histoire de l'Amérique française* 41 (1987–88): 537–52. The cholera epidemics are discussed in Geoffrey Bilson, *A Darkened House: Cholera in Nineteenth-Century Canada* (Toronto: University of Toronto Press, 1980). Barbara Tunis examines the question of smallpox vaccination in "Public Vaccination in Lower Canada, 1815–1823: Controversy and a Dilemma," *Historical Reflections* 9 (1982): 267–76.

Jean-Marie Fecteau analyzes social issues in *Un nouvel ordre des choses: la pauvreté, le crime, l'État au Québec, de la fin du XVIIIᵉ à 1840* (Montreal: VLB Editeur, 1989). Serge Gagnon's research on social history is available in *Plaisir d'amour et crainte de Dieu: sexualité et confession au Bas-Canada* (Ste. Foy, QC: Les Presses de l'Université Laval, 1990), and *Mariage et famille au temps de Papineau* (Ste. Foy, QC: Les Presses de l'Université Laval, 1993). Jean-Pierre Hardy examines body hygiene and other questions linked to daily life in *La vie quotidienne dans la vallée du Saint-Laurent (1790–1835)* (Quebec: Septentrion, 2002). Françoise Noël proposes a useful case study of social organization in *The Christie Seigneuries: Estate Management and Settlement in the Upper Richelieu Valley, 1764–1854* (Montreal/Kingston: McGill-Queen's University Press, 1992). A brief examination of rural life may be found in Serge Courville and Normand Séguin, *Rural Life in Nineteenth-Century Quebec* (Ottawa: Canadian Historical Association, 1989 (Historical Booklet 47).

Material on the history of the judicial system is available in Donald Fyson's unpublished Ph.D. thesis, "Criminal Justice, Civil Society, and the Local State: The Justices of the Peace in the District of Montreal, 1764–1830" (Université de Montréal, 1995); and in Evelyn Kolish, *Nationalismes et conflits de droits: le débat du droit privé au Québec, 1760–1840* (LaSalle, QC: Hurtubise HMH, 1994). Several articles on justice, martial law and state repression during the rebellions may be found in F. Murray Greenwood and Barry Wright, eds., *Canadian State Trials, vol. II: Rebellion and Invasion in the Canadas, 1837–1839* (Toronto: University of Toronto Press, 2002). On the War of 1812, see Martin F. Auger, "French-Canadian Participation in the War of 1812: A Social Study of the Voltigeurs Canadiens," *Canadian Military History* 10(3) (2001): 23–41. On the treatment of the mentally ill, see James E. Moran, *Committed to the State Asylum: Insanity and Society in Nineteenth-Century Quebec and Ontario* (Montreal/Kingston: McGill-Queen's University Press, 2000). The transformation of Lower Canada's landscape by settlers and the consequent emergence of community sentiment and its links with the rise of nationalism are studied in Colin M. Coates, *The Metamorphoses of Landscape and Community in Early Quebec* (Montreal/Kingston: McGill-Queen's University Press, 2000). See also his article on the interest in landscaping of some upper-class Britons in Lower Canada, "Like 'The Thames towards Putney': The Appropriation of Landscape in Lower Canada," *Canadian Historical Review* 74 (1993): 317–43.

A brief synthesis of the rebellions is available in English in Jean-Paul Bernard, *The Rebellions of 1837 and 1838 in Lower Canada* (Ottawa: Canadian Historical Association, 1996 (Historical Booklet 55). A fuller examination may be found in his book, *Les rébellions de 1837–1838* (Montreal: Boréal Express, 1983). Allan Greer challenges earlier analyses of the events of 1837 and their origins in *The Patriots and the People: The Rebellion of 1837 in Rural Lower Canada* (Toronto: University of Toronto Press, 1993), and in "1837–38: Rebellion Reconsidered," *Canadian Historical Review* 76 (1995): 1–18. In "Historical Roots of Canadian Democracy," *Journal of Canadian Studies* 34(1) (1999): 7–26, Greer also contends that "ethnic nationalism" was much more characteristic of the anglophone Tories of Lower Canada than of the French-speaking Patriots. Joseph Schull, *Rebellion: The Rising in French Canada, 1837* (Toronto: Macmillan, 1971) is an older, popular treatment. Jacques Monet, *The Last Cannon Shot: A Study of French Canadian Nationalism, 1837–1850* (Toronto: University of Toronto Press, 1969) contains useful material on both the rebellion and its aftermath. Relations between Britain and Canada are analyzed in Peter Burroughs, *The Canadian Crisis and British Colonial Policy, 1828–1841* (Toronto: Macmillan, 1972); Ged Martin, *The Durham Report and British Policy: A Critical Essay* (Cambridge: Cambridge University Press, 1972); Phillip A. Buckner, "The Colonial Office and British North America, 1801–50," in the *Dictionary of Canadian Biography*, vol. 8, *1851–1860* (Toronto: University of Toronto Press, 1985), pp. xxiii–xxxvii; and James Sturgis, "Anglicisation as a Theme in Lower Canadian History, 1807–1843," *British Journal of Canadian Studies* 3 (1988): 210–29. Yvan Lamonde proposes an intellectual history of the period in *Histoire sociale des idées au Québec. vol. I: 1760–1896* (Montreal: Fides, 2000). Janet Ajzenstat sees Durham as a mainstream liberal but not as a cultural chauvinist in *The Political Thought of Lord Durham* (Montreal/Kingston: McGill-Queen's University Press, 1988). The *Journal of Canadian Studies* devoted its Spring 1990 issue, "Durham and His Ideas," to Lord Durham.

For material pertaining to women in Lower Canada in the early nineteenth century see Micheline Dumont et al., *Quebec Women: A History* (Toronto: Women's Press, 1987). Women's work as domestics is examined in Claudette Lacelle, *Urban Domestic Servants in Nineteenth-Century Canada* (Ottawa: Parks Canada, 1987). Bettina Bradbury et al. look at changing marriage contracts in "Property and Marriage: The Law and the Practice in Early Nineteenth-Century Montreal," *Histoire sociale/Social History* 26 (1993): 9–39. Peter Gossage studies the work of the Grey Nuns with foundlings in "Les enfants abandonnés à Montréal au 19e siècle: la crèche d'Youville des Soeurs Grises, 1820–1871," *Revue d'histoire de l'Amérique française* 40 (1987): 31–59. Allan Greer analyzes the participation of women in the rebellions in *The Patriots and the People: The Rebellion of 1837 in Rural Lower Canada* (Toronto: University of Toronto Press, 1999), pp. 189–218. Urban violence involving women is examined in Mary Anne Poutanen, "Images du danger dans les archives judiciaires. Comprendre la violence et le vagabondage dans un centre urbain du début du XIXe siècle, Montréal (1810–1842), *Revue d'histoire de l'Amérique française* 55 (2002): 381–405; in Sandy Ramos, "'A Most Detestable Crime': Gender Identities and Sexual Violence in the District of Montreal, 1803–1843," *Journal of the Canadian Historical Association/Revue de la Société historique du Canada* 12 (2001): 27–48; and in Donald Fyson, Colin Coates, and Kathryn Harvey, eds., *Class, Gender and the Law in Eighteenth- and Nineteenth-Century Quebec: Sources and Perspectives* (Montreal: Montreal History Group, 1993).

Aboriginal issues are reviewed by Daniel Francis in *A History of the Native Peoples of Quebec, 1760–1867* (Ottawa: Department of Indian Affairs and Northern Development, 1983). On Native history of the St. Lawrence valley, see Jean-Pierre Sawaya, *La Fédération des Sept Feux de la vallée du Saint-Laurent, XVIIe–XIXe siècles* (Sillery: Septentrion, 1998). Individuals mentioned in this chapter are also studied in various volumes of the *Dictionary of Canadian Biography*; see, in particular, Fernand Ouellet's article on Papineau in vol. 10, *1871–1880* (Toronto: University of Toronto Press, 1972), pp. 564–78. Jack Verney has recently written a biography of E.B. O'Callaghan, one of the Patriotes' great English-speaking allies: *O'Callaghan, The Making and Unmaking of a Rebel* (Ottawa: Carleton University Press, 1994).

Useful maps relating to this chapter appear in R. Louis Gentilcore, ed., *Historical Atlas of Canada*, vol. 2, *The Land Transformed, 1800–1891* (Toronto: University of Toronto Press, 1993).

CHAPTER

13

UPPER CANADA, 1815–1840: AN EVOLVING IDENTITY

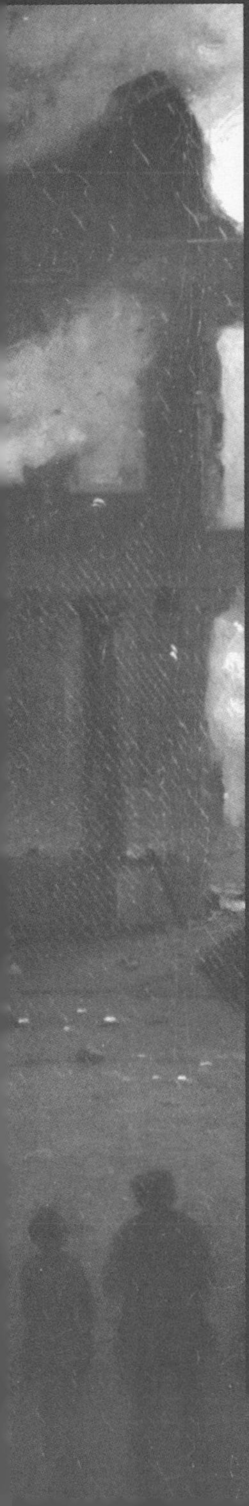

TIME LINE

1816 – Upper Canada introduced the Common School Act, which allocated £6000 annually towards public schools

1817 – The Society for the Relief of Strangers, the first major public welfare agency, established

1818 – Government of Upper Canada agrees to annual payments or annuities in perpetuity for land purchases from the First Nations

1819 – Political activist Robert Gourlay banished from Upper Canada

1824 – William Lyon Mackenzie begins his newspaper, *The Colonial Advocate*, at Queenston, Upper Canada

1826 – Beginning of the Canada Land Company

1827 – Royal Charter establishes King's College in York, the forerunner of the University of Toronto

1829 – Welland Canal open for navigation between Lake Ontario and Lake Erie

Church of Scotland granted a share of the clergy reserves

1830 – Grand Lodge of British North America (the Orange Order) established at Brockville, Upper Canada

1832 – Completion of the Rideau Canal

Major outbreak of cholera in Upper Canada

1834 – William Lyon Mackenzie chosen as Toronto's first mayor

1835 – The opening of the Kingston Penitentiary

1837– William Lyon Mackenzie leads an unsuccessful rebellion against British rule

Battle of the Windmill near Prescott, Upper Canada

From 1815 to 1840 Upper Canada's population quadrupled, from less than 100 000 to more than 400 000. Immigration accounted for much of this increase. Some of the new immigrants came from the United States, but most arrived from the British Isles: northern Irish Protestants, southern Irish Roman Catholics; Lowland and Highland Scots; Welsh and English. The newcomers settled the land; established and refined political, social, and educational institutions; contributed to the colony's economic growth; and participated in its political movements. The British immigrants, with the exception of some Catholic Irish, worked to develop a sense of loyalty to Britain. These newcomers brought British customs and attitudes that eventually mixed, in the years to follow, with those of the settlers already there to create a unique Upper Canadian character.

An early depiction of an African-Canadian woman in the late 1830s, at Lundy's Lane near Niagara Falls, where a number of people of African-American background had settled.

National Archives of Canada/C-93963.

IMMIGRATION AND SETTLEMENT

After the War of 1812, the British government encouraged British over American immigration to Upper Canada. New laws pertaining to "aliens" prevented Americans from obtaining land grants until they had resided in the province for seven years. Nevertheless, some Americans did come, including fugitive slaves from the South and freed ones from the northern states. Most African Americans homesteaded along the border, with the exception of a small group of black veterans of the War of 1812 who settled in Oro township on the western shore of Lake Simcoe.

DIRECTED SETTLEMENT

After 1815, the British settlers that Simcoe had sought in the early years of the province finally arrived. The end of the Napoleonic Wars best explains the migration. Peace brought economic depression and unemployment to Great Britain. It curtailed the army's demand for manpower, and, at the same time, made overseas travel less dangerous. Postwar Britain encouraged emigration. From the government's perspective, it would reduce the population pressure in Britain, provide relief from social unrest, and facilitate expansion and control of its empire.

The British government in the late 1810s and early 1820s assisted the exodus with generous aid, similar to that first given the Loyalists. The assistance included the cost of transportation, free grants of land to family heads, rations for eight months (or until they became established), agricultural supplies at cost, and a minister and school teacher on government salary for each settlement. Initially the British government intended this program mainly for demobilized soldiers and half-pay officers (those officers who received a reduced allowance when not in actual service, or after their retirement).

Some 800 immigrants from four parishes in the Highlands of Scotland settled in Glengarry County, Upper Canada, in 1815. Their early pioneering experiences would be made known through Ralph Connor's popular Glengarry novels after 1900. The government also helped several thousand Scots to settle in Upper Canada, chiefly in the Lanark area in the eastern part of the colony, then others in the Rideau district south of present-day Ottawa. In the 1820s, some 3000 Irish immigrants under government sponsorship and administered by Peter Robinson, the commissioner of Crown lands for Upper Canada, arrived in the Peterborough area. A significant number from North Tipperary, Ireland, also settled in the Bytown (Ottawa) area and, later, around London, attracted by next of kin who had gone before them and had succeeded in acquiring land for their children.

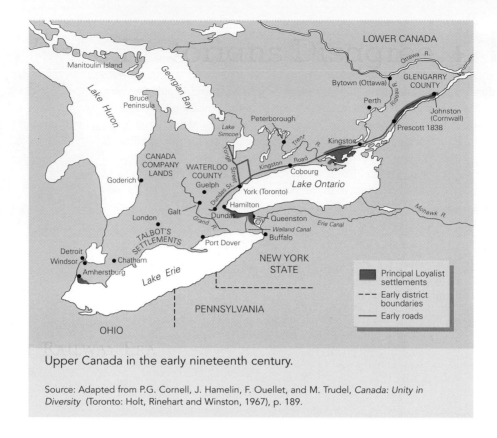

Upper Canada in the early nineteenth century.

Source: Adapted from P.G. Cornell, J. Hamelin, F. Ouellet, and M. Trudel, *Canada: Unity in Diversity* (Toronto: Holt, Rinehart and Winston, 1967), p. 189.

One of the largest of the assisted British emigration schemes was organized by the Rev. Thomas Sockett under the auspices of the Petworth Emigration Committee in the years 1832–37. Some 1800 men, women, and children mostly from the Petworth parish in West Sussex, in the southeast of England, came under Petworth's third Earl of Egremont's sponsorship and under the guidance of the local rector, Rev. Sockett. Most were poor agricultural labourers who arrived in Upper Canada via Montreal and Toronto and were then dispersed to areas of south-central and western Upper Canada, where they were instrumental in building up the colony. The Petworth emigrants represented a transition group — from the older concept in the 1810s and '20s, of government-assisted emigration and settlement, to the concept in the 1840s and '50s, of limited assistance through parishioners or landlords—or else no assistance, expecting immigrants to take care of their own needs through sheer hard work and struggle. "Friendly societies" assisted single women wishing to emigrate — including the London Female Emigration Society, formed in 1850, the British Ladies Emigration Society, formed in 1859, and the Female Middle Class Emigration Society, formed in 1861 — by covering the cost of passage, and also providing a staff of matrons on board the ships.

In the mid-1820s, the British government stopped aiding emigrants, as private charitable associations and landowners, anxious to rid their estates of impoverished tenants, now provided at least minimal assistance. Many immigrants were also willing to come on their own, without government assistance, to escape a desperate situation. This was especially true of the victims of the Irish potato famine.

Upper Canadian landowners, such as Colonel Thomas Talbot, also assisted immigrants in the hope of profiting from government incentives for settlement and land development. Talbot secured 2000 ha on the then-remote northwestern shore of Lake Erie. He subsequently received 81 ha of adjoining land for each colonist he settled on a 20 ha lot of the original grant. Talbot eventually accumulated an estate of nearly 30 000 ha, making him one of the largest landholders in Upper Canada. In return, he contributed to the transformation of more than 200 000 ha of forest into 3000 farm lots in southwestern Upper Canada. His extensive road system made his lands more accessible and hence more valuable.

In 1826, the British government created the Canada Company, the first large-scale Canadian land company, headed by John Galt. The Canada Company purchased over 400 000 hectares of land, consisting of Crown reserves and the huge Huron Tract (the latter in southwestern Upper Canada on the shores of Lake Huron), for the modest price of approximately £350 000 sterling. The Company was allowed to withhold one-third of the price to be used to develop public works and improvements in the Tract. Galt proved incompetent, and the Canada Company initially suffered heavy losses. But it survived into the 1830s when increased immigration enabled it to recover. The Company founded the towns of Goderich, in the Huron Tract, and the town of Guelph in another of its parcels of land east of the Tract. (Galt went on to launch another land company in Lower Canada, known as the British American Land Company, with large holdings in the Eastern Townships.)

These land speculators were only a small fraction of the total number of land speculators in Upper Canada who became rich and rose to positions of social prominence, through land acquisition and sales. In most cases, they paid next to nothing for the land, and then turned around and sold it to poor immigrants at inflated prices. Profits of 50 to 100 percent were not uncommon, although most received returns in the area of 2 to 8 percent.

THE VOYAGE OVERSEAS

Most immigrants came at their own expense. Only a few of the well-to-do could afford the £30 for first-class accommodation on an American frigate, which included a cabin with one or two bunks, a sofa, a window, and full meals. The remainder had to share bunks in the steerage of crowded passenger ships or in the dank holds of timber ships.

Makeshift two-metre-square bunks stacked two or three tiers high lined the sides and ran down the middle of the vessels. The shipowners packed as many as 250 immigrants into a space 28.5 m long by 7.5 m wide and little more than 1.5 m high. Often four people, even complete strangers, were crowded into a single berth. Food was often rancid and clean water and clean air non-existent. Not surprisingly, communicable diseases spread rapidly. Few doctors and medical supplies were available.

The immigrants endured these harsh conditions for up to six weeks — and longer in times of poor sailing. Many had already spent a week or two waiting at dockside for the ship to sail. In his first novel, *Redburn*, Herman Melville describes how the emigrants talked of soon seeing America:

> The agent had told them that twenty days would be an unusually long voyage. Suddenly there was a cry of "Land," and emigrants crowded a deck expecting America, but it was only Ireland.

Some never saw the New World; they died and were buried at sea. Cholera and typhoid spread through Britain and Europe in the 1830s and 1840s, and took its toll with one of every 28 immigrants to Quebec dying on board ship. The wretched and bewildered immigrants who survived the trip were then confronted by unscrupulous "runners," or profiteers at dockside, eager to take advantage of them. They still faced the arduous overland journey to their new homes.

Emigration vessel, between decks. From *The Illustrated London News*, May 10, 1851.

Toronto Reference Library.

The constant need for labour in Upper Canada gave even penniless immigrants an opportunity to earn a living, to adjust to a freer society, and to save for farms of their own. In Upper Canada a landless labourer, in the early 1830s, could still become a landed proprietor — something nearly impossible in Britain.

THE NATIVE PEOPLES

The land came from the First Nations peoples, who, by 1815, were already outnumbered ten to one by non-Natives. After the War of 1812, the First Nations in Upper Canada made seven major land surrenders, opening up much of present-day southern Ontario for settlement. In 1818, the government of Upper Canada changed the method of purchasing the land, offering to make annual payments or annuities in perpetuity, an arrangement that was preferable for the government to a simple one-time payment. Although by this time the First Nations realized that these land-sale agreements were final and irreversible, they lacked the strength in numbers to resist the proposed cessions. In addition, settled areas now divided the bands from one another, a situation which deterred a united response. As well, much of the First Nations' lands near the settlements had been ruined for hunting by the immigrant farmers. Finally, groups like the Mississaugas were influenced by the government's oral promise to help them adjust to farming — a promise not fulfilled, in the case of the Mississaugas at the western end of Lake Ontario, until the mid-1820s.

First Nations migrated north to settle in Upper Canada. They came to escape the American government's removal policy, that dictated that Natives east of the Mississippi must move west of the river. Several thousand Anishinabeg took up residence in Upper Canada in the 1830s and 1840s. Most of the Oneida, one of the Iroquois nations remaining in New York state after the American Revolution, also migrated around 1840 and purchased land on the Thames River west of London. Apart from Governor Francis Bond Head's unsuccessful attempt in 1836–37 to relocate the Anishinabeg of southern Ontario (the Ojibwas, Odawas [Ottawas], and Potawatomis) to Manitoulin Island — a proposal they vigorously opposed — the government of Upper Canada allowed the First Nations to remain on their reserved lands, or reserves. Here they were encouraged to farm in the hopes that they would be acculturated and ultimately assimilated into the dominant society.

COLONIAL OLIGARCHY: THE FAMILY COMPACT

During the years 1815–40, a small, tightly knit elite popularly known as the "Family Compact" ruled Upper Canada. When novelist Charles Dickens visited Toronto in the early 1840s, he described the style of their tight rein on the province as "rabid Toryism." Through political domination of the Executive Council — the governor's "cabinet" — and the Legislative Council (the upper house of the government), this Toronto-centred group controlled government. Through political patronage they appointed like-minded people to the local centres, thus creating, or recognizing already-existing, smaller oligarchies throughout the province. As historian S.F. Wise noted, the Family Compact was "a quasi-official coalition of the central and local élites united for the purpose of distributing honours and rewards to the politically deserving."[1]

Titus Hibbert Ware completed this sketch of Ojibwas at Coldwater north of Lake Simcoe, in 1844. The Native men adjusted to the settlers' style of clothing more easily than did the women, but they still wore moccasins and colourful sashes around their waists in the mid-nineteenth century.

Toronto Reference Library/T14386.

At the centre of the Family Compact stood John Strachan, cleric and educator, as a leading adviser to the governors of Upper Canada. A story circulated in the colony about Strachan's son: One day someone asked him, "Who governs Upper Canada?" "I do," he replied. When asked to explain, he answered, "I govern my mother, my mother governs my father, my father governs Upper Canada."

Around Strachan gathered a group of whom many were his former pupils. Members of this "old boys' network" had strikingly similar backgrounds and views. By far the foremost individual was John Beverley Robinson, who had become acting attorney general of Upper Canada in 1812, at the age of 21, and attorney general in 1818. About half of the Family Compact consisted of descendants of the original Loyalist families. The other half included British immigrants who, like Strachan, had come in the early years of the colony.

Their role in the defence of the province during the War of 1812 heightened their British patriotism. They believed, first, that Upper Canada's strength came from its imperial connection. Secondly, they wanted power to remain in the hands of the governor and his appointed advisers. Thirdly, they wanted the established Church of England to give a "moral underpinning to society." Finally, this elite believed in the economic progress of the province — to be directed by themselves — through commerce, canal building, settlement schemes, and banks.

Sir Peregrine Maitland, lieutenant governor from 1818 to 1828, reinforced the Family Compact's views of Upper Canada. He, too, favoured government through an appointed elite and allied himself with the members of the Executive Council.

The governor and the Family Compact strengthened their hold on the colony through the Crown reserves. By the 1820s — due to increased settlement during the immigration boom — the wealth from the sale of the Crown reserves had become substantial. In 1826, the British government implemented a new policy for the sale of Crown lands. In each district, vacant Crown lands were evaluated and a minimum sale price established. Then the available land was advertised in the newspapers and sold to the highest bidder. The government appointed Peter Robinson as the Commissioner of Crown Lands to oversee the sale of these lands. These payments went directly to

A Methodist camp meeting at Grimsby, just south of Hamilton, Canada West, in 1859.

The United Church of Canada/Victoria University Archives, Toronto/Acc. no. 90.162 P/2019N.

the governor and his Executive Council, much to the resentment of an emerging reform group in the elected Assembly.

The clergy reserves became even more contentious. In 1791, the British government had set aside one-seventh of the land in each township for the support of a "Protestant clergy." John Strachan argued against the claims of the non-Anglican sects for a portion of these "Protestant reserves," maintaining that the Constitutional Act of 1791 had meant by the phrase "Protestant clergy" the Anglican church alone.

RELIGIOUS DISPUTES

The first challenge to the Anglicans' ecclesiastical monopoly came from the Presbyterians. As the established Church of Scotland, this major Protestant denomination demanded a share of the clergy reserves. In 1829, the Colonial Office authorized their inclusion. The Executive Council denied the Methodists the same right. Since Methodism had come into Upper Canada from the United States, Family Compact members suspected it of having radical republican sympathies. Thus, the Methodists had to fight for a portion of the clergy reserves.

Methodism's popularity rested on its appeal to a poor, backwoods frontier community. Through hymns, campfire meetings, and fervent preaching, Methodist preachers reached out to a population untouched by the more aloof and elitist Anglican church. Historian Fred Landon described their camp meetings:

> Sometimes a wave of excitement would sweep over a gathering of this kind and as if moved by one impulse scores would rush to the altar, throwing themselves down, sobbing or groaning. This was the objective of the preaching and far into the night the ministers would move from group to group praying and exhorting the penitents.[2]

Using effective Mississauga preachers such as Peter Jones and John Sunday, a veteran of the War of 1812, the Methodists converted 2000 First Nations people in Upper Canada to Christianity in the late 1820s. Native and white Methodists built missions for Ojibwa-speaking converts at the Credit River, 20 km west of York, and at Grape Island in the Bay of Quinte.

The growth of Methodism led to confrontation with the Anglicans. In 1825, Archdeacon John Strachan used the occasion of a funeral eulogy for Jacob Mountain, the Anglican Lord Bishop of Quebec, to attack certain "uneducated itinerant preachers" of the Methodist church. He described them as ignorant, incapable, idle, and above all, disloyal, because of their emotionally charged and "republican" views.

The Methodists counterattacked through Egerton Ryerson, a 23-year-old preacher of Loyalist background, who wrote a thundering reply in 1826. Raised in a prominent Anglican family but converted to Methodism, Ryerson upheld the educated quality of the itinerant preachers, denied that Methodists held republican views, and challenged the legality of Strachan's position that the Church of England was the established church in the province. So began the public career of Egerton Ryerson. For a half century he would maintain a position of prominence in education and politics in Upper Canada.

Other Protestant denominations and religious sects appeared in the province. Baptists, Quakers, Dunkards, Millerites, Campbellites, Christian Universalists, Mormons, and German-speaking Amish created greater religious pluralism. With the arrival of substantial numbers of Irish Catholics, the Roman Catholic church also strengthened its position.

EDUCATION

Religious disputes extended to education. Prior to 1815, schooling was informal and frequently occurred in the home, conducted by parents, governesses, or tutors. J.G. Hodgins, the late-nineteenth-century historian of education in Ontario, claimed that few children prior to the 1840s received an elementary education. He estimated it to be one in 24.[3] More recent research questions this. Educational historians have noted that in most rural areas and local districts, schooling was considered important enough to be given priority in terms of building a school house or hiring a teacher. By the time of Ryerson's reform of the educational system in Upper Canada in the 1840s (he became superintendent of schools for Canada West in 1844), most townships had at least one and often as many as three or four public schools, not to mention private schools. In addition, Sunday schools began as a means of educating children who had to work the other six days of the week. A few grammar schools, or district schools, existed for the training of boys from well-to-do families who were destined for the professions. Girls fortunate enough to be educated were generally taught at home. In 1816, a committee of the Assembly introduced the Common School Act, which allotted £6000 annually to state-supported, common primary schools intended, at least in theory, for all children. Responsibility for building and maintaining the schools rested in the hands of local boards.

A SECTARIAN VERSUS PUBLIC EDUCATION SYSTEM

Strachan wanted common schools under Church of England control to counteract the use of American textbooks and American-trained teachers. But the Assembly opposed the idea and succeeded in establishing non-sectarian schools. It was a limited victory, however, since financial constraints reduced the annual appropriation for maintaining these schools to only £2500 in 1820.

Thwarted in his efforts for sectarian education in the common schools, John Strachan directed his energy toward the grammar schools. These elite institutions, he believed, could offset the "Americanized" common schools. In 1819, he introduced legislation that required both an annual examination of all the grammar schools in the province and an annual report to the lieutenant governor. He also tried to introduce Andrew Bell's monitorial schools, an English system based on the teaching of Church of England doctrines. The Assembly vetoed the suggestion.

In an attempt to establish an Anglican university to connect higher education with the Church of England, Strachan drew up a royal charter for King's College in York in 1827. The university would hire Anglican professors and house a divinity school for training Anglican clergy. In his enthusiasm, Strachan even offered the Mississauga Methodist leader Peter Jones a place in the proposed divinity school if he would turn Anglican. Jones refused.

John Sunday in the mid-1830s, an engraving by J. Thomson of a painting by W. Gush, which appeared in the March 1839 issue of the *Wesleyan-Methodist Magazine* (London, England). Before his conversion to Christianity, this hardened Mississauga veteran of the War of 1812 apparently knew only three words of English: "pint," "quart," and "whiskey." After he joined the Methodists in 1826, he immediately stopped drinking and won back his self-respect and the respect of the Mississaugas.

The Mississauga village on the Credit River during the winter of 1826–27. The houses, just built, were dressed log cottages with two rooms, of the type erected as a second house by settlers who had been on their farms for 5 to 10 years. Two families occupied each home, and each family had its own room. Originally, 20 of these two-family houses were built.

Egerton Ryerson, *The Story of My Life*, edited by J. George Hodgins (Toronto: William Briggs, 1883), p. 59.

The Assembly opposed these "sectarian tendencies." It refused to support the provincial university. Strachan had to be content with a good preparatory school, modelled on the English classical schools and later known as Upper Canada College. King's College would not come into existence until 1843. By that time, the Methodists had already established their own university, Victoria, in Cobourg, and the Presbyterians had Queen's College in Kingston. Queen's began in 1841, when Thomas Liddell arrived from England with a charter from Queen Victoria to found a Presbyterian theological college. Classes began in a rented house.

SOCIAL, CRIMINAL, AND HUMANITARIAN CONCERNS

The large influx of immigrants, many of whom were destitute, raised the issue of poor relief. Previously, relief had been granted to people in distress only on the recommendation of a magistrate. In 1817, the first major public-welfare agency, the Society for the Relief of Strangers, was established at York. Modelled on a similar society in London, England, this voluntary organization was created "to serve the wants and alleviate the misery" of destitute immigrants. In 1828, the society changed its name to "the Society for the Relief of the Sick and Destitute." The altered name reflected a change in attitude about social assistance: only individuals who were both sick and destitute would be eligible for relief. Able-bodied but unemployed individuals had to work in return for assistance. Those in authority assumed that work was available for everyone and that able-bodied people who did not work were lazy. They needed a moral lesson in frugality, hard work, and self-discipline. The government established two "houses of industry" in 1837 to provide work for all "fit and able inmates," one in Toronto and one in Kingston.

CRIME AND PUNISHMENT IN UPPER CANADA

For the recalcitrant and criminal element in Upper Canadian society, "gaols," an asylum, and the Kingston Penitentiary (opened in 1835) existed. Gaols, or jails, were established early on to deploy shaming punishment, and to deal with social outcasts, such as the mentally ill, the local vagrant, or the habitual drinker, as well as transients who had nowhere else to go. Ill-equipped to retain people for extended periods of time, these unpleasant places, designed not to rehabilitate but to punish individuals, were stop-gap institutions.

Beginning in the 1830s, penitentiaries began to replace gaols as penal institutions. They were built to provide extended incarceration with the intention of using the time to rehabilitate the criminal. The Kingston Penitentiary, the first of its kind in the country, reflected this new perspective. The usual sentence term lasted from one to six years for crimes such as grand and petty larceny, forgery, horse stealing, and assault. Over half of the convicted were under the age of 25 and thus were believed to be young enough to be reformed. The building itself incorporated the most recent design features for penal institutions and had the distinction of being the largest and most expensive building in the country. It served, as well, as a showcase of the "civilizing" nature of Upper Canadian society. Criminal rehabilitation ranked with religion and economic growth as benchmarks of reform and progress in the nineteenth century.

Drunkenness was considered the major cause of crime in Upper Canada. It accounted for most assault cases and was blamed for the breakup of families, poor work habits, and low productivity. Alcohol also contributed to social and political upheaval. Social reformers believed temperance societies were the solution to the problem of drink. The first temperance societies in Upper Canada appeared in the Niagara peninsula, but by the 1830s, district societies existed throughout the province. Most were affiliated with the Methodist, Presbyterian, or Baptist churches. In 1839, these temperance societies of Upper Canada affiliated with the American Temperance Union. The temperance movement aimed at abstinence through self-restraint rather than through government legislation, in the belief that drunkenness was a personal problem requiring a personal solution.

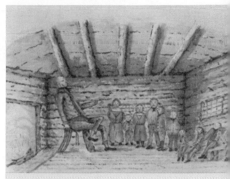

A sketch by William Elliot of an early schoolhouse in the village of Adelaide, west of London, Canada West, in 1845.

J. Ross Robertson Collection/Toronto Reference Library/T16581.

SECTARIAN, ETHNIC, AND POLITICAL TENSIONS

Sectarian, ethnic, and political tensions contributed to violence and crime in Upper Canada. Most pronounced was the hatred between Irish Protestants (Orange) and Irish Catholics (Green) that originated in Ireland and carried over to the New World by Irish immigrants. The Orange Society was founded in Ireland in 1795 and transplanted in British North America in 1830, when Ogle R. Gowan, an Irish Protestant from Dublin known for his anti-Catholic tracts, began the Grand Orange Lodge of British North America in Brockville, Upper Canada. Three years later, in 1833, some 90 lodges existed in the province with an estimated membership of over 8000. While these lodges served as social clubs, in some cases as insurance companies, and as hiring centres for Irish Protestants, they also held meetings designed to arouse hatred against Irish Catholics. Fighting erupted in local bars, in communities where both groups lived in close proximity, and among work crews on the canals or in the lumber camps — especially on Irish festive holidays, such as March 17th, St. Patrick's Day, and July 12th, the anniversary of Protestant William of Orange's defeat of the Irish Catholics at the Battle of the Boyne.

Occasionally, political violence erupted at election time. Before the introduction of the secret ballot, voters had to show their support for candidates publicly. Some candidates hired thugs to intimidate and coerce voters to support them. During the election campaign of 1834 in Toronto, the streets were taken over by mobs brandishing sticks who represented the interests of opposing candidates. The authorities called in the infantry to restore the peace.

Ethnic clashes occurred frequently in the lumber camps in and around Bytown (Ottawa). Irish lumberers, known as "Shiners," fought with French Canadians for jobs. Owners of the lumber camps, especially Peter Aylen, deliberately incited these riots to take control of the lumber industry by undermining their competitors. The "Shiner Wars," as the disputes were called, were worse during springtime, when winter work was over and the lumberjacks had both money and idle time to drink and gamble in Bytown's many bars.

CHOLERA EPIDEMICS

Cholera, which entered the Canadas in the early 1830s as a result of British immigration, posed an immediate and pressing social problem. Near-panic prevailed in the summer of 1832, when the board of health recorded 273 deaths from the dread disease in York alone. In the province as a whole, at least 550 people died that summer. The disease became most people's primary concern; as one Upper Canadian complained, "Nothing is to be heard but the 'cholera.'" In the

Kingston Chronicle of April 7, 1832, a poem appeared that recounted the fear that the disease instilled. The last stanza read:

> The months pass on, and the circle spreads,
> And the time is drawing nigh,
> When each street may have a darkened house,
> Or a coffin passing by.

The government urged each district to establish its own board of health. Such boards became responsible for regulation and, in the case of port cities like Kingston and York, of inspecting immigrant ships. The disease ran its course in 1832, only to return again in 1834 to cause another nearly 350 deaths in Upper Canada. The first major medical breakthrough occurred only in the early 1850s, when cholera was linked to contaminated water or food.

WOMEN IN UPPER CANADA

Women played an integral role in British North American society in the early to mid-nineteenth century, although their importance was seldom acknowledged publicly. Their responsibilities consisted mainly of childbearing, childrearing, and social assistance to others, as well as "domestic employment," which included such tasks in the home as cooking, cleaning, sewing, knitting, spinning, and weaving, in addition to outdoor work, such as taking care of the poultry and the barnyard, the vegetable garden, and fruit growing — thereby freeing the men and boys to work in the fields. When her husband was away, a farm wife often assumed complete responsibility for outdoor work. Beyond the immediate family obligations, some women took in sewing or laundry, or boarders, or were seamstresses, keepers of inns or taverns in their homes, or schoolteachers within their homes.

Women were regulated and restricted by rules, traditions, customs, and laws made by male social elites, church leaders, government officials, and legal authorities. The concept of "domesticity" was taking hold in upper-middle-class families in the early to mid-nineteenth century. It was premised on the belief in a differentiation between women and men in work and lifestyle, with women restricted essentially to the private sphere of the home and family and men to the public sphere of the workplace.

British common law defined women as subordinate to their husbands, fathers, and even brothers. In the eyes of the law, husband and wife constituted one person — the husband. That meant a wife did not have the legal right to sign a "contract" or to run her own business without her husband's permission. A married woman did have the right of a dowry, a lifetime interest in one-third of her husband's property. But even when and where the law was operative, it only applied upon the death of the husband, and not in instances of separation or marriage breakdown. As well, it could be overridden, since the husband had the right to dispose of the family property to whomever he chose as heir, which in most cases was a son, or even a grandson or son-in-law over a wife or a daughter. Divorce was possible but difficult, since in Upper Canada it required a special act of the legislature.

Christian law criminalized abortion and forbade infanticide. The murder of a child was punishable by death, although the ruling was seldom applied. It was considered "criminal" to conceal the birth of a "bastard," a child born out of wedlock. As noted in *Canadian Women: A History*, "[A]ll of the laws affecting sexuality, marriage, and motherhood might be regarded as evidence of new kinds of intrusions into women's lives, as male lawgivers attempted to reinforce or reinterpret traditional male control over, as well as their protection of, women in a changing world."[4]

Despite such restrictions, some women played active roles in education and religion. Some became schoolteachers in tax-supported schools. By 1851, women constituted almost one-fifth of "common" school teachers in Upper Canada. They were most often in rural schools, where few male teachers were available, or in districts where financial restraints necessitated hiring a female teacher, since she could be hired for "half the price." Women were also active in the Sunday school movement and in missionary societies, both of which played a social and educational role. Women were still refused entry into medical and law schools, and into the ministry. A few women did preach and prophesy, especially in the evangelical religious denominations, but even here they could not become ministers because this would imply gender equality. The one possible exception were Quaker women, who were separated from, but considered equal to, men.

Some women were able to exercise their vote in general elections in the early nineteenth century in Upper Canada. But in 1849, a Reform government passed a law excluding women from the franchise in both the Canadas. Still, in the first half of the nineteenth century, politicians' wives played an active role "behind the scenes." Isabel Mackenzie, for example, fought as hard against the Tory elite as her husband, William Lyon Mackenzie, did. Women were also involved in distributing and signing petitions for political change. Women in Upper Canada exercised considerable social power, even if they lacked official authority.

ECONOMIC DEVELOPMENTS

The mass immigration of 1815–40 contributed to economic growth. During this period, Upper Canada became a thriving, complex, and viable society based on an exchange economy, both export and domestic, and financed by both capital and credit. The expansion rested to a large extent on wheat farming. Economic historian John McCallum notes that "close to three-quarters of the cash income of Ontario farmers was derived from wheat, and wheat and flour made up well over half of all exports from Ontario until the early 1860s."[5] Much of this exported wheat, especially in the 1830s and 1840s, went to Lower Canada. Still, in 1830, the average income per household that was dependent on wheat export was only $25.

Timber rivalled wheat as the major export staple of Upper Canada. In the Ottawa valley, with its rich forests of pine and oak and the region's easy access to the St. Lawrence, lumbering, not agriculture, became the primary industry. Economic historian Douglas McCalla calculated that "forest products probably account for at least half of all the province's export earnings between 1815 and 1840."[6] The timber trade was a by-product of farming, since settlers had to clear the forests before being able to farm the land.

CONSERVATION

The early settlers transformed the landscape of Upper Canada ecologically. In general, they had little interest in conservation or in the long-term management of land. They sought only to maximize short-term profits. Thus, they came to see the forests as a monolith to push back.

In the name of "progress," settlers and woodsmen cut down trees at an astonishing rate. Historical geographer J. David Wood argues that more than the railroad, the axe was the agent of radical change of the early Ontario landscape. "The domain of southern Ontario was transformed from woodland to farmland in less than a hundred years by an army of axe-wielding settlers and woodsmen."[7] Journalist William Smith noted at the time the determination by which settlers cleared the Oak Ridges Morraine, north of Toronto: "the universal Canadian practice has been followed in clearing the land, that of sweeping away everything capable of bearing a green leaf. The new settlers look upon trees as enemies."

The Road between York and Kingston, Upper Canada, 1830, a watercolour by James Pattison Cockburn (1779–1847), a British army officer. The painting shows the density of the early Upper Canadian forests.

National Archives of Canada/C-12632.

While such activity did result in a host of productive farms that greatly boosted the economy of Upper Canada, "progress" came at a price: the loss of a large segment of the eastern woodland forests and the plants and animals that lived in these wooded areas. Animals, from bears and deer to the passenger pigeon and the vole, were in retreat. So too were other species of birds and animals, as well as insects. Some areas cleared were at the headwaters of rivers, resulting in soil erosion that caused tonnes of silt to pour into streams that flowed into Lake Ontario. Thus, the water ecology was adversely affected, along with the fish and aquatic animals. Atlantic salmon, for example, lost their spawning grounds, and by the mid-nineteenth century no longer migrated in vast numbers up the St. Lawrence River. The last Atlantic salmon were caught in Ontario in the 1890s. (A century later, in 1988, the Ontario Ministry of Natural Resources began reintroducing the fish to Lake Ontario.)

The settlers' relentless drive to conquer and subdue the wilderness constituted a form of "ecological imperialism," comparable to political and economic imperialism in terms of its devastation to the colony. By the 1850s, over one-third of the forested areas of southern Ontario had been destroyed. Within the next generation, three-quarters were gone, and by 1914 and the outbreak of World War I, over 90 percent.

TRANSPORTATION

Wheat and timber required transportation networks. Native trails soon became roads, giving greater accessibility. More roads were built in the Huron Tract beside Lake Huron, in the Talbot settlement south of London, and by the military settlers in the Ottawa valley and the Kingston area. Around York, a road system was developed to link the capital to outlying regions dependent on it for trade.

In the 1820s, a regular stagecoach line began between York and Kingston. At first, the service was erratic. Coaches required anywhere from two to four days to complete a one-way trip, depending on road conditions. By the 1830s, daily service became available year round. At the same time, coach lines along Yonge Street began to service the towns, villages, hamlets, and farming communities north of York (or Toronto, as the city returned to its original name in 1834).

CANAL BUILDING

The Great Lakes–St. Lawrence natural waterway would provide an effective means of transportation if the natural obstacles, notably Niagara Falls and the rapids at Lachine near Montreal, could be overcome. Canals offered a solution. In 1825, the first canal was completed around the Lachine rapids. Canals also enabled small naval vessels to enter the heart of North America to defend Upper Canada against possible American attacks.

 The British government paid for the province's first megaproject: the Rideau Canal, completed and opened for public use in 1832. The colonial authorities wanted the Rideau Canal to link Bytown (Ottawa) with Kingston for defence purposes, bypassing the rapids along the St. Lawrence and at a safe distance from American territory. In 1826, Lieutenant Colonel John By

Scene on the Welland Canal in the mid-nineteenth century. From G.P. Scrope, ed., *Memoirs of the Life of the Right Honourable Charles Lord Sydenham* (London, 1843).

National Archives of Canada/C-5954.

of the Royal Engineers arrived to oversee the project. Over a 6-year period, By supervised a force of 4000 who worked with shovel and wheelbarrow, sometimes 16 hours a day, 6 days a week. Swarms of mosquitoes and blackflies plagued the workers all spring and summer. In the swamps and marshes, swamp fever and malaria became rampant. A heavy, noxious mist arose from the decaying vegetable matter that had been excavated after stagnant water had been drained off. Trees were cut back in an effort to provide freer air circulation at the work sites, in keeping with the prevailing medical belief that malaria was caused by foul air (in Italian, *mal'aria* — "bad air"). More than 500 men lost their lives in the work camps.

When completed, the waterway, threading through a series of lakes, was more than 210 km in length and contained 47 locks. (The original locks are still in operation today.) It had been an ambitious undertaking to meet an American attack that never materialized; nonetheless, its construction boosted the economy of the eastern part of the province.

The construction of the province's second megaproject, a canal bypassing Niagara Falls and linking Lake Ontario to Lake Erie, began at roughly the same time as the Rideau Canal. It opened, however, three years earlier, in 1829. The incentive behind construction of the Welland Canal was strictly commercial. But, once again, the impetus for action came from the United States.

In 1825 the Americans completed the Erie Canal, which linked the Great Lakes by water with the Hudson River and the ice-free port of New York. The new canal attracted trade from the American West and from Upper Canada. Great Lakes farmers found it cheaper and faster to ship via New York City to Britain. New York City rose to economic primacy in North America, with a population by the early 1830s of a quarter-million — roughly the size of Upper Canada's entire population.

A young St. Catharines merchant and second-generation Loyalist, William Hamilton Merritt, dreamed of building a canal to bypass Niagara Falls and thus make the St. Lawrence–Great Lakes waterway system an effective rival to the Erie Canal. The British government agreed to underwrite one-ninth of the cost of construction in return for the right of government ships to pass through the canal toll-free. John B. Yates, an American investor from Oswego, New York, became the largest shareholder in Merritt's Welland Canal Company, while the government of Upper Canada offered a land grant and a loan of £25 000. In the end, Merritt's "private" project became the biggest publicly financed project of its time, costing an estimated £450 000 in 1833.

What canal builders failed to realize at the time was the environmental impact of canal construction. The building of the Erie Canal, for example, enabled the sea lamprey, a parasite fish that weakens or kills other fish by sucking their blood, to enter Lake Ontario. It put pressure on the lake's native whitefish, trout, and salmon. Then, with the completion of the Welland Canal, the lamprey migrated to the upper Great Lakes, resulting in a dramatic decline in native fish species there too.

EARLY BANKS IN UPPER CANADA

Megaprojects required large amounts of capital, which, in turn, created a need for banks. Banks did not appear in Upper Canada until after the War of 1812. The earliest ones were branches of the Bank of Montreal. These soon proved inadequate for Upper Canadian merchants, who wanted their own banks. In 1819, the merchants of Kingston applied to the government of Upper Canada to charter a provincial bank. Much to their dismay and anger, their appeal was denied in favour of a more recent one from prominent York merchants.

This York bank, known as the Bank of Upper Canada, was controlled by the government. Nine of its fifteen directors belonged to Upper Canada's Executive or Legislative councils. The provincial government also supplied more than one-quarter of the bank's stock. As historian Gerald Craig concluded, "It is no exaggeration to say that the Bank of Upper Canada was a creature of the emerging Family Compact."[8]

The establishment of the first Upper Canadian bank at York rather than at Kingston reflected York's dominance as the provincial capital, a position it had held since 1797, when the seat of government was transferred from Niagara-on-the-Lake to York for security reasons. Through wholesale trade with towns and rural areas within its radius of influence, York became the most influential community in central Upper Canada. In population, York went from 1200 in 1820 to more than 9000 in 1834, the year of its incorporation as the city of Toronto. Economic growth in the 1840s and 1850s further strengthened Toronto's dominance in Upper Canada. The areas immediately adjacent to the city, such as the Home and Gore districts, largely came under its metropolitan control. In 1841, when the Canadas were united, one in five Upper Canadians lived within a 125 km radius of Toronto.

THE RISE OF A REFORM MOVEMENT

In the 1820s, Upper Canada became strongly polarized into conservative and reform camps. Led by the Family Compact, the conservatives favoured British monarchical association, appointed Legislative and Executive Councils, and a stable and hierarchical society free of any political opposition. Their ideology was premised on a strong central government. Economically, they favoured the construction of canals and the establishment of banks, both of which they believed would advance the commercial well-being of the province. The conservatives obtained strong support from the newly arrived middle- and upper-class British immigrants.

The Reform members of the Assembly opposed conservative policies and called for political change. They tended to be "late Loyalists" or recent poorer British immigrants who favoured an elected Legislative Council, or upper house, and an Executive Council that was responsible to the Assembly rather than to the governor. Economically, the Reformers favoured policies that promoted agriculture, since, in large part, they represented the farmers of the central and western areas of the province. They often opposed commercial enterprises such as canal building and banks, which they saw as being either expensive or of limited benefit to farmers.

Thus, there developed in the province a situation roughly parallel to that in Lower Canada. One could class many of the conservatives in both provinces as "reactionary" politically but "progressive" economically, and the Reformers as "radical" politically but "reactionary" economically.

GOURLAY AND MACKENZIE

Robert Gourlay, a 39-year-old Scot who arrived in Upper Canada in 1817, initiated the first serious criticism of the Family Compact and became its most celebrated victim. Soon after his arrival, he complained about the tiny elite's control of the appointed Legislative Council. Vehemently he attacked John Strachan, that "monstrous little fool of a parson," and his "vile, loathsome and lazy" circle. Gourlay favoured township meetings similar to those in New England, where people could voice their grievances. He also advocated more power for the elected Assembly. These radical views led to his prosecution (under a wartime act dating from 1804 that regulated the conduct of immigrants) and his subsequent expulsion from Upper Canada in 1819.

This "banished Briton" left a legacy of political protest. Before his arrest, he circulated a lengthy questionnaire. The last of his 31 questions asked: "What, in your opinion, retards the improvement of your township in particular, or the province in general?" He received a litany of complaints: the bad roads, the clergy and Crown reserves, restrictions on American immigration. These and other complaints continued to be heard throughout the 1820s. As a result, a Reform party began to take shape in the Assembly in 1824 focussing on these concerns.

William Lyon Mackenzie, who arrived in Upper Canada from Scotland in 1820, furthered Gourlay's cause. In 1824, at Queenston, in the Niagara district, he started a newspaper, *The Colonial Advocate*, and relocated it to York the following year. Political scientist S.J.R. Noel noted that Mackenzie brought "exceptional gifts" to his editorship: "The essence of radical journalism is to probe for feet of clay beneath the togas of the high and mighty, and no one probed more fearlessly or relentlessly than he [Mackenzie]."[9]

Mackenzie's attacks enraged several younger members of prominent Family Compact families in York. In 1826, the young men broke into Mackenzie's office and threw his typesetting equipment into Lake Ontario. Such acts only helped to make Mackenzie a hero to the radical Reformers and strengthened his determination to continue his campaign. He succeeded in winning a seat in the Assembly in the election of 1828.

That election returned the first Reform majority to the Assembly. Reformers such as John Rolph, Marshall Spring Bidwell (whose father, Barnabas Bidwell, had been expelled from the Assembly in 1821 under the Alien Act as an American), and William and Robert Baldwin (father and son) led the new group. But in the election of 1830, the Reformers lost their majority to the conservatives, or Tories.

This defeat did not dampen the Reformers' enthusiasm, however. They saw themselves as accomplishing for Upper Canada what like-minded Reformers in Britain and in the United States were doing for their countries. In Britain, the Whig government of Lord Grey fought for reform. In 1832 it introduced the Great Reform Bill, which broadened the franchise. In the United States, President Andrew Jackson led a democratic movement to open up the political process to more people (with the exception of women, African Americans, and the First Nations). The Upper Canadian Reformers who followed William Lyon Mackenzie believed themselves part of a greater progressive movement that would ultimately triumph.

THE MOVE TO REBELLION

www In the early 1830s, the more moderate William Lyon Mackenzie shifted to a radical Reform position, chiefly as a result of a visit to the United States. In 1829, he met President Andrew Jackson

and observed "Jacksonian democracy" in practice. Suspicious of the upper classes and big business, Jackson had favoured the state extending voting rights (for white men at least), and
opened up the political process to the middle and lower classes. Back in Upper Canada,
Mackenzie renewed his attacks on the political elite to the point that he was expelled from the
Assembly, only to be re-elected and expelled three more times. In 1832 he visited England and
met such British reformers as Jeremy Bentham, Joseph Hume, and Francis Place. In London, the
fiery newspaper editor presented the complaints of the Upper Canadian Reformers, as he saw
them, to a sympathetic and receptive British government, which mistakenly believed that
Mackenzie's views represented those of a majority of Upper Canadians.

THE SPLIT AMONG THE REFORMERS

Mackenzie's views were not even representative of the majority of Reformers. A rift occurred by the
mid-1830s between a moderate wing led by Robert Baldwin and a radical wing under Mackenzie
and John Rolph. The moderates desired to preserve Upper Canada's allegiance to the monarchy
and its ties to the British empire, and did not want the American form of elective government that
Mackenzie advocated. Instead, they favoured the British plan of responsible government — a government responsible to the Assembly. To the moderate Reform politicians who had spent years
trying to dissociate reform from republicanism, Mackenzie was an acute embarrassment.

After the Reformers regained control of the Assembly in 1834, the radical Reformers took
action on their own. Mackenzie, just chosen as Toronto's first mayor as well as an Assembly member,
was selected to chair an Assembly grievance committee that produced the famous "Seventh Report
on Grievances" in 1835. It contained a wide-ranging attack on the existing system of colonial government and demanded an elected Legislative Council, an Executive Council responsible to the
Assembly, and severe limitations on the lieutenant governor's control of patronage.

The new governor, Sir Francis Bond Head, appointed in 1836, initially made a positive ges-
ture to the Reformers by appointing two of their members, Robert Baldwin and John Rolph, to
the Executive Council. Then he proceeded to ignore the Council's advice, prompting Reformers
on the Council to resign. They persuaded their fellow members to follow suit. The Assembly
censured the governor and then blocked the granting of supplies, preventing the government
from making expenditures. Head retaliated by refusing to approve any money bills. Then he dissolved the legislature and called an election for the early summer. He actively campaigned in the
election for the Conservatives, warning that the battle was between American republicanism and
the British connection.

The Tories won the election conclusively. Head's intervention in the campaign and his
appeal to the loyalty of recent British immigrants contributed to their victory. A large number in
the colony sided with the governor and the Family Compact, fearing that the Reformers were
dangerously radical and "republican." The Conservatives also used bribery, corruption, the
careful selection of polling places, and the rapid enfranchisement of new British immigrants to
win the election. This convinced Mackenzie and his followers of the impossibility of fair elections and peaceful reform. They underestimated entirely, however, the strength of Upper
Canadian conservatism, as well as the moderate Reformers' opposition to rebellion.

In his recently created newspaper, *The Constitution*, begun symbolically on July 4, 1836,
Mackenzie cited the American Revolution as justification for overthrowing the government. A
group of his followers issued a Toronto Declaration closely modelled on the American
Declaration of Independence. It read in part:

> Government is founded on the authority and is instituted for the benefit of a people;
> when, therefore, any Government long and systematically ceases to answer the great

ends of its foundation, the people have a natural right given them by their Creator to seek after and establish such institutions as will yield the greatest quantity of happiness to the greatest number.

Economic and social forces contributed to unrest in the province. In 1836, an economic downturn occurred throughout the western world. In Upper Canada, this recession led to tight bank credit and even a recall of loans, which hit farmers especially hard. Such action intensified Mackenzie's already deep distrust of banks. Along with hard financial times came a series of crop failures in 1835–37. (Historian Colin Read has argued that no economic crisis existed and that the rebels came, for the most part, from the ranks of the reasonably prosperous agrarian society [see "Where Historians Disagree" in this chapter].)

In the western region of the province, around London, a separate group led by Dr. Charles Duncombe prepared to join the rebels. News of the uprising of Lower Canadian Patriotes under Louis-Joseph Papineau (see Chapter 12) further encouraged the rebels. By early November, no British soldiers remained in Upper Canada because they had been dispatched to quell trouble in Lower Canada. Historian Allan Greer observed that "the Lower Canadian drift towards war provided an impulse, as well as an opportunity, to Upper Canadian radicals."[10]

THE UPPER CANADIAN REBELLION, 1837

During the evening and night of December 4, 1837, about 500 ill-clad and poorly armed rebels gathered at Montgomery's Tavern on Yonge Street (just north of present-day Eglinton Avenue in Toronto) for the attack. The next day, in the late afternoon, Mackenzie led his followers down Yonge Street toward the city. The rest was tragicomedy. At a point just beyond Gallows Hill, near the present site of St. Clair Avenue, they met a party of 20 government men. Mackenzie's front rank fired, then dropped to the ground to let the next rank fire over their heads. Those behind thought their front-rank men had been killed, and they fled in panic.

That same night, Colonel Allan MacNab, a lawyer, land speculator, and loyalist leader, brought reinforcements for the government side from Hamilton. By Thursday, December 7, the loyalist forces were 1500 strong. They marched up Yonge Street to attack Mackenzie's force at Montgomery's Tavern. During the second battle, the rebels were routed within half an hour. The loyalist forces then burned the tavern and marched back to Toronto. Mackenzie's ill-conceived and ill-fated rebellion was over. With a price on his head, he managed to escape to the United States, while some of his followers were captured. Among them were two leaders, Samuel Lount, a former member of Parliament for Simcoe, and Peter Matthews, who were later tried and hanged.

In the western region of the province, Duncombe gathered 500 troops by December 13. MacNab led an opposing group of 500 loyalists. Upon hearing of Mackenzie's defeat, Duncombe's men began to desert the camp. When MacNab attacked on the morning of December 14, he found only a few rebels. Most, including Duncombe, had escaped to the United States.

COUNTERATTACKS FROM THE UNITED STATES

From across the border, the rebel leaders planned further attacks on the government of Upper Canada. Mackenzie found support in the United States

The execution of Samuel Lount and Peter Matthews, for their involvement in the Rebellion of 1837 in Upper Canada. (The date of the drawing and the name of the artist are unknown.) Despite appeals for clemency signed by thousands, the execution went ahead on April 12, 1838, in the courtyard of the Toronto jail. Elizabeth Lount, Samuel's widow, was left to raise their seven children; Hannah Matthews, Peter's widow, was left with eight young children to care for.

National Archives of Canada/C-1242.

Where Historians Disagree

The Causes of the 1837 Rebellion in Upper Canada

Amateur historians were the first to write about the Rebellion of 1837 in Upper Canada. They were both partisan and emotional in their approach because of their closeness to the incident in both time and circumstance. Charles Lindsey, the son-in-law of William Lyon Mackenzie, the leader of the rebellion, blamed the Family Compact's refusal to compromise for driving the moderate Mackenzie to rebellion. In a two-volume work on the rebellion, journalist-cum-historian J.M. Dent challenged Lindsey's view and depicted a diabolical and extreme Mackenzie who led the colony to an unnecessary struggle.[1] These amateur historians all believed that the cause of the rebellion was political — a classic struggle between "democracy" and "privilege." This was the Liberal interpretation of history that held sway in the late nineteenth and the early twentieth centuries. During the 1920s, when Canada was moving toward autonomy, a liberal-nationalist school of historical writing saw the rebellion as an attempt to gain independence from Britain. The rebellion became an important event on the road from "colony to nation."

In the midst of the economic upheaval of the Great Depression of the 1930s, an economic interpretation of the rebellion appeared. Historian Donald Creighton depicted the rebellion in Upper Canada as a struggle between agrarian interests, represented by Mackenzie and his followers, and commercial interests, which controlled the appointed Executive and Legislative Councils. "The rebellions were," Creighton wrote, "the final expression of that hatred of the rural community for the commercialism of the St. Lawrence."[2] Creighton bolstered his economic argument by pointing out that the rebellions broke out in Upper Canada after a succession of crop failures that had brought farmers to the point of starvation and bankruptcy.

Other historians have argued that economic distress was not really at the root of the rebellion. Historian Colin Read pointed out in *The Rebellion of 1837 in Upper Canada* that "the rebels were, for the most part, well-settled members of a reasonably prosperous agrarian society." He saw "no single cause or grand overriding explanation" for their participation. Short-term economic dislocation played a part, as did more individual motivations based on family loyalties or personal friendships and animosities: "So too did specific political grievances as well as the general reform perception that the world was ordered too much in the interests of the few, too little in the interests of the many."[3] The rebels' ignorance of the military strength of the loyalist militia also was a contributing factor, according to Read.

Intellectual historians depict Mackenzie as a man of ideas, who drew his inspiration and his direction from reform movements in both Britain and the United States. They see the rebellion in Upper Canada as part of a general reform impulse that swept western Europe and North America. R.A. MacKay notes: "Few public men in Canadian history have so represented the spirit of their age as did William Lyon Mackenzie, and particularly during the pre-Rebellion stage of his career. This was the age of Catholic Emancipation and the Great Reform Bill, the age of Bentham and Byron, of Cobbett and Edinburgh Reviewers, of O'Connell and Huskisson; the age when the bourgeois monarchy of Louis Philippe triumphed over the last of the Bourbons at Paris, and when 'King' Andrew Jackson succeeded the Adams dynasty at Washington. On both sides of the Atlantic the new wine of liberty and democracy was bursting the old bottles of restriction and privilege.... In the 1820's and 1830's William Lyon Mackenzie was the principal purveyor of these wines of liberty to the backwoods colony of Upper Canada."[4]

In the 1960s, social historians questioned whether the rebellion in Upper Canada was a class struggle. Marxist historian Stanley Ryerson interpreted the rebellion as a bourgeois-democratic revolution caused by oppression and led by men who were fighting for the cause of popular liberty. "Workers ... made up nearly half, and farmers over 40 per cent of the victims of oppression: a significant indication of the social forces that were engaged in action."[5] Fellow Marxist historian Leo Johnson saw the roots of the rebellion in an inequitable

system of land grants designed at the time of Governor Simcoe to create a landed gentry class at the expense of the ordinary farmer. The rebellion was a fight between two different views of land ownership held by two different classes of people.[6]

Read challenges the image of the Upper Canadian rebellion as a "people's revolution." Using the less-known Duncombe uprising in the London area, Read concludes: "There is no basis for arguing that the rebels comprised a clearly disadvantaged sector of society and hence were driven to arms by economic despair or the prospect of plunder." What did distinguish rebels from loyalists, according to Read, was the large number of rebels who were either American-born or born to American parents and who "may well have retained or adopted the deep American dislike of Britain and have been more willing to rebel, hoping to sever the provincial ties to Great Britain."[7] This ideological split was the real cause of the rebellion.

The debate continues, with no interpretation emerging as the definitive one. The net result, however, is a richer and deeper understanding of the decade of the 1830s in Upper Canada, out of which the Rebellion of 1837 arose.

---

[1] J. M. Dent, *The Story of the Upper Canadian Rebellion*, 2 vols. (Toronto: C. Blackett Robinson, 1885).

[2] Donald Creighton, *The Empire of the St. Lawrence: A Study in Commerce and Politics*, [1937]. Reprint with Introduction by Christopher Moore (Toronto: University of Toronto Press, 2002), p. 316.

[3] Colin Read, *The Rebellion of 1837 in Upper Canada* (Ottawa: Canadian Historical Association, 1988), p. 18.

[4] R.A. MacKay, "The Political Ideas of William Lyon Mackenzie," *Canadian Journal of Economics and Political Science*, 3 (1937), p.1.

[5] Stanley Ryerson, *Unequal Union: Confederation and the Roots of Conflict in the Canadas, 1815–1873* (Toronto: Progress Books, 1968), p. 131.

[6] Leo Johnson, "Land Policy, Population Growth and Social Structure in Home District, 1793–1851," *Ontario History*, 63 (1971), 41–60.

[7] Colin Read, *The Rising in Western Upper Canada, 1837–38: The Duncombe Revolt and After* (Toronto: University of Toronto Press, 1982), pp. 207, 208.

among those Americans who saw the rebellion as a Canadian version of the American Revolution — an attempt to end British tyranny. Other Americans saw the uprising as an opportunity for the United States to annex Upper Canada. Some American supporters simply saw participation in a counterattack as an opportunity for looting.

Mackenzie gathered together a motley band of supporters who occupied Navy Island, just above Niagara Falls, on the Canadian side of the Niagara River, where they proclaimed a provisional government. The Upper Canadian militia retaliated by burning the *Caroline*, an American ship used to ferry men and supplies from the American side to Navy Island. Mackenzie's supporters and American sympathizers abandoned Navy Island but did not end their raids. Small, unsuccessful attacks came along the Detroit River.

The most serious counterattack occurred at the Battle of the Windmill along the St. Lawrence River near Prescott, in November, in which 200 invaders barricaded themselves in an old windmill until they were forced to surrender. Thirty men were killed, and the rest were taken prisoner. The government hanged eleven of the rebels for instigating and taking part in the battle. By the end of the Rebellion of 1837, the authorities jailed more than 1000 people on suspicion of treason. Nearly 100 of them were sent to the convict settlements in Australia (more than 70 of these individuals were Americans) and twenty were hanged.

LORD DURHAM'S REPORT

The Rebellion of 1837 in Upper Canada was a minor affair from a military standpoint. Simply put, the populace of Upper Canada did not support revolution. But together with the more extensive uprising in Lower Canada, the troubles in Upper Canada did convince Britain of the need to investigate the causes of the unrest.

The British cabinet responded by replacing Sir Francis Bond Head in early 1838 and sending out one of its most gifted politicians, Lord Durham, or "Radical Jack" (he had earned the nickname due to his support of liberal causes such as parliamentary reform), to inquire into the affairs of the colony and report back to the British government. The prime minister gave Durham broader powers than any of his predecessors, making him governor general of all the British North American colonies. He arrived in May 1838 with a vast entourage, including a full orchestra — which led one observer to suggest that he included it to make "overtures" to the Canadians.

Durham spent only five months in the Canadas, most of the time in Lower Canada. But he made one short visit to Upper Canada, where he consulted with Robert Baldwin, the moderate Reform leader. Despite the brevity of his stay, the time spent was very important, for out of it came one of the most significant documents in Canadian history — his *Report on the Affairs of British North America.*

The Durham Report made a number of important recommendations: It advocated greater colonial self-government. Durham argued that local affairs should be handled by the colonial government and that only larger issues, such as constitutional concerns, foreign relations, trade with Britain and other British colonies, and disposal of public lands, should be decided by the mother country. The Report made two other important recommendations. First, the colonial governor should choose his closest advisers, the members of the Executive Council, from the majority party in the Assembly and abide by the wishes of these elected representatives. Although Durham did not call this "responsible government," it nonetheless came to be known as such. Second, the Report recommended a union of the two Canadas. Durham realized that this would primarily benefit Upper Canada, since it would improve trade for the inland colony and force Lower Canadians to assume part of the debt incurred by Upper Canadians during the building of the canals. Durham also saw such a union of the Canadas as the nucleus of an

THE DISPOSITION OF ARRESTED REBELS, 1837–39

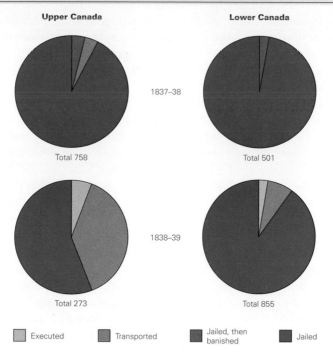

Upper Canada   **Lower Canada**

1837–38

Total 758   Total 501

1838–39

Total 273   Total 855

▢ Executed   ▢ Transported   ▢ Jailed, then banished   ▢ Jailed

Compare the number of arrests in Upper and Lower Canada after the uprising of 1837. Although the crisis in Lower Canada was far more extensive, more arrests were made in Upper Canada.

Source: R. Louis Gentilcore, ed., *Historical Atlas of Canada*, vol. 2, *The Land Transformed, 1800–1891* (Toronto: University of Toronto Press, 1993), plate 23. Reprinted by permission of the University of Toronto Press Incorporated.

eventual amalgamation of all the British North American colonies, which he highly favoured, and as a necessary precursor to the assimilation of the French Canadians. The British government accepted union but rejected responsible government.

Lord Sydenham, Durham's successor, implemented the recommendation for a union of the Canadas in 1840–41. Before it came into effect, Sydenham resolved a long-standing disagreement in Upper Canada. He worked out an arrangement by which the two leading Protestant denominations — Anglicans and Presbyterians — would share half the proceeds of future sales of clergy reserves, while the other half would be divided among the other denominations, according to their numbers.

 By the terms of the Act of Union of 1840, the capital of the new province of Canada became Kingston. English was recognized as the only official language of the Assembly. The united province assumed Upper Canada's debt. And the Assembly consisted of 84 members — 42 from Upper Canada and 42 from Lower Canada. Upper Canada officially ceased to exist. Instead, the area became known as Canada West, part of a larger union of English and French Canadians.

FORMATION OF AN UPPER CANADIAN POLITICAL CULTURE

The elite of Upper Canadian society created a political culture of the colony. It was intellectually based on a belief in the superiority of British values and British ways over that of Americans.

They believed that these values could best be preserved through association with the British monarchy, empire, constitution, and the established Church of England. The possession of land became the outward manifestation of elitism, and the elite of Upper Canada acquired huge tracts — sometimes whole townships — that they believed to be their God-given right to hold. Land wealth also became the ticket to power. As historian John Clarke notes: "The possession of land meant security, wealth, prestige, and the ability to influence events. To be a member of the elite meant, for most, to be landed."[11]

As the dynamics of Upper Canada changed in the early nineteenth century as a result of large-scale immigration and a diversified economy, so too did the nature of its political culture. Rule by an elite gave way to rule by those sufficiently educated to make intelligent judgments, to participate in public debate and political discourse. Social status became less important than intellectual acumen in dictating who had the right to rule. Value was placed on an informed public opinion, which was cultivated through voluntary associations, the periodical press, and political debate, especially in the politically charged atmosphere of the 1830s.

Ironically, this political polarization, particularly around the Rebellion of 1837, led to the demise of the idea of rational public debate and rule by consensus. As groups felt left out of the political process, they resorted to means, other than politics, such as petitioning, riots, effigy burning, and graffiti, to express their opinions and to have political influence. Petitioning, in particular, became a popular form of political protest. Petitions about all sorts of grievances and wrongdoings circulated in Upper Canada in the early nineteenth century. At times, petitioning ended in violence as in 1837. William Lyon Mackenzie had been a petitioner, a means by which he won support for his cause. What was true for Mackenzie was true for the petitioning movement in general; in the words of historian Carol Wilton: "petitioning channelled the energies of thousands of ordinary Upper Canadians into the political process."[12] The result was a more mature and dynamic political culture at mid-century, one that was instrumental in the formation of political parties in the Union period.

The years 1815 to 1840 witnessed a transformation in Upper Canada. Large-scale immigration, chiefly from the British Isles, added some 300 000 people, greatly extended the areas of settlement, and gave the colony a decidedly Upper Canadian orientation, one that rejected violent political change and endorsed the imperial connection.

NOTES

1. S.F. Wise, "Upper Canada and the Conservative Tradition," in Edith G. Firth, ed., *Profiles of a Province: Essays in the History of Ontario* (Toronto: Ontario Historical Society, 1967), p. 27.
2. Fred Landon, *Western Ontario and the American Frontier* (Toronto: McClelland & Stewart, 1967 [1941]), p. 125.
3. J.G. Hodgins, ed., *Documentary History of Education in Upper Canada*, vol. 4 (Toronto: Warwick Brothers and Rutter, 1897), p. 160, cited in Hazel Mathews, *Oakville and the Sixteen* (Toronto: University of Toronto Press, 1953), p. 107.
4. Alison Prentice et al., *Canadian Women: A History*, 2nd ed. (Toronto: Harcourt Brace, 1996), p. 91.
5. John McCallum, *Unequal Beginnings: Agriculture and Economic Development in Quebec and Ontario Until 1870* (Toronto: University of Toronto Press, 1980), p. 4.
6. Douglas McCalla, *Planting the Province: The Economic History of Upper Canada* (Toronto: University of Toronto Press, 1993), p. 64.
7. J. David Wood, *Making Ontario: Agricultural Colonization and Landscape Re-creation before the Railway* (Montreal/Kingston: McGill-Queen's University Press, 2000), p. xviii.

8. Gerald M. Craig, *Upper Canada: The Formative Years, 1784–1841* (Toronto: McClelland & Stewart, 1963), p. 162.

9. S.J.R. Noel, *Patrons, Clients, Brokers: Ontario Society and Politics, 1791–1896* (Toronto: University of Toronto Press, 1990), p. 88.

10. Allan Greer, "1837–38: Rebellion Reconsidered," *Canadian Historical Review* 76 (1995): 14.

11. John Clarke, *Land, Power, and Economics on the Frontier of Upper Canada* (Montreal/Kingston: McGill-Queen's University Press, 2001), p. xxxiii.

12. Carol Wilton, *Popular Politics and Political Culture in Upper Canada, 1800–1850* (Montreal/Kingston: McGill-Queen's University Press, 2000), p. 6.

LINKING TO THE PAST

Settlement Patterns
http://collections.ic.gc.ca/heirloom_series/volume1/chapter5/146-150.htm

A brief illustrated history of settlement in Upper Canada between the early and mid-1800s. Click on the images for more information.

Methodist History
http://www.smokylake.com/history/mission.htm

Information on Peter Jones and the missions to the Mississaugas, as well as the missionaries among the Ojibwa at Lake Simcoe and the political developments accompanying the entry of the Methodist Church into Canada.

The Rideau Canal
http://www.rideau-info.com/canal/history/hist-canal.html

A history of the Rideau Canal.

Towards Confederation: Upper Canada (1791–1841)
http://www.nlc-bnc.ca/2/18/h18-2001-e.html

An overview of the period, including information on the 1837 rebellions. Follow the links for more material on selected topics.

Independence Declaration
http://freenet.victoria.bc.ca/history/etext/mackenzie.independence.declare.html

The text of William Lyon Mackenzie's proclamation to the people on the eve of the Upper Canada Rebellion of 1837.

The Union Act, 1840
http://www.solon.org/Constitutions/Canada/English/PreConfederation/ua_1840.html

The full text of the 1840 Union Act, which united Upper and Lower Canada to create the Dominion of Canada.

RELATED READINGS

The following articles in R. Douglas Francis and Donald B. Smith, eds., *Readings in Canadian History: Pre-Confederation*, 6th ed. (Toronto: Nelson Thomson Learning, 2002), relate to topics covered in this chapter: Jane Errington, "'Woman ...Is a Very Interesting Creature': Some Women's Experiences in Early Upper Canada," pp. 236–52; Cecilia Morgan, " 'Of Slender Frame and Delicate Appearance': The Placing of Laura Secord in the Narratives of Canadian Loyalist History," pp. 252–65; and L.F.S. Upton, "The Origins of Canadian Indian Policy," pp. 296–306.

BIBLIOGRAPHY

The best overview of Upper Canadian society in 1815–40 is Gerald M. Craig, *Upper Canada: The Formative Years, 1784–1841* (Toronto: McClelland & Stewart, 1963). J.K. Johnson critically examines this important book in "Gerald Craig's *Upper Canada: The Formative Years* and the Writing of Upper Canadian History," *Ontario History* 90(2) (Autumn 1998): 117–33. Also useful is R. Cole Harris's chapter "Ontario," in R. Cole Harris and John Warkentin, *Canada Before Confederation* (Ottawa: Carleton University Press, 1991 [1974]), pp. 110–68. Bibliographical suggestions appear in Bryan D. Palmer, "Upper Canada," in M. Brook Taylor, ed., *Canadian History: A Reader's Guide,* vol. 1, *Beginnings to Confederation* (Toronto: University of Toronto Press, 1994), pp. 184–236. J.K. Johnson and Bruce G. Wilson, eds., *Historical Essays on Upper Canada: New Perspectives* (Ottawa: Carleton University Press, 1989), pp. 593–604, contains an extensive annotated bibliography on topics in Upper Canadian history. Also of value are essays in David Keane and Colin Read, eds., *Old Ontario: Essays in Honour of J.M.S. Careless* (Toronto: Dundurn Press, 1990).

Helen Cowan, *British Emigration in British North America: The First Hundred Years*, rev. and enlarged ed. (Toronto: University of Toronto Press, 1961) best describes the experience of immigrating to British North America from Britain. A shorter version is Helen Cowan, *British Immigration Before Confederation* (Ottawa: Canadian Historical Association, 1968). Also useful are H.J.M. Johnston, *British Immigration to British North America, 1815–1860,* Canada's Visual History Series, vol. 8 (Ottawa: Canadian Museum of Civilization, 1974). On the Petworth emigration scheme, see Wendy Cameron and Mary McDougall Maude, *Assisting Emigration to Upper Canada: The Petworth Project, 1832–1837* (Montreal/Kingston: McGill-Queen's University Press, 2000); and Wendy Cameron et al., eds., *English Immigrant Voices: Labourers' Letters from Upper Canada in the 1830s* (Montreal/Kingston: McGill-Queen's University Press, 2000). On immigration to British North America in general, see Ninette Kelley and Michael Trebilcock, *The Making of the Mosaic: A History of Canadian Immigration Policy* (Toronto: University of Toronto Press, 1998). Further studies on Irish immigration and settlement in Upper Canada include D.H. Akenson, *The Irish in Ontario: A Study in Rural History* (Montreal/Kingston: McGill-Queen's University Press, 1984); and Bruce S. Elliott, *Irish Migrants in the Canadas: A New Approach* (Montreal/Kingston: McGill-Queen's University Press, 1988).

Three books best review the experience of African Canadians in Upper Canada: Robin Winks's *The Blacks in Canada*, 2nd ed. (Montreal/Kingston: McGill-Queen's University Press, 1997); Peggy Bristow et al., *"We're Rooted Here and They Can't Pull Us Up": Essays in African Canadian Women's History* (Toronto: University of Toronto Press, 1994); and the more popularly written *The Freedom-Seekers: Blacks in Early Canada* (Agincourt, ON: Book Society of Canada, 1981), by Daniel G. Hill. Roger Riendeau provides a good short summary of the Underground Railway in "Freedom Train," *Horizon Canada* 30 (1985): 704–709.

On crime and criminal justice in early Upper Canada see Peter Oliver, *Terror to Evil-Doers: Prisons and Punishment in Nineteenth-Century Ontario* (Toronto: University of Toronto Press, 1998); John Weaver, "Crime, Public Order, and Repression: The Gore District in Upheaval, 1832–1851," in R.C. Macleod, ed., *Lawful Authority: Readings on the History of Criminal Justice in Canada* (Toronto: Copp Clark, 1988); and the relevant sections in D. Owen Carrigan, *Crime and Punishment in Canada: A History* (Toronto: McClelland & Stewart, 1991). Margaret Atwood's novel *Alias Grace* (Toronto: McClelland & Stewart, 1996) recreates in fiction what life was like in an Upper Canadian penitentiary.

On the Family Compact see Robert E. Saunders, "What Was the Family Compact?" *Ontario History* 49 (1957): 165–78, reprinted in J.K. Johnson, *Historical Essays on Upper Canada* (Toronto: McClelland & Stewart, 1975), pp. 122–40. The origins of an Upper Canadian elite and its transformation over time is the subject of S.J.R. Noel's *Patrons, Clients, Brokers: Ontario Society and Politics, 1791–1896* (Toronto: University of Toronto Press, 1990). On ideological differences in Upper Canada see Jane Errington, *The Lion, the Eagle, and Upper Canada: A Developing Colonial Ideology* (Montreal/Kingston: McGill-Queen's University Press, 1987); David Mills, *The Idea of Loyalty in Upper Canada, 1784–1850* (Montreal/Kingston: McGill-Queen's University Press, 1988); and the essays by S.F. Wise in A.B. McKillop and Paul Romney, eds., *God's Peculiar Peoples: Essays on Political Culture in Nineteenth-Century Canada* (Ottawa: Carleton University Press, 1993).

For the treatment of religion in the context of American immigration and political reform see Fred Landon, *Western Ontario and the American Frontier* (Toronto: McClelland & Stewart, 1967 [1941]). William Westfall's *Two Worlds: The Protestant Culture of Nineteenth Century Ontario* (Montreal/Kingston: McGill-Queen's University Press, 1989) examines the different world views that emerged out of the two dominant religious strains — Anglican and Methodist — in mid-nineteenth-century Upper Canada. An interesting survey is John Webster Grant's *A Profusion of Spires: Religion in Nineteenth-Century Ontario* (Toronto:

University of Toronto Press, 1988). On the role of image in religion and politics in Upper Canada see Cecilia Morgan, *Public Men and Virtuous Women: The Gendered Languages of Religion and Politics in Upper Canada, 1791–1850* (Toronto: University of Toronto Press, 1996). On education see S. Houston and A. Prentice, *Schooling and Scholars in Nineteenth-Century Ontario* (Toronto: University of Toronto Press, 1988); and J. Donald Wilson, "Education in Upper Canada: Sixty Years of Change," in J.D. Wilson, R.M. Stamp, and L.-P. Audet, eds., *Canadian Education: A History* (Scarborough, ON: Prentice-Hall, 1970), pp. 190–213. The best short account of Egerton Ryerson is Clara Thomas, *Ryerson of Upper Canada* (Toronto: Ryerson Press, 1969).

Douglas McCalla's *Planting the Province: The Economic History of Upper Canada, 1784–1870* (Toronto: University of Toronto Press, 1993) is a comprehensive study. The importance of the wheat economy for Upper Canada is discussed in John McCallum, *Unequal Beginnings: Agriculture and Economic Development in Quebec and Ontario until 1870* (Toronto: University of Toronto Press, 1980). For a short overview of the Upper Canadian economy see chapter 6 ("Upper Canada") in Kenneth Norrie and Douglas Owram, *A History of the Canadian Economy*, 2nd ed. (Toronto: Harcourt Brace, 1996), pp. 115–45. Transportation developments and canal building in particular are briefly described in Gerald Tulchinsky, *Transportation Changes in the St. Lawrence–Great Lakes Region, 1828–1860*, Canada's Visual History Series, vol. 11 (Ottawa: Canadian Museum of Civilization, 1974). Peter Baskerville reviews the history of banking in Upper Canada in the introduction to his edited work, *The Bank of Upper Canada: A Collection of Documents* (Toronto: Champlain Society, 1987). On the impact of settlement and economic development on the environment, see J. David Wood, *Making Ontario: Agricultural Colonization and Landscape Re-creation before the Railway* (Montreal/Kingston: McGill-Queen's University Press, 2000).

On early social assistance in Upper Canada see Rainer Boehre, "Paupers and Poor Relief in Upper Canada," in Johnson and Wilson, eds., *Historical Essays on Upper Canada*, pp. 305–40; and Stephen Speisman, "Munificent Parsons and Municipal Parsimony: Voluntary vs. Public Poor Relief in Nineteenth-Century Toronto," in M.J. Piva, ed., *A History of Ontario: Selected Readings* (Toronto: Copp Clark Pitman, 1988), pp. 55–70. On the Shiners' War see Michael Cross, "The Shiners' War: Social Violence in the Ottawa Valley in the 1830s," *Canadian Historical Review* 54 (March 1973): 1–26.

Several studies exist on the development of the Reform movement; besides Craig, *Upper Canada*, and Landon, *Western Ontario* (both cited earlier), see Aileen Dunham, *Political Unrest in Upper Canada, 1815–1836* (Toronto: McClelland & Stewart, 1963 [1927]). William Kilbourn's biography of William Lyon Mackenzie, *The Firebrand* (Toronto: Clarke Irwin, 1956) is a lively account. On the discontent in western Upper Canada see Colin Read's *The Rising in Western Upper Canada, 1837–38: The Duncombe Revolt and After* (Toronto: University of Toronto Press, 1982); and, for the rebellion in general, Colin Read and Ron Stagg, eds., *The Rebellion of 1837 in Upper Canada* (Toronto: Champlain Society, 1985). Colin Read contributes a brief but informative overview of the same topic in his pamphlet, also entitled *The Rebellion of 1837 in Upper Canada* (Ottawa: Canadian Historical Association, 1988). Allan Greer provides an interesting historiographical review of the two Canadian rebellions in "1837–38: Rebellion Reconsidered," *Canadian Historical Review* 76 (1995): 1–18. On the Battle of the Windmill, see Donald E. Graves, *Guns Across the River: The Battle of the Windmill, 1838* (Prescott: The Friends of Windmill Point, 2001).

The standard work on Lord Durham remains C. New, *Lord Durham's Mission to Canada*, with an introduction by H.W. McCready (Toronto: McClelland & Stewart, 1963). Gerald Craig has edited and introduced an abridged version of Durham's Report in *Lord Durham's Report* (Toronto: McClelland & Stewart, 1963). A more up-to-date account is Janet Ajzenstat, *The Political Thought of Lord Durham* (Montreal/Kingston: McGill-Queen's University Press, 1988). A valuable collection of articles, united under the title "Durham and His Ideas," appeared in *Journal of Canadian Studies* 25(1) (Spring 1990).

A good overview of women in Upper Canada (and throughout North America) during this period is Alison Prentice et al., "Carders of Wool, Drawers of Water: Women's Work in British North America," chapter 3 in *Canadian Women: A History*, 2nd ed. (Toronto: Harcourt Brace, 1996), pp. 58–83. For bibliographical references to this topic see Beth Light and Veronica Strong-Boag, *True Daughters of the North, Canadian Women's History: An Annotated Bibliography* (Toronto: Ontario Institute for Studies in Education, 1980). Jane Errington has written on working women in *Upper Canada from 1790 to 1840: Wives and Mothers, School Mistresses and Scullery Maids* (Montreal/Kingston: McGill-Queen's University Press, 1995).

Edward S. Rogers and Donald B. Smith, eds., *Aboriginal Ontario* (Toronto: Dundurn Press, 1994) review the First Nations' history for this period in Ontario. For the Iroquois see also Charles M. Johnston, ed., *The Valley of the Six Nations: A Collection of Documents on the Indian Lands of the Grand River* (Toronto:

Champlain Society, 1964), and for the Mississaugas and other Algonquian groups see Donald B. Smith, *Sacred Feathers: The Reverend Peter Jones (Kahkewaquonaby) and the Mississauga Indians* (Toronto: University of Toronto Press, 1987); Janet Chute, *The Legacy of Shingwaukonse: A Century of Native Leadership* (Toronto: University of Toronto Press, 1998); Peter S. Schmalz, *The Ojibwa of Southern Ontario* (Toronto: University of Toronto Press, 1990); E. Reginald Good, "Mississauga–Mennonite Relations in the Upper Grand River Valley," *Ontario History* 87(2) (June 1995): 155–72; and James A. Clifton, *A Place of Refuge for All Time: Migration of the American Potawatomi into Canada, 1830 to 1850* (Ottawa: National Museums of Canada, 1975). Tony Hall, "Native Limited Identities and Newcomer Metropolitanism in Upper Canada, 1814–1867," in David Keane and Colin Read, eds., *Old Ontario: Essays in Honour of J.M.S. Careless* (Toronto: Dundurn Press, 1990), pp. 148–73, reviews both the Iroquoian and Algonquian history of Upper Canada in the early nineteenth century. On environmental destruction see W. Fraser Sandercombe, *Nothing Gold Can Stay: The Wildlife of Upper Canada* (Erin, ON: Boston Mills Press, 1985).

On the development of an Upper Canadian political culture, see John Clarke, *Land, Power, and Economics on the Frontier of Upper Canada* (Montreal/Kingston: McGill-Queen's University Press, 2001); Jeffrey L. McNairn, *The Capacity to Judge: Public Opinion and Deliberative Democracy in Upper Canada, 1791–1854* (Toronto: University of Toronto Press, 2000); and Carol Wilton, *Popular Politics and Political Culture in Upper Canada, 1800–1850* (Montreal/Kingston: McGill-Queen's University Press, 2000).

Important maps appear in R. Louis Gentilcore, ed., *Historical Atlas of Canada, vol. 2, The Land Transformed, 1800–1891* (Toronto: University of Toronto Press, 1993).

CHAPTER

14

THE UNION OF THE CANADAS: ECONOMIC AND SOCIAL DEVELOPMENTS, 1840–1864

TIME LINE

1843 –	Strike on the Lachine Canal
1845 –	Publication of the first volume of François-Xavier Garneau's *Histoire du Canada*
1846 –	Britain introduces free trade and ends colonial timber and wheat preferences
	Lower Canadian School Act provides for the two state-aided school systems, one Catholic and one Protestant
1849 –	An annexation manifesto to join the United States is prepared in Toronto
	The Anglican-affiliated King's College becomes the non-sectarian University of Toronto
1852 –	Toronto Stock Exchange opens
	Université Laval founded
	Mary Ann Shadd Cary, the first woman publisher and editor of a newspaper, wrote *A Plea for Emigration to Canada West* to appeal to African Americans
	Susanna Moodie's *Roughing It in the Bush* published
1853 –	Completion of the St. Lawrence and Atlantic Railway between Montreal and Portland, Maine
1854 –	British North America enters into a reciprocity agreement with the United States
1855 –	Completion of the Great Western Railway from Niagara Falls via Hamilton and London to Windsor
	School Act of 1855 establishes a full-scale Roman Catholic separate school system in Canada West
1859 –	Completion of the Victoria Bridge over the St. Lawrence River at Montreal
	The Grand Trunk Railway, 1760 km long, is completed

Change, economic and social, transformed the Union of the Canadas during its quarter-of-a-century of existence. In the late 1840s, Britain, the world's industrial pioneer, adopted free trade, an event that led, with the signing of the Reciprocity Treaty with the United States in 1854, to a new north–south orientation in the Canadas' trade. During the 1850s, the new Canadian railway system transformed the agricultural, commercial, and urban character of the province. Travel velocity increased tenfold with the emergence of rail transport, compared with that by horse or canal boat. Large-scale immigration to Upper Canada, or Canada West, and emigration from Lower Canada, or Canada East, altered social and cultural life at mid-century. Education, especially in Canada West, became a much-debated social issue. The mid-nineteenth century marked a real dividing point in the history of the Canadas.

THE COMMERCIAL EMPIRE OF THE ST. LAWRENCE

 In 1937, historian Donald Creighton advanced the Laurentian interpretation of Canadian history: that is, whoever controlled the St. Lawrence could dominate the economic life of the continent.[1] This interpretation also argued that the economic life of British North America was based on "staple" trade, the production and exporting of a few "staple" resources such as fish, furs, timber, and wheat. The American Revolution and the Treaty of 1783 created an artificial political boundary along the St. Lawrence and the Great Lakes, dividing the northern portion of the North American continent into two political units. But the political boundary did not immediately become an economic one. Throughout the early nineteenth century, the British merchants of Montreal vied with those of New York for commercial dominance of the trade of the interior of North America.

Up to the mid-1840s, the British North American commercial bourgeoisie competed successfully against their American counterparts, thanks to the highly favourable mercantile system of trade between the British North American colonies and Britain. The British desired two staples readily available in the United Canadas: timber and wheat.

British shipbuilders needed square-hewed timber, made from Canadian white and red pine, for the masts of sailing ships. In addition, lumber for construction found a lucrative market in Britain. Wood became British North America's most valuable export commodity, making up nearly

"Squaring the timber" — cutting the sides to make the round log into a square one with the use of a broadaxe — was one of the jobs of the shanty workers. The logs were squared to allow them to be fitted tightly into the hold of the ships that transported timber to Britain.

Archives of Ontario/11778-4.

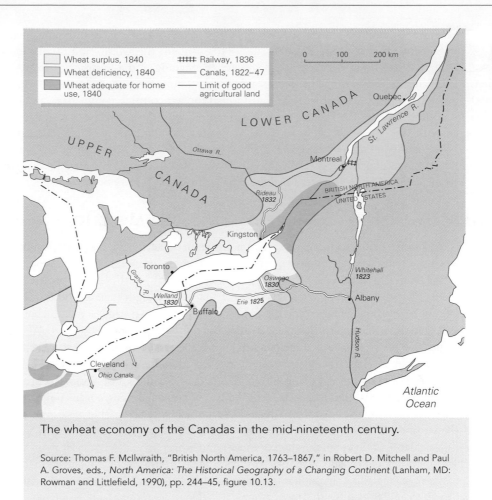

The wheat economy of the Canadas in the mid-nineteenth century.

Source: Thomas F. McIlwraith, "British North America, 1763–1867," in Robert D. Mitchell and Paul A. Groves, eds., *North America: The Historical Geography of a Changing Continent* (Lanham, MD: Rowman and Littlefield, 1990), pp. 244–45, figure 10.13.

two-thirds of the value of the colonies' exports to Britain by the 1840s. But the lumber industry remained vulnerable and volatile, subject to fluctuating demand in Britain, low tariffs after 1842, and overproduction — all of which caused many businesses to go bankrupt during the 1840s and 1850s. Without preferential treatment in Britain, it was difficult for Canadian lumber suppliers to compete with lumber exporters from the Baltic countries with their lower transportation costs.

Within the United Canadas, a second commodity — wheat, in the form of either coarse grain or ground flour — rivalled timber. Canada West was the greatest producer of wheat in British North America. After 1840, a combination of good weather and increased hectarage due to rapid settlement of the rich farmland of Canada West greatly increased total production. The average farmer's export of wheat rose from 45 bushels in the 1840s to 80 bushels in the 1850s, and to as much as 135 bushels in the 1860s. Improved transportation on the St. Lawrence–Great Lakes with the completion of the canal system lowered transport costs and reduced insurance rates. This helped to increase Canadian exports, making Canada West one of the chief suppliers of wheat to feed industrial Britain's growing urban population.

TRANSPORTATION

Exporting bulky staples such as wheat and timber required a sophisticated transportation system. Roads were needed to get wheat to urban centres for local marketing or export. In the

Launch of the Royal William, by J.P Cockburn, 1831. The *Royal William* became the first ship to cross the Atlantic Ocean entirely under steam power.

National Archives of Canada/C-12649.

1840s a series of roads, some of them little more than dirt paths and others gravel-surfaced, crisscrossed the Canadas. By 1852, a comprehensive road system linked Windsor to Montreal, with branches northward to towns on Lake Huron and to Bytown (Ottawa).

 More important for transportation was the canal system linking Lake Erie with Montreal and the Atlantic Ocean. During the 1840s, the government of the Canadas widened and deepened existing canals such as the Welland and the Lachine to accommodate larger steamboats. It built new canals between Montreal and Prescott, where rapids and shallows impeded shipping, and at Beauharnois, Cornwall, and Williamsburg. By 1848, a chain of first-class canals enabled the St. Lawrence–Great Lakes route to rival the Erie–Hudson River route, and Montreal to compete with New York as the major exporting and importing centre for the North American continent.

New York, however, had considerable advantages. It was a larger city, with a heavily populated hinterland based on a diverse economy and, unlike Montreal, with a year-round ice-free port. Shipping rates from New York to Liverpool were also considerably lower than those from Montreal to Liverpool. In addition, in 1845–46 the American government passed the Drawbacks Acts, which allowed Canadian exports and imports to pass in bond through American waterways duty-free, thus making it profitable for Canada West farmers and timber merchants to ship via the United States. Finally, New York had the advantage of being linked to the growing American Midwest by an extensive railway system.

THE ADVENT OF BRITISH FREE TRADE AND REPERCUSSIONS FOR THE UNITED CANADAS

In 1846, Britain adopted free trade. (For the political repercussions of this decision, see Chapter 15). Pressure on the British government to end the old colonial mercantile system came chiefly from British factory owners who wanted reduced tariffs to enable Britain to compete in a world market. They also sought the repeal of the Corn Laws (protective tariffs on grain), arguing that repeal of the laws would mean cheaper food for the industrial working class and hence an opportunity for employers to lower wages.

Liberal economists such as Richard Cobden disproved traditional mercantile theories by pointing out the costs, economic and military, of keeping colonies. They argued persuasively in favour of laissez-faire economics and free trade as benefiting Britain, the industrial world super-power of the day. Britain wanted to purchase raw materials at the lowest possible price and to sell manufactured goods wherever it desired. Historian J.M.S. Careless summarized the economists' argument: "When the whole world was its domain for markets and supplies, what reason was there to guide and husband overseas possessions that cost much more to maintain than they could ever return?"[2]

These free-trade lobbyists convinced Robert Peel's government to repeal the Corn Laws in 1846. Other free-trade measures included the lowering of the timber preference in 1842, which cut the duty on foreign imports in half. Further reductions followed in 1845, 1846, 1848, and 1851. Then, in 1849, Britain repealed the Navigation Laws, which restricted trade with the colonies to British or colonial vessels. As well, the United States obtained access to the Canadian–British trade and to all the Great Lakes trade.

Free trade initially hurt the Canadas. Exports via the St. Lawrence fell by over one-third, from £2.7 million in 1845 to a low of £1.7 million in 1848. Many Canadian merchants regarded the abrupt end of the protected trading system as a treacherous act on Britain's part. They reacted with resentment, especially the Montreal merchants who, with the arrival of free trade, saw the demise of their dream of expanding the commercial empire of the St. Lawrence. The world depression of the same time added to the city's problems as bankruptcies spread. Annexation manifestoes circulated throughout the Canadas proposing union with the United States. Opponents of annexation formed the British–American League in 1849, which advocated tariff protection and a union of the British North American colonies as alternatives to joining the United States. When free traders argued that high tariffs raised the price of consumer goods, Montreal journalist D'Arcy McGee rejoined that protection would "not be to make them dear, but to make them here."

FROM TRANSATLANTIC TO TRANSCONTINENTAL TRADE

The Canadas neither collapsed nor joined the United States. Commerce revived as British North America adjusted to new challenges. Trade increased with the United States. Second, the Canadians now placed a new emphasis on railways as the major means of transportation. These two goals were complementary. Just as the waterways had best facilitated east–west trade across the continent and ultimately with Britain, railways best linked the Canadas and the United States for north–south trade. The transition from transatlantic to transcontinental trade had begun.

This transition came swiftly and dramatically. By the end of 1850, the world depression lifted and prosperity returned through increased trade. Whereas industrialism in Britain had led indirectly to a temporary *decrease* in trade for the British North American colonies, industrialism in the United States led directly to an initial *increase* in markets for the Canadian staple products — timber and wheat. The rapidly growing cities of the eastern seaboard and of the American Midwest needed lumber, the universal building material at the time, to construct houses and commercial buildings, and wheat to feed the growing population. In the 1850s alone, 2.5 million Europeans emigrated to the United States. On the eve of the Civil War, the United States had 31 million people, more than ten times the population of all the British North American colonies combined.

The era of the 1850s inaugurated what historian A.R.M. Lower described as "the North American assault on the Canadian forest."[3] As demand for Canadian lumber increased, American lumber firms and sawmill owners established themselves in Canadian forest areas, especially the Ottawa valley.

Equally, Canadian timber found a rising market in Canada West, with its growing immigrant population. Saw and planing mills, sash and shingle factories, and cabinet making firms arose to serve this local market. Britain also increased its demand for Canadian lumber in the prosperous years of the 1850s. Despite the move to free trade, Britain still remained, in relative terms, the most lucrative market for Canadian timber until into the 1860s, accounting for approximately 80 percent of wood exports.

Canadian wheat did equally well during the prosperous 1850s. Clearly, the removal of the Corn Laws had little adverse effect on Canada's ability to compete in British markets. The demand for wheat during the Crimean War of 1854–56, when Britain prohibited the importation of Russian grain, helped the Canadas. Americans also purchased quantities of Canadian wheat to feed their growing urban population. Exports of Canadian wheat and flour via the St. Lawrence nearly tripled between 1845 and 1856, rising from 4.5 million bushels to 12 million bushels — a figure not surpassed until the next decade. Furthermore, prices tripled in the same period. As a result, agriculture surpassed timber as the major staple of Canadian — indeed, of all British North American — trade in the 1850s.

Farmers in Canada West benefited the most from this increased demand for wheat. Good prices, along with high yields, provided them with capital to increase their hectarage and to diversify their farming. In addition to wheat, they exported wool, meat, eggs, butter, and cheese, especially to the United States.

Farmers in Canada East did not fare as well. Unlike Canada West, where new fertile land remained available until the mid-1850s, a shortage of good agricultural land, combined with problems of climate and fertility, led to serious farm problems. Farmers in Canada East produced little wheat for export, although they did export other grains such as oats and barley, along with dairy products in limited quantities.

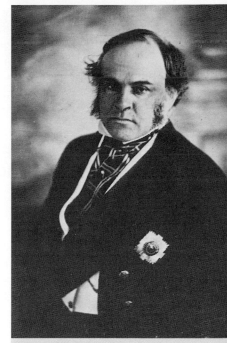

James Bruce, Earl of Elgin and Kincardine, 1848.

National Archives of Canada/C-291.

RECIPROCITY WITH THE UNITED STATES

To expand its lucrative trade with the United States, the Canadas wanted a reciprocal trade agreement. Strong American protectionist sentiment, however, prevented acceptance of the idea. When the Americans finally became receptive to the idea in the early 1850s, Canadian merchants were less enthusiastic because they already enjoyed active trade with the Americans without an agreement. But, as J.M.S. Careless notes, "The emerging economic pattern of the early fifties indicated that if Canada could do without reciprocity, she could do much better with it."[4] The British government endorsed the idea, as a means of easing tensions and reducing Canadian dependence on the mother country. But now the Americans resisted.

Two obstacles remained. The first was the slavery issue in the United States. The divisions between the slave South and the free North affected all aspects of American development at the time, including economic relations with the British North American colonies. Northern senators favoured free trade because they believed it a prelude to annexing the Canadas, which would lead to a preponderance of free states in the Union. Southern senators opposed it for the same reason, until Lord Elgin, who went to Washington in May 1854, convinced them that a prosperous Canada through free trade would be more likely to want independence from, rather than annexation to, the United States.

The other roadblock to reciprocity concerned Maritime fisheries. Britain and the United States had different interpretations of the territorial waters in British North America from which

American fishers were excluded under the Convention of 1818. New England fishers claimed a right to fish in Maritime waters 5 km out from shore, following the shoreline. Nova Scotian and other Maritime fishers claimed a boundary 5 km from headland to headland, thus leaving most of the bays and inlets as exclusive British North American territory. Neither side wanted an armed conflict, and Britain was willing to use the fisheries issue as a negotiating tool for free trade of colonial natural products in the United States. In the end, Britain threatened to withdraw its patrol boats (which prevented American encroachment), unless Nova Scotia agreed to the treaty.

THE RECIPROCITY TREATY

 The Reciprocity Treaty of 1854, approved by the American Senate and ratified by the colonial legislatures, allowed for the free trade of major natural products, such as timber, grain, coal, livestock, and fish, between the British North American colonies and the United States; mutually free navigation on the American-controlled Lake Michigan and the Canadian-controlled St. Lawrence River; and joint access to all coastal fisheries north of the 36th parallel. The agreement ran for a 10-year period commencing in 1855 and was subject to renewal or termination. For Canadians, this reciprocity agreement bolstered the prosperity that had already begun.

THE RAILWAY ERA

Closer economic ties with the United States coincided with the Canadian railway-building era. Suddenly, constructing canals seemed old-fashioned. Increased Canadian–American trade provided the incentive for new rail lines and greater continental economic integration.

The first British North American railway, the Champlain and St. Lawrence Railway, a 23 km line made of wooden rails that linked Montreal and the Richelieu River, was completed in 1836. But the real era of railway building occurred in the 1850s. At the beginning of the decade, only 105 km of track existed in all British North America, compared with 14 500 km in the United States. By the end of the decade, the amount of track had increased to 2880 km in the Canadas alone. By 1856, all the major urban centres in Canada West were linked by railways. Such expansion came as a result of the combination of popular interest, public and private financial support, and private promotion. One of the negative factors was the environmental impact. The railway worked an ecological revolution in the landscape of the Canadas. As new communities arose, both forests and land came under greater assault. The locomotive contributed greatly to the rapid disappearance of the white pine forests of the Canadas.

Governments eagerly courted railways. Railways required large expenditures of public funds and brought governments to the brink of bankruptcy, but these "engines of progress" seemed worth the price. Since Canadians had arrived late in the competition for railways, compared with Britain and the United States, and at a time when the country had hardly begun to industrialize, most of the capital for railway building came from Britain and the United States.

As the British North American colonies had insufficient credit ratings to borrow vast sums abroad, their governments inevitably became involved in railway financing. But unlike canal building, in which the state often took control through public ownership, private companies built railways with extensive government financial assistance. This partnership made possible the construction of rail lines, but at a price. It led to waste, duplication of services, and an excessive drain on the public treasury (in the form of debt). It also contributed greatly to corruption through the granting of railway contracts for political purposes only. In 1849, the government of the Canadas introduced the Railway Guarantee Act, which guaranteed interest at 6 percent on not more than half of the bonded debt of railways over 120 km long, over half of which had already been constructed. Of even more immediate value to railway promoters was the bill introduced in 1850 that permitted municipal governments to buy stock in railway companies and to make loans to them.

Private companies built four key railway lines in the United Canadas in the 1850s. The St. Lawrence and Atlantic line between Montreal and Portland, Maine, completed in 1853, gave Montreal access to a year-round ice-free port on the Atlantic, and made the city once more competitive with New York in continental trade. The second line, the Great Western Railway, completed in 1855, went from Niagara Falls via Hamilton and London to Windsor. In the east, the line joined the New York rail network, while in the west it connected with the Michigan Central. It sought to capture the trade of the American Midwest by offering a quick route from Chicago through to New York by way of the Canadas. Presided over by Sir Allan MacNab and backed by British and American capital, this 575 km railway made a profit from the start. The third major line, the Northern Railway, went from Toronto, on Lake Ontario, to Collingwood, on Georgian Bay — a distance of roughly 160 km. The Northern Railway serviced the rich farmland north of Toronto, opened up the forested area of the Georgian Bay and Muskoka regions, and provided access to Lake Huron. The fourth and most ambitious railway scheme of the decade was the Grand Trunk.

THE GRAND TRUNK RAILWAY

Chartered by Parliament in 1853, the Grand Trunk Railway originally was to run from Windsor, Canada West, to Halifax, Nova Scotia, thus linking the interior of British North America with an ice-free Atlantic port. The railway's name came from the intention to have several small rail lines connect to one main line, much as the branches of a tree join its trunk. When plans to build the Maritime section failed, the company purchased the St. Lawrence and Atlantic line, which ran between Montreal and ice-free Portland, Maine. The scheme proved costly, however, because the St. Lawrence and Atlantic track needed major repairs. Equally expensive was the Grand Trunk

Railway travel in the mid-nineteenth century could be challenging in winter. A Grand Trunk Railway locomotive with snow-clearing machine, Lévis, Quebec, February 1869.

National Archives of Canada/PA-149764.

directorate's decision (taken after it failed in its attempt to purchase the Great Western) to build a competing line through the heart of Canada West from Toronto to Sarnia. As a result, the two railways often ran parallel to each other and serviced the same area.

In 1859, the Grand Trunk completed the Victoria Bridge, one of the great engineering feats of the century. In 1858, its peak year of construction, over 3000 workers helped to build it. This 2700 m bridge, opened by the Prince of Wales in 1860, spanned the St. Lawrence at Montreal and thus allowed for continuous rail connections between Sarnia and Portland.

The Grand Trunk Railway, with 1760 km of track, became the longest railway in the world. This distinction came at great cost to the Canadian public. From the beginning, the company ran into financial trouble, leading its London bankers to approach the provincial government for help. The government bailed it out — six of the railway company's twelve directors belonged to the Canadian cabinet.

By 1859, the Canadian government's debt from railway building exceeded $67 million. The Grand Trunk Railway accounted for a large part of that debt. "This sum alone," economic historians Kenneth Norrie and Douglas Owram note, "was greater than all the money spent on public works — canals, bridges, roads, buildings — by the Province of Canada between the Act of Union in 1841 and Confederation."[5] To make matters worse, this trunk line, designed to tap American trade for the Canadas, had a 1.65 m track gauge — wider than that used in the United States. That meant American goods shipped via the Grand Trunk had to be reloaded at the border, causing the railway to lose most of the trade that it was built to capture. In the 1850s and 1860s, the Grand Trunk Railway never made a profit.

URBAN AND COMMERCIAL DEVELOPMENT

The railways promoted commercial development. They brought in millions of dollars of foreign investment. They required thousands of workers to lay track and then to maintain it. New railway-related industries sprang up across the province — engine foundries, car shops, rolling mills, and metalwork shops — that all needed skilled and unskilled workers. Railway companies themselves often owned many of these businesses. By 1860, Canadian railways had 6660 people on their combined payrolls.

Along with canal building and shipbuilding, railways encouraged the development of a host of secondary industries: flour mills, saw mills, tanneries, boot and shoe factories, textile shops, breweries, distilleries, and wagon and carriage manufacturers. Shipbuilders in Montreal and Quebec City built many of the steamboats that plied the St. Lawrence River and Great Lakes after 1809, using timber from the Ottawa valley. Ironworks were established in Hamilton because of the city's easy access to the American coal fields in Pennsylvania. Significant developments in the manufacturing of agricultural implements occurred, especially in Newcastle, Canada West, where Daniel and Hart Massey produced a combined rake, reaper, and mowing machine in 1855, marking the beginning of a lucrative Canadian industry.

This industrial growth led to the creation of a host of towns, mainly along the rail lines, to service the prosperous agricultural hinterland. In Canada West, the number of towns doubled to more than 80 between 1850 and 1870. Each provided a market centre for local produce and an import centre for manufactured goods. Fewer towns developed in the St. Lawrence River valley, where little good agricultural land remained.

On account of the lack of farmland and their inability to find work in Montreal and Quebec, a number of French Canadians emigrated to neighbouring New England or to the American

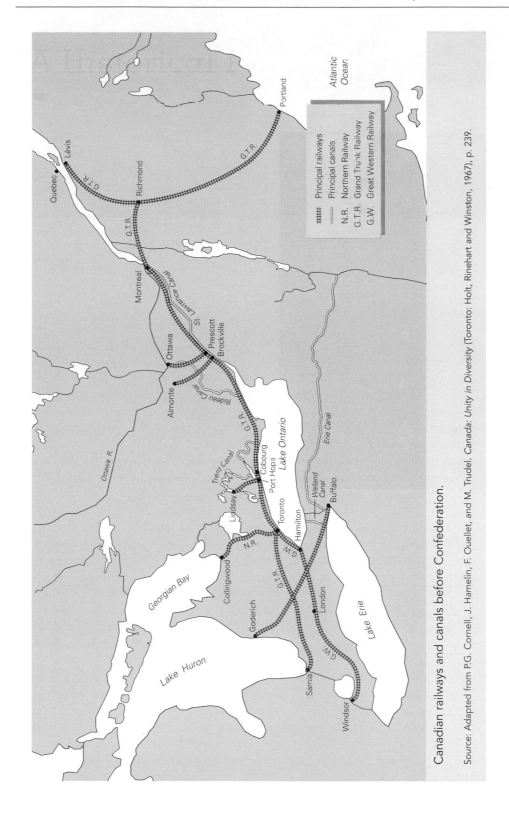

Canadian railways and canals before Confederation.

Source: Adapted from P.G. Cornell, J. Hamelin, F. Ouellet, and M. Trudel, *Canada: Unity in Diversity* (Toronto: Holt, Rinehart and Winston, 1967), p. 239.

The collapse of this railroad bridge over the Desjardins Canal near Hamilton, in 1857, killed 60 train passengers. From *The Illustrated London News*, April 4, 1857.

National Archives of Canada/C-1520.

Midwest, an area that also began to attract farmers from Canada West in the late 1850s. While Canada West's soils tended to be better than those of the St. Lawrence valley, in the assessment of historical geographer R. Cole Harris they "were not nearly as rich as the long-grass prairie soils of parts of the American Middle West."[6] Moreover, by the late 1850s, the best farmland in Canada West had been taken.

Among the hierarchy of towns and cities that developed in the 1840s and 1850s, London became the major centre in southwestern Canada West. Although the artist Daniel Fowler described it in 1843 as "literally dug out of the woods — stumps up to the back doors. A hideous new raw place," yet between 1850 and 1856 its population tripled from 5000 to 15 000. The port of Hamilton dominated the hinterland to the west and south, extending its influence into the Niagara peninsula. Both London and Hamilton became supply depots and manufacturing centres. Hamilton also became an early industrial city. A central location, however, could also have some disadvantages. As urban historian John Weaver noted, "A gang of pickpockets who worked the Great Western Railway and American trains settled in Hamilton on account of its proximity to major urban communities on both sides of the boundary."[7]

On the negative side as well, railways in the 1850s and 1860s were unsafe. During 1854, nineteen serious accidents occurred, the most serious of which killed 52 people and injured 48. That same year, six times as many people were killed on the Great Western Railway as on all British railways, which carried 300 times as many passengers. Railway historian G.R. Stevens noted: "Every railway operation seemed to be conducted in a casual and dangerous manner."[8] In a number of derailments the engine drivers had spotted livestock on the line, but instead of slowing down, speeded up, trying to knock them off the tracks. Signals were ignored, and maintenance of the roadbed was neglected. One accident occurred because a ganger disconnected a rail and then, without setting up a warning flag, went home for dinner. In anguish the editor of the Chatham, Canada West, *Western Planet* wrote: "Better, infinitely better, that the whistle of the locomotive had never woke the echoes of our forests than it should have sounded the death knell of so many human beings, who have dyed this road with their blood." Certainly not all Canadians praised the railway as a symbol of progress, but most did.

RIVALRY BETWEEN TORONTO AND MONTREAL

Toronto serviced a wealthy rural hinterland that extended roughly 20 km to the east, 20 km to the west, and 100 km to the north, to Lake Simcoe. As the city had the advantage of a central location and good harbour facilities on Lake Ontario, it became the railway hub of Canada West, with excellent rail service to various regions of the province. Its leading commerce, the import trade, rose more than fivefold in value, from $1.2 million in 1849 to more than $6.6 million in 1856. Its export trade remained based on grain and wood to external markets, especially the United States but also Britain.

A new urban mercantile elite appeared in Canada West's leading city in the 1850s. Its members founded the Toronto Board of Trade. In 1852 the Toronto Stock Exchange opened, and in 1856 the Bank of Montreal inaugurated its Toronto office. By the end of the decade, the city had become the undisputed regional business centre of Canada West.

Toronto, however, could not supplant Montreal as the largest city in British North America and the dominant metropolitan centre of the Canadas. As one of the oldest centres in British North America, Montreal built upon its initial strengths. After a temporary setback caused by Britain's adoption of free trade in the late 1840s, the city surfaced again as a prosperous centre in the 1850s. Its important location on the St. Lawrence gave it a great advantage over inland Toronto, especially since the canal improvements of the 1840s made it cheaper and more efficient to ship goods by water than by rail.

Even in the competition for rail traffic, Montreal fared well with the completion of the Grand Trunk Railway. The Portland, Maine, branch provided the city with an ice-free port on the Atlantic and access to the agricultural hinterland of Canada West and, to an extent, the American Midwest. Equally, Montreal served as an important import centre for the eastern portion of Canada West, rivalling Toronto for this lucrative market. The city also benefited from the Reciprocity Treaty of 1854, which helped it become a major export centre of Canadian timber and wheat for American markets.

Service industries in Montreal expanded, as footwear manufacturers, furriers, wood-products manufacturers, distilleries, breweries, tobacco factories, brickyards, and sugar refineries opened their doors. Metal-based industries, such as the Victoria Iron Works (the largest industry, with 120 workers), also developed.

SOCIAL DEVELOPMENTS

Annually, 25 000 to 40 000 immigrants entered the Canadas, especially the western section. In 1851, the population of Canada West surpassed that of Canada East for the first time. Overall, the population of the Canadas went from 1.1 million in 1841 to almost 2 million in 1851. Almost half of the people were under the age of 18.

A large number of the new immigrants, estimated to be 90 000, came from Ireland, part of the famine migration resulting from the failure of the potato crop. Traditionally, historians have described these Irish as mainly impoverished Roman Catholics from southern Ireland who lacked farming experience and money, and ended up in ghettos in the cities and towns. Recent research by historian Donald Akenson reveals, however, that by far the largest percentage (more than 75 percent) of Irish immigrants farmed on isolated homesteads in rural areas. Furthermore, more than two-thirds were Protestant.

Clearly, however, the presence of Irish Protestants and Irish Catholics within the cities, or even adjacent rural settlements, resulted in the rise of nativism, the practice of favouring native-born citizens as against immigrants. This was particularly evident in the ports where passengers disembarked, which were mainly Montreal and Toronto for the United Canadas. In Montreal, Irish

Community Portrait

← The Orange Community in Toronto's Cabbagetown

Formed by Irish Protestants in Ireland in 1795, the Orange Order spread rapidly throughout Ireland and England. It came to British North America in the 1820s. The Grand Lodge of British North America was organized in 1830. By 1870 Canada had more than a thousand Orange Lodges, with the largest number in Toronto. Although the Orange Order's membership was spread across all neighbourhoods in Victorian Toronto, Cabbagetown, or East Toronto, had the greatest number of Lodges in the city.

East Toronto emerged in the mid-nineteenth century as an important destination point for British immigrants to Ontario, particularly for Irish Protestants. The growth of railways and industries in Toronto created large numbers of jobs for urban workers north of the new rail and factory complex at the Don River end of the harbour. In the 1840s, after immigrants spread along both sides of King Street East, they settled on the vacant land to the north. There the newcomers built squatters' shacks and planted essential gardens, hence the district's name, "Cabbagetown." Small low-priced houses followed, with some larger buildings.

The largely working-class neighbourhood, close to the adjacent factories and packing houses, soon was the home of a vibrant Orange community. Not all Protestant Irish males belonged, but a substantial number did. Although the initial strength of the Order came from Irish immigrants, the spread of the organization owed much to the support of many non-Irish groups, in particular those of English and Scottish background. While the bulk of the membership came from

Twelfth of July Orange parade along King Street in Toronto, 1874.

the working class, the Toronto Orange community crossed class lines and had a significant middle-class component in the city.

The Orange Lodge celebrated the British Crown and Protestantism. "No Surrender" was the Order's rallying cry. The Orange Order opposed Catholic schools and the use of the French language outside of Quebec. But in the British Protestant fortress of Victorian Toronto, Irish Catholics, not French Canadians, constituted the resident minority group. As John McAree, a prominent Toronto journalist, who was born of Northern Irish parents, wrote in *Cabbagetown Store* (1953), his memoir of his late nineteenth-century Cabbagetown: "Catholics were generally spoken of as Dogans, a term of contempt, I suppose. They were considered as foreign as if they had been Italians, and were viewed with suspicion." In mid-nineteenth-century Toronto, Protestants outnumbered Catholics by three to one. Clearly religion, not "race," was the focus of opposition of the Order; in fact, the Orange Order in Canada allowed Protestant First Nations and Protestant African-Canadian males to join.

The cohesion of Cabbagetown's Orange community came from a system of secret rituals, an internal hierarchy of five "degrees," and the public celebration of July 12th, the date of William of Orange's ("King Billy's") victory at the Battle of the Boyne. The Catholics' defeat in 1690 led to the Protestant minority's maintenance of its domination of Ireland. In the nineteenth century, and well into the twentieth, Cabbagetowners, on "the Glorious Twelfth," crammed with thousands of other Torontonians along downtown streets to catch a glimpse of "King Billy" on his white horse in the Orangemen's huge July 12th Parade, their counterpart to the St. Patrick's Day celebrations.

Some sparring did occur between the Orange community of Cabbagetown and the residents of predominantly Catholic Corktown, located south of Queen and on below King. In the late 1860s, the Orange Young Britons arrived to strengthen the Orange community. Some Young Britons were overly zealous in the late nineteenth century, as John McAree recalled: "A really militant organization was the Orange Young Britons, made up of husky, strutting young men, mechanics and labourers who were extremely provocative. They would parade frequently and always made it a point of invading a neighbourhood east of Parliament Street and south of Queen Street where there was quite a Roman Catholic settlement. These parades always wound up in fist fights and the throwing of stones."

The Orange community in Cabbagetown did a great deal to benefit its members and their families. It served as a social club, and a mutual aid society, which the lower classes could afford to join. Lodge members assisted each other in times of sickness. A primitive insurance system existed to cover burial costs and even to provide lump-sum payments to widows. Orangemen also helped fellow members in the community to find work.

Further Reading

J.M.S. Careless, "The Emergence of Cabbagetown in Victorian Toronto," in Robert F. Harney, ed., *Gathering Place: Peoples and Neighbourhoods of Toronto, 1834–1945* (Toronto: Multicultural History Society of Ontario, 1985): 25–45.

Cecil J. Houston and William J. Smyth, *The Sash Canada Wore. A Historical Geography of the Orange Order in Canada* (Toronto: University of Toronto Press, 1980).

Gregory S. Kealey, "The Orange Order in Toronto: Religious Riot and the Working Class," in Michael J. Piva, ed., *A History of Ontario: Selected Readings* (Toronto: Copp Clark Pitman Ltd., 1988): 71–94.

J.V. McAree, *Cabbagetown Store* (Toronto: The Ryerson Press, 1953).

Harriet Tubman (far left) with some of her "passengers" from the Underground Railway.

Schomburg Center for Research in Black Culture, The New York Public Library, Astor Lennox and Tilden Foundations/SC-CN-92-0675.

Catholics experienced less prejudice due to the commonality of the Roman Catholic faith with the French Canadians. But in Toronto, known at the time as "the Belfast of North America," nativist attitudes were very pronounced, especially after the Irish famine migration, when the city saw its Irish Catholic population increase from one-sixth in 1841 to one-quarter in 1851. Protestants feared that Irish Catholics would undermine the very tenets of British North American self-identity: loyalty to the British Empire and Protestantism. In the presses and in pamphlets, the dominant Protestant population depicted the Irish Catholics as the "ignorant masses," "untameable barbarians," "priest-ridden," and "wretched." Such epithets lingered well after Irish Catholic immigrants had achieved economic success to hinder their social advancement.

African Americans also came to the United Canadas; an estimated 30 000 to 40 000 had arrived by 1861. Some came on the advice of Mary Ann Shadd Cary, the first woman publisher and editor of a newspaper in the Canadas in the 1850s. In 1852, she wrote *A Plea for Emigration to Canada West* to appeal in particular to African Americans by outlining the benefits of emigrating to Canada West. The passage of the Fugitive Slave Act in the United States in 1850 meant that thousands of presumably free African Americans living in the northern states were liable to be captured and sent back into bondage. Instead, many escaped to the Canadas by way of the Underground Railway — a secret, complex network of free blacks, former slaves, and white American and Canadian abolitionists.

With the advent of railroads, it became customary to use railway terminology to describe the secret operations leading slaves to freedom. Those who led the slaves on foot or horseback, or transported them by wagons, barges, or steamers, became "agents" or "conductors." The "passengers" were the runaways. The transfer points or hiding places were called "stations," and the final destination points were "terminals." The largest number of slave fugitives crossed at Amherstburg, situated at the narrowest point of the Detroit River. Other major "terminals" included Windsor, Sandwich, St. Catharines, Niagara-on-the-Lake, Hamilton, Toronto, and Kingston.

One of the most famous "conductors" was the former slave Harriet Tubman, who after escaping to freedom immediately returned to the South to help other slaves. In all she made nineteen trips, bringing out at least 300 slaves, and in 1857 she even succeeded in freeing her parents. Between 1851 and 1857, Tubman made St. Catharines her chief terminal. At one point, a group of slaveholders offered a $40 000 reward for her capture, dead or alive. But she evaded all her would-be captors.

Many African Americans left Canada at the outbreak of the Civil War to help the northern side. Others went home to join friends and relatives after the passage of the Emancipation Act of 1863, having found temporary refuge but no more tolerance than that experienced in the United States. It is estimated one-half stayed, although it is impossible to state an exact figure.

MIGRANT MOBILITY IN THE CANADAS

Within the district of Canada West, people moved frequently. In a case study of rural Peel County, just west of Toronto, social historian David Gagan has shown that prior to 1840 the county had ample cheap land and a relatively self-sufficient population living off its own land and livestock.[9] Two decades later, it had become a major wheat exporting region. Young people moved away from the now overpopulated country areas, either to newer farming areas within the province, to the growing towns and cities of Canada West, or to other areas, such as the American Midwest. Those who stayed in Peel tended to be better off, with larger farms, a higher standard of living, and better-educated children than those who left. In general, people who did not move tended to be more prosperous than the transient in nineteenth-century North America.

Transiency also characterized the urban centres of Canada West. In a quantitative study of Hamilton, social historian Michael Katz noted that the city's population increased in five years (1846–50) by 150 percent.[10] Individuals also moved frequently. According to Katz, more than one-third of those listed in the 1851 census could not be located for the 1861 census. This mobility characterized all social groups, from lower to upper class; people of all groups and all ages sought to improve their living conditions.

In Canada East, people migrated as well. Many went to the United States, especially to New England. With a decline in agriculture and a sluggish timber trade (the two mainstays of the Quebec economy), hard economic times arrived in the 1840s and 1850s. Existing land was depleted, new agricultural land became scarce, seigneuries were subdivided to the point where the habitants could no longer support their families, and unemployment was high in the urban centres. This crisis, along with continued high birth rates, a declining death rate, and increased British immigration, forced many French Canadians to move. An estimated 30 000 emigrants left during the 1840s alone.

The loss of French Canadians to the United States alarmed the Quebec clergy, who feared that the English-speaking population in Quebec (roughly 25 percent of the total population of Quebec in 1861), might one day become the majority in the province if the exodus continued. After 1844, the Roman Catholic church became actively involved in the colonization movement designed to settle the northern areas of Quebec and, more important, to preserve the attributes of traditional family and religious life. "Let us take possession of the soil, it is the best means of preserving our nationality" became the rallying cry of the agrarian nationalism of the 1840s and 1850s. Yet for many French Canadians, the appeal went unheeded. They wanted to escape agriculture, and left for better economic conditions in *"les États."*

URBAN STRUCTURE IN CANADA WEST

Within the towns and cities of Canada West, a fairly rigid social structure existed. A small male elite dominated, socially and politically. A growing commercial middle class, consisting of merchants, shopkeepers, and artisans, led society and was joined by a rising male professional class of clergy, lawyers, doctors, and teachers. Middle-class women were expected to stay at home, in what is now referred to as their "private sphere," where they performed domestic duties and reared children. Increasingly, women obtained positions as teachers (especially of girls at home), but they remained excluded from other professions.

Below the professional class stood the large class of wage labourers, made up mostly of immigrants, both male and female. Few, however, had regular work. Most often, wage-earning employment was temporary (as during a period of apprenticeship) or seasonal. This urban proletariat suffered from poor housing, inadequate sanitation, and seasonal unemployment. Most relied on their own ingenuity to survive, as virtually no help came from government. The prevailing ethos held that success came to those who worked hard; frustration and failure were the result of waste and a lack of individual initiative. Canada West thus remained a society modelled on the agrarian values of hardy "yeoman farmers" and robust, self-reliant pioneers. Many working-class families hired out their children from about the age of 7 or 8 for additional family income; other families expected children of that age to take responsibility at home while older children and the parents worked outside the home.

URBAN DEVELOPMENT IN QUEBEC

In Canada East, urban concentration occurred in only a few centres. Even a long-established town such as Trois-Rivières had a population of only 3000 in the 1840s, while Sorel and Hull remained virtually villages. The educated professional middle class of doctors, lawyers, and teachers constituted the elites in these communities. Sherbrooke was becoming the commercial centre for the predominantly English-speaking area of the Eastern Townships, but at mid-century it was still a village with a population of less than 1000.

Only two urban centres claimed the title of "city" in Canada East in the 1850s: Montreal and Quebec City. The oldest, Quebec, was the centre of the timber trade. The majority of its commercial elite were English-speaking families associated with that trade in some respect. Many of the city's numerous labourers, who inhabited the Lower Town (*basse-ville*) of the city, also worked in the timber industry. Here, in overcrowded and dirty conditions, French-Canadian and Irish workers intermingled. In contrast, the Upper Town, made up predominantly of the English, was considered "one of the cleanest cities in the world." In the northern section, around St. John Street (rue St. Jean), lived merchants, retail traders, artisans, and numerous tavern-keepers, while in the southern part resided officers and government officials.

Montreal was the largest and the most industrialized city in British North America. As factories were built in the 1840s and 1850s, employment prospects attracted workers from the

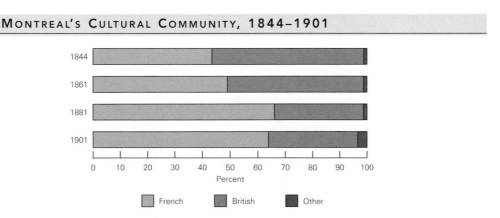

MONTREAL'S CULTURAL COMMUNITY, 1844–1901

Source: R. Louis Gentilcore, ed., *Historical Atlas of Canada*, vol. 2, *The Land Transformed, 1800–1891* (Toronto: University of Toronto Press, 1993), plate 49. Reprinted by permission of the University of Toronto Press Incorporated.

countryside who might otherwise have emigrated to the United States. In the 1860s, the French-speaking population once again outnumbered the English-speaking in Montreal. These French Canadians, along with the Irish immigrants, provided cheap labour for the new industries.

The eastern end of the city remained overwhelmingly working class and predominantly French Canadian, while the west end was decidedly bourgeois and British. The English-Canadian commercial entrepreneurs had begun to move "up the mountain" to build luxurious residences on Mount Royal. Quebec historian Paul-André Linteau argues that "social divisions became so visible in Montreal's industrial sector that the city earned the fitting description 'City of wealth and death.'"[11]

Certainly Montreal's sanitation system contributed to the negative image of the city. Only in 1842 did an underground system replace open sewers on Craig Street. No regular garbage pickup existed. Drinking water was often contaminated.

A WORKING-CLASS CONSCIOUSNESS

A working-class consciousness began to develop in the Canadas by mid-century. In part, industrialization caused this, as impersonal working conditions, due to the expansion of the factory system, became the norm. Skilled and semi-skilled workers joined together in the 1830s to form local trade unions and self-help organizations such as the Ship Labourers' Benevolent Society to deal with changing conditions. With definite skills to offer employers, they enjoyed far more job security than did the labourers. Generally speaking they preferred the strike weapon over the use of spontaneous rioting, which in the 1830s and 1840s was a popular form of protest among unskilled workers. Riots broke out when contractors on canal construction sites or on the developing railways could not pay their labourers. Occasionally, when conditions became desperate, skilled and unskilled workers united to stage riots and strikes.

Labourers organized two early strikes: one on the Lachine Canal in 1843, and the other on the Welland Canal in 1844–45. In both cases, they demanded improved working conditions and higher wages. In 1849, during the protests over free trade, shoemakers in Montreal ravaged a shoe factory and destroyed the sewing machines, in the tradition of the British Luddites, who opposed the mechanization of industry. By the 1860s strikes had generally replaced riots as the main form of labour protest, although they, too, were illegal. (Even trade unions were illegal until 1872.) In contrast to riots, strikes were usually more co-ordinated, longer-lasting, and likely to be less violent. In response to riots and strikes, employers often appealed for municipal or provincial government help (police or troops) to suppress them.

In Canada East, one of the effects of a growing proletariat was the abandonment of children of poorer families to the Grey Nuns' Foundling Hospital. An estimated 12 000 children became wards of the church between 1840 and 1870. The majority died at a young age as a result of their weakened condition upon arrival and the lack of pasteurized milk. The Roman Catholic church also looked after the several thousand Irish orphans whose parents died on the Atlantic crossing, particularly in the worst year of the potato famine, 1847. Most of the Irish orphans were raised as French Canadians and intermarried. The alternative to abandoning children to orphanages or church societies in both the Canadas was infanticide. Some destitute, unmarried, working-class women without family support resorted to such desperate measures, despite the fact that if caught they could be put to death.

Reform of the legal system occurred in the United Canadas. In 1849, William Hume Blake, solicitor general in the Baldwin–LaFontaine government, reformed the Court of Queen's Bench and the Court of Chancery and established a Court of Error and Appeals and a Court of Common Pleas. In 1857, George-Étienne Cartier centralized the legal system and made it more uniform. He also modernized the old Custom of Paris with a new Civil Code that revised contracts and labour law and abolished dower rights unless they were formally registered.

THE PROHIBITION MOVEMENT

The rise of an urban working class had an impact on the prohibition movement throughout British North America. By the 1850s, there was a noticeable shift in emphasis from temperance — abstinence through self-discipline — to prohibition (the use of the power of the state to control and, it was hoped, eliminate alcohol). Social historian Graeme Decarie suggested that this shift in Canada West came about as a result of a perceived threat to traditional Protestant middle-class values from the growing working class (often made up of Irish Catholics). Prohibition became a means for some middle-class Protestants to reassert their position of power and prominence. The Sabbatarian movement, strong among the Protestant churches, advocated all praying and no playing on Sundays. It worked to ban alcohol. Furthermore, Decarie argues, many rural inhabitants saw alcoholism as a predominantly urban phenomenon, another example of urban moral decay. "To them," Decarie noted, "a vote for prohibition was a vote for rural virtue and against urban decadence."[12]

Quebec's great "apostle of temperance" was Charles Chiniquy, a lively and eccentric Roman Catholic priest. He founded the Société de Tempérance in 1840, and by 1844 he had persuaded thousands to take the pledge of abstinence. "Everywhere his zeal goes, intemperance flies," the newspaper *Le Canadien* reported. His "zeal" took him to Kamouraska, Longueuil, and Montreal. His message, according to historian Jan Noel, could be summed up as follows: "The national survival of French Canada depends upon temperance. Giving up drinking might be unpleasant, but it was preferred to the decay and disappearance of a people."[13] (Sexual escapades and charges of embezzlement later led to Chiniquy's excommunication from the Roman Catholic church. In 1856 he became a Protestant and waged a war of slander against his former church until his death at the age of 89, in 1899.)

RELIGION

Religion played an important role in Canada West's society. In the 1840s, the Church of England was the declared church affiliation of 22 percent of the population. The Presbyterians followed at 20 percent, and the Methodists at 17 percent. The Baptists, Quakers, Lutherans, and Congregationalists together had 6 percent. The Roman Catholic population stood at 14 percent in 1841, most of it consisting of Irish Catholic immigrants.

Both the Methodists and the Baptists experienced internal dissension at mid-century. The union of Canadian and British Methodism in 1832 had led to the schism of the Episcopal Methodists and the growth of smaller British Methodist sects. The division appeared to be between the English brand of Wesleyan Methodism and Canadian Methodism. The same was true of the dissension in the Baptist church. As a result, these two churches were more divided by 1850 than they had been in 1830, thus undermining their effectiveness.

The growth of new sectarian movements from within the Methodists and Baptists was accompanied by the rise of external religious sects and "heretical" religious groups that cut into Baptist and Methodist support. Among the largest and most influential of these sects were the Campbellites or Disciples of Christ, Mormons, and Millerites. These new sects received much of their support from the backwoods areas of the province as well as the working class in the towns and cities.

This shift in focus from rural to urban of both mainline churches and sects meant a shift in emphasis from evangelicalism and an emotional approach to religion to an educated clergy, a rational approach to faith, and the valuing of Baconian science. The latter entailed the study and classification of nature as a means to better understand God's design. After 1859, churches also faced the challenge of beliefs coming out of Darwinian science — that all living things had evolved from a primitive form of life through natural selection and the survival of the fittest. Such ideas brought into question Christian belief in humans as beings created in God's image and notions of a benevolent God. As well, urban-oriented society required churches to address issues of social reform with regard to such groups as the poor, the sick, and the mentally ill.

In Canada East, Ignace Bourget, appointed bishop of Montreal in 1840, encouraged French religious orders to come to Quebec to help "Christianize" his diocesans. He also began new indigenous male and female orders that took responsibility for elementary education, the classical colleges, hospitals, and charitable organizations. Bourget was an advocate of ultramontanism, the belief that the state should be linked to and dominated by the church. To this end, he worked with Louis-Hippolyte LaFontaine to ensure that education remained under the control of the Roman Catholic church instead of coming under state control.

The Reverend John Burwash, a Methodist minister, plays a melodeon for a choir, probably in the 1860s.

The United Church of Canada/Victoria University Archives, Toronto/Acc. no. 76.001 P/790N.

EDUCATION AND CULTURE

In the mid-nineteenth century, education entered public debate. Schools grew at a rapid rate to keep pace with the growing population, and the question of separate schools became a contentious issue in Canada West.

State-supported schools developed in the union period. In 1841, the government of the Canadas passed an Education Act extending the common schools throughout the western half of the united province. The act created the office of superintendent of education to oversee educational matters and established local boards of education with powers to tax inhabitants in each district to build and maintain schools. Opposition to the bill arose among those who argued that public funds should also be used to support separate schools for Roman Catholics, just as they were to support Protestant schools in Quebec. The votes of the French-Canadian members for Canada East gave the supporters of the separate-school clause in Canada West the majority they needed in the Assembly. After the clause was passed, Canada West's separate schools received funding in proportion to the number of children in attendance.

At the heart of the separate-school controversy lay the question of the role of education. Roman Catholic leaders believed that education should have a religious component and that religious instruction should be in keeping with the teachings and beliefs of the Roman Catholic church. Catholic bishops argued that the common schools were non-religious or, at best, Protestant in orientation. Only separate schools, they felt, could ensure a proper Catholic and moral education. Furthermore, church leaders such as Armand Charbonnel, bishop of Toronto, argued for the right of Catholic parents to direct the education of their own children.

Opponents of separate schools, such as Egerton Ryerson, the Methodist minister who served as superintendent of education for Canada West (Ontario) from 1844 to 1876, and George Brown, the influential political reformer and editor of the Toronto *Globe*, argued that education should be free, publicly funded, and non-sectarian. They believed that separate schools perpetuated sectarianism — an unhealthy development in education — and undermined the common-school system. Brown further argued that separate schools would allow the church to undermine the educational system and give the pope undue influence in national affairs. The debate between these two approaches to education continued throughout the mid-nineteenth century.

Separate and common schools proliferated in the 1850s and 1860s. By the School Act of 1853, a full-scale Roman Catholic separate-school system came into being. The system had its own separate-school board, with tax support from parents, who were exempt from paying common-school taxes. A share of the provincial grant also paid expenses.

The final pre-Confederation education bill, the Scott Act of 1863, allowed separate schools to receive a share of both the provincial and municipal grants. Separate schools were also extended into rural areas. In return for these concessions, separate schools, like their common-school counterparts, submitted to provincial inspection, centralized control of curriculum and textbooks, and government control of all teacher training.

This system remained in effect when Canada West entered Confederation as the province of Ontario in 1867. Section 93 of the British North America (BNA) Act refers to this system. It states that nothing in any law relating to denominational schools "shall prejudicially affect any right or privilege ... which any class of persons have by law in the province at the Union."

Common or public schools also came under greater centralized control as a result of Superintendent of Education Egerton Ryerson's efforts. His Common School Act of 1846 established a board of education (later the Council of Public Instruction), responsible for assisting the chief superintendent in establishing provincial standards, founded a normal school to train teachers, and held locally elected school boards responsible for operating the schools in their sections. These schools were expected to teach children good moral values — that is, Christian values that included a sense of duty and attachment to Britain, and tolerance toward other ethnic groups and religions — as well as to prepare them for work in an expanding and changing commercial economy. Ryerson believed a centralized and highly regulated system could best achieve these goals. Here lay the foundation of the modern Ontario school system.

In Canada West, a similar process of secularism occurred in higher education. In 1849, under the direction of Ryerson, the government changed the Anglican-affiliated King's College into the non-sectarian University of Toronto. Once King's College had been transformed into the "godless" University of Toronto, John Strachan, Bishop of Toronto, founded the Anglican Trinity University in 1851. (At the turn of the century, Trinity, the Methodists' Victoria University, and St. Michael's, a Roman Catholic college founded in 1852, all became affiliates of the University of Toronto.)

EDUCATION IN QUEBEC

In Canada East, the Lower Canadian School Act of 1846 provided for the two state-aided school systems, one Catholic and one Protestant. Within each Catholic school in Canada East, the *curé* or priest had the right to veto the selection of teachers and textbooks, thus leaving only the task of financing the schools to the provincial authorities.

In 1851, the legislature passed an act to establish a normal school to educate teachers, but it took six years before it became operational. In 1859, it set up the Council of Public Instruction. Consisting of 14 members (ten Catholic and four Protestant) plus the superintendent of education, it assisted the superintendent in making regulations for the normal school, for the organization and administration of common schools, and for the grading of schools and teachers.

At the university level, McGill University, chartered in 1821, became an influential institution. Due to family litigation, however, it did not begin classes until the 1830s. It admitted both English- and French-speaking students (although instruction was in English only) for advanced education in law, medicine, and the arts. Under the guidance of its able principal, William Dawson, appointed in 1855, McGill later acquired a distinguished reputation, especially in scientific research and medicine. In 1852, Université Laval was founded, having developed out of the Séminaire de Québec, founded by Bishop Laval in 1663. Steeped in the French Catholic tradition, the first French-Canadian university soon held a position of respect in Canada East, with its courses in theology, civil law, medicine, and the arts.

CULTURE IN THE CANADAS

With the growth of towns and cities and the expansion of the urban middle class, the range of cultural activities and accomplishments deepened. In Canada East, François-Xavier Garneau wrote his three-volume *Histoire du Canada*, a monumental history of French Canada, as a direct response to Durham's denunciation of French Canadians as a "backward people." Octave Crémazie was the great French-Canadian poet of the period, popular for his nostalgic references to the glories of New France and the miseries that followed after the Conquest. Good-quality newspapers existed, such as Montreal's *La Minerve* and Quebec City's *Le Canadien*. French-Canadian journalists and public figures gave popular lectures on important topics of the day: education, national traits, and *la position de la femme*. In 1843 Ludger Duvernay, the editor of *La Minerve*, organized the Société Saint-Jean-Baptiste de Montréal. Many prominent French Canadians joined this patriotic organization, established to promote the interests of French Canada.

Canadian literature in English had a slow start. In fact, the earliest novel to be written by a British-American–born author and published in the Canadas (Julia Catherine Beckwith's *St. Ursula's Convent*) appeared only in 1824, and the first anthology of poetry in English in 1864. Throughout the 1860s, English-language poetry was popular in the Canadas. William Kirby described the migration of Loyalists to Niagara in his poem *The U.E.L.*, while Charles Sangster captured the beauty of the Canadian landscape in *The St. Lawrence and the Saguenay*. Other writers included Susanna Moodie and her sister Catharine Parr Traill, both of whom obtained publishers, and a readership, in Britain. From 1847 to 1851, George Copway, an Ojibwa from Rice Lake in Canada West, published four books in English in the United States, including the first autobiography by a Canadian Native, and the first history of the Ojibwa people. Peter Jones's *History of the Ojebway Indians* appeared in 1861, four years after the Ojibwa Methodist minister's death in 1856. Amateur historians, such as John Richardson (*The War of 1812*) and Robert Christie (*History of the Late Province of Lower Canada*), praised the early pioneers of the provinces. However, no significant publishing industry existed in the Canadas until the late nineteenth century.

In 1855 John McMullen, a journalist, produced the first history of English Canada, *The History of Canada from First Discovery to the Present Time*. While lacking François-Xavier Garneau's intensity and flair, McMullen did have a justification for his history: "to infuse a spirit of Canadian nationality into the people generally — to mould the native born citizen, the Scotch, the English and the Irish emigrant into a compact whole." Newspapers, among them Toronto's *Globe* and the *Leader*, helped cultivate a national feeling among English Canadians.

In the mid-nineteenth century, Canada's urban music life expanded. Famous artists like Jenny Lind — "the Swedish Nightingale," the finest soprano of the day — and Henri Vieuxtemps, the Belgian violinist and composer, visited and inspired local artists and musicians. Due to the small population of the Canadas, however, few Canadian-born professional musicians could support themselves comfortably with only their performances and teaching. In small towns, local church choirs and brass bands were popular.

Growing prosperity enlarged the market for portrait painters such as G.T. Berthon, landscape painters such as Robert Whale, and exploration artists like Paul Kane. Well-known painters included Cornelius Krieghoff — who around 1860 was probably the best-known artist working in Canada — and Napoléon Bourassa and the recently retired Antoine Plamondon. By 1860, William Notman of Montreal had already established his reputation as a photographer.

The Canadas can also claim Robert S. Duncanson. According to Romare Bearden and Harry Henderson, the authors of *A History of African-American Artists: From 1792 to the Present*, Duncanson was "the first African-American artist to achieve national and international prominence."[14] Raised in Upper Canada, the son of a Scot and a free black woman, Duncanson had

Where Historians Disagree

Who Won the Anishinabeg-Iroquois War in the Late Seventeenth Century?

Usually the lack of Native source material in English or French prevents Canadian historians from learning Native viewpoints. In the case of the Great Lakes Anishinabeg (Ojibwa, Mississauga, and Odawa or Ottawa), however, this is not so. Several Great Lakes Anishinabeg, including Peter Jones, George Copway, William Warren, and Francis Assikinack, wrote important historical accounts in the mid-nineteenth century. These works enable us to supplement the European documentary evidence on the Great Lakes First Nations in the late seventeenth century, especially on the important Anishinabeg–Iroquois wars that continued for half a century after the fall of Huronia in 1649.

William Warren (1825–1853), the son of an American trader and a woman of mixed French and Ojibwa ancestry from the southwestern shore of Lake Superior, provides the shortest description of the struggle. He wrote in the early 1850s: "Their anxiety to open the road to the white traders, in order to procure fire-arms and their much coveted commodities, induced the Ojibways, Ottaways, Pottawatumies, Osaukies, and Wyandots to enter into a firm alliance. They sent their united forces against the Iroquois, and fighting severe and bloody battles, they eventually forced them to retire from Canada."[1]

Francis Assikinack (1824–1863), an Ottawa (or Odawa) from Manitoulin Island, and an Indian Department clerk and former student at Upper Canada College, also made reference to the Odawas' wars with the Iroquois in one of his historical articles in 1858. The Iroquois "used to go out into Lake Huron or Georgian Bay, by the Nahdowa Sahgi-River, until they got two or three severe defeats in the vicinity of the Blue Mountains, by Sahgimah, the most celebrated warrior of the Odahwahs at that time."[2]

George Copway (1818–1869), the Mississauga writer and lecturer of the late 1840s and 1850s, who obtained phenomenal success in the United States between 1848 and 1851, provided the most detailed description of the struggle. In his *History of the Ojibway Nation*, he gives references to the locations of the battles "which terminated in the subjugation of the eastern Iroquois."[3]

Peter Jones (1802–1856), the Mississauga chief and Methodist minister, goes one step further. He not only provides a summary of the battles but also includes evidence that the battles actually took place. He wrote in his *History of the Ojebway Indians*, published posthumously in 1861: "The last battle that was fought was at the outlet of Burlington Bay, which was at the south end of the beach, where the Government House formerly stood (present-day Hamiliton, Ontario). Near to this place a mound of human bones is to be seen to this day; and also another at the north end, close to the residence of the late Captain Brant. Besides these, there are traces of fortifications at short distances along the whole length of the beach, where holes had been dug into the sand and a breastwork thrown round them. They are about twenty or thirty feet in diameter, but were originally much larger. At this finishing battle the Ojebways spared a few of their enemies, whom they suffered to depart in peace, that they might go and tell their brethren on the south side of Lake Ontario — the fate of their nation —

that all the country between the waters of the Ontario, Erie, St. Clair, and Huron, was now surrendered into the hands of the Ojebways."[4]

What primary evidence exists of an Anishinabeg victory in the late seventeenth century over the Iroquois? According to historian José António Brandão and anthropologist William A. Starna, none. In a recent article they argue that the Iroquois "had not been defeated" by the Anishinabeg.[5] The authors add that claims of an Anishinabeg victory are "based on oral traditions published in the mid- to late nineteenth century that remain unconfirmed by the documentary record." In Brandão's exhaustive documentary study of "Iroquois Hostilities to 1701" (a list of nearly 500 Iroquois military encounters in the seventeenth century, published as Table D.I in his recent book),[6] he presents no evidence of an Anishinabeg victory over the Iroquois in southern Ontario.

Historian D. Peter MacLeod argues strongly for greater attention to these Anishinabeg sources in order to correct the documentary approach, which has produced "a distorted vision of post-contact North America in which Amerindians are fully visible only when they interact with Europeans."[7] The academic historians' debate over the use of oral traditions is an old one, but it remains vital to all those concerned about the history of southern Ontario in the late seventeenth century.

[1] William W. Warren, "History of the Ojibways, Based upon Traditions and Oral Statements," reprinted in William W. Warren, *History of the Ojibway Nation* (Minneapolis, MN: Ross & Haines, 1957), p. 146.

[2] Francis Assikinack, "Social and Warlike Customs of the Odahwah Indians," *The Canadian Journal*, new series, 3 (1858): 309.

[3] George Copway, *The Traditional History and Characteristic Sketches of the Ojibway Nation* (London: Charles Gilpin, 1850), p. 85.

[4] Peter Jones, *History of the Ojebway Indians* (London: A.W. Bennett, 1861), p. 113.

[5] José António Brandão and William A. Starna, "The Treaties of 1701: A Triumph of Iroquois Diplomacy," *Ethnohistory* 43, 2 (Spring 1996): 217.

[6] José António Brandão *Your Fyre Shall Burn No More": Iroquois Policy toward New France and Its Native Allies to 1701* (Lincoln: University of Nebraska Press, 1997), pp. 177–278.

[7] D. Peter MacLeod, "The Anishinabeg Point of View: The History of the Great Lakes Region to 1800 in Nineteenth-Century Mississauga, Odawa, and Ojibwa Historiography," *Canadian Historical Review* 73,2 (1992): 209.

A depiction of the Ojibwa defeat of the Iroquois by Mesaquab (Jonathan Yorke) around 1900. It is made from a representation of a rock painting that once stood on Quarry Point, Lake Couchiching.

Ontario Provincial Museum, *Archaeological Report for 1904* (Toronto: King's Printer, 1905).

CIRQUE.

LE CIRQUE COLOSSAL

LEVI J. NORTH!

EXHIBERA ses exercices en cette ville pendant UNE SEMAINE, à commencer de LUNDI 12 JUIN,

En dehors de la Porte St.-Louis,

Sur le champ vis-à-vis du jeu de Crosse de la Garnison.

Cette grande compagnie comprend les premiers talents du monde, parmi lesquels se trouvent les artistes renommés qui suivent:

LEVI J. NORTH, le Grand Écuyer,
    BURNELL RUNNELZ,
        JAMES M'FARLAND,
            GEORGE ARCHER,
                NAT. RODGERS,
                    B. STEVENS,
                        MASTER WILLIE.
                "   JENNINGS.
                "   NAYLOR.
                    La petite VICTORINE NORTH.

CLOWN, BILL JENNINGS.

The circus is coming! Another form of popular culture in the mid-nineteenth century was this entertainment. Here the flier announces the arrival in Quebec City of Levi J. North's colossal circus, for a whole week!

Le Canadien, 5 juin 1854. National Library of Canada.

travelled the Underground Railway in reverse, arriving in Cincinnati, Ohio, in 1841, where he became a highly successful portrait and landscape painter. During the Civil War, he lived in Montreal for a year.

TOURISM AS A FORM OF POPULAR CULTURE

In popular culture, areas of wilderness and wildness began to take on special significance as tourist spots by the mid-nineteenth century, often in juxtaposition to what was meant by their opposite — civilization — in the Victorian mind. As the wilderness began to be "conquered" and subdued and thus lost its threatening nature, as Aboriginal people became more "civilized" and declined dramatically in numbers, and as landscape became imbued with a sense of the romantic and sublime, tourism emerged as a "growth industry." Improved transportation facilities, including canals and railroads, along with other expressions and means of settlement, made it easier for upper- and middle-class individuals to visit exotic or faraway places as tourist sites. As historian Patricia Jasen notes, "The tourist industry was an ally of many forms of economic development in the nineteenth century, such as the growth of railways and steamer companies, and all of these industries were intimately associated with the gospel of expansionism, whereby the fate of the 'unsettled' regions of Canada was identified with the interests of the metropolis."[15] Tourism was, however, the preserve of the upper- and middle-classes. Only they could afford a holiday or even contemplate the "right" to leisure time.

Many romantic tourist places — especially natural landscapes — took on a religious meaning. Tours to places of natural beauty were frequently compared to a secular pilgrimage; tourists went there to worship Nature — and through Nature, God — and to feel their power.

Niagara Falls, above all other tourist attractions, became a special place, attracting as many as 40 000 visitors a year by the later 1840s. To "do" Niagara, along with Boston and Quebec City, became the American equivalent of the European grand tour, a "must" for all affluent North Americans as a status symbol. With the opening of the Erie Canal in 1825 and the Welland Canal in 1832, and especially with the advent of railroads in the 1840s and 1850s, Niagara Falls became more accessible.

From the beginning, Niagara Falls became associated with sexual pleasure, especially as "the Honeymoon Capital of the World." Karen Dubinsky has shown how the "purity" of the natural Falls, its gendered nature as a female icon, evident in such descriptions of the Falls as "the Queen of the Cataracts," "the Queen of Beauty," and "the Water Bride of Time," and the fact that the observer of such beauty was usually depicted as a male, "enhanced the spectatorial pleasure of 'doing' Niagara."[16] Already in the mid-nineteenth century, tourist agents realized the importance of identifying natural sites as places of pleasure — especially sexual pleasure, in a society that suppressed overt expressions of sex — thus enhancing the commercial value.

Between 1840 and 1864, the United Canadas underwent considerable economic and social change. Canadians adjusted to the end of the mercantile system of trade, to the advent of the railway age, and to rapidly changing social conditions in both rural and urban life. This was an age of transition from a British-oriented to an American-oriented economy and from a pioneer to a commercial society. The shift took decades to complete, but it saw its start in the period 1840 to 1860.

Culturally, a French-Canadian identity already existed, but beside it an Upper Canadian or English-Canadian collective identity continued to take shape. Its Protestant variant would be exported westward after Canada's acquisition of the Northwest in the late nineteenth century.

NOTES

1. See Donald Creighton, *The Commercial Empire of the St. Lawrence* (Toronto: Ryerson Press, 1937).
2. J.M.S. Careless, *The Union of the Canadas: The Growth of Canadian Institutions, 1841–1857* (Toronto: McClelland & Stewart, 1967), p. 111.
3. See A.R.M. Lower, *The North American Assault on the Canadian Forest* (Toronto: Ryerson Press, 1938).
4. Careless, *The Union of the Canadas*, p. 136.
5. Kenneth Norrie and Douglas Owram, *A History of the Canadian Economy*, 2nd ed. (Toronto: Harcourt Brace, 1996), p. 189.
6. R. Cole Harris, "Ontario," in R. Cole Harris and John Warkentin, *Canada Before Confederation* (Ottawa: Carleton University Press, 1991 [1974]), pp. 114–15.
7. John G. Weaver, *Hamilton: An Illustrated History* (Toronto: James Lorimer, 1982), p. 77.
8. G.R. Stevens, *Canadian National Railways*, vol. 1 (Toronto: Clarke Irwin, 1960), p. 110.
9. David Gagan, *Hopeful Travellers: Families, Land and Social Change in Mid-Victorian Peel County, Canada West* (Toronto: University of Toronto Press, 1981), p. 20ff.
10. Michael B. Katz, *The People of Hamilton, Canada West: Family and Class in a Mid-Nineteenth-Century City* (Cambridge, MA: Harvard University Press, 1975), p. 2.
11. Paul-André Linteau, "Montreal: City of Pride," *Horizon Canada* 4 (1984): 88.
12. Graeme Decarie, *Prohibition in Canada*, Canada's Visual History Series, vol. 29, Canadian Museum of Civilization, p. 3.
13. Jan Noel, "Dry Patriotism: The Chiniquy Crusade," *Canadian Historical Review* 71(2) (June 1990): 200.
14. Romare Bearden and Harry Henderson, *A History of African-American Artists: From 1792 to the Present* (New York: Pantheon Books, 1993), p. 19.
15. Patricia Jasen, *Wild Things: Nature, Culture, and Tourism in Ontario, 1790–1914* (Toronto: University of Toronto Press, 1995), p. 152.
16. Karen Dubinsky, "'The Pleasure Is Exquisite but Violent': The Imaginary Geography of Niagara Falls in the Nineteenth Century," *Journal of Canadian Studies*, 29, 2 (Summer 1994): 75.

LINKING TO THE PAST www

St. Lawrence River
http://greatcanadianrivers.com/rivers/stlawer/stlawer-home.html

Explore the environmental, economic, political, and cultural importance of the St. Lawrence, from the time of Jacques Cartier to the present.

The St. Lawrence–Great Lakes Canal System (1783–1954)
http://collections.ic.gc.ca/stlauren/hist/hi_slcanals.htm.

An illustrated history of the canal system.

Reciprocity Treaty, 1854
http://www.nlc-bnc.ca/history/18/h18-2996-e.html

An introduction to, and the full text of, the Reciprocity Treaty between the British North American colonies and the United States.

Grand Trunk Railway
http://www.nlc-bnc.ca/2/18/h18-2997-e.html

A brief history of the railway. For other resources, consult The Ontario Railway History Page at http://web.globalserve.net/~robkath.

Fugitives for Freedom: The Black Community in the History of Quebec and Canada
http://www.qesn.meq.gouv.qc.ca/mpages/unit3/u3toc.htm

An overview of the history of the Underground Railway and black settlements in Canada, including brief biographies of Josiah Henson, Harriet Tubman, and others.

Cornelius Krieghoff
http://www.geocities.com/SoHo/Museum/4883/index.html

A look at the life and work of Cornelius Krieghoff. For a more detailed biography, visit http://collections.ic.gc.ca/heirloom_series/volume6/text/vishtml/12-3.html.

RELATED READINGS

R. Douglas Francis and Donald B. Smith, eds., *Readings in Canadian History: Pre-Confederation*, 6th ed. (Toronto: Nelson Thomson Learning, 2002), contains the following articles related to this topic: John McCallum, "Urban and Commercial Development until 1850," pp. 345–58; and Gerald Tulchinsky, "Transportation Changes in the St. Lawrence–Great Lakes Region, 1828–1860," pp. 359–65.

BIBLIOGRAPHY

J.M.S. Careless provides an excellent survey in *The Union of the Canadas: The Growth of Canadian Institutions, 1841–1857* (Toronto: McClelland & Stewart, 1967). Eric Ross reviews life in the Canadas in 1841 in *Full of Hope and Promise: The Canadas in 1841* (Montreal/Kingston: McGill-Queen's University Press, 1991). For Canada East (Quebec), also consult the final chapters in Fernand Ouellet's *Economic and Social History of Quebec, 1760–1850* (Toronto: Macmillan, 1980). Kenneth Norrie and Douglas Owram, *A History of the Canadian Economy*, 2nd ed. (Toronto: Harcourt Brace, 1996), deals with the economy of the United Canadas. For Canada West (Ontario) see the relevant chapters for this period in Douglas McCalla, *Planting the Province: The Economic History of Upper Canada, 1784–1870* (Toronto: University of Toronto Press, 1993). Donald G. Creighton develops the Laurentian thesis in *The Empire of the St. Lawrence: A Study in Commerce and Politics* [1937]. With a new introduction by Christopher Moore (Toronto: University of Toronto Press, 2002). Economic questions are also addressed in Michael Bliss, *Northern Enterprise: Five Centuries of Canadian Business* (Toronto: McClelland & Stewart, 1987); R.T. Naylor, *Canada in the European Age: 1453–1919* (Vancouver: University of British Columbia Press, 1986); G.N. Tucker, *The Canadian Commercial Revolution, 1845–1851* (Toronto: McClelland & Stewart, 1964); and D.C. Masters, *The Reciprocity Treaty of 1854* (Toronto: McClelland & Stewart, 1963). P.J. Cain, *Economic Foundation of British Overseas Expansion, 1815–1914* (London: Macmillan, 1980) explains British economic policies in terms of imperial developments.

Bibliographical suggestions appear in the essays by James H. Lambert, "Quebec/Lower Canada"; Bryan D. Palmer, "Upper Canada"; and J.M. Bumsted, "British North America in Its Imperial and International Context," in M. Brook Taylor, ed., *Canadian History: A Reader's Guide*, vol. 1, *Beginnings to Confederation* (Toronto: University of Toronto Press, 1994), pp. 112–236, 394–447.

On agricultural developments in the Canadas see John McCallum, *Unequal Beginnings: Agriculture and Economic Development in Quebec and Ontario Until 1870* (Toronto: University of Toronto Press, 1980). For Canada East see R.L. Jones, "Agriculture in the St. Lawrence Valley, 1815–1850," in W.T. Easterbrook and M. Watkins, eds., *Approaches to Canadian Economic History* (Toronto: McClelland & Stewart, 1967), pp. 110–26; and Serge Courville and Normand Séguin, *Rural Life in Nineteenth-Century Quebec* (Ottawa: Canadian Historical Association, 1989). For Canada West see R.L. Jones, *History of Agriculture in Ontario, 1613–1880* (Toronto: University of Toronto Press, 1977). A.R.M. Lower reviews the timber trade in *Great Britain's Woodyard: British America and the Timber Trade, 1763–1867* (Montreal/Kingston: McGill-Queen's University Press, 1973). On railway building in the 1850s see G.P de T. Glazebrook, *A History of Transportation in Canada*, vol. 1 (Toronto: McClelland & Stewart, 1964). For an appreciation of the excitement of railway building see T.C. Keefer's *The Philosophy of Railroads* (1849), reprinted with an introduction by H.V. Nelles (Toronto: University of Toronto Press, 1972). The story of the Victoria Bridge is told by Stanley Triggs et al. in *Victoria Bridge: The Vital Link* (Montreal: McCord Museum of Canadian History, 1992).

Urban and commercial development in Canada West is discussed by Jacob Spelt, *Urban Development in South-Central Ontario* (Toronto: McClelland & Stewart, 1972 [1955]); and Douglas McCalla, *The Upper Canada Trade, 1834–1872: A Study of the Buchanans' Business* (Toronto: University of Toronto Press, 1979). For Canada East see G. Tulchinsky, *The River Barons: Montreal Businessmen and the Growth of Industry and Transportation, 1837–1853* (Toronto: University of Toronto Press, 1977). Henry C. Klassen recounts the life of an important Montreal entrepreneur in *Luther H. Holton: A Founding Canadian Entrepreneur* (Calgary: University of Calgary Press, 2000). Peter Baskerville reviews the history of the Bank of Upper Canada in the introduction to his edited work *The Bank of Upper Canada: A Collection of Documents* (Toronto: Champlain Society, 1987).

The chapters "Quebec in the Century After the Conquest," pp. 65–109, and "Ontario," pp. 110–68, in R. Cole Harris and John Warkentin, *Canada Before Confederation* (Ottawa: Carleton University Press, 1991 [1974]) provide an overview of social developments in the United Canadas. For Canada East, see as well, J.I. Little, *State and Society in Transition: The Politics of Institutional Reform in the Eastern Townships* (Montreal/Kingston: McGill-Queen's University Press, 1997). Donald H. Akenson's *The Irish in Ontario: A Study in Rural History* (Montreal/Kingston: McGill-Queen's University Press, 1984) is a valuable study. On nativist attitudes towards Irish Catholics, see Scott W. See, " 'Unprecedented Influx': Nativism and Irish famine immigration to Canada," *American Review of Canadian Studies*, 30, 4 (Winter 2000): 429–53. For the story of blacks in the Canadas in the mid-nineteenth century consult Robin W. Winks, *The Blacks in Canada*, 2nd ed. (Montreal/Kingston: McGill-Queen's University Press, 1997); and Daniel G. Hill, *The Freedom-Seekers: Blacks in Early Canada* (Agincourt, ON: Book Society of Canada, 1981). For immigration in general, see Ninette Kelley and Michael Trebilcock, *The Making of the Mosaic: A History of Canadian Immigration Policy* (Toronto: University of Toronto Press, 1998); and Franca Iacovetta et al., eds., *A Nation of Immigrants: Women, Workers, and Communities in Canadian History* (Toronto: University of Toronto Press, 1998). Two good quantitative studies to consult are David Gagan, *Hopeful Travellers: Families, Land and Social Change in Mid-Victorian Peel County, Canada West* (Toronto: University of Toronto Press, 1981); and Michael Katz, *The People of Hamilton, Canada West: Family and Class in a Mid-Nineteenth-Century City* (Cambridge, MA: Harvard University Press, 1975). On French-Canadian migration see Bruno Ramirez, *On the Move: French-Canadian and Italian Migrants in the North Atlantic Economy, 1860–1914* (Toronto: McClelland & Stewart, 1991). Alison Prentice et al., *Canadian Women: A History*, 2nd ed. (Toronto: Harcourt Brace, 1996) examines changes in the lives of women in the mid-nineteenth century, while Micheline Dumont et al., *Quebec Women: A History* (Toronto: Women's Press, 1987) focusses on women in Lower Canada in the same period. See also Adrienne Shadd, "The Lord Seemed to Say 'Go': Women and the Underground Railroad Movement," in Peggy Bristow et al., eds., *"We've Rooted Here and They Can't Pull Us Up"* (Toronto: University of Toronto Press, 1994), pp. 41–68.

The First Nations' history in the Canadas in the mid-nineteenth century is reviewed in several sources, including Daniel Francis, *A History of the Native Peoples of Quebec, 1760–1867* (Ottawa: Department of Indian Affairs and Northern Development, 1983); and Edward S. Rogers and Donald B. Smith, eds., *Aboriginal Ontario: Historical Perspectives on the First Nations* (Toronto: Dundurn Press, 1994). For biographical treatments see Donald B. Smith, *Sacred Feathers: The Reverend Peter Jones (Kahkewaquonaby) and the Mississauga Indians* (Toronto: University of Toronto Press, 1987); and Janet Chute, *The Legacy of Shingwaukonse: A Century of Native Leadership* (Toronto: University of Toronto Press, 1998). For an in-depth study of a First Nation community in Canada East see Hélène Bédard, *Les Montagnais et la réserve de Betsiamites, 1850–1900* (Quebec: Institut québécoise de recherche sur la culture, 1988). A review of early Native residential schools is provided in J.R. Miller, *Shingwauk's Vision: A History of Native Residential Schools* (Toronto: University of Toronto Press, 1996).

On the history of the working class in the United Canadas consult the relevant essays in Paul Craven, ed., *Labouring Lives: Work and Workers in Nineteenth-Century Ontario* (Toronto: University of Toronto Press, 1995); M.S. Cross, ed., *The Workingman in the Nineteenth Century* (Toronto: Oxford University Press, 1974); and S. Langdon's pamphlet *The Emergence of the Working-Class Movement, 1845–1875* (Toronto: New Hogtown Press, 1975). On strikes see H.C. Pentland, "The Lachine Strike of 1843," *Canadian Historical Review* 29 (1984): 255–77; and Ruth Bleasdale, "Class Conflict on the Canals of Upper Canada in the 1840s," *Labour/Le Travailleur* 7 (1981): 9–39. On labour protest in general consult Bryan Palmer, "Labour Protest and Organization in Nineteenth-Century Canada, 1820–1890," *Labour/Le Travail* 20 (1987): 61–84.

Educational questions are treated in J.D. Wilson, R.M. Stamp, and L.P. Audet, *Canadian Education: A History* (Scarborough, ON: Prentice-Hall, 1970), pp. 167–89, 214–40. For Canada West see also S. Houston and A. Prentice, *Schooling and Scholars in Nineteenth-Century Ontario* (Toronto: University of Toronto Press, 1988); and Franklin A. Walker, *Catholic Education and Politics in Upper Canada*, vol. 1 (Toronto: J.M. Dent and Sons, 1955). William Westfall looks at the creation of Trinity University in Toronto in 1852 in *The Founding Moment: Church, Society and the Construction of Trinity College* (Montreal/Kingston: McGill-Queen's University Press, 2002). For Canada East see Andrée Dufour, *Tous à l'école: État communautés rurales et scolarisation au Québec de 1826 à 1859* (Ville La Salle: Éditions Hurtubise HMH, 1996); and Claude Galarneau, *Les collèges classiques au Canada français* (Montreal: Fides, 1978). The best short biography of Egerton Ryerson remains Clara Thomas, *Ryerson of Upper Canada* (Toronto: Ryerson Press, 1969). On religion see John S. Moir, *The Church in the British Era: From the British Conquest to Confederation* (Toronto: McGraw-Hill Ryerson, 1972); and John Webster Grant, *A Profusion of Spires: Religion in Nineteenth-Century Ontario* (Toronto: University of Toronto Press, 1988).

Cultural aspects of the era are reviewed in George Woodcock, *The Century That Made Us: Canada, 1814–1914* (Toronto: Oxford University Press, 1989). Jan Noel examines the temperance movement in *Canada Dry: Temperance Crusades before Confederation* (Toronto: University of Toronto Press, 1995). Musical developments are reviewed in Helmut Kallmann, *A History of Music in Canada, 1534–1914* (Toronto: University of Toronto Press, 1960); and Timothy J. McGhee, *The Music of Canada* (New York: W.W. Norton, 1985). For information on art in the Canadas in the mid-nineteenth century see Dennis Reid, *A Concise History of Canadian Painting*, 2nd ed. (Toronto: Oxford University Press, 1988). Douglas Fetherling reviews early Canadian journalism in *The Rise of the Canadian Newspaper* (Toronto: Oxford University Press, 1990). Denis Monière has written the biography of an important Montreal newspaper editor: *Ludger Duvernay et la révolution intellectuelle au Bas-Canada* (Montreal: Québec/Amérique, 1987). On tourism as an expression of popular culture see Patricia Jasen, *Wild Things: Nature, Culture, and Tourism in Ontario, 1790–1914* (Toronto: University of Toronto Press, 1995); and Karen Dubinsky, "'The Pleasure is Exquisite but Violent': The Imaginary Geography of Niagara Falls in the Nineteenth Century," *Journal of Canadian Studies*, 29, 2 (Summer 1994): 64–88.

Many portraits of the leading individuals in the Canadas between 1840 and 1864 appear in the *Dictionary of Canadian Biography*, which is now available online at www.biographi.ca. Of particular interest is the sketch by Yves Roby of the colourful Charles Chiniquy (vol. 12, 1891–1900, pp. 189–93). The biographical sketch of John A. Macdonald by J.K. Johnson and P.B. Waite also appears in vol. 12 (pp. 591–612).

Excellent maps of the Canadas in this period appear in R. Louis Gentilcore, ed., *Historical Atlas of Canada*, vol. 2, *The Land Transformed, 1800–1891* (Toronto: University of Toronto Press, 1993).

THE UNION OF THE CANADAS: POLITICAL DEVELOPMENTS, 1840–1864

TIME LINE

1840 – The Act of Union, uniting Upper and Lower Canada, is adopted by the British Parliament

1841 – Governor General Lord Sydenham dies; Sir Charles Bagot becomes governor general of Canada

1848 – British Parliament makes French an official language of Canada

Governor General Lord Elgin asks Louis-Hippolyte LaFontaine and Robert Baldwin to form a government after their electoral victory

1849 – Lord Elgin sanctions the Rebellion Losses Bill; English-speaking protesters burn the Parliament building in Montreal

Manifesto of the Annexation Association published

1854 – Emergence of the Liberal–Conservative alliance led by John A. Macdonald and George-Étienne Cartier

Charter of Grand Trunk Railway adopted by Legislative Assembly

Seigneurial system in Canada East abolished

1857 – "Rep by Pop" becomes the main plank of Reform party's platform

1859 – Ottawa selected as Canada's capital

1860 – Britain transfers all authority over First Nations' matters to the Canadian legislature

1863 – New elections cause a stalemate in the Legislative Assembly

The Act of Union adopted by the British Parliament in July 1840 joined the two Canadas, now renamed Canada East and Canada West. This act gave the old Province of Quebec its fourth constitution since the Conquest. The union had a short but stormy life. Indeed, many latter-day observers have seen it as simply a prelude to Confederation. After all, by 1864, ministerial instability led most members of the united province's Legislative Assembly to agree to work toward the realization of a larger British North American Confederation.

Although ultimately a failure, the union could boast important successes. The government adopted laws providing for the education of children in both sections of the colony. As railway fever swept the nation's business community in the 1850s, solicitous politicians oversaw a multitude of costly and often competing construction projects. They fostered increased trade relations with the United States by negotiating a Reciprocity Treaty covering natural products, which, it was said, was floated through on champagne by Canada's suave governor general, Lord Elgin. They instituted a protective tariff on manufactured goods in an attempt to stimulate industrial growth. In 1854, they finally abolished the seigneurial system in Canada East and even found a solution to the contentious clergy reserves question in Canada West. In addition they oversaw the creation of new government departments and the establishment of a more professional civil service. According to political scientist S.J.R. Noel, "The overall record of governmental accomplishment compares favourably with that of any other era, either before or since."[1]

The union years also saw the resolution of another source of constant feuding between the Legislative Assembly and the governor. Within ten years after the failure of the rebellions, London accepted the principles of responsible government. Henceforth, the governor governed less; his ministers, who were responsible to the Assembly, made decisions in his place. With the coming of responsible government, traditional elites saw their hold on power weaken. They were largely replaced by the new commercial and industrial elites, to whom many of the new brand of politicians were closely allied.

Most significantly, many English-speaking and some French-speaking Canadian historians argue that, in the Union period, French- and English-speaking politicians found common ground on which to co-operate in solving many major political questions. The need to construct a *modus vivendi* also helped restrain ethnic and religious bigotry. French Canada again escaped assimilation. In the 1950s and 1960s, however, several French-speaking historians, including Maurice Séguin and Michel Brunet, took a contrary position. They argued that the union ended the separateness of Lower Canada and fused its destiny with that of Upper Canada. They regarded the union as a disaster, as a second conquest. In their view, Confederation in 1867 only perpetuated Quebec's subordinate position.

FRENCH–ENGLISH RELATIONS

The Colonial Office in London originally intended to use union of the Canadas to punish the French and assure their subjugation, if not their eventual demise, as a linguistic group. Certainly the conditions of union constituted a severe blow for Lower Canada in general and for French Canadians in particular. English became the sole official language of parliamentary documents. The elective Assembly had an equal number of representatives from both halves of the colony, even though in 1841 the largely French-speaking Canada East had 670 000 inhabitants and English-speaking Canada West had only 480 000.[2]

The Act of Union also created "one consolidated revenue fund," making Upper Canada's heavy debt burden the responsibility of the Province of Canada as a whole. Upper Canada could no longer by itself finance costly transportation facilities like roads and canals. It had already borrowed heavily in London, and only union with the virtually debt-free Lower Canada could strengthen its position. Union would bring in higher revenues because the United Canadas could raise tariffs, a measure that Lower Canada, where most goods from Europe entered, could no longer block. It would also recognize that the two Canadas formed a common economic bloc. Montreal's English-speaking merchants had been striving for such a union since the early 1820s.

LORD SYDENHAM

Charles Poulett Thomson, Lord Durham's successor as governor general of Canada, had spent eight years on the Board of Trade in London. This hard-headed administrator wanted to put Canada on a sound financial footing to attract development capital. In his view, investment would assure progress and lessen the appeal of the United States, thus warding off the constant threat of annexation. He also hoped that substantial British immigration would diminish the political and economic influence of French Canadians.

When the vain and strong-willed Thomson arrived in Canada in the autumn of 1839, he sought to convince Upper Canada to agree unconditionally to the proposal for political union. He did not have to convince Lower Canada, which would have no say in the matter. As British prime minister Lord Melbourne had written to Colonial Secretary Lord John Russell to explain his policy, "We feel that we cannot impose this union upon Upper Canada without her consent, and therefore we give her a choice. We give Lower Canada no choice, but we impose it upon her during the suspension of her constitution."

The union was officially inaugurated at the Château de Ramezay in Montreal on February 10, 1841. Thomson, now Baron Sydenham, intoned: "Inhabitants of the Province of Canada: henceforth may you be united in sentiment as you are from this day in name!" Most French Canadians, though, were defiant and bitter. Pierre-Joseph-Olivier Chauveau, a future Quebec premier, condemned the British bankers whom he saw as the force behind union and prophesied: "Today a weeping people is beaten, tomorrow a people will be up in arms, today the forfeit, tomorrow the vengeance."

The French certainly had no reason to trust the assurances of the anti-French Sydenham. Moreover, the union simply had too many elements that they found objectionable. Augustin-Norbert Morin, a Patriote of 1837 and Reform leader Louis-Hippolyte LaFontaine's lieutenant in Quebec City, commented frankly in a letter to Toronto politician Francis Hincks: "I am against the Union and against the main features, as I think every honest Lower Canadian should be." John Neilson, an urbane bilingual Scot who owned the *Quebec Gazette*, formed a committee in the fall of 1840 to work for the election of representatives opposed to union in order to express, by non-violent means, "our reprobation of this injustice which is done to this Province." Unyielding opposition appeared to be the only path open to the French.

Sydenham, however, soon proved himself a masterful strategist. Indeed, he won over most of Canada West to "his" party, with the exception of a few Family Compact Tories such as Sir Allan MacNab (who judged the governor too sympathetic to the doctrine of responsible government), as well as some "Ultra Reformers" (who perceived him as too equivocal in his support of the same doctrine).

In Canada East, *le poulet* (the chicken), as the French disdainfully called Poulett Thomson, laboured under no illusions. He knew the French were hostile to him and would not support his candidates. Apart from areas with important English-speaking populations, he admitted: "We shall not have a man returned who does not hate British connection, British rule, British improvements, and everything which has a taint of British feeling." This unscrupulous political manipulator thus worked to assure the election of a maximum number of English-speaking members. He gerrymandered riding boundaries to eliminate French votes from certain districts and staged polls in English localities situated far from French-speaking towns. As returning officers for the polls he chose partisans, and he used British troops as well as Irish construction labourers to intimidate French-speaking voters in the open voting (the secret ballot was established only in 1874). In LaFontaine's own district, the British candidate hired some strong-armed thugs who took possession of the polling place. Bitterly denouncing Sydenham's "law of the bludgeon," LaFontaine withdrew from the contest to avoid bloodshed and certain defeat that would risk compromising his own leadership. Not surprisingly, the governor won a comfortable working majority in United Canada's first legislature. He was now in a position to be his own prime minister.

TOWARD FRENCH-CANADIAN ACCEPTANCE OF UNION

Sydenham's heavy-handed tactics actually improved the chances for fruitful collaboration between Reformers in Canada East and Canada West. Since 1839 Francis Hincks, a pragmatic and ambitious Irish Protestant immigrant with a passion for journalism, business, and responsible government, assiduously cultivated good relations with LaFontaine. Hincks repeatedly assured the former Patriote that, in return for co-operation in working toward responsible government, his followers would assist French-Canadian efforts to rid the union of objectionable features such as official English unilingualism. Hincks asserted: "You want our help as much as we do yours." At first suspicious, LaFontaine finally concluded that French Canada could obtain more by accepting union than by continuing to oppose it.

THE BALDWIN–LAFONTAINE ALLIANCE

Robert Baldwin, the prominent Toronto Reform leader, endorsed Hincks's overture to LaFontaine. When LaFontaine could not get elected in Canada East, Baldwin arranged for him to run for the Assembly in a safe Reform riding north of York. The Upper Canadian Reform leader championed his new French-Canadian friend against Tory opponents like William Henry Boulton, who became mayor of Toronto in 1845. As mayor, Boulton still condemned the French as "tobacco-smoking, dram-drinking, garlick-eating..., foreign in blood, foreign in race and as ignorant as the ground they stand upon." Despite the opposition, LaFontaine won.

Once elected, this tribune of the French-Canadian Reformers in Canada East represented the farmers of Stouffville and Sharon in the Fourth Riding of York for one term. Later, when Baldwin lost his seat in Canada West, LaFontaine found his new friend and ally a safe seat in Canada East. For one term Baldwin represented the voters of Rimouski, an almost entirely French-speaking area on the south shore of the St. Lawrence River, 300 km east of Quebec City. Symbolically these gestures showed the strength of the English–French coalition.

The particularities of politics in each section of the province created the conditions that brought most French-Canadian leaders to work within the union. The threat represented by the imposed link with Canada West made it necessary for them to work together and to ally themselves with Baldwin and other similarly minded Reformers in Canada West. After 1850, however, when a few radical liberals from Canada East who questioned the Roman Catholic church's prerogatives in temporal matters and opposed the alliance between politicians and business interests took their place in the Assembly, tensions between the left and the right increased among the French. Nevertheless, this potential threat to the unity of the French bloc was successfully contained.

NOTICE.

LOUIS H. LA FONTAINE, ESQ.,

Accompanied by Dr. Baldwin,

WILL MEET THE FREEHOLDERS,

FRIENDLY TO HIS ELECTION,

For the North Riding of the County of York, at
THE FOLLOWING TIMES AND PLACES.

At Sharon--On Monday, 6th September, at noon.
At Bennett's, in North Gwillimbury--Tuesday, 7th, at do
At Johnson's Mills, in Georgina--Wednesday, 8th, at do
At Uxbridge Village--Thursday, 9th, at do
At Stouffville--Friday, 10th, at do.

LESSLIE, BROTHERS, PRINTERS.

An election notice of Louis H. La Fontaine in the north riding of the county of York, 1841. The French-Canadian Reform leader won a seat in the legislature of the Union of the Canadas, in Upper Canada, thanks to the support of Robert Baldwin and the Upper Canada reformers.

Toronto Reference Library.

THE RISE OF A REFORM COALITION

In the early 1840s, Canada West's political spectrum was broad, featuring almost all shades of opinion, from Compact Tories on the right to Ultra Reformers on the left. Basically, Tories vaunted their loyalty to the Crown and to the British connection and, as before the rebellions, they attempted to portray their Reformist opponents as disloyal traitors. In their view, responsible government could only weaken ties with Britain because it challenged the authority of the colonial governor; in any case, Upper Canadian society was too immature to aspire to greater control over its own affairs. It followed that, since the Tories could not recognize the legitimate existence of a loyal opposition in the Assembly, they could not accept party government. In fact, they did not see themselves as a party but rather the embodiment of society's best elements. Tory supporters included business interests, numerous professionals, and the many who benefited from government patronage. Many of the working-class Irish Protestant immigrants who poured into the colony in these years also supported the Tories: in return for Tory largesse, the Orange

Order provided, notably in Toronto, the "votes and strong arms needed in the rough and tumble polling process of the day."[3]

Reformist ambitions were given a powerful boost by Lord Durham's endorsement of responsible government in 1839. In order to prove their loyalty, Reformists worked to place their demands within the framework of the British constitution and British traditions. That the Crown act in non-partisan fashion was accepted British practice, they asserted. They also reminded their opponents that party government existed in Britain. Reformists also denounced the abuses linked to the government's distribution of patronage, although later, when they took power, they would prove themselves to be equally ardent practitioners in the art of dispensing favours.

Theoretically, in the early 1840s, the French Canadians could have aligned with some of Upper Canada's extreme Tories such as Sir Allan MacNab. Like the French, the Tories opposed union, but mutual ethnic and religious animosities precluded even a *mariage de convenance*. An alliance between Reformers and French seemed far more natural, in view of the political goals of both groups throughout the 1820s and 1830s and the growing personal friendship between Baldwin and LaFontaine.

It took time to establish this common front, however. Many so-called Reformers did not want to oppose the government, as the French Canadians had done, for fear of compromising the public-works projects promised for their districts by Lord Sydenham and obviously desired by the voters. The pragmatic Hincks, at least until he, too, defected to the government side, and especially the more principled Toronto Reform leader Robert Baldwin, were virtually alone. Baldwin, for example, never succeeded in bringing Sydenham to appoint French-speaking members to the Executive Council.

Then, the political landscape changed overnight. Sydenham's sudden death from lockjaw in September 1841 (caused by an injury, the result of a fall from his horse), led to the appointment of a new governor, Sir Charles Bagot, a man who lacked Sydenham's resolve to push through the assimilationist objectives of the union.

As disappointed Reformers from Canada West abandoned the new governor and returned to Baldwin's leadership, Bagot, a highly successful diplomat, lobbied for French-Canadian support to bolster his tottering government. His successor, Sir Charles Metcalfe, was likewise convinced that the anti-French assimilationist policies of the union were impractical, although he, too, believed that Anglicization was an appropriate long-term policy.

These governors walked a tightrope in governing the colony without the aid of representatives of the French Canadians, who formed nearly half the united province's population. Yet they were conservatives and strong believers in the British connection, and, in trying to appease the supposedly disloyal and rebellious French, they risked losing support among the English-speaking of both Canadas.

In addition, the governors had difficulty persuading the British government to renounce at least any immediate hopes for assimilation. Bagot reported to Colonial Secretary Lord Stanley that it was all very well to wait for immigration to "hem in and overwhelm French Population and French Power"; in the meantime, he had to solve pressing political problems by giving positions to French members and making other "concessions." When Bagot made good his threat and brought reformers Baldwin and LaFontaine into his government, Lord Stanley was dismayed. On his deathbed, Bagot justified his conduct to his critics in London: "I had no choice in regard to [my measures] if the Union was to be maintained."

On the highly charged question of giving official status to the French language, Governor Metcalfe wanted to act before LaFontaine forced him to do so. Again, Lord Stanley vehemently disagreed, since the Act of Union was designed "to promote the amalgamation of the French and English races," and to authorize bilingualism would be to abandon this goal. Only in 1848, three

The Great Blondin thrills a crowd at the Place d'Armes in Montreal with his skill on a tightrope, drawn across Notre Dame Street between the Old Seminary Church and Notre Dame Church. In the early 1840s, the governors of Canada were just as daring in trying to rule without the aid of French-Canadian representatives. Oil painting by W.H.B. Bartlett, around 1840.

Courtesy of the Royal Ontario Museum, Toronto/954.192.4 © ROM.

years after Metcalfe's request, did the British Parliament amend the Act of Union to end the proscription of the French language.

The achievement of responsible government did not put an end to close co-operation between French- and English-speaking politicians. It did signify the need to build new alliances. In the turbulent early 1850s, when the loosely organized Reform group split into moderate and radical factions, most French-speaking members of the Assembly, representing the moderate Parti bleu, began to co-operate with Conservatives from Canada West to form governments. This coalition, symbolized by the close association of John A. Macdonald and George-Étienne Cartier, carried over into the post-Confederation period.

THE ARRIVAL OF RESPONSIBLE GOVERNMENT

The most important single factor in bridging the ethnic gulf during the 1840s was the arduous, but ultimately successful, struggle for responsible government. In 1840, recognition of this principle still appeared far off. The Act of Union concentrated enormous power in the hands of the colonial governor, appointed by London. The governor, in turn, appointed for life the members of the upper house, or Legislative Council. He could also reward his supporters, since he had the right to name a host of public officials. In Parliament he chose his advisers, dismissing and replacing them at will. He also held broad veto powers over bills adopted by the legislature. Yet, over the course of the union's first decade, the governor's powers were radically curtailed.

Responsible government came only after dramatic battles. The Colonial Office urged Canada's governors to avoid concessions lest things get out of hand and Canada agitate for independence. On his deathbed, Sydenham considered the issue favourably resolved, but his "reign of harmony" implied an active, and often unscrupulous, participation of the governor in politics. In contrast, Bagot, a conciliator, was willing to risk appointing an Executive Council that would have the support of a majority in the Assembly. Taking into account the growing power of the French bloc, he invited LaFontaine to join his council. When the latter shrewdly demanded that Baldwin, too, have a place, the unhappy Bagot again yielded.

London was dismayed. The Duke of Wellington, Bagot's own uncle, called him "a fool." Colonial administrators expressed the strongest regrets — to which the governor replied that, had he acted otherwise, "Canada would have again become the theatre of a widespread rebellion, and perhaps the ungrateful separatist or the rejected outcast from British dominion." Despite Bagot's apparent recognition of the principle that he could only choose ministers who commanded the support of a majority of the members of the Assembly, no guarantee existed that the governor might not some day replace his advisers if he disagreed with them. Moreover, Bagot's government, consisting of a wide variety of personalities of various political hues, did not really constitute a ministry. Party government, though undeniably a little closer, had not yet come to the province.

GOVERNING IN THE CANADAS BEFORE AND AFTER RESPONSIBLE GOVERNMENT

Before   **Responsible Government**   **After**

Before responsible government was introduced, the Legislative Assembly had no effective control over the Executive Council, on whose advice the governor relied. With the coming of responsible government, the Executive Council could remain in office only as long as it had the Legislative Assembly's support.

Source: Adapted from P.G. Cornell, M. Hamelin, F. Ouellet, and M. Trudel, *Canada: Unity in Diversity* (Toronto: Holt, Rinehart and Winston, 1967), p. 143.

Where Historians Disagree
The Impact of the Union of the Canadas

The Union of the Canadas had a brief life, barely a quarter of a century. Many English-speaking historians have viewed it as simply a stepping-stone toward Confederation, or the wider union of all the British North American colonies; each failing of the union, especially each political crisis, simply rendered Confederation more necessary. Describing the resignation in June 1864 of the short-lived ministry headed by Étienne-Pascal Taché and John A. Macdonald, historian William L. Morton commented: "With its defeat the fabric of Canadian politics crumbled." What was the solution? asks Morton. Another shuffle of the "worn and greasy political cards?"[1] Surely not! Only a wider union of the British North American colonies could rescue politics from the morass into which it had sunk.

More recently, British historian Ged Martin has challenged past historiography that argued that the union's difficulties made further constitutional changes necessary. He believes the union should not be perceived as a black night that preceded the dawn of Confederation. The union was "not a political failure which had to be swept away in favour of the new British North American structure."[2] Martin sees no "deadlock" in 1864; rather there was a "logjam" needing to be disentangled. And certainly the rapid growth of Canada West's population made some form of representation by population necessary.

Historians with a special interest in French Canada have offered widely diverging analyses of the impact of union. For Maurice Séguin, the union condemned the French to permanent inequality. It repre-sented a "second conquest" that the French had no choice but to accept.[3] It created a political entity in which French Canadians, despite their large numbers, constituted proportionally a minority. The French were also faced with political inferiority within institutions of government that were largely English-speaking. In addition, economic domination was a painful reality. Few leaders of industry or commerce were French-speaking.

For historian Mason Wade, the very fact that the French avoided assimilation has to be seen as an unqualified triumph. The French Canadians definitely strengthened their position throughout the 1840s. "Faced with the prospect of national extinction," they "closed their ranks and won the peaceful victory which insured their national survival."[4] Moreover, Wade insists that their co-operation with anglophone politicians represented the first hesitant but positive steps toward "Canadian duality."

Historian Jacques Monet has also argued that, despite its original design that foresaw the demise of French Canada, the union benefited both French- and English-speaking Canada. Rephrasing Lord Durham's famous words, Monet affirms that union proved that "both French and English Canadians could live together within the bosom of a single state."[5] Also writing from the bicultural perspective popular in the 1960s, J.M.S. Careless saw union as having bound French and English together, "compelling them to work out new adjustments that were at least as significant as the strains so evident between them.... The union of the Canadas evolved the dual French–English political party, with dual ministerial leadership, and brought the two peoples to self-government in partnership. The major features of institutional growth under the union were produced by their joint efforts — as well as by their inability to escape the one really fundamental Canadian Fact, that they had to live together."[6]

A century and a half later, in spite of the changing dynamics within Canada that may make some of the above historians' comments appear rather dated, the debate about the relationship between French- and English-speaking Canadians continues, giving increased interest to the study of the Union period.

[1] William L. Morton, *The Kingdom of Canada*, 2nd ed. (Toronto: McClelland & Stewart, 1969), p. 315.

[2] Ged Martin, *Britain and the Origins of Canadian Confederation, 1837–67* (Vancouver: University of British Columbia Press, 1995), p. 5.

[3] Maurice Séguin, *L'idée d'indépendance au Québec: genèse et historique* (Trois-Rivières: Boréal Express, 1968), p. 36.

[4] Mason Wade, *The French Canadians, 1760–1967*, rev. ed., *vol. 1 (1760-1911)* (Toronto: Macmillan, 1968), p. 220.

[5] Jacques Monet, *The Last Cannon Shot: A Study of French Canadian Nationalism, 1837–1850* (Toronto: University of Toronto Press, 1969), p. 6.

[6] J.M.S. Careless, *The Union of the Canadas: The Growth of Canadian Institutions, 1841–1857* (Toronto: McClelland & Stewart, 1967), p. xii.

More responsible for this outcome was Sir Charles Metcalfe, who arrived in Canada as governor in March 1843, determined to maintain the British connection. He had succeeded in pacifying Jamaica; now London hoped that he might do equally well in Canada. As the Queen's representative, he did not intend to submit to LaFontaine, and he would certainly not commit himself to taking his advice. The Reformers' distribution of patronage, and their unseemly rush for jobs for their people, greatly disturbed the governor. Metcalfe assured Colonial Secretary Lord Stanley that he would strive to get a majority in Parliament, that if he failed he would dissolve the Assembly and try again, "and that if I fail then, still I cannot submit, for that would be to surrender the Queen's government into the hands of rebels, and to become myself their ignominious tool." Metcalfe proved every bit as steadfast as his confession of faith seemed to indicate. In the rancorous election of 1844, he did obtain a slim majority by inflicting a decisive defeat on the overconfident and "disloyal" Upper Canadian Reformers. He was, however, spectacularly unsuccessful in Lower Canada, where LaFontaine had built up an effective political machine.

The moderate regime that governed the colony from 1844 until 1847, led by the eloquent Conservative "Sweet William" Henry Draper as attorney general for Canada West and virtual prime minister, succeeded in adopting several important pieces of legislation, including school acts for both Canadas, legal reform, a revamped land-grant system that would lessen speculation, and a permanent civil list of salaried officials.

True responsible government did not yet exist, however. Although the Executive Council did have the confidence of the Assembly, the governor's powers remained very broad. Indeed, Conservatives hoped that if the governor's administrative measures were popular, responsible government would lose its appeal. Moreover, Draper's attempts to build significant French support failed utterly. The old Patriote Denis-Benjamin Viger agreed to work with him, but Viger failed to gain the backing of influential French Canadians.

LORD ELGIN AND RESPONSIBLE GOVERNMENT

The pace of events quickened with the arrival of Lord Elgin, the new governor general, in 1847. By this time the British Crown had ceased to play an active part in politics. Moreover, with the British move toward laissez-faire liberalism and the adoption of free trade, it became less imperative for London to control the colonies as there was no longer any need to regulate colonies' trade relations. Indeed, the British government was now convinced that only colonial autonomy could hold the empire together, and it instructed Elgin to accept this principle and to behave in a strictly neutral fashion.

The elections of 1848 produced a strong majority for LaFontaine's group in Canada East and a significant majority for Baldwin's Reform movement in Canada West. The Reformers' victory achieved, Lord Elgin called on LaFontaine and Baldwin to form a government. Henceforth, the governor assented to legislation adopted by Parliament, unless he judged it contrary to the interests of Great Britain. Elgin proved as much in 1849 when he agreed to sign, despite personal reservations, the Rebellion Losses Bill, which compensated those who had lost property during the Rebellions of 1837–38 in Canada East (the question of losses in Canada West had been settled in 1845). The bill proved bitterly controversial since it also compensated "traitorous" rebels for their losses.

Responsible government thus moved Canada forward along the road to democracy and political autonomy. For that reason, most historians have viewed its coming as a great milestone in Canada's history. The voters, through their elected representatives, would now exercise greater control over government — or at least the property-holding male portion would, for in 1849 the Reformers amended the election law to exclude women from the franchise. In spite of the common-law prohibition against female suffrage, a few women had voted. They had even helped a Tory win in 1844 — an incident that the Reformers had not forgotten.

Perhaps more relevant to the politicians' daily preoccupations, responsible government also ensured that the leaders of the governing party would control patronage. Political scientist S.J.R. Noel asserts that the British resisted responsible government in part precisely because they "appreciated the central importance of patronage in the political process."[4] Another consequence of responsible government was to ensure a shift of power and influence away from conservative traditional elites and toward the new commercial and industrial classes. Business and politicians co-operated closely. In fact, a great many politicians were businesspeople who came to politics to advance both their personal interests and those of the business community. In this sense, it would be naïve to claim that responsible government actually gave power to the common people. Yet business domination was not to go unchallenged, and elections did bring members of a variety of other groups to Parliament.

FIRST NATIONS IN THE CANADAS

 As the total percentage of Native people in the Canadas fell to less than 1 percent of the total population, they became more and more invisible to the dominant society. So little attention, in fact, was paid to Native affairs that the Act of Union (1841) omitted to make provision for "Indians," or even to provide for the payment of annuities for earlier land surrenders. Officials only corrected this oversight in 1844.

With responsible government, however, colonial officials did begin to pay more attention to the First Nations. The British government finally transferred all authority over "Indian affairs" to the Canadian legislature in 1860. The Canadian politicians committed themselves to a system of First Nations education based on model farms and industrial or residential schools, in order to bring about the eventual assimilation of the Native population. Christian missionaries would

A Historical Portrait ☞

☞ Nahnebahwequay

Nahnebahwequay is one of the few nineteenth-century First Nations women whose life can be described in some detail, using her own writings and those of others who wrote about her. She was one of the first Great Lakes First Nations women to acquire an English-language education and an understanding of the dominant settlers' society. Thanks to her attendance at a Methodist Indian mission school, a visit to England as a young girl, and her marriage to an English immigrant, she learned enough of the ways of the newcomers to be at ease in their society. Yet, she never compromised her principles on matters of Native land claims or injustice to her people.

The year that Nahnebahwequay, or "Nahnee," as she later called herself, was born, her parents, Bunch and Polly Sunegoo, became Christians. They were among the first Mississaugas to help build the Methodist mission at the Credit River, 20 km west of Toronto. The leading spirit of the mission was her uncle Peter Jones, who became an ordained Methodist minister and a chief of the Mississaugas of the Credit.

Nahnee helped her parents with the chores in their log cabin home and on their farm. As a young child in the 1820s and early 1830s, she lost all her siblings through disease. Once she herself was on the point of death. Throughout this adversity, her mother did not lose her Christian faith. Nahnee, in turn, also became a Christian. Thanks to Nahnee's aunt, Peter Jones's well-educated English wife, Eliza Field, who came to the mission after their marriage in 1833, Nahnee had special advantages. At the Jones's home, Eliza taught her and other

Nahnebahwequay ("Upright Woman").

County of Grey–Owen Sound Museum, Owen Sound, Ontario.

Mississauga girls sewing, and other household skills. When Eliza returned to England for a visit in 1837, Nahnee accompanied her and her uncle. Comfortable in many social settings, Nahnee developed an unusual self-confidence.

Shortly after her return to the Credit, Nahnee, aged 15, married an English immigrant, William Sutton, who was 28. Despite the age gap, theirs was a very successful marriage. Both shared an intense Christian outlook. They left the Credit in the late 1840s for the Owen Sound area to the north, where the energetic William worked with the local Ojibwas as a farm instructor and local preacher. He cleared his own farm on a tract of land given them by the Ojibwas. In these years, Nahnee raised her growing family and helped run the farm.

When William agreed to be a farm instructor at Ojibwa Methodist missions around Sault Ste. Marie, the Sutton family moved north. When they returned they discovered that their land near Owen Sound was for sale. During their absence, the local Ojibwas had signed a treaty with the British, who did not recognize the validity of the Native grant of land to the Suttons. The Indian Department, at the same time, announced that it no longer considered Mrs. Sutton an Indian, "on the ground of her having married a white man."

In 1860, Nahnee, obtaining no redress, took her land claim and the grievances of the Ojibwas, to Queen Victoria herself. Sympathetic Quakers in New York City provided her with passage to Britain. In London, the Quakers assisted her in gaining an audience with the Queen on June 19, 1860. The Queen noted in her journal that her visitor spoke English quite well and had come to present a land petition on behalf of her people. Curiously, however, the Queen made no mention of Nahnee's pregnancy, which must, in her ninth month, have been quite obvious. Nahnee gave birth to a son, Albert, on July 11, 1860, at the home of Quaker friends in London.

Subsequently, the Suttons were allowed to buy back their farm near Owen Sound. This outcome did not appease Nahnee, who relentlessly continued to fight for Native rights. She argued that the Europeans acted "as though their ideas of justice are that 'might is right.' " She severely criticized as "wholesale robbery" the government's attempt, in 1861, to purchase Manitoulin Island on the north shore of Lake Huron for non-Native settlers. A quarter of a century earlier, the Upper Canadian colonial administration had promised the large island, forever, to the Anishinabeg. For the last years of her life, Nahnee suffered from poor health, and died at age 41 in 1865.

administer the schools. It was unquestioningly assumed that the First Nations should be, for their own well-being, absorbed into the settler society.

Ironically, after their hard fight to achieve greater self-government from Britain, Canadian politicians imposed even tighter control over the First Nations population of the Canadas. The government had established and surveyed reserves, but under the legislation adopted in the 1850s and 1860s, Aboriginal people were given little opportunity to administer their remaining lands themselves. A subtle distinction can be seen in the reference to First Nations people in treaties. In an 1819 treaty, they were referred to as a "nation"; later, in the Robinson treaties (concerning the north shores of Lakes Huron and Superior) in 1850, the undoubtedly less prestigious term "tribe" was used.

One group, the First Nations at Kanesatake (Oka), did not receive a reserve. During the Rebellions of 1837–38, the Sulpicians, who were the seigneurs at the Lake of the Two Mountains, had stood loyally by the British. The religious order encouraged Roman Catholics to enlist in British militia units and contributed money to support those units. Immediately after the uprisings, in 1840, the governor's Special Council issued an ordinance that gave title to the land to the Sulpicians.

THE ANNEXATION MOVEMENT

Following the achievement of responsible government, the years 1848–54 saw feverish political activity. When Governor General Lord Elgin sanctioned the Rebellion Losses Bill on April 25, 1849, the fury of Montreal's Tories exploded. A mob invaded Parliament and put it to the torch, then stoned Elgin's carriage, ransacked LaFontaine's house, and rampaged through the town.

Canada West experienced considerable unrest, too. The Tories staged protest meetings to denounce the rewarding of "rebels" and "pardoned traitors," and thousands signed petitions demanding Elgin's recall. Baldwin and William Lyon Mackenzie were burned in effigy, and Lord Elgin met a similar fiery condemnation from a Toronto mob. The *Brockville Statesman* minced no words in its commentary on Elgin: "Without peace there can be no prosperity, and that peace cannot be procured so long as his hated foot presses the free soil, or his lying lungs breathe the pure air of Canada."

For many Tories, this was French domination at its worst, and Elgin and his Reform government were bowing to it. Yet in spite of their bitter denunciations and violent actions, they did not consider themselves disloyal to Britain. On the contrary, they appealed to Queen Victoria to dissolve the Legislative Assembly and veto the hated Rebellion Losses Bill. Nor were they averse to using violence, or to seeing it used on their behalf by their Irish allies, in an era in which political violence was common.

Three Indian Chiefs and Peter McLeod Presenting a Petition to Lord Elgin, by Théophile Hamel (1848). On March 12, 1848, three Montagnais (Innu) chiefs from the Saguenay River, with their interpreter, Peter McLeod, met the governor general and presented their grievances. The newcomers had pushed them further and further into the interior, from Tadoussac, to Chicoutimi, to Lac St. Jean. In Canada East, unlike in Canada West, the government did not conclude treaties with the resident First Nations. The British argued that the Royal Proclamation of 1763 had not designated the valley of the St. Lawrence and surrounding area as "Indian territory."

Private collection/Photo courtesy of the owner.

At the same time, some Tories clearly linked their loyalty to economic opportunity; thus they denounced Britain's move toward free trade because it signified an end to the imperial preferences that gave exporters in the British North American markets an advantage over traders in other nations to which higher tariffs had previously applied. Britain's new trade policies thus helped to push large sectors of Canadian commerce into depression. Shipping activity at Montreal declined by more than 40 percent between 1847 and 1849. Finding none of the much-vaunted benefits of the British connection, some Tories, who had hitherto proclaimed their loyalty and condemned traitors and rebels, campaigned for annexation to the United States.

Montreal became the hotbed of annexationist sentiment. In October 1849, the English-language press published the manifesto of the Annexation Association, signed by 325 citizens, many of them notable businesspeople, such as William Molson and John Redpath. Early in 1850 the formation of the Toronto Annexation Association, supposedly embracing "a large number of the most respectable merchants and inhabitants of this city, of all parties and creeds," was announced.

FRENCH CANADA AND ANNEXATION

Even French Canada displayed some interest in annexation, though obviously for entirely different reasons. Louis-Joseph Papineau, who had returned to Canada from the United States after having been granted amnesty in 1844, was well known for his admiration of American democratic institutions and his hatred of the Canadian union. Radical young intellectuals belonging to the Institut canadien, a literary and debating society in Montreal, or who wrote for the newspaper *L'Avenir*, took up the annexationist cause. They declared that they preferred "Brother Jonathan" (a personification of the United States), with his egalitarian principles, to John Bull (signifying England), with his haughty and aristocratic airs.

This painting by Joseph Légaré depicts the burning of the Canadian Parliament building in Montreal on the night of April 25, 1849. It is believed that rioters, protesting the passage of the Rebellion Losses Bill, smashed the gas mains, then set fire to the escaping gas. Earlier that day, crowds of English-speaking protesters had thrown stones and rotten eggs at Lord Elgin's carriage because the governor general had sanctioned the bill. The riots lasted two days. Subsequently, it was decided that Montreal would no longer be the seat of government, and the capital alternated between Quebec City and Toronto.

McCord Museum of Canadian History, Montreal, M11588.

A naïve but sincere Louis-Antoine Dessaulles, Papineau's nephew, expressed his ardent desire that French Canada follow the path of Louisiana, with its large French-speaking population, in order to obtain the advantages both of a separate state and of American prosperity and democracy. Dessaulles, journalist Jean-Baptiste-Éric Dorion (appropriately nicknamed "*l'enfant terrible*"), and their friends, however, constituted but a tiny group. Their movement had no popular base, and other elites in French Canada vociferously condemned annexation. George-Étienne Cartier echoed conservative sentiment when he warned that American democracy signified that "the dominant power was the will of the crowd, of the masses." The Roman Catholic clergy, for its part, feared that annexation would put an end to the liberty that it enjoyed under British rule.

In Canada West, annexationism, though noisy, made little headway. Newspapers frequently published citizens' statements lauding the benefits of the relationship with Britain. John Strachan, now Anglican Bishop of Toronto, roundly denounced annexation as being opposed to "the plainest and most solemn declarations of the revealed will of God," for it signified union with republicans who sanctioned slavery. Opponents of annexation published their own manifestoes in the press.

In July 1849, Tories, frustrated by the Reform government and by "French domination," gathered at Kingston to launch the British–American League. Future prime minister John A. Macdonald apparently played an active behind-the-scenes role in its organization, but the Toronto *Globe*, edited by George Brown, Macdonald's great political opponent, reported that Macdonald "said little in the convention and indeed he never says much anywhere except in barrooms...." Patriotic delegates overwhelmingly rejected a resolution favourable to annexation. One delegate declared passionately, "It was never intended by Providence that the American, or Gallic, eagles should ever build their nests in the branches of the British oak, or soar over her prostrate lion."

A later convention, held in Toronto in November, voiced support for a union of the British North American colonies, which many delegates viewed as a means of escaping from French domination. Macdonald judged this scheme "premature and impractical for the moment."

With the revival of prosperity in the early 1850s, annexationist sentiment receded rapidly. Although union with the United States had been much discussed, it had little popular support. Also, the Americans' unresponsiveness to annexationist tendencies north of the border hastened the movement's decline.

Louis-Joseph Papineau, a portrait by Napoléon Bourassa, 1858. Bourassa, the most prominent French-Canadian painter in Montreal around 1860, was also Papineau's son-in-law. In 1857, he married Azélie, Papineau's eldest daughter. The famous French-Canadian nationalist Henri Bourassa, founder of *Le Devoir* in 1910 and its editor until 1932, was Papineau's grandson.

Musée du Québec/52.58.

NEW POLITICAL ALLIANCES

While moderate English-speaking Conservatives attempted to find a new basis for unified action, the Reform movement began to splinter. By 1850, with responsible government a reality, tensions arose between moderates and radicals on issues such as political reform, railway policy, financial affairs, and church–state relations. The radical Reformers, with their stronghold in the area west of Toronto, denounced Montreal business interests, actively promoted agrarian democracy, and announced that they were seeking out "only men who are Clear Grit," *grit* being American slang for firmness of character.[5] Under journalist George Brown's leadership, the Clear Grits became vocal champions of "rep by pop," or representation according to population, the implication being that Canada West, with its larger and rapidly increasing population, deserved a greater number of seats — and, therefore, a preponderant influence over government policy — than did francophone Canada East.

At the same time, with Louis-Joseph Papineau's political revival, the French-Canadian Parti rouge made a modest appearance in the Assembly in 1848. The *rouges* gained ground in the elections of 1851 and 1854, especially in the Montreal region. These radical reformers inherited the traditions of the Parti patriote. They tended to be somewhat anti-clerical, republican, strongly nationalistic, and highly critical of the close links between government and business, notably in matters pertaining to the railways. Thus, in addition to its usual arch-Tory adversaries, who had been severely shaken by the crisis over the Rebellion Losses Bill and the annexation question, the governing coalition faced mounting pressures from the *rouges* and the Clear Grits, particularly after the retirement of Baldwin and LaFontaine in 1851. After initial attempts to attract Clear Grit support, the government sought the endorsement of the Conservatives and of Hincks's moderate Reformers. In 1854, the so-called Liberal–Conservative alliance emerged, jointly led by Macdonald and Cartier.

A CAPITAL IS CHOSEN

In the 1850s, politics often seemed divorced from the everyday concerns of common people. The difficulty of choosing a seat of government or a capital for the united province symbolized this apparent detachment. Indeed, between 1841 and 1859, the Legislative Assembly voted no fewer

Construction of the Parliament building on Barrack Hill above the west bank of the entrance locks of the Rideau Canal, 1863. Work began in 1859 and was completed in 1866. The Prince of Wales, the future Edward VII, laid the cornerstone on September 1, 1860. Although destroyed in the fire of 1916, the building was rebuilt and is now called the Centre Block, the home of both the House of Commons and the Senate.

National Archives of Canada/C-773.

than 218 times on this seemingly straightforward matter. Political, ethnic, and geographical rivalries transformed the issue into one of the most divisive confronting the union. In 1841, the British government chose the small town of Kingston as the first capital, because it judged both Toronto and Montreal difficult to defend in the event of American attack; moreover, Toronto was too far west. Quebec, with its largely French-speaking population, was not acceptable either. But according to Lord Sydenham, a capital somewhere in Upper Canada would be good for French members because it "would instil English ideas into their minds, [and] destroy the immediate influence upon their actions of the host of little lawyers, notaries and doctors."

Many liberal-minded members soon found Kingston too deeply permeated by Orangeism and Toryism. The government therefore moved its seat to Montreal. But in 1849, the burning of the Parliament building there again necessitated a move, and the seat of government migrated to Toronto. After stormy debate, the legislators agreed that the capital would remain on the humid shores of Lake Ontario for two years, after which it would alternate every four years between Quebec City and Toronto. Citizens of both cities were reluctant to see the capital depart, but Protestant or Catholic, English or French, the members of this so-called "log-rolling compact" preferred relinquishing the seat temporarily to seeing it settle on a permanent basis in some other city.

Eventually, the Assembly appealed to Queen Victoria to choose a capital. After receiving memorials from all appropriate Canadian towns (and some less appropriate ones as well), the British government selected Bytown, which had recently been renamed Ottawa on being incorporated as a city in 1855. Quebeckers were dismayed. The Toronto *Globe* was outraged by this choice of a city in which more than 60 percent of the population was Roman Catholic and half was French Canadian. After more bickering, the Assembly finally deferred in 1859 to the Queen's decision and, six years later, Ottawa became the capital of the Canadas.

George-Étienne Cartier, John A. Macdonald's great French-Canadian ally.

R. Notman & Son/National Archives of Canada/C-6166.

POLITICS AND BUSINESS

Economic progress and, especially after 1845, railway development most engaged the attention of the legislators. Railways required extensive government financial assistance through tax concessions, guarantees, bonds, the assumption of bad debts, and outright grants when private capital was insufficient, as it always was (see Chapter 14).

RAILWAY PROMOTION

At the time, many politicians had close links with business enterprises and exhibited few scruples about combining personal and state interests. Sir Allan MacNab, co-prime minister in the MacNab–Morin and MacNab–Taché administrations from 1854 to 1856, was one. He affirmed candidly, after consuming "one or two bottles of good port," that "my politics are railroads." The great Reformer Francis Hincks, an unabashed defender of railway schemes, was another. A parliamentary committee studied his conduct but found no evidence of corruption, although Hincks had obviously been in situations involving conflicts of interest. Alexander T. Galt of Sherbrooke, Canada East, named minister of finance in the Cartier–Macdonald ministry in 1858, was also a very pragmatic business leader. He was a major force behind, a large shareholder in, and eventually president of, the St. Lawrence and Atlantic Railway that linked

John A. Macdonald, leader of the Upper Canadian Conservatives, about 1857. When attacked by his rival George Brown for his drinking, Macdonald replied that the country would rather have "John A." drunk than George Brown sober.

National Archives of Canada/C-10144.

Montreal to Portland, Maine, by way of Sherbrooke. The Grand Trunk Railway absorbed the line shortly after its completion in 1853. Galt also sat on the board of directors of the Grand Trunk and, in politics, sought to expand Montreal's influence westward.

None of today's conflict-of-interest legislation existed at that time. George-Étienne Cartier, for instance, actively concerned himself with Montreal business while serving as the director of a host of banking, insurance, transportation, and mining companies. Railways, though, were his main activity. Over many years, he held positions as cabinet minister, chair of the Legislative Assembly's Railway Committee, and solicitor for the Grand Trunk Railway. Cartier guided the Grand Trunk's charter through the Assembly in 1854 and said he was prouder of that action than of any other in his life. Hugh Allan, a banker, shipping magnate, and railway promoter, made large contributions to Cartier's election campaigns. In return for the donations he received railway charters, favourable legislation, and the repeal of laws he disliked.

Politics and business were thus closely entwined. Hugh Allan's lawyer, for example, later testified before the Railway Committee: "On every one of these subjects — steamships, railways, canals — the Government had a policy which was favourable to his [Allan's] views, and in my opinion three times the sum would have been well spent had it been necessary to keep a government in power which had ... the improvement of the country so deeply at heart as this Government appears to." Cartier, who reportedly boasted that Irish voters could be bought for a "barrel of flour apiece and some salt fish thrown in for the leaders," was obviously able to make good use of Hugh Allan's money.

The politicians themselves usually waged fierce verbal battles in committee and on the floor of the Assembly over any business-related decisions that the government made. Representatives from Quebec City, for example, such as Commissioner of Crown Lands Joseph Cauchon and Mayor Hector Langevin, protested vehemently that their pet project, the North Shore Railway to Quebec, was sabotaged by the Grand Trunk and its Montreal political allies Cartier and Galt, who had no intention of allowing trade to be diverted downstream.

"REP BY POP"

As time passed, dissatisfaction with the legislative union grew, particularly in Canada West. Some representatives of both Canadas advocated the double majority vote. This notion implied that government ministers from each section of the colony needed the support of the majority of their section's members and, as a corollary, that controversial legislation could not be imposed upon one section of the colony by a majority composed largely of members from the other. Yet the government frequently had a difficult time building a simple majority, let alone finding majority support in both Canadas. In the 1840s, many measures were indeed imposed on Canada East as a result of majorities in Canada West. After 1850, the shoe was often on the other foot, as large numbers of *bleus* helped adopt laws that were approved by only a minority of members from Canada West. One such law was the Scott Act of 1863, which gave added privileges to Canada West's Roman Catholic schools. The double majority principle was simply unworkable. Only separation of the two sections, albeit within a federal system, could permit development according to each section's special needs and interests.

In the early 1850s, Canada West's population surpassed that of Canada East. The Clear Grits now took up as their campaign slogan "rep by pop," or representation based on population. By 1857, it was the foremost plank in the Reform platform. To this demand, most inhabitants of Canada East responded with a resounding "no." Union had instituted equality of representation in 1841; both languages had official status; governments were headed by co-premiers, one from each of the Canadas; and each section of the province had its own attorney general and solicitor general, its own educational legislation, and its own deputy superintendent of education. Even the old pre-union names — Upper and Lower Canada — remained in common use. Some semblance of equality, indeed a crude sort of federalism, had been achieved in spite of the original intentions of the architects of union. Representation by population, Canada East feared, would only destroy this working system.

Clear Grit leader George Brown, tersely described as "a red-haired, lantern-jawed Lowland Scot — six feet four of backbone and Presbyterian prejudice" by Gordon Donaldson in *Fifteen Men: Canada's Prime Ministers from Macdonald to Trudeau* (Toronto: Doubleday, 1969), p. 8.

National Archives of Canada/C-9553.

TOWARD CONFEDERATION

 At the Reform party's convention in Toronto in November 1859, George Brown began to promote the idea, already advocated by the *rouges* of Canada East, of transforming the legislative union into a highly decentralized federative union of the two Canadas. The Conservatives, however, who governed only because of their large block of French support from Canada East, were opposed. Moreover, they countered with suggestions for a wider British North American union. Alexander Galt entered the ministry only after extracting from the Conservatives a promise to work toward Confederation, but initially the idea aroused only perfunctory interest. The Montreal *Gazette* believed that the proposal had possibilities and suggested forming a new English-speaking province that would join portions of eastern Upper Canada with Montreal and the Eastern Townships. Then the French-speaking East could "stand still as long as it likes" and the West could "rush frantically forward," while the centre enjoyed "that gradual, sure, true progress which is the best indication of material prosperity."

The Reformers were understandably suspicious of any Conservative proposal. After all, they had just witnessed Macdonald's political manoeuvres of 1858 that had permitted him to regain power only a few hours after it had been lost to a Brown–Dorion/Reform–Parti rouge coalition, aptly termed the "Short Administration."

Confederation projects were discussed throughout the early 1860s. Many Upper Canadians were angry at having to pay for the expenditures voted by majorities built on eastern support. At last, a century after the Conquest, as George Brown said in the Canadian legislature, the representatives of the British population might aspire to justice without having to wait while "the representatives of the French population [sit here] discussing in the French tongue whether we shall have it." At the same time, Lower Canadians protested, as the newspaper *L'Ordre* put it, that without Lower Canadian help to pay Upper Canadian debts, Upper Canada today would be "nothing more or less than a forest put up for auction by British capitalists to repay their investments."

The deteriorating external situation seemed to instil a sense of urgency about resolving the political deadlock. Across the border, the Civil War raged and Britain's relations with the soon-to-be-victorious North were strained. Canadians began to fear that the Americans might decide to seek revenge on the British by attacking Canada. In addition, trade relations, which had been greatly stimulated by the Treaty of Reciprocity of 1854 as well as by the North's needs during the Civil War, continued to be endangered.

POLITICAL DEADLOCK

The logjam that virtually paralyzed the union government provided the necessary push for change. In May 1862, the Cartier–Macdonald ministry resigned when, in the face of *bleu* defections over the issue of conscription, the legislature defeated its Militia Bill, much to the chagrin of the British government and "Little Englanders," who wished to shift more of the burden of Canadian defence away from British taxpayers. John A. Macdonald, the minister responsible for militia affairs, was inebriated and unavailable during most of the debate. A Liberal administration under John Sandfield Macdonald and Louis-Victor Sicotte, a moderate liberal, or "*mauve*," took office, but the following year it failed to survive a vote of confidence and went to the people.

The 1863 elections saw the Liberals strengthened in Canada West, while in the East, the *bleus* at least avoided a rout. The Liberal camp, however, was weakened by internal division, and in 1864 Sandfield Macdonald gave up the hopeless task of governing. The Étienne-Pascal Taché–John A. Macdonald regime that replaced it was defeated in June 1864, after barely a few weeks in office. Now that opposing forces were almost evenly balanced, the United Canadas appeared to become ungovernable in their present state.

Any evaluation of the rather brief Union period must be qualified. Certainly there was progress in many areas. The coming of responsible government represented a significant milestone in the movement toward democracy and autonomy. For the French, in particular, the dire prophecies of assimilation made at the birth of union did not materialize, though ethnic and religious prejudice remained rampant throughout the era. Chronic political instability helped seal the fate of the union. By 1864, the Canadas were thus once again in the throes of constitutional change.

NOTES

1. S.J.R. Noel, *Patrons, Clients, Brokers: Ontario Society and Politics, 1791–1896* (Toronto: University of Toronto Press, 1990), p. 175.
2. Statistics vary. These are from J.M.S. Careless, *The Union of the Canadas: The Growth of Canadian Institutions, 1841–1857* (Toronto: McClelland & Stewart, 1967), p. 20.
3. Peter Way, "The Canadian Tory Rebellion of 1849 and the Demise of Street Politics in Toronto," *British Journal of Canadian Studies* 10 (1995): 10.
4. Noel, *Patrons, Clients, Brokers*, p. 151.
5. John Robert Colombo, "Grit," *The Canadian Encyclopedia*, 2nd ed., vol. 2 (Edmonton: Hurtig, 1988), p. 940. Grit is fine sand or gravel, which is often valued for its abrasive quality. The Clear Grits characterized themselves as "all sand and no dirt, clear grit all the way through."

LINKING TO THE PAST   w(w)w

Union and Responsible Government
http://www.canadiana.org/citm/themes/constitution/constitution11_e.html

A description of political developments from the impact of the Durham Report to the introduction of responsible government, with links to original documents and document summaries.

The Evolution of Federal Political Parties in Canada
http://www.cric.ca/en_html/guide/parties/parties.html

A brief history of Canadian federal political parties, including the impact of the Baldwin–LaFontaine alliance.

Self-Government and Federal Union (1841–1867)
http://www.canadianheritage.org/books/canada7.htm

A discussion of responsible government, social changes during this period, and the push for a British North American union.

Treaties with First Nations
http://www.ainc-inac.gc.ca/pr/trts/index_e.html

Full text of many treaties, most of which stipulate that the First Nations tribes will yield parts of their lands to the Crown (see, for example, the "Ojibewa Indians" treaties). For images of the original documents and a chronology, visit http://collections.ic.gc.ca/treaties/code.

Kingston as the Capital
http://www.city.kingston.on.ca/firstcapital/winning.asp

An account of the brief period when Kingston served as the nation's capital.

George Brown
http://www.nlc-bnc.ca/2/18/h18-2309-e.html

A brief biography of George Brown, with links to other relevant topics.

RELATED READINGS

R. Douglas Francis and Donald B. Smith, eds., *Readings in Canadian History: Pre-Confederation*, 6th ed. (Toronto: Nelson Thomson Learning, 2002), contains one article related to this topic: A.I. Silver, "Confederation and Quebec," pp. 469–83.

BIBLIOGRAPHY

The union years are examined in J.M.S. Careless, *The Union of the Canadas: The Growth of Canadian Institutions, 1841–1857* (Toronto: McClelland & Stewart, 1967); and W.L. Morton, *The Critical Years: The Union of British North America, 1857–1873* (Toronto: University of Toronto Press, 1964). Maurice Séguin defends his thesis in *L'idée d'indépendance au Québec: genèse et historique* (Trois-Rivières: Boréal Express, 1968). Paul G. Cornell, *The Alignment of Political Groups in Canada, 1841–1867* (Toronto: University of Toronto Press, 1962), analyzes the rather complex development of party groupings. Carol Wilton's doctoral dissertation, "The Transformation of Upper Canadian Politics in the 1840s" (University of Toronto, 1985), represents a significant contribution to knowledge of the period. S.J.R. Noel studies the art of political brokerage in *Patrons, Clients, Brokers: Ontario Society and Politics, 1791–1896* (Toronto: University of Toronto Press, 1990). R.C. Brown, ed., *Upper Canadian Politics in the 1850s* (Toronto: University of Toronto Press, 1967) contains several informative articles, while J.M.S. Careless, ed., *The Pre-Confederation Premiers: Ontario Government Leaders, 1841–67* (Toronto: University of Toronto Press, 1980) constitutes a valuable addition to the political history of the period. Much material on the development of the state in the Union period is available in Allan Greer and Ian Radforth, eds., *Colonial Leviathan: State Formation in Mid-Nineteenth-Century Canada* (Toronto: University of Toronto Press, 1992). In particular, this book contains an article on women and politics in the Canadas: Lykke de le Cour, Cecilia Morgan, and Mariana Valverde,

"Gender Regulation and State Formation in Nineteenth-Century Canada," pp. 162–91. For biographies of Canada West's two leading politicians see Donald G. Creighton, *John A. Macdonald: The Young Politician* (Toronto: Macmillan, 1956); and J.M.S. Careless, *Brown of the Globe*, 2 vols. (Toronto: Macmillan, 1959 and 1963). Carol Wilton-Siegel has studied the role of Conservative politicians of the era in "Administrative Reform: A Conservative Alternative to Responsible Government," *Ontario History* 78 (1986): 105–25; see also Donald R. Beer, "Toryism in Transition: Upper Canadian Conservative Leaders, 1836–1854," *Ontario History* 80 (1988): 207–25.

Several other works also elaborate on the political developments of the period. On responsible government see George Metcalf's essay, "Draper Conservatism and Responsible Government in the Canadas, 1836–1847," *Canadian Historical Review* 42 (1961): 300–24. A recent analysis may be found in Jeffery L. McNairn, *The Capacity to Judge: Public Opinion and Deliberative Democracy in Upper Canada, 1791–1854* (Toronto: University of Toronto Press, 2000). The annexation movement in Upper Canada is studied by Gerald H. Hallowell, "The Reaction of the Upper Canadian Tories to the Adversity of 1849: Annexation and the British American League," *Ontario History* 62 (1970): 41–56; and by S.F. Wise, "Canadians View the United States: The Annexation Movement and Its Effects on Canadian Opinion, 1837–1867," in A.B. McKillop and Paul Romney, eds., *God's Peculiar Peoples: Essays on Political Culture in Nineteenth-Century Canada* (Ottawa: Carleton University Press, 1993), pp. 115–48. For an examination of the American sympathies of some Canadian conservatives and for reflections on political culture see Jeffrey L. McNairn, "Publius of the North: Tory Republicanism and the American Constitution in Upper Canada, 1848–54," *Canadian Historical Review* 77 (1996): 504–37. Jean-Paul Bernard describes annexationist sentiment in French Canada in *Les Rouges: libéralisme, nationalisme et anticléricalisme au milieu du XIXᵉ siècle* (Montreal: Les Presses de l'Université du Québec, 1971), pp. 61–73. Popular political culture in Upper Canada at the time of Durham is studied in Carol Wilton, "'A Firebrand amongst the People': The Durham Meetings and Popular Politics in Upper Canada," *Canadian Historical Review* 75 (1994): 346–75. More general studies of this aspect of politics are David Mills, *The Idea of Loyalty in Upper Canada, 1784–1850* (Montreal/Kingston: McGill-Queen's University Press, 1988); and Jane Errington, *The Lion, The Eagle, and Upper Canada: A Developing Colonial Ideology* (Montreal/Kingston: McGill-Queen's University Press, 1987). The conflict over the choice of a capital is recounted in all its intricacies in David B. Knight, *Choosing Canada's Capital: Conflict Resolution in a Parliamentary System*, 2nd ed. (Ottawa: Carleton University Press, 1991). Carolyn Young reviews the history of Canada's Parliament buildings, with particular emphasis on the design competition of 1859, in *The Glory of Ottawa: Canada's First Parliament Buildings* (Montreal/Kingston: McGill-Queen's University Press, 1995). On corruption see George A. Davison, "The Hincks–Brown Rivalry and the Politics of Scandal," *Ontario History* 81 (1989): 129–52. Michael J. Piva looks at finances in *The Borrowing Process: Public Finance in the Province of Canada, 1840–1867* (Ottawa: University of Ottawa Press, 1992). Peter Way, "The Canadian Tory Rebellion of 1849 and the Demise of Street Politics in Toronto," *British Journal of Canadian Studies* 10 (1995): 10–30, studies violence in politics in Upper Canada in the late 1840s.

British policy toward Canada is discussed in William Ormsby, *The Emergence of the Federal Concept in Canada, 1839–1845* (Toronto: University of Toronto Press, 1969); Peter Burroughs, *British Attitudes towards Canada 1822–1845* (Scarborough, ON: Prentice-Hall, 1971); Phillip Buckner, *The Transition to Responsible Government: British Policy in British North America, 1815–1850* (Westport, CT: Greenwood Press, 1985); and Ged Martin, "Britain and the Future of British North America, 1841–1850," *British Journal of Canadian Studies* 2 (June 1987): 74–96; and the same author's provocative *Britain and the Origins of Canadian Confederation, 1837–67* (Vancouver: University of British Columbia Press, 1995). On French Canada in particular, see Jacques Monet's *The Last Cannon Shot: A Study of French Canadian Nationalism, 1837–1850* (Toronto: University of Toronto Press, 1969). Biographies of the public figures of this age — including LaFontaine, Baldwin, Hincks, Cartier, and Morin — appear in various volumes of the *Dictionary of Canadian Biography*. It is now available online: www.bibliographi.ca. An inside look at the third generation of the Family Compact is provided by John Lownsbrough in *The Privileged Few: The Grange and Its People in Nineteenth Century Toronto* (Toronto: Art Gallery of Ontario, 1980).

For Native policy during the Union period see John S. Milloy, "The Early Indian Acts: Developmental Strategy and Constitutional Change," in Ian A.L. Getty and Antoine S. Lussier, eds., *As Long as the Sun Shines and Water Flows: A Reader in Canadian Native Studies* (Vancouver: University of British Columbia Press, 1983), pp. 56–64; J.E. Hodgett's chapter, "Indian Affairs: The White Man's Albatross," in his *Pioneer Public Service: An Administrative History of the United Canadas, 1841–1867* (Toronto: University of Toronto

Press, 1955), pp. 205–25; and John F. Leslie, "Buried Hatchet: The Origins of Indian Reserves in 19th Century Ontario," *Horizon Canada* 40 (1985): 944–49. Tony Hall also reviews developments in Canada West in "Native Limited Identities and Newcomer Metropolitanism in Upper Canada, 1814–1867," in David Keane and Colin Read, eds., *Old Ontario: Essays in Honour of J.M.S. Careless* (Toronto: Dundurn Press, 1990), pp. 148–73. Legal issues are examined in Sidney L. Harring's *White Man's Law: Native People in Nineteenth-Century Canadian Jurisprudence* (Toronto: University of Toronto Press, 1998). For overviews of the Native peoples in the two Canadas at this time see also Daniel Francis, *A History of the Native Peoples of Quebec, 1760–1867* (Ottawa: Department of Indian Affairs and Northern Development, 1983); and Edward S. Rogers and Donald B. Smith, eds., *Aboriginal Ontario: Historical Perspectives on the First Nations* (Toronto: Dundurn Press, 1994). Biographical treatments include: Donald B. Smith, *Sacred Feathers: The Reverend Peter Jones (Kahkewaquonaby) and the Mississauga Indians* (Toronto: University of Toronto Press, 1987); and Janet F. Chute, *The Legacy of Shingwaukonse: A Century of Native Leadership* (Toronto: University of Toronto Press, 1998). On Nahnee, the subject of this chapter's Historical Portrait, see John Steckley, "Nahnebahwequay ('Standing Woman') or Catherine Sutton," in his *Beyond Their Years: Five Native Women's Stories* (Toronto: Canadian Scholars' Press, 1999), pp. 140–93; and Celia Haig-Brown, "Seeking Honest Justice in a Land of Strangers: Nahnebahwequay's Struggle for Land," *Journal of Canadian Studies* 36, 4 (2001–2002): 143–70.

Useful bibliographical guides to the historical literature on the Canadas include the essays by James H. Lambert, "Quebec/Lower Canada"; Bryan D. Palmer, "Upper Canada"; and J.M. Bumsted, "British North America in Its Imperial and International Context," in M. Brook Taylor, ed., *Canadian History: A Reader's Guide*, vol. 1, *Beginnings to Confederation* (Toronto: University of Toronto Press, 1994), pp. 112–236, 394–447.

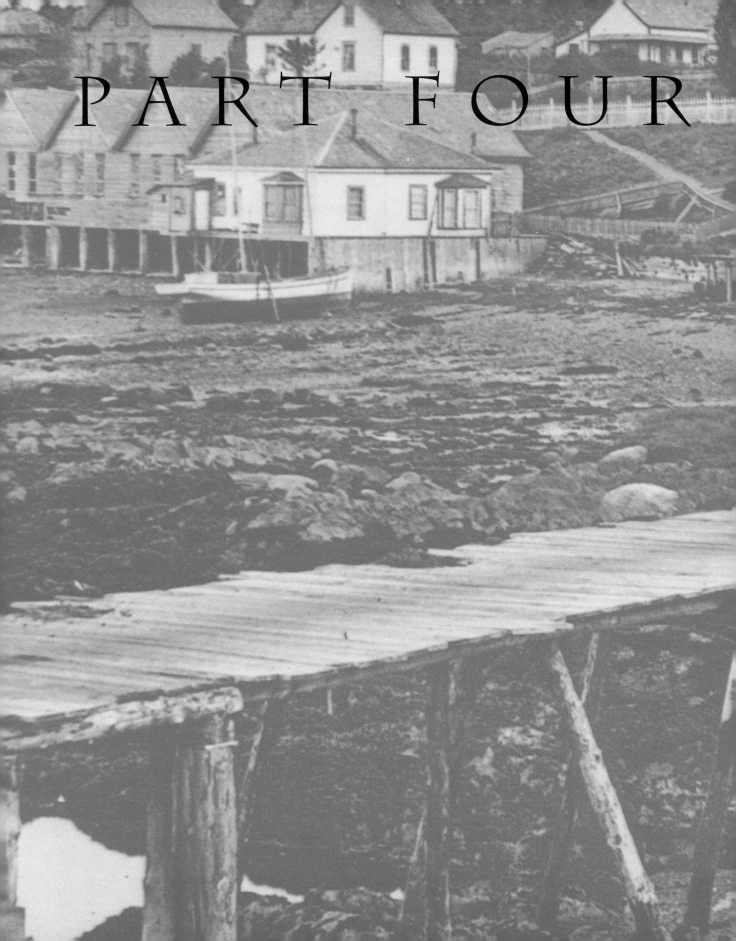

PART FOUR

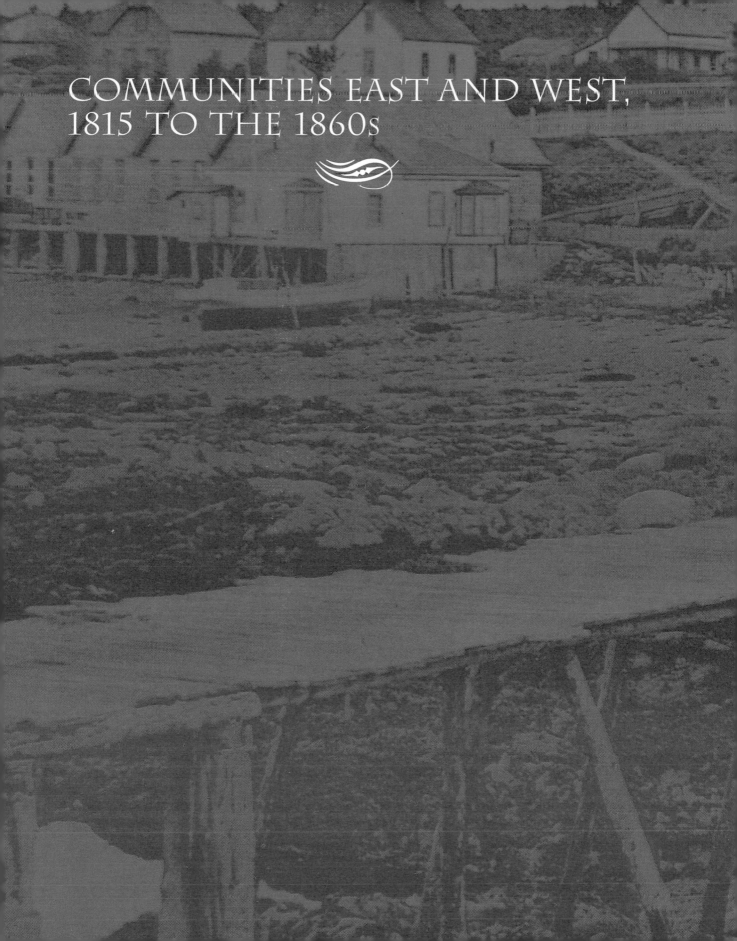

COMMUNITIES EAST AND WEST, 1815 TO THE 1860s

INTRODUCTION

Between 1815 and 1867, distinct British American colonial communities emerged in northeastern North America. In New Brunswick—predominantly Acadian on the north shore and English-speaking in the Saint John River valley—the economy was based on agriculture and lumbering. In Nova Scotia, seaport communities grew along the Bay of Fundy and the Atlantic seaboard. Fishing, shipbuilding, and agriculture in the Annapolis Valley, were the main occupations. Independent communities also developed on Cape Breton Island (which was joined to Nova Scotia in 1820) and Prince Edward Island. The Maritime colonies and Newfoundland pursued an active trade with Britain, the United States, and the West Indies.

In these Maritime colonies, as in the Canadas, conflict erupted between the ruling political elite and the elected members of the Assembly, although it never reached the point of rebellion. But, by the 1850s, each of the Maritime colonies had achieved a form of responsible government.

Newfoundland remained separate and distinct from the other Atlantic colonies. The island's economy was heavily dependent on the cod fisheries of the Grand Banks and on active trade with Britain and the West Indies. The political system evolved slowly in Newfoundland. As late as 1830, no legislature existed and the naval governor had near-dictatorial powers. In 1832, Britain instituted representative government, with an elected Assembly and an appointed Legislative Council, but then suspended it in 1842, due to political deadlock. Representative government was reinstated in 1848 and responsible government implemented in 1855, thus ending direct British rule.

In the Northwest, a community known as the Red River colony emerged at the confluence of the Red and Assiniboine Rivers. It consisted of French Métis (children of French fur traders and First Nations women), the "Country-born" (offspring of British fur traders and First Nations women), and a small number of descendants of the Selkirk settlers who arrived from Britain in the early nineteenth century. The colony's economy was based on a mixture of trade in buffalo hides and small-scale agriculture. Tensions arose within the community in the 1810s when the two rival fur-trading companies, the Hudson's Bay Company and the North West Company, vied for dominance. In 1821, the British government forced them to amalgamate, as the Hudson's Bay Company. The Company attempted to enforce a monopoly of the fur trade, but in the 1840s the Métis resisted, thus strengthening their own identity as a "new nation."

On the north Pacific coast, Britain and the United States competed for control of the area known as Oregon Territory, until they agreed to occupy it jointly. In 1846, the two countries further agreed to extend the boundary from the Rockies along the 49th parallel to the coast, with Britain acquiring all of Vancouver Island.

With the discovery of gold in the Fraser River valley in 1858, Britain created a separate colony on the mainland. In 1866, the mainland colony and Vancouver Island were united into the joint colony of British Columbia, with Victoria as the capital. By the late 1860s, British Columbians had to choose among three future options: remaining a British colony, joining the United States, or becoming part of Canada.

To the north, the land remained in Aboriginal control, visited only by a small number of fur traders and, in the Arctic waters in the mid-1840s and 1850s, by explorers searching for the Northwest Passage.

CHAPTER 16

THE MARITIME COLONIES, 1815–1864

TIME LINE

1818 – Under the Convention of 1818, the Americans lose the privilege of landing and drying their fish in the three Maritime colonies

1820 – Cape Breton and Nova Scotia become one colony

1836 – Thomas Chandler Haliburton's first series of sketches, *The Clockmaker; or, The Sayings and Doings of Sam Slick of Slickville*, is published

1840s – Britain ends its special protection of the timber trade

1842 – The Webster–Ashburton Treaty establishes the present-day New Brunswick–Maine border

1848 – Responsible government is achieved in Nova Scotia, and later in Prince Edward Island (1851) and New Brunswick (1854)

1852 – New Brunswick's famous sailing vessel, the *Marco Polo*, earns the title of the "world's fastest ship"

1854 – The Reciprocity Treaty with the United States is signed

1857 – Nova Scotia allows legal divorce on the grounds of cruelty, such as wife battering

1864 – The governments of New Brunswick, Nova Scotia, and Prince Edward Island agree to meet in Charlottetown to discuss Maritime union

After the Loyalists' arrival, Atlantic British North America consisted of four separate colonies: Nova Scotia, New Brunswick, Prince Edward Island, and Cape Breton. The population lived widely scattered in isolated coastline communities and forested valleys, with only a few larger centres, such as Saint John, Halifax, and Fredericton. Economically, the Maritime provinces depended on fishing and farming, but the full development of the land-based resources began only in the early nineteenth century. While Nova Scotia (to which Cape Breton was reattached in 1820) kept largely to fishing and trade, New Brunswick started to cut its extensive pine forests. On Prince Edward Island, agriculture became the mainstay of the colonial economy. By the mid-nineteenth century, coal mining near Pictou, Nova Scotia, and on Cape Breton Island had also grown in importance. On the eve of Confederation, Nova Scotia, New Brunswick, and Prince Edward Island had healthy economies based on agriculture, fish, forest products, and trade with the West Indies.

The half-century following the Napoleonic Wars also witnessed major political developments. By the 1850s, Nova Scotia, New Brunswick, and Prince Edward Island had achieved responsible government; with the Executive Council (Cabinet) in each colony drawn from the majority party in the Assembly, and responsible to it. Power now passed to the elective branch of government.

ECONOMIC DEVELOPMENTS, 1815–1850

The peace treaty of 1783 granted American citizens fishing privileges in the in-shore waters of the British North American colonies. However, during the negotiations of the Treaty of Ghent, which ended the War of 1812, the British argued that the Americans had abrogated this right by declaring war. Under the Convention of 1818, the Americans lost the privilege of landing and drying their fish in the three Maritime colonies; they retained the right to do so only on unsettled shores in Newfoundland. American vessels continued to enter Maritime harbours to obtain water, purchase wood, or repair damages, but not until the signing of the Reciprocity Treaty in 1854 did Americans regain access to the in-shore fisheries.

After the War of 1812, Maritimers improved their trade ties with the West Indies. Nova Scotia and New Brunswick argued that the privilege of trading with the British West Indies should belong only to loyal British colonies. Initially Britain agreed, and passed several measures favouring the shipping of goods between Saint John and Halifax and the West Indies, but it backed down in the face of subsequent American retaliatory measures. The British West Indies also complained about the higher cost of shipping American imports by the roundabout Maritime route. Finally, in 1830, Britain removed the restrictions on American trade to the islands but left duties on certain essential commodities. This arrangement allowed Nova Scotia and New Brunswick to import American produce duty free and then re-export it to the West Indies as their own. Colonial ships thus maintained much of their share of the trade.

AGRICULTURE

Improved trade relations with the West Indies strengthened the Maritime economy, but agriculture remained weak. While farming flourished on Prince Edward Island, in Nova Scotia's Annapolis valley, and in New Brunswick's Saint John River valley, it did not fare as well in other areas. Nova Scotia and New Brunswick as a whole continued to depend on American foodstuffs to feed their populations well into the nineteenth century. Commercial farming remained very limited, with only Prince Edward Island, the "Garden of the Gulf," exporting large amounts of farm produce. In the case of Nova Scotia and New Brunswick, the lack of good roads, a scattered population, and the absence of protection against American imports accounted for the limited

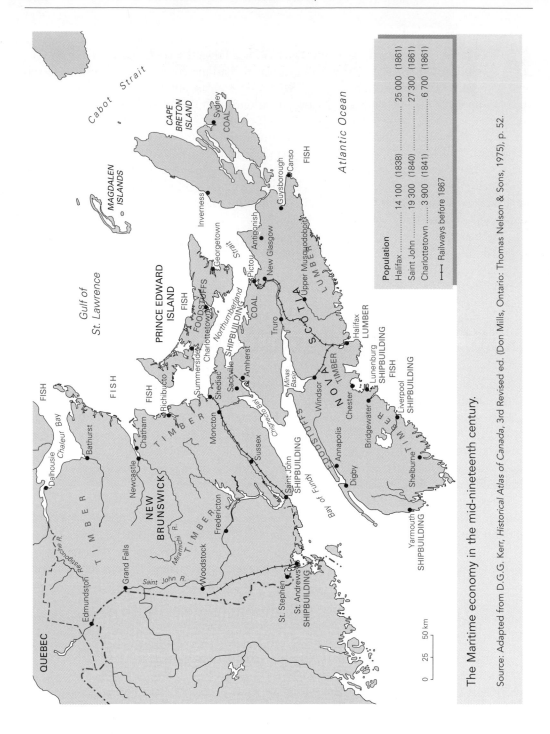

The Maritime economy in the mid-nineteenth century.

Source: Adapted from D.G.G. Kerr, *Historical Atlas of Canada*, 3rd Revised ed. (Don Mills, Ontario: Thomas Nelson & Sons, 1975), p. 52.

Population		
Halifax	14 100 (1838)	25 000 (1861)
Saint John	19 300 (1840)	27 300 (1861)
Charlottetown	3 900 (1841)	6 700 (1861)
Railways before 1867		

agricultural exports. Nevertheless farming, more than either logging or fishing, remained the livelihood of a majority of Maritimers. Even a large number of those employed in logging and fishing worked on a part-time basis in agriculture to support their families.

An increase in immigration after 1815 added to the size of the local market and encouraged greater agricultural production. New Brunswick had roughly 75 000 inhabitants in 1824 and almost 200 000 by 1851. During the same period, Nova Scotia's population rose from

The Axe Falls, painted in 1900 by Robert J. Wickenden (1861–1931).

Musée du Québec/63 38 P.

approximately 100 000 to 275 000. Prince Edward Island's population increased from 23 000 in 1827 to 72 000 in 1855, making it the most densely inhabited colony in British North America, due to its small size.

THE TIMBER INDUSTRY

Forestry became the leading growth industry in the Maritimes after the War of 1812. Local entrepreneurs, many of them farmers and small merchants, began operations in settled or semi-settled areas of the Maritimes. Early on, timber trade also brought into the colonies a new group of British traders and contractors interested in quick profits. Timber companies simply went on Crown land and cut trees, even though the forests belonged to the government. From the 1820s onward, however, the New Brunswick government asserted itself against the timber barons by insisting on timber licences and taxing output.

Forest revenues became vital to New Brunswick's economy. As early as 1826, three-quarters of the province's export revenues came from wood products — square timber, lumber, and ships. By mid-century, one New Brunswick resident noted that the timber trade "has brought foreign produce and foreign capital into the province, and has been the chief source of the money by which its roads, bridges and public buildings have been completed; its rivers and harbours made accessible; its natural resources discovered and made available; its provincial institutions kept up and its functionaries paid."

In the 1840s, New Brunswick survived the gradual reduction of the British preference on colonial timber. British and American demand remained high. By 1865, forest products made up two-thirds of New Brunswick's total exports by value, compared with about 10 percent of Nova Scotia's and Prince Edward Island's exports.

Where Historians Disagree

The Timber Industry in Early New Brunswick: An Environmental Perspective

Environmental history is a relatively new field in Canadian history. In 1989, historian Ramsay Cook lamented the lack of historical interest in the impact of settlement and industry on the natural environment: "Even the no longer so new social history has largely ignored the environment in the rush for class, gender and ethnicity."[1]

In regard to the forests of New Brunswick, however, environmental concerns have long been raised. As early as 1825, for instance, Peter Fisher raised the alarm in his *Sketches of New Brunswick*, the first historical study published in the province:

The persons principally engaged in shipping the timber have been strangers who have taken no interest in the welfare of the country; but have merely occupied a spot to make what they could in the shortest possible time.... Instead of seeing towns built, farms improved and the country cleared and stocked with the reasonable returns of so great a trade, the forests are stripped and nothing left in prospect, but the gloomy apprehension when the timber is gone, of sinking into insignificance and poverty.[2]

A century later, Arthur R.M. Lower developed this same theme of senseless pillage in three books on Canada's forest industries: *Settlement and the Forest Frontier in Eastern Canada* (1936), *The North American Assault on the Canadian Forest* (1938), and *Great Britain's Woodyard: British America and the Timber Trade* (1973). He concluded his last book with this statement: "The Canadian forests contributed to the prosperity of the British timber importer and the enrichment of the American lumberman.... [But] it must be concluded that the new colonies got the minimum out of the wreck of their forests."[3]

In *Northern Enterprise*, a study of five centuries of Canadian business, Michael Bliss took issue with Arthur Lower:

The old idea that the rape of the forests was simply a using up of natural wealth with no compensating benefits is a romantic mockery of the realities and difficulties of colonial development. When A.R.M. Lower wove that theme into his writing about Canadian forest industries, with particular reference to New Brunswick, he was parroting some of the industry's least-informed critics.

Instead Bliss endorsed and cited a New Brunswick contemporary of Peter Fisher, who stated that the timber trade "has brought foreign produce and foreign capital into the Province, and has been the chief source of the money by means of which the country has been opened up and improved; by which its roads, bridges and public buildings have been completed; its rivers and harbours made accessible; its natural resources discovered and made available; its Provincial institutions kept up and its functionaries paid."[4]

Graeme Wynn, who studied the question in depth twenty years ago, takes a middle-of-the-road position. The historical geographer underlines that an export staple was needed to give New Brunswick its economic lift-off. That staple was timber. From 1805 to 1850 the heavy exploitation of the colony's forests transformed the colony from "an undeveloped backwater of 25 000 people to a bustling colony of 190 000." At the same time, Wynn notes the waste and destruction. For example, he commented about early-nineteenth-century sawmilling: "Sawdust dumped into the rivers soon became sodden, sank to the bed of the stream, disturbed the river ecology, and obstructed navigation. In suspension it floated downstream, was deposited on banks and intervales, and drastically reduced fish populations." The debris of bark, slabs, edgings, mill rubbish, and sunken logs was also carried over entire river systems, he noted.

In the end Wynn withholds judgement, claiming the need for further research before definitive statements could be made. With regard to Lower's books, he sees them as "reconnaissance surveys rather than final charts … early interpretations need to be re-examined as more information becomes available."[5]

William Cronon's *Changes in the Land: Colonists and the Ecology of New England*[6]

might be a good model for a follow-up study, as it combines a thorough documentary search with in-depth biological knowledge. A good start in such a direction was made for New Brunswick in 1972 by Gilbert Allardyce, who studied Alma Parish of Albert County in the nineteenth century.[7] At the beginning of the nineteenth century the parish's forests and fishlife appeared inexhaustible. By 1850, however, sawmill dams blockaded the rivers and prevented the passage of salmon toward their headwater spawning grounds all along the Fundy coast. Still, lumbering aggressively increased, which meant more sawdust. Timber killed fishing. When the lumber became exhausted in the early twentieth century, Alma Parish was left with nothing to support settlement, as it had little fertile land for farming. Alma Parish today forms Fundy National Park. In any assessment of the impact of the nineteenth-century timber industry on New Brunswick, both the long-term and short-term consequences need to be considered.

---

[1] Ramsay Cook, "Review of *The Natural History of Canada*," *Canadian Historical Review*, 60 (1989): 386.

[2] Peter Fisher, *Sketches of New Brunswick* (Saint John: Chubb and Sears, 1825), p. 72; reprinted in Arthur R.M. Lower, *Great Britain's Woodyard: British America and the Timber Trade, 1763–1867* (Montreal/Kingston: McGill-Queen's University Press, 1973), p.33.

[3] Lower, *Great Britain's Woodyard*, p. 250.

[4] Michael Bliss, *Northern Enterprise*, (Toronto: McClelland & Stewart, 1987), p. 136.

[5] Graeme Wynn, *Timber Colony: A Historical Geography of Early Nineteenth Century New Brunswick* (Toronto: University of Toronto Press, 1981), pp. 24, 33, 93, and 174.

[6] William Cronon, *Changes in the Land: Indians, Colonists and the Ecology of New England* (New York: Hill and Wang, 1983).

[7] Gilbert Allardyce, "'The Vexed Question of Sawdust': River Pollution in Nineteenth Century New Brunswick," *Dalhousie Review*, 52, 2 (Summer 1972): 177–90.

SHIPBUILDING

 Shipbuilding became a major sideline of the timber industry. Square timber, a bulky commodity, had to be shipped in relatively large vessels, and as Britain could not meet the need for such ships in wartime, so the Maritime shipbuilding industry expanded, making it the first major manufacturing industry in the Maritime region. The Maritimes soon supplied many of the new wooden ships used to ferry timber to Britain.

From the 1820s onward, the Nova Scotia and New Brunswick fleets grew steadily. Maritime timber merchants found they could keep transportation costs low if they owned their own vessels. When prices for vessels rose, they made additional profits by selling the vessel as well as its timber cargo. Other Maritime entrepreneurs saw money to be made in owning ships involved in lucrative coastal trading, particularly in the West Indian trade. By the mid-nineteenth century, Maritime ships carried cotton from New Orleans, rice from India, and molasses from Cuba, as well as timber. From the 1850s to 1870s, the Maritimes and Newfoundland accounted for over two-thirds of the tonnage registered in British North America, which claimed to have the fourth largest merchant marine in the world, after Britain, the United States, and Norway.

The Maritimes gained a reputation as one of the leading centres of the North American shipping industry. In 1851, the James Smith shipyard at Saint John, New Brunswick, launched the *Marco Polo*, which became the colony's most famous ship. The ship had a unique design. It had the underwater body of a clipper and the midship of a cargo carrier. Blest with incredible speed, it cut a week off the previous record for the round trip from Liverpool, England, to Melbourne, Australia, completing that trip in less than six months and earning the title of "the world's fastest ship."

Generally, however, Maritime shipbuilders built broad-beamed vessels designed to maximize carrying capacity, not speed. They increased sail capacity and improved ships' hulls. They extended the average life of Nova Scotia and New Brunswick vessels from a mere 9 years in the 1820s to 15 years by the end of the century. These shipbuilders also constructed their vessels cheaply. An iron steamer in Britain cost four or five times as much in the 1860s as did a wooden vessel from the Maritimes. The popularity of steamers, however, grew rapidly because of their speed and reliability, leaving only a tiny market for wooden ships by the end of the century.

In New Brunswick the major shipowners included many timber exporters, whereas in Nova Scotia the majority were fish exporters, West Indies traders, and import–export merchants. Samuel Cunard, the most famous of the Nova Scotia shipowners, had interests in the West Indies trade, a tea business, a bank, and the sale of imported goods. In 1840, he initiated the first regular steamship service across the Atlantic. Cunard became one of the first Nova Scotians to build a business empire, but he operated his interests from London.

Lumbering and shipbuilding went together. Dorchester, New Brunswick, pictured here in 1875, was one of a hundred shipbuilding villages on the Maritime coast.

National Archives of Canada/C-10103

A number of the shipowners in the 1850s entered new businesses. Thomas Killam of Yarmouth, like his contemporary Samuel Cunard, expanded his business enterprises dramatically. By the time of his death in 1868, his operations included a ship-outfitting business, a marine-insurance company, a telegraph company, a gas-lighting company, and a bank. Enos Collins of Halifax also diversified his shipping interests after the War of 1812. When he died in 1871 at the age of 97, he left behind an estate worth $6 million.

Thousands of men and hundreds of women worked in the Maritime shipyards and in shops making materials for the ships. The sailors were most often in their twenties or early thirties. For most, seafaring was a short-term activity — a means of supplementing the family income, or a job when work was scarce on the mainland. It was a demanding job with long hours, poor pay, and harsh masters. No unions existed on board ship, where the jobs were arduous and often unsafe. On any given voyage, a sailor faced odds of one in 100 of dying.[1] Desertion was one means of protection, and one-quarter of the crew usually deserted during a voyage. Until the sailing industry declined in the late 1870s, the numerous sailors in the ports of eastern Canada lived in what were called "sailortowns."

The *Marco Polo*, New Brunswick's most famous sailing vessel, earned the title "the world's fastest ship" after making the round trip from England to Australia in less than six months in 1852.

New Brunswick Museum, Saint John, N.B./14462.

BANKING

The financial needs of the merchants involved in the timber industry and shipbuilding led to the rise of banks. In Britain, commercial banks developed in the eighteenth century, and in the 1790s scores of them opened in the United States. The Halifax Banking Company, the first bank in Nova Scotia, began trading in money in 1825. A group of merchants founded the Bank of Nova Scotia in 1832, and by 1840 it had branches in Windsor, Annapolis Royal, Pictou, Yarmouth, and Liverpool. New Brunswick's first bank, the Bank of New Brunswick, was chartered in Saint John in 1820; the second, the Commercial Bank, in 1834. Prince Edward Island's first bank opened in the mid-1850s. The banks dealt in foreign-exchange transactions, made loans, and circulated bank notes, on the understanding that the paper notes could always be redeemed, on demand, in real coinage. Depending on the risk the bankers were prepared to take, the banks could generally keep two or three times as many notes in circulation as they had gold or silver coins to redeem them. (The issuing of notes in place of coins allowed the banks to double or triple the amount of interest they collected.)

SAINT JOHN AND HALIFAX

Strong rivalries existed between the two major regional centres in the Maritimes: Saint John and Halifax. Initially Saint John held the advantage, since it was the largest city, controlled the timber trade of the Saint John River valley, had an important shipbuilding industry, and was the natural market for the farmers and fishers on both sides of the Bay of Fundy. Nearly half of the industrial output of New Brunswick was produced in and around Saint John. By the mid-nineteenth century, Saint John had emerged as the Maritimes' major industrial centre, with foundry, clothing, and foot-ware industries. Together they surpassed shipbuilding in value by the 1860s. But the great merchants of Saint John delayed investing in manufacturing iron and steel. Such financial conservatism held back the development of a viable industrial base in New Brunswick by two decades.

Halifax, the military headquarters for the region, had a large, secure, ice-free harbour, very close to major North Atlantic shipping lanes. It also benefited from the Caribbean trade and from its role as Nova Scotia's banking, judicial, and intellectual centre. In terms of industrial

Saint John, New Brunswick, around 1830.

Toronto Reference Library/T14459.

base, it developed a specialization in food-processing industries, such as sugar-refining, brewing, and distilling. But it lacked a readily accessible hinterland. Also, unlike Montreal and Saint John, it lacked a major waterway comparable to the St. Lawrence or the Saint John River. Halifax did succeed in bringing Prince Edward Island, Cape Breton Island, and the Miramichi country of eastern New Brunswick into its commercial orbit, but it lost the important Bay of Fundy region to Saint John.

Urban poverty, particularly in the winter months, constituted a real problem. In both Saint John and Halifax, charitable organizations, staffed by volunteer women and run by churches and ethnic organizations, existed to assist penniless immigrants as well as the urban poor. But they had limited resources. The seasonal nature of North Atlantic shipping meant that labourers, mill hands, sailors, carpenters, and other building-trades workers lost their jobs in the autumn. Only in the 1860s did the colonial governments make a modest entry into the charitable field by establishing orphanages.

THE MARITIMES AND THE UNITED STATES

Issues of borders and trade dominated Maritime–American relations in the mid-nineteenth century. When Britain adopted free trade in the 1840s, many Maritimers looked to continental reciprocity — the free admission into British North America and the United States of each other's natural resources — as a viable alternative. New Brunswick saw reciprocity as the key to gaining entry for its timber into the American market of 23 million people.

THE NEW BRUNSWICK–MAINE BORDER

There could be no hope of reciprocity, however, until a border controversy between New Brunswick and Maine was settled. The Treaty of Paris in 1783 had set the boundary to run north from the St. Croix River to an undetermined height of land. In 1839, New Brunswick and Maine lumber workers almost caused a border war over which group had the right to cut at the head-waters of the Aroostook River, part of the disputed territory. Three years later Daniel Webster, the American secretary of state, and Lord Ashburton, the British envoy, resolved the controversy. The Webster–Ashburton Treaty of 1842 established the present-day New Brunswick–Maine boundary. The treaty left Maine a wedge of land projecting between New Brunswick and the Canadas, yet it kept intact the vital communication route between Quebec and Fredericton via Lake Témiscouata. Reciprocity proposals also met with a favourable response in Nova Scotia with its fish for export, and Prince Edward Island with its farm produce. The Americans, for their part, wanted access to the Maritime in-shore fisheries from which they had been excluded in 1818. The inclusion of the fisheries led the United States to sign a reciprocity agreement with the British North American colonies in 1854.

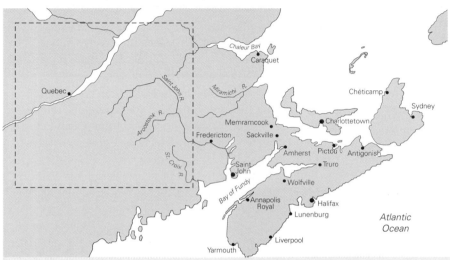

The Maritimes in the mid-nineteenth century. A detail of this map appears below.

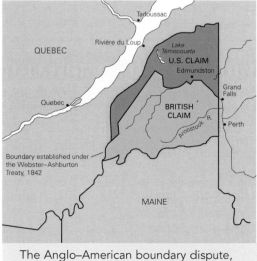

The Anglo–American boundary dispute, settled by the Webster–Ashburton Treaty in 1842.

THE RECIPROCITY TREATY (1854–1866)

 The treaty led to the desired increased trade with the United States. The Maritime colonies now bought one-quarter to one-half of their total imports from the Americans. In return, New Brunswick shipped to the United States increased amounts of lumber; Prince Edward Island shipped more foodstuffs; and Nova Scotia shipped a slightly greater amount of fish. Certainly, the twelve years of the reciprocity treaty proved prosperous, but not solely on account of the treaty. The high demand generated by the American Civil War (1861–65) led to high prices for the Maritimes' fish, timber, and foodstuffs. The carrying trade also benefited.

RAILWAYS

As historian T.W. Acheson has noted in regards to the Maritimes: "The railway was the new technological god that spelled progress and improvement to mid-nineteenth century minds."[2] The leading Maritime cities sought to build railways inland to expand their economic hinterlands. Between 1853 and 1866, New Brunswick built 350 km of railways and Nova Scotia constructed 235 km. Maritime promoters envisaged one day linking the ice-free Maritime ports with the St. Lawrence valley and with the grain-producing American Midwest. Merchants in Halifax and Saint John had visions of their respective cities serving as the focal point from which European commerce could be channelled into the continent and from which American and Canadian exports could be sent abroad.

Yet railways proved expensive both to build and to operate. A single kilometre of track could cost as much as a sizable sailing vessel. Moreover, operating costs were much higher by rail than by sea. To make money, the railway company owners needed both densely populated areas to provide local revenue and the shortest possible direct routes; neither Halifax nor even Saint John had such hinterlands. The larger communities in the interior were too distant, in contrast with those neighbouring Boston, New York, or Montreal, and the land routes passed through long stretches of thinly populated territory.

THE POPULATION OF THE MARITIMES

 In the nineteenth century, thousands of Scottish and Irish immigrants crossed the North Atlantic to British North America to escape overcrowding, famine, and poverty. They joined the already-established resident Maritimers: the Acadians, African Maritimers, First Nations people, and the descendants of the Planters and the white Loyalists, as well as recent English immigrants.

THE ENGLISH AND WELSH

The English of largely Loyalist descent dominated in the Saint John River valley and southeast New Brunswick. The descendants of the Loyalists and the Planters remained numerous in Nova Scotia. Nevertheless, a number of the recent English settlers were public officials and merchants, who obtained good positions in the commercial and political sectors. In the census of 1871, nearly 30 percent of Nova Scotians and New Brunswickers gave their national origin as English or Welsh.

THE ACADIANS

Before the arrival of large numbers of Scots, Irish, and African Americans, many Acadians, who had been deported in 1755, returned from exile. In New Brunswick in the mid-nineteenth century, they made up about 15 percent of the population, and less than 10 percent in Nova Scotia

THE GROWTH OF POPULATION IN THE ATLANTIC REGION, 1806–61

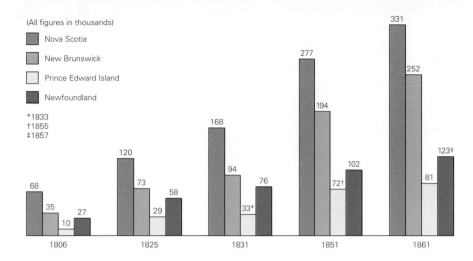

(All figures in thousands)

- Nova Scotia
- New Brunswick
- Prince Edward Island
- Newfoundland

*1833
†1855
‡1857

Source: D.G.G. Kerr, ed., *A Historical Atlas of Canada* (Toronto: Thomas Nelson, 1961), p. 53.

and Prince Edward Island. The Acadians clung tenaciously to the Roman Catholic church as the one institution that took an interest in their well-being. The church established elementary schools and, in 1864, the French-language Collège Saint-Joseph at Memramcook, New Brunswick. The college (which a century later became the nucleus of today's Université de Moncton) furnished the Acadian population with an educated professional elite from which the community drew many of its future political leaders and its sense of Acadian identity.

In the mid-nineteenth century, Acadians felt a new pride in their past. Inspired by Henry Wadsworth Longfellow's poem *Evangeline*, an account of an Acadian woman and her lover separated during the deportation of 1755, many believed that they were a distinct people. The Acadian community in northeastern New Brunswick incorporated, through intermarriage, many Irish, Scots, and English. Their modern-day descendants have British names like McGraw, Finn, McLaughlin, Ferguson, and Kerry, but their mother tongue is French and they consider themselves Acadian. French-Canadian immigrants from Quebec, who arrived in the late nineteenth century, also assimilated into these Acadian communities. In predominantly English-speaking areas, however — Prince Edward Island, for example — some Acadians were themselves assimilated into the English-speaking community. On Prince Edward Island, some Acadians anglicized their names: Aucoin became Wedge, Poirier became Perry, Bourque became Burke.

THE SCOTS

Even though the journey from Scotland was perilous (on one ship that left in 1827, 20 percent of those aboard died), still the Gaelic-speaking Highlanders came, usually in groups or clans. (In the early nineteenth century, Gaelic was the third most common European language spoken in British North America.)

The promise of 40 ha of free land led thousands of landless Scots to immigrate to Nova Scotia. Between 1815 and 1838 about 40 000 Scots came to the colony, particularly to Cape Breton Island. Although the magnificent hills and seacoast of Cape Breton reminded them of

NATIONAL ORIGINS: NOVA SCOTIA (1871), NEW BRUNSWICK (1871), AND PRINCE EDWARD ISLAND (1881)

| | NORTH AMERICAN INDIAN | | ENGLISH AND WELSH | | SCOTS | | IRISH | | FRENCH | |
	NUMBER	%	NUMBER	%	NUMBER	%	NUMBER	%	NUMBER	%
Nova Scotia	1 666	0.4	113 520	29.2	130 741	33.7	62 851	16.4	32 833	8.5
New Brunswick	1 403	0.5	83 598	29.2	40 858	14.3	100 643	35.3	44 907	15.7
P.E.I.	281	0.3	21 568	19.8	48 933	44.8	25 415	23.3	10 751	9.9

| | GERMAN | | DUTCH | | AFRICAN | | SWISS | | TOTAL POPULATION |
	NUMBER	%	NUMBER	%	NUMBER	%	NUMBER	%	
Nova Scotia	31 942	8.2	2 868	0.7	6 212	1.6	1 775	0.5	387 800
New Brunswick	4 478	1.6	6 004	2.1	1 701	0.6	64	—	285 594
P.E.I.	1 076	1.0	292	0.3					108 891

Source: R. Cole Harris and John Warkentin, *Canada Before Confederation: A Study in Historical Geography* (Ottawa: Carleton University Press, 1991 [1974]), pp. 184–85. Data from Census of Canada.

home, the Scots were ill prepared for clearing virgin forest and had many difficulties in establishing their farms. Some left, and some became fishers and boat builders in coastal settlements. Many moved to Prince Edward Island. Nearly half of Prince Edward Island's population (44.8 percent) stated their national origin as Scottish in the Canadian census of 1881. In the census of 1871, one out of three did so in Nova Scotia, and one out of seven in New Brunswick. Generally speaking, the Highlanders belonged to the Catholic church, and the Lowlanders to the Presbyterian.

THE IRISH

Scottish immigrants outnumbered Irish in Nova Scotia and Prince Edward Island, but the reverse was true in New Brunswick. No British American province was more Irish than New Brunswick in the nineteenth century. Between 1815 and 1865, 60 percent of the immigrants to New Brunswick came from Ireland; the newcomers were equally divided in number between Protestant and Catholic. By Confederation the Irish constituted one-third of New Brunswick's population.

Ireland's depressed economy and its overpopulation forced many to emigrate. The potato blight of the 1840s drove out nearly 2 million people. Of the tens of thousands of Irish who boarded timber ships headed for British North America, thousands died en route from cholera and typhoid. Nonetheless 8000 arrived in New Brunswick in 1842, 9000 in 1846, and 17 000 in 1847. Only in 1848 did the numbers fall below 4000.

Although many Irish used New Brunswick as a stepping stone to the United States, a large number stayed. The poverty-stricken congregated in the ports and lumber camps of eastern New Brunswick. The main areas of Irish settlement in New Brunswick before 1850 were the upper Saint John River valley, the Bay of Fundy, and the south shore of Chaleur Bay. Although the Loyalists and their descendants, together with a number of recent English immigrants, controlled the colony's political life, in many communities the Irish outnumbered them.

AFRICAN MARITIMERS

During the War of 1812, Britain received runaway slaves as free citizens. Near the end of the war, some 3000 to 4000 African Americans escaped from Chesapeake plantations during the British raids on Washington and Baltimore. Many of these individuals sought freedom in British North America. Unfortunately, they arrived at a time when abundant, cheap white labour made it very difficult for them to find work. They also faced discrimination and prejudice, especially in Nova Scotia, which had the largest black population (1.6 percent of the total population, according to the Canadian census of 1871), and, to a lesser extent, in New Brunswick (where they formed 0.6 percent of the population). Historian W.A. Spray noted how poorly the 400 refugees were treated in New Brunswick in comparison with the white settlers: "The policy in New Brunswick at this time was to give free grants of at least 100 acres to white settlers.... Yet the black refugees were to get only 50 acres, they were to pay for the surveys, and they were to receive licences of occupation for three years."[3] Furthermore, African Maritimers had no security of possession, since the government could simply refuse to reissue licences after the three-year term expired.

Although people of African descent faced limited economic opportunities and discriminatory treatment, adversity did not extinguish pride, as the story of an African-Martimer family outside Dartmouth indicates. When three armed white trespassers tried in 1818 to force them off their land, the family drove them off, commenting: "We are not in the [United] States, and we can now do as we like."

THE FIRST NATIONS

The Maritimers with the longest residency had the greatest difficulty in adjusting to changing conditions. Unlike the First Nations in Upper Canada after the Proclamation of 1763, the British did not make land agreements with the Maritime First Nations. The Natives thus demanded compensation for territory lost to the settlers. But the British and the Maritime governments held that the Mi'kmaqs' and the Maliseets' title to the land had already been extinguished — first, by the fact that the French had occupied the area and, second, as a result of the Treaty of Utrecht in 1713, which the British claimed gave them sovereign title to Acadia.

The New Brunswick government set aside reserves for the Mi'kmaqs and the Maliseets, but the lack of proper legal descriptions and surveys of the reserve lands encouraged settlers to encroach into these areas. A similar situation developed in Nova Scotia.

By the 1860s, the approximately 1000 Mi'kmaqs and 500 Maliseets in New Brunswick officially had a land base of about 25 000 ha. In Nova Scotia the Mi'kmaqs, who numbered between 1400 and 1800, had only 8000 ha. But the First Nations who faced perhaps the most difficult conditions were the several hundred Mi'kmaqs on Prince Edward Island. Until 1870, they had only a few campsites as reserve land. In that year, however, an English-based organization, the Aborigines' Protection Society, arranged to buy Lennox Island for them, a small island off Prince Edward Island. By the time of Confederation, the First Nations constituted roughly 0.5 percent of the total population of Nova Scotia, New Brunswick, and Prince Edward Island.

Yet the cultures survived. The First Nations spoke their own languages, passed on their traditions and folklore, and practised their crafts. The women produced porcupine quillwork on birchbark, which they then sold in an international market. Mary Christianne Paul Morris was one of the best-known Mi'kmaq quillworkers. Many Mi'kmaq women were employed as furniture makers, ships' carpenters, and builders of small boats.

Mi'kmaq wigwam, probably near Dartmouth, Nova Scotia, in 1860. In late January 1841, the Colonial Office in London received a desperate letter to Queen Victoria from Paul Peminuit, an 85-year-old Mi'kmaq chief from the Shubenacadie community in Nova Scotia. He presented his urgent message: "My people are in trouble. ... No hunting grounds — No beaver — No otter.... All these woods once ours.... White man has taken all that was ours.... Let us not perish."

National Anthropological Archives/Smithsonian Institution/47728.

POLITICAL CHANGES IN THE MID-NINETEENTH CENTURY

After the American Revolution, the British government imposed upon its remaining British American colonies rigid political structures, controlled from above. The governor, his appointed Executive and Legislative Councils, and the judiciary held the reins of power. In contrast, the popularly elected Assemblies had little authority or influence.

With the dismantling of the mercantile system in the late 1840s, a group within the colonies known as the Reformers pressed for responsible government by opposing the small ruling clique that dominated politics. They wanted the members of the Executive Council (or Cabinet) responsible to the majority party in the Assembly. If the Council lost a confidence vote in the Assembly, or lost support in a general election, its members must resign. Secondly, the governor must accept the recommendations of the Executive Council, dependent as it was, on majority support in the Assembly. This is what they meant by responsible government.

Joseph Howe led the Nova Scotia Reformers. Historian Ian Ross Robertson has described him as "a legendary political hero, a first-rate journalist, and perhaps the most renowned public speaker in the colonies during a century that greatly prized the art of oratory."[4] In 1827, Howe purchased the *Novascotian*, a Halifax newspaper, which he remade into the most influential newspaper in the province. Elected to the Nova Scotia Assembly in 1836, Howe organized the Reform attack against the Council of Twelve, an interrelated Halifax-based merchant oligarchy, which controlled both the appointed Legislative Council (the upper house) and the Executive

Council. The Reformers called for an elected upper house and for the Assembly's control over Crown revenues.

The Assemblies elected in 1836 and 1840 favoured reform. In the election of 1847, the Reformers fought on the issue of responsible government, and finally won a majority. On February 2, 1848, the Colonial Office agreed that henceforth the Executive Council must collectively resign if it lost the Assembly's confidence. Nova Scotia thus became the first British North American colony to obtain responsible government. Howe boasted that the Reformers had achieved it peacefully, without "a blow struck or a pane of glass broken." Yet, he should have acknowledged some help from an outside source. The Canadian Rebellions of 1837–38 had gone a long way in convincing Britain of the wisdom of conceding responsible government in British North America.

In New Brunswick, Charles Fisher and Lemuel Allan Wilmot led the Reformers. They faced a situation similar to that in Nova Scotia. Of all the British North American colonies, this province had always been among the easiest to rule. A relatively homogeneous group of Loyalists and their descendants had controlled the colony until the 1830s. Moreover, since Anglicans initially made up a near majority of the population, the position of the Church of England as the established church caused less resentment among New Brunswick's English-speaking population than it did elsewhere. The New Brunswick Assembly in 1837 had even secured control of the revenues of Crown lands, including timber land revenues, in return for the provision of a civil list guaranteeing the salaries of officers of government. As well, the Colonial Office made the Executive Council in the province responsible to the elected representatives in the Assembly. Nonetheless, the colony lacked responsible government until 1848.

Responsible government opened up more than Executive Council seats to the Assembly; it gave the popularly elected body control over patronage — that is, the opportunity to make appointments to public office. Wilmot was one of the Reformers who took full advantage of the opportunity to benefit himself. C.M. Wallace, his biographer, has noted that "his pursuit of office, first on the Executive Council, then on the bench, and finally as lieutenant governor, might well be classed as rapacious."[5]

REFORM IN PRINCE EDWARD ISLAND

The winning of responsible government became an important issue in Prince Edward Island in the 1840s. Initially, the Colonial Office opposed granting internal self-government to such a small colony, but eventually it yielded. The Reformers on the island, politicians such as George Coles and Edward Whelan, insisted on full equality with the mainland colonies. When they won the general election in 1850, they demanded cabinet government, which the Colonial Office granted in 1851. Immediately, the population hoped that the constitutional change would lead to a settlement of Prince Edward Island's land question. The Colonial Office refused, however, to consider escheat (take back) — the cancelling of the large grants to proprietors — and upheld the rights of private property. The island's Executive and Legislative Councils, both controlled by a small group of the leading families in Charlottetown, also protected the proprietors. To challenge this position, the Assembly set up an investigative commission to study the problem. It recommended in 1860 that tenants be allowed to purchase their land and that owners obtain a fair valuation of their property. Progress was slow. As late as 1873, the tenants owned only one-third of the island.

CULTURAL DEVELOPMENTS

As in economic and political life, the Maritime colonies had gained greatly in cultural maturity by the mid-nineteenth century. Throughout the colonies, local church choirs flourished. In the urban centres, the large Anglican and Roman Catholic churches often had organs and skilled musicians. Music societies existed in the cities; among the earliest in British North America were the New Union Singing Society of Halifax (1809) and the Philharmonic Society of Saint John (1824).

Throughout the nineteenth century, theatre was available to audiences in Maritime cities. At first, the Halifax garrison performed plays in makeshift theatres in taverns, but in 1789 it opened the New Grand Theatre. For the opening, the officers and men produced Shakespeare's *Merchant of Venice*. Charlottetown built its first theatre in 1800, and by 1809 Saint John had its own Drury Lane Theatre. Professional companies and leading actors from both the United States and Britain visited in the mid-nineteenth century.

THOMAS CHANDLER HALIBURTON

The Maritimes produced one major North American literary figure in the mid-nineteenth century: Thomas Chandler Haliburton. From 1823 to 1860, the Nova Scotia judge wrote political pamphlets and many works on the history of the province, but he is best remembered for his fiction. Haliburton's classic, *The Clockmaker; or The Sayings and Doings of Samuel Slick of Slickville*, first appeared in 1836 and was followed by two more series of the same humorous stories about the shrewd Yankee peddler who crossed the province selling his poorly produced clocks to easily fooled Nova Scotians. As many as 70 editions of *The Clockmaker* have since appeared, and the book has remained in print for more than 150 years. Haliburton became the first British North American writer to gain an international reputation.

RELIGION AND EDUCATION

By the mid-nineteenth century, the Christian churches remained strong in the Maritime colonies. Considerable religious diversity existed. Among the Protestant denominations, the Anglicans remained numerous and influential, although the Baptists and Methodists made some inroads on their membership. Charles Inglis, the former rector of Trinity Church in New York City, in 1787 had become Nova Scotia's first bishop, with jurisdiction over the colonies of Quebec, New Brunswick, Prince Edward Island, Newfoundland, and Nova Scotia. Inglis sought to make the Anglican church predominant in the Maritimes. But the population, the majority of whom were not of English birth or tradition, resisted. As Maritime historian T.W. Acheson has noted, "The Anglican church was strong in the cities and very strong among the cultivated and politically influential classes, but it never held the support of more than a minority of the free-holders and artisanal and labouring classes of the countryside and towns."[6]

RELIGIOUS DENOMINATIONS

Clearly, by the mid-nineteenth century, the Anglicans had lost some ground to the Baptists, the most active of the Protestant denominations, and to the Methodists. In New Brunswick, the Baptists were the largest denomination, making up nearly one-quarter of the colony's religious population in 1860. In Nova Scotia, the Baptists constituted one-fifth of the population. As a result of their close-knit organizations and high degree of church discipline, the Baptists filled the religious void left in the rural areas of the Maritimes after Henry Alline's death in 1784 (see Chapter 10). Next in strength came the Wesleyan Methodists, who had succeeded by the 1820s in building up an influential following, including converts from the professional classes, taken largely from among the ranks of the evangelical Anglicans. Presbyterians came into their own

Interior of the Academy of Music, Saint John, New Brunswick, engraved from a drawing by Edward John Russell, around 1872.

New Brunswick Museum, Saint John, N.B./W6725. Gift of the New Brunswick Historical Society.

with the large Scottish immigration to the Maritimes. Scottish Presbyterians settled throughout the Maritime colonies, but in large numbers on the north shore of Nova Scotia and in Prince Edward Island. Lutheranism was strong in the German community in Nova Scotia's Lunenburg county; small Quaker and Jewish communities existed as well.

A dynamic Roman Catholic church emerged in the 1840s, strengthened by the arrival of tens of thousands of Irish Catholics. By the mid-nineteenth century, over 40 percent of the population of Prince Edward Island, a third of New Brunswickers, and a quarter of Nova Scotians belonged to the Roman Catholic church. Catholics had gained full civil rights throughout the British Empire in 1829. In the 1840s, the Catholic hierarchy fought the integration of Catholics into the dominant Protestant community. They worked to build Catholic schools, to obtain equality for Catholics in all aspects of society, and to establish the paramount authority of the bishops for all Catholics.

EDUCATION

Maritime Roman Catholics sought state financial support for their church-run schools, whereas the Anglicans, Baptists, Methodists, and Presbyterians favoured publicly funded, state-run primary schools that taught Protestant moral values. Fearful of the electoral consequences among Protestant voters, none of the colonial governments gave separate schools formal legislative approval. Without legal status, denominational schools would not be guaranteed financial aid in any of the three colonies in the 1860s, on the eve of Confederation.

Denominationalism prevailed in higher education. King's College at Windsor, founded by Bishop Inglis, excluded four-fifths of all possible candidates for degrees in the arts because they refused to swear an oath supporting the doctrines of the Church of England. The Anglicans also

Mount Allison Wesleyan College and Academies, Sackville, New Brunswick, 1886.

National Archives of Canada/C-58726.

established the College of New Brunswick (to be reconstituted as the non-secretarian University of New Brunswick in 1859). Governor Dalhousie founded the college in Halifax that still bears his name, to provide an education to students of all religious denominations. But it had effectively become a Presbyterian institution when it finally began to offer classes in the 1860s.

In the early nineteenth century, Presbyterians built Pictou Academy, while in 1828 Baptists established Horton Academy at Wolfville, Nova Scotia (ten years later, it became Acadia College). Between 1838 and 1855, five new universities followed in the Maritimes: Prince of Wales and St. Dunstan's in Prince Edward Island; St. Mary's and St. Francis in Nova Scotia; and Mount Allison in New Brunswick. Each was associated with a religious denomination.

WOMEN IN THE MARITIMES

The Maritimes, in the mid-nineteenth century, as was the case throughout North America, remained a male-dominated society. Men, for instance, owned almost all property and housing. At best, women had only limited rights under the law to protection and safety. In 1836 Prince Edward Island disenfranchised propertied women, as did New Brunswick in 1843 and Nova Scotia in 1851.

Although deprived of the vote, women could, and did, deliver petitions to their legislatures. They played a major role, for example, in petitioning for prohibition. On the positive side as well, after 1849 New Brunswick finally allowed women to attend the provincial Normal School. They numbered close to one-half of New Brunswick's teachers by the late 1850s. Yet, it must be pointed out they were only paid the same wage as a domestic servant, and they were confined to teaching younger school children. And unlike men, who obtained higher wages and could teach the older students, women were still denied entrance to colleges.

On the positive side, Nova Scotia in 1857 became the only British North American province prior to Confederation to allow legal divorce on the grounds of cruelty, such as wife battering. This was indeed an advancement, but New Brunswick and Prince Edward Island took no immediate steps to imitate this legislation. After surveying the status of women in the mid-nineteenth-century Maritimes, historian Ian Ross Robertson reached this conclusion: "It is doubtful whether the status of most women — dependency within a patriarchal world — was improving in the 1850s.... In most cases, the best a woman of the era could hope for was marriage to a man with the means to guarantee her a pedestal from which to supervise other, subordinate women of the household."[7]

By the mid-nineteenth century, the three Maritime colonies had become recognizable economic and political units. Eight of every nine people in the region had been born there. But the inhabitants were far from homogeneous. Religious, ethnic, and provincial divisions remained, and some groups such as the Mi'kmaqs and the African Maritimers and, to a lesser extent, the Acadians, had been pushed to the margins of Maritime society. Women were politically disenfranchised and relegated largely to the domestic sphere. The colonies had become much more consolidated than half a century earlier, but even within their own provincial boundaries, regional loyalties remained strong. Many Maritimers were sceptical of the possibility of Maritime union when politicians first seriously discussed the idea in the early 1860s. Union with the Canadas seemed even more remote.

NOTES

1. Christopher Moore, "Writers of History, Who Killed the Golden Age of Sail?" *The Beaver* 71(5) (October 1991): 61.
2. T.W. Acheson, "The 1840s: Decade of Tribulation," in Phillip A. Buckner and John G. Reid, eds., *The Atlantic Region to Confederation* (Toronto: University of Toronto Press, 1994), p. 331.
3. W.A. Spray, "The Settlement of the Black Refugees in New Brunswick, 1815–1836," in Phillip A. Buckner and David Frank, eds., *The Acadiensis Reader, Atlantic Canada Before Confederation*, vol. 1 (Fredericton: Acadiensis Press, 1985), pp. 152–53.
4. Ian Ross Robertson, "The Maritime Colonies, 1784 to Confederation," in M. Brook Taylor, ed., *Canadian History: A Reader's Guide*, vol. 1, *Beginnings to Confederation* (Toronto: University of Toronto Press, 1994), p. 258.
5. C.M. Wallace, "Lemuel Allan Wilmot," *Dictionary of Canadian Biography*, vol. 10, 1871–1880 (Toronto: University of Toronto Press, 1972), p. 710.
6. T.W. Acheson, "The 1840s: Decade of Tribulation," in Buckner and Reid, eds., *The Atlantic Region to Confederation*, p. 317.
7. Ian Ross Robertson, "The 1850s: Maturity and Reform," in Buckner and Reid, eds., *The Atlantic Region to Confederation*, p. 353.

LINKING TO THE PAST

The Maritime Shipyard
http://www.civilization.ca/hist/canp1/ca18eng.html
An overview of the nineteenth-century shipbuilding industry.

Halifax and Its People, 1749–1999
http://www.gov.ns.ca/nsarm/virtual/halifax
A richly illustrated history of Halifax and its inhabitants.

The Webster–Ashburton Treaty, 1842
http://www.yale.edu/lawweb/avalon/diplomacy/britain/br1842m.htm
The full text of the Webster–Ashburton Treaty of 1842, with related letters and other documents.

Reciprocity and Prosperity
http://collections.ic.gc.ca/peifisheries/history/prosperity.asp

A brief look at the effect of the Reciprocity Treaty of 1854 on the Prince Edward Island fishery. Navigate the site using the sidebar menu to learn more about the history of the PEI fishery.

PEI Census of 1841
http://collections.ic.gc.ca/census

Information on the 1841 census of Prince Edward Island.

The Clockmaker
http://www.canadiana.org/ECO/mtq?id=b3ca8f5bd2&doc=35995

Facsimile of the first edition of Thomas Chandler Haliburton's *The Clockmaker; or The Sayings and Doings of Samuel Slick of Slickville*.

RELATED READINGS

R. Douglas Francis and Donald B. Smith, eds., *Readings in Canadian History: Pre-Confederation*, 6th ed. (Toronto: Nelson Thomson Learning, 2002), has two articles on this topic: Harald E.L Prins, "Survival under Internal Colonialism," pp. 369–387; and Scott W. See, "The Orange Order and Social Violence in Mid-Nineteenth Century Saint John," pp. 387–406.

BIBLIOGRAPHY

The basic study of the Maritimes' history to 1867 is Phillip A. Buckner and John G. Reid, eds., *The Atlantic Region to Confederation: A History* (Toronto: University of Toronto Press, 1994). Margaret R. Conrad and James K. Hiller, *Atlantic Canada. A Region in the Making* (Don Mills, Ontario: Oxford University Press, 2001) is very useful. An older survey is that by W.S. MacNutt, *The Atlantic Provinces: The Emergence of Colonial Society, 1712–1857* (Toronto: McClelland & Stewart, 1965). For New Brunswick see also W.S. MacNutt's *New Brunswick: A History, 1784–1867* (Toronto: Macmillan, 1963); and Graeme Wynn, *Timber Colony: A Historical Geography of Early Nineteenth Century New Brunswick* (Toronto: University of Toronto Press, 1981). A.H. Clark reviews Prince Edward Island's story in *Three Centuries and the Island* (Toronto: University of Toronto Press, 1959). A lively popular history of the island is Douglas Baldwin's *Land of the Red Soil* (Charlottetown: Ragweed Press, 1990). Kenneth Donovan's two edited books, *Cape Breton at 200: Historical Essays in Honour of the Island's Bicentennial, 1785–1985* (Sydney: University College of Cape Breton Press, 1985), and *The Island: New Perspectives on Cape Breton's History, 1713–1990* (Fredericton and Sydney: Acadiensis Press and University College of Cape Breton Press, 1990), review Cape Breton's past two centuries. See also Stephen J. Hornsby's *Nineteenth Century Cape Breton: A Historical Geography* (Montreal/Kingston: McGill-Queen's University Press, 1992). Ian Ross Robertson introduces the historical literature in his essay "The Maritime Colonies: 1784 to Confederation," in M. Brook Taylor, ed., *Canadian History: A Reader's Guide, vol. 1, Beginnings to Confederation* (Toronto: University of Toronto Press, 1994), pp. 237–79.

Economic questions receive attention in Chapter 4 of Kenneth Norrie and Douglas Owram, *A History of the Canadian Economy*, 2nd ed. (Toronto: Harcourt Brace, 1996), pp. 73–93; Michael Bliss, *Northern Enterprise: Five Centuries of Canadian Business* (Toronto: McClelland & Stewart, 1987); S.A. Saunders, "The Maritime Provinces and the Reciprocity Treaty," in George A. Rawlyk, ed., *Historical Essays on the Atlantic Provinces* (Toronto: McClelland & Stewart, 1967), pp. 161–78; Eric W. Sager and Lewis R. Fischer, *Shipping and Shipbuilding in Atlantic Canada, 1820–1914* (Ottawa: Canadian Historical Association, 1986); and Eric W. Sager with Gerald E. Panting, *Maritime Capital: The Shipping Industry in Maritime Canada, 1820–1914* (Montreal/Kingston: McGill-Queen's University Press, 1990).

The social history of the Maritimes in this time period is reviewed in several sources. The three editions of Phillip A. Buckner and David Frank, eds., *Atlantic Canada Before Confederation*, vol. 1, *The Acadiensis Reader* (Fredericton: Acadiensis Press, 1985, 1988, 1998) are invaluable. The first edition contains Judith Fingard's essay "The Relief of the Unemployed Poor in Saint John, Halifax and St. John's,

1815–1860," pp. 190–211. Fingard's "The Winter's Tale: The Seasonal Contours of Pre-industrial Poverty in British North America," appears in the *Canadian Historical Association Historical Papers* (1974): 65–94. Her *Jack in Port: Sailortowns of Eastern Canada* (Toronto: University of Toronto Press, 1982) describes the life of merchant sailors in Saint John and Halifax, and her *Dark Side of Life in Victorian Halifax* (Porters Lake, NS: Pottersfield Press, 1989) focusses on the lives of nearly 100 habitual offenders in Halifax in the mid-nineteenth century. Jan Noel looks at the temperance movement in early-nineteenth-century *British North America in Canada Dry: Temperance Crusades before Confederation* (Toronto: University of Toronto Press, 1995). Several essays in Philip Girard and Jim Phillips, eds., *Essays in the History of Canadian Law: The Nova Scotia Experience* (Toronto: Osgoode Society, 1990) examine aspects of the province's legal history in the nineteenth century. William B. Hamilton reviews the educational history of the three Maritime colonies in "Society and Schools in Nova Scotia" and "Society and Schools in New Brunswick and Prince Edward Island," in J. Donald Wilson, Robert M. Stamp, and Louis-Philippe Audet, eds., *Canadian Education: A History* (Scarborough, ON: Prentice-Hall, 1970), pp. 86–125. An entertaining popular account of Halifax is Thomas H. Raddall's *Halifax: Warden of the North*, rev. ed. (Toronto: McClelland & Stewart, 1971 [1948]). For a more recent survey by three professional historians see: Judith Fingard, Janet Guildford, and David Sutherland, *Halifax, The First 250 Years* (Halifax: Formac Publishing, 1999). T.W. Acheson's *Saint John: The Making of a Colonial Urban Community* (Toronto: University of Toronto Press, 1985) is an in-depth study of New Brunswick's largest city.

A collection of materials relating to Maritime women has been edited by Margaret Conrad, Toni Laidlaw, and Donna Smyth: *No Place Like Home: Diaries and Letters of Nova Scotia Women, 1771–1938* (Halifax: Formac, 1988). See also Janet Guildford and Suzanne Morton, eds., *Separate Spheres: Women's Worlds in the Nineteenth-Century Maritimes* (Fredericton: Acadiensis Press, 1994). Interesting articles include Gail G. Campbell, "Disfranchised but Not Quiescent: Women Petitioners in New Brunswick in the Mid-19th Century," *Acadiensis* 18(2) (Spring 1989), reprinted in Phillip A. Buckner and David Frank, eds., *Atlantic Canada Before Confederation*, 3rd ed. (Fredericton: Acadiensis Press, 1998), pp. 282–314; and Sylvia Hamilton, "Naming Names, Naming Ourselves: A Survey of Early Black Women in Nova Scotia," in Peggy Bristow et al., *"We're Rooted Here and They Can't Pull Us Up": Essays in African Canadian Women's History* (Toronto: University of Toronto Press, 1994), pp. 13–40.

Maritime political developments are examined in Phillip A. Buckner, *The Transition to Responsible Government: British Policy in British North America, 1815–1850* (Westport, CT: Greenwood Press, 1985). The American border dispute, resolved in the Webster–Ashburton Treaty of 1842, is reviewed by Francis M. Carroll, *A Good and Wise Measure. The Struggle for the Canadian–American Border, 1783–1842* (Toronto: University of Toronto Press, 2001). A short sketch of Joseph Howe appears in the *Dictionary of Canadian Biography*, vol. 10, *1871–1880* (Toronto: University of Toronto Press, 1972), pp. 362–70, in an entry by Murray Beck, who has also written the two-volume study Joseph Howe (Montreal/Kingston: McGill-Queen's University Press, 1982–83). John Ross Robertson examines Prince Edward Island's complicated land question in *The Prince Edward Island Commission of 1860* (Fredericton: Acadiensis Press, 1988). Greg Marquis looks at the Maritime colonies during the Civil War years, *In Armageddon's Shadow: The Civil War and Canada's Maritime Provinces* (Montreal/Kingston: McGill-Queen's University Press, 1998). Important portraits of Maritime political, economic, and cultural leaders appear in the volumes of the *Dictionary of Canadian Biography* devoted to the nineteenth century. It is now available online: www.bibliographi.ca.

The peoples of the Maritimes in the late eighteenth and nineteenth centuries are the subject of several studies. On the history of the Native peoples of the Maritimes see Harald E.L. Prins, *The Mi'kmaq: Resistance, Accommodation, and Cultural Survival* (Fort Worth, TX: Harcourt Brace, 1996); and L.F.S. Upton, *Micmacs and Colonists: Indian–White Relations in the Maritimes, 1713–1867* (Vancouver: University of British Columbia Press, 1979). Daniel N. Paul provides an Aboriginal perspective in *We Were Not the Savages* (Halifax: Nimbus Publishing, 1993). For a study of the Acadians on Prince Edward Island see Georges Arsenault's *The Island Acadians, 1720–1980* (Charlottetown: Ragweed Press, 1989). Charles Dunn's classic *Highland Settler: A Portrait of the Scottish Gael in Nova Scotia* (Toronto: University of Toronto Press, 1953); and D. Campbell and R.A. MacLean, *Beyond the Atlantic Roar: A Study of the Nova Scotia Scots* (Toronto: McClelland & Stewart, 1974) deal with the Scots in Nova Scotia. A number of works have appeared on the history of the Irish in British North America. Scott W. See's *Riots in New Brunswick: Orange Nativism and Social Violence in the 1840s* (Toronto: University of Toronto Press, 1993) looks at social violence in the 1840s between Irish Catholics and Protestant Orangemen. Thomas P. Powell has edited *The Irish in Atlantic Canada, 1780–1900* (Fredericton: New Ireland Press, 1991). For a discussion of African

Maritimers consult Robin W. Winks, *The Blacks in Canada: A History,* 2nd ed. (Montreal/Kingston: McGill-Queen's University Press, 1997); and see W.A. Spray's "The Settlement of the Black Refugees in New Brunswick, 1815–1836," in Buckner and Frank, eds., *Atlantic Canada Before Confederation*, vol. 1, *The Acadiensis Reade*r, 1st ed., pp. 148–64. A very interesting study is James W. St. G. Walker, *The Black Loyalists: The Search for a Promised Land in Nova Scotia and Sierra Leone, 1783–1870* (Toronto: University of Toronto Press, 1992 [1976]).

For maps of the Maritimes in this period consult R. Louis Gentilcore, ed., *The Historical Atlas of Canada*, vol. 2, *The Land Transformed, 1800–1891* (Toronto: University of Toronto Press, 1993).

CHAPTER 17
NEWFOUNDLAND TO THE 1860S

TIME LINE

1610 – The English establish Newfoundland's first colony at Cupids

1662 – The French fortify Plaisance (now called Placentia), their fishing colony on the south shore of Newfoundland begun in the 1620s

1699 – Passage of the Newfoundland Act by the English government, the only constitution Newfoundland would have for the next fifty years

1713 – With the signing of the Treaty of Utrecht, Britain gains control of Newfoundland

1729 – The commander of the annual naval convoy to Newfoundland is made the island's governor in the summer months

1784 – The British grant religious freedom in Newfoundland

1800 – The number of permanent residents in Newfoundland reaches 20 000

1809 – Labrador, which had been attached to Quebec in 1774, was returned to Newfoundland's jurisdiction in 1809

1824 – Newfoundland is made a regular British colony

1829 – The last known surviving Beothuk, Shawnadithit, dies

1855 – Britain grants responsible government to Newfoundland

In the sixteenth century, the fleets of four nations — England, France, Spain, and Portugal — sailed to Newfoundland and shared its deep, land-locked eastern harbours. The ships came to one of the world's greatest fishing grounds, the Grand Banks, for codfish — "the beef of the sea" — a diet staple of Roman Catholic Europe, which required abstinence from meat three or more days of the week.

The Beothuks withdrew from the coastal areas where the European newcomers set up shore stations. They did not, as did the Mi'kmaqs in the Maritimes, trade and interact with the Europeans. Consequently, by staying in the interior to avoid the newcomers, they lost access to the valuable food supplies off the coast. They became greatly weakened by starvation and tuberculosis, which the Europeans had inadvertently introduced. Within two centuries of the Europeans' arrival, the Beothuks disappeared completely.

After a half-century of Anglo–French conflict, France ceded Newfoundland to England by the Treaty of Utrecht in 1713. Powerful English merchants, mostly from Devon and Dorset in England's West Country, sought exclusive rights to the fishing grounds. They persuaded British monarchs and parliaments in the late seventeenth century to discourage additional permanent settlement on the island. In the eighteenth century, the merchants' opposition ended and the British government sanctioned settlement. Early in the nineteenth century, the island had a permanent population of more than 40 000 people. Their livelihood depended on exporting fish and on trade with Britain, the Mediterranean countries, the West Indies, and, to a more limited extent, the rest of British North America.

By the mid-nineteenth century, the spirit of political reform that swept through the other British North American colonies arose as well in Newfoundland. This led to intense and bitter disputes. On the eve of Confederation, Newfoundland resembled the other British North American colonies in many respects. Yet, in other ways, it remained quite different.

EARLY SETTLEMENT IN NEWFOUNDLAND

By the early seventeenth century, England became one of the dominant players in the Newfoundland fishery. On the high seas many dangers awaited the English mariners, including fog, floating ice, and pirates. During the early seventeenth century, the "Barbary Rovers" (North African Muslims who travelled the coasts of Europe) allied themselves with France and extended their operations as far as the English Channel. There they waited for the unarmed ships from Newfoundland to return to Britain. They sold into slavery all those sailors they captured who were not needed to work on the pirate ships. The town of Poole in Dorset, which sent out twenty ships annually to Newfoundland, lost twenty ships, or one-quarter of its fleet, in a four-year period. Only after an Anglo–Dutch mission bombarded the pirates' North African headquarters in the late seventeenth century did the danger to English shipping diminish.

The men and boys in the migratory fishing fleet usually came from their ship's home port and its surrounding area. Many had attempted to farm without having enough land to support their families. Others were tradespeople without sufficient work, and others were orphans. On board, they earned wages slightly higher than those of farm workers.

THE LONDON AND BRISTOL COMPANY

In 1610, a group of London and Bristol merchants formed the London and Bristol Company. That same year the merchants sent a governor, John Guy, and 40 men to establish Newfoundland's first colony at Cupids on Conception Bay, 35 km west of St. John's. The Company believed its men would have an advantage over the visiting fishers by being there at the beginning of the fishing season. But the visiting fishers caught just as many fish as did the

A View of a Stage & also of ye manner of Fishing for, Curing & Drying Cod at Newfoundland, an engraving on a map of North America prepared by Herman Moll and published in 1718. This illustration shows the various stages in the cod fishery. The cod was caught and brought to the wharf, where shore crews split, cleaned, and washed it, collected the cod liver oil, and placed the fish on drying racks. Figure A (left) is a typical fisher dressed for North Atlantic weather.

National Archives of Canada/C-3686.

colonists. Moreover, the settlers had to charge as high or higher prices for their fish to cover the colony's expenses. Finally, the rocky land at Cupids had almost no agricultural potential, so settlers could not grow grain and their cattle died from lack of fodder. The failure to discover mineral resources and to begin a commercial trade in furs with the resident Beothuks also contributed to the colony's demise.

Another drawback to colonization was the weather. Lord Baltimore, for example, founded Ferryland, south of St. John's, in 1621. But after wintering on the island in 1628–29, he wrote of his wife and family: "I have sent them home after much sufferance in this wofull country, where with one intolerable wynter were we almost undone. It is not to be expressed with my pen what wee have endured." Lord Baltimore redirected his colonizing efforts southward to Virginia, where just after his death in 1632 his son received a charter to what became known as Maryland. Some of the Newfoundland settlers remained behind after the colony disintegrated.

Today Ferryland has roughly 700 inhabitants, making it one of the oldest continuously inhabited settlements of English origin in the Americas.

Still England attempted to secure a permanent foothold in Newfoundland, believing that whoever controlled settlement would hold the fisheries. Newfoundland ranked second only to Virginia as a chosen location for early British settlement in North America.

The French also began a colony in Newfoundland. In the 1620s they established a fishing settlement at Plaisance (now called Placentia), on the southern coast of Newfoundland. It remained a small community with only approximately 250 permanent residents at the end of the century. By the time the French commenced their colony, the first English settlement, on the Avalon Peninsula (on the easternmost part of Newfoundland), had, in effect, already failed.

The permanent non-Native population of the island grew slowly. By 1650, an estimated 500 English-speaking residents, including 350 women and children, lived in about 40 settlements scattered along the eastern coast between Cape Bonavista and Trepassey. The population rose to an estimated 2000 by 1680 and consisted of two groups: descendants of settlers brought out by colonizers such as John Guy and Lord Baltimore, and "bye-boatmen" from England's West Country, who came out as passengers on the fishing ships and returned in the autumn. They worked for the settlers or merchants who owned the bye-boats, the small fishing boats left in Newfoundland harbours for use in the spring. As time went on, many of these skilled fishers remained in Newfoundland during the winter. Frequently they stayed for several years, and some became permanent settlers.

Without an organized government on the island, the settlers and the bye-boatmen faced difficult times. They had to earn their living during the short season of cod fishing in the summer, for there was no employment in the winter. When the fishing fleet departed in

The remains of Fort Royal, built in the 1690s to protect the French settlement of Plaisance (now the town of Placentia), and the beach used for drying fish.

Photo courtesy of Dawn Maddock Parsons.

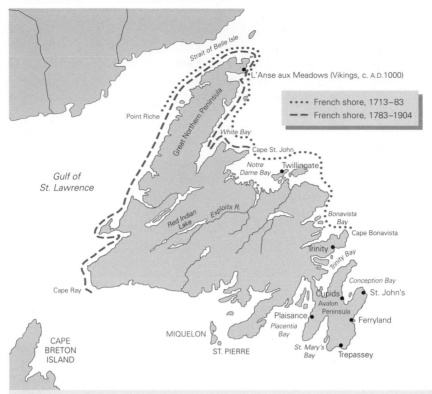

Early Newfoundland.

Source: Adapted from P.G. Cornell, J. Hamelin, F. Ouellet, and M. Trudel, *Canada: Unity in Diversity* (Toronto: Holt, Rinehart and Winston, 1967), p. 111.

September or early October, it left the isolated communities on their own until the following spring. If food ran out, they starved. If illness occurred, no medical people could be called. No births, marriages, or burials could be legally registered, since no clergy lived on the island between 1650 and 1702. The island had no law officers or courts because it had no official status as a colony.

The English government faced a difficult problem in the late seventeenth century. It wanted to prevent settlement on the island, as the Royal Navy relied on the annual fishing voyages to train its crews and maintain ships. In addition, the British feared that a Newfoundland resident fishery would end the English migratory fishery, as had been the case in New England. Yet, if Newfoundland had no settlers or resident fishers, France might seize it. According to historian Frederick W. Rowe, three-quarters of the island's 10 000 km coastline "was already, in effect, almost wholly under the control of the world's most powerful country [France]. How long would it be before France would be occupying the entire Island of Newfoundland?"[1] England resolved this dilemma in 1699. It formally recognized the permanent settlers on the island, but forbade them to encroach on the fishing areas of the migratory fishers. It also announced that no government would be established on the island. The Act to Encourage Trade to Newfoundland, or the Newfoundland Act, the first English statute pertaining to the island, remained the only constitution Newfoundland would have for the next 125 years, until it became a British colony in 1824.

THE ANGLO–FRENCH STRUGGLE FOR NEWFOUNDLAND

Just as the English began settlements on the eastern Avalon Peninsula, the French claimed Newfoundland's south shore. In 1662, the French fortified Plaisance (Placentia). The deep, ice-free harbour offered an excellent refuge for French ships. Fish could be dried on its beaches. But the rocky soil was not suited for agriculture. To build up settlement, the French government initially provided free passage and one year's financial support to settlers migrating to Plaisance. As in New France, however, large-scale French assistance ceased in the early 1670s. The colony grew very slowly after that, and its population remained much smaller than that of the English colony.

Conflict between English and French settlements seemed inevitable. War broke out in 1689, and seven years later Pierre Le Moyne d'Iberville, New France's greatest soldier, with his troops, laid waste the English settlements in Newfoundland, killing 200 people and taking 700 prisoners. But an English expedition in 1697 recaptured all the settlements. From that point on, the English presence remained secure, thanks to its superior naval power.

By the Treaty of Utrecht in 1713, England gained control of the entire island. The French ceded Plaisance, their evacuation of the port being complete by 1714, except for a small number of residents who accepted English rule and stayed behind. Many of the Plaisance evacuees were relocated to Île Royale (Cape Breton Island). France left Plaisance and renounced its claim to Newfoundland, but retained the right to dry cod on what came to be known as the French Shore, between Cape Bonavista and Point Riche (in the northeastern bays and around Newfoundland's Great Northern Peninsula, to a point located about a quarter of the way down the west coast, an area including approximately one-third of Newfoundland's coastline).

By an Anglo–French agreement in 1783, Cape Ray, on the island's southwestern tip, was substituted for Point Riche and the eastern boundary moved from Cape Bonavista to Cape St. John. The French Shore now encompassed the entire west coast, the Great Northern Peninsula, and White Bay. British or Newfoundland fishers were not allowed to interrupt the French fishery in that area, and the French disputed their right to settle there. The question of the French Shore troubled Anglo–French relations for nearly two centuries, until England purchased French landing rights in 1904.

Although the French settlement at Plaisance became British, the French still held New France and the great fort of Louisbourg on Cape Breton Island. On account of France's naval strength, Newfoundland was in danger of a French naval attack until the 1760s. In 1762, the French actually took St. John's, although the English recaptured the town the following year. The Treaty of Paris in 1763 reaffirmed France's Newfoundland landing rights. In addition, to compensate for the loss of French fishing bases in Cape Breton, Britain ceded the islands of St. Pierre and Miquelon off Newfoundland to France, "to serve as a shelter to the French fisherman."

LAW AND ORDER IN EIGHTEENTH-CENTURY NEWFOUNDLAND

 As early as the seventeenth century, competition for favourable harbours reached such a high level that the fishing fleets worked out the "fishing admiral system," a rough-and-ready means of keeping some kind of order in the harbours.

THE FISHING ADMIRAL SYSTEM

To the first ship in a port, regardless of nationality, went the right to take the best fishing room, or strip of beach. The first ship's captain became the "fishing admiral," with the responsibility to

A Fishing Station, by Gerard van Edema (c. 1652–c. 1700), shows a harbour in Placentia Bay about 1690.

Courtesy of the Royal Ontario Museum, Toronto/ 957.91. © ROM.

maintain law and order in each harbour. Much of the admiral's authority rested on his strength. If he had a sizable and well-armed vessel and a large crew, he could enforce his will.

In 1634, the English government confirmed the admiral system in the First Western Charter, the first regulation issued concerning the Newfoundland fishery. The Newfoundland Act of 1699 again affirmed the rights and the authority of the fishing admirals. The system had several serious defects, however. First, the admirals stayed for only three or four months in the spring and summer; for the rest of the year, no one was authorized to maintain law and order. Second, even when present, the admirals had no way of enforcing their rulings, and, as settlement grew, the problems they had to resolve became more complex. Third, as the admirals received no payment for presiding over the courts and, since they had come primarily to fish, they had little interest in enforcing the law. Conditions on the island degenerated rapidly under the fishing admiral system. In the long period between the departure of the ships in the late summer and their return the next year, those guilty of murder, rape, and robbery had ample opportunity to escape.

Historian Keith Matthews offers two explanations for England's delay in establishing a proper legal system.[2] He claims that the establishment of law and other services on the island would have encouraged further permanent settlement, something the government opposed. Second, he points out that the placement of law-enforcement officers in many parts of the island would have involved enormous expenditures for the British government.

In 1729, Britain made a modest improvement in the system. The commander of the annual naval convoy to Newfoundland became the island's governor and commander-in-chief, but he lived on a ship and remained in Newfoundland only during the summer fishing season. Whenever the governor deemed a local regulation desirable, he could issue a proclamation, and his word became law. As governor, he also had the right to appoint magistrates from among the most respected local residents. The magistrates gained an increasing jurisdiction, both in terms of the nature of the cases they could hear and the time of year they would hear them.

THE BEOTHUKS

The Beothuks, Newfoundland's original inhabitants, suffered greatly from the presence of the newcomers. *Beothuk* means "people," and it is the term that the Aboriginal Newfoundlanders applied to themselves. The Beothuks first encountered European fishers in the sixteenth century. From their use of red ochre on their bodies, clothing, and utensils, the early Europeans called them "Red Indians" — an expression still used in Britain to describe the First Nations.

Unlike the Mi'kmaqs in the Maritimes, who adjusted to living near the French, the Beothuks withdrew from the newcomers. With the increasing number of European fishers on the Newfoundland coast, it became difficult in the mid-seventeenth century for the Beothuks to gain access to their seaside summer campsites and, hence, to their food resources, particularly on the eastern and southern coasts. It was very difficult to live in the interior, especially without firearms. Starvation became common, and made the Beothuks much more vulnerable to European diseases.

The pressure on the Beothuks grew in the early 1700s. Several factors contributed to increased European settlement in the northeast and the interior: a salmon fishery developed near the river mouths of northeastern Newfoundland; settlers began to trap fur-bearing animals in the interior; and the spring seal hunt, which was best operated from the northeastern coast, grew rapidly. The British settlers became seal hunters in the spring, salmon catchers in the summer, and trappers in the winter, thus depriving the Beothuks of their traditional sources of food and clothing.

CONFLICT BETWEEN THE BEOTHUKS AND THE EUROPEANS

When the Beothuks encountered the Europeans on the northeastern coast, violence often erupted. The settlers harassed them and raided their camps. George Cartwright, a prominent merchant in Labrador, warned the Colonial Office in 1784:

> Instead of a friendly intercourse with these Indians, our people dispossessed them from beaches and salmon rivers and it is now well known, that the poor Indians are put to the greatest difficulties to procure a scanty subsistence. If some effectual measures will not be taken, that unhappy race of mortals will soon be extirpated, to the disgrace of our Government, our country and our religion.

The Beothuks retaliated. According to contemporary reports and oral traditions, the Beothuks killed about a dozen settlers and wounded nearly as many more between 1750 and 1790. The settlers took their own revenge, killing and wounding Beothuks and destroying their wigwams. The Beothuks' lack of firearms weakened their ability to defend themselves.

The violence continued unchecked. Neighbours and employers were reluctant to become involved in the prosecution of the British criminals, especially since it could mean missing out on the summer's fishing and having to pay for the return expenses from St. John's. As a result, the culprits remained at large, unpunished. Even when murder trials were held at St. John's in the mid-eighteenth century, the court made few convictions.

Several naval officers and settlers in the late eighteenth and early nineteenth centuries worried about the Beothuks' fate. A number of attempts to reach the Beothuks, who lived and hunted along the Exploits River from the interior down to Notre Dame Bay, failed, but one, in 1811, succeeded. After trekking for twelve days up the Exploits River in heavy snow and sub-zero temperatures, Captain David Buchan and his party of 27 made contact with a band of about 40 Beothuks. The Beothuks, though, remained suspicious and killed the two men left behind with them as hostages.

Attempts made to locate the Beothuks the following summer failed. Many of them apparently died, most likely from starvation and tuberculosis. From evidence accumulated by anthropologist Ingeborg Marshall, it appears that a few Beothuks joined the Mi'kmaqs in the southern part of the island, either voluntarily or because they were kidnapped.[3]

Demasduwit, a young woman, was taken captive in 1819 and lived for one year. Then, in 1823, three starving Beothuk women were captured. Both the mother and one of her two daughters died shortly afterward of tuberculosis. But the second daughter, Shawnadithit, called Nancy, a young woman between 16 and 20, survived for six years. She lived at first as a servant in the household of a justice of the peace, but spent the last year of her life in St. John's, informing William Cormack, a champion of the Beothuks, about her people's culture, history, and language. Shawnadithit died in 1829. Apart from two or three Beothuks who may have lived with the Newfoundland Mi'kmaqs, she was the last of the Beothuks.

A Historical Portrait

☞ Demasduwit

The story of Demasduwit, or Mary March as she was named in English, is one of the best-authenticated of all Beothuk captivity stories. In March 1819, a group of ten armed settlers from Notre Dame Bay, out on a mission to recover what they regarded as stolen property, encountered a small party of Beothuks at Red Indian Lake in the interior. A fight ensued, in which the settlers killed Nonosbawsut, the chief, and captured his wife. The settlers took the woman in the hope that she could be taught to speak English and might become an agent of contact with her people. In carrying her off they separated her from her only child, a young baby. Taken to Twillingate on Notre Dame Bay, Demasduwit was placed in the care of the local Anglican missionary, the Rev. John Leigh. Demasduwit was named Mary March, her second name referring to the month of her capture. Twice she tried to escape, but after some weeks the young Beothuk woman appeared to accept her situation. When spring navigation opened on the coast she was brought to St. John's, where she met the governor, Vice-Admiral Sir Charles Hamilton.

The governor was genuinely concerned about the fate of the Beothuk. Appalled by the killing of the Beothuks, he brought the perpetrators of the deed before the grand jury. But the jury accepted the settlers' story that they had not intended to kill the Beothuks but had acted in self-defence. While Demasduwit stayed in St. John's, the governor's wife, Lady Henrietta Hamilton, a skilled artist, painted a watercolour portrait of her.

Sir Charles decided that summer to return Demasduwit to her people. He hoped

Demasduwit, painted by Henrietta Hamilton, wife of the governor of Newfoundland, in 1819.

National Archives of Canada/C-87698.

that she would become an intermediary between the settlers and the Beothuks. She was returned to Notre Dame Bay, but in a greatly weakened state. She had tuberculosis, a disease she had contracted either among her own people or from the English. Although in very poor physical condition, she joined several search parties looking for Beothuks at their summer stations near the mouth of the Exploits River. After these expeditions proved unsuccessful, the English decided that they would travel directly to Red Indian Lake. But Demasduwit died in early January. The military expedition returned her body, which they left in early February at the deserted Beothuk camp where she had been captured the previous year.

Shawnadithit, Demasduwit's niece, was taken captive three years later, in 1823. She learned a considerable amount of English during the six years that she remained among the settlers, until her death from tuberculosis in 1829. Thanks to her testimony, the story of Demasduwit's people is better known. She had witnessed her aunt's capture and her uncle's killing. The mystery of their child was solved — Shawnadithit explained that the baby had died several days after being separated from its mother.

In 1976 a painting of a First Nations woman came up for sale in a New York auction house. The National Archives of Canada authenticated it as Lady Hamilton's miniature of Mary March, the only known portrait of a Beothuk. Now in the National Archives of Canada, Lady Hamilton's sensitive portrait, showing Demasduwit's gentle and melancholy eyes, reminds us of her personal tragedy as well that of her people, the Beothuk of Newfoundland.

POPULATION GROWTH AND SETTLEMENT

At the end of the eighteenth century, Newfoundland's population grew rapidly. The number of permanent residents rose from approximately 2300 in 1730 to about 20 000 by 1800, and about 40 000 in 1830. As late as 1797, resident men outnumbered women five to one. As the settlers built dwellings and warehouses and used increasing amounts of firewood, the forests rapidly disappeared. According to geographer Grant Head, a "clutter of stages, flakes, boats, ships, warehouses, dwellings, vegetable patches, wandering cattle, and snaking trails"[4] replaced the coastal forests. Historical geographers R. Cole Harris and John Warkentin suggest that "the influence of Europeans on the native flora and fauna of the northeastern rim of North America may have been almost as devastating as in the islands and perimeter of the Caribbean."[5]

Much of the population growth came from a large influx of immigrants, chiefly Irish. The first potato famines in the 1720s and 1730s led thousands of Irish to seek refuge across the Atlantic. Newfoundland became the first place in the New World to receive large numbers of Irish immigrants. Cheap transportation, the promise of work, and poor conditions at home brought them to the island. By the 1750s, Irish Catholics comprised probably half the Avalon Peninsula's total population, and by the 1830s they numbered half the entire island's population.

The Irish Catholic immigrants had little love for England, which had invaded Ireland repeatedly, seized Irish lands, and then proscribed the Roman Catholic religion. The Irish came with respect for, and strong loyalty to, their priests, but found that the English would not allow Roman Catholic priests on the island. Not until 1784 did the governor grant religious freedom. That same year, the first "legal" priest arrived in St. John's to minister openly to the Irish Catholics.

Mistrusting each other, the Irish and the English communities segregated themselves geographically. In the larger towns, such as St. John's, they lived in separate neighbourhoods. Intermarriages were rare. When the Catholic Irish moved away from the Avalon Peninsula, they settled in harbours not occupied by English Protestants.

As the population expanded, the economy diversified from the sole reliance on the shore cod fishery. The development of salmon fishing, sealing, and the fur trade led to an expansion of settlement to the northern bays of the island. Settlers occupied hundreds of coves, harbours, and islands chosen for their proximity to the fishing grounds. They began to farm the Avalon Peninsula's scattered pockets of fertile land.

THE RISE OF ST. JOHN'S

In the late eighteenth century, St. John's became the dominant urban centre on the island. It had become the island's capital in 1729, when the British naval convoy commander was made governor. A number of St. John's settlers left the fishery to open taverns and stores catering to the needs of the thousands of fishers who came to the island annually. An English garrison was also located in the town. As a result, St. John's population rose from about 1000 in 1790 to more than 5000 in 1810.

At first glance, St. John's, situated at the extreme eastern tip of the island, seems an odd choice as the island's great commercial centre. In fact, however, it was located in Newfoundland's most densely populated area — the Avalon Peninsula, which is larger than Prince Edward Island. The peninsula itself was strategically located, being almost equidistant between the chief ports of New and Old England. In historian William Menzies Whitelaw's words, it was "the natural stepping stone between the old world and the new."[6] In addition, the peninsula lay immediately west of the North Atlantic's best fishing grounds — the Grand Banks.

The importance of St. John's increased in the late eighteenth and early nineteenth centuries. The governor made his headquarters there. The establishment of the Newfoundland Supreme Court in 1792 and of customs and naval offices further raised the town's standing. After the American Revolution, merchants involved in the Canada and West Indies trade established themselves in St. John's. The town's merchants and shipowners financed the fishing trade, marketed dried cod, and distributed foodstuffs and manufactured goods to the outports. The merchants at St. John's, who were involved in exporting cod, directed the island's affairs by acting as suppliers to the smaller merchants and fishers in the outports. A small group of generally Protestant St. John's merchants controlled the fishery in the mid-nineteenth century.

As the town's wealth grew, newspapers, health services, and schools were established. Consequently, St. John's became the only community on the island with an educated and moderately wealthy middle class. The capital, though, could not escape its past, and continuing, livelihood. George Warburton, an Irish soldier and writer, visited St. John's in the mid-1840s on a tour of British North America. In his book, *Hochelaga; or, England in the New World* (1846), he described it as the "fishiest" capital in the world.

> In trying to describe St. John's there is some difficulty in applying to it an adjective sufficiently distinctive and appropriate. We find other cities coupled with epithets which at once give their predominant characteristic: London the richest, Paris the gayest, St. Petersburg the coldest. In one respect the chief town of Newfoundland has, I believe, no rival: we may therefore call it the fishiest of modern capitals. Round a great part of the harbour are sheds, acres in extent, roofed with cod split in half, laid on like slates, drying in the sun, or rather the air, for there is not much of the former to depend upon. Those ships, bearing nearly every flag in the world, are laden with cod; those stout weatherly boats crowding up to the wharves have just now returned from fishing for cod; those few scant fields of cultivation, with lean crops coaxed out of the barren soil, are manured with cod; those grim, snug-looking wooden houses, their handsome furniture, the piano and the musical skill of the young lady who plays it, the satin gown of the mother, the gold chain of the father, are all paid for in cod; the breezes from the

The town and harbour of St. John's from Signal Hill, 1831. The fortification on the hill protected the capital of Newfoundland and offered a shelter for the inhabitants in case of attack. Painted by William Eagar.

National Archives of Canada/C-41605.

shore, soft and warm on this bright August day, are rich not with the odours of a thousand flowers but of a thousand cod. Earth, sea and air are alike pervaded with this wonderful fish.

THE OUTPORTS

Life was harsher in the outports than in St. John's. Jacob Mountain, a young Anglican priest, discovered as much during his seven years of missionary work on Newfoundland's south coast. There is no such thing, he wrote in his posthumously published *Some Accounts of a Sowing Time on the Rugged Shores of Newfoundland* (1857), as a typical Newfoundland fishing village:

In one place you will find them clean, tidy, thriving; houses neatly and substantially built, and a certain air of sobriety and self-respect about the people, the children a picture of delight, with their beautiful eyes, well-formed faces, soft flaxen hair. In another close by, the very reverse of all this; houses, or rather hovels of studs, the crevices gaping wide or filled with moss, the roof covered with rinds of trees and sods, the entrance constructed by heaps of dirt, often nothing that deserved the name of door, the aperture so low that one must stoop to enter, the interior without any furniture but a low table and rough stool, scarcely raised three inches from the ground, the children wretchedly ragged and dirty, crouching round, or creeping into the smoky wood fire, an old sail and a few more studs forming the only partition between the kitchen and sleeping-room, if such terms can be applied to such miserable dens.

A Newfoundland coastal fishing village at low tide, about 1857. Note the absence of trees, where once a coastal forest had stood.

Paul-Émile Miot/National Archives of Canada/photographie acquise avec le support financier du ministère du Patrimoine dans le cadre de la loi sur l'importation et l'exportation de biens culturels/PA-188225.

Scattered along 10 000 km of coast, the population of almost all of Newfoundland's distant and remote coves and harbours lived without clergy or schoolteachers. A rich and varied language developed on account of this isolation. Numerous words and phrases survive today in Newfoundland that are found only — if anywhere — in dialects of the British Isles. Residents of various Newfoundland outports can still be distinguished from one another by their accents, which all hark back to western England or Ireland.

In the outports, women had a better chance of equality than those in many other parts of British North America, on account of their important role in the fishery. As historian Ian Ross Robertson has written, "The colony depended on the export of saltfish, or salted dried cod fish, and it was often women who processed on shore the fish that men caught."[7] In effect, they ran the fisheries on shore.

RELIGION AND EDUCATION

www Organized religion came to the island in the eighteenth century. The Anglicans arrived in 1703 with the appointment of John Jackson as the first missionary in Newfoundland for the Society for the Propagation of the Gospel in Foreign Parts (SPG). During the 1700s, two or three Anglican clergy were stationed on the island. Roman Catholic priests had probably arrived and worked secretly on the island before freedom of worship was granted in 1784. After this date, other Protestant churches, such as the Methodists and the Congregationalists, also organized on the island. On the Labrador coast, Moravian missionaries began their work among the Inuit in 1771.

No school is known to have existed in Newfoundland until the eighteenth century, when the SPG established a few schools for the poor and underprivileged. Later, the Wesleyan Methodists and other groups opened schools as well. Most children, however, had no schooling and remained illiterate. The availability of education improved with the foundation of the Newfoundland School Society in 1823. The society, which was closely identified with the

Church of England, provided free grants of land on which to build schools, and free passages to the colony for teachers. It would operate 40 schools in the decades to follow. In the larger towns, particularly St. John's, the upper classes had private tutors and private schools and, in a few cases, sent their children off to be educated in England, since "respectable classes" did not want their children mixing with the "lower orders" in the SPG or Methodist schools. A rigid class structure existed in the capital.

THE MIGRATORY FISHERY BECOMES RESIDENT

Both the American and the French revolutions and the subsequent Napoleonic Wars influenced Newfoundland's trade patterns. With New England's departure from the British empire in 1783 and Britain's subsequent exclusion of Americans from the empire's carrying trade, Newfoundland became the British West Indies' major supplier of fish. Fishery production expanded, creating new jobs and, in turn, causing a sharp decline in emigration from Newfoundland to New England. Newfoundland ships, operating out of Newfoundland ports, became an integral part of the triangular trade with Britain and the West Indies. As it now became illegal for British subjects to own American-built ships, the island began to construct its own vessels.

The outbreak of the last and longest of the wars between Britain and France, the Napoleonic Wars (1793–1814), also contributed to the new prosperity on the island. The price of dried fish rose substantially during the later years of the war because the French had to abandon their Newfoundland fishery. France simply could not protect its fishing fleet in wartime when the country needed to mobilize all of its naval resources to fight England. English vessels also stayed at home. Fears of press-gangs in England forcefully seizing sailors for service in the Royal Navy also convinced many of the bye-boatmen to remain on the island instead of returning to Britain. The resident population, and the fisheries, grew. By 1815, residents owned almost the complete fishing fleet and produced the entire yield of saltfish, whereas immediately before the Napoleonic Wars the English migratory fishery produced more than half the total English–Newfoundland catch.

During these prosperous years, shipowners, settlers, and St. John's entrepreneurs invested heavily in the fishery, creating a resident Newfoundland fleet. They began sending ships to less crowded parts of the coast, to the northern part of the island, and on to Labrador. Each June, thousands of Newfoundland fishers sailed for Labrador to catch cod. Those who fished out of fixed locations with a "room" on shore became known as the "stationers" (or "squatters" or "roomers"); those who lived aboard their schooners and followed the fish were the "floaters" (or "green fish catchers"); those who chose to settle permanently on the Labrador coast became "the livyeres" (most likely a corruption of "live here"). As the Labrador fishery expanded, Britain reattached Labrador to Newfoundland, taking it out of Lower Canada's control in 1809.

The sense of independence and the outlook of these hardy Newfoundlanders on the Labrador coast echoes forth today in one of Newfoundland and Labrador's favourite chanteys, "Jack Was Every Inch a Sailor," a retelling of the Biblical story of Jonah in the whale with a Newfoundlander as the hero.

'Twas twenty-five or thirty years since Jack first saw the light.
He came into this world of woe one dark and stormy night.
He was born on board his father's ship as she was lying to.
'Bout twenty-five or thirty miles southeast of Bacalieu.

Chorus
Jack was every inch a sailor, five and twenty years a whaler,
Jack was every inch a sailor, he was born upon the bright blue sea.

Dory and Crew Setting Cod Trawl-Lines on the Bank, by H.W. Elliott and Captain J.W. Collins (1887).

G.B. Goode, *The Fisheries and Fishing of the United States* (Washington, 1887), plate 26. Reproduced in R. Louis Gentilcore, ed., *Historical Atlas of Canada*, vol. 2, *The Land Transformed, 1800–1891* (Toronto: University of Toronto Press, 1993), plate 37. Reprinted by permission of the University of Toronto Press Incorporated.

When Jack grew up to be a man, he went to the Labrador.
He fished in Indian Harbour, where his father fished before.
On his returning in the fog, he met a heavy gale,
And Jack was swept into the sea and swallowed by a whale.

Repeat Chorus

The whale went straight for Baffin's Bay, about ninety knots an hour,
And every time he'd blow a spray he'd send it in a shower.
"O, now," says Jack unto himself, "I must see what he's about."
He caught the whale all by the tail and turned him inside out.

Repeat Chorus

THE RISE OF THE SEAL FISHERY

Sailors entered the waters off Newfoundland and Labrador's northern coasts to harvest the seal herds on the ice floes. Mammals and fish provided the bulk of the world's industrial oil in the early nineteenth century, and young seals had an excellent fat for fine-quality oil. Their skins could also be sold in England. The industry grew rapidly. Between 1831 and 1833, the seal fishery averaged between 30 and 40 percent of Newfoundland's total exports. More than 600 000 seals were harvested in 1831 alone. By the 1850s, 13 000 men were employed annually in the seal hunt. It supplemented the production of salt cod. In the 1860s, however, a decline set in due to overharvesting.

POLITICAL CHANGES IN THE NINETEENTH CENTURY

Until 1832, Newfoundland was unique among the British North American colonies in that it had no legislature and the naval governor still had near-dictatorial powers. But by the early nineteenth century, the new mercantile and professional elite of St. John's led the struggle for social and political reform. Cut off from regular communication with the capital, the outports

Sealers "copying" the floes, c. 1920. "Copying" in Newfoundland and Labrador means leaping from floe to floe.

Provincial Archives of Newfoundland and Labrador.

remained removed from the discussion. The campaign for self-government was thus led by a group of first-generation arrivals who were anxious for political power but knew little about the island — except for what happened in St. John's.

THE RISE OF A REFORM MOVEMENT

A Scottish physician, William Carson, who had come to St. John's in 1808, led the Reform movement. In his first tract, written three years after his arrival, he argued against the system of naval governors and called for constitutional reform. The first advance came in 1817, when Newfoundland officially became more than a summer fishery. The Colonial Office decided that the governor should remain on the island all year round and not just for two or three months in the summer. Then, in 1824, Britain recognized Newfoundland as a regular colony and abolished the naval government. It repealed the old fishing laws, an action that, among other things, allowed residents to hold clear title to land. In addition, in 1832 Britain instituted representative government. Parliament made provision for a Newfoundland legislature with elected and appointed chambers. Almost all of the male residents of the island gained the franchise.

Political reform heightened internal dissension between Protestants and Catholics (now almost evenly divided in number), between English and Irish, between radicals and conservatives, between merchants and fishers, and between St. John's and the outports. In 1842, Britain suspended Newfoundland's constitution in order to end political deadlock. The Colonial Office then formed a new integrated legislature consisting of eleven elected members and ten Crown appointees. This reduced the Reformers to a small minority, at least until Britain restored the two-chamber system in 1848.

With William Carson's death in 1843, the Reform movement lost much of its momentum, but it revived in 1850 with a platform of obtaining responsible government. Carson's successors, such as John Kent, a fiery Reform politician, demanded that the island obtain cabinet, or responsible, government. This goal was achieved in 1855, finally ending direct British rule. The first premier, the Reform, or Liberal, leader Philip Francis Little, a Roman Catholic, tried to bridge the divisions between the two religious communities by inviting both Roman Catholics and Protestants into his Cabinet, a goal that a Conservative successor, Frederick Carter, a Protestant, also pursued.

On the eve of the discussions for British North American federation, Newfoundland looked eastward toward Britain, not westward toward the mainland. Newfoundland's patterns of trade and settlement linked it to Europe, the West Indies, and the United States. The development of the western part of the island, which contained the land most suitable for agriculture, would have served as a bridge to Canada. Until 1904, however, the French held on to their treaty rights to dry fish on the western coastline.

Newfoundland's geography and distinctive history placed it very much apart from the Canadas and even from the three Maritime colonies. As historian William Menzies Whitelaw wrote of nineteenth-century Newfoundland, "In many ways it was an integral part of British North America, but in others it remained as remote as Bermuda had been from the thirteen colonies."[8]

NOTES

1. Frederick W. Rowe, *A History of Newfoundland and Labrador* (Toronto: McGraw-Hill Ryerson, 1980), p. 109.
2. See Keith Matthews's comments on the growth of law in Newfoundland in *Lectures on the History of Newfoundland, 1500–1830* (St. John's: Breakwater Books, 1988), pp. 131–50.
3. Ingeborg Marshall, *A History and Ethnography of the Beothuk* (Montreal/Kingston: McGill-Queen's University Press, 1996), pp. 157–58.
4. C. Grant Head, *Eighteenth Century Newfoundland: A Geographer's Perspective* (Toronto: McClelland & Stewart, 1976), p. 245.
5. R. Cole Harris and John Warkentin, *Canada Before Confederation: A Study in Historical Geography* (Ottawa: Carleton University Press, 1991 [1974], p. 6.
6. William Menzies Whitelaw, *The Maritimes and Canada before Confederation* (Toronto: Oxford University Press, 1966 [1934]), p. 29.
7. Ian Ross Robertson, "The 1850s: Maturity and Reform," in Phillip A. Buckner and John G. Reid, eds., *The Atlantic Region to Confederation* (Toronto: University of Toronto Press, 1994), p. 353.
8. Whitelaw, *The Maritimes and Canada*, p. 28.

LINKING TO THE PAST w(w)w

The Colonization of Newfoundland
http://www.heritage.nf.ca/exploration/sponsored.html

An illustrated overview of sponsored colonization of Newfoundland—from early settlement schemes, through the Cupids colony, to the French settlement of Placentia—as well as voluntary settlement in the seventeenth and eighteenth centuries.

Placentia, Newfoundland
http://collections.ic.gc.ca/placentia/

Extensive information on the geography and history of Placentia, including the Beothuks, the fishers, and settlers from various European countries. This site also discusses the area's justice system, church history, individual forts, and more.

History of Law and Government in Newfoundland
http://www.heritage.nf.ca/law/default.html

An illustrated history of Newfoundland's government up to the time of Confederation. Go to http://www.heritage.nf.ca/law/admirals.html to read about the fishing admirals.

The Beothuks
http://www.delweb.com/nfmuseum/notes1.htm

From the Newfoundland Museum, an illustrated overview of what is known about these early inhabitants of Newfoundland.

1800s Newfoundland: A Pictorial
http://collections.ic.gc.ca/nfld

An extensive collection of photographs, most likely taken by Simeon H. Parsons (1844–1908), one of Newfoundland's earliest professional photographers.

Religion, Society & Culture in Newfoundland and Labrador
http://www.ucs.mun.ca/~hrollman/

This extensive site offers information on the major religions of Newfoundland and includes an outline of the history of the Beothuk, information on Bishop Inglis's interview with Shawnadithit, and *An Account of the State of the Schools in the Island of Newfoundland, Established or Assisted by the Society for the Propagation of the Gospel in Foreign Parts from 1827.*

RELATED READINGS

For a short survey of early Newfoundland history see Keith Matthews's "The Nature and the Framework of Newfoundland History," in R. Douglas Francis and Donald B. Smith, eds., *Readings in Canadian History: Pre-Confederation*, 6th ed. (Toronto: Nelson Thomson Learning, 2002), pp. 113–119.

BIBLIOGRAPHY

Frederick W. Rowe's *A History of Newfoundland and Labrador* (Toronto: McGraw-Hill Ryerson, 1980) remains the most complete study of Newfoundland's history. Peter Neary and Patrick O'Flaherty provide a short introduction to the island's history in their popular work *Part of the Main: An Illustrated History of Newfoundland and Labrador* (St. John's: Breakwater Books, 1983). Margaret R. Conrad and James K. Hiller, *Atlantic Canada. A Region in the Making* (Don Mills, Ontario: Oxford University Press, 2001) contains valuable references to Newfoundland and Labrador. Mark Kurlansky's popular "biography of the fish that changed the world" is delightful: *Cod* (New York: Penguin, 1998). For an invaluable biographical guide to the historical literature consult Olaf Uwe Janzen's essay, "Newfoundland and the International Fishery," in M. Brook Taylor, ed., *Canadian History: A Reader's Guide*, vol. 1, *Beginnings to Confederation* (Toronto: University of Toronto Press, 1994), pp. 280–324. Important maps of Newfoundland and the fisheries before 1800 appear in R. Cole Harris, ed., *Historical Atlas of Canada*, vol. 1, *From the Beginning to 1800* (Toronto: University of Toronto Press, 1987). G.O. Rothney has written a short survey, *Newfoundland: A History* (Ottawa: Canadian Historical Association, 1964). .

Studies on the history of Newfoundland in the pre-nineteenth-century period include Gillian T. Cell, *English Enterprise in Newfoundland, 1577–1660* (Toronto: University of Toronto Press, 1969); and Keith Matthews, *Lectures on the History of Newfoundland, 1500–1830* (St. John's: Breakwater Books, 1988). Specific information on Lord Baltimore's colony is contained in Luca Codignola's *The Coldest Harbour in the Land: Simon Stock and Lord Baltimore's Colony in Newfoundland, 1621–1649* (Montreal/Kingston: McGill-Queen's University Press, 1987). W. Gordon Handcock reviews English settlement in Newfoundland in *Soe Longe as There Comes No Women* (St. John's: Breakwater Books, 1989). Several essays on early Newfoundland appear in G.M. Story, ed., *Early European Settlement and Exploitation in Atlantic Canada: Selected Papers* (St. John's: Memorial University of Newfoundland, 1982).

For the eighteenth century see C. Grant Head, *Eighteenth Century Newfoundland: A Geographer's Perspective* (Toronto: McClelland & Stewart, 1976). Several sections of Phillip A. Buckner and John G. Reid, eds., *The Atlantic Region to Confederation: A History* (Toronto: University of Toronto Press, 1994); and the older study, W.S. MacNutt's *The Atlantic Provinces: The Emergence of a Colonial Society, 1712–1857* (Toronto: McClelland & Stewart, 1965) contain extensive references to Newfoundland. Frederic F. Thompson's *The French Shore Problem in Newfoundland* (Toronto: University of Toronto Press, 1961) examines this complex question. Patrick O'Neill reviews the history of the economic and political capital of the island in *The Story of St. John's, Newfoundland* (Erin, ON: Boston Mills Press, 1975). Sean T. Cadigan looks at merchant–settler relations in Newfoundland from 1785 to 1855 in *Hope and Deception in Conception Bay* (Toronto: University of Toronto Press, 1995). John P. Greene has written *Between Damnation and Starvation: Priests and Merchants in Newfoundland Politics, 1745–1855* (Montreal/Kingston: McGill-Queen's University Press, 1999). For the history of St. John's, consult Patrick O'Neill, *The Story of St. John's, Newfoundland* (Erin, Ontario: Boston Mills Press, 1975).

The mid-nineteenth-century political history of the island is reviewed in Keith Matthews, "The Class of '32: St. John's Reformers on the Eve of Representative Government," in Phillip A. Buckner and David Frank, eds., *Atlantic Canada Before Confederation*, vol. 1, *The Acadiensis Reader* (Fredericton: Acadiensis Press, 1985), pp. 212–26; and Gertrude E. Gunn, *The Political History of Newfoundland, 1832–1864* (Toronto: University of Toronto Press, 1966). The first volume of a projected series on the political history of Newfoundland has recently appeared, Patrick O'Flaherty's *Old Newfoundland. A History to 1843* (St. John's: Long Beach Press, 1999). P.B. Waite has written a sketch of John Kent, the Reform politician, in the *Dictionary of Canadian Biography*, vol. 10, *1871–1880* (Toronto: University of Toronto Press, 1972), pp. 398–401. Other important biographies of prominent Newfoundlanders appear in this invaluable biographical series, now available online at www.biographi.ca.

An entertaining collection of references to Newfoundland in the nineteenth century is R.G. Moyles's *"Complaints Is Many and Various, But the Odd Divil Likes It"* (Toronto: Peter Martin Associates, 1975). James Hiller and Peter Neary have edited a collection of articles, *Newfoundland in the Nineteenth and the Twentieth Centuries: Essays in Interpretation* (Toronto: University of Toronto Press, 1980). Shannon Ryan reviews nineteenth-century economic developments in "Fishery to Colony: A Newfoundland Watershed, 1793–1815," in Buckner and Frank, eds., *Atlantic Canada Before Confederation*, vol. 1, pp. 130–48. Shannon Ryan has also written *Fish Out of Water: The Newfoundland Saltfish Trade, 1814–1914* (St. John's: Breakwater, 1986). For the history of the Newfoundland seal hunt consult Shannon Ryan, *The Ice Hunters: A History of Newfoundland Sealing to 1914* (St. John's: Breakwater, 1984); and James E. Candow, *Of Men and Seals* (Ottawa: Canadian Parks Service, Environment Canada, 1989). A short introduction to Newfoundland dialects appears in Phillip W. Rogers, "The Dictionary of Newfoundland English," *Queen's Quarterly* 91 (1984): 832–37. A fascinating look at Newfoundland English is G.M. Story, W.J. Kirwin, and J.D.A. Widdowson's edited work, *Dictionary of Newfoundland English*, 2nd ed. with supplement (Toronto: University of Toronto Press, 1990).

A substantial literature exists on Newfoundland's Native population. Book-length treatments include the essential study by Ingeborg Marshall, *A History and Ethnography of the Beothuk* (Montreal/Kingston: McGill-Queen's University Press, 1996); and James P. Howley's *The Beothucks or Red Indians: The Aboriginal Inhabitants of Newfoundland* (Toronto: Coles, 1974 [1915]); and Frederick W. Rowe, *Extinction: The Beothuks of Newfoundland* (Toronto: McGraw-Hill Ryerson, 1977). L.F.S. Upton has written a valuable article, "The Extermination of the Beothucks of Newfoundland," *Canadian Historical Review* 58 (1977): 133–53. For the Mi'kmaqs' history see also Dennis Bartels, "*Ktaqamkuk Ilnui Saqimawoutie*: Aboriginal Rights and the Myth of the Micmac Mercenaries in Newfoundland," in Bruce Alden Cox, ed., *Native People, Native Lands: Canadian Indians, Inuit and Metis* (Ottawa: Carleton University Press, 1988), pp. 32–36. Titles on both the Mi'kmaqs' and the Beothuks are listed in Ralph Pastore's "Native History in the Atlantic Region during the Colonial Period," *Acadiensis* 20(1) (Autumn 1990): 200–25. Ralph Pastore and G.M. Story provide a valuable sketch of Shawnadithit, the last known survivor of the Beothuks, in the *Dictionary of Canadian Biography*, vol. 6, *1821–1835* (Toronto: University of Toronto Press, 1987), pp. 706–709. In *Beyond Their Years. Five Native Women's Stories* (Toronto: Canadian Scholars Press, 1999), pp. 96–173, John Steckley includes an essay on Shawnadithit. G.M. Story completed the sketch of Demasduwit in the *Dictionary of Canadian Biography*, vol. 5, *1801–1820* (Toronto: University of Toronto Press, 1983), pp. 243–44.

Interesting maps of Newfoundland appear in the first two volumes of the *Historical Atlas of Canada*: vol. 1, R. Cole Harris, ed., *From the Beginning to 1800* (Toronto: University of Toronto Press, 1987); and vol. 2, R. Louis Gentilcore, ed., *The Land Transformed, 1800–1891* (Toronto. University of Toronto Press, 1993).

THE NORTHWEST TO THE 1860s

The Blackfoot-speaking peoples occupied the rich buffalo ranges of present-day southern Alberta and northern Montana in the mid-eighteenth century. The horse, brought to Mexico by the Spanish, reached them about 1730, at about the same time that Cree middlemen brought them guns. Apart from possibly one or two "northern white men," as they later termed the English, the only Europeans that the Blackfoot speakers encountered on the northern plains in the 1740s and 1750s were French traders from Canada, whom they called "real white men."

After the fall of New France in 1760, hundreds of Europeans ventured into the interior from the north, the east, and the south. The best furs came from the Northwest, and independent fur traders from Montreal came to buy them. In the early 1780s, these Scottish and American fur traders formed the North West Company (whose agents came to be called Nor'Westers) to challenge the Hudson's Bay Company, already more than a century old. Thirty years of competition between the two companies ended with their merger in 1821. Even after the Métis broke the Hudson's Bay Company monopoly in the Red River in 1849, the company remained the leading commercial power in Rupert's Land.

The buffalo were the great wonder in the region: 50–60 million roamed on the Great Plains in the early nineteenth century. John Tanner, a Virginia boy kidnapped and later adopted by the Ottawa (Odawa), recalled that around 1800 near Pembina in the Red River area, he held his ear to the ground and heard the sound of a distant herd. Later he discovered that the herd at that point was 30 km away. Half a century later, in southern Alberta, John Palliser heard a gigantic herd before he saw them: "Their particular grunt sounded like the roar of distant rapids in a large river." Yet, by the mid-1860s, the bounty of nature had been strained to the limit. Due to the increased kill by newcomers and First Nations, the buffalo had become scarce in many areas of the Plains. As historian Olive Dickason writes: "The bison, once 'countless' because they were so many, were rapidly becoming 'countless' because there were none left."[1] Once the Plains First Nations lost their economic independence with the loss of the buffalo, their political independence was threatened too.

THE FRENCH AND THE ENGLISH IN THE INTERIOR

 The French came west in search of a short route to China. Since Verrazzano's voyage in 1524, the French had believed in the existence of a gulf that cut deeply into the continent from the Pacific, like Hudson Bay or the Gulf of Mexico. When René-Robert Cavelier de La Salle travelled inland in 1669 in search of China, his neighbours named his land grant on the south bank of Montreal Island "La Chine" (China), in recognition of his ambition to reach the Orient by way of "La Mer de l'Ouest" (the Western Sea). Half a century later, the French still hoped that somewhere between the 40th and 50th parallels of latitude a navigable strait joined the Western Sea to the Pacific Ocean.

THE FRENCH SEARCH FOR THE "WESTERN SEA"

In 1717, the French Crown approved expeditions to discover the Western Sea, but would not pay for them. Profits from fur-trade posts west of Lake Superior had to cover the exploration costs. Then, in 1730, Pierre Gaultier de Varennes et de La Vérendrye, commander of the fur-trading post on Kaministiquia (present-day Thunder Bay), offered to establish a post on Lake Winnipeg. He agreed to conduct explorations for the Western Sea from this base, at no expense to the Crown.

From Kaministiquia, La Vérendrye travelled westward in the 1730s, building fur-trading posts in the Lake of the Woods district and around Lakes Winnipeg and Winnipegosis. The

---

Indian Greeting White Man, a painting by the American illustrator Frederic Remington (1861–1909). "Real white men" is what the Blackfoot of Alberta call the French in the Blackfoot language, probably because traders from New France were the first Europeans to make contact with them.

Glenbow Collection, Calgary, Canada/60.2.20.

Chevalier de La Corne, a successor, founded a fort farther west, near the forks of the north and south branches of the Saskatchewan River, in 1753. The French never found "La Mer de l'Ouest," but they did locate the key to the interior — the Saskatchewan River, whose twin branches flow through the central plains in a huge, wavering Y.

One of the best summaries of the French advance westward came later from the pen of an English visitor who travelled across Alberta in 1914. "Cross the whole vast plain of Central Canada and reach the mountains. What is that called, you ask? That is Mount Miette. And that? That is Tête Jaune. And that lake? It is Lake Brûlé. They were more than scouts in front of an army. They were so far ahead that the army will take a century before it reaches their outposts...." The visitor was writer Sir Arthur Conan Doyle, creator of Sherlock Holmes.

THE HUDSON'S BAY COMPANY'S INLAND EXPEDITIONS

The English established trading posts in the late seventeenth century at the mouths of rivers emptying into Hudson Bay. From these forts they carried on a profitable trade with the Cree and Assiniboine, who, acting as middlemen, brought furs to them and came to dominate the exchange of furs. They charged the First Nations in the interior a considerable markup on the European goods they obtained from the English and, until 1713, from the French.

The English sponsored only two inland expeditions southwest of York Factory, their major post on Hudson Bay. In 1690–91 they sent Henry Kelsey, a young employee, just out of his teens, known to the Hudson's Bay Company's committee in London as "a very active lad, delighting much in Indians' company, being never more pleased than when he is travelling amongst them," to explore the interior. He travelled from York Factory with a Cree band and reached the prairies, probably in present-day east-central Saskatchewan. But upon his return the company decided not to establish costly forts in the interior. As long as the Crees and the Assiniboines brought good furs to them, the English would stay on Hudson Bay.

Then a series of armed clashes occurred on Hudson Bay between the French and the English. By the Treaty of Utrecht in 1713, France recognized England's possession of the coastline of Hudson and James Bay. But the French continued to trade in the interior. So, more than half a century after Kelsey's journey, the English changed their minds. They now felt the effect of strong French competition. In 1754, they sent Anthony Henday inland to convince the First Nations to give up their trade at the French posts and to come to the bay. In his journal, which is far more precise than Kelsey's, Henday identified the specific groups in the interior and provided notes on their way of life. The young trader became the first Englishman to describe the buffalo hunt. Henday returned to York Factory with a Native wife who had helped him immeasurably as an interpreter, an assistant, and a reliable source of information.

THE IMPACT OF THE EUROPEANS ON THE FIRST NATIONS

The arrival of the Europeans greatly altered the First Nations' way of life through the introduction of guns, horses, and new trade patterns. It also led to the rise of a mixed people: the Métis.

The impact of firearms differed for the Woodland peoples and those on the Plains. The Woodland peoples came to rely on guns much more than those on the Plains, who really only used them in warfare. For the Woodland First Nations, specialists in hunting furs, the gun generally proved more efficient than the bow and arrow as it eliminated long hours of trapping, waiting for the animal to weaken through loss of blood. Moreover, they had access to the service centres where gunsmiths could repair them; for instance, at York Factory on Hudson Bay, in what is now northeastern Manitoba. Hence, the Woodland groups, despite certain disadvantages — the awkward loading of powder and shot, barrels that were prone to explosion, and the firearms' easy breakage in cold weather — used them a great deal. This reliance on firearms tied them closely to the fur-trading posts.

Distant from service centres, the Plains peoples could not easily have their firearms repaired. In addition, the First Nations in the interior could not obtain ammunition easily, since the traders did not stock large supplies. Moreover, for buffalo hunting, the Native peoples preferred sinew-backed bows with metal-tipped arrows, which did not make a noise that prematurely stampeded a herd. Their experienced hunters could easily reload a bow on horseback. But in battle, the Plains peoples did use firearms. Guns had obvious advantages. Bullets went a longer distance than arrows and had greater killing power. Rawhide shields and armour offered little protection against a musket ball. In addition, the gun's loud report gave its user a psychological advantage in battle.

In the early eighteenth century, the Chipewyans, armed with guns, moved further into the woodlands immediately north of the Woodland Crees. Directly supplied by the English at Churchill, the Chipewyans sold European goods to interior nations. The Chipewyan woman, Thanadelthur, became an invaluable interpreter and envoy for the Hudson's Bay Company in the 1710s. Like the Woodland Crees farther south, the Chipewyans became the traders' middlemen. In addition, European guns gave them an advantage in their struggle with the Inuit to the north and the Crees. In 1770–72, Samuel Hearne, a Hudson's Bay Company explorer, made an epic journey with a group of Chipewyans across the barren lands from Churchill to the Arctic Ocean. His account, *A Journey from Prince of Wales's Fort, in Hudson's Bay, to the Northern Ocean*, remains one of the classics of North American travel literature, although now it is recognized that Hearne's publisher embellished the original text, and apparently invented entire scenes.

Migration and the adoption of new ways characterized the experience of the Lakota, or Sioux, farther to the south. In the eighteenth century, they moved out onto the plains. No consensus exists about the reason for the move; according to historian Peter Iverson, the Sioux and their neighbours, the Ojibwa, have their own explanations. "The Ojibwas, for example, say they forced the Sioux, their word for 'enemy,' out of Minnesota, but the Lakota people do not subscribe to this story. Instead, they speak of their imagination and initiative in following the bison and tell how they sought out opportunities for trade and expansion, which could be realized only in the West."[2]

Apparently, the Cree already lived along the North Saskatchewan River in the late eighteenth century, but their repeated intrusions ended their initially friendly relations with the Blackfoot or "Prairie People." Individual Cree bands travelled over the plains independently. No single chief co-ordinated the expansion. As historian Hugh Dempsey writes, the chiefs "did not order their people to move, they simply told them their own plans. A good chief had a faithful following, and they would go with him; but if for any reason his people disagreed with him, they were free to make their own decisions."[3]

The horse had a greater impact than the gun on the Native peoples of the prairies. The Blackfoot used horses for hunting buffalo. Horse-mounted warriors replaced those on foot in driving and luring the animals into buffalo pounds or over cliffs (buffalo jumps). Mounted hunters rushed straight into a herd, singled out an animal, rode beside it, and killed it at close range with two or three arrows from their bows.

The Blackfoot sought five qualities in their buffalo horses: the ability to sustain a high speed over a distance of several kilometres; instant response to commands; quick movement alongside a buffalo while staying clear of it and its horns; the ability to run swiftly without stumbling over uneven ground; and finally, the ability to remain controlled in face of stampeding buffalos. A trained horse was worth several simple riding or pack animals.

The horse caused a cultural revolution on the Great Plains. It became a symbol of wealth. Some rich individuals owned up to 100 horses. By giving away or even lending horses, individuals enhanced their prestige. Horses were borrowed for hunting and for war parties, with the borrower returning in payment a portion of the game killed or of the goods seized. The horse thus contributed to a class structure among the Native peoples of the prairies, based on the number of horses owned.

The introduction of the horse had other effects. It intensified warfare between First Nations. Combat on horseback with a bow and arrow, lance, war club, or knife — or a European rifle — led to increased casualties. The horse also enabled the Woodland Assiniboines and many of the Woodland Crees to hunt buffalo on the prairies, thus lessening their dependence on European guns and trade goods. In general, life became very mobile for the First Nations of the Great Plains, particularly for the equestrian Blackfoot-speaking communities.

THE FUR TRADE AFTER THE FALL OF NEW FRANCE

After the fall of New France in 1760, the Hudson's Bay Company anticipated a trade monopoly in the Northwest. But the company soon faced new rivals: aggressive Scottish and American traders operating out of Montreal. In the early 1770s, these traders employed large numbers of French-speaking voyageurs and sent large shipments of goods to the West.

Their arrival on the prairies led to clashes with the First Nations population. In 1779, the Plains Cree attacked a trading post on the North Saskatchewan River, killing two traders. Other incidents occurred, including a battle at a post on the Assiniboine River in 1781, in which three traders and 30 First Nations people died. Only a smallpox epidemic in 1781–82 saved the traders from large-scale Native retaliation.

In the early 1780s, the Montreal traders combined their capital to form the North West Company, a decentralized fur-trading operation that soon expanded beyond the French fur trade in the West to include the Peace, Mackenzie, and Columbia River districts.

THE EMERGENCE OF THE NORTH WEST COMPANY

The North West Company employed experienced French-Canadian, Métis, and Iroquois canoeists. These hardy voyageurs would cross half a continent. As a rule, they were short (long legs were a definite disadvantage in a birchbark canoe), with great strength and endurance. On the journey, they slept only 5 to 6 hours a day. They paddled from 12 to 15, even 18, hours a day, if they had to. With their light paddles and rapid strokes, they made 40 to 60 strokes a minute. They regularly portaged loads of 80 kg, sometimes 120 kg, on their backs over rocky trails.

The North West Company underwent great expansion in the 1780s and 1790s. In 1778, fur trader Peter Pond reached the Athabasca and Peace River country (in present-day northern Alberta), rich with fur-bearing animals. In 1789, Alexander Mackenzie journeyed down the Mackenzie River and, in 1793, reached the Pacific Ocean. The company then opened up posts in the Mackenzie Basin and, later, along the Columbia River.

The cost of sending goods over a supply line that stretched from Montreal to Fort Chipewyan on Lake Athabasca greatly curbed the North West Company's profits. Still the Nor'Wester organization grew and, in 1804, incorporated the XY Company (formed in the late 1790s by independent Montreal fur traders).

Despite its opponent's great size, the Hudson's Bay Company had the advantage of a shorter, hence less expensive, transportation route — Hudson Bay was considerably closer than Montreal to the inland posts. The smaller company could take trade goods to the Athabasca country at about one-half the cost. The Hudson's Bay Company's York boats, although slower and much heavier than a canoe, could carry greater amounts of trade goods in, and more fur bundles out, than could the Nor'Westers' canoes.

Hudson's Bay Company employees with their stock and canoes. Voyageurs with a tumpline around their foreheads normally carried two, or sometimes three, of these 40-kg packages of furs or merchandise over a portage. Since warm or wet weather drew out the smell of any unscraped fat on the pelts, the fur bundles often were rancid travelling companions.

National Archives of Canada/C-82974.

The Hudson's Bay Company developed the durable York boat, which allowed them to compete effectively with the North West Company.

Hudson's Bay Company Archives, Archives of Manitoba.

A Historical Portrait ☜

☞ George Nelson

If asked to name the most celebrated fur traders of the late eighteenth and early nineteenth centuries, most historians would immediately mention Samuel Hearne, David Thompson, Alexander Mackenzie, Simon Fraser, Peter Fidler, or Peter Pond. A host of names would follow, but most likely it would be a long while before the name of the lowly, underpaid North West Company clerk George Nelson would surface. He produced no great maps or surveys, made no great voyages of exploration, rose to no great administrative heights. He achieved no fame in his lifetime at all, in contrast to his younger brothers, Wolfred Nelson, a Patriote in the Lower Canadian Rebellion of 1837 — and later mayor of Montreal; and Robert Nelson, the Patriotes' leader in 1838 and later a very successful surgeon in the United States.

But for the attention of fur-trade historians Jennifer Brown, Robert Brightman, and Sylvia Van Kirk, George Nelson might still be unknown to students of the Canadian fur trade. His chief distinction, as Brown and Brightman point out in their edited work, *"The Orders of the Dreamed": George Nelson on Cree and Northern Ojibwa Religion and Myth, 1823*[1] comes from his sensitive recording, in a memoir written nearly two centuries ago, of western Cree and Ojibwa beliefs. He listened to the people and carefully recorded their stories. Sylvia Van Kirk describes his memoir as "one of the finest early ethnographic documents of its kind."[2]

George Nelson (1786–1859) was the son of Loyalists from New York who fled to Quebec to escape the American Revolution. As the son of an English Protestant schoolmaster, George received a good education.

From the age of 16, when he entered the fur trade, he lived among First Nations people. From 1802 to 1823 Nelson served as a clerk in present-day Wisconsin, northwestern Ontario, Manitoba, and Saskatchewan. He married Mary Ann, an Ojibwa woman, who was a valuable helpmate in his work. Upon his retirement from the fur trade they settled with their four daughters at Sorel, just east of Montreal.

During his years in the Northwest, Nelson wrote constantly. Many of his fur-trade journals and his reminiscences (written 10 to 40 years after the events they describe) have survived and are valuable for an understanding of the Native peoples of the Northwest. But his memoir of 1823, written in his last year in the fur trade, while Nelson was stationed at Lac la Ronge in northeastern Saskatchewan, is the greatest ethnological treasure because it offers insight into the religion and myth of the Cree and Ojibwa.

In the text, Nelson provided "detail of their private life," including an account of the shaking tent ceremony used by religious leaders to provide a glimpse into the future. Nelson also discussed the importance of dreams to the Native peoples. Attention is given to the mythical being the Windigo: "Suffice it to say that they are of uncommon size — Goliath is an unborn infant to them: and to add to their dread, they are represented as possessing much of the Power of Magicians. Their head reaching to the tops of the highest Poplars (about 70, or 80, feet)."[3]

Nelson's life in Lower Canada after his retirement was not happy. His wife died in 1831. Only one of their children survived into adulthood. Nelson became estranged from his brothers, Wolfred and Robert, on account of their participation in the Rebellions of 1837–38. He regarded their activities as treason. As a farmer he had little success. Probably his greatest joy after his wife's death came from writing his reminiscences of his days in "Indian country." He died in 1859 at the age of 73.

[1] Jennifer S.H. Brown and Robert Brightman, *"The Orders of the Dreamed": George Nelson on Cree and Northern Ojibwa Religion and Myth, 1823* (Winnipeg: University of Manitoba Press, 1988).

[2] Sylvia Van Kirk, in collaboration with Jennifer S.H. Brown, "George Nelson," *Dictionary of Canadian Biography*, vol. 8: *1851–1860* (Toronto: University of Toronto Press, 1985), p. 653).

[3] Nelson, *"The Orders of the Dreamed,"* p. 86.

RIVALRY BETWEEN THE NORTH WEST COMPANY AND THE HUDSON'S BAY COMPANY

Competition from the North West Company forced the Hudson's Bay Company to go farther inland to obtain the best furs. The expansion of the two companies led to the elimination of the Cree and Assiniboine middlemen, as both the Nor'Westers and the Hudson's Bay Company

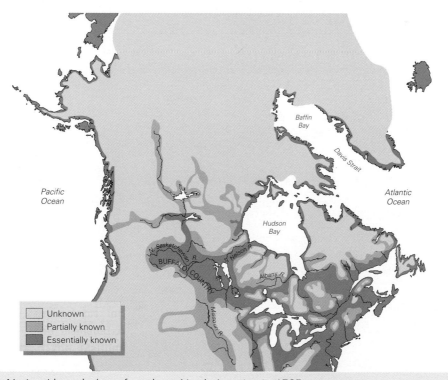

Non-Natives' knowledge of northern North America in 1795.

Source: Adapted from Richard I. Ruggles, *A Country So Interesting: The Hudson's Bay Company and Two Centuries of Mapping, 1670–1870* (Montreal/Kingston: McGill-Queen's University Press, 1991), p. 73.

Where Historians Disagree
The First Nations' Role in the Fur Trade

For years, many fur-trade historians argued that the First Nations were passive agents in a trade dominated by more dynamic European traders. In *The Fur Trade and the Northwest to 1857*, for instance, E.E. Rich wrote that "within a decade of their becoming acquainted with European goods, tribe after tribe became utterly dependent on regular European supplies. The bow and arrow went out of use, and the Indian starved if he did not own a serviceable gun, powder, and shot; and in his tribal wars he was even more dependent on European arms."[1]

In the 1970s and early 1980s, Arthur J. Ray, Robin Fisher, Daniel Francis, Toby Morantz, and Paul C. Thistle challenged this interpretation. They underlined the independence of the Native peoples and their power in the trade. Historian Olive Dickason summarized the new approach in a review of Paul C. Thistle's *Indian–European Trade Relations in the Lower Saskatchewan River Region to 1840*: "Common to all of these works is the theme that Amerindians were as aware as Europeans in matters of self-interest, and during the early days of the fur trade at least, were able to manipulate matters to their own advantage. As long as they held the monopoly in fur production, they were also able to dictate the terms by which they were willing to trade. It was only when the exploitative nature of the fur trade began to affect the availability of resources, coupled with the widening technological gap that was a consequence of the Industrial Revolution, that Europeans were able to gain the upper hand."[2]

This led to a recognition of the First Nations' role in the fur trade as partners and initiators, as well as consumers. They became involved by their own choice. As historian Robin Fisher notes, concerning the early West Coast maritime fur trade, "The Indians of the northwest coast exercised a great deal of control over the trading relationship and, as a consequence, remained in control of their culture during this early contact period."[3] He added: "Even in these early years, the Indians were not passive objects of exploitation. Rather, they vigorously grew accustomed to the presence of the Europeans; they also became shrewder in trading with them."[4]

The absence of Native peoples' narratives remains the great weakness of research into the fur trade. Daniel Francis questions whether this has led historians to overemphasize the importance of the trading exchanges. In his *Battle for the West: Fur Traders and the Birth of Western Canada*, he observed that "the two groups met briefly at the posts to exchange goods, each receiving from the other things it could not produce for itself. Then they parted, the Indians returning to a world the trader never entered or understood, a world with its own patterns of trade, its own religion and social relations, its own wars and alliances.... [For] the most part traders were peripheral to the real concerns of the Indian people."[5]

Native-written studies have partially compensated for the absence of earlier First Nations accounts, including George Blondin's *When the World Was New: Stories of the Sahtú Dene* and Edward Ahenakew's *Voices of the Plains Cree.*[6]

[1] E.E. Rich, *The Fur Trade and the Northwest to 1857* (Toronto: McClelland & Stewart, 1967), pp. 102–103.

[2] Olive Dickason, "Review of *Indian–European Trade Relations in the Lower Saskatchewan River Region to 1840* by Paul C. Thistle," *Western Canadian Publications Project Newsletter,* 21 (May 1987): 2.

[3] Robin Fisher, *Contact and Conflict: Indian–European Relations in British Columbia, 1774–1890* (Vancouver: University of British Columbia Press, 1977), p. 1.

[4] Ibid., p. 4.

[5] Daniel Francis, *Battle for the West: Fur Traders and the Birth of Western Canada* (Edmonton: Hurtig, 1982), p. 62.

[6] George Blondin, *When the World Was New: Stories of the Sahtú Dene* (Yellowknife: Outcrop Books, 1990); and Edward Ahenakew, *Voices of the Plains Cree,* ed., Ruth M. Buck (Regina: Canadian Plains Research Center, 1995; originally published, 1973).

established direct contact with the interior hunting bands. The Woodland Assiniboine and the Woodland Cree bands moved out onto the prairie and became provisioners, supplying the two trading companies with pemmican (dried buffalo meat mixed with buffalo fat and berries). Pemmican was easy to transport, kept well, and provided a nutritious, balanced diet. The demands for pemmican were enormous: a voyageur would consume nearly a kilogram a day — the equivalent of approximately three kilograms of fresh meat.

THE RISE OF THE MÉTIS

 French fur traders were established in the upper Great Lakes by the 1690s. As they intermarried with Native women, a group of "mixed-bloods," or Métis, appeared. The number of mixed marriages grew steadily. After a generation or two, Métis settlements extended from the upper Great Lakes west to the Red River and south through the Great Plains to the Arkansas River. Their culture uniquely blended Native and European customs. They saw themselves as constituting a "new nation." In 1818, William McGillivray of the North West Company commented that the Métis "one and all look upon themselves as members of an independent tribe of natives, entitled to a property in the soil, to a flag of their own, and to protection from the British government."

French and Métis voyageurs travelled throughout the area that is present-day western Canada and the United States. They introduced a number of French words to describe the new terrain: "coulee" (from *coulée*) for a deep gulch or ravine; "butte" for a flat-topped hill; and "prairie" (from *pré*) for meadow. The French also left a permanent record of their presence in the pronunciation of place names — for instance, in the silent terminal "s" of Arkansas and Illinois.

One of the earliest photographs taken in the Canadian
West: a portrait of Susan, a
Swampy Cree mixed-blood
woman. Photographer
Humphrey Lloyd Hime, then
24 years old, took this shot
while accompanying the Hind
expedition in 1858.

Toronto Reference Library/T14359.

The Métis's blending of French and Native worlds led to the development of a new language — French Cree, or, as the Métis call it, "Michif."
John C. Crawford, a linguist, has described the language as follows: "The
extraordinary characteristic of Michif is the manner in which French and
Cree components combine; the noun phrase is a French domain; verb
structure is clearly and thoroughly Cree, and syntax is Cree with French
and probably English influence."[4] "Bungee," a dialect of English with a
strong Cree and Ojibwa component, evolved among the Aboriginal peoples who lived close to the Scottish settlement in the Red River.

THE MÉTIS AT THE RED RIVER

In the early nineteenth century, encampments of the French and their
mixed-blood descendants developed at the junction of the Red and the
Assiniboine rivers (at present-day Winnipeg). The increasing number of
intermarriages furthered the growth of the "new nation" of the Métis. Like
the mixed-bloods on the upper Great Lakes, the Red River Métis built
homes of squared logs covered with bark roofs. They made a special
baking-powder biscuit called "bannock," still a staple food in Métis communities today. Although they farmed a little, growing peas and potatoes
in small gardens behind their cabins, they lived essentially off the buffalo
hunt in the early nineteenth century.

They also introduced European technology to prairie life. For
example, they introduced the small wagons used by the French Canadians
in Quebec. These "Red River carts," built entirely of wood and tied
together with leather, were easy to repair and very efficient. To cross a
river, one simply took off the wheels, some of which were 2 m in diameter, strapped them underneath the cart, and used the vehicle as a raft. But
the carts' constant rubbing of wood against wood made a terrible noise
(one observer described it as the sound of a thousand fingernails being
drawn across a thousand panes of glass at the same time). As well, the carts
stirred up clouds of dust that could be seen several kilometres away. Still,
the Red River carts aided the Métis during the buffalo hunt. An ox-drawn cart could carry a load
of 400 kg more than 30 km in a day. Several carts could be tied together in a caravan, enabling
one driver to handle five oxen and carts. Soon the Red River cart trails rivalled the rivers as
transportation routes.

ABORIGINAL WOMEN IN THE FUR TRADE

By the late eighteenth and early nineteenth centuries, many North West Company and Hudson's
Bay Company employees had Native wives. Besides providing companionship and emotional
support, Native wives offered voyageurs economic benefits too: the daughter of a leading hunter
or chief brought to her new husband the trade of his new father-in-law, as well as his immediate
relations. Native wives also taught the traders the customs and languages of the First Nations.
As well, Native women acted as guides and interpreters for their husbands. Moreover, they made
pemmican, gathered berries, fished, dressed skins, and made moccasins and snowshoes, all
essential skills for the fur traders' survival.

By the early 1800s, interracial marriage between Europeans and the First Nations had
become so common that about 1000 First Nations women and Métis children lived at North

West Company posts. The company encouraged its labourers to marry the mixed-blood daughters of the older employees rather than First Nations women, in an effort to reduce the number of dependants at its posts, and thereby the demands for assistance. Many young Métis women had the ideal background for life as wives at a fur-trading post: they knew both the skills of their Native ancestors and the domestic duties required at the post — cleaning, planting, and harvesting.

THE RED RIVER COLONY

In 1811, Lord Douglas, the Fifth Earl of Selkirk, and a leading shareholder in the Hudson's Bay Company, persuaded the company to establish a European agricultural colony at the forks of the Red and Assiniboine rivers. The colony would provide a home to retire in for Hudson's Bay Company employees and their Native wives and families. It would also become an agricultural centre to supply provisions for the company's workforce in the interior. As well, the colony could serve as a refuge for evicted Scottish tenant farmers.

The following year, Selkik recruited the majority of his settlers from Kildonan, Sutherlandshire, where the evictions of the tenant farmers to make sheep runs had been particularly brutal. Earlier, he had settled 800 displaced Highlanders on Prince Edward Island and had begun a less successful settlement at Baldoon on Lake St. Clair in Upper Canada. After his family acquired a controlling interest in the Hudson's Bay Company, Selkirk obtained from the company an enormous land grant of 300 000 km² in the Red River valley — five times the size of Scotland — that he named Assiniboia. The location was contentious because it lay across the North West Company's vital pemmican supply line in the heart of the Red River valley, thus threatening to curtail its supply of pemmican. But the North West Company failed to prevent the founding of the colony.

THE ESTABLISHMENT OF THE SELKIRK COLONY

The advance party of 18 of Selkirk's settlers reached the Red River from Hudson Bay in late August 1812, and another 120 joined them in late October. Miles Macdonell, Selkirk's choice as governor, established the settlers near the junction of the Red and the Assiniboine rivers (now downtown Winnipeg).

The idealistic and impractical Lord Selkirk sent them off without ploughs, with only hoes and spades to use for cultivation. As well, the colony's lifeline of communication stretched back more than 1000 km to a tiny fort on Hudson Bay, visited once a year by ships from Britain. To survive the first winter, the newly arrived colonists had to travel 125 km south to encamp near the Hudson's Bay Company post at Pembina. The following year, only their potatoes yielded well, thus forcing the settlers to spend another rugged Red River winter at Pembina, this time in log huts. Only the assistance of the local Métis and North West Company traders enabled the Selkirk settlers to survive those first two years.

Then Macdonell unwittingly antagonized the Métis. He issued a "pemmican proclamation" in January 1814 that placed an embargo on the export of pemmican from the Red River settlement. This action hurt the North West Company because it depended on Red River pemmican to feed its voyageurs in the interior. The proclamation confirmed the Nor'Westers' suspicions that the Hudson's Bay Company had planted the Red River colony to ruin them. They retaliated first by offering the Selkirk settlers free transport to new homes and better land in Upper Canada. Two-thirds of the 200 settlers accepted in 1815. Then, the Nor'Westers arrested Miles Macdonell, forced the remaining settlers to withdraw, and burned the settlement. Selkirk retaliated by sending more settlers to reoccupy the colony, along with a new governor, Robert Semple.

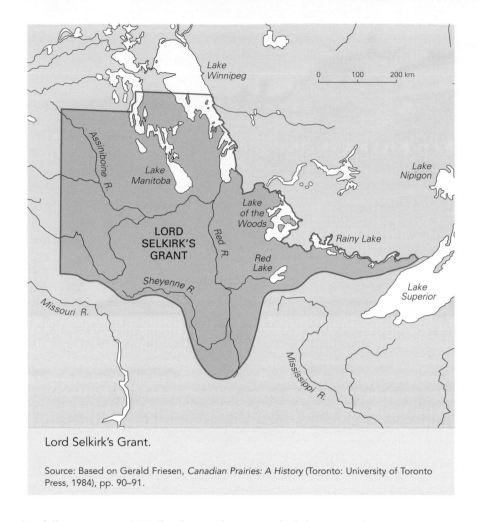

Lord Selkirk's Grant.

Source: Based on Gerald Friesen, *Canadian Prairies: A History* (Toronto: University of Toronto Press, 1984), pp. 90–91.

The following year (1816), the rivalry intensified between the two companies. The Nor'Westers selected young Cuthbert Grant, the son of a Scottish Nor'Wester and a Cree mother, then in his early twenties, and three French-speaking Métis to head a movement of French-speaking Métis to drive out the Selkirk colonists.

SEVEN OAKS

On June 19, 1816, on a field called Seven Oaks, Grant and a party of some 60 or 70 Métis confronted Governor Robert Semple and some 25 settlers and Hudson's Bay Company employees. Fighting broke out, and Semple and 20 of his men lost their lives. Only one of Grant's men was killed.

The victory strengthened Métis unity by reinforcing an identity that had already existed among the French-speaking Métis in the Red River valley. Within hours, the conflict was retold in the "Chanson de la Grenouillère," or "Song of Frog Plain," by Pierre Falcon, the Prairie Métis bard. That song became the French-speaking Métis's national anthem. Their collective memory of the victory gave the French-speaking Métis in the Red River a cohesion and a common identity that the English-speaking mixed-bloods (called the Country-born) around the Hudson's Bay Company posts to the north lacked.

THE MERGER OF THE NORTH WEST AND HUDSON'S BAY COMPANIES

w(w)w The violence at Red River prompted the British government to seek a forced solution to the rivalry. It pressured the two financially exhausted companies to unite. In 1821, the Hudson's Bay and North West companies merged. The consolidated company, the Hudson's Bay Company, ended the North West Company's trade route via Montreal and shipped its furs through Hudson Bay. After 1821, only 5 percent of the furs exported from British North America passed through Montreal.

George Simpson, nicknamed "the Little Emperor" by his employees, became the governor of the newly-restructured Hudson's Bay Company for the next forty years, until his death in 1860. He had jurisdiction over an area that included Hudson Bay, the Arctic and Pacific Oceans, and the Missouri River. Simpson introduced strict conservation measures in areas that had been overtrapped, laid off hundreds of redundant employees, kept salaries down, and closed unnecessary posts.

RED RIVER SOCIETY IN THE MID-NINETEENTH CENTURY

The Red River Scottish colonists and mixed-blood farmers faced many environmental challenges throughout the early nineteenth century. Grasshoppers destroyed their crops in 1818–19, and a great flood levelled their settlement in 1826. Whenever the Red River overflowed its banks, the water spread quickly over huge areas because of the flatness of the valley. In 1826, in just one day, the flood waters rose nearly three metres, transforming the settlement into a lake. Houses were swept away that winter; the survivors dug cellars in the prairie, roofed them with sod, and lived underground. Floods would strike the Red River colony twice more during the century, in 1852 and 1882. Frosts destroyed the colony's crops totally or partially at least once every decade from 1810 to 1870.

Only by the 1840s, did the settlement of some 6000 inhabitants achieve a level of stability and prosperity. The Métis, almost half the total population, resided south and west of the forks of the two rivers. To the north, down the Red River toward Lake Winnipeg, lived the Country-born, the descendants of English-speaking fur traders and their Native wives; they comprised about a third of the settlement. Their neighbours, the original Selkirk settlers, were about a tenth of the Red River population, and the First Nations comprised another tenth.

THE COUNTRY-BORN

The English-speaking mixed-bloods, the "Country-born," came from the northern Hudson's Bay Company posts. Many of their European ancestors came from the Orkney Islands, northwest of Scotland. Before 1800, the Hudson's Bay Company recruited more than 80 percent of its personnel there. Most of them were under 21 years of age. They worked as contract labourers for three or four years before returning home. Some, however, remained much longer; a few stayed for more than 20 years. These individuals fathered large families. Many used their savings to provide for their "country wives" and Native children before leaving to retire in the Orkneys or in Scotland. With the establishment of Selkirk's permanent settlement, many retired employees of the company now stayed in the Red River colony with their Native families. Their children were introduced to farming. Many also joined the Anglican church, first established by John West in 1820. A few obtained positions in the Hudson's Bay Company. Although racial bonds and the common use of the Cree or Ojibwa languages united the Country-born and the French-speaking Métis, religion and their place of residence in the Red River colony divided them.

Métis Encampment on a Buffalo Hunt, a painting by Paul Kane.

Courtesy of the Royal Ontario Museum, Toronto/912.1.25. © ROM.

Canadian historian John Foster wrote of the Country-born that a number "moved comfortably among the Métis. Others were more at home with the Indians.... Still others served a leadership role among the Kildonan Scots. Equal diversity could be found in terms of occupation and wealth."[5]

THE FRENCH-SPEAKING MÉTIS

The French-speaking Métis created a cohesive community, unified, in particular, by their Roman Catholic faith. The arrival of the first French-speaking priests in the Red River settlement in 1818, followed by the first Oblate missionaries and the first sisters, the Grey Nuns, in the 1840s, strengthened the Métis's Christian faith as well as their knowledge of the language and culture of their French-Canadian ancestors.

The Métis also obtained a sense of community through participation in their expanding buffalo hunt. In the 1840s, they went on two annual hunts from the Red River — in June and in September or October. These expeditions included more than 1000 people. The Métis elected ten captains by vote at a general council, one of whom they named "chief of the hunt," or "governor." Each captain had ten "soldiers" under his command who helped the governor of the hunt maintain order. After the Métis elected the officers, they drew up regulations and the crier announced them. Such rules as "no person or party to run buffalo before the general order" show the discipline of the hunt. Rigid discipline prevented the premature stampede of the herds and was essential in the resistance to raids by the Sioux.

THE SAYER TRIAL, 1849

The Métis, the largest group in the Red River colony, came to resent the Hudson's Bay Company's tight control over the settlement. The test case of Métis power came during the trial of Pierre-Guillaume Sayer, a Métis trader arrested in 1849 on a charge of illegally trafficking in furs. The

Hudson's Bay Company argued that Sayer violated its monopoly by selling goods to the colonists and trading with the First Nations. The Métis, who had not yet left on the spring hunt, organized an informal self-defence committee. Between 200 and 300 Métis, including committee member Louis Riel, Sr., gathered outside the courthouse during the trial. After hearing the evidence, the court found Sayer guilty as charged. The judge, however, imposed no sentence. It would have been difficult to do so, because the Métis hunters constituted the most powerful military force in the colony. When Sayer emerged from the courthouse a free man, the Métis knew that they had broken the Hudson's Bay Company's monopoly. "*Vive la liberté, le commerce est libre*," they shouted. After the trial, the Hudson's Bay Company recognized French as an official language in the Red River colony.

Pierre-Guillaume Sayer (left) and Louis Riel, Sr.

Provincial Archives of Manitoba/N1445.

THE BATTLE OF GRAND COTEAU, 1851

The second test of Métis power came two years later. As the Métis moved farther to the southwest to hunt buffalo, they came into conflict with the Sioux. The Métis–Sioux wars intensified in the 1840s and came to a head in 1851, at the battle of Grand Coteau ("big hillock"), southeast of present-day Minot, North Dakota. During the clash, in which the Métis fought from behind a circular barricade made with their carts, packs, and saddles, at least 20 of the Sioux, but only one Métis, died. The Métis victory over a numerically larger party of Sioux demonstrated their growing military supremacy in the Red River and surrounding areas.

THE END OF THE RED RIVER COLONY'S ISOLATION

By the 1840s, the Red River Métis had developed a largely self-sufficient economy based on the buffalo hunt, some small-scale farming, and seasonal labour for the Hudson's Bay Company. But it was in the 1850s that the colony's horizons grew enormously, mainly as a result of its more frequent contacts with St. Paul, Minnesota, to the south.

St. Paul gradually replaced York Factory on Hudson Bay as the Red River's major entrepôt. From 1851 to 1869, the number of Red River carts journeying to St. Paul, Minnesota, to sell furs and purchase supplies rose from 100 to 2500. Mail service to the Red River colony came through St. Paul after 1853, rather than by the slower and more cumbersome route through York Factory on Hudson Bay. A railway reached St. Paul in 1855, and within a year the Hudson's Bay Company itself used it to bring in supplies. The establishment of a regular steamboat connection with St. Paul and to the Red River colony in 1859 made the ties with Minnesota (with a population of nearly 200 000 by 1860) all the more binding. Indeed, only the depression of 1857, the American Civil War in 1861–65, and the outbreak of war between the Americans and the Sioux in 1862–64 prevented Minnesota's annexation of all the Red River country.

The settlement changed rapidly in the 1860s. Louis Goulet, a Métis who grew up in the Red River valley during that decade, left a colourful account of the region and the Red River Métis immediately before union with Canada. "Everything had been improved, from transportation to food on the table. Craftsmanship was considerably improved, thanks to superior tools that could now be bought in almost any ordinary general store and at prices most people could afford." Most houses had floors, pane glass windows, and partitioned rooms. Spinning wheels and weaving looms were also present in many Métis homes.

Many Métis moved farther west in the early 1860s attracted by rising opportunities in the buffalo-hide trade. Those who spent the winter on the prairies to be nearer the herds became

Red River carts by the North Saskatchewan River, 1871.

National Archives of Canada/PA-138573.

known as *hivernants* ("winterers"). The growing Métis involvement in the buffalo-robe trade led them to establish settlements at the forks of the Saskatchewan River, in the North Saskatchewan River valley, in the Cypress Hills area of present-day southwestern Saskatchewan, and at Lac Ste. Anne, about 80 km northwest of Fort Edmonton. Lac Ste. Anne became the largest Métis settlement in the Northwest outside of the Red River colony until St. Albert (about 15 km northwest of Edmonton) was founded in 1862. By the mid-1860s, the buffalo herds had migrated so far from present-day Manitoba that the Red River-based hunt had almost ended.

In 1871, approximately 2000–4000 mixed-bloods lived along the North Saskatchewan River between the Red River and the Rockies, and about 11 000 at the junction of the Red and the Assiniboine rivers. The Métis and Country-born population of 13 000–15 000 was approximately one-half of the estimated number of Plains First Nations in British North America. The mixed-bloods' increasingly frequent intrusions into the First Nations' hunting grounds in search of buffalo bred resentment.

THE PLAINS FIRST NATIONS IN THE MID-NINETEENTH CENTURY

While the Métis and Country-born population doubled in the Red River every 15–20 years, that of the Plains First Nations seriously declined in the mid-nineteenth century.

THE IMPACT OF DISEASE

In 1837–38, smallpox ravaged the Great Plains nations, just as it had a half-century earlier (in 1780–82). Such diseases tended to be carried along the trade routes — the drainage systems of the Missouri and Saskatchewan rivers. Non-Native crews usually carried the smallpox viruses. The boat brigades' tight schedules often caused crews to be dispatched while the men were still infectious. They moved into the interior and infected the First Nations who had gathered in their large summer camps. They, in turn, carried the disease farther inland.

The First Nations' way of life inadvertently contributed to the spread of the new diseases. They lived in close-knit family groups in very small living areas. In addition, the Native peoples had no idea that the disease was spread simply by contact; they insisted on visiting the sick, and in doing so, unknowingly spread the illness. As one Peigan told David Thompson, "We had no belief that one Man could give it to another, any more than a wounded Man could give his wound to another."

Thanks to the efforts of the Hudson's Bay Company traders, however, many of the Cree around the company's posts were saved. The discovery of a smallpox vaccine in Europe around 1800 checked the spread of the epidemic. The Hudson's Bay Company began an extensive vaccination program among the western Canadian Native peoples. The vaccinated population constituted an effective barrier, and the highly contagious disease spread no farther north than the Hudson's Bay Company posts on the northern fringes of the prairies. Saved from smallpox, the Cree became the most numerous First Nations group on the Canadian prairies. After the epidemic had run its course, the Crees could more readily move farther onto the prairies because the strength of the Blackfoot-speaking nations had been so reduced. But, smallpox continued to take its toll. In 1870 alone, more than 3500 First Nations, Métis, and Country-born on the Canadian Plains died because of the absence of vaccine at this time.

Other infectious killer diseases also ravaged the Native peoples. In 1864–65, an outbreak of scarlet fever killed more than 1000 Blackfoot-speaking people. A measles epidemic hit the Cree. Influenza and whooping cough also spread through their communities. A new disease — tuberculosis — arrived in the 1860s, brought by refugee Sioux from the United States and by Red River people moving west (both groups had already been exposed to the deadly bacterium).

THE ARRIVAL OF THE WHISKEY TRADERS

In the mid-1860s, the Blackfoot experienced another assault: that of the American whiskey traders. In the 1850s and the early 1860s, the Blackfoot had traded with both the Hudson's Bay Company and the American Fur Company. At Fort Edmonton and Rocky Mountain House they exchanged pemmican and horses, as well as the few beaver furs they trapped, for British trade goods. At Fort Benton, in Montana, they traded bulky buffalo hides and robes (which were difficult for the Hudson's Bay Company to transport profitably in their York boats) for American goods. The hides made excellent coats and robes. They could also be tanned into a very tough and durable leather suitable for making industrial machinery belts. The American Fur Company bought all that it could, shipping the furs down the Missouri by steamer to St. Louis.

The stability of the Missouri River fur trade suddenly ended, however, in 1864 with the collapse of the American Fur Company. Then, just after the end of the American Civil War in 1865, the discovery of gold brought a flood of prospectors and merchants to the mountains of Montana. With them came a flourishing whiskey trade. After U.S. marshals began to enforce laws against the trade, many of the traders moved north to present-day southern Alberta and Saskatchewan to make their fortunes. Their arrival led to great social disruption among groups that had little acquaintance with alcohol and no social controls in place to deal with its consequences.

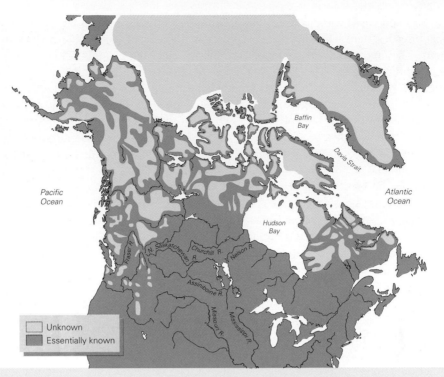

Non-Natives' knowledge of northern North America in 1870.

Source: Adapted from Richard I. Ruggles, *A Country So Interesting: The Hudson's Bay Company and Two Centuries of Mapping, 1670–1870* (Montreal/Kingston: McGill-Queen's University Press, 1991), p. 119.

THE NORTHWEST ON THE EVE OF CANADIAN SETTLEMENT

Until the late 1850s, the fur traders and the early visitors to the Northwest had all reported that the treeless prairies, which stretched as far as the eye could see, were unsuitable for farming. Wreford Watson, a historical geographer, has noted: "There developed in the minds of Europeans an equation that went as follows: bareness equals barrenness equals infertility equals uselessness for agriculture."[6] This perception changed in the late 1850s, and by the 1860s, Canadians had come to covet the Northwest. The lack of good agricultural land in the United Canadas made the western lands more inviting. In the early 1860s, both the Canadian and the British expeditions to the Northwest published their findings. Of the two, the British-sponsored expedition led by John Palliser is the best known. Dispatched in 1857, it was commissioned to report on the possibilities for agricultural settlement. In the same year, the Canadians sent out an expedition with Henry Youle Hind, a professor of geology and chemistry at Trinity University in Toronto, as scientific observer. Both expeditions reported on the magnificent possibilities for European agriculture, particularly in the Red River area and in the "fertile belt" of the North Saskatchewan River valley. These findings provided the incentive for the westward expansion of the eastern British North American colonies.

The First Nations remained the dominant group on the Plains until the late nineteenth century. By the 1860s, however, their political power had been reduced by severe population losses through epidemics, the rapidly diminishing buffalo herds, and the rise of a new mixed-blood

The two Royal Navy ships, HMS *Assistance* and HMS *Pioneer* under the command of Sir Edward Belcher, engaged in the search for Franklin. Shown in winter quarters, Devon Island, 1853.

National Archives of Canada/C-041305.

population who now intruded into their hunting grounds. And, in the Red River area at least, small numbers of Canadians began to arrive.

NORTH OF THE PRAIRIES

The majority of the North's indigenous peoples, the First Nations and the Inuit, enjoyed uncontested political control of their homelands until the late nineteenth century and, in many more isolated areas, into the twentieth. Arctic explorers, fur traders, and Christian missionaries were the first non-Native newcomers to come north. A very small number of Christian missionaries, Roman Catholic and Anglican, arrived around 1850, or about half a century after the fur traders. Until the late nineteenth century, however, the number of church workers in the North remained quite small.

A decade or so after Alexander Mackenzie's voyage, in 1789, down the river that now bears his name, the North West Company had established its first posts in the Mackenzie River valley. Fort of the Forks (later renamed Fort Simpson) was built just after 1800; it was followed by Fort Good Hope, the first post on the lower Mackenzie, in 1805. After the merger of the North West and Hudson's Bay Companies in 1821, the revitalized Hudson's Bay Company extended its operations throughout the Mackenzie River valley as far as Fort McPherson, founded in 1840 as Peel's River Post. By the 1840s, the company was expanding over the Mackenzie Mountains into the Yukon River valley.

European epidemics, brought north by the fur traders, devastated Native communities. Anthropologist Shepard Krech III has written that the Gwitch'in (Kutchin) in the northern Yukon and adjacent area, for example, had a population of about 5400 people in the early nineteenth century. By the 1860s, this number had been reduced to around 900. "In the 1860s, one Kutchin was alive where six had been originally."[7] That ratio can possibly be applied to other First Nations groups in the Mackenzie River valley and the Yukon.

In the early nineteenth century, British naval parties resumed the search for the Northwest Passage — not for economic reasons but for the international prestige of locating it. Sir John Franklin became one of the most famous explorers of all time. Sent off, in 1844, with the latest technological assistance, with ships heated by pipes fired from steam boilers, and with a three-year supply of canned food, the expedition seemed guaranteed of success. Yet Franklin, on this, his third Arctic expedition, refused to adapt to indigenous technology. He took no dogs, sleds, pemmican, or Inuit clothing. Within two years, the entire expedition of 129 men perished, as their ships became locked in pack ice near King William Island in the central Arctic. Even their great source of food, the canned provisions, turned out to be a liability, as the seams, soldered with lead, leaked toxic lead into the food.

Over 30 expeditions searched for Franklin and his missing party between 1847 and 1859: first, unsuccessfully, for survivors; and second, after evidence surfaced of their deaths, for explanations of the expedition's failure. The intensive search resulted in a large part of the Canadian Arctic Archipelago being charted and the northern limits of the North American continent established. Their sailing in and out of Arctic bays and inlets, and their wintering over on Arctic ice, led the English to claim sovereignty over the Inuit's homeland.

The fur trade attracted first the French to the Northwest, and later the British. Two rival companies in the British period — the Hudson's Bay Company (founded in 1670) and the North West Company (established in the 1780s) — vied for monopoly over the fur trade in the region. In 1821, the British government forced a merger of the two companies under the Hudson's Bay Company name. Settlement grew in the area, first at the junction of the Red and Assiniboine rivers, and later, in the 1860s, farther west, nearer the diminishing buffalo grounds. The intermarriage of fur traders and First Nations had led to the creation of two new peoples, the Métis and the Country-born. By the end of the 1860s, these two mixed-blood groups numbered from 13 000 to 15 000 in the Northwest, roughly half of the Plains First Nations population, estimated to be 25 000. It was the Métis, with their sense of constituting "a new nation," who would confront the Canadians when they tried to take control of the region in the late 1860s.

NOTES

1. Olive Patricia Dickason, *Canada's First Nations*, 2nd ed. (Toronto: Oxford University Press, 1997), p. 266.

2. Peter Iverson, "Native Peoples and Native Histories," in Clyde A. Milner II, Carol A. O'Connor, and Martha A. Sandwiess, *The Oxford History of the American West* (New York: Oxford University Press, 1994), p. 31.

3. Hugh A. Dempsey, *Big Bear* (Vancouver: Douglas & McIntyre, 1984), p. 48.

4. John C. Crawford, "What Is Michif?: Language in the Métis Tradition," in Jacqueline Peterson and Jennifer S.H. Brown, eds., *The New Peoples: Being and Becoming Métis in North America* (Winnipeg: University of Manitoba Press, 1985), p. 233.

5. John Foster, "The Country-Born in the Red River Settlement (c. 1820–1870)," Ph.D. thesis, University of Alberta, 1973, p. 264.

6. Wreford Watson, "The Role of Illusion in North American Geography: A Note on the Geography of North American Settlement," *Canadian Geographer* 13 (Spring 1969): 16.

7. Shepard Krech III, "On the Aboriginal Population of the Kutchin," *Arctic Anthropology* 15(1) (1978), reprinted in Kenneth S. Coates and William R. Morrison, eds., *Interpreting Canada's North* (Toronto: Copp Clark Pitman, 1989), p. 66.

LINKING TO THE PAST

The Canadian West
http://www.archives.ca/05/0529/052901_e.html

A lavishly illustrated and cross-referenced history of the West. The section "Anticipation: Expectations for the New Land" covers some of the material discussed in this chapter.

Arctic Dawn: The Journeys of Samuel Hearne
http://web.idirect.com/~hland/sh/title.html

This site features an illustrated hypertext version of Hearne's own account of his travels, *A Journey from Prince of Wales's Fort, in Hudson's Bay, to the Northern Ocean.*

Fur Trade and Mission History
http://collections.ic.gc.ca/abpolitics/alberta/fur_trade/index.html

Historical overview of the exploration, fur trade, and religious missions in the West, with a focus on present-day Alberta.

An Overview of the Métis
http://www.geocities.com/SoHo/Atrium/4832/metis.html

An overview of Métis history and culture.

Transfer of Power
http://www.canadiana.org/hbc/hist/hist8_e.html

A brief look at the merger of the Hudson's Bay Company and the North West Company. Navigate this extensive Website, which explores the history of the fur trade and HBC, for historical information, biographies of explorers, maps, stories, and more.

Images of the West
http://www.ucalgary.ca/applied_history/tutor/calgary/imagewest.html

Information on John Palliser's and Henry Youle Hind's expeditions.

RELATED READINGS

Four useful essays on this topic appear in R. Douglas Francis and Donald B. Smith, eds., *Readings in Canadian History, Pre-Confederation*, 6th ed. (Toronto: Nelson Thomson Learning, 2002): Arthur J. Ray, "Fur Trade History as an Aspect of Native History," pp. 51–60; Sylvia Van Kirk, "'Women in Between': Indian Women in Fur Trade Society in Western Canada," pp. 61–74; Frits Pannekoek, "The Flock Divided: Factions and Feuds at Red River," pp. 416–434; and Irene M. Spry, "The Métis and Mixed-Bloods of Rupert's Land before 1870," pp. 409–416.

BIBLIOGRAPHY

The literature on the Northwest is voluminous. For the archaeological background see Olive P. Dickason's "A Historical Reconstruction for the Northwestern Plains," *Prairie Forum* 5 (1980): 19–37, reprinted in R. Douglas Francis and Howard Palmer, eds., *The Prairie West: Historical Readings*, 2nd ed. (Edmonton: University of Alberta Press, 1992), pp. 39–57. Gerald Friesen's *The Canadian Prairies: A History* (Toronto: University of Toronto Press, 1984) provides an excellent overview of the entire period; as does Sarah

Carter, *Aboriginal People and Colonizers of Western Canada to 1900* (Toronto: University of Toronto Press, 1999). John Warkentin has written "The Western Interior: 1800–1870," in R. Cole Harris and John Warkentin, *Canada Before Confederation* (Ottawa: Carleton University Press, 1991 [1974]), pp. 232–88. Two beautifully illustrated books are William R. Morrison, *True North: The Yukon and Northwest Territories* (Toronto: Oxford University Press, 1998); and John Herd Thompson, *Forging the Prairie West* (Toronto: Oxford University Press, 1998), both in Oxford's new "Illustrated History of Canada" series. For the Mackenzie River basin see Kerry Abel's *Drum Songs: Glimpses of Dene History* (Montreal/Kingston: McGill-Queen's University Press, 1993). Changing perceptions of the Northwest are reviewed by R. Douglas Francis in *Images of the West* (Saskatoon: Western Producer Prairie Books, 1989). Kerry Abel provides a complete bibliographic guide to the historical literature in "The Northwest and the North," in M. Brook Taylor, ed., *Canadian History: A Reader's Guide*, vol. 1, *Beginnings to Confederation* (Toronto: University of Toronto Press, 1994), pp. 325–55.

For information on the First Nations in the eighteenth and nineteenth centuries consult Arthur Ray, *Indians in the Fur Trade* (Toronto: University of Toronto Press, 1974). John Ewers's history *The Blackfeet* (Norman: University of Oklahoma Press, 1958), and his *The Horse in Blackfoot Indian Culture* (Washington, DC: Smithsonian Institution Press, 1955) are essential. The impact of the horse and the gun on Blackfoot culture is reviewed by Oscar Lewis in *The Effects of White Contact Upon Blackfoot Culture: With Special Reference to the Role of the Fur Trade* (Seattle: University of Washington Press, 1966 [1942]). On cultural change on the northern Plains, an essential work is Theodore Binnema's *Common and Contested Ground. A Human and Environmental History of the Northwestern Plains* (Norman: University of Oklahoma Press, 2001). Deanna Christensen has written a valuable community study, *Ahtahkakoop. The Epic Account of a Plains Cree Head Chief, His People, and Their Struggle for Survival 1816–1896* (Shell Lake, Saskatchewan: Ahtahkakoop Publishing, 2000). Hugh Dempsey's biographies of three Plains chiefs offer a vivid portrait of Blackfoot, Blood, and Cree life in the nineteenth century: *Crowfoot* (Edmonton: Hurtig, 1972); *Red Crow* (Saskatoon: Western Producer Prairie Books, 1980); and *Big Bear* (Vancouver: Douglas & McIntyre, 1984). John Milloy reviews the history of the Cree from 1790 to 1870 in *The Plains Cree* (Winnipeg: University of Manitoba Press, 1988). Laura Peers looks at the Ojibwa in *The Ojibwa of Western Canada: 1780 to 1870* (Winnipeg: University of Manitoba Press, 1994). In his provocative monograph *Eighteenth-Century Western Cree and Their Neighbours* (Ottawa: Canadian Museum of Civilization, 1991), Dale R. Russell questions the belief that the Cree and the Assiniboine came onto the Plains only after their contact with the European fur traders. For background on the impact of disease, see the early section of Maureen K. Lux, *Medicine that Walks: Disease, Medicine, and Canadian Plains Native People, 1880–1940* (Toronto: University of Toronto Press, 2001). Hugh Dempsey's recent study, *Firewater. The Impact of the Whiskey Trade on the Blackfoot Nation* (Calgary: Fifth House, 2002) reviews the topic of substance abuse.

E.E. Rich provides an overview of the fur trade in western Canada in *The Fur Trade and the North West to 1857* (Toronto: McClelland & Stewart, 1967); as does Frits Pannekoek, *The Fur Trade and Western Canadian Society, 1670–1870* (Ottawa: Canadian Historical Association, 1987). Glyndwr Williams has written a short survey, "The Hudson's Bay Company and Fur Trade: 1670–1870," *The Beaver* 314(2) (Autumn 1983): 4–86. Another interesting survey is that by Dan Francis, *Battle for the West: Fur Traders and the Birth of Western Canada* (Edmonton: Hurtig, 1982). A more in-depth treatment is Dan Francis's book, written with Toby Morantz: *Partners in Furs: A History of the Fur Trade in Eastern James Bay, 1600–1870* (Montreal/Kingston: McGill-Queen's University Press, 1983). A very useful collection of essays on the nineteenth century in Western Canada is Theodore Binnema, Gerhard J. Ens, and R.C. Macleod, eds., *From Rupert's Land to Canada* (Edmonton: University of Alberta Press, 2001).

For short sketches of the most important European fur traders see the essays on Kelsey, La Vérendrye, Henday, Hearne, Thompson, and others in the 14 volumes of the *Dictionary of Canadian Biography* (Toronto: University of Toronto Press, 1966–1998). It is now available online: www.biographi.ca. Barry Gough has recently written a biography of Alexander Mackenzie, *First Across the Continent* (Toronto: McClelland & Stewart, 1997). Short biographies of many of the important Arctic explorers and fur traders appear in Richard C. Davis, ed., *Lobsticks and Stone Cairns: Human Landmarks in the Arctic* (Calgary: University of Calgary Press, 1996). Excerpts from the original narratives appear in Germaine Warkentin, ed., *Canadian Exploration Literature: An Anthology* (Toronto: Oxford University Press, 1993). Dennis Combet, ed., *In Search of the Western Sea. Selected Journals of La Vérendrye/À La Recherche de la Mer de l'Ouest*, (Winnipeg: Great Plains Publications, 2001), provides transcriptions of the original French texts of La Vérendrye's journals as well as English translations of them. *In A Year Inland* (Waterloo, Ontario: Wilfrid Laurier University Press, 2000), Barbara Belyea presents all four surviving versions of Anthony Henday's report on his 1754–55 journey into the interior of Western Canada.

The Métis are the subject of numerous studies. One popular work is D. Bruce Sealey and Antoine S. Lussier, *The Métis: Canada's Forgotten People* (Winnipeg: Manitoba Métis Federation Press, 1975). George Woodcock translated Marcel Giraud's classic *Le Métis Canadien* (Paris: Institut d'ethnologie, Université de Paris, 1945) into English, under the title *The Métis in the Canadian West*, 2 vols. (Edmonton: University of Alberta Press, 1986). Jacqueline Peterson and Jennifer S.H. Brown have edited *The New People: Being and Becoming Métis in North America* (Winnipeg: University of Manitoba Press, 1985). In *Cuthbert Grant of Grantown* (Toronto: McClelland & Stewart, 1963), M.A. MacLeod and W.L. Morton recount the life story of the first prominent leader among the prairie Métis. Guillaume Charette's *Vanishing Spaces: Memoirs of a Prairie Métis* (Winnipeg: Editions Bois Brûlés, 1980) contains the memoirs of Louis Goulet, who was born in the Red River valley in 1859. D.N. Sprague reviews Red River Métis history in his introduction to *The Genealogy of the First Métis Nation: The Development and Dispersal of the Red River Settlement, 1820–1900*, comp. D.N. Sprague and R.P. Frye (Winnipeg: Pemmican Publications, 1983), pp. 11–28. Gerhard Ens reviews the movement of the Métis westward in "Dispossession or Adaptation? Migration and Persistence of the Red River Métis, 1835–1890," *Canadian Historical Association Historical Papers* (1988): 120–44. His study, *Homeland to Hinterland: The Changing Worlds of the Red River Métis in the Nineteenth Century* (Toronto: University of Toronto Press, 1996), expands on this theme. Unlike Sprague, Ens sees the Métis's movement west of the Red River as a response to "new economic opportunities," a pull westward rather than a push by outside forces.

Frits Pannekoek discusses Red River society in the mid-nineteenth century, in his *A Snug Little Flock: The Social Origins of the Riel Resistance, 1869–70* (Winnipeg: Watson & Dwyer, 1991). Contrary conclusions about Red River society are reached by Irene Spry in "The Métis and Mixed-Bloods of Rupert's Land before 1870," in Peterson and Brown, *The New People*, pp. 95–118. A specific study of a Red River community is Robert J. Coutts, *The Road to the Rapids: Nineteenth-Century Church and Society at St. Andrew's Parish, Red River* (Calgary: University of Calgary Press, 2000).

For the "atmosphere" of the 1860s in the Northwest see fur trader Isaac Cowie's *The Company of Adventurers: A Narrative of Seven Years in the Service of the Hudson's Bay Company during 1867–1874* (Lincoln: University of Nebraska Press, 1993; originally published in 1913). James MacGregor provides a comprehensive review of the mid-nineteenth century in his *Senator Hardisty's Prairies, 1849–1889* (Saskatoon: Western Producer Prairie Books, 1978). The story of the Oblate Roman Catholic missionaries is told by Raymond J.A. Huel in *Proclaiming the Gospel to the Indians and the Métis* (Edmonton: University of Alberta Press, 1996).

The story of Native women and the fur trade is told by Jennifer S.H. Brown in *Strangers in Blood: Fur Trade Company Families in Indian Country* (Vancouver: University of British Columbia Press, 1980); and by Sylvia Van Kirk in *"Many Tender Ties": Women in Fur Trade Society in Western Canada* (Winnipeg: Watson & Dwyer, 1980). Brian Gallagher questions the argument that increasing racism in the period before 1870 caused a decline in the marriage rate between European officers of the Hudson's Bay Company and Métis women: "A Re-examination of Race, Class and Society in Red River," *Native Studies Review* 4(1–2) (1988): 25–65. Edith I. Burley provides a detailed look at the labourers of the Hudson's Bay Company in *Servants of the Honourable Company: Work, Discipline, and Conflict in the Hudson's Bay Company, 1770–1879* (Toronto: Oxford University Press, 1997).

For an introduction to the northernmost area of the Northwest in this period consult Keith J. Crowe's *A History of the Original Peoples of Northern Canada*, rev. ed. (Montreal/Kingston: McGill-Queen's University Press, 1991); also see Alan Cooke and Clive Holland, *The Exploration of Northern Canada: A Chronology* (Toronto: Arctic History Press, 1978). Two interesting books containing Native perspectives are Julie Cruikshank, *Reading Voices* (Vancouver: Douglas & McIntyre, 1991), on oral and written interpretations of the Yukon's past; and George Blondin, *When the World Was New: Stories of the Sahtú Dene* (Yellowknife: Outcrop Books, 1990). Two volumes contain valuable information on the Inuit and First Nations: David Damas, ed., *Handbook of North American Indians*, vol. 5, *Arctic* (Washington, DC: Smithsonian Institution, 1984); and June Helm, ed., *Handbook of North American Indians*, vol. 6, *Subarctic* (Washington, DC: Smithsonian Institution, 1981). The story of Arctic exploration in the mid-nineteenth century is well told in Hugh N. Wallace, *The Navy, the Company, and Richard King: British Exploration in the Canadian Arctic, 1829–1860* (Montreal/Kingston: McGill-Queen's University Press, 1980).

Valuable maps of the Northwest appear in R. Cole Harris, ed., *Historical Atlas of Canada*, vol. 1, *From the Beginning to 1800* (Toronto: University of Toronto Press, 1987); R. Louis Gentilcore, ed., *The Historical Atlas of Canada*, vol. 2, *The Land Transformed, 1800–1891* (Toronto: University of Toronto Press, 1993); and Richard I. Ruggles, *A Country So Interesting: The Hudson's Bay Company and Two Centuries of Mapping, 1670–1870* (Montreal/Kingston: McGill-Queen's University Press, 1991).

CHAPTER 19

THE PACIFIC COAST TO THE 1860s

TIME LINE

1774 – The Spanish expedition led by Juan Pérez encounters the Haida off the Queen Charlotte Islands

1778 – Captain Cook visits Nootka Sound on the west coast of Vancouver Island

1793 – The Pacific coastline is mapped by George Vancouver for the Royal Navy

Fur trader Alexander Mackenzie becomes the first European to cross the continent via Lake Athabaska to the Pacific Ocean

1821 – Union of the Hudson's Bay Company and the North West Company

1827 – Fort Langley is built by the Hudson's Bay Company near the mouth of the Fraser River

1843 – The Hudson's Bay Company builds Fort Victoria on Vancouver Island

1846 – Under the Oregon Treaty, the 49th parallel becomes the international boundary between British and American claims from the Rocky Mountains to the Pacific

1849 – The colony of Vancouver Island is established by the Hudson's Bay Company at the request of the British Crown

1858 – The Fraser River gold rush leads to the establishment of the mainland colony of British Columbia, separate from the colony of Vancouver Island

1862 – The construction of the Cariboo Road begins

1866 – The two colonies of British Columbia and Vancouver Island are united

The First Nations population of present-day British Columbia lived along the major salmon rivers, at scattered village sites along the ocean, and inland along the river systems. Europeans did not begin to explore the northwestern coast of North American until the 1770s.

Initially, Spain, Russia, Britain, and the United States competed for control. Eventually, however, only Britain and the United States contested the sector between Russian Alaska and Spanish California. In 1818, they agreed to joint occupancy of the area. Twenty-eight years later, in 1846, the two countries consented to extend the international border along the 49th parallel from the prairies to the Pacific, and to include Vancouver Island in Britain's jurisdiction.

Immigrants first settled at the southern tip of Vancouver Island in the 1840s and then at the mouth of the Fraser River during the gold rush of 1858. In the 1860s, the newcomers claimed ownership of the entire coast and interior of British Columbia, even though well into the nineteenth century, the First Nations outnumbered them.

THE FIRST NATIONS OF THE NORTHWEST COAST

The First Nations had been living on the Pacific coast for thousands of years. One of the oldest archaeological sites to be found on the North Pacific coast is in the Fraser River canyon; it dates back at least 8500 years. The Native peoples probably arrived in successive waves, for nineteen distinct languages are represented on the British Columbia coast today. Hemmed in by towering mountains, the narrow coastline was heavily populated. It is estimated that nearly half of the total First Nations population of Canada lived in British Columbia at the moment of European contact. For these maritime people, salmon was the main food resource. They used red cedar for the construction of their plank houses, canoes, containers, and carved masks, as well as their most famous creations — totem poles.

NOTIONS OF PROPERTY

In several respects, the Northwest Coast peoples had a notion of property similar to that of Europeans. A large group of kinspeople, or a lineage — a group of people who shared a common ancestor in the real or mythological past — formed the primary unit of their societies. One or several kin groups might occupy the same winter village, and these villages in turn constituted independent units within the larger nation. Local kin groups claimed ownership of the fishing stations, berry patches, cedar groves, and stretches of beach. When they left their permanent winter villages for the salmon fisheries, they went to their own recognized stretches of the rivers. When the Europeans came, the chiefs or leaders of the kin groups made them pay for the wood and even the fresh water they used.

THE POTLATCH AND SOCIAL STRUCTURE

Northwest Coast Native society had an elaborate hierarchical social structure. At the bottom were the slaves, acquired in war or by purchase. Above them, stood everyone else, in a very careful ranking. Anthropologist Philip Drucker notes that "each society consisted not of two or more social classes, but of a complex series of statuses graded relatively, one for each individual of the group."[1] The rankings were evident in social functions such as the potlatch, which involved a distribution of gifts according to each person's status.

European society had no direct equivalent for the potlatch. Anthropologist Wilson Duff described it as "a large gathering to which important people were invited in order to witness some event, such as a young person assuming a new name or the completion of a new house

The beautiful sea-going canoes of the Northwest Coast were usually made of a single felled cedar, which was hollowed and shaped to meet specified requirements.

National Archives of Canada/C-30193.

and erection of a totem pole. On such an occasion the host would display his wealth and present gifts to his guests. The more he gave away, the more prestige he acquired."[2] Honour came in giving, not in receiving. In the late nineteenth century, European missionaries succeeded in outlawing the potlatch ceremonies. They regarded such ceremonies as an immoral squandering of wealth and a barrier to the Natives' conversion to Christianity.

The Northwest Coast Native peoples had other unique traditions. Each local kin group, for example, had identifiable privileges indicating its members' common origins. One lineage of the Nimpkish, a village group among the Kwakwaka'wakw (Kwagiulth, or Kwakiutl), on northeastern Vancouver Island, believed themselves descended from a giant halibut and a thunderbird that transformed themselves into human beings. People in this lineage proudly displayed the thunderbird and the halibut as crests on their houses, dance blankets, and painted screens. Today, the Nimpkish can point out the rock where the thunderbird first landed.[3] The kin group also had the right to specific prerogatives in their intricate ceremonial system, such as the right to certain names, songs, and dances.

FIRST NATION IMPRESSIONS OF THE EUROPEANS

The Squamish of the Capilano reserve at Vancouver tell about the first time their ancestors encountered the newcomers, a century and a half earlier. As Chief Mathias told the story, the warriors hesitated going on board the floating island with cobwebs hanging from the sticks growing on it, until, with great misgivings, the bravest climbed the rope ladder onto the deck. The pale-faced captain, who looked like a corpse, advanced with outstretched hand. Never

Captain George Vancouver visited Chief Cheslakee's village on the Nimpkish River in July 1792. Each of the several dozen Kwakwaka'wakw (Kwagiulth or Kwakiutl) villages was socially and politically autonomous. This illustration is reproduced from Vancouver's *Voyage of Discovery*.

Glenbow Archives, Calgary, Canada/NA-528-1.

having heard of the handshake, the chief thought they were being challenged to a Native finger-wrestling match. He therefore waved away the man with whom the captain was trying to shake hands and called for the Squamish strongman to accept the challenge. Seeing he was misunderstood, the captain shrugged and approached the chief with outstretched hand. The chief then said to the strongman, "He doesn't want you. He thinks you are not strong enough." With that, the chief refused to consider the captain's "challenge." The strangers' gifts also greatly puzzled Mathias's ancestors. It appeared to them that they had received snow in a sack (flour) and buttons (coins).

EUROPEAN EXPLORATION OF THE NORTHWEST COAST

Although Spain was the first European power to reach the Pacific Ocean, it took the Spanish two and a half centuries to advance northward from Mexico. Apostolos Valerianos, a Greek captain who spent 40 years serving Spain in the Americas, better known by his Spanish name of Juan de Fuca, allegedly sailed north along the Pacific coast and, in about 1590, entered a vast gulf or wide inlet between the 47th and 48th parallels that led into a broader sea with many islands. Fuca believed this to be the western outlet of the fabled Straits of Anian, a body of water that could provide a convenient, practical sea passage between Europe and Asia. But the Spanish took so little interest in the expedition that they failed to preserve any authentic record of it, and only Fuca's later statement that he made the voyage survives.

Crippled by economic depressions, epidemics, and defeats on European battlefields, Spain lost its pioneering spirit. Rival European empires had seized Spanish islands in the West Indies, but luckily for Spain, its European rivals seldom ventured to the Pacific, until Russians arrived in the eighteenth century.

RUSSIAN ACTIVITY IN THE NORTH PACIFIC

Vitus Bering, a Danish navigator in the Russian service, made the first documented Russian voyage to present-day Alaska. In 1728, he sailed along the eastern coast of Siberia until he found the strait that now bears his name. Then, in 1741, he explored an area in present-day south-eastern Alaska. His return, however, proved disastrous: the 60-year-old mariner died of scurvy after having been shipwrecked on an island off the Siberian coast. Nevertheless, his ill-fated voyage established Russia's claim to the Alaskan Panhandle and led to Russian economic expansion in the Pacific. The survivors from Bering's ship brought back a cargo of 900 sea-otter pelts. These brought high prices in Chinese markets, since the Chinese upper classes prized the furs for their warmth and their glossy beauty. Within a half-century, the highly profitable sea-otter trade led to an international rivalry among Russia, Spain, and later Britain and the United States.

Rumours of the Russian activity prompted Spain to advance northward to protect Mexico. In 1767, the Spanish developed a major port at San Blas on Mexico's west coast and established settlements in California at San Diego, Monterey, and San Francisco. They also sponsored expeditions to investigate Russian advances along the Northwest Coast and to assert Spanish sovereignty north of Mexico. Juan Pérez sailed from San Blas in late January 1774 to Alaska, but bad weather forced him to turn back just north of the Queen Charlotte Islands. Pérez met 150 Haidas off the Queen Charlottes — the first recorded meeting between Europeans and British Columbian First Nations. The meeting was friendly, and the Spaniards traded small shipboard objects for Native artifacts (now displayed in the Museo de América in Madrid).

THE ARRIVAL OF THE BRITISH

Instead of the Russians, the British became the Spaniards' greatest rival on the Pacific Northwest Coast. Captain James Cook, already renowned for his discoveries in Australasia and Antarctica, and who had been present at the French surrender of Louisbourg in 1758 and had helped to guide the English armada to Quebec, visited the Northwest Coast on his third expedition to the Pacific in the spring of 1778. Cook's two vessels, *Discovery* and *Resolution*, arrived at Nootka Sound, which had been sighted by Pérez four years earlier. Here, Cook spent a month refitting his ships. Since no other European power knew of the Spaniard's previous visit, Cook (who was killed in January 1779 by Natives in Hawaii) was credited with "discovering" Nootka, and the British claim to the Northwest Coast received international recognition.

To strengthen their claim to the Northwest Coast, the Spanish in 1789 established a colony at Nootka Sound and maintained a garrison of 200–250 men for six years, with only a brief absence during the winter of 1789–90. The dispute over territorial jurisdiction, known as the Nootka Sound Controversy, brought Spain and Britain to the brink of war. Spain argued that it had the exclusive right to trade and to control the coast, while Britain claimed that navigation was open to any nation. But, in 1795, Spain agreed to share the northern ports because it badly needed British assistance in its war against France. Thus ended Spain's attempts to exert a Spanish presence north of California. Today, about 100 Spanish geographical names, such as Valdes and Galiano islands, remain to remind us of the early Spanish expeditions.

The publication, in 1784, of the official account of Cook's third voyage proved a turning point. Captain James King, who had taken command shortly after the death of Cook, recounted in *A Voyage to the Pacific Ocean* (1784) how sea-otter pelts obtained in trade on the Northwest Coast had brought as much as $120 each at Canton, China. Other mariners saw their opportunity. The first was the sea captain James Hanna, who sailed in a British vessel appropriately named *Sea Otter*. Several other British and American ships followed.

IMPERIAL RIVALRY ON THE NORTHWEST COAST

The withdrawal of Spain in the mid-1790s left the Northwest Coast open to three contenders: Russia, Britain, and the newly independent United States. In 1784, the Russians established a base at Three Saints Harbor on Kodiak Island in the Gulf of Alaska. North of the present-day Alaskan boundary, the Russians now encountered intense British and American competition for sea-otter pelts. The Russian traders, however, laboured under several major handicaps. In contrast to both the Americans and the English, they possessed fewer and poorer trade goods and inferior trading vessels. The Russian advance slowed down in the Alaska Panhandle, where they faced strong competition from British and American traders and from Tlingit middlemen, who traded European goods to the interior First Nations in what is now Yukon and northwestern British Columbia.

New tools and pigments became available to the Native peoples after contact with the fur traders. Carving became more elaborate and colourful. This photo, taken by C.F. Newcombe in 1901, shows the Kwakwaka'wakw village of Blunden Harbour.

Royal British Columbia Museum/PN 258.

Britain strengthened its claim with the dispatch of a three-year expedition under George Vancouver, a naval officer who had served with Cook's expedition in 1778. From 1792 to 1794, Vancouver methodically and painstakingly charted the intricate coastline from Oregon to Alaska. This thorough survey proved that Juan de Fuca Strait was not the entrance to the great inland sea that Fuca had reported. Vancouver later wrote in *Voyage of Discovery to the North Pacific Ocean*: "I trust the precision with which the survey ... has been carried into effect, will remove every doubt, and set aside every opinion of a *north-west passage*, or any water communication navigable for shipping, existing between the north Pacific, and the interior of the American continent, within the limits of our researches."

Before leaving the Northwest Coast, the navigator named a huge island "Quadra's and Vancouver's Island" (sharing the honour with his friend Juan Francisco de la Bodega y Quadra, the Spanish commander at Nootka Sound). Later, it became known simply as Vancouver's Island, and finally as Vancouver Island.

The outbreak of war between Britain and France in 1793, which lasted until 1815, curtailed British voyages to the Northwest Coast. As Britain withdrew men from its merchant ships for service in the Royal Navy, American entrepreneurs captured Britain's trade in the North Pacific. After the mid-1790s, American traders dominated the coastal trade until the mid-1820s, by which time the sea otter was virtually extinct due to overhunting.

THE FIRST NATIONS AND THE MARITIME FUR TRADERS

The Northwest Coast First Nations welcomed the European fur traders with their iron trading goods. They wanted the metal to construct tools. The Spanish discovered that the First Nations coveted iron so much that they even removed the metal strapping from the sides of Spanish ships. Not even the rudder chains were safe. Some Natives horrified the friars when they tore down a large cross to take out the nails that held it together. They paid careful attention to the quality of goods they purchased and refused iron that contained flaws or was too brittle. They also bought muskets.

In addition to purchasing iron goods, the Native peoples bought cloth, clothing, and blankets. They also developed a liking for rum and molasses.

The coastal First Nations initially exercised considerable control over the early European fur trade, preventing the Europeans from coming into contact with the inland groups. Often the Native traders were middlemen who added a 200–300 percent markup to the furs and goods they traded. Women traders participated actively in the transactions with the newcomers. Anthropologist Loraine Littlefield notes "the many historical accounts that document the presence of women in trade transactions, their shrewdness and skill in bargaining, and their role as chief negotiators."[4] Historians, she argues, have underplayed their contribution.

Although the linguistic diversity of the Pacific coast exceeded that of Europe, a single trade language called the Chinook jargon came into use along the West Coast in the 1830s. In its vocabulary of about 300 key words are borrowings from First Nations languages, as well as English and French: "skookum" means powerful or fast, "chuck" — water; "cheechako" — newcomer; "Kinchotsh" (King George Man) — Englishman. It was spoken as well in the inland districts, and the middlemen knew that language. The entry around 1810 of European traders into the interior, however, took away much of the First Nations middlemen's trade. For nearly 40 years, the maritime fur trade prospered, but by 1825 the sea-otter population neared extinction.

The fur trade enriched the coastal peoples' culture. The tools they made from their new supplies of iron allowed them to produce better and more refined headdresses, costumes, and masks for feasts and ceremonies. As well, new dyes and pigments became available through the traders. Although the First Nations carvers favoured the traditional colours, weavers supplemented the original pigments — red and yellow ochres, black and blue-green copper oxide — with the whole spectrum of European trade colours. Wood carving expanded. During these years the totem poles, which displayed individual families' genealogies, underwent much elaboration and reached greater heights.

Although the Northwest Coast peoples enjoyed a higher standard of living after European contact, they also died in large numbers. The absence of accurate statistics makes it difficult to provide even rough estimates of the casualties, but European infectious diseases such as measles, mumps, and, especially, smallpox took their toll, as they did elsewhere in the Americas. Anthropologist Wilson Duff estimates that the smallpox epidemic that started in Victoria in 1862 killed about one-third of the First Nations population within two years.[5] Although some historians argue that no evidence exists to prove losses this high, they do not deny the occurrence of the epidemic or its catastrophic impact on the First Nations' society.

SECURING THE INLAND FUR TRADE

After European navigators reached the Northwest Coast by sea, European fur traders arrived by land. Anxious to find a short supply line to the Pacific Ocean, the North West Company searched for a route westward from Lake Athabasca to the Pacific. The Nor'Wester Alexander Mackenzie, the first European to canoe the northern river that now bears his name and to reach the Arctic Ocean, completed the first crossing of North America (north of Mexico) in 1793 by travelling down what is now called the Fraser River, then over to the Bella Coola River, and down to the Pacific. On a seaside rock he simply wrote, "From Canada. By Land." The arduous route proved useless for transporting furs, but the journey made the 24-year-old Mackenzie's reputation as a fearless and daring trader-explorer.

Two other Nor'Westers worked to find a commercial route to the Pacific. In 1808, Simon Fraser, who had first opened up fur-trading posts in the interior of what is now British Columbia, travelled with a small party down the treacherous river named after him. He succeeded, but concluded that the route was unnavigable.

Finally, in 1811, David Thompson, a partner of the North West Company, followed the Columbia River, and thereby connected the North West Company trade route from east of the Rockies to the Pacific Coast. A sea expedition sent by John Jacob Astor's Pacific Fur Company had arrived in late March 1811, just months before Thompson. On the basis of having founded Fort Astoria, the Americans claimed the Oregon country.

THE JOINT OCCUPATION OF THE OREGON TERRITORY

As a temporary compromise, Britain and the United States agreed in 1818 to occupy the Columbia country jointly and to decide its fate later. The agreement left commerce open to both British and American traders between latitudes 42° and 54°40' (from the northern boundary of California to the southern limits of Alaska).

With the merger of the North West Company and the Hudson's Bay Company in 1821, the new Hudson's Bay Company under the management of Sir George Simpson began to exploit the rich fur resources of the Northwest Coast. Having obtained from the British Crown a 21-year lease to the exclusive trade of the "Indian Territory" (the lands between the Rocky Mountains and the Pacific), Simpson located a Pacific depot at Fort Vancouver, in an area of good farmland 150 km up the Columbia River. Other forts followed. The three most important were Fort Langley, near the mouth of the Fraser River, built in 1827; Fort Simpson, on the boundary of the Russian territory to the north, in 1831; and Fort Victoria, strategically located on the southern tip of Vancouver Island, in 1843. The Hudson's Bay Company's energetic commercial activities established a strong British presence on the Pacific coast.

American interest in the Columbia country increased in the early 1840s. Americans began arriving in the 1830s, and by 1843 they numbered about 1000. In the next three years, another 5000 settlers arrived in the Columbia River valley. But thanks to the Hudson's Bay Company's network of posts, inland trails, and shipping routes, Britain dominated north of the Columbia River.

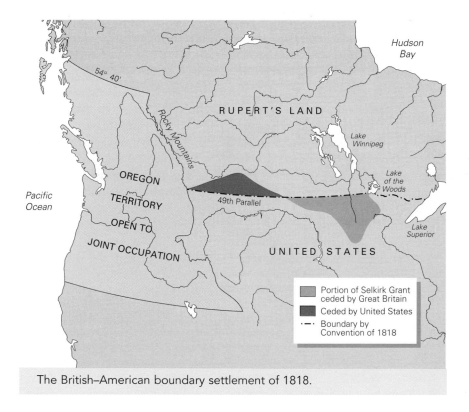

The British–American boundary settlement of 1818.

Nanaimo, Vancouver Island's "second city," around 1866. On the extreme right of this photo, the octagonal bastion built by the Hudson's Bay Company still stands today.

Toronto Reference Library/T14258.

Nevertheless, American president James Polk, who won the presidential election in December 1844 with the electoral slogan "54° 40' or fight," demanded all of "Oregon," up to the Russian border.

In his inaugural address in March, President Polk reaffirmed his position that the United States's title to Oregon was "clear and unquestionable." Great popular support existed for his stand. In the summer of 1845, the expansionist newspaper, *The United States Magazine and Democratic Review*, introduced in an editorial the phrase, "manifest destiny." The paper argued that foreign governments were attempting to check "the fulfillment of our manifest destiny to overspread the continent allotted by Providence for the free development of our yearly multiplying millions." Within months, the phrase became common usage throughout the United States.

Fortunately for Britain's claim, the Americans began a war with Mexico in 1846 over Texas (and later New Mexico and California), and Polk did not want a war with both Mexico and Britain. To avoid conflict, Britain retracted its claim to all the land south of the Columbia River. The Anglo–American treaty signed in June 1846 extended the 49th parallel (which had become the international border across the prairies in 1818) from the Rocky Mountains to the Pacific Ocean, and left all of Vancouver Island in British hands.

Anxious to counter the threat of American squatter settlement in its Pacific territory, the British government asked the Hudson's Bay Company to colonize, as well as to manage, Vancouver Island for ten years. A royal grant of 1849 stipulated that the company had to develop the island, make lands available to settlers at reasonable prices, and safeguard Aboriginal rights. By the end of 1849, Fort Victoria served as the company's western headquarters, its shipping depot, and its provisioning centre, as well as the capital of the colony of Vancouver Island. In 1852, the Colonial Office extended the jurisdiction of the governor of Vancouver Island to include the Queen Charlotte Islands.

At the time of the first census in 1855, less than 1000 non-Native inhabitants lived in the Pacific colony of Vancouver Island. The discovery of coal at Nanaimo on the east coast of the island had led to the founding of a small permanent European settlement there. But until the Fraser River gold rush in 1858, the colony continued primarily as a fur-trading region, with its centre at Fort Victoria.

The fur traders consisted of immigrants from places as diverse as the Orkney Islands and Hawaii, along with French Canadians, Iroquois, and mixed-bloods. Many of the non-Natives were married to First Nations, Country-born, or Métis women. The existence of virtually free land in Oregon and Washington attracted settlers there; on Vancouver Island, land had to be purchased. At the time, perhaps as many as 200 Europeans lived in the various fur-trading posts on the mainland. On Vancouver Island and the mainland, the Aboriginal peoples outnumbered the Europeans by roughly fifty to one.

JAMES DOUGLAS

James Douglas became governor of the colony of Vancouver Island in 1851, replacing Richard Blanshard, the first governor, who resigned one year after arriving in Fort Victoria. A "Scotch West Indian," Douglas was born in British Guiana (now Guyana), the son of "a free coloured woman" and a Scottish merchant. Sent to Scotland for his schooling at age twelve, James later left school at the age of sixteen and joined the North West Company as an apprentice. After the union of the two rival companies, he entered northern "Oregon," or New Caledonia, as the company called it. There, in 1828, he married Amelia Connolly, the daughter of William Connolly, a fur trader from Lower Canada, and his Cree wife. In 1830, the company transferred James to Fort Vancouver, and nine years later he became a chief factor. With his promotion to Fort Victoria in 1849, he became the senior company officer west of the Rocky Mountains.

James Douglas played such an important role in the early history of British Columbia that he is called "the father of British Columbia." He and his wife, Amelia Connolly Douglas, had multi-ethnic backgrounds — Douglas was of Scottish and African origin, and his wife of Irish, French-Canadian, and First Nations descent.

The British Columbia Archives/HP 2656.

JAMES DOUGLAS'S ABORIGINAL POLICY

Douglas refused to intervene in quarrels among the First Nations, but he did use his power, including Royal Navy gunboats, to settle disputes between them and Europeans. Shortly before he became governor, Douglas wrote that, in all his dealings with First Nations, he had "invariably acted on the principle that it is inexpedient and unjust to hold *tribes* responsible for the acts of *individuals*." The governor meted out stern discipline to individuals he perceived as warranting such treatment, but not to their communities. Unlike many of the early settlers on the island, Douglas tried to understand First Nations society. Above all, he did not want the open warfare that had broken out between the American settlers and the Native peoples in the Washington Territory to spill over the border.

To avoid conflict between the First Nations and the settlers, Douglas purchased land from the First Nations before new settlement occurred. Between 1850 and 1854, he made fourteen treaties with groups living in areas that Europeans wanted to settle. In all, he purchased roughly 1000 km² of land, or about 3 percent of the total area of Vancouver Island. Douglas allowed the communities to select the land they wanted for their reserves and instructed the surveyors to meet the First Nations peoples' wishes.

In hindsight, Douglas was not overly generous with the amount of land allotted to reserves on Vancouver Island and later on the mainland. Just before he retired as governor of the mainland colony of British Columbia in 1864, he told the legislature, "The areas thus partially defined and set apart, in no case exceed the proportion of ten acres [4 ha] for each family concerned."

At the first elections to the Vancouver Island Assembly in 1856, some 40 voters elected 7 members to North America's smallest legislature. Painting by Charles W. Simpson for a book celebrating the Diamond Jubilee of Confederation in 1927.

National Archives of Canada/C-013947.

Some of the settlers complained that although Douglas handled First Nations well, he did not handle the colonists properly. They protested that he had not carried out his obligation to settle the island, that he ruled autocratically, and that he relied too heavily on the company's officials for advice. Most of all, they objected to his setting the price of land at £1 for one acre (0.4 ha) when land in the neighbouring American Pacific Northwest went for one-quarter the price. The rising business class in Victoria objected to his "family-Company compact," composed of former Hudson's Bay Company officials and members of his own family, in particular, his brother-in-law, David Cameron (appointed to the Supreme Court and the Legislative Council); and his son-in-law, Dr. John Sebastian Helmcken, the first speaker of the Assembly.

When settlement on Vancouver Island grew in the late 1850s, Douglas made determined efforts to purchase the First Nations' land and to set aside reserves in the areas into which settlers were moving. Lack of funds, however, made the process more difficult. In 1858, the governor left the Hudson's Bay Company and no longer had access to the company's storehouses. Moreover, the Aboriginal communities wanted larger payments for their land, as they had come to realize its true value to the newcomers. The Vancouver Island House of Assembly, established in 1856, asked Britain to lend it money for First Nations land payments. The Colonial Office refused and replied that the funds should be raised locally. As the colonial legislature considered itself unable to buy out Native title on Vancouver Island, it gave the First Nations no compensation for their lands after 1859. Without negotiating treaties, the Europeans settled along the Pacific coast. Their settlements were interspersed among small, autonomous Aboriginal villages. The government of Vancouver Island (and later British Columbia) set aside Native reserves without extinguishing the First Nations' title to the land. (Only a century and a half later, in the 1990s, would the treaty process resume on Vancouver Island and on the coastal mainland.)

New Westminster, British Columbia, around 1863.

F.G. Claudet/The British Columbia Archives/HP 9326.

DOUGLAS AND THE CREATION OF THE COLONY OF BRITISH COLUMBIA

When word of the discovery of gold on the lower Fraser River reached California in the spring of 1858, the rush began. Nine years earlier, in 1849, 80 000 people entered the California gold fields in one year alone. By 1858, though, the California gold rush had lost its momentum, and the gold seekers headed north. Seemingly overnight, a tent town arose at Victoria. Many new businesses or branches of American firms, financed by San Francisco capital, were established. One witness counted 225 new commercial buildings in Victoria in 1858.

Once in Victoria, the miners faced the challenge of reaching the gold fields in the interior. They needed boats to cross the Strait of Georgia to the mouth of the Fraser. Lacking the necessary boat-building skills, many launched their own hastily made vessels. Not surprisingly, some swamped, and their owners drowned. Once the would-be prospectors reached the mouth of the Fraser, they faced an additional 250 km journey up the river to the first big strike, just south of Yale, an old trading post. In the last two weeks of May, 10 000 men travelled up the Fraser by canoe, sailboat, and raft. Another 15 000 arrived by the end of the year.

The arrival of thousands of Americans threatened British sovereignty on the mainland and raised the danger of a war between prospectors and the First Nations. As the senior British official in the area, Douglas claimed the mainland and its minerals for the Crown. He drew up mining regulations, licensed miners, and hired constables. The Colonial Office praised Douglas, even though, strictly speaking, he lacked legal authority on the mainland. The British government quickly established a second colony on the mainland, British Columbia, separate from that of Vancouver Island.

James Douglas became British Columbia's first governor while still serving as governor of Vancouver Island (which in 1859 came under the direct control of the Colonial Office, after the royal grant to the Hudson's Bay Company ended). Col. Richard Clement Moody, the first lieutenant governor of British Columbia, established the colony's new capital near the mouth of the Fraser River at New Westminster.

Since no assembly was granted on the mainland — the British government did not wish to extend the electoral system to transients from California and Oregon — James Douglas retained great powers, including the power to legislate by proclamation. In May 1861, John Robson, the

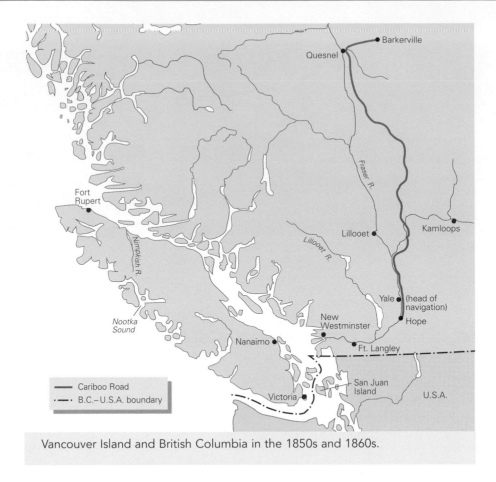

Vancouver Island and British Columbia in the 1850s and 1860s.

editor of New Westminster's *British Columbian*, wrote of the lack of political liberty: "We are in a state of veriest serfdom."

James Douglas, together with Matthew Baillie Begbie, British Columbia's first chief justice, established a uniform judicial system for the colony. Historian Margaret Ormsby gives us this portrait of Begbie: "A Cambridge graduate of considerable intellectual attainment, a man with a natural hauteur, an accomplished teller of anecdotes, and something of a musician, Begbie had the distinction of mind and manner so much admired by Douglas."[6] Judge Begbie's circuit court tours established a frontier version of British law in the scattered mining camps.

In 1860, about 4000 gold miners (the majority from California and Oregon; the rest from eastern Canada, Britain, Europe, and even China) proceeded eastward, pushing into the Thompson, Lillooet, and then the southern Cariboo regions. By 1861, with big strikes at Richfield, at Barkerville, and at Lightning on Williams Creek, the Cariboo region became the major mining field. The gold resources could not be exploited, however, without road links to the coast. Roads were also needed to guarantee British commercial and military control of the interior. Using public funds, James Douglas built the 650 km Cariboo Road, completed in 1863, which connected the gold towns of Yale and Barkerville.

Apart from doing some backpacking and some work at the diggings, the First Nations obtained little economic benefit from the gold rush. The miners had no intention of sharing the area's rich lands and resources with the original inhabitants. Although James Douglas had allowed the First Nations to choose the locations of their reserves, he made no treaties with them on the

Where Historians Disagree

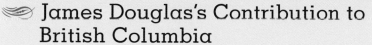 James Douglas's Contribution to British Columbia

In the historiography of British Columbia, James Douglas is a figure comparable to Champlain in Quebec and to Simcoe in Ontario. Few historians have been more laudatory of his contribution to British Columbia than historian Margaret Ormsby. In a biographical sketch of Douglas written in 1972, she states: "A man of iron nerve and physical prowess, great force of character, keen intelligence, and unusual resourcefulness, Douglas had had a notable career in the fur trade. As colonial governor his career was even more distinguished. Against overwhelming odds, with indifferent backing from the British government, the aid of a few Royal Navy ships, and a small force of Royal Engineers, he was able to establish British rule on the Pacific Coast and lay the foundation for Canada's extension of the Pacific seaboard. Single-handed in the midst of a gold-rush he had forged policies for land, mining, and water rights which were just and endurable."[1]

Recently, reassessments of Douglas have appeared, and his contribution, while still acknowledged as significant, is being judged more critically. In her study *The West beyond the West: A History of British Columbia*, Jean Barman introduced several criticisms of Douglas's administration. She noted his "overbearing style of governing" and the fact that he readily extended his authority beyond his legitimate power. Moreover, "he alienated newcomers from Ontario and the Maritimes through his haughty demeanour and preference for Britons over Canadians."[2] His feverish road-building program, she added, left the mainland colony of British Columbia burdened by debt.

Douglas's Aboriginal policies have also been questioned. Political scientist Paul Tennant argued that the governor was far less generous to the First Nations than was formerly believed.[3] Earlier commentators such as Robert Cail,[4] Robin Fisher,[5] and Wilson Duff[6] have regarded the governor's Native policies favourably. Anthropologist Wilson Duff, for instance, wrote in *The Indian History of British Columbia*: "As colonization progressed, his main concerns, in addition to maintaining law and order, were to purchase the Indian ownership rights to the land and to set aside adequate reserves for their use."[7] Tennant himself does admit that "at a time when aboriginal peoples elsewhere were routinely being forced from their lands and often actively exterminated, Douglas displayed a spirit of tolerance, compassion, and humane understanding."[8] Nonetheless, with the exception of fourteen small treaties signed between 1850 and 1854 on Vancouver Island, Douglas made no further attempts to negotiate the transfer of land title with the First Nations peoples. Moreover, the man who had complete control of the mainland from 1858 to 1864 made no treaties there at all. He, in fact, no longer supported the principle of Aboriginal land title. Instead, he spent large sums of money, principally on roads, to take miners in and out of the interior.

Tennant does acknowledge, however, that at least inadvertently, James Douglas made an enormous contribution to the survival of Aboriginal British Columbia. The governor's decision to set aside reserves for First Nations communities at locations of their own choosing helped to protect these groups from cultural extinction. As Tennant writes, "The surviving members of traditional communities could thus remain resident on preferred sites within their ancestral homelands and so could retain a sense of communal unity and an active connection with historic places and communal memories. Confined to their small reserves, they could nurture a deepening sense of injustice as they witnessed the takeover of their surrounding traditional lands without regard to aboriginal title. Douglas's approach thus facilitated the retention of the communal and tribal group identities that he assumed would vanish."[9]

Recently, after over a century of resistance, British Columbia has begun discussing land claims with Aboriginal groups. This has created much interest in James Douglas's early treaties on Vancouver Island, and, as well, in the reasons for his failure to complete further treaties on the Island and on the mainland of British Columbia. Historical assessment of Douglas's First Nations policies will lead, no doubt, to further discussion of his role in British Columbian history.

[1] Margaret Ormsby, "Sir James Douglas," *Dictionary of Canadian Biography*, vol. 10, *1871–1880* (Toronto: University of Toronto Press, 1972), p. 248).

[2] Jean Barman, *The West Beyond the West: A History of British Columbia* (Toronto: University of Toronto Press, 1991), pp. 80, 97.

[3] Paul Tennant, *Aboriginal Peoples and Politics: The Indian Land Question in British Columbia, 1849–1989* (Vancouver: University of British Columbia Press, 1990), p. 29.

[4] Robert Cail, *Land, Man and the Law: The Disposal of Crown Lands in British Columbia, 1871–1913* (Vancouver: University of British Columbia Press, 1974).

[5] Robin Fisher, *Contact and Conflict: Indian–European Relations in British Columbia, 1774–1890*, 2nd ed. (Vancouver: University of British Columbia Press, 1992 [1977]).

[6] Wilson Duff, *The Indian History of British Columbia*, vol. 1, *The Impact of the White Man* (Victoria: Royal British Columbia Museum, 1992 [1965]), p. 61.

[7] Ibid., p. 61.

[8] Tennant, *Aboriginal Peoples and Politics*, p. 29.

[9] Ibid., p. 38.

mainland. They received no compensation for the expropriation of their lands. Moreover, the miners intruded on their village sites, fishing stations, and cultivated areas. The increased number of non-Natives also resulted in the outbreak of disease, such as the smallpox epidemic of 1862 that claimed the lives of many First Nations living both along the coast and in the interior.

JAMES DOUGLAS'S ACCOMPLISHMENTS

Douglas remained in office as governor of both British Columbia and Vancouver Island until 1864. The settlers long complained about his autocratic ways and his "despotism," but in their haste to condemn him, they overlooked his accomplishments. On the mainland, he had confronted the Americans and firmly established British institutions. By building the Cariboo Road, he solved the problem of inland communication.

The governor's First Nations policy constituted another achievement. Thanks largely to him, Vancouver Island and British Columbia were spared the fierce wars between First Nations and settlers that raged in the United States. The real test came in the Fraser River valley and the

Cariboo country during the gold-rush days in the late 1850s and early 1860s. Apart from an attack in 1864 by Chilcotins on a road-building crew who had entered their territory uninvited, no major acts of First Nations armed resistance occurred. Perhaps this is explained in part, as historian J.I. Little writes, by the fact that "they were too dispersed and culturally diverse to take effective action during the period in which they still held the numerical upper hand."[7]

BRITISH COLUMBIA IN THE MID-1860S

www British Columbia experienced a post–gold-rush slump in the mid-1860s. Gold production fell, and people left the colony. Still, the region was rich in many natural resources. British Columbia's stands of Douglas fir produced ten times more wood per hectare than would New Brunswick's Miramichi or the Canadas' Ottawa valley.[8] But in the 1860s, high transportation costs ruled out large-scale exploitation. Beginnings had been made in lumber and fishing as export industries, but coal mining at centres like Nanaimo was still the most important industry, despite its decline. Some farming had begun, with specialization in wheat in the upper Fraser region, and with dairy and market gardening under way on the island. High American tariffs also reduced British Columbia's and Vancouver Island's trade with the United States, although Vancouver Island did sell some coal to San Francisco.

In the late 1860s, about 12 000 non-Natives lived in British Columbia and on Vancouver Island, more than half of them in the southwestern corner of the island. Between 1000 and 2000 lived in the lower Fraser valley, with the remainder along the routes to the gold fields or at fur-trading posts. Since most Americans had left, at least three-quarters were British or Canadians and, of these, males predominated. A small community of African-American settlers from San Francisco, and a few settlers from the Caribbean, resided in Victoria and on the lower mainland. More than 1000 Chinese from California, mostly men, remained to work finds in the Cariboo. As late as 1871 there were only 53 Chinese women in the entire province. Most of the Chinese men came originally from poor rural backgrounds in southeastern China and could not bring over their families. (Other reasons for the small number of females include prejudices in Chinese society against emigration, and the hostile reception often given to Asians in British Columbia.)

CHRISTIAN MISSIONARIES AND THE PACIFIC COAST PEOPLES

Missionaries sought to convert the First Nations to Christianity in the 1850s. William Duncan began his work at Fort Simpson in 1857 and continued it at neighbouring Metlakatla, where he built a model mission. Other Anglican missionaries followed. Methodists from Canada West also came; Thomas Crosby worked on Vancouver Island and along the northern coastline. In the late 1850s, the Oblate Fathers established Roman Catholic missions along the south coast, in the Okanagan, and in the Fraser valley.

The missionaries tried to convert the First Nations into good European Christians. This attempt was revealed in early church architecture. Historian Robin Fisher wrote that "in the main, the churches expressed the missionaries' overall intent to replace that which was Indian with that which was European."[9] In their zeal, the missionaries even banned totem poles. In 1900, the annual report of the federal Department of Indian Affairs noted that roughly 80 percent of British Columbia's First Nations were reported to be Christians.

It is difficult to judge the extent to which European settlers disrupted First Nations culture. Anthropologist Rolf Knight pointed out that many Native people near the settlements adjusted to the new economic conditions.[10] Independently of both mission and government direction, some First Nations tended potato gardens in the 1850s, and in the decades to follow, they started mixed farming. As early as the mid-1850s, independent Native loggers delivered logs to sawmills. Many

Community Portrait

The Black Community of Victoria

Canadians have long congratulated themselves on the improved state of race relations in Canada, and earlier in British North America, in contrast with that in the United States. While it is true that the British Empire abolished slavery in 1833, approximately one-third of a century before the United States, did African British North Americans achieve equality and full participation in their society? The existence of a vibrant, thriving community of people of African descent in Victoria, Vancouver Island, in the late 1850s and 1860s allows for comparisons to be made.

In the 1850s, African Americans faced increasing persecution and denial of civil rights in California. Several members of the African-American community in San Francisco sent a letter of enquiry to the government of the colony of British Columbia. Back came a favourable reply, they would be welcomed. It is interesting to note that James Douglas, the governor of Vancouver Island, had some African ancestry from his West-Indian mother.

The response that African Americans would be welcomed prompted the emigra-

When American forces threatened Vancouver Island in 1860 (during the dispute between Britain and the United States over the ownership of the strategic San Juan Island, near Fort Victoria), the black community formed a volunteer militia regiment to protect the colony. In 1872, international arbitration settled the boundary dispute in favour of the Americans, and San Juan Island became part of the United States.

Charles Gentile/National Archives of Canada/C-22626.

tion of approximately 400 people of African background from California to Victoria in 1858 and 1859. Since California was not a slave state, those moving to Vancouver Island were already free. A number came with business experience, and with the advantage of knowing a trade. A few, such as Mifflin Gibbs, brought capital with them. Without a doubt one of the central figures in the migration was Gibbs, a free-born African American, originally from Philadelphia, the son of a Wesleyan Methodist minister. As a young man in his mid-twenties he had moved to San Francisco and, within a year, became a partner in a clothing business. But the discrimination against blacks rankled him. He became one of the first to emigrate northward. Once in the colony, he joined the Victoria Pioneer Rifle Corps, an all-black volunteer militia, known familiarly as the African Rifles, formed to protect the colony against possible American aggression.

In Victoria the newcomers pushed for integration. They sought what was denied to them in the United States: equal access to institutions, services, and the political process. Gibbs himself became a naturalized British subject, which allowed him to register as a voter. Elected to the Victoria city council in 1866, he served two terms — one as the chair of the important finance committee.

Unfortunately, full equality was not achieved. It soon became apparent that the African-American immigrants still suffered prejudice in their new home. Some churches established segregated sections. Some saloons and other public facilities refused service to them. Theatres made them sit for performances in the balcony seats. These divisions were backed up by physical intimidation. Even the loyal Pioneer Rifle Corps suffered humiliation, as they were barred from parades and public ceremonies. Legal equality prevailed, and some African Americans achieved acceptance, but the colour line remained.

By the late 1860s, a number of African Americans left the colony and returned to the United States. Gibbs himself departed in 1869, and settled in Little Rock, Arkansas. The Civil War had ended, and opportunities surfaced for many in the country of their birth, but the persistence of the colour bar in British North America had also contributed to the exodus. In their new home on Vancouver Island, African Americans had contended with much of the same bigotry that they had tried to escape in pre-Civil War California.

Further Reading

Sherry Edmunds-Flett, "Mifflin Wistar Gibbs," *Dictionary of Canadian Biography*, vol. 14: *1911–1920* (Toronto: University of Toronto Press, 1998): 398–399.

Crawford Kilian, *Go Do Some Great Thing. The Black Pioneers of British Columbia* (Vancouver: Douglas and McIntyre, 1978).

James W. St.G. Walker, *Racial Discrimination in Canada: The Black Experience, Canadian Historical Association Booklet No. 41* (Ottawa: The Canadian Historical Association, 1985).

of the Hudson's Bay Company supply ships and several private trading schooners employed First Nations as crew members throughout the nineteenth century. They worked as hunters and crew on European sealing ships and, on occasion, wintered in Japan. First Nations-owned schooners began to appear in the 1870s, some of which they themselves had constructed. From the 1870s on, the First Nations entered the commercial fishing and canning industry. Thus, despite difficult circumstances, a number of them adjusted to the new conditions.

View of Metlakatla, British Columbia, in the 1870s. The magnificent Church of St. Paul's, shown in the upper right, was dedicated in 1874. It sat 1200 people.

The British Columbia Archives/HP 20388.

THE UNION OF THE TWO COLONIES

Major economic problems faced the two colonies of British Columbia and Vancouver Island in the mid-1860s. With the end of the gold rush, the economy was depressed and the two governments almost bankrupt. Anxious to save money, Britain promoted union of the two colonies, which would allow substantial reductions in administrative costs. In 1866, the colonies joined together and New Westminster became the capital. (A vigorous lobby, however, led by John Sebastian Helmcken, James Douglas's son-in-law, convinced the governor to move the capital to Victoria in 1868.) Despite the political consolidation of the two colonies, the depression continued. In 1867, a new issue arose: the American purchase of Alaska. This put in doubt the independence of British Columbia. As Helmcken noted in his diary, the Americans "boasted they had sandwiched British Columbia and could eat her up at any time!"

In 1867, the new united colony of British Columbia, only one year old, was the youngest of Britain's North American colonies. With the exception of a handful of fur traders, none of the approximately 8000 British Columbians of European descent in the colony had lived more than 25 years on Britain's Pacific coast. Thanks to the Hudson's Bay Company, Britain had retained this huge territory against Russian, and particularly against American, advances. But what would be the province's fate?

As the Canadas, New Brunswick, and Nova Scotia completed the final arrangements for their union, British Columbia's settler population debated its future. At no point did they consult the colony's 25 000 First Nations; rather, they proceeded as if the original inhabitants did not exist. British Columbia had three options: Britain, the United States, or Canada. Emotionally, most favoured the province's continuation as a British colony. Those seeking to increase British

Columbia's trade with its most important trading partner, however, endorsed annexation to the United States. Many British Columbians who had been born in the Canadas and the Maritimes favoured union with Canada, as did those who saw Confederation as the best means of protecting British institutions on the Northwest Coast and of developing British Columbia's resources.

NOTES

1. Philip Drucker, "Rank, Wealth, and Kinship in Northwest Coast Society," in Tom McFeat, ed., *Indians of the North Pacific Coast* (Toronto: McClelland & Stewart, 1966), p. 137.
2. Wilson Duff, *The Indian History of British Columbia*, vol. 1, *The Impact of the White Man* (Victoria: Royal British Columbia Museum, 1992 [1965]), p. 21.
3. Peter L. Macnair, *The Legacy: Continuing Traditions of Canadian Northwest Coast Indian Art* (Victoria: British Columbia Provincial Museum, 1980), p. 21.
4. Loraine Littlefield, "Women Traders in the Maritime Fur Trade," in Bruce Alden Cox, ed., *Native People, Native Lands: Canadian Indians, Inuit and Métis* (Ottawa: Carleton University Press, 1988), p. 173.
5. Duff, *Indian History*, p. 43.
6. Margaret Ormsby, *British Columbia: A History* (Toronto: Macmillan, 1958), p. 171.
7. J.I. Little, "The Foundations of Government," in Hugh J.M. Johnston, ed., *The Pacific Province: A History of British Columbia* (Vancouver: Douglas & McIntyre, 1996), p. 80.
8. Donald MacKay, *The Lumberjacks* (Toronto: McGraw-Hill Ryerson, 1978), p. 160.
9. Robin Fisher, "Missions to the Indians of British Columbia," in W. Peter Ward and Robert A.J. McDonald, eds., *British Columbia: Historical Readings* (Vancouver: Douglas & McIntyre, 1981), p. 123.
10. Rolf Knight, *Indians at Work: An Informal History of Native Indian Labour in British Columbia, 1858–1930* (Vancouver: New Star Books, 1978), pp. 7–27.

LINKING TO THE PAST www

Northwest Coast Native Culture
http://www.civilization.ca/aborig/grand/grandeng.html

The on-line version of this exhibition housed in the Canadian Museum of Civilization's Grand Hall features descriptions and photographs of artifacts related to Northwest Coast First Nations cultures. Check out the links at the bottom for additional artifacts and historical information.

Gifting and Feasting in the Northwest Coast Potlatch
http://www.peabody.harvard.edu/potlatch

An illustrated overview of the potlatch on the Northwest Coast.

Totem Poles: An Exploration
http://users.imag.net/~sry.jkramer/nativetotems

This site explains the meaning of totem poles and answers some of the most commonly asked questions about them.

Hudson's Bay Company at Fort Victoria
http://collections.ic.gc.ca/fortvictoria

An on-line exhibition on the inhabitants of and the daily life in Fort Victoria, with a virtual tour of the fort.

Douglas Treaties: 1850–1854
http://www.gov.bc.ca/tno/history/douglas.htm

Information on the fourteen treaties made by James Douglas and First Nations.

British Columbia Archives
http://www.bcarchives.gov.bc.ca/index.htm
The archives' extensive on-line collection includes images (photographs, paintings, drawings, and prints), government and private documents and records, and cartographic documents and maps of British Columbia from its beginnings to the present.

RELATED READINGS

Two articles in R. Douglas Francis and Donald B. Smith, eds., *Readings in Canadian History: Pre-Confederation*, 6th ed. (Toronto: Nelson Thomson Learning, 2002), are useful for this topic: Sylvia Van Kirk, "Tracing the Fortunes of Five Founding Families of Victoria," pp. 437–458; and Barry M. Gough, "The Character of the British Columbia Frontier," pp. 458–466.

BIBLIOGRAPHY

Two excellent overviews of the history of the two Pacific colonies are Jean Barman's *The West beyond the West: A History of British Columbia* (Toronto: University of Toronto Press, 1991; revised edition, 1996) and Hugh J.M. Johnston, ed., *The Pacific Province: A History of British Columbia* (Vancouver: Douglas & McIntyre, 1996). R. Cole Harris provides a geographical overview, in "British Columbia," in R. Cole Harris and John Warkentin, eds., *Canada Before Confederation* (Ottawa: Carleton University Press, 1991 [1974]), pp. 289–311. A wealth of information on British Columbia can be found in Daniel Francis, ed., *Encyclopedia of British Columbia* (Madeira Park: Harbour Publishing, 2000). Tina Loo provides a very useful bibliographical guide in her essay "The Pacific Coast," in M. Brook Taylor, ed., *Canadian History: A Reader's Guide*, vol. 1, *Beginnings to Confederation* (Toronto: University of Toronto Press, 1994), pp. 356–93.

Reviews of British Columbia's Aboriginal past appear in Wilson Duff, *The Indian History of British Columbia*, vol. 1, *The Impact of the White Man* (Victoria: Royal British Columbia Museum, 1997 [1965]); Robin Fisher, *Contact and Conflict: Indian–European Relations in British Columbia, 1774–1890*, 2nd ed. (Vancouver: University of British Columbia Press, 1992 [1977]); and two volumes by historical geographer Cole Harris, *The Resettlement of British Columbia. Essays on Colonialism and Geographical Change* (Vancouver: University of British Columbia Press, 1997); and *Making Native Space. Colonialism, Resistance, and Reserves in British Columbia* (Vancouver: University of British Columbia Press, 2002). Two interesting studies of First Nations women are included in Wendy Mitchinson et al., *Canadian Women: A Reader* (Toronto: Harcourt Brace, 1996): Loraine Littlefield, "Women Traders in the Maritime Fur Trade," pp. 6–19; and Carol Cooper, "Native Women of the Northern Pacific Coast: An Historical Perspective, 1830–1900," pp. 89–119. An essential source on the culture of the Native peoples is Wayne Suttles, ed., *Northwest Coast*, vol. 7 of the *Handbook of North American Indians* (Washington, DC: Smithsonian Institution, 1990). Two studies of slavery are Robert H. Ruby and John A. Brown, *Indian Slavery in the Pacific Northwest* (Spokane, WA: Arthur H. Clark, 1993); and Leland Donald, *Aboriginal Slavery on the Northwest Coast of America* (Berkeley: University of California Press, 1997). Aldona Jonaitis has published the beautifully illustrated *From the Land of the Totem Poles* (Vancouver: Douglas & McIntyre, 1988) on Northwest Coast Native art. Paul Tennant's, *Aboriginal Peoples and Politics: The Indian Land Question in British Columbia, 1849–1989* (Vancouver: University of British Columbia Press, 1990) is very useful.

First Nations statements include *The Spirit in the Land* (Gabriola, BC: Reflections, 1987), which provides a summary of the land claim of the hereditary chiefs of the Gitskan and Wet'suwet'en people to nearly 60 000 km^2 in northwestern British Columbia. First Nations traditions on the Northwest Coast are reviewed in Ruth Kirk, *Wisdom of the Elders* (Victoria: Royal British Columbia Museum, 1986). Chief Mathias Capilano presents a Squamish version of the Europeans' arrival in "Strangers Appear on English Bay," in *Romance of Vancouver*, vol. 2, compiled by the Native Sons of British Columbia (n.p., 1926), pp. 5–6. A similar version, "How the Squamish Remember George Vancouver," was presented by Chief Philip Joe at the Vancouver Conference on Exploration and Discovery in April 1992; see Robin Fisher and Hugh Johnston, eds., *From Maps to Metaphors: The Pacific World of George Vancouver* (Vancouver: University of British Columbia Press, 1993), pp. 3–5. On the impact on the First Nations of European infectious disease, see: Robert Boyd, *The Coming of the Spirit of Pestilence: Introduced Infectious Diseases and Population Decline among Northwest Coast Indians, 1774–1874* (Vancouver: University of British Columbia Press, 1999).

A bibliographical guide has been compiled by Robert Steven Grumet: *Native Americans of the Northwest Coast* (Bloomington: Indiana University Press, 1979).

Warren L. Cook's *Flood Tide of Empire: Spain and the Pacific Northwest, 1543–1819* (New Haven: Yale University Press, 1973), and three articles by Christen Archer — "The Transient Presence: A Re-appraisal of Spanish Attitudes Toward the Northwest Coast in the Eighteenth Century," *B.C. Studies* 18 (1973): 3–32; "Spanish Exploration and Settlement of the Northwest Coast in the 18th Century," *Sound Heritage* 7(1) (1978): 33–53; and "Cannibalism in the Early History of the Northwest Coast: Enduring Myths and Neglected Realities," *Canadian Historical Review* 61 (1980): 453–79 — provide the background on Spanish activities. In *The Men with Wooden Feet: The Spanish Exploration of the Pacific Northwest* (Toronto: NC Press, 1985), John Kendrick also reviews the Spanish experience. Donald Cutter examines the Spanish expeditions of 1791 and 1792 in his *Malaspina and Galiano* (Vancouver: Douglas & McIntyre, 1991).

For a survey of Russian and American activities in the North Pacific see James R. Gibson's *Otter Skins, Boston Ships and China Goods: The Maritime Fur Trade of the Northwest Coast, 1785–1841* (Montreal/Kingston: McGill-Queen's University Press, 1992). Barry Gough reviewed early British contact in *The Northwest Coast: British Navigation, Trade, and Discoveries to 1812* (Vancouver: University of British Columbia Press, 1992); and he studied the later period in *Gunboat Frontier: British Maritime Authority and Northwest Coast Indians, 1846–90* (Vancouver: University of British Columbia Press, 1984). *The Dictionary of Canadian Biography*, vol. 4, *1771–1800* (Toronto: University of Toronto Press, 1979) contains sketches of James Cook by Glyndwr Williams, pp. 162–67, and of George Vancouver by W. Kaye Lamb, pp. 743–48. Many aspects of Vancouver's voyage are reviewed in Robin Fisher and Hugh Johnson, eds., *From Maps to Metaphors: The Pacific World of George Vancouver* (Vancouver: University of British Columbia Press, 1993). The coastal fur trade is examined by Richard Somerset Mackie in *Trading Beyond the Mountains: The British Fur Trade on the Pacific, 1793–1843* (Vancouver: University of British Columbia Press, 1997). For a survey of the inland fur trade see Theodore J. Karamanski, *Fur Trade and Exploration: Opening the Far Northwest, 1821–1852* (Vancouver: University of British Columbia Press, 1983).

Other items can be cited for the nineteenth century. Margaret Ormsby concisely reviews the life of James Douglas in the *Dictionary of Canadian Biography,* vol. 10, *1871–1880* (Toronto: University of Toronto Press, 1972), pp. 239–49. Clarence G. Karr has written an interesting article on Douglas, "James Douglas: The Gold Governor in the Context of His Times," in E. Blanche Norcross, ed., *The Company on the Coast* (Nanaimo: Nanaimo Historical Society, 1983): 56–78. *Old Square Toes and His Family* by John Adams (Victoria, B.C.: Horsdal and Schubart Publishers Ltd., 2001) contains full biographical portraits of James and Amelia Douglas. W. Peter Ward and Robert A.J. McDonald, eds., *British Columbia: Historical Readings* (Vancouver: Douglas & McIntyre, 1981) includes James E. Hendrickson's "The Constitutional Development of Colonial Vancouver Island and British Columbia," pp. 245–74. Richard Mackie has written "The Colonization of Vancouver Island, 1849–1858," *B.C. Studies* 96 (Winter 1992–93): 3–40. Tina Loo's *Making Law, Order, and Authority in British Columbia, 1821–1871* (Toronto: University of Toronto Press, 1994), is the first comprehensive legal history of British Columbia in the colonial period. Dorothy Blakey Smith provides a sketch of J.S. Helmcken in her introduction to *The Reminiscences of Doctor John Sebastian Helmcken* (Vancouver: University of British Columbia Press, 1975). An interesting look at early Victoria is provided by Peter A. Baskerville in *Beyond the Island: An Illustrated History of Victoria* (Burlington, ON: Windsor Publications, 1986).

Economic history is a growing field of research. A lively account of the British Columbia gold rushes is contained in Douglas Fetherling's *The Gold Crusades: A Social History of Gold Rushes, 1849–1929* (Toronto: Macmillan, 1988). John Douglas Belshaw has written two articles on coal mining on Vancouver Island: "Mining Technique and Social Division on Vancouver Island, 1848–1900," *British Journal of Canadian Studies* 1 (1986): 45–65; and "The Standard of Living of British Miners on Vancouver Island, 1848–1900," *B.C. Studies* 84 (Winter 1989–90): 37–64. Lynne Bowen has completed an interesting study of labour unrest on Vancouver Island in 1849: "Independent Colliers at Fort Rupert," *The Beaver* 69(2) (April–May 1989): 25–31. Paul A. Phillips's essay, "Confederation and the Economy of British Columbia," in W. George Shelton, ed., *British Columbia and Confederation* (Victoria: University of Victoria, 1967), pp. 43–60, is very useful.

In the field of gender and race history, Adele Perry has written *On the Edge of Empire. Gender, Race, and the Making of British Columbia, 1849–1871* (Toronto: University of Toronto Press, 2001). Interesting accounts of non-Aboriginal and non-European groups in British Columbia in the nineteenth century include Crawford Killian, *Go Do Some Great Thing: The Black Pioneers of British Columbia* (Vancouver:

Douglas & McIntyre, 1978); James Morton, *In the Sea of Sterile Mountains: The Chinese in British Columbia* (Vancouver: J.J. Douglas, 1974); and Tom Koppel, *Kanaka: The Untold Story of Hawaiian Pioneers in British Columbia and the Pacific Northwest* (Vancouver: Whitecap Books, 1995).

For important maps consult the first two volumes of the *Historical Atlas of Canada*: vol. 1, R. Cole Harris, ed., *From the Beginning to 1800* (Toronto: University of Toronto Press, 1987); and vol. 2, R. Louis Gentilcore, ed., *The Land Transformed, 1800–1891* (Toronto: University of Toronto Press, 1993).

PART FIVE

TOWARD CONFEDERATION

INTRODUCTION

The idea of a union of the British North American colonies had been considered on a number of occasions since the 1790s. The British government had encouraged the idea since the 1830s. Yet only in the early 1860s were the conditions right for such action. Those "conditions" included: externally, a threat of American takeover of the British North American colonies at the end of the Civil War, and direct British pressure through its political representatives in the colonies, the lieutenant governors; and internally, political deadlock in the United Canadas, public debt as a result of overzealous schemes of railway building, and the possibility of acquiring the Northwest from the Hudson's Bay Company,

Yet in 1867, only three of the colonies — the United Canadas, Nova Scotia, and New Brunswick — agreed to experiment with union, and even within these colonies, the debate proved acrimonious, and the decision tenuous. Why was there such opposition, especially in Quebec and the Maritimes? And why, in the end, did they agree to unite? Why, too, was there a sense of haste in the process?

While the Fathers of Confederation clearly hoped this initial union would be the nucleus of a larger transcontinental nation (the very motto for the new country *"A Mari Usque ad Mare"* — "From Sea to Sea" — reflected their aspiration), no assurance existed in 1867 that this would be the case. Only in retrospect do we look back at Confederation as the making of a larger Canada.

THE ROAD TO CONFEDERATION

TIME LINE

1861 – Outbreak of the American Civil War

Trent affair: the seizure of two Confederate envoys from the British mail-steamer *Trent*

1864 – Confederate raid on St. Alban's, Vermont from British North American territory

Britain sends 14 000 soldiers to British North America, the largest detachment since the War of 1812

Political deadlock in the Canadas leads to the defeat of the Macdonald–Taché coalition government

Formation of the "Great Coalition" to work towards British North American federation

Canadian and Maritime delegates discuss a possible plan for union at the Charlottetown Conference in September

The terms of the British North American federation are agreed upon at the Quebec Conference in October

1865 – Canadian legislature approves the Quebec Resolutions, but only a narrow majority of French-Canadian members endorse them

Premier Leonard Tilley defeated by anti-Confederationists in New Brunswick election

Joseph Howe writes "The Botheration Letters" appealing to Nova Scotians to oppose joining a union of the British North American colonies

1866 – The United States government terminates the Reciprocity Treaty of 1854

Fenian invasion of New Brunswick is threatened, and the Fenians raid the Niagara peninsula in Canada West

Leonard Tilley's pro-Confederation party wins the election in New Brunswick

Westminster Conference in London, England prepares the passage of the British North America Act through the British Parliament

1867 – The British North America Act is passed, creating the Dominion of Canada

The Dominion of Canada is born with the union of the colonies of Nova Scotia, New Brunswick, Canada East (Quebec), and Canada West (Ontario)

John A. Macdonald becomes Canada's first prime minister

Historian P.B. Waite notes that "the Confederation movement followed Newton's first law of motion: all bodies continue in a state of rest or of uniform motion unless compelled by some force to change their state."[1] Proposals for British North American union had been considered well before the 1860s, but they never became reality. By the 1860s, however, threats of an American takeover as a result of the Civil War, pressure from Britain for unification of the British North American colonies, internal problems in the colonies, such as heavy public debt from extensive railway building and, in the case of the Canadas, political deadlock (and the desire to acquire the Northwest), led both Canadians and Maritimers to consider union. These immediate circumstances, more than a spirit of nationalism, prepared the way for Confederation.

THE IMPACT OF THE AMERICAN CIVIL WAR

Fear of an American takeover during the Civil War contributed to British North American unification. Historian F.H. Underhill once suggested that "somewhere on Parliament Hill in Ottawa ... there should be erected a monument to this American ogre who has so often performed the function of saving us from drift and indecision."[2]

THE *ALABAMA* AND *TRENT* AFFAIRS

Although Britain was officially neutral during the American Civil War, many Britons backed the Confederacy because of their dependence on southern cotton for the textile industry. The international rules of neutrality prevented the legal construction of Confederate warships in British shipyards, but the South secretly had a swift and powerful cruiser built in a shipyard near Liverpool. The Southern strategists had the ship launched in a hurry, just one step ahead of outraged Union diplomats in England. On the North Atlantic the C.S.S. *Alabama*, as it was now named, hoisted the Confederate ensign of Stars and Bars, and a brass band broke into "Dixie" as the men cheered. In the 22-month rampage on three oceans that followed, the *Alabama* burned or captured 64 Northern merchant vessels and a Union warship — until the U.S.S. *Kearsarge* cornered and sank the Confederate raider off the coast of Normandy in June 1864. The United States held Britain responsible for the destruction of ships and cargoes by the *Alabama* and other British-built Confederate vessels. Northern leaders argued that since Britain knew the uses to which the South put these ships, it was effectively a contributor to the war and should pay for damages incurred. One Northern proposal included all of British North America as compensation.

Another incident during the Civil War that heightened Anglo–American antagonism was the *Trent* affair. In November 1861, an American warship stopped the British steamer *Trent* and forcibly removed two Confederate envoys on their way to England to secure assistance for the Southern cause. Tempers flared on both sides, with Britain threatening retaliation if the North did not free these Confederate agents, seized in neutral waters, and the North denouncing Britain for aiding the Southern cause. In the end, President Abraham Lincoln released the prisoners on Christmas Day, 1861, to avoid war with Britain.

THE ST. ALBAN'S RAID

As the Union army continued its victorious march south in 1864, the Confederacy planned attacks on the North via Canada. At St. Alban's, Vermont, on October 19, 1864, 26 Confederate sympathizers terrorized the town, robbed three banks of $200 000, set several fires, wounded two men and killed another, and then fled to Canada. The government arrested them, but

The *Trent* affair, 1861, was the most serious diplomatic crisis between Britain and the United States during the American Civil War. It arose after the Union warship *San Jacinto* (shown on the right) seized, on the high seas, two Confederate envoys from the British mail-steamer *Trent*. This drawing appeared in *The Illustrated London News*, December 7, 1861.

National Archives of Canada/C-18711.

Charles Joseph Coursol, a Montreal magistrate, released them — and even returned the money to them — on a legal technicality.

More than the raid itself, this act of leniency infuriated Northerners. The Canadian government quickly condemned Coursol's action. As well, in January 1865, the Canadian Assembly passed legislation that provided for the deportation of aliens involved in acts against a friendly foreign state. Nevertheless, Canada once again became suspect. General John A. Dix, commander of the American military district in the east, threatened Canada with retaliation if it refused to turn Southern raiders over to American authorities immediately.

These hostilities inevitably affected the British North American colonies. Fear of an impending American attack led Britain to send 14 000 soldiers to British North America, the largest detachment of troops dispatched since the War of 1812. But Britain was anxious to withdraw its expensive garrisons from North America as soon as possible, and thus London encouraged the colonies to provide for their own defence. This was more likely to occur if the colonies were united.

The colonies realized the need for a railway that would extend from an ice-free port on the Atlantic into the interior, within British North American territory. Militarily, British North America undoubtedly needed a rail link — many of the 14 000 reinforcements sent to the Canadas were forced to make an epic journey by sled across New Brunswick because no rail link existed to the seaboard; and economically it would enhance intercolonial trade.

THE GREAT COALITION

In this tense atmosphere the politicians in the United Canadas tried to solve the problem of political deadlock in their Assembly. Neither the Conservatives nor the Reformers could form a stable government. Between 1861 and 1864, for example, the Canadas experienced two elections and three changes of administration. On June 14, 1864, the most recent administration, the Macdonald–Taché coalition, went down to defeat. Macdonald requested dissolution of the Assembly, but rather than accept his request, Governor General Monck urged the Conservative leader to open negotiations with George Brown, leader of the Reform party, with the possibility of forming a coalition. Brown and Macdonald were arch-enemies. Their hostility resulted from a combination of conflicting personalities, ideological differences, and support for rival urban centres — Brown for Toronto and Macdonald for Montreal. Nevertheless, the two men agreed to negotiate. On June 30, a jubilant Assembly heard Brown announce that he would enter a coalition cabinet along with two others from his Reform party, Oliver Mowat and William McDougall, and work for federation. Thus was born the "Great Coalition of 1864."

Brown made three demands in return for his support. First, he insisted that the coalition government work toward a federation of all the British North American colonies and, if this wider aim proved unattainable, toward a federation of the two Canadas alone. Second, he demanded representation by population, or "rep by pop," as it became popularly known. The Clear Grits believed that representation in the Canadian assembly should be based on population distribution, rather than on equality between the two sections. By 1861, Canada West had almost 1.4 million people, compared with the 1.1 million of Canada East.

Third, Brown called for the incorporation of Rupert's Land into Confederation. He insisted that westward expansion accompany the entry of the Maritimes into a federal union. For nearly a decade, Brown's newspaper, the Toronto *Globe*, had kept Upper Canadians informed about developments in the Northwest. The *Globe* provided generous excerpts from the reports of the two scientific expeditions in the late 1850s — the British Palliser and the Canadian Hind expeditions. Brown's interest in the Northwest lay in its potential for the development of Canada West. On January 22, 1863, for example, the Toronto newspaper editor outlined his imperial vision:

> If Canada acquires this territory it will rise in a few years from a position of a small and weak province to be the greatest colony any country has ever possessed, able to take its place among the empires of the earth. The wealth of 400 000 square miles of territory will flow through our waters and be gathered by our merchants, manufacturers and agriculturists. Our sons will occupy the chief places of this vast territory, we will form its institutions, supply its rulers, teach its schools, fill its stores, run its mills, navigate its streams.

THE CHARLOTTETOWN CONFERENCE

In the early 1860s, the Maritime colonies of Nova Scotia, New Brunswick, and Prince Edward Island considered union among themselves, endorsed by the Colonial Office in Britain. Although all three governments had some reservations about the suggestion, they had agreed to meet. No date or place had yet been set for the meeting when, in July 1864, the government of the Canadas asked permission to attend and to present a proposal for a wider British North American federal union. The Maritimers agreed, and arranged the meeting for September 1, 1864, in Charlottetown.

At the Charlottetown conference, the Canadian delegation presented an impressive *tour de force*. John A. Macdonald and George-Étienne Cartier set out the arguments in favour of Confederation and the general terms of the Canadian proposal, particularly those aspects dealing with the division of powers between the central and provincial governments. Alexander Galt, the minister of finance in the Canadas, dealt with economic issues, while George Brown handled constitutional concerns. The main features of their proposal included continued loyalty to the British Crown through membership in the British empire; a strong central government

The banquet and ball, the final night of the Charlottetown Conference, at Province House. The assembly chamber — now decorated with evergreens, flowers, and flags — became the ballroom. Under brilliant gaslight, delegates and their partners danced to the music of two Charlottetown bands from the gallery. At the front and centre of the re-creation by artist Dusan Kadlec appear John A. Macdonald and George-Étienne Cartier.

The Ball at the Legislature, 1864, by Dusan Kadlec. © Parks Canada.

within a federal union in which the provinces retained control over their own local affairs; and representation in a lower house based on population and an upper house based on regional representation. Thomas D'Arcy McGee, the gifted poet-politician, spoke eloquently in terms of the need for a common British North American vision.

Within four days, the Canadians had presented such a convincing case that the Maritime delegates abandoned their talk of Maritime union. Before the conference adjourned on September 7, the delegates agreed to meet again on October 10 at Quebec City to explore in greater detail the nature of a British North American federation.

THE QUEBEC CONFERENCE

In the interim, the Canadian delegates reworked the broad general principles of Charlottetown into specific resolutions. They presented them at Quebec in the form of the Seventy-Two Resolutions. The magnitude of what they attempted is impressive. Over a two-week period, they established the political framework for a union of the British North American colonies. Their plan incorporated aspects of the British unitary and the American federal systems. The Maritime and Canadian delegates debated the resolutions, finally reaching agreement on the terms of what, with only a few minor alterations, would become the British North America Act.

Community Portrait

The Charlottetown Conference as a Political Community

On September 1, 1864, twenty-three political leaders from the Atlantic colonies and from the United Canadas met in Charlottetown to discuss the possibility of a British North American union. They came together as strangers to one other. So the success of the conference depended on the ability to create a sense of community—for the representatives to come to know and to trust one another, and to believe that they had something in common. In this respect social events became as important as the political meetings. The wives of the politicians, especially the wives of the Island hosts who organized the social gatherings, made a very important contribution by helping to create a sense of community at the Charlottetown Conference. As historian Gail Cuthbert Brandt points out: "Mrs. Dundas, wife of the Lieutenant-Governor of Prince Edward Island, and the wives of Maritime politicians such as Mercy Haine Coles and Mrs. Haviland used their social skills to help transform the mutual ignorance and suspicion of Canadians and Maritimers into the personal bonds of esteem and friendship which facilitated political accommodation and new constitutional arrangements."[1] As well, the presence of women reminded the politicians that their decisions affected all members of the community, including women and children. As a result, historians have now come to identify these women as the "Mothers of Confederation."

The politicians who met at Charlottetown came with quite different agendas, interests, and hopes. Indeed, initially, the Charlottetown Conference was called to discuss Maritime union only. Then the politicians from the Canadas asked to attend to put forward a proposal for a wider British North American union, and the focus shifted. Thus mistrust, divisiveness, and differences had to be overcome in order to find points of common interests, to cultivate a feeling of community. Luncheons, dinners, banquets, and balls, dutifully organized and arranged by the wives of the Maritime representatives, became common occurrences during the seven days of deliberations at Charlottetown. These social events fostered the feeling among the politicians that they belonged to a community. In a letter to his wife and confidante Anne Nelson, daughter of publisher William Nelson,* George Brown from Upper Canada noted the change that came over the delegates as they wined and dined: "Cartier and I made eloquent speeches, and whether as the result of our eloquence or of the goodness of our champagne, the ice became completely broken, the tongues of the delegates wagged merrily, [and] the banns of matrimony between all the provinces of British North America were formally proclaimed."

Brown failed to note in his letter the important role that the women played in forging this sense of political community. But at the final banquet, the delegates made the last toast to Mrs. Dundas and the other ladies present as acknowledgement of their important role in making the Charlottetown Conference a success. The Conference had shaped a political community of the leaders who would go on to forge the new nation of Canada.

Further Reading

Moira Dann, *Mothers of Confederation*. CBC Transcript (Toronto: Canadian Broadcasting Corporation, 1989).

Gail Cuthbert Brandt, "National Unity and the Politics of Political History," Presidential Address, *Journal of the Canadian Historical Association* (1992): 3–11.

Christopher Moore, *1867: How the Fathers Made a Deal* (Toronto: McClelland & Stewart, 1997).

J.M.S. Careless, "George Brown and the Mother of Confederation, 1864," Canadian Historical Association *Annual Report*, (1960): 57–73.

[1] Gail Cuthbert Brandt, "National Unity and the Politics of Political History," Presidential Address, *Journal of the Canadian Historical Association* (1992): 7.

* Nelson, the publisher of your textbook, is a direct descendant of William Nelson's publishing firm.

The delegates to the Charlottetown Conference, September 1864.

George P. Roberts/National Archives of Canada/C-733.

From left to right:

1. Charles Drinkwater, private secretary to John A. Macdonald
2. Hewitt Bernard, secretary to John A. Macdonald
3. Alexander T. Galt, Canada
4. Charles Tupper, Nova Scotia
5. Edward B. Chandler, New Brunswick
6. Hector-Louis Langevin, Canada
7. Edward Palmer, Prince Edward Island
8. John Hamilton Gray, New Brunswick
9. Robert Dickey, Nova Scotia
10. George-Étienne Cartier, Canada
11. Thomas D'Arcy McGee, Canada
12. William A. Henry, Nova Scotia
13. John A. Macdonald, Canada
14. William H. Steeves, New Brunswick
15. John Hamilton Gray, Prince Edward Island
16. John M. Johnson, New Brunswick
17. Samuel L. Tilley, New Brunswick
18. Adams G. Archibald, Nova Scotia
19. Andrew A. Macdonald, Prince Edward Island
20. William Campbell, Canada
21. William MacDougall, Canada
22. George Coles, Prince Edward Island
23. William H. Pope, Prince Edward Island
24. Jonathan McCully, Nova Scotia
25. George Brown, Canada

Macdonald clearly favoured a legislative union or a strong central government, arguing that the Civil War in the United States was the result of overly powerful state governments. In the discussions, references to the American Civil War — with its death toll equal to the entire population of the Maritime colonies in the 1860s — constantly surfaced. The Colonial Office in Britain and its appointees, the Maritime governors, also favoured a strong central government to make all major decisions, as was done in the United Kingdom. The Maritime delegates, however, feared a loss of their identity in a legislative union and favoured a federal union with their own powerful local governments. The French Canadians, through their spokesman, George-Étienne Cartier, equally insisted on a local government in Quebec strong enough to protect their language, civil law, and customs.

The delegates reached a compromise. They granted some of the powers requested to the provincial governments, but gave the central government residuary powers (powers not specifically assigned to the provinces). Second, they included, as a right of the central government, the power "to make laws for the peace, order and good government of Canada." The federal government also gained the power of disallowance — the right to reject provincial laws of which it did not approve.

In the mid-1970s, the Prince Edward Island Legislative Council was restored to its original state, that of 1864, when it served as the meeting place for the Charlottetown Conference and thus became the birthplace of Confederation. Province House is now a national historic site.

Canadian Heritage (Parks Canada), Atlantic Region.

THE DEBATE OVER THE SEVENTY-TWO RESOLUTIONS

The delegates confirmed their previous agreement at Charlottetown on a federal lower house based on representation by population and an upper house based on regional representation. But they strongly disagreed on the number of representatives from each region in the upper house — the Senate. The disagreement almost destroyed the conference. The issue became contentious because the smaller Maritime provinces saw the Senate as a means of strengthening their regional representation to offset their numerical weakness in the lower house. In the end, the delegates agreed that the Maritimes would have 24 seats, the same number given to each of Ontario and Quebec. They also disagreed over the means of choosing senators. After discussing and eliminating a number of proposals, it was decided on appointment for life by the central government. (In hindsight, that decision destroyed the possibility of the Senate ever becoming an effective voice for regional or provincial interests. In only a few instances has the appointed Senate challenged the views of the elected House of Commons.)

After acrimonious debate, the delegates accepted the financial arrangements proposed by A.T. Galt. He recommended that the new federal government assume the public debts — up to a specified maximum amount — of each province that joined. In addition, the federal government would finance the Intercolonial Railway, linking the Maritimes to the Canadas. This agreement was written directly into the British North America Act.

Galt also argued successfully for the central government, with its heavy financial obligations, to control the main sources of revenue. It would have unlimited taxing powers, including the collection of both direct taxes and indirect taxes, such as customs and excise duties, one of the main sources of revenue at the time. In contrast, the provinces could levy only direct taxes. To compensate the provinces for the cost of education, roads, and other local obligations, Galt proposed that the federal government pay annual subsidies based on 80 cents per head of their population. The provinces could raise additional revenue by direct taxation or by selling their natural resources (public lands, minerals, and waterpower), which would remain in provincial hands.

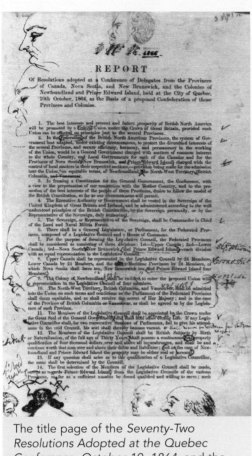

The title page of the *Seventy-Two Resolutions Adopted at the Quebec Conference, October 10, 1864,* and the basis of the British North America Act. This copy shows doodles by John A. Macdonald.

National Archives of Canada/C-95155.

RESPONSES TO THE CONFEDERATION PROPOSALS

When the Quebec Conference ended, the delegates returned home to secure approval for the resolutions. The Fathers of Confederation considered submitting the draft constitution for popular approval but later decided to follow the British procedure of ratification by the politicians only. They worried about public opposition to the scheme. The positive side of this procedure was the ability to get the resolutions approved relatively quickly and without much opposition and therefore with no undue delay of the political process. The negative side was that only a limited number of people had a voice in the constitutional debate. The elected politicians represented a very restricted constituency that excluded unpropertied males and all women. As a result, the Confederation agreement did not at the time (or since) form the basis of a political community with a clear sense of itself and its political rights and constitutional freedoms.

Absent entirely from the constitutional process were the First Nations. To the Fathers of Confederation, the First Nations were wards of the state, upon whom sovereignty could be imposed. They were not people with rights of their own or members of the political community. As political scientist Peter Russell notes, "Aboriginal peoples were treated as subjects, not citizens, of the new dominion."[3]

In the legislatures of the Canadas, considerable debate ensued. George Brown and his Reformers expressed concern about a wider union with the Maritimes, favouring instead a revised union of the Canadas as being more advantageous to Upper Canadians. They also believed that the Intercolonial Railway would be another expensive publicly funded railway like the Grand Trunk. Nevertheless, Brown agreed to overlook both these reservations, since the proposed federation was to be based on "rep by pop." In general, Upper Canadian politicians favoured Confederation, realizing that they had the most to gain from the union.

DEBATE OVER CONFEDERATION IN CANADA EAST

Members of the Parti rouge, under the leadership of Antoine-Aimé Dorion, had serious reservations. Dorion argued that "It is not at all a confederation that is proposed to us, but quite simply a Legislative Union disguised under the name of a confederation. How could one accept as a federation a scheme ... that provided for disallowance of local legislation?" Furthermore, he pointed out that in the proposed House of Commons the English-Canadian representation from Canada West and the Maritimes would greatly outnumber the French-Canadian representation. Dorion also pointed out that the British North American union would heighten rather than diminish possible tension with the United States, as it would add the nearly 1000 km New Brunswick–American border to Canada's political boundary. Finally, this nineteenth-century liberal denounced the Fathers of Confederation for refusing to allow the people to make their views known on the proposed union, either through a plebiscite or by an election. In a prophetic statement, Dorion summarized his misgivings:

> I greatly fear that the day when this Confederation is adopted will be a dark day for Lower Canada. ... I consider it one of the worst measures which could be submitted to us and if it happens that it is adopted, without the sanctions of the people of the province, the country will have more than one occasion to regret it.

George-Étienne Cartier countered Dorion's criticisms. He emphasized that in the new federal union, French Canadians would control their own provincial government and legislature, have their own local administration, and retain the Civil Code. Furthermore, the French language would be official in the province of Quebec as well as in the federal administration, and the rights of religious minorities for separate schools would be recognized in all the provinces. On the question of English-Canadian dominance, Cartier pointed out that the "new nationality" would be a "political nationality" only, not a "cultural nationality," and therefore did not require French Canadians to suppress their cultural differences for the sake of some common pan-Canadian nationalism. He also reminded his French-Canadian compatriots of the importance of the British connection to offset the threat of American annexation and the loss of identity that would ensue. (Cartier had an almost morbid fear of the Americans and an equally strong dislike of republicanism.)

Finally, Cartier presented Confederation to French Canadians as their best hope for cultural survival in a world of limited possibilities. The existing union, crippled by deadlock, could not go on; for French Canadians, union with the United States would be the worst possible fate. The independence of Lower Canada was not feasible. Only a larger federation of British North American colonies, Cartier concluded, offered French Canadians possibilities beyond their own provincial boundaries at the same time as it protected their affairs within their own province. Cartier's close association with the Grand Trunk Railway (as one of the company's directors) and his desire to play a larger role as a statesman on a national stage no doubt contributed to his enthusiasm for Confederation.

Cartier faced a difficult struggle promoting Confederation in Quebec. He turned to the clergy for support, despite his personal concerns about mixing politics and religion. He could not, however, count on unreserved support. Ignace Bourget of Montreal, the most powerful French-Canadian bishop, feared for the future of the church in a new political union with other English-speaking colonies with large Protestant populations. He kept silent about his misgivings, however, since the other Quebec bishops were more favourably disposed, at least in principle. For the church to have opposed Confederation would have put them in the camp of their arch-enemies, the *rouges*, who were strongly anti-clerical.

The Confederation debates in the Canadas lasted just over a month, from February 3 to March 11, 1865. In a final vote, 91 favoured and 33 opposed Confederation. In the breakdown of votes in the two sections, 54 of the 62 members from Canada West favoured the proposal, as did 37 of the 62 members from Canada East. Of the 48 French-Canadian members present, 27 voted for and 21 against. Overall, Confederation won overwhelmingly, but among French Canadians the victory was narrow, indicating serious reservations on their part.

NEW BRUNSWICK INITIALLY REJECTS CONFEDERATION

In New Brunswick, Samuel Leonard Tilley, a son of a Loyalist, a leader of the temperance forces in the 1850s, and a Saint John druggist who had been premier since 1857 and who had represented the province at both the Charlottetown and Quebec conferences, argued the advantages of Confederation for New Brunswickers: Saint John would be a year-round, ice-free port for the export of Canadian goods, and a lucrative market would exist in central Canada for Maritime coal and manufactured goods. The promised Intercolonial Railway would make such trade possible.

The opposition to Confederation in the Maritimes was as strong as it was among French Canadians in Canada East. A.J. Smith, the opposition leader, headed the anti-Confederate forces. He argued that the terms of union with the Canadas, particularly in the Quebec Resolutions, offered few — if any — benefits to New Brunswick. No guarantee existed that the Intercolonial Railway would be constructed and, if it were built, where it would run and which area of the province, the north shore or the southern Saint John River valley, would benefit from it. One member of the Assembly asked derisively: "Mr. Tilley, will you stop your puffing and blowing and tell us which way the Railway is going?"

The opposition also pointed out that New Brunswick's economic trade pattern, especially since the Reciprocity Treaty of 1854, had been north–south rather than east–west. Commercial interests in the province had no economic ties with the Canadas. Furthermore, union with Canada could lead to a flooding of the New Brunswick market by Canadian imports, and a high tariff structure. In addition, New Brunswickers would be forced to assume a portion of the heavy Canadian debt from canal and railway building. Finally, Smith argued that Confederation would diminish New Brunswick's political power by giving the province representation of only 15 members of Parliament in a House of Commons with 194 members. The Roman Catholic clergy in the province also opposed Confederation based on the Quebec Resolutions, believing that a Canada dominated by Protestant "extremists" like George Brown could threaten Roman Catholic schools and the church itself throughout the proposed union.

These arguments formed the basis of debate in the election campaign of early 1865, an election fought chiefly on the issue of Confederation. New Brunswickers responded clearly and decisively — the Tilley pro-Confederation government lost heavily.

OPPOSITION IN NOVA SCOTIA

 In Nova Scotia, Charles Tupper faced a challenge at least equal to Tilley's in New Brunswick. Here opposition to the Quebec Resolutions and to Confederation transcended party lines and centred on Joseph Howe, "Father of Responsible Government," now no longer a member of the Assembly but still the most powerful political figure in Nova Scotia. The "voice of Nova Scotia" saw Confederation as restricting the colony's potential by reducing it to a backwater province in an insignificant North American nation. While Howe was an enthusiast of railways and an advocate of the Intercolonial Railway, he favoured Nova Scotia's autonomy from the Canadas and preferred closer economic ties to Britain and the United States.

In early 1865, Howe presented his position in a series of letters written anonymously and entitled "The Botheration Letters." He argued that if Nova Scotia joined Confederation it would lose its identity and cease to be an important colony in the great British empire. Furthermore, Howe pointed out that the province looked eastward to the Atlantic Ocean and Britain, rather than westward to the continent and the Canadas. As he vividly expressed it, "Take a Nova Scotian to Ottawa, away above tide-water, freeze him up for five months, where he cannot view the Atlantic, smell salt water, or see the sail of a ship, and the man will pine and die." Like

Antoine-Aimé Dorion, Howe also objected to Confederation being imposed without consulting the electorate.

Within the province, Howe's arguments won particular support in those areas of the colony that looked to the sea and depended on ocean trade, shipbuilding, and fishing for their livelihood. In contrast, Charles Tupper drew his main support from the interior, where the coal, steel, and railway interests saw greater economic benefits from transcontinental, as opposed to oceanic, trade.

In the winter of 1866–67, Howe went to England to present his case for Nova Scotia staying out of Confederation to the colonial secretary and the British Parliament. Dissent in the province against Tupper's School Act of 1864, which placed the cost of education on the localities themselves rather than on the provincial government, aided Howe in this anti-Confederation campaign. Knowing full well that he could not win an election on the Confederation and schools issues, Tupper encouraged the British North American leaders to conclude their discussions and achieve union before he had to face an election in 1867. In the meantime, Tupper, under pressure from the new lieutenant governor, Sir William Fenwick Williams, introduced the issue of Confederation into the legislature in April 1866, although he made no reference to the Quebec Resolutions or any other specifics of the union under consideration.

THE REJECTION OF CONFEDERATION IN PRINCE EDWARD ISLAND

Joseph Howe, Nova Scotia's determined opponent to Confederation.

National Archives of Canada/C-22002.

In Prince Edward Island, support for Confederation went from modest to none. At the Charlottetown and Quebec conferences, the island's representatives had driven the hardest bargain, pressing for better terms on representation in the Senate and the House of Commons and for better economic terms.

Their enthusiasm and interest declined when the delegates returned home. Disagreement broke out across party lines, as personal feuds and in-party fighting erupted. Within the governing Conservative party, chaos occurred when Premier Gray resigned in mid-December 1864 over his own party's opposition to Confederation. He was replaced by an anti-Confederate, J.C. Pope. Ironically, the new premier's brother, W.H. Pope, the new provincial secretary, supported British North American union.

The real opposition, however, came from the islanders themselves. Their opposition centred on a number of issues. One was the age-old issue of absentee landlordism. From the late 1760s onward, absentee British landlords had controlled the island, much to the resentment of the local population. In 1860, a British commission appointed to investigate the question issued a report favourable to the islanders, only to have it rejected by the proprietors and the Colonial Office. Thus, when the Colonial Office pressured Prince Edward Islanders to adopt Confederation, they resisted. Also, many islanders saw Confederation as simply replacing one set of distant landlords in Britain with another in Ottawa. In addition, islanders believed that Confederation would give them very little. Union would mean higher taxes to support the enormous Intercolonial Railway project and higher tariffs to create interprovincial trade — neither of which would greatly benefit Prince Edward Island. They also disliked the proposed form of representation in the Senate and House of Commons, which would deny them a major voice in distant Ottawa.

In the end, the majority of islanders saw few if any benefits in Confederation. As the Charlottetown *Islander* wrote on December 30, 1864: "The majority of people appear to be wholly averse to Confederation.... We have done our duty. We have urged Confederation — the people have declared against it."

DEBATE OVER CONFEDERATION IN NEWFOUNDLAND

Newfoundland failed to support Confederation out of apathy, not opposition. Newfoundland had not participated in the Charlottetown Conference, but it had sent two representatives — Ambrose Shea, a liberal Roman Catholic, and F.B.T. Carter, a conservative Protestant — to the Quebec Conference, at which both delegates had endorsed Confederation. They returned to a colony that was initially mildly interested but soon became largely indifferent. The initial enthusiasm came as a result of Newfoundland's destitute condition. Fishing, the chief industry, was in decline throughout the 1860s. Agriculture and the timber trade, while distant seconds to fishing as commercial activities, also experienced hard times. Although Newfoundlanders initially hoped that if they joined Confederation it might solve their economic ills, they soon thought otherwise. Most Newfoundlanders concluded that Canada was simply too far away to be of benefit to them. Essentially, the island continued to look eastward to Britain rather than westward to Canada.

The politicians never overcame the Newfoundlanders' indifference to Canada. Premier Hugh Hoyles, who had also been premier at the time of the Quebec Conference, favoured Confederation, as did most members from both parties in the Legislative Council and the Assembly. But few people outside government circles endorsed the idea. In April 1865, Hoyles retired and was replaced by F.B.T. Carter. He allied with his political opponent, Ambrose Shea, to form a coalition government to persuade Newfoundland to join Confederation. They obtained the enthusiastic support of the pro-Confederation governor, Anthony Musgrave. But even this impressive political coalition could not stir up popular interest in the subject. R.J. Pinsent, a representative of the Legislative Council, spoke for many Newfoundlanders when he noted, "There is little community of interest between Newfoundland and the Canadas. This is not a Continental Colony."

EXTERNAL PRESSURES

By the end of 1865, public support for British North American Confederation had apparently vanished, except in Canada West. All four of the Atlantic colonies opposed it, while Canada East had serious reservations. Two external developments, however, altered the situation: British intervention and the American threat.

BRITISH SUPPORT FOR CONFEDERATION

In *Britain and the Origins of Canadian Confederation, 1837–67*, historian Ged Martin argues that Britain's role in bringing about Confederation was not so much one of cajoling and pressuring as one of gently and persuasively arguing that the time was right for union of the British North American colonies, an idea that Britain had advocated since the 1830s. Certainly one reason why the Britain government resurrected the idea again in the mid-1860s was Britain's desire to rid itself of the expense of defending British North America by seeking to ease tension in its relations with the United States. Thus, when a pro-Confederation delegation from the Canadas arrived in London in the autumn of 1865, it was warmly welcomed; a counter-delegation from Nova Scotia under Joseph Howe was not. The British government also replaced the governor of Nova Scotia with a new appointee, one more sympathetic to Confederation. As well, the Colonial Office ordered New Brunswick Governor Arthur Gordon to intervene in his province's politics to ensure the success of Confederation. Finally, Britain agreed to guarantee the loan interest for the proposed Intercolonial Railway should Confederation come about, thus giving the Maritime provinces an additional incentive to unite with the Canadas.

THE AMERICAN CONTRIBUTION TO CONFEDERATION

While Britain applied direct pressure, the United States did so indirectly. When the Civil War ended in 1865, Northern extremists proposed that the Northern army be mobilized to annex the British North American colonies. Moreover, influential politicians in the American Midwest, such as Senators Alexander Ramsey of Minnesota and Zachariah Chandler of Michigan, advocated annexation of the British Northwest. Other American politicians, such as Congressman Nathaniel Banks, Senator Charles Sumner, and even Hamilton Fish, the secretary of state in Ulysses S. Grant's administration, wanted possession of all the British territory in North America. The New York *Herald* and the Chicago *Tribune* called for the annexation of Canada.

Amidst such talk, the American government terminated the Reciprocity Treaty of 1854. American protectionist interests had advocated abolition of the treaty as early as 1862. In December 1865, Congress passed a motion to end the Reciprocity Treaty as of March 1866. American annexationists argued that the treaty's abrogation would lead to such economic hardship among the British colonies as to force them to join the United States. Ironically, instead of forcing the British colonies into the arms of the United States, the announced abrogation of reciprocity encouraged the colonies to consider an alternative commercial union among themselves.

FENIAN RAIDS

A direct American military threat also furthered the cause of Confederation. Fanatical republican Irishmen known as Fenians had formed a brotherhood in 1859 in the United States to fight for the independence of Ireland. They devised a grandiose scheme by which they would capture the British North American colonies and use them as ransom to negotiate with the British government for the liberation of Ireland. Their marching song explicitly set out their goals:

> We are the Fenian Brotherhood,
> skilled in the art of war,
> And we're going to fight for Ireland,
> the land that we adore.
> Many battles we have won, along with
> the boys in blue,
> And we'll go and capture Canada for
> we've nothing else to do.

The Fenians expected the sympathy and support of Irish Catholics in the British colonies to the north, but they were disappointed. Few supported them, and prominent individuals such as Thomas D'Arcy McGee came out strongly against them.

The Fenians posed little threat until the end of the American Civil War. In the summer of 1865, the Union army released thousands of Irish-American soldiers, who were trained, receptive to mobilizing in defence of their native country, and now idle. Furthermore, the Fenians met

In May 1866, the Fenians invaded the Niagara peninsula. Their banners bore the initials "I.R.A." (Irish Republican Army).

National Archives of Canada/C-18737.

with little resistance and even had muted support from an American government that sympathized with their anti-British sentiments. Many American politicians also feared that if they failed to support the Fenians they would alienate the large number of American Irish Catholic voters.

The Fenian threat tended to be more psychological than physical. The actual military activities were few and restricted to border skirmishes. The Fenians did, however, make two significant attacks that alarmed British North Americans. The first took place in New Brunswick. In April 1866, small bands of Fenians moved into the coastal towns of eastern Maine. New Brunswick mobilized its volunteer soldiers. The Fenians only succeeded in stealing the flag from a customs house before the militia and British regulars forced them back across the border. The raid helped the Confederation cause in the New Brunswick election that took place at that time. In April, the New Brunswick legislature passed the Confederation resolutions.

In late May, a much more serious incident occurred on the Niagara frontier, when 1500 Fenians crossed the Niagara River into Canada West. At Ridgeway on June 2 the Fenians defeated the Canadian militia, but then they withdrew. They never returned, although they continued to pose a threat to Canada until 1870.

CONFEDERATION OPPOSED AND ACCEPTED

In New Brunswick, A.J. Smith's anti-Confederationist government, which took office in 1865, soon ran into considerable difficulties. It contained many conflicting interests and lacked internal unity. The first blow came in the autumn of 1865, when R.D. Wilmot and T.W. Anglin,

Where Historians Disagree
Why Nova Scotia and New Brunswick Joined Confederation

Why did the two Maritime provinces of Nova Scotia and New Brunswick, which appeared to have so little to gain from union and in which opposition to Confederation was so pronounced, agree in the end to join with the Canadas? This question has generated considerable debate. In the 1920s, when separatist sentiments were strong in the region, Maritime historians focussed on the opposition to Confederation. They explained it in terms of the desire on the part of local communities to maintain the status quo and the absence among them of any feeling of identity with the distant communities of the Canadas. In essence, an inherent conservatism prevailed that worked against Confederation. How, then, did these historians account for Confederation? George Wilson attributed the success of the pro-Confederationists in the election of 1866 to the Fenian raids (which led many New Brunswickers to fear for the security of their colony) and to the financial contribution of the Canadas to the election campaign.[1] William Menzies Whitelaw, on the other hand, stressed the manipulative tactics of the Canadian politicians at the Quebec Conference of 1864 that won Maritime leaders over to Confederation.[2]

In the 1960s, historians believed that the greatest pressure for union came from Britain and the United States. Donald Warner emphasized the American military threat along with British imperial pressure as the decisive factors in overcoming Maritime opposition to union.[3] P.B. Waite argued that Confederation was "imposed on British North America by ingenuity, luck, courage, and sheer force."[4]

Waite also added a new explanation. Writing on the eve of the Canadian centennial, he interpreted the Maritimers' support for Confederation as a desire to overcome parochialism by becoming part of a larger and greater transcontinental nation. In other words, he believed that a nascent Canadian nationalism was stirring. Kenneth Pryke later challenged this assumption. "Support for union ... did not always indicate a broadsighted vision," he wrote, "nor did opposition to it necessarily indicate a reactionary sectionalism."[5] Instead, Pryke argued, acceptance of Confederation in Nova Scotia was simply an acquiescence to colonial realities — it was an acceptance of the inevitable.

Historian Del Muise shifted the debate from politics (and the pressures exerted on Maritime politicians) to economics. He noted that the political divisions that arose in Nova Scotia over Confederation coincided with the economic divisions that existed in the province. Anti-Confederationists supported the old maritime economy, based on "wood, wind and sail" — those who looked to Britain and the ocean for their livelihood. Pro-Confederationists favoured a continental economy — they were a younger generation who saw a better future for the province in railways, coal, and industrialization. In the end, the latter outfought the former.[6] With regard to New Brunswick, Alfred G. Bailey associated the main opposition to Confederation with the "business fraternity who had been endeavouring for a decade to integrate the commerce of the province more closely with that of the United States."[7] By implication, the supporters of

Confederation envisioned a brighter economic future for the province within a Canadian transcontinental economy.

Other historians have seen the division between the anti- and the pro-Confederationists as a cultural one, between native-born and British-born Maritimers. Ethnic historians have found the greatest opposition to Confederation among Irish Catholics and Acadians, and the strongest support among the English elite. There are, however, sufficiently significant exceptions to these generalizations to put their validity in question.

In *Britain and the Origins of Canadian Confederation, 1837–67*, historian Ged Martin examines Britain's role in bringing about Confederation. He argues that Britain did not put pressure on the recalcitrant colonies, such as Nova Scotia and New Brunswick, to accept the type of union proposed at Charlottetown and Quebec, but rather encouraged them to accept the idea of union as one that had been around for some time and whose time had now come, due to a variety of circumstances in the 1860s.[8]

Historian Phillip Buckner shifted the debate away from the subject of opposition and toward that of the union. He noted that "if one turns the traditional question on its head and asks not why were so many Maritimers opposed to Confederation but why so many of them agreed so easily to a scheme of union that was clearly designed by Canadians to meet Canadian needs and to ensure Canadian dominance . . . , then the Maritime response to the Canadian initiative looks rather different." Buckner pointed out how weak and ineffective Maritime opposition to Confederation was. He also argued that it would have taken more than external pressure to push the Maritimes into a union they did not really want, and concluded that there had to have been internal support for the cause. Buckner suggested that such popular support was evident in "those who equated consolidation with material progress and modernization."

Buckner called for studies of the "intellectual milieu in which literary figures and the growing number of professionals functioned, of clerical thought, and indeed of changing views of the role and function of the state held by entrepreneurs and by other groups in society" to see to what extent support for Confederation came from those groups seeking "the emergence of larger and more powerful institutional units of government."[9] This is indeed a neglected subject of study and one that might shed new light on the ongoing debate about the Maritimes and Confederation.

[1] George Wilson, "New Brunswick's Entrance into Confederation," *Canadian Historical Review*, 9 (1928): 4–24.

[2] William Menzies Whitelaw, *The Maritimes and Canada before Confederation* (Toronto: Oxford University Press, 1966 [1934]).

[3] Donald Warner, *The Idea of Continental Union* (Lexington: University of Kentucky Press, 1960).

[4] P.B. Waite, *The Life and Times of Confederation, 1864–1867* (Toronto: University of Toronto Press, 1962), p. 323.

[5] Kenneth Pryke, *Nova Scotia and Confederation, 1864–1871* (Toronto: University of Toronto Press, 1979), p. 6.

[6] Del Muise, "The Federal Election of 1867 in Nova Scotia: An Economic Interpretation," *Nova Scotia Historical Society, Collection* (1968): 327–51.

[7] Alfred G. Bailey, "The Basis and Persistence of Opposition to Confederation in New Brunswick," *Canadian Historical Review*, 23 (1942): 382–83.

[8] Ged Martin, *Britain and the Origins of Canadian Confederation, 1837–67* (Vancouver: University of British Columbia Press, 1995).

[9] Phillip Buckner, "The Maritimes and Confederation: A Reassessment," *Canadian Historical Review,* 71 (1990): 14–15, 22.

two of Smith's ablest cabinet ministers, resigned. Wilmot was converted to the Confederation cause during a visit to the Canadas in September 1865. Anglin left for another reason: he opposed his government's decision to assist a private company to build an important provincial railway. (He wanted the New Brunswick government itself to construct it.) A second blow came in November, when the Smith government lost an important by election in York County to Charles Fisher. The pro-Confederation forces interpreted the win in York as a victory, especially since the pro-Confederation government of the Canadas had contributed handsomely to Fisher's campaign fund. Finally, Smith failed in his bid to persuade the American government to renew the Reciprocity Treaty of 1854. In addition to these setbacks, Smith had to fight Governor Arthur Gordon who, at the British government's insistence, was pressuring New Brunswickers to support Confederation.

THE ELECTION OF 1866 IN NEW BRUNSWICK

In exasperation, the Smith government resigned in April 1866. In the ensuing election campaign, Samuel Leonard Tilley resurrected his earlier arguments for Confederation and added a few new ones. He pointed out to the people of New Brunswick what they could expect from Confederation: lower taxes, the Intercolonial Railway, a fair share in the running of the nation, a market for their raw materials and manufactured goods — in other words, material progress and modernization. He argued that union would "open up and colonize immense tracts of fertile lands ... lying unreclaimed and desolate. It will multiply the sources of industry and intensify the demand for labour. It will tend to keep our young men at home and allure those of other lands to our shores." Such views reflected the more cosmopolitan attitudes in the Maritimes by the mid-1860s.

Parliament Buildings, Ottawa, by Frances Anne Hopkins (1867).

Art Gallery of Ontario, Toronto. Purchased with assistance from the Government of Canada through the Cultural Property Export and Import Act, 1989.

During the campaign, both parties benefited from external funds. The anti-Confederates received money from Nova Scotia and possibly the United States, while the pro-Confederates obtained financial support from the government of the Canadas. "Give us funds," a desperate Tilley cabled John A. Macdonald. "It will require some $40 000 or $50 000 to do the work in all our counties." Macdonald agreed. He did not want Confederation to go down to defeat in New Brunswick simply for lack of money. Direct British intervention and threatened Fenian raids also assisted Tilley's cause.

These circumstances, along with an ineffective campaign on Smith's part (he had lost his only viable alternative to Confederation — reciprocity with the United States), resulted in a resounding victory for Tilley. Tilley immediately had the New Brunswick legislature endorse Confederation without referring it directly to the populace.

THE WESTMINSTER CONFERENCE

In the autumn and winter of 1866, delegates from Nova Scotia, New Brunswick, and the United Canadas met in London to prepare the passage of the British North America Act. The Quebec Resolutions served as the starting point for this last round of negotiations. Although the Maritime delegates pressed for modifications of those aspects of the resolutions that provided for a strong central government, in the end the resolutions were accepted as final except for a few minor but significant changes. Rather than a "federation," the union would be known as a "confederation." Subsidies to the provinces would be increased beyond the agreed 80 cents a head by a fixed grant

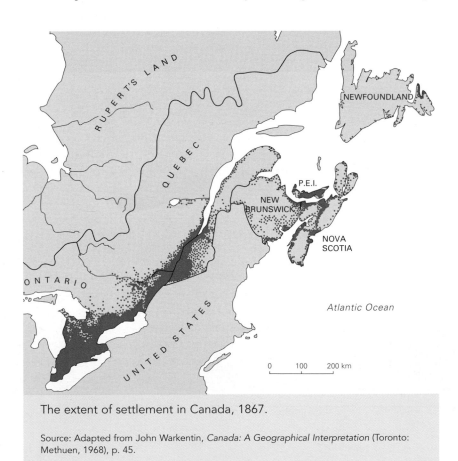

The extent of settlement in Canada, 1867.

Source: Adapted from John Warkentin, *Canada: A Geographical Interpretation* (Toronto: Methuen, 1968), p. 45.

from the federal government. The contentious issue of separate schools, which had been heatedly debated in the legislature of the Canadas in the spring of 1865, was settled by applying the Quebec clause on education, which safeguarded the Protestant separate schools in Quebec, to all other provinces in the union, or to new provinces that had separate schools "by law" at the time they joined Confederation. Furthermore, religious minorities had the right of appeal to the federal government if the provincial government threatened their school systems, as they existed before Confederation.

Right up to the time that Confederation was ratified in the British Parliament, opposition continued in Nova Scotia. While the delegates were meeting in London to finalize the terms of Confederation, Joseph Howe was meeting British officials to convince them to reject the union. He denounced British and Canadian politicians as attempting to force Confederation against the popular will. But the British government refused to retract its support. When the British North America Act was signed on March 29, 1867, Howe returned to Nova Scotia cured "of a good deal of loyal enthusiasm" and embittered against the Canadians. He was not alone. Many Nova Scotians saw Confederation as the beginning of the end for Nova Scotia. Elsewhere, Confederation was accepted, although not with enthusiasm, except in Ontario.

John A. Macdonald wanted to call "the new nation" the "Kingdom of Canada," but the British government objected because they feared the term would further offend the Americans, implying as it did a more autonomous country. Leonard Tilley had chanced upon an alternative title, as well as an appropriate motto, for the new country — A *Mari Usque Ad Mare* (From Sea to Sea) — while reading Psalm 72:

> He shall have dominion also from sea to sea,
> and from the river unto the ends of the earth.

 On July 1, 1867, the Dominion of Canada was born.

NOTES

1. P.B. Waite, "Confederation," in *The Canadian Encyclopedia*, 2nd ed., vol. 1 (Edmonton: Hurtig, 1988), p. 488.
2. F.H. Underhill, *The Image of Confederation* (Toronto: Canadian Broadcasting Corporation, 1964), p. 4.
3. Peter H. Russell, *Constitutional Odyssey: Can Canadians Become a Sovereign People?* 2nd ed. (Toronto: University of Toronto Press, 1993), p. 32.

LINKING TO THE PAST

Canadian Confederation
http://www.nlc-bnc.ca/2/18/index-e.html
This site from the National Library of Canada offers extensive information on Confederation, the events that led up to it, and the people behind it. The site includes biographies of John A. Macdonald, George-Étienne Cartier, George Brown, Charles Tupper, and Alexander Tilloch Galt. For information on the influence of the American Civil War, go to http://www.nlc-bnc.ca/2/18/h18-2003-e.html. Also check out the full text of the Seventy-Two Resolutions, the British North America Act, and related historical documents at http://www.nlc-bnc.ca/2/18/h18-2600-e.html.

1850–1867: On the Road to Confederation
http://www.canadiana.org/citm/themes/constitution/constitution12_e.html
A description of political developments during this period, including the impact of the American Civil War, the Charlottetown and Quebec conferences, Fenian raids, and the Westminster Conference.

The Charlottetown Conference, 1864
http://collections.ic.gc.ca/charlottetown/

An extensive site that presents background material; a day-by-day summary of the conference, including description of the social events that took place; and a collection of newspaper clippings, paintings, and photographs.

Nova Scotian Separatism
http://www.uni.ca/ns_sep.html

A brief summary of Nova Scotia separatism, with an excerpt from Joseph Howe's speech against Confederation.

The Fenian Raids of Upper and Lower Canada
http://www.doyle.com.au/fenian_raids.htm

A history of the Fenians and their raids, including the Battle of Ridgeway.

The Dominion of Canada, 1867
http://www.atlas.gc.ca/site/english/maps/historical/territorialevolution/1867

A map of the Dominion of Canada in 1867. Click on "Read Map Description" for more information.

RELATED READINGS

R. Douglas Francis and Donald B. Smith, eds., *Readings in Canadian History: Pre-Confederation*, 6th ed. (Toronto: Nelson Thomson Learning, 2002), includes two important articles on the subject of Confederation: A.I. Silver, "Confederation and Quebec," pp. 469–83; and Phillip Buckner, with P.B. Waite and William M. Baker, "CHR Dialogue: The Maritimes and Confederation: A Reassessment," pp. 483–515.

BIBLIOGRAPHY

The three best general texts on Confederation, all written in the 1960s, are Donald Creighton, *The Road to Confederation: The Emergence of Canada, 1863–1867* (Toronto: Macmillan, 1964); W.L. Morton, *The Critical Years: The Union of British North America, 1857–1873* (Toronto: McClelland & Stewart, 1964); and P.B. Waite, *The Life and Times of Confederation, 1864–1867: Politics, Newspapers, and the Union of British North America* (Toronto: University of Toronto Press, 1962). The Canadian Historical Association has published a number of pamphlets on aspects of Confederation by leading scholars in their fields: J.M. Beck, *Joseph Howe: Anti-Confederate* (Ottawa, 1966); J.-C. Bonenfant, *The French Canadians and the Birth of Confederation* (Ottawa, 1966); P.G. Cornell, *The Great Coalition* (Ottawa, 1966); W.L. Morton, *The West and Confederation, 1857–1871* (Ottawa, 1962); P.B. Waite, *The Charlottetown Conference* (Ottawa, 1963); and W.M. Whitelaw, *The Quebec Conference* (Ottawa, 1966). Christopher Moore takes a more recent look at the topic in *1867: How the Fathers Made a Deal* (Toronto: McClelland & Stewart, 1997). Peter H. Russell looks at the history of the constitutional process from Confederation to the Charlottetown Accord in *Constitutional Odyssey: Can Canadians Become a Sovereign People?* 2nd ed. (Toronto: University of Toronto Press, 1993).

Ramsay Cook has edited and written an introduction to *Confederation* (Toronto: University of Toronto Press, 1967), a collection of interpretive essays on the subject. Also useful are the articles included by Ged Martin in his edited work *The Causes of Canadian Confederation* (Fredericton: Acadiensis, 1990). A good primary source is P.B. Waite, ed., *The Confederation Debates in the Province of Canada, 1865* (Toronto: McClelland & Stewart, 1963). J.M. Bumsted provides a bibliographical guide to Britain's response to the Confederation idea, and to British North America's imperial ties in general, in "British North America in Its Imperial and International Context," in M. Brook Taylor, ed., *Canadian History: A Reader's Guide*, vol. 1, *Beginnings to Confederation* (Toronto: University of Toronto Press, 1994), pp. 394–447.

Confederation can also be studied through biographies of the protagonists; relevant biographies include D.G. Creighton, *John A. Macdonald*, vol. 1, *The Young Politician* (Toronto: Macmillan, 1952); J.M.S. Careless, *Brown of the Globe*, vol. 2, *Statesman of Confederation, 1860–1880* (Toronto: Macmillan, 1963);

Brian Young, *George-Étienne Cartier: Montreal Bourgeois* (Montreal/Kingston: McGill-Queen's University Press, 1981); O.D. Skelton, *Life and Times of Sir Alexander Tilloch Galt*, rev. ed. (Toronto: McClelland & Stewart, 1966 [1920]); and J.M. Beck, *Joseph Howe*, vol. 2, *The Briton Becomes Canadian, 1848–1873* (Montreal/Kingston: McGill-Queen's University Press, 1983). Important biographical sketches can be found in the volumes of the *Dictionary of Canadian Biography* devoted to the late nineteenth century. It is now available online: www.biographi.ca. On women's role in the Confederation process see Moira Dann, *Mothers of Confederation* (Montreal: CBC Transcripts, 1989).

On the Maritime provinces and Confederation in 1867 see Phillip A. Buckner, "The 1860s: An End and a Beginning," in Phillip A. Buckner and John G. Reid, eds., *The Atlantic Region to Confederation: A History* (Toronto: University of Toronto Press, 1994), pp. 360–86; Martin, *The Causes of Canadian Confederation* (cited above); Kenneth Pryke, *Nova Scotia and Confederation, 1864–1874* (Toronto: University of Toronto Press, 1979); W.S. MacNutt, *New Brunswick: A History, 1784–1867* (Toronto: Macmillan, 1962); F.W.P. Bolger, *Prince Edward Island and Confederation, 1863–1873* (Charlottetown: St. Dunstan's University Press, 1964); and H.B. Mayo, "Newfoundland and Confederation in the Eighteen-Sixties," *Canadian Historical Review* 29 (1948): 125–42. On Quebec see J.-C. Bonenfant, *La Naissance de la Confédération* (Montreal: Leméac, 1969); and Marcel Bellavance, *Le Clergé québécois et la Confédération canadienne de 1867* (Sillery, QC: Septentrion, 1992).

On the American and British influence on Confederation consult Robin Winks, *Canada and the United States: The Civil War Years* (Montreal: Harvest House, 1971 [1960]); John A. Williams, "Canada and the Civil War," in H. Hyman, ed., *Heard Round the World: The Impact Abroad of the Civil War* (New York: Alfred A. Knopf, 1969), pp. 257–98; C.P. Stacey, *Canada and the British Army, 1841–1871*, rev. ed. (Toronto: University of Toronto Press, 1963 [1936]). On the influence of the American Civil War on the Maritimes, see Greg Marquis, *In Armageddon's Shadow: The Civil War and Canada's Maritime Provinces* (Montreal/Kingston: McGill-Queen's University Press, 1998). A study of a specific incident that almost led to war between Britain and the North is Norman B. Ferris, *The Trent Affair: A Diplomatic Crisis* (Knoxville: University of Tennessee Press, 1977). Max Guérout has written a popular illustrated account of the most famous Confederate ship, "The Wreck of the C.S.S. Alabama, Avenging Angel of the Confederacy," *National Geographic* 186(6) (December 1994): 66–83. On the Fenian raids consult Hereward Senior, *The Last Invasion of Canada: The Fenian Raids, 1866–1870* (Toronto: Dundurn Press, 1991). Studies of Britain's influence on the British North American federation include the new volume by Ged Martin, *Britain and the Origins of Canadian Federation, 1837–67* (Vancouver: University of British Columbia Press, 1995); and John T. Saywell, "Backstage at London, 1864–1867: Constitutionalizing the Distinct Society?" *National History*, 1 (4) (Summer 2000): 331–46.

Index